Criminal Litigation Handbook

Criminal Litigation Handbook

MARTIN HANNIBAL

LISA MOUNTFORD

OXFORD
UNIVERSITY PRESS

OXFORD
UNIVERSITY PRESS

Great Clarendon Street, Oxford OX2 6DP

Oxford University Press is a department of the University of Oxford.
It furthers the University's objective of excellence in research, scholarship,
and education by publishing worldwide in

Oxford New York

Auckland Cape Town Dar es Salaam Hong Kong Karachi
Kuala Lumpur Madrid Melbourne Mexico City Nairobi
New Delhi Shanghai Taipei Toronto

With offices in

Argentina Austria Brazil Chile Czech Republic France Greece
Guatemala Hungary Italy Japan Poland Portugal Singapore
South Korea Switzerland Thailand Turkey Ukraine Vietnam

Oxford is a registered trade mark of Oxford University Press
in the UK and in certain other countries

Published in the United States
by Oxford University Press Inc., New York

British Library Cataloguing in Publication Data
Data available

Library of Congress Cataloging in Publication Data
Data available

Typeset by Newgen Imaging Systems (P) Ltd., Chennai, India
Printed in Great Britain
on acid-free paper by
Ashford Colour Press Ltd, Gosport, Hants.

ISBN 0-19-928957-3   978-0-19-928957-8

10 9 8 7 6 5 4 3 2 1

CONTENTS

PREFACE

We suggested in the preface to the first edition of the *Criminal Litigation Handbook* that the project had been a challenging undertaking, not least because of the incremental implementation of a number of important and wide-ranging reforms introduced by the Criminal Justice Act 2003. Writing the second edition has proven to be equally challenging – not least because the criminal justice system in England and Wales is dynamic and fast moving! A number of significant reforms under the CJA 2003 have yet to be implemented and it is often a calculated guess to decide whether to write about a topic from a pre-CJA or post-CJA perspective. Other important legislative changes have also been implemented such as the reforms to the powers of arrest and classification of offences under the Police and Criminal Evidence Act 1984 introduced by the Serious Organised Crime and Police Act 2005.

In spite of these uncertainties our aim from the outset has been to deliver a text that is comprehensive but which provides a highly practical, innovative and contextual learning resource for those students who are studying the compulsory Criminal Litigation element on the Legal Practice Course and/or an elective in Advanced Criminal Litigation. The feedback to the first edition appears to suggest that we have successfully achieved this aim, and we sincerely thank our teaching colleagues from other institutions, our practitioner friends and the students for their highly constructive and useful comments. We always welcome your invaluable advice and comments.

The Handbook is accompanied by an innovative Online Resource Centre, which contains a number of pedagogical features and includes videoclips of selected portions of the case studies that form the basis of ongoing exercises throughout the text.

One issue with which we struggled long and hard was where to include the all-important rules of criminal evidence. Rather than have the rules at the end of the book, we have sought to integrate them throughout the text.

The Handbook is divided into six sections:

Part I is an introduction to criminal litigation.

Part II considers the process of investigation up to the decision to charge, including relevant rules of criminal evidence.

Part III considers post-charge procedures up to and including trial.

Part IV considers the remaining rules of criminal evidence.

Part V considers the post-conviction matters of sentencing and appeals against conviction and/or sentence.

Part VI considers youth justice issues.

The writing of the course manual and the production of the video case studies and the Online Resource Centre could not have been achieved without the cooperation and assistance of a great many people.

In relation to the video case studies of Lenny Whyte/William Hardy and Roger Martin we say a special thank you to the following:

Milena Srdanovic (CPS lawyer)
Celia Laing (defence lawyer)
Heather Drew (defence lawyer)
Alison Bailey (legal adviser)

Vicky Priestly (legal adviser)
John Peel (CPS designated caseworker)
Jason Jamil (LPC student 2003–2004)
Mark Woolsey (LPC student 2003–2004)
Samantha Jewel (LPC student 2003–2004)
Carol Hawthorne (magistrate)
Dr Mike Carter (magistrate)
Rev Christopher Dalton (magistrate)
Nick Hannibal

In relation to the Peter West Police Station Scenario we would sincerely like to thank the following:

DC Keith Pagett (Staffordshire Police)
DS Angus Parker (Staffordshire Police)
Sgt Ian Cantrill (Staffordshire Police)
Lisa O'Shea (Accredited Police Station Representative with the Public Defender Service)
Peter Gould (LPC student 2004–2005) who gave an outstanding and entirely convincing performance as Peter West, the suspect!

Each of these individuals very kindly gave up their time and volunteered their services for free, thereby allowing us to bring our case studies to life.

We thank Alison Bailey additionally for her helpful comments on a number of draft chapters.

Special thanks go to the camera crew:

Ray Johnson (professor of film heritage and documentary, Staffordshire University)
Darren Teale (final year media student 2004)
Richard Edwards (final year media student 2004)
Gary Robinson (final year media student 2004)
Peter Robinson (senior technician, Staffordshire Law School)
Adam Johnson

We are indebted to Ray Johnson for his tremendous help in directing the filming of our case studies, undertaking the voiceover and the editing of *R v William Hardy*. Special thanks also go to Darren Teale for undertaking the editing of *R v Lenny Whyte* and *R v Roger Martin*. We would like to thank Peter Robinson (Staffordshire Law School's senior IT technician) for helping us to film our Police Station Scenario and for his very patient editing of the same!

Also thanks to the Chief Constable of Staffordshire, John Giffard, for permission to involve Staffordshire Police and to the staff at Uttoxeter Police Station in rural Staffordshire who allowed us to take over their police station for a day in November 2005.

We would like to thank Dr NJF Smalldridge BA (Oxon), BM, MRC Psych for the time and effort he undertook in devising and writing a psychiatric report on behalf of our fictional defendant Lenny Whyte.

Also, Lisa O'Shea (Accredited Police Station Representative) for her helpful comments on the police station chapters; former colleague Margaret Brown for her comments on draft chapters and Robin Lichfield, partner and defence solicitor with Lichfield Reynolds Solicitors, North Staffordshire, for answering all our questions and providing us with some very valuable comments on our case studies and draft chapters.

We thank the entire team at OUP (particularly Lucy Graham and Anna Read). Special thanks go to Kate Hilton (OUP's IT guru) for her fantastic work on building and maintaining the Online Resource Centre. We also acknowledge the tremendous hard work of our former assistant commissioning editor Rebecca Webb and Stephanie Orr, our production editor on the first edition.

Most of all we thank our families (Merryn, Matt, Nick and Charlie Hannibal, Nick and Alexandra Mason) for their enduring patience!

Any errors or omissions are entirely ours.

The law is stated at 10 April 2006.

Lisa Mountford
Martin Hannibal
Staffordshire Law School

GUIDED TOUR OF THE BOOK

The *Criminal Litigation Handbook* by Hannibal and Mountford is a pedagogically rich text which has been designed to facilitate your learning and understanding of criminal litigation. This 'Guided Tour of the Book' will explain how to fully utilise your text by illustrating each of the features used by the authors to explain the practical aspects of the criminal litigation process.

20.1 Introduction
20.2 The indictment
20.3 Supporting the defence counsel at trial
20.4 Last-minute checklist
20.5 First day of trial
Conference with counsel

CHAPTER CONTENTS

A detailed contents list at the start of each chapter enables you to anticipate what will be covered and identify what the main topics of the chapter will be. Use this feature to also gain an understanding of how the topics fit together in the wider subject area.

Consider the following examples of s. 36 an

☼ Example

Andrew is implicated in a recent offence of assault
Andrew tells you he has no knowledge of the incid
the bruising visible on his face. A failure to off
adverse inference being drawn under s. 36.

EXAMPLES

Look for the example icon to find relevant, practical examples of how the law has been or could be applied in common situations. These examples bring the subject to life and allow you to examine how principles, rules and statutes work in practice.

occasion prevents him from offending fron

⚖ Looking ahead

When in force, s. (2) CJA 2003 inserts para. 9AA
the defendant is under 18 years. Bail may be refuse
would commit an offence if he was granted bai
that the present offence was committed while the

'LOOKING AHEAD' BOXES

These boxes are used to highlight areas where the law may change. Potential reforms are considered ensuring that once you go into practice, you're already aware of how things might change.

R v Imad Al Khawaja [2006] 1 Cr App R 9

The defendant, a doctor had been convicted of ind
included hypnotherapy. Prosecution witness one (W
W1 committed suicide shortly before the trial. Her v
in the exercise of the trial judge's discretion under
and *Kostovski* in that the defendant had not bee

CASE OUTLINES

These case outlines give you an awareness of relevant case law in the subject area. Use these explanations to point you towards the most relevant case reports in your law library or to better inform your knowledge of how the law has been applied in court.

CASE STUDIES

Throughout the book, the authors refer to three fictional case studies, which provide a practical focus to the law and procedures described in the text. The documentation for these case studies appears on the Online Resource Centre. See the 'Guided Tour of the Online Resource Centre' at p xxii for more information.

> 5. I[n ...] of case will it normally be approp[r...]
>
> **Case study: R v [...]nny Whyte**, Appendix 1
>
> You will recall tha[t ...]nny Whyte has been committe[...]
> has been set for [...] Plea and Case Management H[...]
> [...]sed material, in compliance with [...]
> you loo[...] at the defence statement in relation to Le[...]

ONLINE RESOURCE CENTRE ICON

Wherever this icon appears in the margin, more information is available on the Online Resource Centre which accompanies this text. This may be video footage, case study documentation or links to other useful web sites or guidance. See the 'Guided Tour of the Online Resource Centre' at p xxii for more information.

> [...]dures;
>
> **online resource centre** [...]ower to take [fi]ngerprints; int[...]
> [...]ation evidence given by e[...]
> [...]s references will be made [...]
> [...]d from the Home of[fi]ce web [...]
> [...]ode D.

END OF CHAPTER FEATURES

KEY POINTS SUMMARY

The key points covered are summarised in a user-friendly list at the end of each chapter. Look to these summaries to help you consolidate your learning or to check your knowledge at revision time.

> **KEY P[OI]NT SUMMAR[Y]**
> - Be a[wa]re that most crimin[al c]ases involve inve[...]
>   which [... a] statutory powe[r] of search, seizure [...]
> - Criminal [...] will co[mm]ence either by the iss[...]
>   suspect.
> - The CPS or other prosecuting agency prosecu[...]

SELF-TEST QUESTIONS

These questions allow you to test yourself on particular areas of the law in preparation for your exams or to assess your learning throughout the duration of the course. Use these questions to highlight areas where you might need to improve your understanding by re-reading the text or asking your lecturer.

> b[... bec]ome more onerous under the CJA
> [i]mplemente[d ...]
>
> **SELF-TEST Q[UE]STION**
>
> [C]onsider the fo[llo]wing scenario and attempt to
> [...]ny (ag[e ...]) is charged with rape contrary [...]
> 15. The attack is alleged to have occurred in s[o...]

FIGURES

Flowcharts, shaded boxes or example forms provide a visual representation of what has been described within the chapter

> **FIGURE 28.1** STRU[CTU]RED APPROACH TO SE[N...]
> - Sentence i[s ba]sed on the serio[us]ness of the offe[...]
>   committi[ng t]he offence and th[e ri]sk of harm cau[...]
> - A court w[ill h]ave a sentencing [pur]pose in mind [...]
>   sentence.
> - The seriousnes[s ...]e/s is determined b[...]

GUIDED TOUR OF THE ONLINE RESOURCE CENTRE

Online Resource Centres are developed to provide students and lecturers with ready-to-use teaching and learning resources. They are free-of-charge, designed to complement the text and offer additional materials which are well-suited to electronic delivery.

All these resources can be downloaded and are fully customisable allowing them to be incorporated into your institution's existing virtual learning environment.

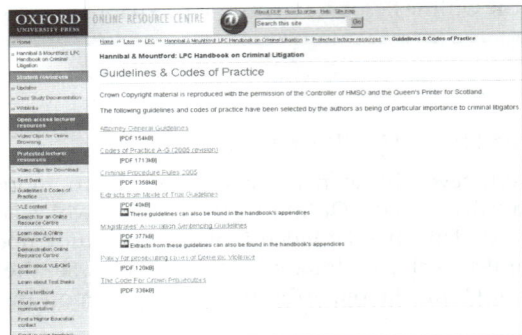

STUDENT RESOURCES

All the resources in this area of the site are freely accessible to all, with no password required. Simply visit the site at: www.oxford-textbooks.co.uk/orc/lpccrimhandbook2e/.

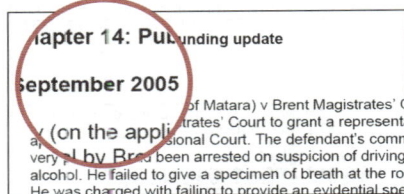

UPDATES

Updates are posted on the website when the law changes or when an important case passes through the courts, allowing you to keep fully informed of developments. The updates are freely accessible to all and offer an easy way to keep abreast of changes in this rapidly changing subject area.

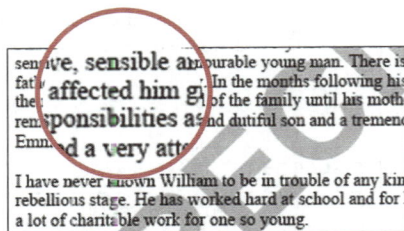

CASE STUDY DOCUMENTATION

The three fictional case studies in the book are accompanied by all of the documentation you would expect to see in reality. This allows you to see what a solicitor's file might typically contain and prepares you for what to expect when you go into practice.

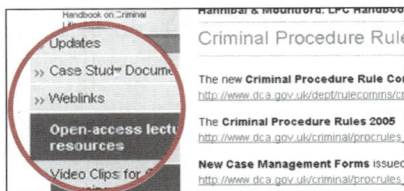

LINKS TO LEGISLATION, RULES AND OTHER DOCUMENTATION

This part of the website provides links to useful information which is freely accessible elsewhere on the internet. Use this resource to find relevant guidelines, statutes, codes of practice and other documentation quickly and easily.

CHAPTERS ON REGULATORY CRIME AND FRAUD

For students whose course has a City focus, corporate crime will be an important topic. Written by two leading barristers in this area, Nicholas Yeo and Sarah Le Fevre, two online chapters on regulatory crime and fraud enable you to get to grips with aspects of criminal law which are key for City lawyers.

LECTURER RESOURCES

These resources are available solely to lecturers and are accessed with use of a free password. To obtain a password, follow the links on the main site at: www.oxfordtextbooks.co.uk/orc/lpccrimhandbook2e/; our web team will contact you with a password within 2 working days. All of the resources on this part of the site can be downloaded into your institution's virtual learning environment.

VIDEO CLIPS

High resolution video footage showing fictional criminal proceedings allows you to emphasise the practical application of what you describe in your teaching. Included on the site is video footage of:

- all three case studies;
- our 'free-standing' police station video scenario.

(Selected, low resolution video clips of the *R v Lenny Whyte* case study are available to lecturers without a password.)

TEST BANK OF QUESTIONS

A bank of questions covering all aspects of the book is available to download into your virtual learning environment (VLE). Also available in Word format, the multiple choice questions give you the ability to provide a resource which your students can use to test themselves, or which you can use to assess their learning. Once included in your VLE, the questions are entirely customisable, enabling you to remove questions which are less relevant to your course, or to change the order of the questions to match the order in which topics are taught at your institution.

Each question is accompanied by feedback which shows why the selected answer is correct or incorrect and then points the student towards the relevant page of the textbook if they need to re-read.

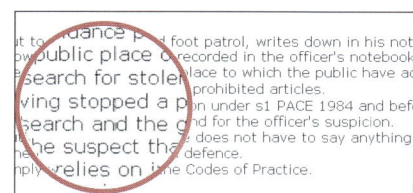

LINKS TO GUIDELINES AND CODES OF PRACTICE

Use this resource to easily find documents important for criminal litigators. Collected together in one place, this resource provides you with all the important documents to which you may want to refer your students.

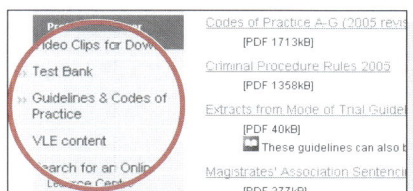

GLOSSARY

Listed below are some of the terms and abbreviations that you will encounter in the *Criminal Litigation Handbook* and later as part of training in criminal practice.

Access to Justice Act 1999	AJA 1999.
Accused/defendant	The natural or legal person against whom a criminal case is brought. In practice, the terms 'the accused' and 'the defendant' are used interchangeably.
Appeal	A request to a higher court to reconsider the defendant's conviction and/or sentence.
Appellant	The natural or legal person who is appealing against the conviction and/or the sentence.
Attorney-General	A-G – Appoints the DPP, initiates some prosecutions and issues guidelines.
Bail	The release of a person from custody by the police or the court with a duty to surrender to custody at a specified time, date and location.
Bail Act 1976	BA 1976.
Co-accused/co-defendant	The natural or legal person who is jointly charged with a criminal offence.
Criminal Defence Service	CDS.
Criminal Prosecution Service	CPS.
Crime and Disorder Act 1998	CDA 1998.
Criminal Evidence Act 1898	CEA 1898.
Criminal Justice Act 1967	CJA 1967.
Criminal Justice Act 1988	CJA 1988.
Criminal Justice Act 2003	CJA 2003.
Criminal Justice and Public Order Act 1994	CJPOA 1994.
Criminal Procedure and Investigations Act 1996	CPIA 1996.
Criminal Procedure Rules	Crim PR.
Crown Court Rules	CCR.
Detainee/suspect	A person arrested and detained by the police when investigating a criminal offence. 'Detainee' is used interchangeably with the word 'suspect'.
Director of Public Prosecutions	DPP – head of the CPS.
District Judge	Professional lawyer who tries cases in the magistrates' court.
Either-way offence	An offence that can be tried either in the Crown Court or in the magistrates' court.
European Convention on Human Rights 1950	ECHR 1950.

European Court of Human Rights	ECtHR.
Human Rights Act 1998	HRA 1998.
Indictable offence	Refers to both indictable-only and either-way offences.
Indictable-only offence	An offence that can only be tried in the Crown Court.
Indictment	The document detailing the charge the defendant pleads to at a Crown Court trial.
Indictment Act 1915	IA 1915.
Information	The document containing the charge that the defendant pleads to in summary cases.
Justices of the Peace Act 1997	JoPA 1997.
Legal Services Commission	LSC.
Magistrates' Courts Act 1980	MCA 1980.
Magistrates' Court Rules	MCR.
Oaths Act 1980	OA 1980.
Plea and Case Management Hearing	PCMH.
Police and Criminal Evidence Act 1984	PACE.
Powers of Criminal Courts (Sentencing) Act 2000	PCC(S)A 2000.
Prosecution of Offences Act 1985	POA 1985.
Road Traffic Act 1988	RTA 1988.
Road Traffic Act 1991	RTA 1991.
Road Traffic Offenders Act 1988	RTOA 1988.
Summary-only offence	An offence that can only be tried in the magistrates' court.
Summons	A court order which requires the defendant or witness to attend court at a specified time and date.
Volunteer	A person who is helping the police with inquiries but who has not been arrested.
Warrant of arrest	A document issued by the court ordering the person specified should be arrested.
Youth Justice and Criminal Evidence Act 1999	YJCEA 1999.

TABLE OF CASES

TABLE OF CODES OF PRACTICE AND PROFESSIONAL CONDUCT RULES

TABLE OF EUROPEAN LEGISLATION

TABLE OF STATUTES

TABLE OF STATUTORY INSTRUMENTS

Part I

INTRODUCTION TO CRIMINAL LITIGATION

Part I equips the reader with the background information that will inform the substantive areas covered in later Chapters.

Chapter 1 explains the aims of the *Criminal Litigation Handbook* and its pedagogical features.

Chapter 2 introduces some key terms, including the classification of criminal offences and the personnel involved in the criminal justice system.

Chapter 3 provides an overview of the criminal litigation process, according to the classification of the offence.

Chapter 4 identifies the pervasive areas that commonly arise in criminal cases, including the European Convention on Human Rights and aspects of the Solicitor's Professional Conduct Rules. This chapter further considers the importance of good advocacy skills.

Finally, Chapter 5 provides an introduction to criminal evidence.

1.1   INTRODUCTION

The *Criminal Litigation Handbook* provides a new and innovative approach to criminal litigation for those studying both the compulsory litigation element of the Legal Practice Course (LPC) and an elective in Advanced Criminal Litigation. The law and procedure covered by the Handbook not only covers the Law Society's written standards, but each chapter also contains additional explanation and analysis to assist the reader's knowledge and understanding of this dynamic subject.

In preparing the Handbook, our intention has been to provide an integrated and practical approach to the study of Criminal Litigation. As experienced Criminal Litigation teachers, we are aware of the need for a textbook that gives students an accessible and comprehensive explanation of the key substantive, procedural and evidential issues, while also providing a learning resource that illustrates, through practice-based examples, diagrams, self-test exercises and case studies, the operation of the law in a very practical context.

Our experience has shown that utilising a wide range of interrelated learning resources is the most effective way to reinforce student understanding of the key legal issues. It also assists students to prepare for their written assessments (and where appropriate, their skills assessment in Criminal Litigation) as well as briefly introducing other issues encountered during training and later as practitioners.

1.2   WHAT DO WE MEAN BY TAKING AN INTEGRATED APPROACH?

The integrated approach is reflected in our belief that LPC students should be aware that the constituent parts of criminal procedure, the rules of criminal evidence, professional conduct and legal skills are not discrete elements, but are part of the integrated picture that is involved in representing a client in a criminal case. Our treatment of the rules of criminal evidence highlights this integrated approach. It is our belief that an understanding of the key evidential issues is relevant at all stages of the case, even during the solicitor's earliest representation of his client at the police station or during the first interview in the office. Chapter 5, An Introduction to Criminal Evidence, provides an overview of the main evidential issues in a criminal case and is designed to encourage you to think about evidence before the law is examined in more detail later in the Handbook.

We cover a number of substantive evidential rules in Part II dealing with the investigation of criminal offences and the role of the solicitor at the police station. The other rules of evidence are covered in Part IV.

An integrated approach is also taken when explaining the rules of professional conduct, legal skills and human rights as well as the rules of criminal procedure.

1.3 WHAT DO WE MEAN BY TAKING A PRACTICAL APPROACH?

The practical approach is achieved through a variety of means. We have attempted to explain the law and procedure in an accessible and reader-friendly style. The substantive content of each chapter is supplemented by practical examples and diagrams, as well as self-test questions and answers to test students' knowledge and understanding. The three case studies which run throughout the book are an essential part of our practical approach. The case studies are:

Case study 1: *R v Lenny Whyte*.

Case study 2: *R v William Hardy*.

Case study 3: *R v Roger Martin* (**web-based only**).

Case study 4: Peter West (**which can be accessed as a protected lecturer resource only**).

A selection of documentation supporting case studies 1 and 2 is included in Appendices 1 and 2 of the Handbook and form the basis of ongoing exercises throughout the text. The exercises are designed to give you the opportunity to apply your knowledge of criminal procedure and evidence in the context of a 'real' case. You will be asked to consider some of the documentation in support of case studies 1 and 2 at the conclusion of this introductory chapter, before going on to Chapter 2. We ask you to keep the case studies in mind as you work through the various stages of the criminal litigation process. Treat these fictional creations as your clients.

Case study 1, *R v Lenny Whyte*, is based on a not guilty plea and illustrates many of the key stages of a typical case from Lenny's first appearance before the magistrates' court through to trial in the Crown Court. Some important rules of criminal evidence are also considered in a practical context.

Case study 2, *R v William Hardy*, is based on a guilty plea. It features a plea in mitigation and illustrates sentencing practice and procedure.

online resource centre

Case study 3, *R v Roger Martin*, can only be accessed through the Online Resource Centre. This case study is also based on a guilty plea and highlights sentencing practice and procedure in road traffic cases.

Case study 4 features Peter West, who has been arrested and detained at the police station in connection with an allegation of rape. The case study depicts the key stages of a suspect's detention and interrogation at the police station through to the decision whether or not to charge.

Our comprehensive Online Resource Centre brings the case studies to life through video clips which illustrate the following:

R v Lenny Whyte: mode of trial enquiry and contested application for bail;

R v William Hardy: plea before venue and sentencing hearing including a plea in mitigation;

R v Roger Martin (web-based only): sentencing hearing, including a plea in mitigation.

Case studies 1, 2 and 3 were filmed in March 2004 and feature principal participants who all have professional experience of the magistrates' courts, either as advocates or legal advisers.

The cases are heard before a bench of serving lay magistrates. All the participants very kindly agreed to give up their valuable time in order to assist us in making the films. The video clips should be viewed as learning aids in that they seek to illustrate, in a practical way, certain important stages of a criminal case in the magistrates' court. The videos are not necessarily a depiction of how cases always proceed and they should not be regarded as definitive examples of how advocacy might be conducted before a magistrates' court. Commentary on the clips is provided and transcripts (based for the most part on the principal submissions made by the advocates) are included in the documentation that supports the case studies.

Case Study 4 was filmed on location at an operational police station in November 2005. Documentation supporting this case study is available in the protected lecturer resource area. The case study depicts the key stages of a suspect's detention and interrogation at the police station through to the decision whether to charge, including the booking in procedure with the custody officer; the disclosure interview between the legal adviser and investigating officers; the interview between legal adviser and client; the police interview with the suspect, and the charging decision. The roles are played by serving police officers and an accredited police station legal adviser.

1.4 ONLINE RESOURCE CENTRE

Our Online Resource Centre can be accessed at www.oxfordtextbooks.co.uk/orc/lpccrim handbook2e/.

Features included on the website are fully explained in the 'Guided tour to the website' at page x, but it will be useful to introduce the resource here also. The website is divided into useful sections to help the individual reader, and includes the following resources:

Section 1: Password protected lecturer resources   A test bank of multiple choice questions test students' knowledge and understanding. High-quality video clips bring to life the key procedural stages of the Handbook's case studies and are formatted for download through broadband, suitable for viewing on a computer or intranet. Alternatively this resource is available as a higher resolution file on CD in order to project the clips onto a large screen in lectures. The clips include accompanying selective transcripts broadly based on the principal submissions made by the advocates. A selection of Codes of Practice and Guidelines, including the Magistrates' Court Sentencing Guidelines 2004.

Section 2: Open access lecturer resources   The video clips of court scenarios are available for online browsing intended for lecturers to review the material available.

Section 3: Student resources   These are freely available resources and include updates to cover recent developments in criminal litigation and criminal evidence, accompanied by useful web-links. There will also be complete documentation supporting case studies 1, 2 and 3.

Wherever you see this symbol there is a link to our Online Resource Centre.

In order to derive maximum benefit from the Handbook, we recommend you make full use of the learning and information resources of the Online Resource Centre.

1.5 LOOKING AHEAD – REFORMING THE LAW OF CRIMINAL LITIGATION AND EVIDENCE

You are studying criminal litigation and evidence at a time of profound change – the most radical for a generation. The main focus of the reforms has been the Criminal Justice Act 2003 (CJA 2003) which is largely based on the recommendations in Lord Justice Auld's *Review of the Criminal Courts*, which was published in October 2001. At various times during the last two years, the CJA 2003 has reformed some of the well-established rules of criminal evidence, sentencing and procedure. From 1 January 2006 the Serious Organised Crime and Police Act 2005 (SOCPA 2005) revised many of the investigatory powers used by the police on a daily basis, including the classification of criminal offences for the purposes of arrest, the powers of arrest and the issue of search warrants. Also, with effect from April 2005, the conduct of all criminal cases have been governed by the Criminal Procedure Rules (Crim PR) which has introduced a radical reformulation to the philosophy and management of criminal litigation and which is discussed in more detail at 1.9 below.

It is anticipated that during 2006/07 the CJA 2003 will introduce further important reforms to the procedure for determining the place of trial for either-way offences as well as extending the magistrates' powers to impose a custodial sentence of 12 months for any offence. Any proposed changes will be highlighted in the text by the heading 'Looking Ahead' and the following symbol.

A particular difficulty encountered by criminal practitioners and criminal litigation students is keeping up-to-date with these legislative developments as well as understanding the ways in which the courts are interpreting and applying the new provisions. As a matter of good practice, a LPC Criminal Litigation student should be aware of any changes not only for assessment and learning purposes but also job interviews. In addition to your own research, our Online Resource Centre will bring you any significant developments during 2006/07.

In addition the reforms introduced by the CJA 2003, you should also be aware that the Criminal Defence Service Act 2006 aims to change the criteria for eligibility for public funding in criminal cases. Looking further ahead, at the time of writing the Police and Justice Bill is before Parliament proposing changes to the legal powers exercised by the newly created Community Support Officers, as well as amending the law on police bail and extending stop and search powers. Finally, the Violent Crime Reduction Bill gives the police and local authorities increased powers to control the causes of alcohol-related violence and disorder and to deal the possession of real and imitation firearms. Expect further initiatives from the Prime Minister's office during the summer of 2006 as law and order will no doubt be high on the political agenda!

1.6 THE LPC MARKET

Communicating with colleagues who teach Criminal Litigation at other institutions has uncovered a diverse range of teaching strategies and approaches to satisfying the Law Society's requirements for both the core criminal litigation course and an advanced criminal litigation elective. We therefore encourage teachers and students not to use the Handbook in a prescriptive way, but to adapt the written materials, the case studies and the other learning resources to suit their specific needs.

1.7 RESEARCH SOURCES

Legal research is an integral part of your studies on the LPC. It is also an important skill that you will be required to apply in practice. While our Online Resource Centre provides invaluable links to related websites from which you can access further useful information, we also recommend the use of practitioner texts and practitioner journals.

1.7.1 PRACTITIONERS' WORKS

Blackstone's Criminal Practice

Also published by Oxford University Press, *Blackstone's Criminal Practice* is an established leading research source for criminal practitioners. Annually updated and written in an accessible and user-friendly way, *Blackstone's* provides a detailed explanation of the main substantive criminal offences, the key stages of criminal procedure and the rules of criminal evidence. *Blakestone's* is also available on CD-ROM.

Archbold Criminal Pleading and Practice

This well-established authoritative practitioner text is specifically directed to the practice and procedure of trials on indictment. *Archbold* now publishes a companion volume for proceedings in the magistrates' court.

Stone's Justices Manual

This is the most authoritative text for proceedings in the magistrates' court. *Stone's* is an indispensable source of reference for all criminal practitioners.

1.7.2 TEXTBOOKS

Defending Suspects at the Police Station (Ed Cape; published by the Legal Action Group)

This book offers a clear explanation covering all aspects of representing a client at the police station, including a detailed exposition of police powers and invaluable advice about the strategies to be adopted by the legal adviser.

Active Defence (Ede and Shepherd; Law Society Publications)

This is an excellent, informative guide to representing a client at the police station.

The Golden Rules of Advocacy (Keith Evans; Oxford University Press)

An informative, short and entertaining book!

1.7.3 JOURNALS

Journal articles provide an invaluable source of information on current issues and recent developments in criminal procedure and evidence.

Justice of the Peace

Published weekly, *Justice of the Peace* contains articles of interest and case analyses on issues of particular relevance to proceedings in the magistrates' court.

Criminal Law Review

You will have encountered this authoritative journal already during your academic studies. Published monthly, the *Review* contains articles on recent developments in substantive criminal law, procedure and evidence as well as informed analysis of recent cases.

Legal Action Group Magazine

This is a monthly publication from the Legal Action Group which contains articles of topical interest for the criminal practitioner and summaries of important cases.

General legal journals such as the *Solicitor's Journal, Counsel*, the *Legal Executive* and the *Law Society Gazette* may also contain articles of interest on criminal litigation and evidence and summaries of important developments and cases.

1.7.4 ELECTRONIC RESEARCH SOURCES

Electronic research sources from some of the key criminal justice organisations can be accessed via the web-links section from our Online Resource Centre.

online resource centre

1.8 A MATTER OF STYLE

The use of the masculine he/his should be taken to include she/her. In using the masculine we do not want to give the impression that all advocates within the criminal justice system and those who stand accused of committing criminal offence are male – far from it!

1.9 THE CRIMINAL PROCEDURE RULES

As we explained at section 1.5 above, you are studying Criminal Litigation and Evidence at a time of profound change. An important purpose of recent reforms has been an attempt to modernise the conduct and management of criminal cases. An important part of this strategy is the implementation of the Criminal Procedure Rules (Crim PR). The Rules have their origin in the Courts Act 2003, which established the Criminal Procedure Rule Committee. This was charged with task of creating a comprehensive procedural code for governing the conduct of all criminal cases. An integral part of the code is the creation of the Criminal Procedure Rules which came into force on 4 April 2005 and are intended to have the same effect on the conduct of criminal cases that Lord Woolf's *Access to Justice* report (July 1996) had on civil litigation through the creation of the Civil Procedure Rules.

The aim of the Criminal Procedure Rules is to bring about an evolutionary cultural change to the management of criminal cases. The Rules can be accessed from our Online Resource Centre (web-links section). In most situations the Criminal Procedure Rules simply consolidate and adopt the existing criminal procedure rules which had been located in various statutory instruments. All these rules are now brought together in a unified set covering all of the criminal courts. What is new however, is the identification of an overriding objective in Part 1 which pervades the application of the Rules.

The overriding objective under the new Code is that all criminal cases must be dealt with justly. Part 1.1 defines this to include:

(a) acquitting the innocent and convicting the guilty;

(b) dealing with the prosecution and the defence fairly;

(c) recognising the rights of a defendant, particularly those under Article 6 of the European Convention on Human Rights;

(d) respecting the interest of witnesses, victims and jurors and keeping them informed of the progress of the case;

(e) dealing with the case efficiently and expeditiously;

(f) ensuring that appropriate information is available to the court when bail and sentence are considered; and

(g) dealing with the case in ways that take into account –

   (i) the gravity of the offence alleged,

  (ii) the complexity of what is in issue,

 (iii) the severity of the consequences for the defendant and others affected, and

 (iv) the needs of other cases.

Each participant in a criminal case must prepare and conduct the case in accordance with the overriding objective, ensure compliance with the Criminal Procedure Rules and directions made by the court, and at once inform the court and all parties of any significant failure to take any procedural step required by the Rules.

The most significant aspect of the Criminal Procedure Rules is Part 3, which for the first time gives courts explicit powers to manage and progress criminal cases. It is the application of the rules in Part 3 that are intended to bring about an evolutionary change in culture. Part 3 requires courts to exercise their powers in accordance with the overriding objective. It makes clear the duties and responsibilities of all those engaged in the criminal justice system.

Part 3 further requires criminal courts to exercise effective case management procedures to ensure, *inter alia,* the early identification of the real issues in the case; the early identification of witness needs in every case; delay being discouraged, and the progress of cases monitored closely. Under the Rules for example, each party is now required to nominate an individual responsible for progressing the case. The court will also be required to nominate a court officer responsible for the progression of the case.

The Rules are intended to make the administration of criminal justice more efficient, with greater use being made of information technology. They are complemented by the Criminal Case Management Framework produced by the Department of Constitutional Affairs in July 2004. It can be accessed at http://www.cjsonline.gov.uk. Its purpose is to provide guidance on how adult cases prosecuted by the CPS might be managed most effectively and efficiently from pre-charge through to conclusion. The Criminal Procedure Rules are likely to be the subject of much comment and will continue to develop and be revised. Any significant developments will be included on the updating section of our Online Resource Centre.

SELF-TEST QUESTIONS

online
resource
centre

The documentation you are about to read can be found on our Online Resource Centre, and in Appendices 1 and 2 in this Handbook. All we would like you to do at this stage is to begin to familiarise yourself with our fictional clients Lenny Whyte and William Hardy and the nature of the accusation that has been made against each of them.

Case study 1: *R v Lenny Whyte.*

Read document 1 (Lenny Whyte's initial statement given to his solicitor) and documents 18(A)–(P) which comprise the nature of the prosecution's evidence against Lenny. What offence is Lenny Whyte charged with having committed?

Case study 2: *R v William Hardy.*

Read document 1 (William Hardy's initial statement given to his solicitor) and documents 10(A)–(E) which comprise the nature of the prosecution's evidence against William. What offence is William Hardy charged with having committed?

2

THE TERMINOLOGY OF CRIMINAL LITIGATION AND ITS PERSONNEL

2.1 INTRODUCTION

In your LPC studies and later in practice, you will need to understand and be able to use the terminology of the criminal justice system. Chapter 2 provides a brief overview of the classification of criminal offences according to their venue for trial, plus the jurisdiction and personnel of the criminal courts. Many of the points discussed in this chapter are considered in more detail later in the text.

2.2 CLASSIFICATION OF CRIMINAL OFFENCES ACCORDING TO THEIR TRIAL VENUE

The classification of an offence is important because it determines whether the case will be dealt with in the magistrates' court or Crown Court.

As Figure 2.1 shows, all criminal offences fall within one of three classifications. The classifications are:

- summary offences;
- offences triable either way; and
- indictable-only offences.

You should always check the classification of an offence you are dealing with, whether in an examination or in real life. After a while, you will start to remember the classification of the more common offences. The classification of all criminal offences can be researched in a practitioner work, such as *Blackstone's Criminal Practice*.

Summary offences

The least serious offences are known as summary offences and are dealt with summarily in the magistrates' court, whether the defendant pleads guilty or not guilty. The offence of common assault, under s. 39 Criminal Justice Act 1988, is a summary only offence. Under s. 127 Magistrates' Courts Act 1980, prosecution of a summary offence must normally be commenced within six months of the offence's commission.

Offences triable either way

Offences triable either way are middle-ranking offences in terms of their seriousness, and can be tried either summarily before magistrates or on indictment before a judge and jury in the Crown Court. An example of an either-way offence is theft, s. 1 Theft Act 1968. It is the defendant's indication of plea which determines where an either-way offence will be dealt with.

Where the defendant indicates a not guilty plea, the decision as to where an either-way offence will be tried is made at the mode of trial enquiry conducted in the magistrates' court under ss. 17–21 Magistrates' Courts Act 1980. Unless the magistrates decide that trial on indictment in the Crown Court is more appropriate or the defendant elects for trial in the Crown Court having been given the choice, the case will be tried summarily.

If the defendant indicates an intention to plead guilty, the case will remain in the magistrates' court, which will then consider the appropriate sentence with the possibility of committing the defendant for sentence in the Crown Court.

Indictable-only offences

The most serious crimes are known as indictable-only offences, they will be tried at the Crown Court before a judge and jury. The common law offence of murder and the statutory offence of robbery under s. 8 Theft Act 1968 are indictable-only offences. While the defendant's trial will be held in the Crown Court, the prosecution will commence in the magistrates' court. Following the defendant's initial appearance before a magistrates' court, his case is sent forthwith to the Crown Court for trial under s. 51 Crime and Disorder Act 1998.

2.3 THE INVESTIGATING AND PROSECUTING ORGANISATIONS

The responsibility for investigating and prosecuting a criminal offence is shared between several organisations.

The investigation of most criminal offences is undertaken by the police. Upon the completion of the investigation, the crime file is passed to the Crown Prosecution Service, which decides whether there is sufficient evidence to charge the suspect. The Crown Prosecution Service (CPS) is divided into 42 areas, which are aligned to the police forces of England and Wales.

The conduct of most day-to-day prosecutions in the magistrates' court or the Crown Court will be dealt with at a local CPS office by a Senior Crown Prosecutor or a Crown Prosecutor working in a Trial Unit or in a Criminal Justice Unit. A Senior Crown Prosecutor and a Crown Prosecutor will be either a solicitor or a barrister. As a criminal defence solicitor, you will have daily contact with Crown Prosecutors at the pre-trial stage and during the proceedings in the magistrates' court.

You will also deal with other CPS staff, including a Designated Caseworker and a Caseworker. A Designated Caseworker (DCW), who is not a formally qualified lawyer, is allowed to review and to present a limited range of cases in the magistrates' court. A Caseworker will assist the Crown Prosecutor by preparing cases, attending court, liaising with witnesses and criminal justice agencies as well as post-trial administration.

While the CPS clearly plays a dominant role in the prosecution of criminal offences (in 2002/03, the CPS dealt with 1.4 million cases sent by the police and prosecuted 1.08 million defendants in the magistrates' courts and 80,000 cases in the Crown Court), other state agencies also investigate and prosecute criminal offences in specific areas of responsibility:

- The Health and Safety Executive (HSE) investigates and prosecutes criminal offences arising from accidents in the workplace under the Health And Safety At Work Act 1974.
- Local authorities investigate and prosecute offences under the Trade Descriptions Act 1968, Education Act 1996, environmental law cases and prosecutions relating to food and hygiene.
- the Department of Trade and Industry investigates and prosecutes a large number of offences involving companies and company officers, including directors.
- The Environmental Agency investigates and prosecutes environmental crime in all its forms.
- The Serious Fraud Office investigates and prosecutes serious or complex fraud.
- HM Revenue and Customs prosecutes offences relating to evasion of tax and customs duties.
- The Serious Organised Crime Agency has recently been created by the Serious Organised Crime and Police Act 2005. The agency will assume responsibility for the investigation and conduct of cases previously dealt with by the National Criminal Intelligence Service, the Home Office Immigration Crime Unit and HM Revenue and Customs.

2.4 THE LEGAL SERVICES COMMISSION AND THE CRIMINAL DEFENCE SERVICE

In some cases, most notably road traffic offences, the costs of your client's legal representation will be privately funded out of his income and/or capital unless he has legal expenses insurance or the costs are being paid for by a third party such as his employer.

Where your client is charged with a more serious offence it is likely that the costs of his legal representation at various stages of the case will be paid for or subsidised by the state under various funding schemes. A detailed examination of the various legal aid schemes is considered in Chapter 14.

Criminal legal aid is supervised by the Legal Services Commission with the day-to-day administration of the scheme undertaken by the Criminal Defence Service (CDS). There are approximately 2,900 solicitors' firms having contracts with the Legal Services Commission to provide criminal legal aid through the CDS. In 2002/03 almost £1.1 billion was spent on criminal legal aid.

Where a solicitors' firm is franchised to provide criminal legal aid, the firm receives block monthly payments from the CDS for undertaking work under the scheme. The firm then submits monthly reports to enable the CDS to adjust the block payments up or down, to correspond with the amount of work undertaken.

2.5 THE PUBLIC DEFENDER SERVICE

The recently established Public Defender Service (PDS) provides an alternative to a criminal client seeking advice and representation from a solicitor in private practice. Through the Legal Services Commission, the PDS employs criminal defence solicitors to provide advice and assistance to clients. As part of the pilot project eight PDS offices are located in Liverpool, Chester, Birmingham, Middlesbrough, Darlington, Swansea, Pontypridd and Cheltenham to assess the effectiveness of the scheme.

2.6 THE CRIMINAL COURTS

It is likely that you will have studied the hierarchy of the criminal courts during your academic studies. This section and Figure 2.2 are intended to briefly remind you of the jurisdiction of the courts within the criminal justice system.

2.6.1 MAGISTRATES' COURT

As a criminal defence solicitor, the vast majority of your time will be spent preparing for and appearing in cases listed in the magistrates' court (also referred to as summary proceedings).

The magistrates' court is the workhorse of the criminal justice system. Virtually all criminal prosecutions commence in the magistrates' court, and magistrates try approximately 98 per cent of all criminal cases. Only two per cent of contested cases are heard in the Crown Court. The practice and procedure in the magistrates' court is governed by the Magistrates' Courts Act 1980 and the Criminal Procedure Rules.

The magistrates' court has the following jurisdictions:

- tries summary offences;
- tries offences triable either way that are considered suitable for summary trial by the magistrates where the defendant has consented to summary trial;
- deals with certain preliminary matters during the early stages of all prosecutions including:
  - the defendant's application for a representation order under the Access to Justice Act 1999;
  - the defendant's bail application;
  - ordering the disclosure of prosecution evidence against the defendant;
- hears mode of trial proceedings under ss. 17–21 Magistrates' Courts Act 1980 to decide where either-way offences should be tried;
- commits a defendant under ss. 3 and 4 Powers of Criminal Courts (Sentencing) Act 2000 to the Crown Court for sentence where he has pleaded guilty or has been found guilty of an either-way offence and the magistrates consider their sentencing powers are too limited to deal with the defendant;
- hears committal proceedings under ss. 6 (1) or 6 (2) Magistrates' Courts Act 1980 in respect of an either-way offence which the magistrates believe is suitable to be tried at the Crown Court, or where the defendant has elected trial at the Crown Court;
- sends indictable-only offences to the Crown Court for trial under s. 51 Crime and Disorder Act 1998.

2.6.2 MAGISTRATES

A magistrate is either a justice of the peace or a district judge. Lay magistrates are unpaid, and while they are not required to hold any formal legal qualifications, all magistrates undergo a period of induction and training. They are required to 'sit' for a prescribed number of days each year. There are approximately 30,000 active lay magistrates in England and Wales, who normally try cases sitting as part of a Bench of three.

District judges are appointed from solicitors and barristers who have been qualified for at least seven years and are paid a salary. A district judge hears a case sitting alone and can exercise all the powers of a Bench of lay magistrates. Section 65 of the Courts Act 2003 now enables district judges to exercise some of the powers of recorders who sit as judges in the Crown Court in certain cases.

2.6.3 THE JUSTICES' LEGAL ADVISER

When conducting a summary trial, the lay justices will be assisted by an adviser, who will usually be a solicitor or barrister. The law maintains a strict division of responsibilities between the magistrates and their adviser. The magistrates are the sole arbiters of law and fact. The *Practice Direction (Criminal Proceedings: Consolidation)* [2000] 1 WLR 2870 provides that the adviser will sit with lay magistrates to advise the Bench on matters of law, evidence, human rights points and procedure. The adviser will also put the charge to the accused, take a note of the evidence in the case and help an unrepresented accused present his case.

When the justices retire to consider their verdict the adviser may only advise them on points of law and evidence (*Stafford Justices, ex parte Ross* [1962] 1 WLR 456).

2.7 THE YOUTH COURT

As a general rule, where the defendant is under 18, he should be dealt with in the youth court. All magistrates' courts have a youth court panel of specially trained magistrates who have been appointed because of their suitability for dealing with juvenile cases. The practice and procedure is more informal and less intimidating than in the adult court.

The youth court has the following characteristics:

• it will be a 'closed' court, as the public are excluded from the court proceedings;
• only those involved in the proceedings will be present;
• the young person will not sit in the dock but will sit with a parent or guardian in front of the magistrates;
• the court must consist of no more than three magistrates, one of whom must be a man and one a woman;
• the young person will be addressed by his first name;
• a young person is asked whether he admits or denies the offence;
• the Bench records a finding of guilt against the juvenile, not a conviction.

A district judge (who has undertaken the required training) may also sit alone in the youth court.

2.8 THE CROWN COURT

The Courts Act 1971 created the Crown Court to deal with cases to be tried on indictment before a judge and jury. The practice and procedure in the Crown Court is now governed by the Supreme Court Act 1981 and the Criminal Procedure Rules and has the following jurisdictions:

• tries offences triable either way committed for trial at the Crown Court;
• tries indictable-only offences;
• sentences offenders committed for sentence by the magistrates' courts in relation to an either-way offence under ss. 3 and 4 Powers of Criminal Courts (Sentencing) Act 2000;
• hears appeals against conviction by a magistrates' court and/or against sentences imposed by the magistrates.

Section 66 Courts Act 2003 now enables a Crown Court judge to exercise the powers of a district judge (magistrates' court).

The following types of judge preside over sittings of the Crown Court:

- High Court judges;
- circuit judges; and
- recorders and assistant recorders, who are part-time judicial officers.

2.9 THE HIGH COURT (QUEEN'S BENCH DIVISION)

The Queen's Bench Division of the High Court has a limited jurisdiction in criminal matters. An action in judicial review can be commenced in the Queen's Bench Division against a public body such as the CPS for exceeding or misusing its legal powers or for not following the correct procedure or for exercising its legal powers in an 'irrational' way.

The Divisional Court of the Queen's Bench Division hears appeals by way of case stated under s. 111 MCA 1980 from either the prosecution or defence in criminal cases heard in the magistrates' court. Appeal by way of case stated is appropriate where it is submitted that the magistrates have misinterpreted a point of law or evidence.

2.10 THE COURT OF APPEAL (CRIMINAL DIVISION)

The jurisdiction of the Court of Appeal (Criminal Division) requires that the Court hears appeals against conviction and/or sentence from those cases tried in the Crown Court, and hears points of law referred by the Attorney-General. The work of the Court is presided over by the Lord Chief Justice. Cases are normally heard by the Lord Chief Justice sitting with two puisne judges, or a Lord Justice of Appeal sitting with two ordinary judges.

The Court of Appeal hears appeals against conviction and/or sentence from the Crown Court and gives guidance on the procedures and practices of the criminal courts.

2.11 THE HOUSE OF LORDS

The judicial work of the House of Lords is presided over by the Lord Chancellor. It is the highest court in the criminal jurisdiction and hears appeals from the Court of Appeal on points of law of public importance. Leave to appeal is required.

2.12 PERSONNEL AND THE CRIMINAL PROCEDURE RULES

All those involved in the conduct of criminal cases must discharge their duties and responsibilities in accordance with the overriding objective in Part 1 of the Criminal Procedure Rules (highlighted in Chapter 1), which is that all criminal cases be dealt with justly.

KEY POINT SUMMARY

- Understand that all criminal offences are classified as either summary, either-way or indictable-only offences.
- Research the classifications of the offence/s you are dealing with.
- Criminal litigation examiners often set questions on the procedure to be followed in the prosecution of either-way offences!
- Know the jurisdiction of the main criminal courts.

1. How are the following offences classified according to place of trial? (You may have to do some legal research to discover the answer. A good place to start is *Blackstone's Criminal Practice*.)

    (i)   Criminal damage where the value of the damaged property is less than £5,000, s. 1 Criminal Damage Act 1971.

    (ii) Criminal damage where the value of the damaged property is more than £5,000.

    (iii) Possession of a controlled drug, s. 5 Misuse of Drugs Act 1971.

    (iv) Careless driving, s. 3 Road Traffic Act 1988.

    (v)   Murder.

FIGURE 2.1 CLASSIFICATION OF OFFENCES ACCORDING TO PLACE OF TRIAL

- **Summary offences**
  - least serious offences;
  - tried summarily in the magistrates' court;
  - e.g. taking a conveyance without consent, s. 12 Theft Act 1968;
  - e.g. careless and inconsiderate driving, s. 3 Road Traffic Act 1988;
  - e.g. common assault, s. 39 Criminal Justice Act 1988;
  - e.g. causing harassment, alarm or distress, s. 5 Public Order Act 1986.

- **Either-way offences**
  - middle-ranking offences;
  - e.g. theft, s. 1 Theft Act 1968;
  - e.g. affray, s. 3 Public Order Act 1986;
  - e.g. burglary, s. 9 Theft Act 1968;
  - e.g. assault occasioning actual bodily harm, s. 47 Offences Against the Person Act 1861.
  - tried either summarily or on indictment in the Crown Court;
  - decision as to trial venue taken at the mode of trial where D indicates a not guilty plea or makes no indication of plea.

- **Indictable-only offences**
  - most serious offences;
  - e.g. murder;
  - e.g. robbery, s. 8 Theft Act 1968;
  - e.g. rape, s. 1 Sexual Offences Act 2003.
  - case commences in the magistrates' court;
  - trial takes place on indictment before a judge and jury in the Crown Court.

FIGURE 2.2 THE CRIMINAL COURTS

MAGISTRATES' COURT

- tries summary offences;
- tries either-way offences considered suitable for summary trial;
- sends indictable-only offences the Crown Court for trial, s. 51 Crime and Disorder Act 1998;
- hears mode of trial proceedings in either-way offences, ss. 17–21 Magistrates' Courts Act 1980;
- holds committal proceedings in either-way offences to be tried on indictment, s. 6(1) or s. 6(2) MCA;
- deals with preliminary matters including bail and representation orders.

CROWN COURT

- tries indictable-only offences;
- tries either-way offences committed for trial on indictment;
- sentences those committed from the magistrates' court for sentence;
- hears appeals against conviction and / or sentence from the magistrates' court.

HIGH COURT (QUEEN'S BENCH DIVISION)

- hears appeals by way of case stated, s. 111 Magistrates' Courts Act 1980;
- hears judicial review cases.

COURT OF APPEAL (CRIMINAL DIVISION)

- hears appeals against conviction and/or sentence from the Crown Court;
- issues practice directions on criminal procedure and sentencing.

HOUSE OF LORDS

- hears appeals on a points of law of public importance in cases referred from the Court of Appeal (Criminal Division).

3   AN OVERVIEW OF A CRIMINAL CASE

3.1   INTRODUCTION

This overview chapter explains:

- the police investigation;
- prosecuting a summary offence;
- prosecuting an either-way offence;
- prosecuting an indictable-only offence.

The various stages mentioned in this chapter are covered in considerably more detail later in the text.

3.2   THE POLICE INVESTIGATION OF THE OFFENCE

A criminal case usually begins with a police investigation into whether an offence has been committed. When investigating the offence, the police will interview witnesses and anyone suspected of being involved in the offence. Written statements will be taken which will form the basis of the prosecution case if the matter proceeds to trial. To assist in the criminal investigation and to uncover sufficient evidence to charge the suspect or to eliminate him from their enquiries, the police will use various statutory powers, including:

- the power to stop and search the suspect's person or motor vehicle;

- the power to search his property;
- the power of arrest;
- the power to detain the suspect at the police station;
- the power to interview a suspect on tape or by recording the interview in writing;
- the power to interview a witness;
- the power to take fingerprints and intimate or non-intimate samples;
- the power to convene an identification procedure such as holding an identification parade, a video identification or a group identification.

Many of these powers are exercised where an individual is suspected of having committed the offence and has been arrested. Alternatively, a person may voluntarily assist the police without being arrested. This is commonly known as 'helping the police with their enquiries'.

Where the suspect is detained at the police station after arrest or as a volunteer, he will be entitled to have a legal adviser present to ensure that his rights under the Police and Criminal Evidence Act 1984 are respected by the police. The legal advice given at the police station is free of charge for the most part. The role of the legal adviser at the police station is both crucial and influential. We consider this role in some detail in Chapter 12.

3.3 THE DECISION TO CHARGE

The decision to charge a suspect at the police station will be taken by the CPS or in some limited circumstances by the custody officer. Where a decision is taken to charge the suspect he will be issued with a charge sheet. The charge sheet constitutes the 'information' on which the defendant will be tried. The charge sheet will include a date upon which the defendant must make his initial appearance before a magistrates' court.

If the defendant has been charged at the police station he may be released on police bail or kept in custody until his first appearance in the magistrates' court. Where there is insufficient evidence to charge, the police may release the suspect on police bail while enquiries continue.

3.4 COMMENCING THE PROSECUTION

Sometimes, instead of charging an individual at the police station, a prosecution is commenced by the prosecution 'laying an information'. The 'information' is a written document alleging the commission of an offence by a particular individual which requires the magistrates' court to issue a summons or warrant for arrest against the person named. The decision to commence a prosecution by laying an information is most commonly used in the case of minor summary offences. The summons is a document addressed to the accused containing particulars of the offence together with the time and date when he must appear before the magistrates' court.

Looking Ahead

When ss. 28–31 CJA 2003 come into in force, references to an 'information' are to be construed as references to a written charge, and references to a summons are to be construed as references to a requisition. Under these provisions all public prosecutions will commence by the prosecutor issuing a written charge and 'requisition' requiring the person to appear before a magistrates' court to answer the written charge. Each of these documents will need to be served on the defendant and the court. A public prosecutor includes the police, CPS and various government agencies.

3.5 PROSECUTING A SUMMARY OFFENCE

The prosecution of a summary offence such as common assault or careless driving can begin with the defendant being charged at the police station or by the issue of a summons.

In some straightforward cases, the accused may be in a position to plead guilty to the summary offence at a very early stage in the proceedings (possibly at his first appearance before magistrates). In other cases, the defence may seek an adjournment and request disclosure of the prosecution's evidence so that an evaluation of the prosecution's case can be undertaken before offering a client advice on the appropriate plea.

As you will see, the prosecution must disclose the nature of the evidence it intends to use to prove the defendant's guilt. The obligation is made clear in the Attorney-General's Guidelines on Disclosure. This evidence is referred to as 'used' material, as the CPS will use the evidence against the defendant at trial. The disclosure of this evidence by the CPS is commonly known 'Advance Information'.

3.5.1 PLEADING GUILTY TO A SUMMARY OFFENCE

A defendant may plead guilty to a summary offence. If a guilty plea is entered, the magistrates will proceed to sentence him. At the sentencing hearing, the Crown Prosecutor or Designated Caseworker will present the facts of the case and the defendant's previous convictions to the magistrates. The defendant's solicitor or the court duty solicitor will then address the court about any factors which are relevant to the offence or about the defendant's personal circumstances. This is known as a plea in mitigation, and its purpose is to persuade the court to impose a less severe sentence that might otherwise be imposed. The defendant may then be sentenced by the magistrates, or, where the court needs more information about the defendant, the probation service may be instructed to prepare a pre-sentence report and sentence will be passed at the next hearing.

3.5.2 PLEADING NOT GUILTY TO A SUMMARY OFFENCE

Where the defendant indicates a not guilty plea to a summary offence, the case will be adjourned and a date set for the defendant's summary trial.

If a not guilty plea is entered in relation to a summary offence, the CPS comes under further disclosure obligations under the Criminal Procedure and Investigations Act 1996 (CPIA). This Act requires the prosecution to disclose any 'unused' evidence to the defence. 'Unused' evidence consists of witness statements or other material obtained by the police during the criminal investigation which will not form part of the prosecution case at trial as it may undermine the prosecution case or assist the defence case. The issue of the pre-trial disclosure of evidence is of fundamental importance within the criminal justice system. We consider disclosure in its entirety in Chapter 17.

At a summary trial, the prosecution will open the proceedings by making a brief opening speech and by calling its witnesses. Each prosecution witness will be cross-examined by the defence. At the close of the prosecution case the defence will call its witnesses, who in turn will be cross-examined by the prosecutor. The defence advocate may then make a closing speech. The justices retire to consider their verdict. On a finding of guilt, the defence advocate will make a plea in mitigation and the defendant may be sentenced immediately or the decision may be adjourned until a later date where a pre-sentence report is requested by the court.

3.5.3 AN APPEAL FROM SUMMARY PROCEEDINGS

An appeal against conviction and / or sentence from a decision of the magistrates will usually be heard in the Crown Court. Where the appeal is against conviction, there will be a complete rehearing of the case.

Appeals are considered in more detail in Chapter 33.

The progress of a typical summary-only case is illustrated in Figure 3.1.

3.6 PROSECUTING AN EITHER-WAY OFFENCE

The prosecution of an either-way offence such as burglary will normally commence after the suspect has been arrested and charged at the police station. The charge sheet will detail the criminal offence(s) alleged against the accused. He will then either be released on police bail or kept in custody until his first court hearing in the magistrates' court.

3.6.1 THE DEFENDANT'S FIRST COURT HEARING

An important procedure that will be dealt with at this stage is the defendant's absolute right to the disclosure of used material. This is known as advance information.

The rules relating to this disclosure are contained in Part 21 Crim PR. The material that will be disclosed at this stage by the CPS must include:

* a précis of the prosecution witness's evidence against the accused; or

* copies of the prosecution witness statements;

Advance information will also usually include a summary of or copy of any tape-recorded interview and details of the defendant's criminal record.

Advance information may not be available in time for the defendant's initial appearance before a magistrates' court. Often the defendant's initial appearance in connection with an either-way offence is likely to be adjourned to allow the CPS time to serve advance information on the defence.

At this initial hearing, the magistrates may also deal with the defendant's application for public funding by granting or refusing a representation order and his entitlement to be released on bail, unless the court concludes the defendant should be remanded in custody.

3.6.2 PLEA BEFORE VENUE AND MODE OF TRIAL

The next court hearing usually decides whether the trial will be held in the magistrates' court or in the Crown Court.

The proceedings begin with the plea before venue where the defendant indicates to the court whether he would plead guilty or not guilty if the case were to proceed to trial. If he indicates that he would plead guilty the case is dealt with summarily and a guilty plea is entered.

Where the defendant indicates that he will plead not guilty if the case proceeds to trial, a mode of trial hearing will be held. Unless there is agreement as to the place of trial, both the Crown Prosecutor and the defence advocate will address the court on whether the trial should be held in the magistrates' court or in the Crown Court.

The decision about where the defendant ought to be tried lies initially with the magistrates, who take into account the submissions made by the prosecution and the defence, guidance contained in the National Mode of Trial Guidelines and a number of 'statutory' factors contained in s. 19 Magistrates' Court Act.

Where the magistrates consider that trial on indictment in the Crown Court is appropriate, the proceedings will be adjourned until a committal hearing can be held. If the magistrates believe that the case may be tried summarily, the defendant has the right to elect trial either in the Crown Court or before magistrates. If trial on indictment is chosen, the case will be adjourned for a committal hearing to be held. Where the defendant chooses summary trial, the case will be listed for a summary trial.

Once committed for trial, the procedure is the same as for indictable-only considered below. The progress of a typical either-way case is illustrated in Figure 3.2.

Important changes to the mode of trial procedure and the abolition of committal for trial are contained in the Criminal Justice Act 2003. The latest date for implementation of these changes is November 2006.

3.7 PROSECUTING AN INDICTABLE-ONLY OFFENCE

The prosecution of an indictable-only offence will begin in the magistrates' court.

3.7.1 THE DEFENDANT'S INITIAL APPEARANCE

At this first hearing, the court will deal with the defendant's application for a representation order and bail. The magistrates will then send the case to the Crown Court for trial under s. 51 Crime and Disorder Act 1998.

3.7.2 THE DEFENDANT'S FIRST APPEARANCE IN THE CROWN COURT

The defendant will make his first appearance before a Crown Court judge either at a preliminary hearing or at a Plea and Case Management Hearing.

3.7.3 SERVICE OF PROSECUTION EVIDENCE

After the case has been sent for trial, the CPS is required to serve the witness statements and other evidence upon which they will rely at trial on the defence. This is known in many CPS areas as the 'case sent bundle' and comprises 'used' material (defined above in the context of either-way offences).

At the same time, s. 3 Criminal Procedure and Investigations Act 1996 requires the prosecution to provide the accused with initial disclosure of 'unused' evidence. Such evidence is defined as any evidence which will not be used by the prosecution at trial which has not previously been disclosed and which would, reasonably be considered capable of undermining the case for the prosecution, or of assisting the case for the accused.

After initial prosecution disclosure, s. 5 CPIA 1996 requires the accused to file a defence statement, indicating which aspects of the prosecution case he takes issue with and for what reasons and also giving particulars of any defence or alibi he intends to rely on at trial. The filing of a defence statement is obligatory for cases tried on indictment. It is optional where cases are to be tried summarily. Once a defence statement has been filed, s. 7A CPIA 1996 provides that the CPS must look again at any previously undisclosed evidence and decide whether any of it falls within the definition of evidence that could reasonably be said to assist the defendant having regard to what he has said in his defence statement.

3.7.4 THE PLEA AND CASE MANAGEMENT HEARING

In preparing for trial there will be a Plea and Case Management Hearing (PCMH). At the PCMH, the defendant will be arraigned, i.e. required to plead guilty or not guilty.If the defendant pleads not guilty, final arrangements will be made for the trial, and based on information provided by all parties to the case, a trial date will be set. Binding decisions on matters of law and evidence may also be made.

If the defendant pleads guilty at the PCMH, the defendant may be sentenced at the hearing or the case may be adjourned for pre-sentence reports to be compiled.

3.7.5 CROWN COURT TRIAL

At the Crown Court trial where the defendant pleads not guilty, the prosecutor will make an opening speech once the jury has been sworn, after which he will call his witnesses. Each witness will be cross-examined by the defence advocate.

At the close of the prosecution case, the defence may make a submission of no case to answer where the prosecution has failed to prove an essential element of the offence or the prosecution evidence has been manifestly discredited, as in *R v Galbraith* [1981] 2 All ER 1060.

Where the submission is not made or is unsuccessful, the defence will call its witnesses who will then be cross-examined by the prosecution. At the close of the defence case, the prosecutor will make a closing speech; the defence will then make a closing speech and the judge will direct the jury on points of law and evidence. The jury will then retire to consider its verdict. On a finding of guilty, the defendant may be sentenced forthwith or the sentencing hearing may be adjourned for the preparation of pre-sentence reports.

3.7.6 APPEALS AGAINST CONVICTION AND/OR SENTENCE FROM THE CROWN COURT

Appeals arising out of conviction and sentence in the Crown Court are heard by the Court of Appeal. Leave to appeal must be sought.

The progress of a typical indictable-only offence is illustrated by Figure 3.3.

KEY POINT SUMMARY

- Be aware that most criminal cases involve investigation by the police and other state agencies which use statutory powers of search, seizure, arrest and detention against a suspect.
- Criminal cases will commence either by the issue of a summons or by the police charging a suspect.
- The CPS or other prosecuting agency prosecutes the case through court.
- All offences are classified as summary-only, either-way or indictable-only, and this determines their place of trial.
- All prosecutions begin in the magistrates' court where preliminary matters relating to legal aid, the early disclosure of evidence by the prosecution and bail are determined.
- The prosecution must make available to the defence all the evidence it intends to use against the defendant at trial and in a number of instances will be required to disclose unused material.
- Be aware of the procedures that a case follows from investigation to trial.
- All the areas introduced in this chapter are dealt with in more detail at appropriate places elsewhere in the text.

SELF-TEST QUESTIONS

1. Who decides whether there is sufficient evidence to charge a suspect?
2. Does the prosecution have to disclose the evidence it intends to use at trial in summary cases?
3. In what kind of case will a mode of trial hearing be held?
4. Before which court will a defendant charged with an indictable-only offence make his first appearance?
5. Which court will generally hear a defendant's appeal against conviction in summary proceedings?

FIGURE 3.1 SUMMARY OFFENCE

INVESTIGATION

↓

CHARGE	SUMMONS

↓

Initial appearance before magistrates' court

↓

If pleading guilty at initial appearance, likely to be sentenced immediately or following an adjournment for pre-sentence report

↓

If pleading not guilty, matters of bail and legal aid will be dealt with at the initial appearance. The initial hearing will be adjourned to facilitate the service of prosecution evidence and to check on the availability of witnesses in the case. At the subsequent hearing, a date ought to be set for a summary trial.

FIGURE 3.2 EITHER-WAY OFFENCE

INVESTIGATION

↓

CHARGE   SUMMONS

↓

Defendant will make Initial appearance in magistrates' court. If pleading guilty straight away, the defendant is likely to be sentenced immediately or following an adjournment for pre-sentence report

↓

If pleading not guilty or if unsure as to plea, matters of bail and legal aid will be dealt with. Advance information should be requested if unavailable. If it is not available at the initial appearance, an adjournment will be ordered pending service of advance information. The next appearance should be the plea before venue/mode of trial enquiry

↓

If advance information has been made available and instructions have been taken on it, the defendant should be in a position to indicate his plea. If guilty, the defendant will be sentenced immediately or following an adjournment. If not guilty, a mode of trial enquiry will be held. Magistrates may decline jurisdiction, in which case the matter will be adjourned for a committal hearing to take place. If the magistrates consent to a summary trial, the defendant may choose to elect trial by jury, in which case the matter will be adjourned for a committal hearing. If magistrates accept jurisdiction, and the defendant consents to a summary trial, an adjournment will follow and a date will be set for a summary trial

↓

At the committal hearing, if there is a case to answer, the matter will be committed to the Crown Court where a date will be set for a Plea and Case Management Hearing (PCMH)

↓

At the PCMH the defendant will enter his plea. If guilty he may be sentenced there and then or following an adjournment. If not guilty an adjournment will follow and a date will be set for a Crown Court trial

FIGURE 3.3 INDICTABLE OFFENCE

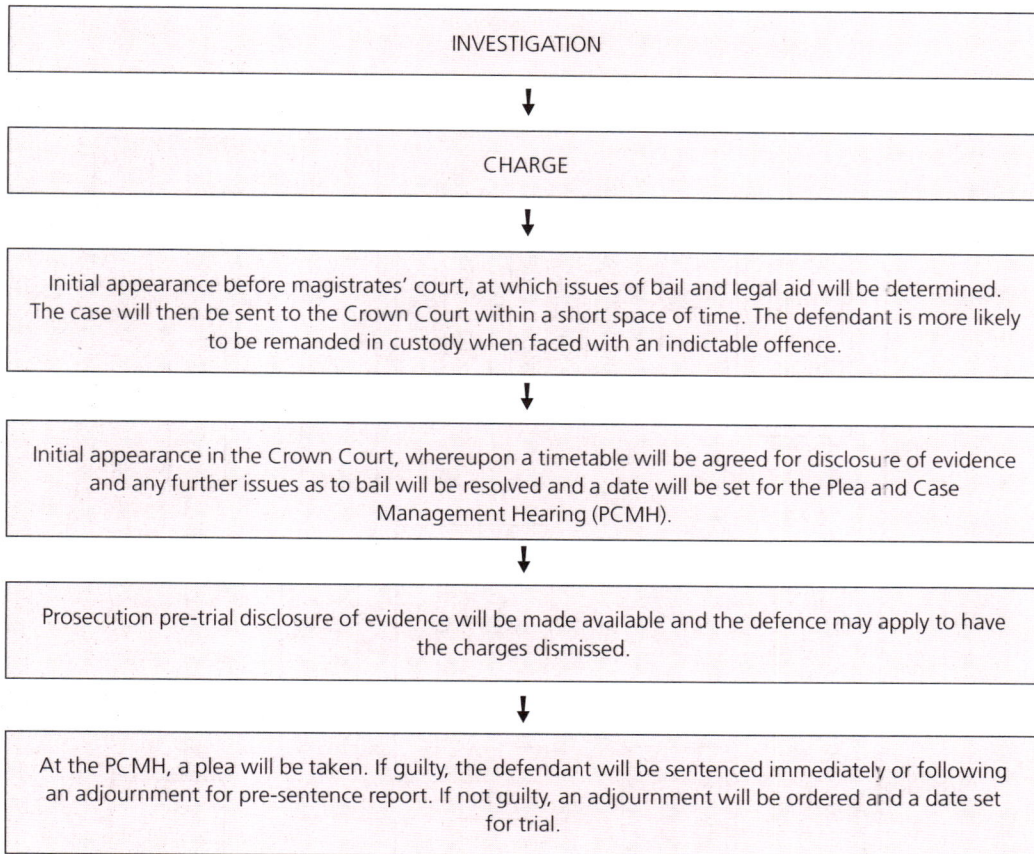

INVESTIGATION

↓

CHARGE

↓

Initial appearance before magistrates' court, at which issues of bail and legal aid will be determined. The case will then be sent to the Crown Court within a short space of time. The defendant is more likely to be remanded in custody when faced with an indictable offence.

↓

Initial appearance in the Crown Court, whereupon a timetable will be agreed for disclosure of evidence and any further issues as to bail will be resolved and a date will be set for the Plea and Case Management Hearing (PCMH).

↓

Prosecution pre-trial disclosure of evidence will be made available and the defence may apply to have the charges dismissed.

↓

At the PCMH, a plea will be taken. If guilty, the defendant will be sentenced immediately or following an adjournment for pre-sentence report. If not guilty, an adjournment will be ordered and a date set for trial.

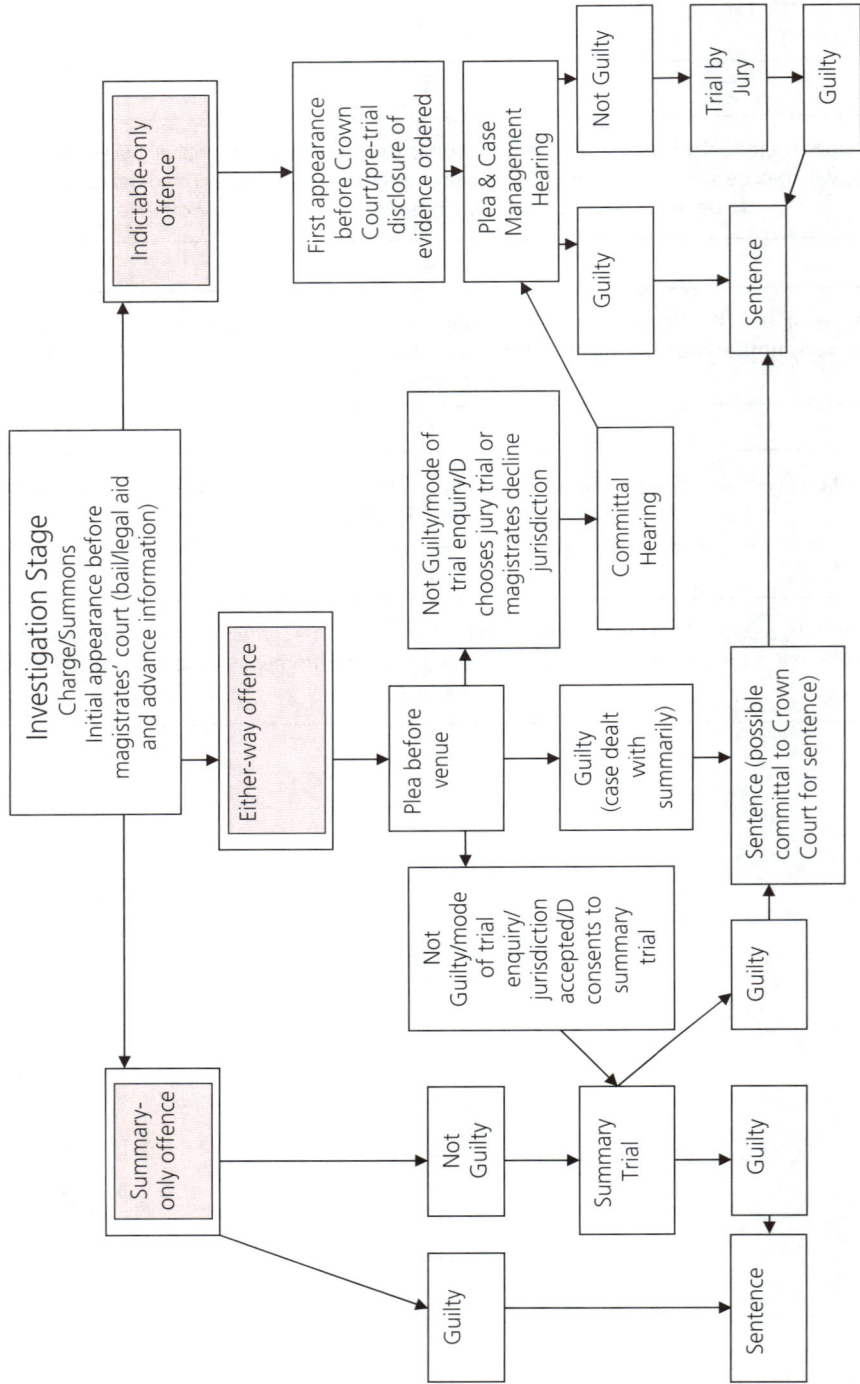

FIGURE 3.4

4.1   INTRODUCTION

In addition to studying litigation, business law and property, the LPC syllabus requires students to have an understanding of those topics which pervade the LPC.

The pervasive subjects are European Community law, revenue law, the European Convention on Human Rights, and professional conduct. This chapter explains the two pervasive subjects most relevant to Criminal Litigation – the European Convention on Human Rights 1950 and professional conduct.

The third topic featured in this chapter is advocacy. Advocacy is an LPC skill which is commonly assessed as part of the Criminal Litigation course.

In this chapter we specifically consider:

- the European Convention on Human Rights 1950;
- protecting your client's rights under the Human Rights Act 1998;
- professional conduct;
- the principles of good advocacy.

4.2 **THE EUROPEAN CONVENTION ON HUMAN RIGHTS (ECHR) 1950**

As a pervasive subject, an ECHR point may arise in any of the core subjects, or in the electives or as part of a skills assessment. However, since its implementation in domestic law in October 2000 by the Human Rights Act (HRA) 1998, the ECHR has had a greater influence on criminal procedure and evidence than in any other area of legal practice. To deal successfully with the demands of the Criminal Litigation course, the LPC student should have a good working knowledge of the following ECHR Articles.

Article 3 – the prohibition of torture

'No one shall be subjected to torture or inhuman or degrading treatment or punishment.'

This provision is of limited importance but may be invoked when challenging the admissibility of your client's confession on the ground that it had been obtained by 'oppression' under s. 76(2)(a) PACE 1984. Article 3 will be relevant when arguing that the manner in which the police interrogated your client – for example by shouting or making threats – breached Convention law.

Article 3 is an absolute right from which no derogation is permitted.

Article 5 – the right to liberty and security

'1. Everyone has the right to liberty and security of person. No one shall be deprived of liberty save in the following cases and in accordance with a procedure prescribed by law:

(a) the lawful detention of a person after conviction by a competent court;

(b) the lawful arrest or detention of a person for non-compliance of a lawful order of a court . . . ;

(c) the lawful arrest and detention of a person except for the purpose of bringing him before a court of competent legal authority on reasonable suspicion of having committed an offence or fleeing after having done so; . . .

2. Everyone who is arrested shall be informed promptly, in a language which he understands, of the reasons for his arrest and of any charge against him.

3. Everyone arrested or detained in accordance with paragraph 1c shall be entitled to trial within a reasonable time or to release pending trial. Release may be conditioned by guarantees to appear for trial

4. Everyone who is deprived of his liberty by arrest or detention shall be entitled to take proceedings by which the lawfulness of his detention shall be decided speedily by a court

5. Everyone who has been the victim of arrest or detention in contravention of the provisions of this article shall have an enforceable right to compensation.'

Article 5 is a qualified right allowing a state to derogate from it in defined circumstances.

Article 5 may be invoked where your client has been unlawfully arrested or otherwise detained by the police. For example, Article 5 will be relevant when challenging the decision of the police or the court to refuse your client bail.

Article 6 – the right to a fair trial

'1. In the determination of his civil rights and obligations, or of any criminal charge against him everyone is entitled to a fair and public hearing within a reasonable time by an independent and impartial tribunal established by law. Judgment shall be pronounced publicly but the press or public may be excluded in the interests of morals, public order or national security in a democratic society, where the interests of juveniles or the protection of private life of the parties so require, or to the extent strictly necessary in the opinion of the court in special circumstances where publicity would prejudice the interests of justice.

2. Everyone charged with a criminal offence shall be presumed innocent until proved guilty according to the law.

3. Everyone charged with a criminal offence has the following minimum rights:

(a) to be informed promptly, in a language which he understands and in detail of the nature and cause of the accusation against him;

(b) to have adequate time and facilities for the preparation of his defence;

(c) to defend himself in person or through legal assistance of his own choosing or, if he has not sufficient means to pay for legal assistance, to be given it free when the interests of justice so require;

(d) to examine or have examined witnesses against him and to obtain the attendance and examination of witnesses on his behalf under the same conditions as witnesses against him;

(e) to have the free assistance of an interpreter if he cannot understand or speak the language used in court.'

Article 6 is the most significant Article for criminal litigators and is relevant at all stages of a criminal case, including:

- the defendant's right to have legal representation at the police and at trial;
- the procedural and evidential rules adopted by the court at trial; and
- the principles applied when passing sentence.

The right to a fair trial in Article 6(1) is drafted in absolute terms. What constitutes a fair trial, however, is not defined. The presumption of innocence in Article 6(2) and the provisions of Article 6(3) are specified minimum general components of a fair trial. The jurisprudence of the European Court of Human Rights has implied a number of rights into Article 6, including the privilege against self-incrimination. In deciding the fair trial provisions under Article 6, it should be stressed that the European Court of Human Rights is not concerned with the actual guilt or innocence of the accused but rather whether the whole trial process was in accordance with Article 6.

It is always open to a defence advocate to argue that the admissibility of a particular piece of evidence in a case will violate the defendant's right to a fair trial in accordance with Article 6. Sometimes evidence is obtained by the police in violation of Article 8 which guarantees an individual's right to privacy. Article 8 is a qualified right. A defence advocate could nonetheless try to argue that his client's right to a fair trial has been compromised because the evidence has been obtained in violation of a Convention right.

4.3 THE GENERAL PRINCIPLES OF LAW OF THE ECHR

In addition to the substantive rights of the ECHR, regard must also be had to the general principles of law that have been developed under the ECHR.

4.3.1 THE RULE OF LAW

Any restriction in domestic law of a person's rights under the ECHR must be prescribed by law, and not as the result of an arbitrary decision.

In *The Sunday Times v United Kingdom (No. 1)* [1979–1980] 2 EHHR 245, it was held that for the interference to be in accordance with the law:

- there must be some legal regulation permitting the interference;
- the regulation must be readily accessible; and
- the regulation must be formulated with such precision as to enable the person to regulate his conduct.

Thus while arresting a person during a criminal investigation is *prima facie* in breach of that person's rights to liberty under Article 5, provided the arrest was made under the authority of a recognised legal power such as s. 24 PACE 1984, the rule of law principle will not be breached.

4.3.2 LEGITIMACY OF AIM

Where domestic law is permitted to derogate from a legal right of the ECHR, any interference with the right must be directed towards a legitimate, identifiable aim such as the prevention of disorder or crime. Once again, the interference with a person's right to liberty under Article 5 is permitted as it is directed at investigating or preventing crime.

4.3.3 PROPORTIONALITY

Any interference in domestic law with a legal right under the ECHR must be a proportionate response when measured against the objective the interference is intended to address. In colloquial terms, this means that the State 'cannot use a sledgehammer to crack a nut'.

When applying the principle of proportionality, the court considers whether the interference with a Convention right is 'necessary in a democratic society' or is based on 'a pressing social need'. In determining the components of a fair trial under Article 6, the principle of proportionality is evident both in the application of domestic law and in decisions of the European Court of Human Rights.

4.4 WHAT IS THE RELATIONSHIP BETWEEN THE HUMAN RIGHTS ACT (HRA) 1998 AND THE ECHR?

The HRA 1998 provides the legal framework for using the ECHR in UK domestic law. Section 1 of the HRA 1998 formally incorporates ECHR law into UK domestic law. This means that points of ECHR law can be cited in the criminal courts in support of your client's case.

4.4.1 ARE THE DOMESTIC COURTS REQUIRED TO HAVE REGARD TO THE ECHR?

Section 3 of the HRA 1998 places an obligation on the criminal courts to interpret all legislation 'as far as possible' to comply with ECHR law. This is known as the interpretive obligation.

In discharging the interpretive obligation, the courts must apply ECHR law as determined by the decisions of the European Court of Human Rights. Therefore when citing a relevant ECHR point in support of your legal argument where, for example, you seek to challenge the admissibility of prosecution evidence or to exclude a confession then, under its interpretive obligation, the court must take into account the ECHR when making its decision.

4.4.2 WHAT IS THE POSITION WHERE IT IS NOT POSSIBLE TO GIVE EFFECT TO ECHR LAW?

The HRA 1998 does not give the courts the power to strike down legislation which is contrary to the ECHR. So, where it is not possible to give effect to the ECHR law in a case, s. 4 HRA 1998 requires the superior courts such as the Court of Appeal and the House of Lords to make a declaration of incompatibility. The declaration gives Parliament the opportunity to amend the domestic provision which conflicts with Convention law. It is a matter for Parliament to decide whether or not to amend the offending legislation.

4.4.3 DOES THE HRA 1998 OFFER ADDITIONAL PROTECTIONS TO THE DEFENDANT'S LEGAL RIGHTS?

The most significant additional protection is provided by s. 6 HRA 1998, which places a duty on a public authority such as the police, the Crown Prosecution Service and the courts, to discharge its legal duties in compliance with the ECHR. Article 6(1) provides:

'It is unlawful for a public authority to act in a way which is incompatible with Convention rights.'

A range of remedies in the civil courts apply where a public authority acts in breach of its duties under s. 6 HRA 1998, including actions in tort and/or judicial review. Section 8 of the HRA 1998 requires that where a court finds that a public authority has acted unlawfully, it must grant a remedy that is 'just and appropriate'.

4.5 THE ECHR AND THE RULES OF CRIMINAL PROCEDURE AND EVIDENCE

While generally the practice and procedure of the English criminal trial satisfies the obligations laid down by the Convention, since the implementation of the HRA 1998, a number of important decisions have been made by the courts where Article 5 or Article 6 have been directly invoked. These decisions include:

- *R (on the application of the DPP) v Havering Magistrates' Court* [2001] 2 Cr App R 2 confirmed that proceedings under the Bail Act 1976 were governed by Article 5.

- *T and V v United Kingdom* (2000) 30 EHRR 121 decided that the boys who had been tried for the killing of Jamie Bulger had not had a fair trial in the Crown Court under Article 6 because their young age and the formality of the Crown Court procedures had prevented them from participating effectively in the trial process.

- *R (Anderson) v Secretary of State for the Home Department* [2003] 1 Cr App R 32, the House of Lords decided that to comply with Article 6, where a prisoner was sentenced to life imprisonment, the decision as to how long the prisoner should serve in prison (known as the tariff) should be taken by a judge, not by the Home Secretary.

- *Murray v United Kingdom* (1996) 22 EHRR 29, the European Court of Human Rights held that adverse inferences could not be drawn from a suspect's silence at the police station where he had not been offered legal advice. United Kingdom domestic law was found to be in breach of Article 6(3) of the Convention.

These and other important decisions influenced by the ECHR are considered in more detail at appropriate places in the text. The recognition of a defendant's rights under Article 6 is specifically identified in Part 1 of the new Criminal Procedure Rules as a component of the overriding objective of dealing justly with criminal cases.

4.6 PROFESSIONAL CONDUCT

Underpinning your work as a criminal lawyer are your professional conduct duties. Criminal cases are conducted in an adversarial system of enquiry where the aim of each side is to win. This requires the lawyer to represent his client's interests at all times and to be a partisan advocate for his case – subject to the rules of professional conduct.

The rules apply at all stages and impose upon the solicitor ethical responsibilities not only to his client but to the wider criminal justice system as a whole. The rules of professional conduct in relation to criminal litigation are to be found in *The Guide to the Professional Conduct of Solicitors* published by the Law Society. At the point of going to press the rules we are about to refer to are in draft form only. They are expected to come into force in 2006. The rules pertaining to Litigation and Advocacy are contained in Rule 11 and the Guidance thereto.

The purpose of this section is to provide a brief overview of and introduction to these professional conduct duties. Specific aspects of professional conduct are highlighted further at appropriate places in the text. The implementation of the Criminal Procedure Rules in 2005, with their overriding objective and active case management powers given to the courts (highlighted in Chapter 1), will significantly increase the pressures on all those involved in the conduct of criminal cases as they will be significantly more accountable to the court for a failure to actively progress a case. However, Note 4 of the Guidance to Rule 11 is worth highlighting. It states:

'As an officer of the court you should take all reasonable steps to assist in the smooth running of the courts but only in so far as this is consistent with your duties to your client, in particular the duty of confidentiality. For example, if your client fails to attend a hearing you may properly state that you are without instructions, but you could not disclose your client's whereabouts.'

Professional conduct issues in relation to criminal clients are most likely to arise in the following contexts:

- duties to the court;
- confidentiality;
- conflict of interest;
- interviewing witnesses;
- specific duties on advocates.

4.6.1 DUTIES TO THE COURT

Although you have a duty to represent the interests of your clients, you have a wider obligation to the criminal justice system as a whole which may, on occasion, conflict with the obligations owed to your client. Rule 1.03 provides:

'You must treat the interests of your client as paramount, provided they do not conflict with:

- your obligations in professional conduct; or
- the public interest in the administration of justice.'

In the case of the prosecutor, he has a duty to act as a minister of justice. In other words, the prosecutor is under a duty not to secure a conviction at all costs. The nature of the role of the Crown Prosecution Service is considered in Chapter 13. The onerous nature of the prosecutor's duty to make disclosure of relevant material that undermines the case for the prosecution or assists the defence is considered in Chapter 17.

You will soon discover that some defendants will lie or be economical with the truth. What should you do if you become aware that your client intends to lie to the police or to the court?

4.6.2 KNOWINGLY MISLEADING THE COURT

While you have a basic duty to act in the best interest of your client, you have an overriding duty not to mislead the court. Rule 11.01 could not be more explicit. It states:

'You must never deceive or knowingly mislead the court.'

The rules acknowledge that you may mislead the court inadvertently. If you become aware of this during the course of the proceedings, you must, with his client's consent, immediately inform the court. If your client does not consent, you must cease to act. The obligation not to knowingly deceive a court is further defined in paragraphs 9–13 of the Guidance to Rule 11. You may believe that your client is being untruthful. However, suspicion is not the same as knowledge. If you allowed a witness to be called whose evidence you knew to be untrue, this would constitute serious breach of professional conduct (Rule 11.01 Guidance Note 10). If your client were to admit to you, during ongoing proceedings, that he misled the court or committed perjury, you must not act further unless your client agrees to disclose the truth (Rule 11.01 Guidance Note 13).

Your duty not to deceive the court will arise where, for example, you are satisfied that your client is adopting false particulars (name or address or date of birth) with the intention of deceiving a court by avoiding the revelation of previous convictions, perhaps to achieve a more favourable sentence or bail outcome. In such circumstances you would need to explain to your client that you cannot allow such a course to be pursued and that unless your client is willing to correct the details or is willing to change his mind, you will have to withdraw from the case (Rule 11.01, Guidance Note 11).

The overriding duty upon an advocate to assist the court extends to referring the court to a relevant point of law even though it might go against your case (Rule 11, paragraph 15 (a)). However, it does not extend to imposing an obligation upon a defence lawyer to correct information given by a prosecutor which you know may allow the court to make a mistaken assumption, provided you do not indicate your agreement with the information (Rule 11.01 Guidance Note 12). Nor does it extend to an obligation to disclose facts or witnesses that may be of assistance to an adversary (Rule 11.01 Guidance Note 15 (b)).

4.6.3 WHAT ACTION SHOULD YOU TAKE WHERE YOUR CLIENT CHANGES HIS VERSION OF EVENTS?

A commonly encountered professional conduct issue occurs where your client keeps changing his version of the facts in the case. There is no general duty upon a solicitor to enquire in every case as to whether your client is telling the truth. If your client makes inconsistent statements, this is not a ground for refusing to act. However, you need to be wary and you must cease to act where it is clear that your client is attempting to put forward false evidence as this will conflict with your duty as an officer of the court (Rule11, paragraph 14). You should never suggest a defence to your client to fit the facts nor must you fabricate a defence. This extends to taking witness statements. You must never put words into a witness's mouth.

4.6.4 WHAT IS THE POSITION WHERE YOUR CLIENT ADMITS HIS GUILT TO YOU?

A problem that might be encountered is where your client admits his guilt to you but wishes to plead not guilty. This could of course occur at the police station as well as at court. Can you continue to act? The previous edition of the Professional Conduct Rules included Rule 21.20, which provided:

> 'A solicitor who appears in court for the defence in a criminal case is under a duty to say on behalf of the client what the client should properly say for himself or herself if the client possessed the requisite skill and knowledge. The solicitor has a concurrent duty to ensure that the prosecution discharges the onus placed upon it to prove the guilt of the accused.'

Rule 21.20 is not reproduced in the 2006 draft edition of the Rules. In answer to the question posed above, you can continue to represent your client on a not guilty plea, as it is your professional duty to require the prosecution to prove its case beyond reasonable doubt. However, you must not do anything to positively assert your client's innocence. If at the close of the prosecution's case, your client sought to give evidence on oath or to call witnesses with a view to making a positive assertion of innocence (i.e. which expressly or by implication suggests that someone other than your client committed the crime) you would be knowingly misleading the court. In these circumstances, if your client persisted in such a course, you would be required to withdraw from the case (Rule 11.01, Note 9).

In those cases where you cease to act for a client, do not forget that your duty of confidentiality towards your client precludes you from informing the court of the reason for your decision.

4.6.5 CONFIDENTIALITY

You will be aware that in accordance with Rule 4, a solicitor is under a strict duty to keep confidential the affairs of his client. This duty continues for all time unless your client agrees to waive confidentiality. There are certain exceptional instances when the duty of confidentiality can be overridden. These are set out in the Guidance to Rule 4, paragraphs 10–20.

Communications between a solicitor and his client are additionally protected from disclosure even to the court by means of legal professional privilege. The privilege extends in criminal cases to communications passing between a solicitor and a third party, such as a barrister or expert witness, provided the communication was made in connection with actual or contemplated litigation. The rules of evidence relating to legal professional privilege are considered further in Chapter 27.

Issues of confidentiality are likely to arise in criminal cases where professional embarrassment (see your overriding duty to the court above) forces you to withdraw from a case. You cannot in these circumstances explain to a court the reason why you are no longer acting.

The issue of confidentiality may also arise at the police station. In Chapters 8 and 12 we explain how the right to silence at the police station has been modified by s. 34 Criminal Justice and Public Order Act 1994. Where a defendant fails to mention facts in interview which he subsequently relies on in court in his defence, a court can choose to draw an adverse inference in circumstances where it considers it was reasonable for the defendant to have mentioned the facts he now relies on in his defence. Before an adverse inference is drawn however, a court shall have regard to any explanation for remaining silent that the defendant advances: this might include legal advice given at the time to remain silent. Obviously, any advice given by the solicitor at the time is protected from disclosure by client confidentiality and legal professional privilege. In these circumstances, the defendant must be prepared to waive his legal professional privilege so that the reasons for the advice can be properly considered by the court.

The confidentiality rule is allied to the rules regarding conflict of interest.

4.6.6 CONFLICT OF INTERESTS

Rule 3.01–3.02 provides that a solicitor should not accept instructions to act for two or more clients where there is a conflict or significant risk of a conflict between the interests of those clients. Rule 3.03 states that a solicitor must not continue to act for two or more clients where a conflict of interests arises between those clients. You can continue acting for one of the clients providing that the duty of confidentiality to the other client is not put at risk.

A conflict of interest can commonly arise when the solicitor is called upon to represent two or more suspects at the police station who are being investigated for the same offence. This potential conflict may also extend to a case where both clients are charged in the same proceedings as co-accused where, at trial, one co-accused decides to plead guilty and give evidence that implicates the other co-accused. When acting for two or more co-accused it is important to ensure there is no conflict of interest between them. Such a conflict may not be immediately apparent. If having taken instructions from two co-accused, it becomes apparent that there is a conflict of interest, the rules of professional conduct require you to cease to act for both.

In the Guidance to Rule 3, paragraphs 25–35 makes specific provision in relation to acting for co-defendants. For reasons of space we do not include a full text but strongly recommend you read through the guidance notes. They can be downloaded from the Law Society's website at: http://www.lawsociety.org.uk. A link to our Online Resource Centre will take you to them.

4.6.7 INTERVIEWING WITNESSES

You will frequently encounter the phrase 'there is no property in a witness'. In a criminal case, this means that the defence solicitor may interview a prosecution witness and the prosecution may interview a defence witness. The Guidance to Rule 11, paragraph 16 provides:

'You are permitted, even when acting as an advocate, to interview and take statements from any witness at any stage in the proceedings, whether or not that witness has been interviewed or called as a witness by another party. You must not tamper with the evidence of a witness or attempt to pressurise the witness into changing their evidence. To avoid such allegations it would be wise, when seeking to interview a witness for the other side, to offer to interview them in the presence of the other side's representative.'

If a defence solicitor wishes to interview a prosecution witness, it is sound professional practice to contact the prosecution, in order to ascertain whether a member of the prosecution team wishes to be present at the interview.

4.6.8 SPECIFIC PROFESSIONAL DUTIES ON ADVOCATES

There are further professional conduct rules which apply specifically to the solicitor acting as an advocate. They are detailed in Rule 11.05 and Guidance Notes 24–26. They cover the situation where an advocate or a member of the advocate's firm could be called as a witness at trial. They also govern the way in which an advocate should treat a witness while giving evidence.

Rule 11.06 states quite simply that you must not make, or offer to make payments to a witness dependant upon the outcome of the case or the nature of the evidence the witness should give. It is, however, permissible to pay reasonable witness expenses (Guidance Note 27).

4.7 ADVOCACY

Advocacy is the legal skill most often associated with criminal litigation. Put simply, advocacy is the art of communication. Having come this far on your journey to become a solicitor you will hopefully have begun to develop your oral communication skills and an ability to put forward structured and coherent arguments. Those skills now need to be harnessed and applied in a different context.

The most readily identifiable areas where a criminal advocate's oral presentation skills come to the fore are at contested bail hearings, pleas in mitigation of sentence and, of course, in conducting trials. It will be some time before you undertake any of these independently, although trainee solicitors do have rights of audience before Crown Court judges in chambers and may therefore represent a defendant on an appeal against magistrates' refusal to grant bail. In this short section on advocacy we identify some of the key components of persuasion.

4.7.1 EFFECTIVE ADVOCACY

Effective advocacy depends on:

- good preparation; and
- persuasive oral communication skills.

Good preparation presupposes a thorough knowledge of both the facts in the case and the relevant law. For example, when making a bail application, you would be expected to have a good working knowledge of the Bail Act 1976 and to apply the facts of your client's case thereto. The submission of a plea in mitigation presupposes a thorough knowledge of sentencing principles and practice.

Similarly, if you were to make an application to have evidence excluded at trial, your preparation would have alerted you to the relevant legal basis of your submission and the facts that you would need to be proved in order to substantiate your submission.

While knowledge and understanding of the relevant law and facts are important, you must also be able to present your legal argument in a structured, coherent and persuasive way.

4.7.2 WHAT MAKES AN ORAL PRESENTATION PERSUASIVE?

The following checklist is based on our experience of developing and assessing advocacy skills on the LPC. Whatever the context for your presentation, awareness of what may be termed 'credibility factors' may help.

Eye contact

Eye contact greatly enhances an oral presentation. It shows you are confident enough to move away from a prepared script and enables you to assess and gauge the reaction your submission is having on your listener. If you want to get your message across you must engage your listener. Maintaining eye contact is an obvious way of helping to achieve this.

Posture

Do not slouch. Stand up straight with your head slightly elevated. Posture affects the resonance of your voice. Your posture should make you appear relaxed and confident.

Voice

Accents are not a problem, providing you are clear in your enunciation of words. The acoustics vary from courtroom to courtroom so you may need to explore your voice audibility levels. Avoid being too loud and aggressive, or too softly spoken. The latter does not inspire confidence. Deep breathing (from the diaphragm) can help your voice to resonate more, thereby making you more audible. If you think you have a monotone delivery, try to get some vocal variety into your voice. Try reading a children's story to a young relative: you will soon find out ways to make your delivery more interesting.

Pace

It is very important to correctly pace your submission. True advocacy is not about reading from a prepared script, as this will make it more likely that you will read too quickly and consequently your audience will be unable to follow your argument. Too slow a delivery can have a stultifying effect upon your audience. Experiment, and choose a pace that is suitable.

Pause

The pause is a simple but very effective persuasive device. Use it for dramatic effect. If you have a particularly telling point to advance, make the point and then . . . pause momentarily. Allow the point to be considered by your listener. Used in combination with voice inflection, the effect should resonate with your audience.

Distracting mannerisms

We all have them. You will be the best judge of what distracting mannerisms you have. If you have the opportunity, why not record yourself making an oral submission? When you review your performance, ask yourself: does my body language detract from the message I am putting across? Are you fiddling with the loose change in your pocket or juggling a pen in your hands? Do you sway from side to side? Are you constantly touching your face or your hair? Look at the expression on your face. Is it the face of someone who feels relaxed and confident in the submission they are making? Do you look up and smile occasionally or are you frowning/perplexed/refusing to make eye contact? All of these mannerisms distract from the message you are trying to put across.

Structure

A persuasive argument will be delivered in a structured fashion. Devising a structure should help you to avoid unnecessary repetition. The simplest and most effective structure for any submission is for it to have a beginning, middle and end. Break up your submission into listener-friendly portions, e.g.:

> 'Ma'am, I have three points I would like to make this morning: My first point is this. . . . . my second point is this . . . . my third and final point is this. . . . . In summary, Ma'am . . . .'

Sometimes the nature of your submission will determine its structure. When devising and delivering a submission on bail, for example, the Bail Act 1976 provides a logical structure within which to work.

Keep your submission concise. Cut down on the verbiage. Try to avoid reading out sections from statute and case law. Copy and highlight the relevant sections/passages and then hand them in for the bench/judge to read.

Brevity

You will soon come to realise that a court's time is very precious. With this in mind, always try to make your submission succinct. Developing a logical structure to your submission will assist. Try to avoid unnecessary repetition.

Persona

It is important when appearing as an advocate that you should look confident – even if you do not feel confident. Dressing suitably and smartly helps an advocate to step into the role. It also helps to inspire confidence in your client and it conveys the correct impression to the court. First impressions really do count. Without being dramatic, your opening address needs to capture the attention of the court. What sort of individual engages you? The more open and the more interesting the personality is, the more likely the audience will listen. Behavioural psychology has much to teach the aspiring advocate!

Be prepared to make appropriate concessions. Avoid being arrogant or patronising. Organise yourself and your notes so that your composure and professionalism comes across.

Language

Persuasion is as much about your choice of language as anything else. Words can be very powerful tools with which to convey a message. Think carefully about the choice of words you make. Can you find a more powerful adjective to advance the point you are making? Try to use language which includes your audience. For example, you might say: 'Let's examine together the circumstances in which the defendant's confession was obtained. . . .' Personalise the situation: 'Ma'am, I invite you to consider what you would have done in the same situation as my client. . . .'

Some individuals are natural advocates. They have charm and exude confidence. If they combine their natural ability with knowledge and application of the law, they are capable of making a persuasive submission even in the most hopeless of cases. Other individuals might initially be less comfortable in the spotlight which the art of advocacy demands. Advocacy skills can be developed with practice and reflection.

If you are accessing our Online Resource Centre you will be able to see some examples of advocacy in our filmed case studies. *R v Lenny Whyte* contains a fully contested application for bail. *R v Hardy* and *R v Martin* both comprise pleas in mitigation. The specifics of each of these submissions are considered in the chapter on bail and the chapters on sentencing.

online resource centre

KEY POINT SUMMARY

- Arguments based on Article 6 ECHR can arise in relation to many aspects of criminal litigation, including procedure and evidence.

- The right to a fair trial in Article 6 comprises many rights, some of which are specifically defined in Article 6, some of which are implied.

- Domestic courts must as far as possible, interpret our law in accordance with Convention rights.

- In determining rights under the Convention, regard must be had to the jurisprudence of the European Court of Human Rights.

- Human rights issues are pervasive – they can arise at any time. As a Legal Practice Course student, always look for potential human rights arguments.

- Have a thorough working knowledge of the rules of professional conduct and know the typical instances where professional conduct dilemmas are likely to arise in the context of criminal litigation.

- You may not be asked specifically about a professional conduct point – nevertheless if, in your view, a professional conduct issue arises, deal with it.

- A solicitor is an officer of the court and should always conduct himself appropriately.

- If in doubt about your professional conduct obligations, always ask.

SELF-TEST QUESTIONS

1. Explain how Convention rights are incorporated into domestic law and how a defence solicitor might make use of such Convention rights.

2. What are the potential consequences of failing to spot and deal with an aspect of the Solicitor's Professional Conduct Rules?

FIGURE 4.1 EUROPEAN CONVENTION ON HUMAN RIGHTS 1950 AND
CRIMINAL LITIGATION

ARTICLE 3

- prohibition of torture – to challenge the admissibility of a confession under 'oppression', s. 76(2)(a) PACE.

ARTICLE 5

- the right to liberty and security – to challenge the decision of the police and/or the court not to grant a client bail.

ARTICLE 6 – THE RIGHT TO A FAIR TRIAL

- The defendant's rights under Article 6 are pervasive at all stages of a criminal case, including

    - the defendant's right to legal advice at the police station;
    - the presumption of innocence at trial;
    - the right to be present at his trial and to be legally represented;
    - the principles governing sentencing;
    - exclusion of evidence at trial.

GENERAL PRINCIPLES OF ECHR LAW

Absolute rights permit no derogation.

Qualified rights do permit derogation but any derogation must:

- be in accordance with the rule of law;
- pursue a legitimate aim;
- be a proportional response.

AN INTRODUCTION TO THE LAW OF CRIMINAL EVIDENCE

5.1   INTRODUCTION

On most LPC programmes the designation of a course in 'Criminal Litigation' is potentially misleading. A more accurate description would be 'Criminal Litigation and Evidence' because on the LPC, as in criminal practice, it is impossible to divorce the rules of criminal litigation from the rules of criminal evidence. Consequently every LPC student (and criminal lawyer) requires a thorough understanding of the rules of evidence and the way in which the principles are applied as part of the prosecution and the defence case.

It is also important to appreciate that the rules of evidence are relevant not only when preparing for trial and during the trial but are pervasive and significant throughout the whole case. One of the aims of this book is to try to reflect the integration of the rules of criminal evidence with procedure. For example, the way in which the police gather evidence against an accused during the investigation may have important evidential consequences if the substantive provisions of PACE and the Codes of Practice are not complied with. The legal adviser at the police station needs to understand the rules of evidence in order to evaluate the strength of the evidence the police claim to have and to be able to advise his client accordingly: that might include advising him to exercise his right to remain silent.

Some of you will have encountered the rules of evidence at the academic stage of your studies, and your understanding of the rules is therefore assumed. Your challenge will be to recognise and apply the rules of evidence in the more practical context of the LPC. For those studying evidence for the first time, a steep learning curve is about to be encountered. You must simultaneously learn the rules and be able to recognise and apply them in the

particular factual context. This chapter provides an overview of and a very simplified introduction to the main evidential rules. In particular, it addresses the following:

- the purpose of the law of evidence;
- the core concepts of relevance, admissibility, and weight;
- the different types of evidence.

Later chapters will explain the rules of evidence in more detail.

5.2 THE PURPOSE OF THE LAW OF CRIMINAL EVIDENCE

The law of evidence is the body of rules which prescribe the ways in which evidence is
presented in a criminal trial. The rules regulate how the prosecution proves its case to the
court and, in exceptional situations, how the defendant might prove his innocence. The law
of evidence also seeks to ensure that the accused receives a fair trial and operates in close
conjunction with the right to a fair trial under Article 6 ECHR.

5.3 FACTS IN ISSUE

Where the defendant pleads not guilty, the facts in issue identify what has to be proven by
the prosecution for the defendant to be found guilty, or exceptionally what the defendant has
to prove in order to establish his innocence. The facts in issue are determined by reference
to the *actus reus* and the *mens rea* of the offence with which the defendant is charged. Your
knowledge of substantive criminal law is assumed. The burden of proving your client's guilt
beyond reasonable doubt rests, for the most part, on the prosecution. You can and indeed
should research the required elements of the offence/s with which your client is charged so
that you know the elements of the offence the prosecution must prove. In a charge of theft
under s. 1 Theft Act 1968 the facts in issue are:

Actus reus	Mens rea
Appropriates	Dishonestly
Property	Intention to permanently deprive
Belonging to another	

The prosecution has to prove each element of the *actus reus* and the *mens rea* of the offence for
the defendant to be found guilty. This is known as discharging the legal burden of proof. The
prosecution will discharge the legal burden of proof by putting evidence before the court in
support of each fact in issue. This is known as discharging the evidential burden. Legal and
evidential burdens of proof are considered in greater detail in Chapter 21.

5.4 CORE CONCEPTS

There are three core concepts relating to evidence. They are relevance, admissibility and
weight.

5.4.1 RELEVANCE

For evidence to be put before the court, it must be relevant or probative of a fact in issue. There
are no special rules to decide the question of relevance – it is a matter of common sense. For
example, on a charge of theft of a bottle of wine from a supermarket, it is not relevant for
the prosecution to put forward evidence that the defendant rode to the supermarket on a

bike with defective lights, or that he has recently been divorced. It is relevant, however, for a prosecution witness to tell the court that she saw the accused put a bottle of wine under his coat and walk out of the defendant's supermarket without paying.

The relevance of evidence sometimes arises in the context of the admission of a defendant's past bad character. For example, X is on trial for sexual assault alleged to have been perpetrated on an 11-year-old boy. He denies the offence. How relevant would it be to make it known to the jury or to magistrates that two years ago X received a conditional discharge for downloading indecent images of children from an internet site? Where an argument arises as to the relevance of a particular piece of evidence, the decision whether or not to admit the evidence is ultimately taken by the judge in the Crown Court and by the magistrates in the magistrates' court.

5.4 2 ADMISSIBILITY

For the court to receive evidence it not only has to be relevant to a fact in issue but must also be admissible. Admissible evidence means evidence which as a matter of law can be received by the court. Evidence will be admissible unless it is excluded either under a mandatory rule of exclusion or in the exercise of the court's discretion to ensure the defendant enjoys a fair trial. Mandatory rules of exclusion apply to the opinion evidence of a lay witness and include the general rule that hearsay evidence is inadmissible unless the hearsay evidence falls within a recognised common law or statutory exception.

Every defendant enjoys the right to a fair trial. Such a right has many facets, sometimes the right will require the exclusion of evidence which the prosecution seeks to have admitted. This may be because of the manner in which the evidence has been obtained (this could apply to evidence of a confession and evidence of identification, or indeed any evidence yielded by the investigating authorities in the exercise of their statutory powers of stop, search and seizure). Evidence may also have to be excluded if its admission would prejudice a fair trial. By prejudice we mean the damaging effect the admission of a particular piece of evidence might have on the minds of the jury or magistrates. Relevance and admissibility are closely entwined. Would a jury or magistrates attach too much significance to a particular piece of evidence to the neglect of other evidence in a case which might raise a reasonable doubt? Consider the prejudice that could be engendered by the admission of the previous conviction for downloading child pornography at the trial of X for sexual assault in the earlier example. The power to exclude evidence is contained in s. 78 PACE (unfairness) and/or s. 82(3) PACE (probative value outweighed by prejudicial effect).

Where the admissibility of evidence is disputed, the decision to admit or exclude evidence rests with the judge in the Crown Court and with the magistrates in the magistrates' court. A decision to admit disputed evidence which results in a conviction may provide grounds for an appeal against conviction. Equally, a decision to exclude a particular piece of evidence may have profound implications for the prosecution's ability to discharge its legal burden of proof beyond reasonable doubt.

5.4.3 WEIGHT

Even where a piece of evidence is relevant and admissible, this does not mean that the jury or magistrates will find the evidence convincing or persuasive. For example, a witness may state in court that she only caught a fleeting glimpse in poor light of a person accused of a crime as he ran down the street at night. Unless supported by other independent evidence, the court might attach little weight to this evidence. However, where the witness recognised the defendant as an old acquaintance, and saw the defendant in broad daylight from a short distance, then the court might give considerable weight to the identification. The statistical odds that are attached to modern-day DNA evidence often give such evidence huge probative value in the eyes of the jury or magistrates. The weight to be attached to a particular piece of evidence is a matter for the jury in the Crown Court and magistrates in magistrates' court. Advocates on either side will wish to make representations about the degree of weight to be attached to particular evidence in the case.

In some instances (particularly in relation to identification evidence), the defendant's right to a fair trial requires the judge (in the Crown Court) to warn the jury about the dangers of relying on certain types of evidence. In other instances (relying on the evidence of certain types of witnesses) the requirement to give a warning lies in the discretion of the judge. Where a conviction results in part from a failure to give an appropriate warning, the defendant may have grounds for an appeal against conviction.

5.5 ASSESSING THE EVIDENCE – THE PROSECUTING SOLICITOR'S ROLE

In deciding whether a prosecution should be pursued, the Code for Crown Prosecutors requires the CPS lawyer to determine whether there is sufficient evidence to secure a conviction. In making this assessment, the CPS lawyer will be mindful of the rules of evidence. The CPS lawyer has no active investigative role and therefore must make an assessment of the evidence gathered by the police. This will include consideration of witness statements and items of real evidence which may have been subject to forensic analysis. The CPS lawyer has no direct access to witnesses. Based on the assessment of the evidence, the CPS lawyer might suggest further investigation is needed.

5.6 ASSESSING THE EVIDENCE – THE DEFENCE SOLICITOR'S ROLE

Irrespective of whether your client is to be tried summarily or on indictment, the rules relating to pre-trial disclosure of evidence mean the defence solicitor will know the nature of the evidence against his client before trial. In assessing the strength of evidence as disclosed by the prosecution witness statements and other material, you need to have in mind the core concepts of relevance, admissibility and weight of evidence. There is one important advantage to a defendant pleading guilty at an early stage in the proceedings, in that he is entitled to a sentencing discount of up to one third. Where a defendant pleads guilty, the evidence against him is never tested in open court. A defence solicitor should not of course advise his client to plead guilty unless the evidence against him is particularly strong and admissible.

5.7 PROCEDURE FOR DETERMINING ADMISSIBILITY OF DISPUTED EVIDENCE AND THE ROLE OF THE TRIAL JUDGE

The primary role of the trial judge is to ensure the defendant enjoys a fair trial. On occasions this will require the judge to exclude evidence from the jury's consideration. In the Crown Court, a strict separation of function exists between judge and jury. The judge determines all issues of law (including disputed evidence) in the absence of the jury. The jury determines issues of fact. In the magistrates' court, the magistrates are the ultimate arbiters of both fact and law. Legal advice on the law is provided by the magistrates' clerk or legal adviser. On occasion a *voir dire* (or trial within a trial) may need to be held to resolve a dispute as regards the admissibility of evidence. Such a procedure would involve the judge/magistrates hearing evidence about the manner in which the disputed evidence was obtained before applying the law and either excluding or admitting the evidence. The *voir dire* procedure works more effectively in the Crown Court given the separation of function between judge and jury. If, after hearing evidence and argument, the trial judge decides that the disputed evidence must be excluded, the jury will be immunised from the knowledge that it ever existed. A further and very important function of the trial judge is to sum up the evidence for the jury at the conclusion of the trial and to direct the jury in accordance with the law. This will require the trial judge to direct the jury in accordance with the rules of evidence. Judges are greatly assisted in this respect by the Judicial Studies Board specimen directions (www.jsboard.co.uk) which contain precedents on directing a jury on all aspects of criminal law and evidence.

5.8 TYPES OF EVIDENCE

Where evidence is relevant and admissible, it will be presented to the court in one of the following forms.

5.8.1 ORAL TESTIMONY

This is the evidence of a witness given orally in court and presented by the party calling the witness on factual matters within the witness's personal knowledge and experience. An example of a witness giving factual evidence would include the witness stating that: 'I saw the defendant break the car window and drive the car away at speed.' In the criminal trial, direct oral testimony is the preferred way for evidence to be put before the court and is likely to be the type of evidence that the court will find the most persuasive.

5.8.2 OPINION EVIDENCE

A witness is called at a trial to give evidence of fact based on the witness's personal knowledge and experience. The witness is not called to the witness box to offer an opinion on what he or she saw or heard. The general rule is that where a witness gives opinion evidence, it will be inadmissible. It would not be possible for a witness to state: 'It's obvious that the defendant killed him.'

There are two exceptions to this general rule:

1. An expert may give opinion evidence on a matter that goes beyond the ordinary competence of the court. In criminal cases it is very common for the prosecution to rely on the evidence of a forensic scientist. Expert evidence is considered in more detail in Chapter 24.

2. A lay person may state his opinion on a matter not requiring expertise as a way of conveying facts that he has personally perceived. A witness will be allowed to say that when she saw the accused 'he appeared to be drunk', or 'the car was speeding immediately before the car hit the pedestrian'.

5.8.3 DOCUMENTARY EVIDENCE

Relevant and admissible evidence may be contained in a document. A witness statement is an example of documentary evidence. Other types of documentary evidence include:

- photographs;
- maps;
- plans;
- videocassettes;
- computer print-outs;
- business documents;
- expert report.

5.8.4 REAL EVIDENCE

Real evidence comprises objects produced in court so the court may draw inferences from the condition and existence of the object. In a murder trial, a knife produced as the murder weapon, or the defendant's bloodstained clothing, would be examples of real evidence. In a public order offence, CCTV footage of the incident would constitute real evidence.

5.8.5 DIRECT AND CIRCUMSTANTIAL EVIDENCE

In whatever form evidence is admitted, it will have either direct or circumstantial relevance. Direct evidence requires nothing more of the jury or magistrates than an acceptance or rejection of the evidence that has been given. If X testifies that he saw Y walk up to Z, take out a knife and stab Z, this is direct evidence of the *actus reus* of murder. At his trial for murder, however, Y calls a witness who states she was with Y at the time of the alleged murder some 30 miles away. If accepted, this constitutes direct evidence of alibi. Circumstantial evidence requires the court not only to accept the witness's account but to draw an inference from the evidence. If X testifies that he saw Y running away from Z and that he observed Y had bloodstains on his clothing, this would constitute circumstantial evidence linking Y to the murder of X. Expert forensic evidence may suggest that the blood on Y's clothing matches that of the victim Z. Again, if the evidence is accepted by the court, it provides circumstantial evidence that Y was in close contact with the victim of the crime at the relevant time. A criminal case may be based entirely on circumstantial evidence. The trial of Ian Huntley for the murders of Holly Wells and Jessica Chapman is one of many high profile convictions based on circumstantial evidence.

5.9 CLARIFYING THE EVIDENTIAL ISSUES

In any contested criminal case there is bound to be a multiplicity of evidential issues. It is important, however, not to lose sight of the 'big picture'. Advocates need to make sense of the evidence and to develop a theory of the case which is supported by the evidence. In this way a coherent and focused case can be put before the jury or magistrates. The core issues in a case need to be distilled from the mass of detail and if the case is to be contested, a defence theory needs to be developed.

The defence theory is a clear and concise explanation of why the case should be resolved in the defendant's favour. In devising a plausible defence theory, the evidence that needs to be challenged and marshalled will become clear. On a charge of theft, for example, it may be that the defendant denies a dishonest intent. If this is the case, you should be marshalling your evidence and argument with this central issue in mind. Perhaps the defendant will challenge the prosecution's suggestion that he was responsible for the crime, on the basis that the case is one of mistaken identification. If this is the defence theory of the case, you should be concentrating on challenging the prosecution's evidence of identification and presenting any evidence which tends to support the theory advanced by the defendant such as evidence of alibi. The development of a defence theory will determine the nature of your cross-examination of each witness. This is why it is important to crystallise the facts in issue.

5.10 CONCLUSION

This chapter has introduced you to some of the core concepts that apply in the context of criminal evidence. Later chapters will examine the evidential considerations that arise in the context of:

- a confession being made to the police;
- obtaining and relying on eye-witness identification;
- a defendant exercising his right to remain silent at the police station who subsequently advances a defence at trial;

- a desire to adduce hearsay evidence;

- a desire by the prosecution to adduce evidence of a defendant's bad character;

- a desire by either side to adduce opinion evidence;

- reliance upon the uncorroborated evidence of a witness with a purpose of his own to serve in giving false evidence;

- the evidence of a child or mentally handicapped witness;

- prosecution evidence that has been obtained in a dubious or unlawful manner;

- the desire of the prosecution to withhold certain evidence from the defence.

The rules are significant at all stages of a criminal case and a good understanding of the law and the ability to apply the principles in a practical way to the facts of the case is important for the successful criminal litigation student. The rules of criminal evidence cannot be ignored – so in a determined and purposeful way, after carefully reading this introductory chapter, move on to the other chapters which deal with evidential rules in practice.

KEY POINT SUMMARY

- For the most part the prosecution bears the legal burden of proving a defendant's guilt beyond reasonable doubt. The elements of the offence charged determine what the prosecution needs to prove if it is to secure a conviction.

- To be admissible, evidence must be relevant to the facts in issue but not all relevant evidence is admissible.

- Evidence can be excluded by the application of mandatory rules and through the exercise of judicial discretion in the interests of ensuring a fair trial.

- In the Crown Court, matters of relevance and admissibility of evidence are determined by the judge in the absence of the jury. Matters of fact are determined by the jury. There is no separation of function in the magistrates' court and so magistrates determine matters of fact and law.

- An accused person is entitled to pre-trial disclosure of the evidence to be used against him enabling his advocate to evaluate the strengths and weaknesses of the case against him.

- Where an accused person chooses to plead guilty, the evidence against him is not tested in open court.

SELF-TEST QUESTION

Case study 1: *R v Lenny Whyte*

Consider documents 1 and 18 (A)–(P) in Appendix 1. Given that we have yet to cover the rules of criminal evidence in detail, simply list the nature of the evidence that is said to link Lenny Whyte to the burglary allegation. In doing so, can you identify any issues of evidence this scenario is likely to give rise to? In simplistic terms at this stage, consider how Lenny will challenge the nature of the evidence against him and in doing so, start to formulate a theory of the defence case.

FIGURE 5.1 AN OVERVIEW OF CRIMINAL EVIDENCE

PURPOSES OF THE LAW OF EVIDENCE

- The law of evidence regulates how the prosecution or the defence proves its case to the court.

- The rules determine what evidence may be received and what evidential use can be made of that evidence, and in so doing they seek to ensure the defendant receives a fair trial.

- In the Crown Court, the judge determines the admissibility of disputed evidence in the absence of the jury.

- In a summary trial, issues relating to the admissibility of disputed evidence are resolved by the magistrates with legal advice provided by their legal adviser.

FACTS IN ISSUE

- The issues that have to be proven for the prosecution (or exceptionally the defence) to succeed at trial.

- The facts in issue are the *actus reus* and the *mens rea* of the offence charged.

- The facts in issue can also include secondary facts which are relevant to the facts in issue such as the admissibility of a piece of evidence.

BASIC EVIDENTIAL RULES

- To be heard at trial, evidence must be:
- **relevant** to a fact in issue; and
- **admissible** (i.e. as a matter of law, the evidence can be put before the court).
- The **weight** to be afforded to a particular piece of evidence is a question of fact for the jury/magistrates.

TYPES OF ADMISSIBLE EVIDENCE

- Relevant and admissible will be presented at trial as one of the following types:
- oral testimony;
- documentary evidence;
- real evidence.

Part II
INVESTIGATION AND CHARGE

Part II examines the process of investigation of criminal offences and the decision to charge.

In this Part we consider the general and specific powers of the police to investigate criminal offences (Chapter 6) and the process of detention and questioning (Chapter 7).

We also consider rules of evidence relating to a decision by a suspect to remain silent (Chapter 8) and the rules of evidence relating to unlawfully obtained evidence (Chapter 9), the admissibility of confession evidence (Chapter 10) and the admissibility of evidence of identification (Chapter 11).

Chapter 12 seeks to bring Part II together by considering the practical steps legal advisers might take at the police station. Finally, the decision to charge a suspect or to offer an alternative course is considered in Chapter 13, which also looks at the role of the Crown Prosecution Service (CPS).

6 THE POWERS TO STOP, SEARCH AND ARREST

6.1   INTRODUCTION

The police have extensive statutory powers to stop and search and to arrest a person in connection with the investigation of a criminal offence. Under the Police and Criminal Evidence Act 1984 (PACE), the power to stop and search and arrest are general powers, which can be used in a wide range of situations. The police may also use a vast array of specific powers to stop, search and arrest granted to them under various statutes, including the Terrorism Act 2000, the Misuse of Drugs Act 1971 and the Serious Organised Crime and Police Act 2005.

In this chapter we examine:

- the common law and statutory powers of stop and search before arrest;
- the statutory power of arrest under PACE 1984;
- the statutory powers to search a person and his property after arrest;
- the power to grant street bail; and
- the pervasive influence of the European Convention on Human Rights 1950 and the right to liberty under Article 5.

6.2 STOP AND SEARCH BEFORE ARREST

The primary purpose of stop and search is to enable an officer to allay or confirm his suspicion about a person being in possession of stolen or prohibited articles or drugs without arresting him. Stop and search has long been one of the most controversial aspects of police powers and consequently the law provides detailed guidance as to what action the officer may take when questioning or searching a person in the street before arrest.

6.3 STOP AND SEARCH AT COMMON LAW

At common law, an officer does not have the right to stop or detain a person unless the person freely volunteers to cooperate with the officer (*Rice v Connelly* [1966] 2 All ER 64). Code A, Notes for Guidance, para. 1, recognises that an officer may speak to a member of the public in the normal course of his duties without detaining the person or exercising any compulsion over him. The person being questioned has a civic but not a legal duty to assist the officer to prevent crime and to discover offenders.

In the absence of the officer exercising a statutory power to stop and search or arrest, the person cannot be compelled to remain with the officer.

6.4 STATUTORY POWERS TO STOP AND SEARCH IN THE STREET BEFORE ARREST

Reference will be made throughout this chapter to Code A issued under PACE 1984. Code A can be freely accessed online from the Home Office. Our Online Resource Centre includes a link taking you to the PACE Codes of Practice.

The police have wide statutory powers to stop and search a suspect's person and/or his motor vehicle. Code A, Para. 1.5 stipulates that an officer may only stop and search a person in the lawful exercise of a statutory power to do so even where the person consents to being stopped and searched.

Statutory stop and search can be exercised either under a general or a specific legal power.

6.4.1 THE GENERAL POWER TO STOP AND SEARCH – S. 1 PACE 1984

Section 1 PACE (as supplemented by Code A) gives the police the general power to stop and search a person in a public place or a place to which the public have access before arrest, where the officer has reasonable grounds for suspecting the person is in possession of stolen or prohibited articles. The power of search under s. 1 PACE extends to a vehicle.

Paragraph 1.1 Code A, requires that stop and search must be used 'fairly, responsibly, with respect for those being searched and without unlawful discrimination'.

To be a lawful stop and search under s. 1 PACE, the following factors must be present:

(1) The stop and search must be connection with stolen or prohibited articles

Stop and search under s. 1 PACE may be exercised in respect to:

- stolen articles; or
- prohibited articles; or
- an article relevant to the commission of an offence under s. 139 Criminal Justice Act 1988 (possession of a bladed instrument); or
- a prohibited firework.

What are stolen articles?

'Stolen' articles are given the same meaning as in the Theft Act 1968 and include items arising out of the offence of theft, burglary, robbery or criminal deception.

What are prohibited articles?

'Prohibited' articles include offensive weapons; or articles made or adapted for use or intended use in an offence under the Theft Act 1968 and under s. 1 Criminal Damage Act 1971.

An offensive weapon is based on a definition similar to that under s. 1 Prevention of Crime Act 1953 as being an article made or adapted for use for causing injury to a person or intended for such use. It includes articles that are offensive weapons in themselves such as knives and guns and everyday articles that have been made or adapted for use as an offensive weapon. An example of this first type of offensive weapon would be a bottle that has been deliberately broken to give it a jagged edge or the end of a screwdriver sharpened to a point. Articles used or adapted for or intended for use in connection with the following offences under the Theft Act 1968 to include theft (s. 1), burglary (s. 9), taking a motor vehicle without consent (s. 12) or obtaining property by deception (s. 15), will cover diverse items such as a crow-bar, car keys, a credit card or any relevant item provided the user has the necessary intent to commit an offence under the 1968 Act.

(2) The requirement for reasonable suspicion

Under s. 1 PACE, reasonable suspicion will be present where:

- the officer has actual suspicion that the person is in possession of stolen or prohibited articles (the subjective test); and
- there are reasonable grounds for that suspicion (the objective test).

Detailed guidance on the meaning of reasonable suspicion is found Code A, para. 2.2–2.11. Code A stipulates that:

- reasonable suspicion will be determined on the facts of each case, including the time and the place the power was exercised and the suspect's behaviour, for example, where the suspect is seen by the officer on the street late at night and appears to be hiding something;
- reasonable suspicion can never be determined on the basis of the suspect's personal factors alone such as his race, ethnic background, religion, appearance or that the suspect is known to have previous convictions;
- reasonable suspicion should normally be based on good, reliable and recent police intelligence.

For judicial guidance on the reasonable suspicion test, see *O'Hara v Chief Constable, RUC* [1997] AC 286, at 6.8.6 below.

(3) Where can the stop and search take place?

The officer may only stop and search in a 'public place or a place to which the public has access,' s. 1(1) PACE. This wide definition includes the street or in a park or in a cinema, which is a place to which the public has access. The power cannot generally be exercised in the suspect's home or any other dwelling without the occupier's consent.

While the police do not enjoy a general right to search in a person's house under s. 1 PACE, the power may be exercised in a garden or yard attached to a house where the officer reasonably believes that the suspect does not live at that address and is not on the land with the express or implied permission of the occupier.

(4) Additional rights under s. 1 PACE and Code A:

- The suspect is entitled to a written record of the officer's reasons for the stop and search, Code A, Paragraph 3.10; recording requirements are detailed in paragraph 4.
- The officer must tell the suspect his name and police station, the purpose of the search and the reason for it.
- S.1 PACE not only applies to stopping a suspect on foot but also covers an officer stopping a suspect's vehicle in order to check on who is travelling in the vehicle.
- The search must be conducted at or near the place where the suspect was first detained.
- Generally, only the suspect's outer clothing should be searched – where the search requires the removal of more than the outer clothing it should be conducted in private.

Consider the following example of a search conducted under s. 1 PACE.

PC Atherton is on night patrol when he sees Danny walking through the town centre carrying a tool bag. There have been several burglaries in the locality in recent months. When the officer stops and questions Danny, he is exercising his powers under s.1 PACE. He will be acting lawfully if the following conditions are present:

- Danny has been stopped in a public place or a place to which the public has access;
- the officer had reasonable suspicion based on objective grounds;
- the purpose of the stop and search was to discover whether Danny was in possession of stolen or prohibited articles or articles to be used in connection with an offence of criminal damage;
- the procedural requirements of Code A were complied with.

6.5 SPECIFIC POWERS TO STOP AND SEARCH BEFORE ARREST

There are additional stop and search powers available to the police to use in specific situations granted under various statutes. A summary of the main stop and search powers are contained in Annex A of Code A and include the power to search for drugs (Misuse of Drugs Act 1971).

6.6 THE CONSEQUENCES OF AN UNLAWFUL STOP AND SEARCH

If a suspect has been unlawfully stopped and searched, where, for example, the police officer cannot prove the 'reasonable suspicion test', the admissibility of any resulting evidence may be challenged at any subsequent trial by the defence under s. 78 PACE on the basis that the admission of the evidence would have 'an adverse effect on the fairness of the proceedings' or under s. 82(3) PACE on the basis that 'the prejudicial effect of the evidence outweighs the probative value'. These provisions are considered more fully in Chapter 9. It might also afford a defence to a person accused of obstructing/ resisting or assaulting a police constable in the execution of his duty.

6.7 A DUTY TO GIVE INFORMATION PRIOR TO ARREST?

A number of statutes impose a legal duty on a person to answer police questions. Various provisions under the Road Traffic Act 1988 (ss. 164–172) impose a legal duty on motorists to provide certain information and documents when they have been stopped by the police or have been involved in an accident/incident on a public road.

6.8 POWERS OF ARREST

An arrest will occur during a criminal investigation where the police have the legal and factual grounds to justify depriving the suspect of his liberty. The most important reason for arresting a suspect is to question him about his possible involvement in or knowledge of a criminal offence.

6.8.1 WHAT IS AN ARREST?

While there is no legal definition of 'arrest', in *Christie v Leachinsky* [1947] AC 573, it was suggested that an arrest was 'the beginning of imprisonment'. On a factual basis, a person will be under arrest where he is deprived of his liberty, usually, though not exclusively, by physical restraint, so that he is not free to go where he pleases.

Common law and statutory powers of arrest exist in the following situations:

- at common law an officer can arrest the suspect in respect of a breach of the peace;
- an arrest can be made under an arrest warrant obtained from a magistrate, s. 1 Magistrates' Courts Act 1980;
- arrest without a warrant by a police constable in connection with a criminal offence where the legal grounds under s. 24(1), (2) or (3) and s. 24(5) PACE 1984 apply;
- arrest without a warrant by a citizen in connection with an indictable offence where the legal grounds under s. 24A PACE 1984 apply;
- preserved powers of arrest continue to apply to a limited range of offences listed in Schedule 2 PACE 1984, e.g. s. 7 Bail Act 1976 and the power to take fingerprints/samples in certain circumstances (ss. 27, 61 and 63 PACE).

6.8.2 ARREST AT COMMON LAW

Arrest may be made at common law in connection with an anticipated or an actual breach of the peace. The arrest may be made a police officer or a member of the public.

6.8.3 ARREST WITH A WARRANT – S. 1 MAGISTRATES' COURTS ACT 1980

Arrest under an arrest warrant is now a less common method of detaining a suspect. Section 1 of the Magistrates' Courts Act 1980 states that a justice of the peace may issue a warrant for arrest provided that:

- the accused has attained the age of 17;
- the offence alleged is indictable or punishable with imprisonment; or
- the suspect's address cannot be sufficiently established for the service of a summons.

6.8.4 **STATUTORY POWER OF ARREST – S. 24 PACE AS AMENDED BY SOCPA 2005**

Important changes to the power of arrest have been introduced by ss. 110–111 of the Serious Organised Crime and Police Act (SOCPA) 2005. The changes coincide with the revision of the PACE Codes of Practice and the introduction of a new Code G which covers the new powers of arrest. Code G can be accessed via the weblinks section of our Online Resource Centre. There is now a single, generic power of arrest for all offences contained in s. 24 PACE, as amended. The distinction between arrestable and non-arrestable offences no longer applies.

6.8 5 **ARREST WITHOUT A WARRANT BY A CONSTABLE**

The main power of arrest without a warrant under s. 24(1)–(3) PACE 1984 is exercisable by a police officer in connection with any criminal offence on the following grounds:

24 (1) A constable may arrest without a warrant

(a) anyone who is about to commit an offence; or

(b) anyone who is in the act of committing an offence; or

(c) anyone whom he has reasonable grounds for suspecting to be about to commit an offence; or

(d) anyone whom he has reasonable grounds for suspecting to be committing an offence.

24 (2) If a constable has reasonable grounds for suspecting that an offence has been committed, he may arrest without a warrant anyone whom he has reasonable grounds to suspect being guilty of it.

24 (3) If an offence has been committed a constable may arrest without a warrant

(a) anyone who is guilty of the offence;

(b) anyone whom he has reasonable grounds for suspecting to be guilty of it.

For the arrest to be lawful not only must one of the grounds in s. 24 (1)–(3) PACE 1984 be made out, the officer must additionally prove that he had reasonable grounds for believing that an arrest was *necessary* (s. 24(4)) for one or more of the reasons listed in s 24(5) PACE.

The reasons include (s. 24(5) PACE 1984):

(a) to enable the person's name to be ascertained where the constable does not know and cannot readily ascertain the person's name or has reasonable grounds for doubting the name given by the person is his real name;

(b) to enable the person's address to be ascertained;

(c) to prevent the person in question

(i) causing physical injury to himself or another;

(ii) suffering physical injury;

(iii) ausing loss or damage to property;

(iv) committing an offence against public decency;

(v) causing unlawful obstruction of the highway;

(d) to protect a child or vulnerable person from the person; or

(e) to allow the prompt and effective investigation of the offence or, of the conduct of the person;

(f) to prevent the prosecution for the offence from being hindered by the disappearance of the person in question.

The Government has suggested that the new legal framework provides a 'straightforward, universal framework' that relates to all offences. While it is too early to judge whether this justification is correct, a number of concerns are apparent about the new powers. First, the revised s. 24 PACE 1984 represents a considerable extension of police powers to arrest a person without a warrant in connection with any criminal offence. Under the 'old' s. 24 PACE 1984, the main power of arrest without a warrant could only be exercised in relation to an arrestable offence. The definition of an arrestable offence included all serious and middle ranking offences. An arrest without a warrant in connection with a non-arrestable offence (most minor and regulatory offences) could only be made under s. 25 PACE 1984 where one or more of the arrest conditions applied which generally related to the officer doubting the identity or the address of the arrested person.

The amended s. 24 PACE has radically extended the range of offences for which arrest is permitted without a warrant without any reference to the nature or seriousness of the offence in question. Having said this, operational discretion is given to individual police officers to determine whether an arrest is necessary. Paragraph 2.6 Code G provides:

> 'Extending the power of arrest to all offences provides a constable with the ability to use that power to deal with any situation. However, applying the necessity criteria requires the constable to examine and justify the reason or reasons why a person needs to be taken to the police station for the custody officer to decide whether the person should be placed in police detention.'

Relevant circumstances will include such things as the situation of the victim; the nature of the offence; the circumstances of the offender and the needs of the investigation (Code G 2.8). Instead of arresting an individual, a police officer could decide to report the person for summons, grant street bail (see below) or issue a fixed penalty notice.

A further associated concern with the abolition of the 'new' power of arrest is that a number of powers ancillary to arrest including, for example, searching the suspect's house, are likely to be exercised over a much broader range of offences.

A third cause for concern is the broad terms in which the 'necessity' grounds under s. 24(5) PACE are drafted. The test to decide whether the officer acted lawfully will include whether he had reasonable grounds for believing that one of the criterion in s. 24(5) applied at the time the arrest was made. Some of those grounds, especially where an arrest is necessary to allow the prompt and effective investigation of the offence, are almost unchallengeable from a defence perspective and this therefore reduces further the opportunity to challenge the prosecution case at trial in connection with police investigation of the offence.

6.8.6 THE REQUIREMENTS OF A LAWFUL ARREST UNDER S. 24 PACE

In order to justify an arrest, a constable must have 'reasonable grounds' for suspecting that a particular individual has committed or is committing or is about to be commit a criminal offence and that he has reasonable grounds for believing that any one of the arrest conditions in s. 24(5) is made out.

While the test of 'reasonable grounds' for suspicion is not defined, it implies both an objective and a subjective element. The subjective element will be satisfied where on the facts known to the officer and in the circumstances existing at the time of the arrest, the officer actually believed the suspect was at some stage of committing an offence or had committed an offence and objectively, the reasonable person would also have formed the necessary reasonable grounds for suspicion.

In *O'Hara v Chief Constable, RUC* [1997] AC 286, the House of Lords confirmed that the test was in two parts:

- first, there must be actual suspicion on the part of the officer (or member of the public) that an offence was at some stage of commission; and

- second, there must be reasonable grounds for that suspicion.

The House of Lords' decision in O'Hara was cited with approval by the European Court of Human Rights in *O'Hara v United Kingdom* [2002] 34 EHHR 32.

O'Hara v Chief Constable, RUC [1997] AC 286

The prosecution was brought under the Prevention of Terrorism (Temporary Provisions) Act 1984, which contained an identical provision to that in the Police and Criminal Evidence Act 1984. The Prevention of Terrorism Act provided that a person could be arrested by a police officer applying the 'reasonable grounds' test. On the instructions of a senior officer, O'Hara had been arrested by a policeman on suspicion of being a terrorist. O'Hara was later released without charge and sued the police on the basis there had never been any suspicion on the part of the arresting officer that O'Hara was a terrorist and so there had been no lawful basis for the arrest.

The House of Lords held that the test of reasonable grounds for suspicion fell into two parts. First, there must be actual suspicion on the part of the arresting officer and secondly, there must be reasonable grounds for that belief. This test is judged objectively. It was not enough to say that the arresting officer was acting on instructions from his superior as the arresting officer must show 'reasonable groundsfor suspicion'. On the facts of O'Hara there was sufficient evidence to show that the officer had formed a genuine suspicion as a result of the briefing from his superior and that the suspicion was reasonable. The arrest had therefore been lawful.

A lawful arrest further requires the application of s. 28 PACE. Upon arrest the suspect must be told at the time or as soon as practical thereafter who the arresting officer is, which station they are from, the fact that the suspect is under arrest and what are the grounds for the arrest. What the suspect should be told on arrest is further articulated in G paragraph 2.2 and in Note 3 of Code G.

Upon arrest, a person must be cautioned (see Code G paras. 3.1–3.7) in the following terms:

'You do not have to say anything. But it may harm your defence if you do not mention when questioned something which you later rely on in court. Anything you do say may be given in evidence.'

The suspect must be taken to a designated police station as soon as is reasonably practicable (s. 30 PACE), unless he is granted street bail (see below).

6.8.7 THE USE OF REASONABLE FORCE

Section 3(1) of the Criminal Law Act 1967 allows reasonable force to be used when making an arrest or when preventing a criminal offence. The 'reasonable force' test is decided by the magistrates or by the judge on the specific facts of each case.

6.8.8 CITIZEN'S POWER OF ARREST – S. 24A PACE 1984

Section 24A PACE 1984 now regulates a citizen's power of arrest, which may be made in the following circumstances. The reference in s. 24 A to indictable offences includes either-way offences.

Section 24A(1) PACE 1984 provides:

'A person other than a constable may arrest without a warrant

(a) anyone who is in the act of committing an indictable offence; or

(b) anyone whom he has reasonable grounds for suspecting to be committing an indictable offence.'

Section 24A(2) PACE 1984 further provides that:

'Where an indictable offence has been committed a person other than a constable may arrest without a warrant

(a) anyone who is guilty of the offence or

(b) anyone whom he has reasonable grounds for suspecting him to be guilty of it.'

Section 24A(3)(a) PACE 1984 requires that *in addition* to satisfying one of the grounds above in s. 24A(1)–(2) PACE 1984, the arrest will only be lawful if the citizen has reasonable grounds for believing that an arrest is necessary for one or more of the reasons listed in s. 24A(4) PACE below *and* it appears to the person making the arrest that it is not reasonably practicable for a constable to make the arrest instead.

Section 24A(4) PACE 1984 defines the grounds to include:

(a) causing injury to himself or any other person;

(b) suffering physical injury;

(c) causing loss or damage to property;

(d) making off before a constable can assume responsibility for him.

6.8.9 PRESERVED POWERS OF ARREST

The following statutory powers of arrest are preserved by the amendments to PACE 1984:

- arrest in connection with the taking of fingerprints at a police station, s. 27 PACE;
- arrest for the taking of samples in certain circumstances, s. 63A PACE;
- arrest for a failure to surrender to police bail, s. 46A PACE;
- arrest of a person who has broken or is likely to break a condition of bail, s. 7 Bail Act 1976;

6.8.10 WHAT IS THE POSITION WHERE THE POLICE NEED TO ARREST A SUSPECT IN A PRIVATE PLACE?

The position is clear where the person is arrested on the street or in another place to which the public have access. What is the position, however, where the police need to arrest a person in private place such as his home or business premises? Section 17 PACE provides that a police officer may enter and search premises without a warrant to *inter alia*:

(1) execute a warrant of arrest or a warrant of committal to prison;

(2) arrest a person for an indictable offence (this includes an either-way offence);

(3) arrest in respect of certain public order offences (e.g. possession of offensive weapons at public meetings and processions);

(4) where the officer is in uniform, for any offence under the Criminal Law Act 1977 ss. 6, 7, 8 or 10 (these relate to entering and unlawfully remaining on property);

(5) recapture a person unlawfully at large and whom he is pursuing, or

(6) to save life or limb or prevent serious damage to property.

Except in relation to s. 17(6) above, a police constable must have reasonable grounds for believing that the person he is seeking is on the premises.

6.8.11 TAKING ACTION AGAINST AN 'UNLAWFUL' ARREST

A failure to comply with the correct procedure renders the arrest unlawful—although an unlawful arrest can be remedied after the proper formalities have been complied with (*Lewis v Chief Constable of South Wales* [1991] 1 All ER 206.) Where the police have made an unlawful arrest, the defence may challenge the admissibility of prosecution evidence obtained as a result of it. The defence could submit that admitting the prosecution evidence would have an 'adverse effect on the fairness of the proceeding' (s. 78 PACE) and/or the 'probative value of the prosecution evidence is outweighed by its prejudicial effect' (s. 82(3) PACE) – see Chapter 9 for consideration of the principles that apply to the exclusion of unlawfully obtained evidence.

Where a suspect has not been properly cautioned, application can be made by the defence at trial to have any resulting evidence excluded.

6.9 THE POWER TO GRANT STREET BAIL

The traditional position has been that PACE has required an arrested person to be taken to the police station as soon as possible. It was then a matter for the custody officer to decide whether to charge the suspect or to detain him without charge or to release him on police bail.

Section 4 of the Criminal Justice Act 2003 created a new s. 30A PACE which provides that where a suspect is arrested at the scene of the offence, the suspect may be given 'street bail' without the suspect being taken to the police station to be bailed. The provision permits the police to decide when an arrested person should attend the police station. No conditions can currently be imposed on the grant of street bail; however, the Police and Justice Bill 2006 contains provisions which will allow the police to impose conditions. The suspect is then required to attend a specified police station at a later date. The suspect must be given a written notice stating the offence for which he was arrested and the time and date of the police station at which he is required to attend. There is a power of arrest for non-compliance.

6.10 POLICE POWERS TO SEARCH THE SUSPECT'S PERSON AND/OR PROPERTY

Where the suspect has been arrested, the police have a wide range of legal powers to search any property or premises owned or occupied by him for evidence relating to the offence(s) under investigation. The power of the custody officer under s. 53 PACE 1984, to search the suspect on arrival at the police station and to seize and retain property is addressed in Chapter 7 where the process of detention and questioning of suspects is considered.

6.10.1 SEARCHING WITH THE SUSPECT'S PERMISSION

The detained person may agree to his home or business premises being searched. Where consent is not given, however, the police have a wide range of legal powers to carry out a lawful search.

6.10.2 SEARCH OF AN ARRESTED PERSON AWAY FROM THE POLICE STATION: S.32(1) PACE 1984

Where the suspect has been arrested away from the police station, s. 32(1) PACE permits a constable to search an arrested person if he has reasonable grounds for believing that:

- the arrested person may present a danger to himself or others; or
- may have concealed on him anything which he might use to assist him in escape from lawful custody; or
- may have concealed on him anything which might be evidence relating to an offence.

Section 32(1) gives the police wide discretion in the way in which the power to search is exercised. It means that a police officer may search an arrested person for 'anything' on him. In practice it means that the officer can search an arrested person for items which might be wholly unrelated to the reason why the initial arrest was made as the words 'relating to an offence' do not necessarily relate to the offence for which the arrest is made. These wide powers are limited to some extent insofar as the officer must have reasonable grounds for believing that a search is necessary. Simply making a search at the time of arrest would be unlawful unless the officer could prove the necessary 'reasonable grounds' for his belief.

A police officer may not require a person to remove any of his clothing in public other than an outer coat, jacket or gloves, although it can include the search of a person's mouth (s. 32(4) PACE).

6.10.3 SEARCH AT PREMISES WHERE THE SUSPECT HAS BEEN ARRESTED: S. 32 PACE 1984

Section 32 PACE confers on a police officer the power to enter and search any premises where the suspect was at the time of his arrest or immediately before his arrest, for evidence relating to the offence for which he is being arrested. The power of search is restricted unless the officer has reasonable grounds for believing that there is such evidence on the premises.

In every case it is a question of fact where entry is made under s. 32 PACE, whether the officer considered that reasonable grounds existed for his belief that evidence might be found as a result of the search.

Where the reasonableness of the officer's belief and/or the admissibility of any evidence discovered as a result of the search is disputed by the defence, the issue will be decided prior to trial or through means of a *voir dire* (trial within a trial). Evidence obtained as a result of an unlawful search remains admissible subject to the court's dicretion to exclude under ss. 78 and 82 PACE (see Chapter 9).

6.10.4 THE POWER OF SEIZURE: S. 19 PACE 1984

Section 19 provides that a constable who is lawfully on any premises has power to seize anything which is on the premises if he has reasonable grounds to believe that it has been obtained in consequence of the commission of an offence, or that it is evidence in relation to an offence, and that it is necessary to seize it in order to prevent it from being concealed, lost, altered or destroyed.

The power of seizure does not extend to items the constable has reasonable grounds to suspect are subject to legal privilege (see 6.10.8 below). An additional power of seizure has been granted to the police under ss. 50 and 51 Criminal Justice and Police Act 2001. These new powers enable the police to remove material which cannot be practicably examined on the premises with a view to determining whether it contains evidence capable of being seized or whether the material may be subject to excluded categories of material (see 6.10.8 below). The most obvious example of this would be a personal computer containing material that might disclose evidence of the commission of an offence or contain evidence relevant to an offence.

6.10.5 SEARCH OF AN ARRESTED PERSON'S PREMISES: S.18 PACE 1984

Section 18 PACE deals with the search of premises occupied or controlled by a person who is under arrest for an indictable offence (which includes all offences triable either way) and permits a search if there are reasonable grounds for suspecting that there is evidence on the premises (other than items subject to legal privilege) that relate either to the indictable offence or some other connected or similar indictable offence. Section 18(2) confers a power of seizure of such evidence.

6.10.6 PRESERVED POWERS OF ENTRY

A number of statutes provide police officers with a power to search a suspect's premises to obtain evidence in relation to the investigation of a specific offence. Section 23(3) of the Misuse of Drugs Act 1971 allows the police to enter and search premises in connection with an investigation under the 1971 Act.

6.10.7 **SEARCH WARRANTS: S. 8 PACE 1984**

The powers of search discussed so far give the police the power to search premises owned by the arrested person or to search the premises where the person was arrested. What can the police do where it is not possible or practicable to contact the person who could allow the police to enter premises to search for evidence in connection with an offence? In these circumstances, the police will make a written application to a justice of the peace under s. 8 PACE for a warrant authorising the officer to enter and search the premises specified in the application.

To be granted a search warrant, the officer must satisfy the justice of the peace that there are reasonable grounds for believing that:

- an indictable offence has been committed; and
- there is material on the premises which is likely to be of substantial value to the investigation of the offence; and
- the material is likely to be relevant evidence; and
- the evidence does not include items subject to legal professional privilege, excluded material, or special procedure material; and
- *inter alia*, it is not practicable to communicate with any person entitled to grant entry, or if it was, it is likely that the purpose of the search will be frustrated or seriously prejudiced.

Two types of warrant may now be issued. First, the traditional specific premises warrant may be issued authorising the police to search the address specified on the warrant. Alternatively, s. 8 (2)–(4) SOCPA 2005 has introduced an all-premises warrant which covers all premises owned or occupied by the person named in the application but where it is not reasonably practicable to specify all such premises at the time of the application. The application for an all premises warrant will specify that:

- because of the offence(s) specified in the application there are reasonable grounds for believing that it is necessary to search the premises owned or controlled by the person which are not specified in the application to find material which is likely to be of substantial value to the investigation; and
- it is not reasonably practicable to specify in the application all the premises which the person owns or controls which might need to be searched.

The warrant will allow access to all premises occupied or controlled by the person whether they are specified on the application or not. Where the terms of the warrant permit, an all-premises warrant authorises the police to make multiple visits on multiple occasions to the list of premises specified in the warrant – subject to the requirement that any second and subsequent visits must be authorised by an officer of at least the rank of inspector.

The entry and search under the warrant must be completed within three months of issue. From a defence perspective, it is likely that the exercise of power under an all premises warrant will be challenged under Article 8 ECHR 1950 as infringing the owner's right to privacy. We anticipate that this provision will be the subject of case law in the near future.

6.10.8 **MATERIAL THAT MAY NOT BE SEIZED**

It is important to note that certain categories of 'material' cannot be seized by the police. These items are subject to legal professional privilege; 'excluded material' and 'special procedure material'.

(1) Items subject to legal professional privilege

These are defined by s. 10(1)(a) PACE and include any communication containing legal advice. The doctrine of legal professional privilege requires that any written and/or oral legal advice passing between a lawyer and his client in connection with a case is privileged and cannot be divulged to a third party without the client's consent.

(2) 'Excluded' material

'Excluded material' is defined by s. 11 PACE and consists of personal records held in confidence by the person who created them. Personal records are defined as medical records, records of spiritual healing and files kept by social workers and probation officers about their clients.

(3) 'Special procedure material'

Section 14 PACE defines 'special procedure material' as material which has been acquired by a person in the course of his trade, business or profession or other occupation or office and who holds it subject to an express or implied undertaking to keep it confidential. It also extends to journalistic material unless it had been acquired in confidence, in which case it will be regarded as excluded material under s. 11 PACE.

6.10.9 **SAFEGUARDS**

Sections 15 and 16 of PACE provide certain safeguards against potential misuse of the warrant by the police under s. 8 PACE (above), and any non-compliance with the sections renders a search and entry of premises unlawful. At trial the defence advocate could apply to have prosecution evidence obtained as a result of the unlawful search excluded either under s. 78 PACE on the grounds that to admit the evidence 'would have an adverse effect on the fairness of the proceedings' or under s. 82(3) PACE on the basis that the probative value of the evidence is outweighed by its prejudicial effect.

6.11 **THE PERVASIVE INFLUENCE OF THE EUROPEAN CONVENTION ON HUMAN RIGHTS (ECHR) 1950**

Powers of arrest and stop and search are subject to the protections afforded by Article 5 ECHR (the right to liberty and security of the person including the right not to be detained by the police without lawful authority) and Article 8 ECHR (the right to privacy).

When exercising stop and search powers, the police will be required to show that:

- the power to stop and search was prescribed by law; and
- the power was exercised in pursuance of a legitimate aim; and
- the exercise of the power was proportionate to the aim to be achieved.

An arrest will satisfy the requirements of Article 5 ECHR where the person is brought before a competent legal authority such as a court either on reasonable suspicion of having committed an offence or to prevent him from committing an offence or from escaping after having committed an offence (*Fox, Campbell and Hartley v UK* [1990] 13 EHHR 157).

The lawfulness of an arrest may also be judged according to whether:

- the legal authority for the arrest is precise and accessible; and
- is procedurally fair and not arbitrary; and
- proportionate to the aim of depriving a person of his liberty.

The test of reasonable suspicion will satisfy Article 5 provided that an objective observer would be satisfied that the suspect may have committed an offence (*Fox, Campbell and Hartley v UK* [1990] 13 EHHR 157).

KEY POINT SUMMARY

- Know the legal grounds that permit a person to be stopped and searched before arrest (s.1 PACE 1984).

- Where appropriate, be prepared to challenge the legality of stop and search and any evidence obtained as a result of the unlawful exercise of power. The challenge may be made to the police or the Crown Prosecution Service or to the court at the defendant's trial.

- Know the legal grounds under which a person can be arrested (s. 24 and 24A PACE 1984).

- Where appropriate, be prepared to challenge the legality of an arrest and any evidence obtained as a result of an unlawful arrest. The challenge may be made to the police or the Crown Prosecution Service or to the court at the defendant's trial.

- Have a good working knowledge of the law governing the powers to search the suspect and/or his property after arrest.

- Where appropriate, be prepared to challenge the legality of the power of search and any evidence obtained as a result of an unlawful search.

- Be aware of the pervasive influence of the ECHR in relation to stop and search and arrest and cite ECHR case law to support your submissions.

SELF-TEST QUESTIONS

1. Where can you find guidance on the reasonable suspicion or belief test?

2. Which caution should be given to the suspect on arrest?

3. Where are the police powers to search a person and his property after arrest contained?

4. In what circumstances will the police apply to a justice of the peace for a warrant to be issued under s. 8 PACE?

5. Police are called to a public order disturbance in town. By the time they arrive, the incident appears to be over. CCTV operators have provided a description of a male individual wearing a football top who appears to have been the instigator of the trouble and who appeared to be waving some kind of bottle or weapon in his hand. One of the police officers notices a male wearing such a top walking towards a taxi-rank. On approaching the male (Trevor), he runs off. He is apprehended within a matter of minutes. What powers do the police have in this regard?

6. A short, factual scenario based on the exercise of police powers appears at the end of Chapter 9 (scenario 1); although the focus of the question is based on the admissibility of unlawfully obtained evidence, you may wish to consider what aspects of police procedure relating to stop and search and arrest might be considered unlawful.

FIGURE 6.1 POLICE POWERS OF STOP/SEARCH/SEIZURE AND ARREST

STOP AND SEARCH BEFORE ARREST

Section 1 PACE and Code A

- A person may be stopped and/or searched in a public place or in a place to which the public has access where:
  - the officer reasonably suspects the person is in possession of
    - stolen articles; or
    - prohibited articles.

SEARCHING THE SUSPECT AFTER ARREST

- with the suspect's consent; or
- under s. 32 PACE where the officer:
  - has reasonable grounds for believing the suspect may present a danger to himself or others; or
  - has concealed anything on him he might use to escape from custody; or
  - has concealed on him evidence which might be related to an offence.

SEARCH OF PREMISES AFTER ARREST

- search with the suspect's consent;
- search with a warrant in connection with an indictable offence, s. 8 PACE;
- search the premises at which the suspect is arrested, s. 32 PACE;
- search premises owned/controlled by the suspect, s. 18 PACE;
- preserved powers of entry, e.g. s. 23 Misuse of Drugs Act 1971.

POLICE OFFICER ARREST WITHOUT A WARRANT

- s. 24 PACE where a police officer has reasonable grounds for suspecting that the person:
  - is about to commit an offence; or
  - is committing an offence; or
  - has committed an offence AND
  - it is necessary to arrest the individual for any of the following reasons (s. 24(5)):
    - to enable the person's name to be ascertained where the constable does not know and cannot readily ascertain the person's name or has reasonable grounds for doubting the name given by the person is his real name; or
    - to enable the person's address to be ascertained;
    - to prevent the person in question
      - causing physical injury to himself or another;
      - suffering physical injury;
      - causing loss or damage to property;
      - committing an offence against public decency; or
      - causing unlawful obstruction of the highway;
  - to protect a child or vulnerable person from the person; or
  - to allow the prompt and effective investigation of the offence or of the conduct of the person;
  - to prevent the prosecution for the offence from being hindered by the disappearance of the person in question.

FIGURE 6.1 (CONTINUED)

CHECKLIST FOR A LAWFUL ARREST – S. 28 PACE

- There must be a legal ground for the arrest, e.g. s. 24 PACE.

- There must be the factual grounds for the arrest, e.g. reasonable grounds for believing that an offence has been committed.

- The person must be cautioned as follows:
  - 'You do not have to say anything. But it may harm your defence if you do not mention when questioned something which you later rely on in court. Anything you do say may be given in evidence.'

- The person must be informed of the reason for his arrest.

- The person should be taken to a designated police station as soon as is reasonably practicable.

7   DETENTION AND INTERROGATION

7.1 **INTRODUCTION**

Following his arrest, the suspect should be brought to a designated police station as soon as is reasonably practicable. At this point, the suspect becomes the centrepiece of the police investigation. It is likely that the police will want to question their detainee and undertake certain investigatory procedures, including obtaining from the detainee:

* fingerprints;
* a non-intimate sample;
* an intimate sample;
* photographs;
* requesting the detainee participate in a formal identification procedure.

In this chapter, we consider the process of detention, questioning and charge. The procedures associated with obtaining identification of a suspect are considered in Chapter 11.

A detailed legal framework for the treatment of suspects at the police station is provided by the substantive provisions of PACE and the Codes of Practice, particularly Code C. The provisions define the extent of the power of the police in relation to a detainee and importantly provide a number of safeguards for suspects. A copy of Code C is freely accessible from the Home Office website – our Online Resource Centre includes a link taking you to the Codes of Practice.

online
resource
centre

The safeguards contained in PACE and its accompanying Codes of Practice exist to ensure the suspect enjoys fair treatment while in detention but also to promote investigative integrity on the part of the police, thereby ensuring the quality and reliability of evidence obtained at the police station. Evidence obtained at the police station in breach of PACE and Code C is vulnerable to challenge, and a defence lawyer might seek exclusion of any resulting evidence under s. 78 PACE (see Chapter 9) and under s. 76 PACE, in the case of a confession (see Chapter 10). Section 67(11) PACE allows the Codes of Practice to be admissible in evidence if relevant to a matter to be decided by a court.

It is the duty of the legal adviser at the police station to advance and protect the rights of his client while in custody. To do this, the legal adviser needs a detailed knowledge of PACE and the Codes of Practice so that he is in a position to constantly challenge the police if they do not play by the rules.

Be aware that there are more extensive powers relating to the process of detention and interrogation in relation to persons suspected of involvement in terrorist activities. Such provisions are contained in the Codes of Practice and the Terrorism Act 2000, and are outside the scope of this work. More details can be found in *Blackstone's Criminal Practice.*

As part of the second edition of this text, we are pleased to offer a 'stand alone' video case study, entitled the Peter West Police Station Scenario, which, together with relevant supporting documentation, can be accessed via password on our Online Resource Centre. The video is lengthy and is split into a number of different sections. It explores all aspects of detention at the police station, including the role of the legal adviser, and illustrates many of the points covered in this and Chapter 12.

In this chapter, we explain the process of detention and charge including the following:

* the role of the custody officer;
* the importance of the custody record;
* the circumstances in which a suspect can be detained without charge;
* the length of time a suspect can be in custody;

- the obligation to keep continued detention under review;
- the right of a suspect to have someone informed of his arrest;
- the right of a suspect to have access to a solicitor;
- the basic rights of a suspect in custody;
- specific safeguards in relation to vulnerable suspects;
- the conduct of an interview; and
- the decision to charge and withhold bail.

We begin, however, by mentioning those who voluntarily attend at the police station.

7.2 THE RIGHTS OF A VOLUNTEER AT THE POLICE STATION

It is often reported in the media that a person is 'helping the police with their enquiries'. You may recall that during the murder investigation into the death of Holly Wells and Jessica Chapman, Ian Huntley and Maxine Carr 'assisted the police with their enquiries' prior to their arrests. This expression means that a member of the public is voluntarily assisting the police in the criminal investigation without having been arrested. A volunteer is entitled to leave police custody at any time (Code C para. 3.21).

If the police wish to detain the volunteer, he must be arrested, at which point his legal status changes to that of a detainee.

7.2.1 QUESTIONING A VOLUNTEER

If the police wish to put questions to a volunteer for the purpose of obtaining evidence which may be put before a court, the volunteer must:

- be cautioned before replying;
- be told that he is not under arrest;
- be told that he is free to leave if he wishes; and
- be told that he may obtain free and independent legal advice (Code C para. 3.21).

7.3 ARREST AND ARRIVAL AT THE POLICE STATION

Section 30 PACE requires an arrested person to be taken to a designated police station as soon as practicable after arrest. A designated police station is equipped with the appropriate facilities for dealing with a suspect in detention.

Once the suspect arrives at the police station he will be taken to the custody suit for 'booking-in'. This will be carried out by the custody officer on duty.

7.4 THE ROLE OF THE CUSTODY OFFICER

The custody officer plays an essential role in ensuring that the suspect's legal rights at the police station are complied with (s. 39 PACE). The officer should always remain independent and impartial of the criminal investigation. He should not question the suspect about his involvement in the alleged offence. The custody officer is the person responsible for taking some important decisions in relation to the suspect, including whether he should be detained or released and, in conjunction with the CPS, whether he should be charged.

7.4.1 THE CUSTODY RECORD

The custody officer is also responsible for compiling the suspect's custody record. A custody record must be opened as soon as is reasonably practicable for each person brought to a police station (Code C para. 2.1). The suspect's legal adviser and/or appropriate adult have a right of access to the custody record 'at any time while the person is detained' (Code C para. 2.4). When a detained person leaves the police station, they are entitled to a copy of the custody record upon request (Code C para. 2.4A).

online
resource
centre

The custody record is a very important document in evidential terms to both the prosecution and defence. It should provide a detailed record of all aspects of the suspect's detention. (We have included extracts from the custody record in relation to our case study *R v Lenny Whyte* in Appendix 1. The complete documentation, including the full custody record can be accessed on our Online Resource Centre.)

The custody record will include details of the suspect's arrest, the reason for his detention, authorisation of search procedures or continued detention, requests for legal advice/medical advice, reviews of the suspect's detention, details of meals and refreshments given to the suspect and any complaints made by the suspect. The custody record should be carefully considered to ensure the detainee's rights have been respected.

Where questions of the admissibility of evidence obtained during the investigation arise, the custody record may be adduced in evidence at trial. For this reason, the solicitor or legal adviser should ensure that any representations he makes regarding his client's detention are recorded in the custody record.

7.4.2 WHAT RIGHTS MUST THE CUSTODY OFFICER INFORM THE SUSPECT OF ON HIS ARRIVAL AT THE POLICE STATION?

Upon arrival at the police station, and in accordance with Code C para. 3.1, the custody officer should explain to the suspect that he has the following rights which may be exercised at any stage:

1. the right to have someone informed of his arrest;

2. the right to consult in private with a solicitor, such advice being free and independent;

3. the right to consult the Codes of Practice.

The custody officer is also required, under Code C paras. 3.5–3.10, to undertake a risk assessment to consider the specific needs of each detainee. This will include asking the suspect on his arrival at the police station whether he:

• wants legal advice;

• wants to inform someone of his arrest;

• might be in need of medical treatment;

• requires the presence of an appropriate adult;

• requires an interpreter.

7.4.3 SEARCH UPON ARRIVAL AT THE POLICE STATION

The custody officer is obliged to ascertain a detainee's property when brought into custody (s. 54 PACE). Property and clothing may be seized and retained if it could cause physical injury, damage to persons or property or could be used to assist an escape from lawful custody. Strip searches and intimate searches require special justification (see Code C, Annex A).

7.4.4 IMMEDIATE DECISION MAKING OBLIGATIONS ON THE CUSTODY OFFICER – IS THERE SUFFICIENT EVIDENCE TO CHARGE?

Following the arrested person's arrival at the police station and having completed the formalities, the custody officer, in conjunction with a CPS lawyer on rota at the police station, has a duty to determine whether there is sufficient evidence to charge the suspect with the offence for which he has been arrested.

The CJA 2003 has made some significant changes to the charging procedure at the police station, considered further in Chapter 13. For the most part, the decision to charge a suspect rests with the Crown Prosecution Service (s. 28 and Sch. 2 CJA 2003, amending s. 37 of PACE). As an alternative to charging the suspect, the CPS has discretion to offer a simple caution or conditional caution.

If there is sufficient evidence to charge, s. 37(7) PACE requires that the suspect shall either be:

- released without charge and on bail for the purpose of enabling the Director of Public Prosecutions to make a decision under section 37B;
- released without charge and on bail but not for that purpose (i.e. to allow for enquiries to continue);
- released without charge and without bail; or
- charged.

Where the decision to charge is not taken immediately and the file is passed to the CPS for review (s. 37B), a suspect can be released on bail under s. 37(7)(a), pending a decision to charge. Bail granted for this purpose can be conditional (s. 37(D)). Any breach of bail granted in these circumstances carries a power of arrest (s. 37(C)). The provision gives a measure of public protection in a case where the police have released a suspect on bail pending a charging decision by the CPS. However, it also means that some suspects will have to comply with onerous pre-charge bail conditions for some considerable time, which can amount to a significant restriction on a suspect's liberty. Legal advisers at the police station need to be aware of this and be prepared to negotiate manageable bail conditions. Application may be made to a magistrates' court (s. 47(1)(e)) to vary conditions of bail imposed under s. 37(7)(a). Provision is made in the Police and Justice Bill 2006 for conditions to be attached to the grant of police bail under s. 37(7)(b), where the suspect is released without referral to the CPS, pending further enquiries. Police bail and the circumstances in which conditions can be attached to the grant of police bail are further considered at paragraph 7.14.2 below.

A failure to surrender or a failure without reasonable cause to abide by any conditions imposed under s. 37(7)(a) can precipitate the suspect being charged for the original offence for which he was arrested, and will of course be relevant to any subsequent bail hearing before a court.

If charged, the suspect may be kept in police custody (s. 38 PACE) pending first appearance before a magistrates' court, or released on bail with or without conditions attached to that bail (s. 47(1A) PACE). The defendant's charge sheet will contain the date of the defendant's initial appearance before a magistrates' court. A failure to answer police bail granted in these circumstances entitles the police to arrest without warrant (s. 46(A) PACE).

7.5 DETENTION WITHOUT CHARGE

The continued detention of a person arrested, but not charged, is allowed under s. 37(2) PACE where the custody officer has reasonable grounds for believing that his detention without charge is necessary:

- to secure or preserve evidence relating to an offence for which he is under arrest; or
- to obtain such evidence by questioning him.

Where the custody officer decides that continued detention without charge is necessary, the justification for doing so must be noted in the custody record. The grounds are easily made out in a case where the investigating officer needs to interview witnesses or the suspect, or to undertake personal searches. Where the custody officer becomes aware at any time that the detention grounds have ceased to exist, there is an obligation on the custody officer to release the suspect immediately (s. 34(2) PACE) without bail, unless it appears that there is a need for further investigation (s. 34(5) PACE).

7.5.1 FOR HOW LONG CAN A SUSPECT BE DETAINED WITHOUT CHARGE?

There are strict time limits on how long a detained individual can be kept at a police station without charge. Unauthorised detention beyond the requisite time is unlawful.

7.5.2 INITIAL DETENTION PERIOD OF 24 HOURS

The general position is that the suspect can be detained at the police station without charge for 24 hours (s. 41 PACE). The 24-hour period begins to run, for the most part, from the time of the suspect's arrival at the police station, which must be noted in the custody record.

At the end of the 24-hour period the suspect must either be charged or released unconditionally or on bail.

7.5.3 DETENTION WITHOUT CHARGE BEYOND 24 HOURS?

The basic 24 hours of detention without charge can be extended up to 36 hours for an indictable offence (which includes either-way offences) where the provisions of s. 42(1) PACE apply. These are that:

- a senior officer of at least the rank of superintendent authorises the suspect's continued detention; and
- the officer has reasonable grounds for believing that it is necessary to detain the suspect without charge to secure or preserve evidence by questioning him; and
- the investigation is being conducted diligently and expeditiously.

Where these conditions apply, the suspect can be detained for an additional period of up to 12 hours. This is a total of 36 hours from the time of arrival at the police station. Where the suspect's basic period of detention has been extended, the reasons for doing so must be noted on the custody record. Continued detention is easily justified where investigating officers wish to interview or reinterview a suspect or to undertake searches of an intimate nature or to arrange an identification procedure.

7.5.4 DETENTION BEYOND 36 HOURS – WARRANT OF FURTHER DETENTION

Where the police wish to detain the suspect without charge beyond 36 hours, an application under s. 43 PACE must be made to the magistrates' court for a warrant of further detention. An application for continued detention beyond 36 hours can only be made in relation to an indictable offence (which includes either-way offences).

The suspect has the right to be present at the hearing and to be legally represented. The defence solicitor may make a submission to the magistrates about the suspect's continued detention. In practice, the application for a warrant of further detention is invariably granted by the magistrates.

Where the police establish a case that the suspect should be detained for a further period without charge, the court may authorise detention for a further period of up to 36 hours, i.e. making a total 72 hours from his arrival at the designated police station.

At the end of 72 hours, where the police wish to continue holding the suspect without charge, a further application can be made to the magistrates requesting that the suspect should be detained for a further period of up to 24 hours, making a total of 96 hours from the time of the suspect's arrival at the police station.

At the end of 96 hours, the suspect must either be charged, or released unconditionally, or on police bail (s. 44 PACE).

In making an application for a warrant of further detention before a magistrates' court, the police must set out their reasons. In so doing, the police will need to explain the circumstances of the suspect's arrest, what investigatory steps have been undertaken so far and what further enquiries are needed. They will need to establish why the suspect's detention is necessary each time an application is made to have the detention period extended up to the maximum of 96 hours.

Where an individual has not been charged but has been released on police bail, the custody time limit clock freezes at this point. It resumes ticking once the suspect answers his police bail.

7.6 OBLIGATION TO REVIEW A SUSPECT'S DETENTION

Section 40 PACE requires the police to carry out periodic reviews of the suspect's detention, the details of which must be recorded in the custody record. The purpose of the review is to ensure the suspect's continued detention is lawful.

Where the suspect has not be charged, the review of his detention must be carried out by an officer of at least the rank of inspector who has not been directly involved in the investigation. This officer is known as the 'review officer'. Provision is made under s. 40 PACE and Code C, paras. 15.9–15.11, for reviews to be conducted over the telephone or via video-link in some instances. However, the suspect always has a right to make representations.

Where the suspect has been arrested and charged, the review can be carried out by the custody officer.

7.6.1 WHEN MUST THE REVIEWS BE CONDUCTED?

The first review of detention must be made no later than six hours after the detention was first authorised by the custody officer and thereafter every nine hours to ensure that the reasons for detaining the suspect's detention continue to apply.

The legal adviser should be satisfied that the suspect's detention was lawful at all times. The custody record should help to determine this. If the detention ground under s. 37(2) PACE ceased to exist or never existed in the first place, or if a review of detention was not carried out, continued detention becomes unlawful.

7.7 WHAT RIGHTS DOES A SUSPECT IN CUSTODY ENJOY?

The importance of the rights we are about to cover cannot be overstated. Where incriminating admissions or inferences from silence have been obtained in breach of these rights, exclusion of such evidence can be sought under ss. 76/78 PACE (see Chapters 9 and 10).

7.7.1 THE SUSPECT'S RIGHT TO INFORM SOMEONE OF HIS ARREST: S. 56 PACE

Section 56(1) PACE provides that where a person has been arrested and held in custody, he shall be entitled to inform a friend, relative or some other person likely to be interested in his welfare of his arrest as soon as is reasonably practicable. For some detainees, especially those who might be termed 'vulnerable', the right of intimation under s. 56 PACE is an important right.

Guidance on the right is contained in Code C para. 5 (supplemented by Annex B).

Contact can extend to the detainee speaking on the telephone to a particular individual (although this is unlikely to be a private call) and writing to the person concerned (though such correspondence is likely to be read). At the discretion of the custody officer, it can include a visit by the individual concerned.

7.7.2 WHEN CAN THE RIGHT TO HAVE SOMEONE INFORMED OF YOUR ARREST BE DELAYED?

The suspect's general right to inform someone of his arrest may be delayed where the grounds in s. 56(2)–(5) PACE Code C Annex B are made out.

Section 56 provides that:

- the suspect must have been arrested in connection with an indictable offence; and
- an officer of at least the rank of inspector authorises the delay on the basis that the officer has reasonable grounds for believing that telling the suspect's relative, friend or other person likely to take an interest in his welfare of the arrest will:
  - lead to interference with or harm to evidence connected with a serious arrestable offence; or
  - lead to interference with or physical injury to other persons; or
  - lead to the alerting of other persons suspected of having committed such an offence but not yet arrested for it; or
  - hinder the recovery of any property obtained as a result of such an offence.

The authorisation for the delay may be given to the suspect orally or in writing. The reason for the delay must be noted in the custody record and if justified, may not exceed 36 hours from the time the suspect arrives at the designated police station.

7.7.3 THE SUSPECT'S RIGHT TO LEGAL ADVICE: S. 58 PACE

The general right to legal advice under s. 58 PACE (supplemented by Code C para. 6 (Annex B)) is one of the most important protections against the abuse of the suspect's civil liberties by the police. The importance of ensuring a suspect has access to legal advice while being detained has been underlined many times by the European Court of Human Rights: *Murray v UK* (1996) 22 EHRR 29 and *Condron v UK* (2001) 31 EHRR 1.

7.7.4 WHO PAYS FOR LEGAL ADVICE GIVEN AT THE POLICE STATION?

The Police Station Advice and Assistance Scheme administered by the Legal Services Commission enables a suspect to have legal advice free of charge in the vast majority of cases. The suspect may request the services of a solicitor of his choice or from the Duty Solicitor Scheme.

7.7.5 THE OBLIGATION ON THE POLICE TO FACILITATE ACCESS TO LEGAL ADVICE

Code C places strict obligations on the police to ensure access to legal advice. The obligations include the following:

- All detainees must be informed that they have the right to consult and communicate with a solicitor in private and at any time, free of charge (Code C para. 6.1).
- Nothing must be said or done by the police with the intention of dissuading a detainee from obtaining legal advice (Code C para. 6.4).
- Any request for legal advice must be noted in the custody record.
- If the detainee declines to speak to a solicitor in person, it should be explained to him that he has a right to speak with that person on the telephone and if the detainee continues to waive his right, the custody officer should ask the detainee why and the reasons should be recorded on to the custody record (Code C para. 6.5).
- When a solicitor arrives at the police station to see the suspect, the suspect must be informed of the solicitor's arrival and asked if he would like to see him. This is so even if he has earlier declined legal advice (Code C para. 6.15).

- A detainee who wants legal advice may not be interviewed until they receive such advice unless the circumstances listed in Code C para. 6.6 apply.
- Where the suspect has access to legal advice, he must be allowed to have his solicitor present for the interview.
- If the solicitor requested is on his way to the station or about to set off, an interview should not normally be started until he arrives (note 6A).
- Where the suspect requests legal advice during an interview, there should be no further questioning until the suspect has spoken to his legal adviser (Code C para. 6.5).

The police are also required to remind the suspect about his right to legal advice at the following stages of his detention:

- immediately before the commencement or recommencement of any interview at the police station (Code C para. 11.2);
- before a review of detention takes place (Code C para. 15.4);
- after the suspect has been charged, if a police officer wishes to draw the suspect's attention to any written or oral statements made by any other person (Code C para. 16.4);
- after the suspect has been charged, if further questions are to be put to the suspect about the offence (Code C para. 16.5);
- prior to an identification parade, group identification or video identification is held Code D para. 3.17);
- prior to the taking of an intimate body sample (Code D para. 6.3).

7.7.6 IN WHAT CIRCUMSTANCES CAN A SUSPECT'S RIGHT OF ACCESS TO LEGAL ADVICE UNDER S. 58(8) PACE BE DELAYED?

The decision by the police to delay a detainee's access to legal advice is a serious step and must be justified, as it can have very serious implications for evidence obtained from a suspect as a result (see Chapter 10). On numerous occasions, the European Court of Human Rights has stressed the fundamental importance of the right to legal advice at the police station (*Murray v UK* (1996) 22 EHRR 29; *Averill v UK* (2001) 31 EHRR 36 and *Condron v UK* (2001) 31 EHRR 1).

The right to delay access to a solicitor can only be exercised in accordance with the conditions laid down in s. 58(8) (Annex B Code C) i.e. when:

- the suspect has been arrested in connection with an indictable offence; and
- an officer of at least the rank of superintendent authorises the delay on the ground that he has reasonable grounds for believing that if the suspect was permitted to exercise his right to receive legal advice it will:
  - lead to interference with or harm to evidence connected with a serious arrestable offence or interference with or physical injury to other persons; or
  - lead to the alerting of other persons suspected of having committed such an offence but not yet arrested for it; or
  - will hinder the recovery of any property obtained as a result of such an offence.

The reason for the delay must be noted in the custody record and, if justified, may not exceed 36 hours from the time the suspect arrived at the designated police station. The suspect must be informed of the reason for the denial of legal advice, s. 58(9) PACE. If the grounds for delaying access to legal advice cease to apply, the suspect must be asked whether he wants to see his legal adviser (Code C Annex B A.6).

The police may not delay access to a particular solicitor on the grounds that he may advise the suspect not to answer questions or that the solicitor was initially asked to attend the station by someone else (Code C Annex B, A.4).

If the authorising officer concludes that any of the risks identified above apply to the particular solicitor requested, the detainee must be allowed to choose another solicitor (Code C Annex B A.3).

7.8 WHAT ARE A SUSPECT'S BASIC RIGHTS WHILE IN POLICE DETENTION?

Code C, paras. 8–9 and 12 recognise that a detainee is entitled to certain fundamental rights while detained at the police station. They include:

- A right to an adequately heated, cleaned and ventilated cell; access to toilet facilities.
- At least two light meals and one main meal in any 24-hour period, taking account of special dietary requirements, and regular refreshments.
- A requirement that a detainee receives appropriate clinical attention as soon as reasonably practicable if the person appears to be suffering from physical illness, is injured, appears to need clinical attention or appears to be suffering from a mental disorder. If a detainee requests medical attention, a health care professional must be called. If a detainee needs to take prescribed medication, an appropriate health care professional must be called, and in some instances, may be the only person who can administer the medication.
- The requirement that in any 24-hour period, the suspect must be allowed at least eight hours' continuous rest, preferably at night and free from questioning (Code C para. 12.2).
- Breaks during the interview should occur at normal meal times, and short breaks should be held approximately every two hours (Code C para. 12.8).

7.9 THE TREATMENT OF VULNERABLE SUSPECTS

Code C makes specific provision for the identification and treatment of vulnerable suspects. Annex E provides a detailed summary of the important provisions in relation to detainees under 17, the mentally disordered or mentally vulnerable suspect. The risk assessment which the custody officer is required to undertake at the outset of the detention process in relation to all detainees should identify those detainees who might be described as being 'vulnerable'. Aspects of criminal procedure specifically relevant to juveniles (those under the age of 18) are considered in Chapter 34.

A key right in protecting the vulnerable suspect is access to an appropriate adult. The custody officer must inform an appropriate adult as soon as possible about the detention and request the appropriate adult to attend the police station as soon as practicable (Code C para. 3.15).The appropriate adult is likely to be the vulnerable person's parent or guardian, a social worker, or another responsible adult. The role of the appropriate adult is to protect the vulnerable person's interests and to ensure that his legal rights are respected by the police. The right of access to an appropriate adult is additional to the right of access to legal advice. Code C para. 11.5 stipulates that in the case of a juvenile or mentally vulnerable person, no interview should be undertaken in the absence of the appropriate adult.

7.10 INTERVIEWING THE SUSPECT

The police investigation will involve questioning the suspect and interviewing other witnesses with a view to gathering sufficient evidence to charge the suspect or to exclude him from their investigations. Interviewing a person suspected of committing the crime is the centrepiece of many police investigations. Even for those people who are experienced at dealing with the police, being interviewed can be a very intimidating and unsettling experience. Vulnerability may lead some suspects to admitting to crimes they have not committed, or being susceptible to a particular line of police questioning, bullying or inducements. For these reasons, the substantive provisions of PACE and Codes C and E closely regulate the conduct of police interviews with the suspect. The duties of the police and the custody officer and the corresponding rights of the suspect in custody, exist to try and ensure the reliability and fairness of evidence resulting from the detention process. The admissibility of evidence, particularly confession evidence, is vulnerable to challenge under s. 76(2)(a) or (b), s. 78 and s. 82(3) PACE where it has been obtained in breach (accidental or otherwise) of PACE and the Codes of Practice. The Codes of Practice are admissible in evidence for this purpose under s. 67(11) PACE.

7.10.1 WHAT CONSTITUTES AN INTERVIEW?

Code C para. 11.1A defines an interview as:

> 'the questioning of a person regarding his involvement in a criminal offence where there are grounds to suspect him of such an offence or offences which, by virtue of paragraph 10.1 of Code C must be carried out under caution.'

All interviews must be carried out at a police station. The only exception to this is in the circumstances narrowly defined in Code C para. 11.1 where delay in conducting an interview would lead to interference with or harm to evidence connected with an offence, interference with or physical harm to other persons, or serious loss of or damage to property. In such a case, contemporaneous written notes must be kept.

The effect of Code C para. 11.1A is to permit an informal conversation between an investigating officer and a suspect, providing it does not relate to the circumstances of an offence which the police are investigating. This would cover such matters as verifying someone's identity, but would certainly not cover a prolonged conversation with a view to securing admissions capable of being used in evidence.

7.10.2 WHEN MUST AN INTERVIEW CEASE?

Code C para. 11.6 provides that an interview should cease when the officer in charge of the investigation:

- is satisfied all the questions they consider relevant to obtaining accurate and reliable information about the offence have been put to the suspect, including allowing the suspect an opportunity to give an innocent explanation and asking questions to test this;
- has taken account of any other available evidence; and
- the officer in charge of the investigation, or in the case of a detained person, the custody officer, reasonably believes that there is sufficient evidence to provide a realistic prospect of conviction.

7.11 THE REQUIREMENT TO CAUTION

At the beginning of the interview the suspect must be cautioned. Where the interview recommences after a break, the investigating officer must remind the suspect that he remains under caution and, where he considers it to be appropriate, the caution should be read to the suspect again.

There are two ways in which the suspect may be cautioned, depending whether or not an adverse inference from the suspect's silence may be drawn under ss. 34, 36 and 37 Criminal Justice and Public Order Act 1994 (see Chapter 8).

Where an adverse inference may be drawn at trial from the suspect's silence at the police station, the caution should be given as follows:

> 'You do not have to say anything. But it may harm your defence if you do not mention when questioned something which you later rely on in court. Anything you do say may be given in evidence.'

This caution will be appropriate where the suspect has been offered and/or received legal advice.

Under Code C the police are required to administer an alternative caution where:

- a person has been denied a solicitor under s. 58(8) PACE; or
- a superintendent authorises an interview to proceed under Code C para. 6.6(b) before the suspect has been given an opportunity to receive legal advice; or
- the suspect is to be interviewed after charge.

The revised caution reads:

> 'You do not have to say anything. But anything you do say may be given in evidence.'

The revised caution was introduced to comply with the European Court of Human Rights decision in *Murray v UK* (1996) 22 EHHR 29 and is given statutory effect in s. 58 Youth Justice and Criminal Evidence Act 1999.

7.12 WHAT CONSTITUTES A FAIR INTERVIEW?

7.12.1 OPPRESSIVE INTERVIEWS

It is an essential requirement of fairness that when interviewing a suspect about his involvement in an offence, the police do not abuse their position of trust by conducting the interview in an 'oppressive' manner. This requirement is recognised by Code C para. 11.3, which provides:

> 'No police officer may try to obtain answers to questions or to elicit a statement by the use of oppression.'

'Oppression' is not defined in Code C, but is partially defined by s. 76(8) PACE, to mean torture, inhuman or degrading treatment and the use or threat of violence. Section 76(2)(a) PACE requires the court to exclude a confession that has been obtained through oppression and is considered further in Chapter10.

Code C para. 11.4 requires the interviewing officer, at the beginning of the interview, to put to the suspect any significant statement or silence which occurred in the presence or hearing of a police officer before the start of the interview. A significant statement is one which appears capable of being used in evidence against the suspect.

7.12.2 INDUCEMENTS TO CONFESS

Code C para. 11.5 makes it clear that no interviewer shall indicate, except to answer a direct question, what action will be taken by the police if the person being questioned answers questions, makes a statement or refuses to do either.

7.12.3 FITNESS TO BE INTERVIEWED

Before any detainee is interviewed the custody officer must assess whether the detainee is fit to be interviewed (Code C para. 12.3). This would be particularly pertinent to detainees who are drunk or under the influence of an illicit substance. In some instances, the custody officer will need to consult an appropriate health care professional in order to determine the suspect's fitness to be interviewed. As previously indicated, vulnerable suspects have the right to have an appropriate adult present during the interview (Code C para. 11.15).

7.12.4 PHYSICAL CONDITIONS OF THE INTERVIEW

An interview should take place in a room which is properly, heated, lighted and ventilated (Code C 12.4). There are no limits on the number of officers who may be present during the interview, but the officer in charge must identify them to the suspect and he should be aware of the possibility that the presence of too many officers might be seen as oppressive.

7.12.5 THE ROLE OF THE LEGAL ADVISER DURING INTERVIEW

Code C Notes for guidance para. 6D acknowledges the nature of the legal adviser's role in the interview:

'A detained person has a right to free legal advice and to be represented by a solicitor. The solicitor's only role in the police station is to protect and advance the legal rights of his client. On occasions this may require the solicitor to give advice which has the effect of his client avoiding giving evidence which strengthens a prosecution case. The solicitor may intervene in order to seek clarification or to challenge an improper question to his client or the manner in which it is put, or to advise his client not to reply to particular questions or if he wishes to give his client further legal advice.'

We consider in some detail the practical aspects of the role of the legal adviser at the police station in Chapter 12.

Save with regard to a restricted number of exceptions, a suspect who wants legal advice may not be interviewed or continue to be interviewed until they have received it (Code C para. 6.6).

7.13 HOW SHOULD AN INTERVIEW BE RECORDED?

7.13.1 THE REQUIREMENT TO TAPE RECORD POLICE INTERVIEWS

An interview in the investigation of indictable and either-way offences must be tape recorded (Code E para. 3.1). It is also common practice to tape record interviews in connection with the majority of summary offences. The practice and procedure of tape recorded interviews are governed by Code E of the Codes of Practice and the *Practice Direction (Crime Tape Recording Police Interviews)* [1989] 1 WLR 631. Interviews should be recorded with the full knowledge of the person to be interviewed and will be recorded on two tapes. One is a working copy, with the other being sealed at the completion of the interview. A transcript of the interview is produced from the working tape and is required to be a 'balanced' version of the interview. The tape and the transcript must record where the interview took place, the identity of the people present and the time the interview commenced, the time of any breaks and the time the interview finished. (The transcripts of interview in relation to two of our case studies (*R v Lenny Whyte* and *R v William Hardy*) can be located within Appendices 1 and 2 respectively.) (In relation to *R v Roger Martin* (our web-based only case study), a transcript of interview is included.)

A written summary of the tape-recorded interview will be sent to the defence as part of the requirements of Advance Information under Part 21, Criminal Procedure Rules. The defence has the right to have access to a copy of the tape to check the accuracy of the summary prepared by the prosecution. If the defence agrees that the summary served by the prosecution is accurate (subject to any legal arguments about the admissibility of the evidence at trial) the written summary will be part of the evidence in the case. If the defence does not agree with the summary, the tape will be transcribed in full for use at the trial. If necessary, the tape will be played in full at the trial.

online resource centre

A new Code F provides for the video recording of interviews with the suspect. The practice is the subject to pilot projects in a number of police force areas prior to expected national implementation.

7.13.2 HOW SHOULD AN INTERVIEW OUTSIDE THE POLICE STATION BE RECORDED?

Where an interview takes place outside a police station (in the limited circumstances set out in Code C para. 11.1), or where the interview is not tape recorded, the police are required to make an accurate written record of the interview which the suspect must be given the opportunity of reading and signing as correct (Code C para. 11.7–11.14). Code C para. 11.13 requires an officer to make a note of any comments made by a suspect, including unsolicited comments, which are made outside the context of the interview but are relevant to the offence. The note should be dated and timed and the suspect should be invited to sign the documented record and to make any amendments to it as he deems necessary.

The failure to accurately record an interview with a suspect as required by Code C and E has been consistently used for excluding evidence of the interview at trial (*R v Keenan* [1990] 2 QB 54) (see Chapter 10).

7.14 CHARGING A SUSPECT

As we have already seen, as soon as there is sufficient evidence to charge a suspect, s. 37(7) PACE requires the custody officer to charge or release the suspect. The decision to charge will, for the most part, be made by the CRS, in accordance with the statutory charging regime under the CJA 2003. As an alternative to charging, you might seek to persuade the custody officer to offer your client a caution instead. A caution is an alternative to a prosecution and Code C Notes for Guidance 16A requires the custody officer to take account of alternatives to prosecution. The use of a caution and the conditional caution under the CJA 2003 as an alternative to prosecution are considered in Chapter 13.

7.14.1 QUESTIONING AFTER HAVING BEEN CHARGED

On charging or informing the suspect that he might be prosecuted for an offence, no further questions may be asked of the detainee except in the circumstances provided for in Code C para. 16.5. They include where an interview is necessary:

- to prevent harm or loss to some other person, or the public;
- to clear up an ambiguity in a previous answer or statement;
- in the interests of justice for the detainee to have put to them, and to have an opportunity to comment on, information concerning the offence which has come to light since they were charged, or to be informed that they might be prosecuted.

Before such an interview is undertaken, the detainee must be cautioned that he does not have to say anything, but that anything he does say may be given in evidence. The adverse inference provision under s. 34 CJPOA 1994 has no application in this situation.

7.14.2 POLICE BAIL AFTER CHARGE AND BEFORE CHARGE

Once the defendant has been charged, the decision as to whether to remand or release him pending his first appearance before a magistrates' court is made by the custody officer. Section 38 PACE requires the custody officer to have regard to the same considerations as those which a court is required to have regard to, in taking a decision under the Bail Act 1976. Bail as a substantive topic in its own right is considered in detail in Chapter 15. A custody officer can refuse bail if one or more of the grounds under s. 38(1) PACE apply. They include:

- The suspect's name or address cannot be ascertained, or the custody officer has reasonable grounds for doubting whether a name or address furnished by him is his real name or address.
- The custody officer has reasonable grounds for believing that the person arrested will fail to attend court to answer bail.
- In the case of a person arrested for an imprisonable offence, the custody officer has reasonable grounds for believing that the detention of the person arrested is necessary to prevent him from committing an offence.
- In the case of a person arrested for a non-imprisonable offence, the custody officer has reasonable grounds for believing that the detention of the person arrested is necessary to prevent physical injury to any other person or causing loss or damage to property.
- The custody officer has reasonable grounds for believing that the detention of the person arrested is necessary to prevent him from interfering with the administration of justice or with the investigation of offences or a particular offence.
- The custody officer has reasonable grounds for believing that the detention of the person arrested is necessary for his own protection.

These grounds are virtually the same to those applied by a court under Schedule 1 Part 1 para. 2 Bail Act 1976. In determining whether the accused is likely to abscond, commit further offences or interfere with the course of justice, the custody officer will have regard to the factors set out in s. 9 Bail Act 1976, including:

- the defendant's bail record;
- the nature of the offence;
- the defendant's community ties;
- the defendant's criminal record.

Instead of remanding a defendant into custody pending his first appearance before a court, the custody officer may impose conditions on the grant of police bail post-charge in accordance with s. 47(1A) PACE in much the same way as a court. This includes conditions of residence, reporting at intervals to a police station, the imposition of a curfew, prohibiting contact with a particular individual or access to a particular place. A custody officer may not, however, impose a condition requiring the defendant to reside in a bail hostel. Conditions may only be imposed where the custody officer considers them to be necessary to ensure the defendant surrenders to custody, does not commit an offence while on bail, or interfere with witnesses or obstruct the course of justice. Conditions may also be imposed for the defendant's own protection or welfare. A failure by an accused to abide by the conditions of post-charge police bail will result in the accused being arrested and brought before a magistrates' court (s. 7(3) Bail Act 1976). A proven failure to abide by such conditions would be a significant factor in determining whether the accused should be remanded into custody throughout the currency of the proceedings. The accused has the right to apply to a magistrates' court to vary bail conditions imposed by the police under s. 43B, Magistrates Court Act 1980.

As a consequence of the statutory charging regime under the CJA 2003 (outlined in paragraph 7.4.4 above), conditions can now be attached to the grant of bail pre-charge where the matter under investigation has been referred to the CPS for a charging decision (s. 37(7)(a) PACE). If a defendant has been released on conditional bail during this time and has not breached any of the conditions, there is no reason why the custody officer should not then grant the defendant bail subject to the same conditions if the defendant is subsequently charged.

The legal adviser at the police station may well be required to make representations to the custody officer where it is proposed to remand the defendant in custody pending his first appearance before a magistrates' court or as to the appropriateness of bail conditions.

7.14.3 DRUG TESTING AT THE POLICE STATION

Section 63B PACE, as amended by s. 7 Drugs Act 2005, gives the police the power to demand a urine sample from suspects upon arrest or after charge in order to test for the presence of a Class A drug. The power to take a sample arises in relation to certain 'trigger offences'. In addition, s. 9 Drugs Act 2005 gives the police the power to require a person who has tested positive to undergo an initial assessment to see if the person has a propensity to misuse Class A drugs and would be suitable for treatment. Where the test shows the presence of a Class A drug, the information will be passed onto a court which must take it in to account when making a bail decision under the Bail Act 1976 (Chapter 15, para. 4.7). A failure to give a sample or to consent to undergo an initial assessment or follow-up treatment results in the commission of an offence. The testing procedure is currently being piloted in several police force areas.

KEY POINT SUMMARY

- Be aware of the custody officer's extensive duties and responsibilities.
- Understand the suspect's right to legal advice and to have someone informed of their arrest at the police station and the circumstances in which the exercise of these rights can justifiably be delayed.
- Understand that the safeguards contained in PACE and in Code C not only seek to protect the suspect while in custody but that they also seek to promote the integrity of the investigative process so as to ensure the reliability of evidence obtained in consequence.
- Understand the importance of the custody record containing everything relevant to your client's detention at the police station, including the justifications for the decisions taken.
- Be aware of detention time limits and the obligation to charge or release when there is sufficient evidence etc.
- Know the definition of a vulnerable suspect and the additional rights that such a suspect enjoys.
- Know which caution should be administered in which situation.
- Understand that evidence obtained as part of the investigation into a criminal offence in breach of PACE/Code C is vulnerable to challenge under s. 78 PACE and/or s. 76 PACE. Under s. 78 PACE such evidence can be excluded in the exercise of the court's discretion to ensure the defendant enjoys a right to a fair trial.
- Know the circumstances in which conditions can be imposed on the granting of police bail, both pre-charge and post-charge.
- Know the grounds upon which a custody officer can refuse police bail post-charge (s. 38 PACE).

SELF-TEST QUESTIONS

The self-test questions that support this chapter are located at the conclusion of Chapter 10, which considers the admissibility of confession evidence. Chapter 10 also includes analysis of the admissibility of the confession in our case study, *R v Lenny Whyte*.

FIGURE 7.1 MAXIMUM PERIODS OF DETENTION WITHOUT CHARGE AT THE POLICE STATION

Non-indictable offence – 24 hours maximum, after which defendant must be released (unconditionally or on police bail) or charged, s. 41 PACE.

↓

Indictable offence (which includes an either-way offence) – 24 hours unless a superintendent or above authorises detention for further 12 hours (24 + 12 = 36 hours) where the officer has reasonable grounds for believing that:

• the detention is necessary to secure or preserve evidence; or
• to obtain such evidence by questioning the suspect; and
• the investigation is being conducted diligently and expeditiously, s. 42 PACE.

↓

Detention beyond 36 hours

• Section 43 PACE permits detention without charge beyond 36 hours.
• Police must apply to a magistrates' court for a warrant of further detention where:

  – the detention is necessary to secure or preserve evidence; or to obtain such evidence by questioning the suspect; and

• the offence is an indictable offence offence; and
• the investigation is being conducted diligently and expeditiously.

The warrant authorises detention for a further 36 hours (24 + 12 + 36 = 72 hours).
The police may apply for a further warrant of detention for 24 hours (24 + 12 + 36 + 24 = 96 hours).
At the end of 96 hours, the suspect must either be released on police bail or unconditionally, or charged (s. 44).

SUMMARY OF RIGHTS WHILE IN CUSTODY

• right to legal advice in private (s. 58 PACE);
• right to have someone informed of your arrest (s. 56 PACE);
• continual review of detention (s. 40 PACE);
• right to an appropriate adult if you are vulnerable (Code C);
• right to medical advice (Code C);
• right to basic human rights (food/sleep/refreshments) (Code C).

8 THE RIGHT TO SILENCE AT THE POLICE STATION

8.1 INTRODUCTION

As we saw in the preceding chapter, the formal interview provides a significant opportunity for obtaining evidence against the suspect and remains the centrepiece of most criminal investigations. In some cases, the answers a suspect gives in the interview will lead to him being eliminated from the investigation. In other cases, the suspect's answers may well provide evidence in support of the prosecution's case. Interrogation is a cheap and effective resource. Tactically, the police might reason that by engaging the suspect in answering their questions, he may well talk himself into trouble.

A suspect has a number of options open to him so far as the formal interview is concerned. He may:

- admit his guilt;

- answer questions and perhaps advance a defence to the allegations made against him;

- exercise his right to remain silent (which may include putting forward a prepared statement);
- choose to be selectively silent (answer some questions but not others)

The last option is never to be recommended, as it creates a very poor impression of the defendant in court.

In Chapter 12 we explore in detail the practical considerations a legal adviser will have regard to when advising a client which course to take and how to prepare for the interview process accordingly.

In preparing a client for interview, the legal adviser may well consider that silence is the best strategy to adopt. However, silence is not without evidential consequences and a legal adviser must fully understand the law relating to the right to silence, if silence is to be advised.

8.2 WHAT ARE THE RISKS ASSOCIATED WITH REMAINING SILENT?

A suspect enjoys the right to silence at the police station. He cannot be compelled to answer police questions or otherwise respond to the allegations that have been made against him. However, if a suspect remains silent and is subsequently charged and then advances a defence at trial, there is a danger that the court may draw adverse inferences against his silence under s. 34 of the Criminal Justice and Public Order Act 1994 (CJPOA). Adverse inferences may also be drawn where a suspect fails to account for objects etc found on his person (s. 36 CJPOA 1994) and/or from his failure to account for his presence at a particular place (s. 37 CJPOA).

The purpose of this chapter is to explain the substantive law under the 'silence' provisions of the CJPOA 1994.

8.3 WHAT DOES S. 34 CJPOA 1994 STATE?

Section 34 provides:

'(1) Where, in any proceedings against a person for an offence, evidence is given that the accused:

(a) at any time before he was charged with the offence, on being questioned under caution by a constable trying to discover whether or by whom the offence had been committed, failed to mention any fact relied on in his defence in those proceedings; or

(b) on being charged with the offence or officially informed that he might be prosecuted for it, failed to mention any such fact, being a fact which in the circumstances existing at the time the accused could reasonably have been expected to mention when so questioned, charged or informed, as the case may be . . .

(c) the court, in determining whether there is a case to answer; and

(d) the court or jury, in determining whether the accused is guilty of the offence charged, may draw such inferences from the failure as appear proper.'

8.3.1 WHAT IS THE EFFECT OF S. 34?

Section 34 does not abolish a suspect's common law right to silence. Its effect is much more restrictive. It will apply where:

- on being questioned about an offence or being informed that he is to be charged for an offence or on being charged;
- the defendant fails to mention a fact which he later relies on at trial in his defence;
- in circumstances where a court (jury/magistrates) conclude it was reasonable in the circumstances which existed at the relevant time for the defendant to have mentioned the fact.

Section 34 is based on the simple rationale that if a suspect has an explanation to put forward in answer to an allegation made against him, he ought to put it forward at the first opportunity, namely in interview. If he does not, but later chooses to rely on facts in his defence which he could reasonably have mentioned at the police station, an adverse inference may be drawn. The evidential effect of s. 34 is to undermine the accused's defence at trial.

Section 34 is not limited solely to the suspect being questioned. An adverse inference can arise at the charging stage (s. 34(1)(b) (see *R v Dervish* (2002) 2 Cr App R 105)).

8.4 WHAT ARE THE CONDITIONS FOR DRAWING ADVERSE INFERENCES UNDER S. 34 CJPOA?

There are a number of conditions that need to be satisfied before the court may draw adverse inferences under s. 34. The leading case of *R v Argent* [1997] 2 Cr App R 27 provides that the following conditions must be met.

1. There must proceedings against a person for an offence.

2. The alleged failure to answer questions must occur before the defendant was charged or on being charged with the offence or officially informed that he might be prosecuted for it.

3. The failure must occur during questioning under caution by a constable (i.e. 'You do not have to say anything. But it may harm your defence if you do not mention when questioned something you later rely on in court. Anything you do say may be given in evidence.').

4. The questioning must be directed towards trying to discover whether, or by whom, the alleged offence has been committed.

5. The alleged failure by the defendant must be to mention any fact relied on in his defence in the proceedings. This raises two questions of fact: first is there some fact the defendant has relied on in his defence; and secondly, did the defendant fail to mention it to the constable when questioned in accordance with the section?

6. The fact that the defendant failed to mention must be a fact which, in the circumstances existing at the time, he could reasonably have been expected to mention when questioned.

Section 34 has generated a considerable amount of case law in its relatively short history. Some of the cases further develop the prerequisites for drawing an adverse inference established in *R v Argent* (1997).

Under s. 34(2A) CJPOA an adverse inference cannot be drawn in circumstances where access to a solicitor has not been made available in accordance with s. 58 PACE. In these circumstances, the suspect must be cautioned as follows: 'You do not have to say anything, but anything you do say may be given in evidence.' (Code C Annex C).

What follows is intended to provide you with a simplified and succinct précis of what has become a complex and technical area of evidence law. Paragraphs 8.4.1–8.4.5 below seek to summarise the relevant case law.

8.4.1 '. . . IF YOU DO NOT MENTION WHEN QUESTIONED *SOMETHING YOU LATER RELY ON* IN COURT . . .'

Adverse inferences may only be drawn against a fact which the defendant fails to mention at the police station but which he 'later relies on' in his defence. What is meant by 'something you later rely on?'

A defendant does not need to remain completely silent in interview for s. 34 to be triggered. It is the defendant's failure to mention *any fact* which he subsequently relies on in his defence. If a defendant puts forward facts or an explanation at the police station but then departs from that version at trial or advances new facts, he is still at risk of an adverse inference.

Neither does a defendant have to give evidence on oath in order to trigger s. 34. There are a number of ways in which a defendant can be said to rely on facts in his defence. This includes facts elicited through cross-examination of prosecution witnesses (*R v Bowers* [1998] Crim LR 817) and by the defendant calling witnesses in his defence. If, through either or both of these means, the defendant is relying on facts not previously mentioned, he is at risk of an adverse inference.

Some further useful guidance on what constitutes 'a fact relied on' for the purposes of s. 34 is provided by the decision of the House of Lords in *R v Webber* [2004] 1 All ER 770. The House of Lords concluded that the word 'fact' should not be given a narrow or pedantic meaning. If a defendant advances at trial any pure fact or exculpatory explanation or account which, if it were true, he could reasonably have been expected to advance earlier, then s. 34 is potentially operational. This applies when an advocate, acting on his client's instructions, puts a specific and positive case to a prosecution witness, as opposed to asking questions intended to probe or test the prosecution case. It is immaterial whether or not the prosecution witness accepts the assertions made.

Where a defendant does no more at trial than put the prosecution to proof of its case, s. 34 has no application (*R v Moshaid* [1998] Crim LR 420).

8.4.2 *FAILS TO MENTION A FACT* THAT HE LATER RELIES ON FOR HIS DEFENCE

A second important element to be considered is that the defendant must fail to mention a fact which he later relies on for his defence. For adverse inferences to be drawn, the failure to mention must relate to a fact, and not, for example, a theory or a hypothesis.

R v Nickolson [1999] Crim LR 61

The defendant had been arrested on suspicion of having raped his stepdaughter. In interview he denied the offence. He did say in interview that he was in the habit of masturbating in the bathroom. The girl's nightdress had been seized as part of the investigation. It was not appreciated at the time of the interview that traces of seminal fluid would subsequently be found on it. Asked at his trial to account for the seminal staining on the girl's nightdress, the defendant stated he had masturbated in the toilet on the evening of the alleged rape and that shortly after, the girl had gone to the toilet. Any semen on the toilet seat could well have innocently found its% way onto the girl's nightdress. The prosecution maintained the defendant was offering this explanation as a fact which he had not previously advanced. The trial judge agreed and directed the jury in accordance with the requirements of s. 34. The Court of Appeal held the defendant's statement had been offered as a theory or a possible explanation, and was therefore speculative in its nature.

If facts are not known at the time of the interview and the defendant subsequently offers an explanation for them at trial, s. 34 has no application.

R v B (MT) [2000] Crim LR 181

The defendant was on trial for raping his stepdaughter. He had failed to mention in interview that his stepdaughter might have been motivated by jealousy, which would explain why she had falsely accused him of raping her. In fact, whilst the defendant may have had suspicions as to his stepdaughter's motives, he did not know this as a fact. He actually learned it was a fact when the victim herself gave evidence. The defendant pursued the victim's jealousy further in his evidence. The Court of Appeal concluded this was not a fact the defendant could reasonably have been expected to mention at the police station. He may have had his suspicions as to his stepdaughter's motives, but this was not the same as knowing it as a fact.

In the Crown Court, the trial judge is required to identify to the jury the facts that can properly be said to have been relied on which were not mentioned in interview (*R v B* (2003) unreported).

8.4.3 ANY QUESTIONING MUST BE DIRECTED TO TRYING TO DISCOVER WHETHER OR BY WHOM THE ALLEGED OFFENCE WAS COMMITTED (S. 34(1)(a))

Suppose the police have already made up their minds to charge your client before commencing an interview? Your client remains silent but subsequently relies on facts at his trial. Is an inference permitted in these circumstances? In what sense would questioning during such an interview be directed at trying to discover whether or by whom the alleged offence was committed?

Code C para. 11.6 provides that an interview should cease when the officer in charge of the investigation:

- is satisfied all the questions they consider relevant to obtaining accurate and reliable information about the offence have been put to the suspect, including allowing the suspect an opportunity to give an innocent explanation and asking questions to test this;
- has taken account of any other available evidence; and
- the officer in charge of the investigation, or in the case of a detained person, the custody officer, reasonably believes that there is sufficient evidence to provide a realistic prospect of conviction.

This provision clearly gives the police greater leverage on the need to hold an interview before taking a decision as to whether there is in fact sufficient evidence to charge. Solicitors who choose to advise silence on the basis that there is sufficient evidence to charge without the need for an interview must therefore act with care.

8.4.4 WHAT INFERENCE MAY A COURT DRAW UNDER S. 34 CJPOA 1994?

The answer is, 'such inferences as appear proper' (s. 34(2) CJPOA). The jury or magistrates do not have to draw an adverse inference. If they choose to draw an adverse inference, they may conclude that the defendant remained silent because he had no answer to the allegations being made against him, or none that he was prepared to put forward and have subjected to critical questioning by investigating officers. They may conclude that he has since made up his defence to fit the facts as disclosed by the prosecution.

8.4.5 'ADVERSE INFERENCES WILL ONLY BE DRAWN WHERE, IN THE CIRCUMSTANCES EXISTING AT THE TIME THE ACCUSED *COULD REASONABLY HAVE BEEN EXPECTED TO MENTION. . . .'*

What is meant by the expression 'could reasonably have been expected to mention?'

The all-important question of reasonableness is a question of fact for the jury or magistrates (*R v Condron* [1997] 1 WLR 827; *R v Argent* [1997] 2 Cr App R 27). If a defendant wishes to persuade the court not to draw an adverse inference, tactically he needs to adduce evidence (perhaps by offering his explanation in the witness box or calling the legal adviser who gave him the advice at the police station) to explain his reasons for remaining silent at the relevant time. This will almost certainly require your client to waive his legal professional privilege (see below, paragraph 8.5.1). It will then be a matter for the jury or magistrates to decide whether it was reasonable in the circumstances for the defendant to have remained silent and if not, whether to draw an adverse inference.

What amounts to 'reasonable' will depend on the particular circumstances of each case.

In *R v Argent* [1997] 2 Cr App R 27, the Court of Appeal identified the following non-exhaustive list of factors on the issue of reasonableness:

- the time of day;
- the defendant's age;
- the defendant's experience at dealing with the police;

- the defendant's mental capacity;
- the defendant's state of health;
- the defendant's sobriety;
- the defendant's tiredness;
- the defendant's personality;
- whether the defendant remained silent on the basis of legal advice;
- the extent of the disclosure of the police case gainst the defendant.

The court or jury must consider these factors from the subjective perspective of the defendant at the time of his detention at the police station, not from the position of the reasonable man. If the court or jury concludes that it was reasonable for the defendant to have remained silent for the reason(s) given, an adverse inference should not be drawn.

8.5 DO ANY SPECIAL CONSIDERATIONS APPLY WHERE THE DECISION TO REMAIN SILENT IS BASED ON LEGAL ADVICE?

The reasonableness of a defendant's decision to remain silent is, as we have seen, a question of fact for a jury or magistrates to decide. Consequently, a defendant is not insulated from having an adverse inference drawn against him, where he gives as his reason for remaining silent the fact that he relied on the advice of his solicitor.

In *R v Hoare and Pierce* [2005] 1 Cr App R 22, Lord Justice Auld made the following observations as regards s. 34:

'It is not the purpose of section 34 to exclude a jury from drawing an adverse inference against a defendant because he genuinely or reasonably believes that, regardless of his guilt or innocence, he is entitled to take advantage of that advice to impede the prosecution case against him. In such a case the advice is not truly the reason for not mentioning the facts. The section 34 inference is concerned with flushing out innocence at an early stage or supporting other evidence of guilt at a later stage, not simply with whether a guilty defendant is entitled, or genuinely or reasonably believes that he is entitled, to rely on legal rights of which his solicitor has advised him. Legal entitlement is one thing. An accused's reason for exercising it is another. His belief in his entitlement may be genuine, but it does not follow that his reason for exercising it is . . . .'

How is a court to assess the reasonableness of the defendant's decision to remain silent unless it is told of the reason/s for the advice? This has clear implications for legal professional privilege.

8.5.1 ADVISING SILENCE AND LEGAL PROFESSIONAL PRIVILEGE

Communications between solicitor and client are of course protected from disclosure in evidence by legal professional privilege. The privilege belongs to the client and, as such, only the client may choose to waive it. In *R v Condron* [1997] 1 WLR 827, the Court of Appeal observed that for the defendant to simply assert in the witness box, 'I chose not to answer questions on the advice of my solicitor', would be unlikely to impress the jury. If sufficient weight were to be given to the defendant's reasons for not mentioning relevant facts, more explanation would almost certainly have to be given. In order to achieve this, the defendant would need to waive legal professional privilege in order to explain the basis on which his solicitor's advice had been given. Having waived privilege, the defendant could expect to be subjected to cross-examination on precisely how much he told his solicitor at the relevant time. The Court of Appeal explained the position as follows:

'Communications between an accused person and his solicitor prior to interviews by the police are subject to legal professional privilege. But the privilege can be waived by the client, though not the solicitor. If an accused person gives as a reason for not answering questions, that he has been advised by his solicitor not to do so, that advice, in our judgment, does not amount to a waiver of privilege.

But, equally, for reasons which we have already given, that bare assertion is unlikely by itself to be regarded as a sufficient reason for not mentioning matters relevant to the defence. So it will be necessary, if the accused wishes to invite the court not to draw an adverse inference, to go further and state the basis or reason for the advice. Although the matter was not fully argued, it seems to us that once this is done that it may well amount to a waiver of privilege so that the accused, or if his solicitor is also called, the solicitor, can be asked whether there were any other reasons for the advice, and the nature of the advice given, so as to explore whether the advice may also have been given for tactical reasons.'

The implication for legal professional privilege are considered further in Chapter 12 which examines the practical steps a legal adviser might take in advising a suspect at the police station.

In *R v Bresa* [2005] EWCA Crim 1414, the Court of Appeal observed in a case where no reason is put forward as to the basis for the legal advice given, the jury should be reminded that the defendant is under no obligation to reveal what transpired between himself and his legal adviser; however, he has a choice as to whether to make such revelation. The overriding question which always has to be answered is: could the defendant have reasonably been expected to mention the facts he is now relying on?

8.5.2 DIRECTING THE JURY ON THE EFFECT OF SILENCE CONSEQUENT UPON LEGAL ADVICE

The relationship between silence and legal advice has been influenced by decisions of the European Court of Human Rights (*Condron v UK* (2001) 31 EHRR 1 and *Beckles v UK* (2002) 36 EHRR 162). An important decision of the Court of Appeal in this regard is to be found in *R v Betts and Hall* [2001] 2 Cr App R 16, in which Lord Justice Kay, delivering the judgment of the Court of Appeal, held it is not the correctness of the legal advice with which the court is concerned but the genuineness of the suspect's reliance on it, and that if the jury concluded that the defendant's reason for silence was his genuine reliance upon legal advice, an adverse inference must not be drawn. However, *R v Betts and Hall* must be reconsidered in the light of the decision of the Court of Appeal in *R v Howell* which provides that the defendant's decision to remain silent must be both genuine and reasonable.

R v Howell [2005] 1 Cr App R 1

Howell was suspected of involvement in a serious assault on his flat-mate. He told his solicitor, as he would later tell the jury, that he had acted in self-defence when he stabbed his flat-mate. His solicitor asked the investigating officers if the victim of the attack had made a written statement. He had not. He had however given the investigating officers a detailed verbal account, including the specific allegation that the defendant had attacked him with a knife. The defendant had indicated to his solicitor that the victim might withdraw his allegation. Consequently the solicitor advised him to make no comment in interview. No evidence was forthcoming from the solicitor as to the reasons for his advice. The defendant was asked in cross-examination, why, if he was an innocent man, had he not taken the opportunity of putting forward his version of events. The defendant gave as his reason for not answering questions, the fact that he had simply followed the advice of his solicitor. In his summing-up the trial judge instructed the jury to consider whether the defendant had been right to act upon the advice of his solicitor.

On the facts of *Howell*, the Court of Appeal concluded that the solicitor had been wrong to advise silence on the basis of the absence of a written complaint from the victim, especially as adequate oral disclosure had been given. This was not a case where it would have been difficult for the defendant to recall events. The defendant had been there in the flat. He must have known whether he acted in self-defence or not. In the circumstances it had been permissible for the jury to draw an adverse inference on the basis that it had been reasonable to have expected the defendant to mention such facts, notwithstanding the advice of his solicitor.

8.5.3   REMAINING SILENT ON LEGAL ADVICE AFTER *R v HOWELL*

In *Howell*, the Court of Appeal talked of the important responsibility defence solicitors have when giving advice at police stations:

> 'there must always be soundly based objective reasons for silence, sufficiently cogent and telling to weigh in the balance against the clear public interest in an account being given to the suspect by the police. Solicitors bearing the important responsibility of giving advice to suspects at police stations must always bear that in mind.'

As examples of the type of instance in which a solicitor could justifiably advise silence, the Court of Appeal cited such matters as the suspect's mental condition and his ability to recollect events without reference to documents or some other source.

The all important question is what does not amount to a sound objective reason for remaining silent. Suppose your client genuinely relies on your advice but it later transpires that your advice was wrong or ill-conceived? How fair is it for an adverse inference to be drawn against your client in these circumstances? A suspect, particularly one who is inexperienced in police station procedure, is hardly going to question your professional judgment in this respect. We will further consider the issues raised by this case in Chapter 12 when we explore the practical steps a legal adviser might take when advising at the police station, with particular emphasis on the circumstances in which the advice to remain silent might safely be given.

In the later cases of *R v Hoare and Pierce* [2005] 1 Cr App R 22 and *R v Beckles* [2005] 1 All ER 705, the Court of Appeal gave a ringing endorsement of its earlier decision in *R v Howell*, and could in fact see no conflict between the decision in *R v Howell* and *R v Betts and Hall*. The critical test under s. 34 remains: was the fact which the defendant failed to mention one that the defendant could reasonably have been expected to mention notwithstanding genuine reliance on legal advice? You are reminded of the quotation taken from Lord Justice Auld's judgement in *R v Hoare* and *Pierce* that appears on page 91.

The fact that legal advice was relied on does not automatically prevent an adverse inference from being drawn. The Judicial Studies Board specimen direction to the jury on this aspect of s. 34 reads:

> 'The defendant has given evidence that he did not answer questions on the advice of his solicitor/legal representative. If you accept the evidence that he was so advised, this is obviously an important consideration: but it does not automatically prevent you from drawing any conclusion from his silence. Bear in mind that a person given legal advice has the choice whether to accept or reject it; and that the defendant was warned that any failure to mention facts which he relied on at his trial might harm his defence. Take into account also (here set out any circumstances relevant to the particular case, which may include the age of the defendant, the nature of and/or reasons for the advice given, and the complexity or otherwise of the facts on which the defendant has relied at the trial). Having done so, decide whether the defendant could reasonably have been expected to mention the facts on which he now relies. If, for example, you considered that he had or may have had an answer to give, but genuinely and reasonably relied on the legal advice to remain silent, you should not draw any conclusion against him. But if, for example, you were sure that the defendant remained silent not because of the legal advice but because he had no answer or no satisfactory answer to give, and merely latched onto the legal advice as a convenient shield behind which to hide, you would be entitled to draw a conclusion against him, subject to the direction I have given you.'

The complete version of JSB's specimen direction can be accessed from the web-links section on our Online Resource Centre. Ensure you access the most up-to-date version of the direcions on s. 34 by following the updates link: August 2005, Direction 40.

online
resource
centre

8.6 **THE RIGHT TO SILENCE AND PROTECTING THE DEFENDANT'S RIGHT TO A FAIR TRIAL**

The law relating to the right to silence has been influenced by the European Court of Human Rights. Although not specifically guaranteed under Article 6, the right to silence is an implied right. The fundamental importance of the right was stated in *Murray v United Kingdom* (1996) 22 EHRR 29:

> 'Although not specifically mentioned in Article 6 of the Convention, there can be no doubt that the right to remain silent under police questioning and the privilege against self-incrimination are generally recognised international standards which lie at the heart of the notion of a fair procedure under Article 6. By providing the accused with protection against improper compulsion by the authorities, these immunities contribute to avoiding miscarriages of justice and to securing the aims if Article 6.'

Is the decision to draw adverse inference compatible with Article 6 of the ECHR? The short answer is yes – providing numerous safeguards are met. Some of the required safeguards apply at the questioning stage, such as the need to correctly caution the suspect. Others apply at trial (particularly in relation to the judge's direction to the jury). The safeguards are all contained in the Judicial Studies Board specimen direction on s. 34 which forms the basis for the trial judge's crucial directions to the jury on the operation of s. 34. The essential safeguards are set out below:

(1) Adverse inferences cannot be the sole reason for finding a defendant guilty. Under s. 38 CJPOA 1994, no person shall have a case to answer or be convicted solely on an adverse inference drawn under s. 34. This important safeguard has been developed further with European Court of Human Rights jurisprudence. In *Murray v UK* (1996) 22 EHRR 29, the ECtHR stated quite categorically that it would be contrary to Article 6 to base a conviction solely or mainly on a defendant's silence.

(2) Adverse inferences may not be drawn where the police have delayed a detainee's access to a solicitor under PACE s. 58 and Code C para. 6.6. This amendment to the Criminal Justice and Public Order Act 1994 was enacted to take account of decisions of the ECtHR in *Murray v UK* (1996) 22 EHRR 29, *Condron v UK* (2001) 31 EHRR 1 and *Averill v UK* (2001) 31 EHRR 36. All these decisions have consistently stressed the fundamental importance of access to a solicitor at the police station. In such instances, the suspect will be cautioned that he does not have to say anything, but that anything he does say may be given in evidence.

(3) An adverse inference may only be drawn when, having listened to any explanation put forward by the defendant for his failure to mention facts and being satisfied that a sufficiently a strong case against the defendant is made out, the jury or magistrates conclude that the only sensible explanation for his silence is that he had no answer at the time or none that would stand up to scrutiny.

(4) The jury or magistrates should regard an adverse inference as providing additional support only in a situation where the prosecution's case, aside from the defendant's silence, is so strong, as to call for an answer from the accused.

The appropriate direction in relation to reliance upon legal advice is set out above in full (8.5.3).

A failure by the trial judge to correctly direct the jury on all aspects of s. 34 gives rise to a potential right of appeal in the event of conviction (*R v Webber* [2004] 1 WLR 404). The importance of the trial judge discussing his direction on s. 34 with the trial advocates in advance of his summing-up has been stressed time and time again. If you find yourself sitting behind counsel in the Crown Court, it is essential that you take a verbatim note of the trial judge's direction.

8.7 HOW SHOULD A COURT PROCEED WHERE S. 34 IS INOPERATIVE?

It appears that the court should revert to the common law position, exemplified in *Hall v R* [1971] 1 WLR 298. The defendant is entitled to a direction that no adverse inference should be drawn from the fact that he exercised his right to silence (*R v McGarry* [1999] 1 Cr App R 377). In this particular case, the prosecution conceded that s. 34 has no application on the facts. A failure to give a 'McGarry' direction, however, is not always fatal to a conviction (*R v Francom* [2001] 1 Cr App R 237).

8.8 CONCLUDING REMARKS ON S. 34

The trial judge has the responsibility for ensuring a fair trial, and on occasion this may require him to exercise discretion to exclude prosecution evidence under s. 78 PACE (see Chapters 9 and 10). If the s. 34 caution was incorrectly administered or deliberately misrepresented, or the interview took place in blatant breach of the safeguards in Code C, s. 78 PACE (see Chapter 9), the defence advocate should submit that no adverse inference should be drawn.

For a summary of the precise conditions that a jury or magistrates must find before an adverse inference can safely be drawn, we invite you to consider the Judicial Studies Board (JSB) specimen direction on s. 34. The specimen directions are issued by the JSB to all Crown Court judges in an effort to promote consistent application of the rules relating to criminal law, evidence and procedure when summing-up to the jury. The updated directions can be accessed online from www.jsboard.co.uk.

It will be apparent from all that has been said above that the practical operation and effect of s. 34 are complex. There are a considerable number of hoops through which a conscientious jury or magisterial bench must jump before adverse inferences may be drawn under s. 34. The extent to which a jury understands the directions on s. 34 is open to debate, and you may well wonder whether utilising s. 34 CJPOA 1994 is worth it? In *R v Brizzalari* [2004] EWCA Crim 310, the Court of Appeal called for prosecutors to refrain from too readily seeking to activate s. 34.

8.9 SUBMITTING A PREPARED STATEMENT TO THE POLICE AS AN ALTERNATIVE TO REMAINING SILENT

An alternative approach to advising a suspect to remain silent is to put forward his denial and/or defence in a written statement prepared and read out during the interview by his legal adviser. This approach prevents a s. 34 CJPOA 1994 inference being drawn against a defendant at a subsequent trial, provided the facts disclosed in the written statement are consistent with the defendant's case at trial. Such statements do, however, need to be very carefully drafted, as any omission in the statement (which is then reinforced at trial with further information), or any departure from it at trial, would leave the defendant vulnerable to an adverse inference under s. 34 CJPOA 1994. In *R v Knight* [2004] 1 Cr App R 9, the Court of Appeal held that, provided the defendant mentioned in his prepared statement all the facts he later relied on in court, adverse inferences would not be drawn, as this practice fulfilled the purpose of s. 34, i.e. the early disclosure of the suspect's account.

R v Knight [2004] 1 Cr App R 9

The defendant was convicted of an indecent assault on a girl. At the beginning of the police interview his solicitor read out a prepared statement denying the allegation. Thereafter the defendant refused to answer police questions on legal advice. At his trial the prepared statement was read to the jury and the defendant gave evidence consistent with what he had said in his prepared statement. The judge directed the jury that it could choose to draw the inference that the defendant had refused to answer police questions because he did not want his prepared statement to be subject to critical scrutiny by the police.

It was argued by the prosecution on appeal that on a literal interpretation of the wording in s. 34, the defendant had failed to mention facts when being questioned. The Court of Appeal disagreed, stating:

> 'We have come to the clear conclusion that the aim of ss. 34(1)(a) does not distinctly include police cross-examination of the suspect upon his account over and above the disclosure of that account. Had that been intended, it seems to us that Parliament would have used significantly different language. The relevant failure could readily be described as a failure 'to answer questions properly put to him under caution by a constable trying to discover whether or by whom the offence had been committed', rather than a failure to mention any facts relied on in his defence. But the point is not merely linguistic. A requirement to submit to police cross-examination (so long as the questions are proper), or at any rate an encouragement to do so on pain of later adverse inferences being drawn, is a significantly greater intrusion into a suspect's general right of silence than is a requirement, or encouragement, upon the suspect to disclose his factual defence. We by no means suggest that such an intrusion could not properly be legislated for without offence to Article 6 of the European Convention on Human Rights; but it would, we think, require a much sharper expression of the legislature's will than can be found in the words of the statute as enacted.'

In *Knight*, the Court of Appeal cautioned that the use of a prepared statement should not of itself be regarded as an 'inevitable antidote to later adverse inferences'. An inference is still possible where the prepared statement proves to be incomplete or inconsistent with what the defendant later relies on in evidence.

The danger of inconsistencies between the defendant's case at trial and the prepared statement at the police stations was underlined by the Court of Appeal in *R v Turner* [2004] 1 All ER 1025:

> '. . . such a statement is not an inevitable antidote to later adverse inferences. It may be incomplete in comparison with the defendant's later account at trial, or it may be inconsistent with that account. This court notes a growing practice, no doubt on advice, to submit a pre-prepared statement and decline to answer any questions. This in our view may prove a dangerous course for an innocent person who subsequently discovers at the trial that something significant has been omitted. No such problems would arise following an interview where the suspect gives appropriate answers to the question.'

Legal advisers ought to give careful consideration to the use of a prepared statement. It may prove to be the safest course of action in some circumstances. In *R v Knight*, the facts of the accusation were straightforward. The accused denied the offence of indecent assault and was able to fully and simply articulate his defence in his prepared statement. He articulated precisely the same defence before the jury. Section 34 requires your client to do no more than this.

8.10 DRAWING INFERENCES FROM A FAILURE TO ACCOUNT FOR OBJECTS, SUBSTANCES OR MARKS: S. 36 CJPOA

While most judicial attention has been focused on the application of s. 34 Criminal Justice and Public Order Act 1994, the potential for adverse inferences being drawn from the defendant's silence under ss. 36 and/or 37 should not be forgotten. As with s. 34, a competent criminal lawyer will have a good understanding of the ambit of ss. 36 and 37 and the relevant case law and be prepared to apply this knowledge in support of his client's case. Consider each section below.

Section 36

'(1) Where

  (a) a person is arrested by a constable, and there is

    (i) on his person; or

    (ii) in or on his clothing or footwear; or

    (iii) otherwise in his possession; or

    (iv) in any place in which he is at the time of his arrest, any object, substance or mark, or there is any mark on any such object; and

  (b) that or another constable investigating the case reasonably believes that the presence of the object, substance or mark may be attributable to the participation of the person arrested in the commission of an offence specified by the constable; and

  (c) the constable informs the person arrested that he so believes, and requests him to account for the presence of the object, substance or mark; and

  (d) the person fails or refuses to do so, then . . .

(2) . . . (c) the court, in determining whether there is a case to answer; and (d) the court and the jury, in determining whether the accused is guilty of the offence charged, may draw such inferences from the failure or refusal as appear proper

(3) Subsections (1) and (2) above apply to the condition of clothing or footwear as they apply to a substance or mark thereon.'

8.11 DRAWING INFERENCES FROM A FAILURE TO ACCOUNT FOR ONE'S PRESENCE AT A PARTICULAR PLACE: S. 37 CJPOA

Section 37

'(1) Where –

(a) a person arrested by a constable was found by him at a place at or about the time the offence for which he was arrested is alleged to have been committed; and

(b) that or another constable investigating the offence reasonably believes that the presence of the person at that place and at that time may be attributable to his participation in the commission of the offence; and

(c) the constable informs the person that he so believes, and requests him to account for that presence; and

(d) the person fails or refuses to do so, then if, in any proceedings against the person for the offence, evidence of those matters is given . . . .

(2) . . .

(c) the court, in determining whether there is a case to answer; and

(d) the court or the jury, in determining whether the accused is guilty of the offence charged, may draw such inferences from the failure or refusal as appear proper.'

8.12 WHAT IS THE EFFECT OF SS. 36 AND 37?

An adverse inference may only be drawn under s. 36 or s. 37 in accordance with the precise wording in the statutory sections. The suspect must be cautioned in these strict terms. It is not the job of the legal adviser to correct the caution if it is mistakenly put. A failure to properly caution the suspect under either s. 36 or s. 37 will mean that an adverse inference cannot be drawn, and the defendant's replies should be edited out of the transcript that is eventually placed before the court.

The evidential effect of an inference drawn under either section is to strengthen the prosecution's case, irrespective of any defence subsequently advanced by the defendant in court. Section 38(3) CJPOA 1994 applies, in that no one will have a case to answer, or be convicted of an offence, based solely on an inference drawn from a failure or refusal as prescribed in s. 36(2) and s. 37(2). In accordance with s. 58 Youth Justice and Criminal Evidence Act 1999, an adverse inference under s. 36(4A) and s. 37(3A) CJPOA cannot be drawn where access to a solicitor has not been made available under s. 58 PACE.

Consider the following examples of s. 36 and 37.

Example 1

Andrew is implicated in a recent offence of assault. On his arrest, he has visible bruising about his face. Andrew tells you he has no knowledge of the incident alleged. Andrew is bound to be asked to account for the bruising visible on his face. A failure to offer some explanation for the bruising may lead to an adverse inference being drawn under s. 36.

Example 2

Leon is arrested on suspicion of the burglary of an optician's premises. In the course of the burglary a pane of glass was smashed. An eye-witness gives a description of the suspect. Leon is stopped by the police in the vicinity some 20 minutes later. His shoes are seized and subject to forensic examination. Shards of glass are found embedded in the soles of the shoes. Leon denies involvement with the burglary. Leon will be asked to account for the presence of glass in his shoes. A failure to offer an explanation for its presence may result in an adverse inference being drawn under s. 36.

Example 3

The police are investigating an attempted arson offence at a school. Kevin is arrested in the school playing fields shortly after the alarm was raised. Kevin denies any involvement in the matter. In interview, Kevin is bound to be asked to account for his presence on the school fields. A failure to offer an explanation may result in an adverse inference being drawn under s. 37. If it later transpires that Andrew's trousers disclose traces of petrol, he can expect to be asked to account for its presence in interview in accordance with s. 36.

Very few cases have gone to appeal on ss. 36 and 37. One case which did is *R v Compton* [2002] EWCA Crim 2835. In this case, the defendants were accused of drug trafficking. The police had found a substantial quantity of used banknotes in their possession. When tested, a substantial number of the banknotes were found to be contaminated with heroin, far above the level likely to be found on banknotes in general circulation. Both defendants denied drug trafficking at their trial and insisted that the banknotes represented the funds of a jewellery business in one case, and an antiques business in the other. Both defendants suggested at their trial that the contamination was attributable to their personal drug habit. Both defendants had made largely no comment interviews, although one of the defendants had explained the presence of heroin based on the fact that he was a drug user. A s. 36 inference was rightly left to the jury since the 'bare statement' that each was a drug user did not 'account for' the presence of substantial contamination as put to them by the investigating officer.

In this case, the Court of Appeal reiterated the importance of the trial judge giving a correct direction on s. 36.

8.12.1 **ANTICIPATING ADVERSE INFERENCES UNDER SS. 36 AND 37 CJPOA**

A legal adviser at the police station must try to anticipate questions likely to form the basis of a s. 36 or 37 inference. It reaffirms the importance of checking the custody record very carefully to see what has been seized from your client or his property and what searches have been undertaken and whether final or preliminary results are available. You may need to ask your client some searching questions about the state of the evidence against him. Your client needs to be prepared for the sort of questioning that could form the basis of an inference under ss. 36 or 37.

KEY POINT SUMMARY

- If a defendant advances facts at his trial which he failed to mention in interview, he may have an adverse inference drawn against him if the court considers it was reasonable, at the time, for the defendant to have advanced the particular facts.

- The reasonableness of a defendant's decision depends upon a number of factors (some of them are listed in *R v Argent*).

- It matters not that the defendant's decision to remain silent was based on legal advice given at the time – it is still a matter for the jury/magistrates.

- An inference can only be drawn if, having worked through a number of specified safeguards in the JSB's specimen directions, the jury comes to the conclusion that the defendant remained silent because he had no answer to the allegations, or none that he was prepared to have subjected to critical scrutiny.

- An adverse inference may not be drawn where the court concludes the accused genuinely and reasonably relied on legal advice.

- Legal advisers must consider whether there are sound objective reasons for advising silence.

- Where a defendant is to rely on legal advice as the reason for seeking to avoid an adverse inference, he must expect to waive his legal professional privilege.

- Where an adverse inference is drawn, it is a contributing evidential component of the prosecution's case and a conviction cannot be based wholly or mainly on the fact of silence.

SELF-TEST QUESTIONS

Consider the following short scenarios and decide whether ss. 34/36 or 37 are engaged.

Scenario 1

Karl is being questioned on suspicion of manslaughter. He refuses to answer questions put by the police. At his trial Karl gives evidence to the effect that he acted in self-defence.

Scenario 2

Stan is arrested on suspicion of murder. During his interview he puts forward a defence of provocation. At trial he gives evidence consistent both with provocation and self-defence.

Scenario 3

Jason is arrested on suspicion of attempted rape. The victim of the attack retaliated, scratching her assailant's face. In interview Jason is cautioned and asked to account for scratch marks that can be seen on his face. Jason chooses not to reply. In fact, he remains silent through out the interview. Giving evidence at his trial, Jason states he has been mistakenly identified in that he has an alibi.

Scenario 4

Following a burglary, Rio is arrested a few hours later. It is clear that the burglar exited the property along a muddy track and over a wall topped with metal spikes. The police inform Rio that he is under arrest on suspicion of burglary. In interview Rio advances a defence of alibi. In the course of the interview he is cautioned and asked to account for a tear on the sleeve of his jacket and mud on his shoes. Rio is unable to offer any explanation for either.

Scenario 5

Jane is arrested on a Sunday evening on suspicion of criminal damage. She is found by a police officer near to a field where genetically modified maize is under cultivation. Several crops have been uprooted. When questioned under caution about the alleged offence, Jane is asked to account for her presence near to the field. Jane refuses to reply. She also refuses to give evidence at her trial.

Scenario 6

Carley is arrested on suspicion of being in possession of a controlled drug with intent to supply. She admits to being in possession, but denies intent to supply. Her solicitor is of the view that she is unfit to be interviewed by the police due to drug withdrawal symptoms. The police doctor disagrees. Carley takes the advice of her solicitor and chooses not to answer questions during the interview. She is charged with possession with intent to supply. At trial she will give evidence denying intent to supply. Does she have anything to fear from her failure to answer questions at the police station?

FIGURE 8.1 DRAWING ADVERSE INFERENCES FROM SILENCE

ADVERSE INFERENCES: S. 34 CJPOA 1994

- Section 34 CJPOA 1994 does not abolish the right to silence.

- Section 34 CJPOA 1994 applies where a defendant
    - is questioned under caution; or on being charged; or
    - fails to mention a fact that he later relies on in his defence.

- An adverse inferences may only be drawn where:
    - defendant has been offered legal advice, s. 34(2A) CJPOA 1994;
    - if the court considers it would have been reasonable for the defendant to have mentioned the fact; see *R v Condron; R v Argent*.

- The reasonableness test includes the defendant's:
    - age and experience of dealing with the police;
    - mental capacity;
    - state of health; and whether legal advice was given.

- It is a matter for the jury/magistrates as to whether an adverse inference should be drawn.

- In a jury trial, the judge must direct the jury in accordance with the JSB's specimen direction on s. 34, which includes a host of safeguards, including:
    - conviction cannot be based wholly or mainly on a failure to mention;
    - the court must consider the reason for the defendant remaining silent;
    - an adverse inference may only be drawn if the jury concludes that the real reason for the defendant's failure was that he had no answer to the allegation, or none that would withstand critical scrutiny.

- A court may not draw an adverse inference where the defendant reasonably and genuinely relied on legal advice; see *R v Howell; R v Hoare and Pierce*.

- A solicitor advising silence at the police station must make his client fully aware of the risks.

- A prepared statement containing all the defence facts may prevent adverse inferences form being drawn; see *R v Knight*.

ADVERSE INFERENCES: S. 36 CJPOA 1994

- Adverse inferences may be drawn where, after arrest, the defendant refuses to account for any object, substance or mark on his person; or in his clothing; or otherwise in his possession; and

- the officer has a reasonable belief that the object etc may be attributable to his participation in the offence; and

- the possible effect of his failure or refusal to account for the object was explained to the defendant, Code C para. 10.11.

ADVERSE INFERENCES: S. 37 CJPOA 1994

- Adverse inferences may be drawn where, after arrest, defendant refuses to account for his presence at a particular place; and

- the officer has a reasonable belief that his presence may be attributable to his participation in the offence; and

- the possible effect of his failure or refusal to account for his presence was explained to the defendant, Code C para. 10.11.

9 UNLAWFULLY AND UNFAIRLY OBTAINED EVIDENCE

9.1 INTRODUCTION

Part II of this book is concerned with the investigation of criminal offences. However, the process of investigation is part of a continuum that often culminates in a trial or guilty plea. The manner in which the police obtain evidence during an investigation may have implications for the admissibility of evidence at any subsequent trial. While the rules of evidence are applied for the most part at trial, they also underpin the construction of a criminal case. The police should be aware that evidence obtained by them in breach of the rules is open to challenge.

Every defendant enjoys the right to a fair trial, which is explicitly guaranteed in Article 6 ECHR. The right to a fair trial has a very broad application, however, and is not solely considered in relation to unlawfully obtained evidence. The court has power to exclude any prosecution evidence, the admission of which would prejudice a fair trial.

In this chapter, we consider the defendant's right to a fair trial in the context of the rules relating to the admissibility of unlawfully or unfairly obtained evidence by examining the position at:

- common law and;
- under s. 78 Police and Criminal Evidence Act 1984.

9.2 WHAT IS UNLAWFULLY OBTAINED EVIDENCE?

Unlawfully or unfairly obtained evidence is apt to describe any prosecution evidence which has been obtained pre-trial in a 'questionable' manner. Unlawfully obtained evidence could include evidence obtained as a result of an unlawful search of a person or his property. It can also include evidence obtained through the use of an *agent provocateur* or an undercover police officer and evidence of incriminating admissions obtained through unauthorised surveillance methods. It should be emphasised that this list is by no means exhaustive.

Unlawfully obtained evidence also embraces a confession or evidence of identification obtained in breach of the safeguards under the Police and Criminal Evidence Act 1984 (PACE) and the Codes of Practice that accompany it. The law relating to the admissibility of confession evidence is separately considered in Chapter 10. The law relating to the admissibility of identification evidence is considered in Chapter 11. The exercise of discretion to exclude evidence both at common law and under s. 78 PACE apply equally to such types of evidence.

The use of 'underhand' methods of investigation or the occasional 'bending of the rules' can yield highly relevant evidence of a suspect's guilt. This poses a dilemma for the court. To exclude such evidence may mean a guilty defendant walking free, but to admit such evidence would be to condone unlawful activities by the police.

9.3 INTERRELATIONSHIP OF RULES OF PROCEDURE AND RULES OF EVIDENCE

Although arguments surrounding the admissibility of evidence will occur at trial, we have chosen to consider the law relating to unlawfully obtained evidence at this juncture because it is most likely to arise in the context of evidence obtained as part of the investigative process. In Chapters 6 and 7, we set out the legal requirements of lawful stop and search, arrest, detention, and questioning of suspects. The question which lies at the heart of this chapter is whether or not evidence obtained in unlawful circumstances or in breach of the Codes of Practice can be excluded in the exercise of judicial discretion? The answer to this question is yes, as the power exists at common law and under s. 78 PACE. Perhaps the more important question we should ask is: will a court exercise its power to exclude such evidence? The answer to this question can only really be explored in the context of some case law examples.

9.4 COMMON LAW DISCRETION

The criminal courts have always retained the power at common law to exclude evidence capable of prejudicing a fair trial.

In relation to the admissibility of unlawfully obtained evidence, however, the common law has always adopted a narrow stance. Provided the evidence is relevant and reliable, its admission is not generally regarded as prejudicing the defendant's right to a fair trial. The following cases exemplify the common law position.

Kuruma Son of Kainu v R [1955] AC 197

The accused was on trial for unlawful possession of ammunition during a period of emergency in Kenya. The police had found the ammunition during an unlawful search. The Privy Council was quite adamant that such evidence remained admissible, notwithstanding the manner in which it has been obtained.

In the leading common law case of *R v Sang* [1980] AC 402, a case based on entrapment by the prosecuting authorities, Lord Diplock summarised the position at common law as follows:

'(1) A trial judge in a criminal trial has always a discretion to refuse to admit evidence if in his opinion its prejudicial effect outweighs its probative value. (2) Save with regard to admissions and confessions and generally with regard to evidence obtained from the accused after commission of the offence, he has no discretion to refuse to admit relevant admissible evidence on the ground that it was obtained by improper or unfair means. The court isn't concerned with how it was obtained.'

Earlier in his judgment, Lord Diplock stated:

'The function of a judge at a criminal trial as respects the admission of evidence is to ensure the accused has a fair trial according to the law. It is no part of a judge's function to exercise disciplinary powers over the police or prosecution as respects the way in which the evidence to be used at the trial is obtained by them. . . .'

Although the common law has now been largely superseded by s. 78 of PACE, it is still used in legal argument. Section 82(3) of PACE specifically preserves the common law discretion to exclude evidence the prejudicial effect of which outweighs its probative value.

9.5 DISCRETION UNDER S. 78 PACE

Section 78(1) provides:

> 'In any proceedings the court may refuse to allow evidence on which the prosecution proposes to rely to be given if it appears to the court that, having regard to all the circumstances, including the circumstances in which the evidence was obtained, the admission of the evidence would have such an adverse effect on the fairness of the proceedings that the court ought not to admit it.'

Section 78 gives a court the power to exclude prosecution evidence where that evidence would have an adverse effect on the fairness of the proceedings. The exercise of the power is discretionary. The fairness of the proceedings is not however defined, although the court is invited, by the wording in the section, to have regard to the circumstances in which the evidence was obtained.

In theory at least, s. 78 PACE looks as though it might be applied to exclude evidence on a wider basis than the discretion exercised at common law. Case law illustrations showing the exercise of judicial discretion under s. 78 in relation to unlawfully obtained evidence strongly suggest otherwise. The notable areas of exception in this regard are confession evidence and evidence of identification, which are considered in Chapters 10 and 11.

In practice, an application to have evidence excluded under s. 78 is more likely to succeed in relation to confession evidence and evidence of identification than most other types of evidence for the simple reason that the many safeguards that regulate the manner in which such evidence is obtained under Code C and D, exist to ensure the quality and reliability of such evidence. The integrity of confession evidence and evidence of eye-witness identification may well be compromised if breaches occur. In these circumstances it is much easier to argue that the prejudicial effect of admitting such evidence outweighs its probative value in the case. In the interest of fairness, such evidence ought to be excluded.

9.6 CATEGORIES OF UNLAWFULLY OBTAINED EVIDENCE OTHER THAN CONFESSIONS AND EYE-WITNESS IDENTIFICATION

There are many different ways in which the police might obtain evidence in a dubious or unlawful manner, including:

- evidence yielded as a result of an unlawful search;
- evidence found pursuant to an unlawful arrest;
- evidence obtained through means of entrapment;
- evidence obtained through use of unlawful surveillance;
- evidence obtained by deception or trickery;
- evidence obtained in the course of committing trespass to premises;
- evidence obtained in breach of an individual's right to privacy;
- evidence obtained in violation of the privilege against self-incrimination; or
- evidence obtained in violation of legal professional privilege.

We include a small selection of case law examples based on some of these categories.

9.6.1 USE OF TRICKERY OR DECEPTION BY THE POLICE

There are other ways in which evidence of a self-incriminating nature might be obtained from a suspect than through the formal police interview procedure. These include the use of covert listening devices and covert surveillance operations. Code C has little, if any, application to evidence of a self-incriminating nature obtained in such circumstances. What is clear, however, is that the use of such methods should not be adopted with the express intention of deliberately avoiding the Codes of Practice. The principles in this regard were established in *R v Christou* [1992] 4 All ER 559. Undercover officers posed as 'shady jewellers', willing to receive stolen items of jewellery. The purpose of the operation had been to recover stolen goods and identify thieves and handlers. On the basis of information gathered, the defendant and others were prosecuted. Upholding the conviction in this case, the Court of Appeal concluded the appellant was not being questioned by police officers and that the conversation was on equal terms. Consequently, Code C had no application in this particular context. The Court of Appeal went on to say that:

> 'It would be wrong for police officers to adopt or use an undercover pose or disguise to enable themselves to ask questions about an offence uninhibited by the requirement of the Code and with the effect of circumventing it. Were they to do so, it would be open to the judge to exclude the questioning and answers under section 78 of PACE.'

R v Bailey and Smith [1993] 3 All ER 365

The two accused were arrested in connection with an armed robbery. Both were legally represented and chose to exercise their right to remain silent. They were charged and brought before a magistrates' court where they were remanded into police custody for the purposes of attending an identification parade. The questioning of suspects after charge is prohibited under Code C. The investigating officers decided to put the defendants in the same cell, in an attempt to obtain further useful evidence. The cell was bugged. The officers had sought authorisation for their proposed course of action from a senior officer. The officers invented a charade, telling the defendants that it was not their choice to have them share a cell but that they had been forced into it by an uncooperative custody officer. The defendants were taken in, notwithstanding the fact that their solicitor had warned them that the bugging of police cells was not uncommon. While together in the cell, they made incriminating admissions which were used in evidence against them.

The Court of Appeal held the trial judge had rightly admitted the evidence. Lord Justice Simon Brown summed up his reasoning as follows:

> 'Where, as here, very serious crimes have been committed . . . by men who have not shrunk from using trickery and a good deal worse, and where there has never been the least suggestion that their covertly taped confessions were oppressively obtained or were other than wholly reliable it seems to be hardly surprising that the trial judge exercised his discretion in the way he did. . . .'

9.6.2 UNAUTHORISED SURVEILLANCE METHODS

The increasing sophistication of technological surveillance devices allows the police to obtain evidence in many different covert ways. For the most part, such surveillance operations are regulated by the Regulation of Investigatory Powers Act 2000 (RIPA), an immensely complicated piece of legislation. Where the use of such surveillance is unauthorised or involves the police acting in breach of the criminal and or the civil law, should the evidence be admitted?

R v Khan [1996] 3 All ER 298

Khan was under suspicion of drug smuggling. In an attempt to obtain evidence against him, investigating officers attached a listening device to a property visited frequently by Khan, of which neither Khan or the flat's owner had any knowledge. There were Home Office Guidelines in existence regarding the use of covert surveillance, but there was no statutory authorisation for the use of such devices at the time, although the officers had sought and obtained permission of the Chief Constable. As a consequence of the operation, the police obtained a tape recording that proved Khan was involved in the importation of heroin. They sought to use it in evidence against him at his trial.

At his trial the prosecution accepted that there was no statutory authority for the use of the device and that placing it on the property without the owner's permission constituted a civil trespass. Khan conceded that the tape was authentic and that it was his voice which could be heard. On appeal it was argued on his behalf that the evidence had been obtained in violation of Article 8, guaranteeing a right of privacy and that the trial judge should have excluded the tape-recorded conversations in the exercise of his discretion either at common law or under s. 78 PACE.

Notwithstanding there may have been a violation of Article 8, the House of Lords concluded that the evidence was rightly admitted at common law and under s. 78. The evidence was especially relevant and could not be said to have adversely affected the fairness of the proceedings.

Mr Khan subsequently took his case to the European Court of Human Rights, in *Khan v United Kingdom* (2001) 31 EHRR 45. Whilst finding the UK to be in violation of Article 8, the ECtHR determined that there had been no violation of Article 6, guaranteeing the right to a fair trial.

As regards Article 6(1), the ECtHRs observed:

'It is not the role of the Court to determine, as a matter of principle, whether particular types of evidence, for example, unlawfully obtained evidence may be admissible or, indeed, whether the applicant was guilty or not. The question which must be answered is whether the proceedings as a whole, including the way in which the evidence was obtained, were fair. This involves an examination of the 'unlawfulness' in question and, where violation of another Convention right is concerned, the nature of the violation found.'

The ECtHRs concluded the applicant had enjoyed a fair trial, notwithstanding the main evidence against him had been obtained in breach of a Convention right. In particular, the ECtHR's noted there had been no doubt as to the authenticity of the tape and the strength and reliability of the evidence it had yielded. There had been no inducement to confess or entrapment. Furthermore, s. 78 PACE had afforded Khan the opportunity to challenge the admissibility of the evidence. In these circumstances his trial had been fair.

9.6.3 UNLAWFUL SEIZURE AND SUBSEQUENT USE OF REAL EVIDENCE

R v Sanghera [2001] 1 Cr App R 299

Evidence was admitted following an unlawful search, contrary to Code B of the Codes of Practice. There had been a robbery at a post office which was owned by the defendant. As part of the investigation into the crime, the police omitted to obtain the defendant's written consent to search his premises. In the course of their search, the police had found a hidden box containing a substantial quantity of cash, as a result of which their suspicion that the robbery was a sham was aroused. The money from the box was removed and a hidden camera installed. The defendant was arrested a few days later having been seen to look in the hidden box. The defendant did not contest the reliability of the evidence that the unlawful search had yielded. However, he maintained he would have wanted to be present at the time of the search, as this would have afforded him the opportunity of offering an immediate explanation of the presence of the money found in the box. In the circumstances, he argued the evidence should have been excluded under s. 78 of PACE. The trial judge rejected this submission and the defendant was convicted.

The Court of Appeal dismissed his appeal, summarising the relationship between breaches of the Codes of Practice and the exercise of discretion under s. 78 as follows:

'In relation to section 78, it is of importance, in our judgment, that each particular case is considered on its facts and that no broad generalisation is made as to its application. However, there are clearly different situations with which the courts have to deal under section 78. There are situations where a serious breakdown in the proper procedures has taken place in the whole of the prosecution process. In such a situation, the courts may well take the view that the nature of the breakdown is so significant that it would not be appropriate to allow the evidence to be admitted. There are also situations lower down the scale where there has been a breach of the Code which can be regarded as being significant but not serious. That is not of the same gravity as indicated by the first category of situations. There may be cases where breaches of the Code can be said to be venial or technical. In the case of the latter category the court will almost inevitably come to the conclusion that there has been no injustice or unfairness involved and will exercise its discretion in favour of allowing the evidence to be given. There are difficulties with regard to the middle category, the category where it could be said the breach was significant but not serious. In that situation section 78 leaves the matter to be evaluated by the judge concerned, looking at all the circumstances.'

On the facts, and given that the police had acted in good faith, it could not be said that the defendant had been prejudiced in any way. The evidence yielded was both relevant and reliable and the defendant had been afforded the opportunity of both explanation and challenge at his trial.

In *R v Cooke* [1995] 1 Cr App R 318, the defendant claimed that a non-intimate sample of his hair had been taken from him unlawfully. The sample yielded hugely compelling DNA evidence which convicted the defendant of rape and kidnap. The Court of Appeal held that the evidence had not been obtained unlawfully and that, even if it had, s. 78 would not require the court to exclude it, because such illegality would not have cast doubt on the reliability and probative strength of the resulting evidence. In this sense, the evidence could be distinguished from confession evidence obtained in breach of PACE and the Code of Practice, which tends to be of a more inherently unreliable nature.

9.6.4 EVIDENCE OBTAINED IN VIOLATION OF THE PRIVILEGE AGAINST SELF-INCRIMINATION

Allan v UK (2002) 236 EHRR

Allan and his co-accused were suspected of murder. All the defendants had been charged with an unrelated robbery and remanded into custody. Some days later, Allan was arrested on suspicion of murder. He refused to answer questions in interview. Authorisation was obtained to secure the 'services' of a long-standing police informant known as H who had a criminal record and who was under arrested on unrelated matters. H was placed in Allan's cell for the express purpose of gaining Allan's trust and eliciting information from Allan regarding the murder. At a later stage, H was fitted with a recording device. Telephone conversations between the investigating officers and H included comments by the police encouraging H to 'push him for what you can'. H eventually made a 59-page witness statement detailing his conversations with Allan. He was then released on police bail pending sentencing which was due to occur after he had given evidence at Allan's trial. In his evidence, H stated that in one conversation which had not been recorded, Allan had admitted his presence at the murder scene. This was disputed by Allan.

The ECtHR had no hesitation in concluding that Allan had not enjoyed a fair trial because his right to silence had been completely undermined. The use of an undercover informant by the police had been the functional equivalent of an interview without any of the safeguards under PACE and Code C. Furthermore, the alleged admissions constituted the main and decisive evidence against Allan, and the unavailability of an audio record of the alleged conversation clearly compromised the quality of the evidence.

9.6.5 ENTRAPMENT

Law enforcement often requires the police to use the services of an *agent provocateur*, such as an undercover police officer or an informer, who infiltrates a criminal enterprise in an attempt to gather evidence. This is known as entrapment. Evidence obtained in this way is susceptible to challenge both at common law and under s. 78 PACE; but entrapment *per se* does not afford a defence in English law to a criminal charge.

The difficulty for the courts, in choosing to exercise this discretion, is where to draw the line. At what point do the prosecuting authorities overstep the mark dividing the legitimate collection of evidence of a criminal enterprise and inciting someone to commit a crime they might not otherwise have committed?

The difficulties associated with the admissibility of this type of evidence have exercised the courts on a number of occasions. In *R v Christou* [1992] 4 All ER 559, the facts of which were mentioned earlier, in answer to the claim that the defendant had been entrapped by the police officers posing as shady jewellery dealers, the Court of Appeal observed that the defendant had not been forced, persuaded or encouraged to sell the goods. If he had not used the officers' shop, he would have gone elsewhere.

Lord Taylor explained the defendant's position as follows:

> 'Nobody was forcing the defendants to do what they did. They were not persuaded or encouraged to do what they did. They were doing in that shop exactly what they intended to do and, in all probability, what they intended to do from the moment they got up that morning. They were dishonestly disposing of dishonest goods. If the police had never set up the jeweller's shop, they would, in my judgment, have been doing the same thing though of course they would not be doing it in that shop, at that time. They were not tricked into doing what they would not otherwise have done . . . I do not think that is unfair or leads to an unfairness in the trial.'

The law relating to the admissibility of evidence yielded by the process of entrapment has steadily evolved. A definitive statement of the relevant principles which takes account of relevant case law and the jurisprudence of the ECtHR on this issue (*Teixeira de Castro v Portugal* (1998) 28 EHRR 242) was provided by the House of Lords in the following case, combining two appeals.

R v Loosely; Attorney-General's Reference (No. 3 of 2000) [2001] 1 WLR 2060

In Loosely's case, an undercover officer posed as a prospective buyer of drugs. His actions were part of an authorised surveillance in the Guildford area, which had seen a rise in the supply of heroin. The focus of suspicion fell on a particular public house in which the undercover officer had been given the defendant's contact number as a possible source of supply. On contacting the defendant, the officer asked if he could 'sort us a couple of bags'. The defendant responded willingly to the solicitation and immediately made arrangements to take the undercover officer to a place where he was able to obtain the drugs.

In the matter of the Attorney-General's reference, undercover officers offered the defendant contraband cigarettes. After a lengthy conversation about the cigarettes, one of the officers asked the defendant if he could 'sort him some brown'. It was only after numerous conversations, much persuasion and the offer of further contraband cigarettes, that the defendant eventually obtained a quantity of heroin for the officers. On handing the drug over to the undercover officers, the defendant was recorded as saying: 'I am not really into heroin myself.' In interview he maintained he had nothing to do with heroin and had only supplied the officers because of their requests and as a favour for the contraband cigarettes.

The House of Lords concluded that in entrapment cases, the application to have the evidence excluded is in reality an application to stay the proceedings for an abuse of process since the evidence obtained through the use of entrapment usually forms the entire basis of the prosecution's case. If the evidence of entrapment were to be excluded the prosecution would collapse. For this reason, an abuse of process application was the appropriate remedy. Accordingly the relevant test to be applied in English law was that set out in *R v Latif and Shazard* [1996] 1 WLR 104: namely, whether the conduct of the prosecuting authorities had been so shameful and unworthy as to constitute an affront to the public conscience.

In *Loosley*, their Lordships accepted the need for prosecuting authorities to use undercover officers in the detection and prosecution of crime. The use of entrapment, however, or 'state-created crime', is an abuse of process. Where is the line to be drawn in this regard?

Lord Hoffmann identified the relevant factors of entrapment as follows:

1. Whether the police caused the defendant to commit the crime or merely provided him with an unexceptional opportunity.

2. Whether the accused would have committed the offence with someone else.

3. Whether the police suspect the accused might commit an offence-In relation to this factor, Lord Hoffmann observed: 'The only proper purpose of police participation is to obtain evidence of criminal acts which they suspect someone is about to commit or in which he is already engaged. It is not to tempt people to commit crimes in order to expose their bad characters and punish them.' Relevant to this factor is the question of whether or not the particular police operation had been authorised.

4. The nature of the offence, i.e. whether the deployment of an undercover officer is the only way of achieving the desired result.

Ultimately, each case depends on its individual facts. Applying these guiding principles to the appeals before them, their Lordships concluded that Loosely's appeal should be dismissed. His arrest had come about as a result of legitimate concern in the rising supply of hard drugs in the Guildford area and from one public house in particular. As Loosely expressed himself keen to arrange a supply, the undercover officer had not needed to undertake any persuasion, and therefore his actions clearly fell within the bounds of acceptable conduct. In relation to the *Attorney-General's Reference*, the House of Lords concluded it would not interfere with the trial judge's exercise of discretion. The defendant in that case had come under considerable and sustained pressure by officers to supply them with a Class A drug and could be said to have been induced to commit the offence based on the continued supply of contraband cigarettes to him.

9.7 ABUSE OF PROCESS

In addition to discretion to exclude evidence at common law and under s. 78 PACE, the criminal courts have an inherent jurisdiction to stay proceedings for abuse of process. This would be a very serious step for a court to take as its effect is to bring the trial to a premature end, although a stay does not have the same legal effect as an acquittal. In the rare instances where a stay is ordered, the court is saying either that the defendant cannot enjoy a fair trial or, as a result of the actions of the prosecuting authorities, that it is not fair to try the accused.

A defendant might argue a stay in a case where there has been considerable delay in bringing charges with the result that the defendant would find it difficult to advance a defence. It could also cover a case where:

- extensive pre-trial publicity makes a fair trial impossible;

- there is a repeat prosecution where a previous trial was aborted;

- there is a decision to commence a prosecution in circumstances where the prosecution agreed an alternative course of action, i.e. to caution instead of prosecute (see *R v Dobson* [2000] EWCA 1606);

- the prosecution have lost or failed to secure evidence relevant to the crime which might have assisted the defendant; or

- the prosecution have withheld relevant evidence.

The above list is not exhaustive. In *R v Loosley* (above), the House of Lords held that the issue of entrapment was more appropriately dealt with as abuse of process rather than s. 78 PACE, as a successful assertion that the actions of the police amounted to entrapment effectively brings the trial to an end.

Where proceedings are stayed on account of the unlawful activities of the prosecuting authorities, the court is effectively sending out the message that such activities will not be tolerated and cannot be condoned. The exercise of discretion under the abuse of process is therefore wider than the discretion exercised under s. 78 PACE. However, the type of misconduct involved for an abuse of process application to succeed must be such that it would be an affront to public conscience for the proceedings to continue or for the conviction to stand (*R v Latif* [1996] 1 WLR 104).

R v Edward Grant [2005] 3 WLR 437

The defendant was charged with conspiring with others to murder his wife's lover, who had been shot dead after answering a knock at his door. The defendant accepted that there had indeed been a conspiracy to assault the victim but not to murder him. It was suggested that the victim might have been killed by criminal contacts of his own. Before the trial began an application was made to stay the proceedings as an abuse of process. It transpired that the police had installed a covert listening devise in the exercise yard of the police station where the defendant was being held. The installation was properly authorised for the purpose of recording conversations between the detainees implicated in the murder investigation. The effect, however, had been to record inadvertently conversations between solicitor and client while in the exercise yard. No prejudice was caused to the defendant as the prosecution placed no reliance on the tape-recorded conversations. The Court of Appeal upheld the abuse of process application, however, firmly endorsing the absolute sanctity of legal professional privilege and holding that in some instances, no prejudice to the defendant had to be proved in order for an abuse of process application to succeed.

'We are in no doubt but that in general unlawful acts of the kind done in this case, amounting to a deliberate violation of a suspected person's right to legal professional privilege, are so great an affront to the integrity of the justice system, and therefore the rule of law, that the associated prosecution is rendered abusive and ought not to be countenanced by the court . . .' (Per Laws LJ)

9.8 CONCLUSION

In conclusion, we can safely suggest that the exercise of judicial discretion under s. 78 PACE is comparable to the exercise of discretion at common law. With the exception of confession evidence and evidence of identification where s. 78 is more likely to be successfully argued, evidence obtained in excess of the powers available to the police is likely to be admitted if it yields relevant and reliable evidence.

The current state of the law in relation to the exercise of judicial discretion under s. 78 should not inhibit a defence advocate from making an application to have unlawfully obtained evidence excluded. As the saying goes-nothing ventured, nothing gained. If the argument as to admissibility fails, the unlawful nature of the activities can still be put to the police in cross-examination with a view to undermining that witness's credibility.

KEY POINT SUMMARY

- Every accused enjoys the right to a fair trial and a component of that right includes the ability to challenge any evidence that might be said to have been obtained unlawfully or in a dubious manner.

- The power to exclude evidence in the interests of securing a fair trial exists at common law and under s. 78 PACE – both are exercised on a discretionary basis.

- Section 78 PACE has largely superseded the common law.

- Section 78 PACE applies to all types of prosecution evidence, including prosecution evidence that has been obtained unlawfully.

- Evidence obtained in breach of PACE and/or the Codes of Practice can be said to have been obtained unlawfully and is therefore vulnerable to the risk of exclusion.

- With the exception of confession evidence and evidence of identification, the power to exclude unlawfully obtained is exercised restrictively.

- This chapter should be read in conjunction with Chapters 10 and 11 in order to gain the widest possible understanding of s.78 discretion and the discretion exercised at common law.

SELF-TEST QUESTIONS

Scenario 1

Ranjit Singh will state as follows:

'Shortly before midnight last night I was driving home in my mother's Ford Escort Cabriolet, registration number R457 KYE. I had just parked the car and was removing my sport's bag from the boot. It contained my squash equipment. I was wearing my black tracksuit trousers and hooded sweatshirt. I was searching for my mobile phone in the back of the car when two men approached me. One reached into the car and grabbed me by the arm. It was dark. I could not see what they were wearing. Fearing a racial attack, I just lashed out and hit one of them. I extricated myself and started to run. One of them shouted: 'Stop we're police officers.' I was grabbed in a matter of seconds. The other man began to search my bag and then me. The other searched my car. Finally, I heard one of them say, 'Let's teach him a lesson.' With that I was handcuffed. They emptied my pockets and removed my trousers, socks and shoes. They found a small quantity of cocaine tucked inside my sock. I was then arrested and subsequently charged with (a) possession of a controlled drug and (b) assaulting a police officer in the execution of his duty.'

Do you feel you can challenge the admissibility of the evidence in the case? If so, upon what grounds?

Scenario 2

Stan is charged with possession of cocaine with intent to supply. He has no previous convictions, although he has the reputation for being able to acquire goods on the cheap. He is approached one evening by an acquaintance, accompanied by two men. The acquaintance tells Stan the two men are looking to be supplied with cocaine. At first Stan says he cannot help. The two men then appear to make a phone call and increase their price. At this point Stan makes several telephone calls and tells the men to come back next day. They do so and are supplied with a quantity of cocaine. The two men then reveal themselves to be undercover drug squad officers. They arrest and subsequently charge Stan with possession of drugs with intent to supply.

Does the manner in which the evidence has been obtained provide Stan with an argument for seeking to have the evidence excluded?

FIGURE 9.1 UNLAWFULLY AND UNFAIRLY OBTAINED EVIDENCE

WHAT IS IT?

- Any evidence obtained unlawfully or in an underhand manner, which can include:
  - evidence obtained in breach of Codes of Practice under PACE;
  - evidence obtained through the use of an *agent provocateur*;
  - evidence obtained in breach of rights under PACE – unlawful search/seizure;
  - evidence obtained in violation of Article 8 – the right to privacy;
  - evidence obtained in violation of the privilege against self-incrimination.

CHALLENGING THE ADMISSIBILITY OF UNFAIRLY OBTAINED EVIDENCE

COMMON LAW PRESERVED BY S. 82(3 PACE)

- illustrated in *R v Sang* and *R v Khan*;

- restrictive in its application;

- save for evidence of a self-incriminating nature obtained by means of trickery/deception after commission of offence, evidence obtained unlawfully or unfairly remains admissible if it is relevant and reliable;

- basically, if the probative value of the evidence exceeds its prejudicial effect, the evidence will be admitted.

SECTION 78 PACE 1984

- gives courts discretion to exclude **ANY** prosecution evidence, the admission of which would have an adverse effect on the fairness of the proceedings;

- s. 78 is not confined to unlawfully obtained evidence;

- application of s. 78 is discretionary;

- used most successfully to exclude confession evidence obtained in breach safeguards of PACE and Code C (*R v Aspinall*; *R v Walsh*; *R v Canale*);

- also used to exclude identification evidence obtained in breach of safeguards under Code D (*R v Finley*);

- less successfully used in relation to other types of evidence i.e. unlawful arrest/search/seizure, unauthorised surveillance/underhand tactics where the evidence yielded is relevant, reliable and authentic (*R v Khan*);

- on the use of an *agent provocateur* see *R v Loosely* and the application of abuse of process;

- unless the reliability of the evidence is tainted by the illegality or unfairness, making it more difficult for the defendant to challenge the evidence, it is likely to be admitted.

10 CONFESSION EVIDENCE

10.1   INTRODUCTION

In many criminal cases, the police interview with the suspect is the centrepiece of the investigation. In a significant number of cases the prosecution will wish to place reliance on the interview as it will have some evidential relevance. Where a suspect makes statements of an incriminating nature in interview, the interview is said to constitute a confession. A confession can be persuasive prosecution evidence against an accused. In this chapter, we consider:

• the definition of a confession;

• the dangers associated with confession evidence;

• the recording requirements for police interviews;

• the requirements under PACE and Code C and their relationship to confession evidence;

• the rules which regulate the admissibility of confession evidence;

• the procedure by which the admissibility of a confession would be determined;

• the relationship between confession evidence and the rule against admitting hearsay evidence;

• the admissibility of mixed statements.

10.2 WHAT IS THE LEGAL DEFINITION OF A CONFESSION?

Section 82(1) PACE 1984 defines a confession as:

> 'Any statement wholly or partly adverse to the person who made it, whether made to a person in authority or not and whether made in words or otherwise.'

The definition of a confession is extremely wide and covers any statement by the accused which the prosecution seeks to rely on for an evidentially adverse purpose. Such statements do not have to be made to a person in authority, e.g. a police officer. It is possible to secure a conviction on the basis of confession evidence alone. You may recall that Michael Stone's conviction for the double fatal hammer attack on Lin and Megan Russell in 1996, was based on a confession he was alleged to have made in earshot of a convicted, serving prisoner while on remand awaiting trial.

The suspect needs to be careful about how he answers questions in interview if he does not wish to incriminate himself. The role of the legal adviser at the police station is critical in this regard. The police are well versed in the psychology of interrogative technique. Indeed the entire interview process is geared to persuading the suspect to talk. By talking, the suspect is more likely to say something of a revealing, incriminating or self-contradictory nature, especially over the course of several interviews. We saw in Chapter 8 that the provisions in ss. 34–36 and 37 Criminal Justice and Public Order Act 1994 have placed increased pressure on suspects to speak, and that a failure to put forward facts subsequently relied on in court may result in an adverse inference being drawn against the accused, in circumstances where it was reasonable for the accused to have mentioned those facts.

10.3 WHY IS CONFESSION EVIDENCE PROBLEMATIC?

It is a fact borne out of numerous miscarriages of justice and extensive psychological research that suspects do sometimes confess for reasons other than the truth. Detention inside a police station is a demeaning, often bewildering experience. Whether out of a sense of fear, frustration, desperation, desire to please or because a suspect is vulnerable to suggestion, some detainees will make incriminating admissions for reasons of short-term expediency, in order to relieve the pressure of the situation and in the hope that matters will be sorted out in their favour in the long term. It is for this very important reason that the law makes specific provision for the admissibility of confession evidence. The main provision is contained in s. 76 PACE. In addition, the admissibility of a confession can also be challenged under s. 78 PACE. Section 78 gives the court the power to exclude any prosecution evidence (including confession evidence) if its admission would have an adverse effect on the fairness of the proceedings. We have already considered the application of s. 78 PACE outside the context of the formal interview in Chapter 9.

10.4 THE IMPORTANCE OF THE CODES OF PRACTICE IN RELATION TO FORMAL INTERVIEWS

Crucially relevant to the admissibility of confession evidence are the safeguards contained in PACE and the Codes of Practice, including ss. 56 and 58 PACE 1984, Codes C and E. The majority of the safeguards were identified and considered in Chapter 7. (At the conclusion of this chapter, we include a set of self-test questions designed to test your knowledge of Code C safeguards in the context of the admissibility of confession evidence.)

Code C seeks to promote integrity in the investigative process. Although Code C does not have the force of law, as with the other Codes of Practice issued under s. 67(11) PACE they are admissible in criminal proceedings where they are relevant to any question arising in the proceedings.

A breach of PACE and/or the Codes will not automatically lead to the court excluding a resulting confession. However, a breach of PACE or the Codes (which has contributed to a person making incriminating admissions) enables the advocate to make the argument that the confession ought to be excluded either under ss. 76 and/or 78 PACE. A causal link must always be established between the breach alleged and the resulting confession. In challenging the admissibility of a confession, the role of the custody officer and the evidential significance of the custody record cannot be overstated.

10.5 RECORDING REQUIREMENTS OF INTERVIEWS

The provisions requiring the recording of interviews are contained in Code E. An account of any interview undertaken at the police station should be reliable, impartial and accurate. The best way of ensuring this is to have the interview tape recorded. Code E para. 3.1 stipulates that a tape recording shall be used at police stations for any interview with a person who is under caution in respect of any indictable offence, including an offence triable either way. Although no specific mention is made of summary-only offences, it is also common practice for the police to interview under tape recorded conditions. Provision is made under Code E for the manner in which tape recorded interviews are to be carried out. Code F contains guidance on the visual recording of police interviews which is currently being piloted in a number of different police areas.

In circumstances where an interview is not tape recorded, Code C paras. 11.7–11.4 requires the interviewing officer make and complete a verbatim record of what was said in the interview. The record should be completed during the interview unless this would be impracticable. If a written record is not made during the interview, it must be made as soon as practicable thereafter and the suspect must be given the opportunity to read the interview and to sign it as correct or to indicate how he considers it to be inaccurate. As a matter of good practice, any legal adviser attending the police station should of course be keeping an accurate written record of what took place, the questions asked and the answers given, during the course of the interview.

It is not unusual for suspects to make unsolicited comments off record, which are outside the context of a formal interview which may be relevant to the investigation of an offence. Code C para. 11.13 requires the police to keep a written record of such comments which should be signed and dated. Ordinarily, the suspect should be given the opportunity to read the record and to sign it as being an accurate record of what was said.

The recording requirements of interviews are of practical importance, in that they ought to provide an accurate account of what took place. The recording requirements assist the police as much as anyone else in that they are protected to a degree from accusations that they have 'verballed' the suspect (in other words, they have attributed comments to the suspect which he denies were ever made). Any departure from the norm in terms of recording immediately compromises the integrity of the police officers concerned and may form the basis of a challenge to exclude disputed evidence of incriminating admissions.

10.5.1 ENTITLEMENT TO A COPY OF THE TAPE RECORDED INTERVIEW

Legal advisers are entitled to a copy of all recorded interviews, on request. Under the various rules relating to the disclosure of used material (Criminal Procedure Rules, Part 21), the prosecution will normally provide the accused with a written summary of the recorded interview. Except in the most straightforward of cases (and especially where an accused was unrepresented at the police station), it is good practice to request a copy of the tape recorded interview.

10.6 CHALLENGING ADMISSIBILITY UNDER S. 76 PACE 1984

Section 76(2) provides two limbs under which a confession can be excluded – oppression and unreliability:

'If, in any proceedings where the prosecution proposes to give in evidence a confession made by an accused person, it is represented to the court that the confession was or may have been obtained—

(a) by oppression of the person who made it; or

(b) in consequence of anything said or done which was likely, in the circumstances existing at the time, to render unreliable any confession which might be made by him in consequence thereof,

the court shall not allow the confession to be given in evidence against him except in so far as the prosecution proves to the court beyond reasonable doubt that the confession (notwithstanding that it may be true) was not obtained as aforesaid.'

Where the defence (or the court) raise the issue of the admissibility of a confession, the prosecution has the legal burden of proving that the confession was not obtained through oppression (s. 76(2)(a)) and/or is not unreliable (s. 76(2)(b) PACE). If the prosecution cannot prove beyond reasonable doubt that the confession has not been obtained by oppression or is not unreliable, it must be excluded notwithstanding that it may be true.

Each provision will now be considered in turn.

10.6.1 OPPRESSION: S. 76(2)(a)

Oppression is partially defined in s. 76(8) to include torture, inhuman or degrading treatment, and the use of threat of violence (whether or not amounting to torture).

In the important case of *R v Fulling* [1987] QB 426, the Court of Appeal felt that oppression should be defined by its dictionary definition as being 'the exercise of authority or power in a burdensome, harsh or wrongful manner; unjust or cruel treatment of subjects, inferiors, etc; the imposition of unreasonable or unjust burdens.' The case of *Fulling* provides that for conduct to amount to oppression within the meaning of s. 76(8), there must be deliberate misconduct by the police. Oppression is a question of degree. What is oppressive as regards one individual may not be oppressive as regards another. To this end, the personal characteristics of the accused, including his mental strengths and weaknesses will be relevant.

What amounts to 'oppressive' conduct was found to have occurred in *R v Paris, Abdullah and Miller* (1993) 97 Cr APP R 99, in which the defendants appealed against their conviction for murder. During the investigation, M was interviewed a total of 13 hours over five days. A solicitor was not present during the first two interviews and M consistently denied his involvement in the crime during the first seven interviews. During interviews eight and nine, M accepted that he was present at the crime scene. He was then pressed to say who had stabbed the victim. M finally confessed that he had. Having denied his involvement over 300 times on tape, he later agreed with the officer's suggestion that he may have been under the influence of drugs and stabbed the victim without knowing what he was doing. He finally admitted: 'I just stabbed, not stabbed her . . . just thumped her in the face I mean.' Allowing the appeal, the Court of Appeal held that, short of physical violence, it was hard to conceive of a more hostile and intimidating environment. There was no doubt that the police conduct was 'oppressive' within the meaning of s. 76(2)(b).

10.6.2 UNRELIABILITY: S. 76(2)(b)

The key issue under s. 76(2)(b) is whether the confession is unreliable, not whether it is true or false. A confession may well be true, but if it has been obtained in circumstances rendering it unreliable, it must be excluded. The wording in s. 76(2)(b) (notwithstanding that it may be true) makes this perfectly clear. If the circumstances existing at the time were likely to induce an unreliable confession (notwithstanding it might actually be reliable and true), the actual confession must be excluded (*R v Proulx* [2001] 1 All ER 57).

In determining whether a confession should be excluded on the ground that it is 'unreliable', s. 76(2)(b) requires the court to consider 'anything said or done to the accused . . . in the circumstances existing at the time.'

A court determining the admissibility of a confession under s. 76(2)(b) must therefore examine all the relevant circumstances of the accused's detention and interrogation and take account of what was said or done to the accused.

As well as the suspect's subjective characteristics, breaches of PACE and the Codes of Practice are often highly relevant to excluding a confession on the ground of unreliability. Although a breach will not render a confession automatically inadmissible, the safeguards under PACE and the Codes exist to try and ensure reliability of confession evidence by protecting the suspect's basic rights.

The presence or absence of bad faith on the part of the police is largely irrelevant to a s. 76(2)(b) enquiry. What is important is the effect any breach had on the particular suspect at the time. A failure by the police to spot a particular vulnerability perhaps due to a medical condition or substance abuse and to make a appropriate provision, may provide grounds for seeking the exclusion of a confession under this section. Subtle or not so subtle inducements offered by the police to encourage the suspect to confess, such as promises of bail or a lesser charge, are also relevant considerations. For s. 76 PACE to apply, there must be a proven causal link between what was said and done at the police station and the resulting confession.

The following selection of cases illustrates the sort of factors courts have regard to when assessing admissibility under s. 76(2)(b). While it is possible to extract some general principles the outcome of each case is largely dependant on its facts.

R v Delaney [1988] 86 Cr App R 18: failure to secure legal representation in relation to a vulnerable suspect

The defendant was convicted of the indecent assault of a three-year-old girl. The only evidence against him was his confession. He had been interviewed at length, having declined the services of a solicitor. Although he was 17 he had an IQ of only 80 and was educationally subnormal. The entire scenario was described by the Court of Appeal as being a set of circumstances 'in which, *par excellence*, any interrogation should have been conducted with meticulous care and with meticulous observance of the rules of fairness.' There was evidence from an educational psychologist, which if accepted, established the defendant to be a vulnerable suspect. The interview had been conducted on a sympathetic basis with the officers being at pains to minimise the seriousness of the defendant's position. On several occasions during the interview reference was made to the defendant's need for treatment rather than punishment. Given the nature of the questioning on such a vulnerable suspect, who was not legally represented, the risk of it producing a false confession was too high.

R v Howden-Simpson [1991] Crim LR 49: inducement to confess

The appellant was an organist and choirmaster. His duties included paying junior choir members for their services at weddings. He failed to pay the money to the choristers and was charged with theft. His confession was excluded under s. 76(2) because of an inducement to confess. The investigating officers had indicated that they would proceed on two non-payments charges only if he admitted the theft. However, if he did not admit the two charges they would interview every chorister not paid and make a separate charge for each. In the circumstances the Court of Appeal had no hesitation in deciding that the confession ought to have been excluded under s. 76(2)(b). The predicament the appellant was placed in by the officers rendered his confession unreliable.

The physical condition and mental characteristics of the accused are part of the circumstances existing at the time for the purposes of s. 76(2)(b).

R v McGovern (1991) 92 Cr App R 228

The defendant was arrested on suspicion of murder. She was aged 19 and was six months pregnant. She had been sick in her cell shortly before the interview and according to a psychologist's evidence she had a mental age of a 10-year-old. The police were anxious to interview her because the victim in the investigation was still missing and it was not known whether she was alive or dead. The defendant was interviewed twice. She made damaging admissions in both interviews. As regards the first interview, she was wrongly denied access to a solicitor, in breach of s. 58 of PACE. There were further breaches, in that there was a failure to keep a contemporaneous note of what was said. It was apparent from the beginning that the defendant had comprehension difficulties. She did not understand the caution, which had to be explained to her several times. She was upset, and her distress increased as further questions were put. Ultimately she confessed to stabbing the victim. There was no doubt that had a solicitor been present, the outcome of the first interview would have been different. Indeed the interview would probably have been halted. During the second interview, this time in the presence of a solicitor, the defendant gave a much more coherent account of her involvement in the killing.

Notwithstanding the confession in the first interview was true, as the defendant herself admitted in her second interview, the Court of Appeal concluded her admissions had been made in consequence of her being denied access to a solicitor. The second interview had been tarnished by the conduct of the officers in the first interview, and consequently both interviews were inadmissible.

R v Walker [1998] Crim LR 211

The defendant, a prostitute, was convicted of robbery. She told the police doctor she was a heroin addict. She was prescribed methadone and valium. In interview she made a number of incriminating admissions. At her trial she maintained her victim had not been frightened, and sought exclusion of the interview. At the enquiry into the admissibility into her confession, the defendant gave evidence that she had smuggled some crack cocaine into the police station. She had smoked the drug and was under its influence when interviewed. Psychiatric evidence was called to establish that she had a severe personality disorder, making her prone to provide inaccurate elaboration on events without appreciating the consequences. The defendant's mental state would have been made worse by the use of drugs. The trial judge rejected much of the evidence but allowed the confession into evidence, finding that nothing had been said or done to the defendant within the meaning of s. 76(2)(b). Allowing the appeal, the Court of Appeal held that the wording in s. 76(2)(b) did not require any wrongdoing on the part of the police. The defendant's mental state was one of the circumstances to be taken into account, and there was nothing in any of the earlier decided cases limiting mental conditions exclusively to intellectual impairment. Given the defendant's mental state, her confession could not be said to be reliable.

10.6.3 CAN A DEFENDANT RELY ON SELF-INDUCED UNRELIABILITY?

In the case of *R v Goldenberg* (1988) 88 Cr App R 285, it was held that s. 76(2)(b) does not apply to a situation where what was said or done was by the accused himself. In this case, the accused maintained he had only admitted the offence out of a desperate desire to obtain bail, as he was suffering drug withdrawal symptoms. It was not possible in these circumstances to establish a causal link between anything said or done to the accused and the resulting confession.

Where a suspect perceives some advantage to his self and is thereby motivated to confess, then in the absence of anything said or done, a causal link cannot be established. The position was summarised by Lord Lane C.J. in *R v Rennie* [1982] 1 WLR 64, where he stated:

'Very few confessions are inspired solely by remorse. Often the motives of an accused are mixed and include a hope that an early admission may lead to an earlier release or a lighter sentence. If it were the law that the mere presence of such a motive, even if prompted by something said or done by a person in authority, led inexorably to the exclusion of a confession, nearly every confession would be rendered inadmissible. This is not the law. In some cases the hope may be self- generated. If so, it is irrelevant, even if it provides the dominant motive for making the confession. In such a case the confession will not have been obtained by anything said or done by a person in authority. More commonly the presence of such a hope will, in part at least, owe its origin to something said or done by such a person. There can be few prisoners who are being firmly but fairly questioned in a police station to whom it does not occur that they might be able to bring both their interrogation and their detention to an earlier end by confession.'

10.6.4 CAN A SOLICITOR BE THE CAUSE OF SOMETHING SAID OR DONE?

This point was considered in the case of *R v Wahab* [2003] 1 Cr App R 15, in which the defendant tried to argue that the advice he had been given by his solicitor to confess had been negligent advice and accordingly, his confession should have been ruled inadmissible as being unreliable.

In this case the defendant alleged investigating officers had been putting pressure on him to confess, by making reference to members of his family who were also in custody. At a later stage in the investigation, the defendant asked his solicitor to see whether an accommodation could be reached with the police. His solicitor relayed the substance of what the officers had told him: namely, that they could not give any guarantees, but that they would look again at the situation regarding his relatives if admissions were forthcoming. After carefully considering all the circumstances (which the solicitor had documented and recorded), including the risk of conviction, the involvement in the investigation of his family and the availability of a sentencing discount for an early guilty plea, the defendant chose to make a number of admissions.

In determining the case, the Court of Appeal held that the wording in s. 76(2)(b) – '*having regard to anything said or done . . .*' – was not confined to the actions or omissions of police officers. However, the Court of Appeal held that s. 76(2)(b) did require something extraneous to the person making the confession. Can a solicitor's advice constitute something extraneous? It could, said the Court of Appeal, depending on the particular facts such as advice to confess given to a particularly vulnerable suspect. On the facts of this case the Court of Appeal concluded that the appellant had not been influenced by anything said or done by anyone else and indeed, it had been the defendant who had requested his solicitor to see if an accommodation could be sought. The Court of Appeal underlined the point that s. 76(2)(b) PACE is not concerned with the defendant's motives for confessing, except and in so far as such motive affected the reliability of what was said.

10.7 'UNFAIRNESS': S. 78 PACE/COMMON LAW

We have, of course, already considered the effect of s. 78 PACE in the context of unlawfully obtained prosecution evidence outside the sphere of confession evidence in Chapter 9. The judicial discretion available under s. 78 can be applied to any prosecution evidence in a case where it is contended that the admission of such evidence would prejudice the defendant's right to a fair trial.

Confession evidence clearly falls within the sphere of s. 78 PACE. To remind you, the section provides:

'In any proceedings the court may refuse to allow evidence on which the prosecution proposes to rely to be given if it appears to the court that, having regard to all the circumstances, including the circumstances in which the evidence was obtained, the admission of the evidence would have such an adverse effect on the fairness of the proceedings that the court ought not to admitted.'

Section 78 might be applied to incriminating admissions that have been obtained as a result of unfair conduct by the police, including:

- a failure to secure access to a solicitor;
- a failure to properly record an interview;
- a failure to provide safeguards in relation to a vulnerable suspect;
- deceiving a suspect into making a confession or offering inducements;
- acting in deliberate breach of Code C.

An illustration of the application of s. 78 is provided by *R v Mason* [1988] 1 WLR 139. The defendant (M) was in custody on suspicion of having petrol-bombed the car of his ex-girlfriend's father. M and his solicitor were told (untruthfully) by two police officers, that M's fingerprints had been found on pieces of glass from the petrol bombs that had shattered near the car. As a result of this deception, and perceiving his position to be hopeless, M made a confession statement, which led to his conviction for arson. The Court of Appeal quashed his conviction. It appears from the judgment that the deception practised on the solicitor (an officer of the court) was particularly objectionable, and that the trial judge ought to have exercised his discretion to exclude the confession, as its admission had had an adverse effect on the fairness of the proceedings.

There is some overlap between the type of factors justifying exclusion under s. 76(2)(b) and under s. 78 PACE. As with excluding a confession under s. 76(2)(b), breaches of PACE and the Codes of Practice are highly relevant to the exercise of judicial discretion under s. 78 of PACE. The importance the appellate courts attach to the suspect's access to a solicitor while being detained at the police station (a right under s. 58 PACE) has been underlined in a number of cases including the Court of Appeal's decisions in *R v Samuel* [1988] QB 615 and in *R v Walsh* (1990) 91 Cr App R 161, where it was stated:

> 'To our minds it follows if there are significant and substantial breaches of section 58 or the provisions of the Code, then *prima facie* at least the standards of fairness set by Parliament have not been met. So far as this defendant is concerned . . . to admit evidence against him which has been obtained in circumstances where these standards have not been met, cannot but have an adverse effect on the fairness of the proceedings. This does not mean of course that in every case of a significant or substantial breach of section 58 or the Code of Practice evidence will automatically be excluded. Section 78 does not so provide.' (Saville J.)

Breach of Code C does not guarantee that the confession will be excluded under s. 78 PACE. If there is no causal connection between the breach and the resulting confession, there is no unfairness (*R v Alladice* [1988] 87 Cr App R 380).

The application of s. 78 PACE in relation to a confession purported to have been obtained in breach of reporting requirements is illustrated by *R v Canale* [1990] 2 All ER 187. In this case the interviewing officers failed to make contemporaneous notes of two of the interviews they had with the defendant as required by Code C. The defendant alleged he had been tricked and induced to confess. This was denied by the police. The Court of Appeal described the breaches of the Code of Practice as being 'flagrant, deliberate and cynical' and concluded the admissions were inadmissible in accordance with s. 78. The absence of contemporaneous notes had deprived the trial judge of the very evidence that would have enabled him to resolve the conflict. The absence of the record severely prejudiced the defendant.

The fact that the police have acted in bad faith so far as compliance with the Codes is concerned is a factor the courts will consider. In *Walsh* (above), it was stated that:

> 'although bad faith may make substantial or significant that which might not otherwise be so, the contrary does not follow. Breaches which are in themselves significant and substantial are not rendered otherwise by the good faith of the officers concerned.'

One further excellent illustration of the application of s. 78 PACE in relation to a confession is provided by *R v Aspinall* [1999] Crim LR 741. The defendant, a schizophrenic, was arrested and ultimately convicted on drug charges. Two police surgeons pronounced him fit to be interviewed. During the enquiry into the admissibility of his confession, the defendant's consultant psychiatrist gave evidence to the effect that A might well have been tired and stressed, contributing to a degree of passivity and lack of assertiveness on his part. When asked by the officers whether he wanted to see a solicitor, the defendant had replied: 'No I want to get home to my missus and kids.' The defendant was interviewed without the presence of a solicitor or appropriate adult. The trial judge rejected a s. 78 submission, concluding the defendant had been lucid at the time of interview.

In allowing his appeal and quashing his conviction, the Court of Appeal held the defendant had been unable to judge what was in his best interests. The absence of an appropriate adult (a specific requirement under Code C for vulnerable persons) rendered the confession unfair. The Court of Appeal concluded there had been a breach of Article 6 occasioned by the delay in access to legal advice; the duty solicitor had been otherwise engaged at the relevant time.

10.8 SPECIAL PROVISION FOR MENTALLY HANDICAPPED SUSPECTS

Provision is made under s. 77 PACE for confessions made by mentally handicapped persons:

> ' . . . where at a trial—
>
> (a) the case against the accused depends wholly or substantially on a confession by him; and
>
> (b) the court is satisfied—
>
>   (i) that he is mentally handicapped;
>
>   (ii) that the confession was not made in the presence of an independent person, the court shall warn the jury that there is a special need for caution before convicting the accused in reliance on the confession, and shall explain that the need arises because of the circumstances mentioned in the paragraphs above.'

10.9 ADMISSIBILITY OF CONFESSION EVIDENCE IN CIRCUMSTANCES WHERE CODE C HAS NO APPLICATION

There are other ways in which evidence of a self-incriminating nature might be obtained other than through the formal police interview procedure. These include the use of covert listening devices, covert surveillance operations and *agent provocateurs*. The admissibility of evidence of a self-incriminatory nature obtained in this way is considered in Chapter 9 which examines the operation of s. 78 PACE outside the context of the formal interview.

10.10 THE PROCEDURE FOR DETERMINING THE ADMISSIBILITY OF A CONFESSION

In the Crown Court, where the admissibility of a confession is disputed, the issue will most usually be resolved by means of a *voir dire* (trial within a trial) at a pre-trial hearing.

In some cases, however, where an accused simply denies making a confession at all (by maintaining that his signature has been forged or by denying words attributed to him which were never in fact recorded) a question of fact only arises. On a trial in the Crown Court, the issue of who is telling the truth will be decided by the jury without the need to hold a *voir dire* (*R v Flemming* (1988) 86 Cr App R 32).

10.10.1 THE *VOIR DIRE*

In most indictable cases where the admissibility of evidence arises, the dispute will normally be resolved at a pre-trial hearing at which the judge can make binding decisions on law. The name given to the type of hearing that determines the admissibility of a confession is a *voir dire*, or a trial within a trial. Such a hearing is always conducted in the absence of the jury. The trial judge will hear evidence as to how the confession was obtained and will listen to legal arguments advanced by both sides. The burden of proving the admissibility of a confession under s. 76 PACE rests with the prosecution. In discharging that burden, the prosecution may well call the interviewing officers and custody officer/s to give evidence and will submit the custody record into evidence. The evidence adduced by the prosecution will be subject to cross-examination by the defence. The defendant may testify at the *voir dire* and adduce expert evidence if appropriate. The judge will consider the evidence, apply the law and reach a decision as to whether the confession should be admitted. If it is excluded, the jury will be kept in ignorance of it ever having been made. If the confession is ruled admissible, the accused is still entitled to repeat his allegations as to how it was obtained in the hope of persuading the jury that the confession carries little evidential weight.

Section 45 (Sch. 3) of the Courts Act 2003 now permits binding rulings to be made at pre-trial hearings in criminal cases heard in the magistrates' court. The power to make pre-trial binding rulings is available following a not guilty plea up to the commencement of the trial and extends to issues of law and admissibility of evidence. The rulings made by one bench of magistrates will bind the bench which subsequently tries the defendant. As the two benches will be differently composed, the risk of prejudice to the defendant is minimised. The risk of prejudice is only likely to arise where the admissibility of confession evidence is challenged during the course of the trial itself: in this case if the magistrates excluded the confession, they would continue to hear the case and have to put it to the back of their minds.

10.11 EDITING A CONFESSION

If an admissible confession contains material which is inadmissible under some other rule of evidence (e.g. hearsay or a reference to the accused's previous convictions) the accused is entitled to have the offending material edited out. The current rules are established by *Practice Direction (Crime: Tape Recording of Interviews)* [1989] 1 WLR 631. The Practice Direction allows the prosecution and defence to attempt to agree a transcript of any tape-recorded interview that is to be admitted in evidence. The defence is under an obligation to notify the prosecution whether or not a transcript of a tape-recorded interview is acceptable. In the event that it is not, various rules are encompassed in the Consolidated Practice Direction Part IV to give effect to the attempt to try to resolve difficulties. The practical effect is that where at all possible it is desirable for an edited transcript to be agreed.

10.12 THE RELATIONSHIP BETWEEN CONFESSIONS AND HEARSAY EVIDENCE

Full consideration is given to the difficult topic of hearsay evidence in Chapter 25. The general rule is that hearsay evidence in criminal cases is inadmissible unless it can be brought within a recognised statutory or common law exception. Confession evidence is a well established common law exception. A confession is only admissible against its maker. The confession itself cannot be used in evidence to implicate another co-accused in the crime. The confession is hearsay evidence for this purpose in that it constitutes a statement made on an earlier out-of-court occasion being relied on in court to prove the truth of facts asserted (*R v Gunewardene* [1951] 2 KB 600).

A co-accused who has confessed might of course choose to give evidence for the prosecution at the trial of the other co-accused. In this situation the co-accused becomes an accomplice and his evidence could attract a corroboration warning (see Chapter 24). To illustrate the point, consider the following example:

🔆 Example

Shirley and Debbie are jointly indicted on a charge of arson. In the course of the investigation Shirley confesses her limited involvement placing most of the blame on Debbie. Debbie denies the offence. Shirley's confession by itself constitutes evidence against Shirley only. As against Debbie it amounts to hearsay evidence and is inadmissible. If however Shirley were to plead guilty and give evidence against Debbie there would be no question of hearsay evidence as Shirley's evidence constitutes a direct first hand account.

Special problems arise where one accused seeks to rely on the confession of another co-accused in circumstances where the prosecution choose not to adduce the confession as part of the prosecution case. Varying the facts above, let's say that Shirley confesses and in so doing exonerates Debbie. Shirley is mentally vulnerable and was not represented at the police station by a solicitor nor an appropriate adult. She wishes to retract her confession and pleads not guilty. The CPS chooses not to rely on Shirley's confession. In other words, it will not be adduced into evidence at the trial. It is not clear whether Shirley will give evidence in her defence. What is Debbie to do in such circumstances? She would clearly like to rely on Shirley's earlier confession as evidence of the truth of what it asserts but in doing so it constitutes hearsay evidence. In *R v Myers* [1998] AC 124, the House of Lords created a further judge made exception to the hearsay rule by concluding that a co-accused in Debbie's position is able to rely on the confession providing the confession was not inadmissible under s. 76(2) PACE.

As a result of s. 128 CJA 2003, the provisions of s. 76 PACE apply not only to the prosecution but also to any co-accused who seeks to rely on the admissions of a fellow co-accused.

10.13 EVIDENCE OBTAINED IN CONSEQUENCE OF AN INADMISSIBLE CONFESSION

Where a confession has been ruled inadmissible, it does not mean that evidence obtained as a result of the confession must also be excluded. The position is governed by s. 76(4) PACE, which provides:

'The fact that a confession is wholly or partly excluded in pursuance of this section shall not affect the admissibility in evidence—

(a) of any facts discovered as a result of the confession; or

(b) where the confession is relevant as showing that the accused speaks, writes or expresses himself in a particular way, of so much of the confession as is necessary to show that he does so.'

Section 76(5) goes on to provide that where a confession has been excluded in whole or in part:

'Evidence that a fact . . . was discovered as a result of a statement made by the accused person shall not be admissible unless evidence of how it was discovered is given by him or on his behalf.'

An important point to stress is that the prosecution will not be allowed to point to the inadmissible confession in order to explain how the incriminating evidence was found. Where incriminating facts cannot be adduced without the necessity of referring to the inadmissible confession, neither the confession, nor the facts discovered, will be admissible.

10.14 MIXED STATEMENTS (PART CONFESSION/PART EXONERATION)

It is not unusual for a defendant to give a mixed statement to investigating officers. Such a statement is partly incriminating and partly self-serving. A mixed statement would be something like: 'I murdered him but I acted in self-defence', or 'I admit I took the goods but I always intended to return them . . . .' An admissible confession can be relied on as evidence of the truth because it is an admission against the maker's self-interest. A denial by the defendant however generally carries little evidential weight because it is self-serving in its nature. Such self-serving statements constitute hearsay evidence when they are relied on as proof of the facts they state and as such they are inadmissible. Where however, the defendant gives evidence in support of his own defence at trial and puts forward a defence he mentioned at an earlier stage, the earlier statement may be admitted for the limited evidential purpose of showing the defendant's consistency as a witness (see *R v Storey* (1968) 52 Cr App R 334). This principle however has no application where the defendant chooses not to give evidence at his trial but simply wishes to rely on a self serving statement made by him at the police station.

The evidential problem of the mixed statement only arises where the defendant chooses not to give evidence at his trial. The incriminating part of the statement is admissible as a confession but what of the self-serving portions of the statement? In fairness to the accused the entire statement must be put before the jury. The matter was considered by the Court of Appeal in *R v Duncan* (1981) 73 Cr App R 359 and by the House of Lords in *R v Sharp* [1988] 1 WLR 7. In short, the judge should direct the jury to consider the whole statement, in deciding where the truth might lie. The judge is entitled to point out that the incriminating aspects of the statement might carry more weight than the non-incriminating aspects, as these can be easily manufactured.

KEY POINT SUMMARY

- Except in the clearest of cases request a copy of any police interview (especially if the defendant was unrepresented at the police station).

- The vast majority of interviews conducted at the police station have some evidential value whether because the defendant remained silent and is now raising new facts in his defence or because he makes incriminating admissions or tells lies.

- In some cases there will be an advantage in your client making a full and frank confession to the police. It is therefore important that you ascertain and evaluate the nature of the evidence against your client, that you take your client's instructions on the evidence, and advise accordingly.

- A confession is very widely defined and will cover any incriminating admissions made by your client.

- Breaches of PACE and the Codes of Practice are important in determining the admissibility of confession evidence where such evidence is disputed, although a breach does not automatically entitle a defendant to have a confession excluded.

- Oppression, within s. 76(2)(a) is narrowly defined and will invariably involve some deliberate misconduct on the part of the police.

- Unreliability under s. 76(2)(b) has a much wider application. Breaches of Code C and E are relevant and deliberate impropriety on the part of the police is unnecessary.

- The enquiry under s. 76 PACE 1984 is as to the admissibility of the confession. The fact that the confession may well be true is immaterial to the question of its admissibility.

- Even if a confession is admissible under s. 76 PACE, it may be excluded under s. 78 PACE if its admission would have an adverse affect on the fairness of the case.

SELF-TEST QUESTIONS

A reminder of Code C safeguards

Exercise 1

In order to refresh your memory in this regard, see if you can answer the following short questions. The answers can be found in Appendix 5.

1. At what stages does the suspect have to be cautioned? Would a confession that has been obtained following a failure to properly caution an individual, be admissible?

2. On arrival at the police station what rights should be explained to the suspect by the custody officer?

3. What initial assessment must the custody officer undertake in relation to each suspect and who might be said to constitute a vulnerable suspect?

4. The right of access to a solicitor is governed by the all important s. 58 PACE. In what circumstances may access to a solicitor be delayed? If access was delayed and a confession was obtained, would the confession be admissible?

5. Can the investigating officers begin to question a suspect when he/she has requested a solicitor?

6. What are the maximum periods of detention and at what intervals should detention be reviewed? (It goes without saying that the longer an individual is detained in custody the more they may be tempted to confess in order to relieve the pressure of the situation.)

7. What basic human rights are suspects entitled to while in custody, including rest periods?

8. What actually constitutes an interview under Code C?

9. What is the procedure if the suspect appears to be unfit to be interviewed?

10. What safeguards apply as regards the conduct of an interview in relation to non-vulnerable and vulnerable suspects?

Exercise 2

Case scenario: *R v Lenny Whyte*

Consider the Lenny Whyte scenario. We have begun the process of evaluating the evidence against him. You will see from Document 18 E (included in Appendix 1) that Lenny makes a confession. What he states in his interview satisfies the statutory definition of a confession under s. 82(1) PACE. His interview is tape recorded in accordance with the requirements of Code E para. 3.1. Having regard to Lenny's initial statement (Document 1) and the custody record (Document 9) consider the following questions:

- Do you feel you have grounds for challenging the admissibility of Lenny's confession in due course? If so, what will be the legal basis for your submissions?

- What arguments will you put forward in support of your submissions?

- Consider the manner in which the confession was obtained. Can you point to any specific breaches of Code C?

- How will the admissibility of Lenny's confession be resolved and what evidence will need to be adduced and challenged in this regard?

- Guidance on all the above questions can be found in Appendix 5: Analyis of self-test questions to Chapter 10.

FIGURE 10.1 CONFESSION EVIDENCE

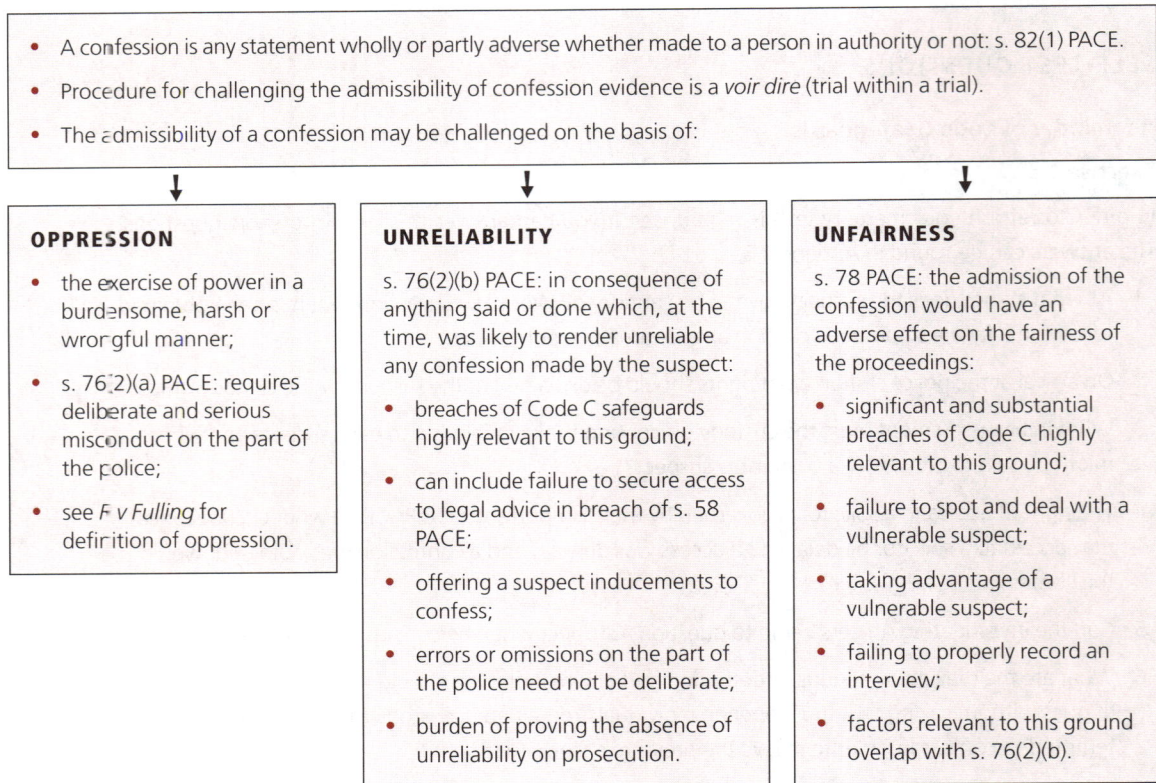

- A confession is any statement wholly or partly adverse whether made to a person in authority or not: s. 82(1) PACE.

- Procedure for challenging the admissibility of confession evidence is a *voir dire* (trial within a trial).

- The admissibility of a confession may be challenged on the basis of:

OPPRESSION

- the exercise of power in a burdensome, harsh or wrongful manner;

- s. 76(2)(a) PACE: requires deliberate and serious misconduct on the part of the police;

- see *R v Fulling* for definition of oppression.

UNRELIABILITY

s. 76(2)(b) PACE: in consequence of anything said or done which, at the time, was likely to render unreliable any confession made by the suspect:

- breaches of Code C safeguards highly relevant to this ground;

- can include failure to secure access to legal advice in breach of s. 58 PACE;

- offering a suspect inducements to confess;

- errors or omissions on the part of the police need not be deliberate;

- burden of proving the absence of unreliability on prosecution.

UNFAIRNESS

s. 78 PACE: the admission of the confession would have an adverse effect on the fairness of the proceedings:

- significant and substantial breaches of Code C highly relevant to this ground;

- failure to spot and deal with a vulnerable suspect;

- taking advantage of a vulnerable suspect;

- failing to properly record an interview;

- factors relevant to this ground overlap with s. 76(2)(b).

11 OBTAINING IDENTIFICATION EVIDENCE

11.1 INTRODUCTION

Proof of the defendant's presence at the scene of a crime is presented at trial in a number of different ways, including:

- visual identification of a suspect by an eyewitness;

- real evidence: the widespread use of closed circuit television surveillance has led to increasing use of videotape footage and photographic stills at trials. The admission of such real evidence can give the court a direct view of the incident enabling the fact finder to determine whether the defendant standing in the dock is the person seen participating in the criminal activity captured on film;
- forensic evidence: identification may also be provided by the opinion of a forensic scientist establishing a connection between the defendant and the crime scene based on the scientific comparison of forensic samples (fingerprints/DNA) found at the scene with evidence found on the defendant or otherwise in his possession.

In this chapter, we consider:

- how identification evidence is obtained by the police during the police investigation;
- the pre-trial safeguards contained in Code D of PACE which seek to ensure the reliability and fairness of eye-witness identification obtained by the police;
- the admissibility of eye-witness evidence obtained in breach of Code D;
- the practical steps a legal adviser can take to ensure the fairness of identification procedures;
- the power to take fingerprints; intimate and non-intimate samples at the police station.
- identification evidence given by expert witnesses.

online resource centre

Numerous references will be made in this chapter to Code D. A copy of Code D can be freely accessed from the Home Office website – our Online Resource Centre provides a link to the full text of Code D.

11.2 WHAT ARE THE DANGERS ASSOCIATED WITH EYE-WITNESS IDENTIFICATION?

Eye-witness identification has been proved to be unreliable by a number of psychological experiments and by past miscarriages of justice. Identification is often made in less than ideal circumstances. A typical crime-related incident is often over in a matter of seconds or minutes, in circumstances of heightened awareness and quite possibly fear. Safeguards are needed to ensure such evidence is gathered in a scrupulously fair manner and is treated with caution at trial. The principal safeguards are afforded pre-trial by PACE Code D and at trial by the Turnbull Guidelines (*R v Turnbull* [1977] QB 224). The Turnbull Guidelines and their considerable importance are considered in Chapter 24.

11.3 HOW IS EYE-WITNESS IDENTIFICATION ACTUALLY OBTAINED?

Eye-witness identification may come about in many different ways. A witness to a crime will usually give an initial statement to the police, which will include a description of those involved. Code D para. 3.1 requires the police to make a record of the suspect's description as first given by a potential witness and for the suspect or his legal adviser to be given a copy of the record.

The police may compile a photofit of a suspect they wish to speak to and circulate it to various media. On occasions a witness may be taken on a tour of the area to see if he is able to spot the person/s he considers was involved. In some instances the police will show a witness 'mug shots' of convicted offenders to see if the witness is able to identify the culprit and in other instances the use of video footage or photographic stills can assist.

11.4 MAKING A DISTINCTION BETWEEN KNOWN AND UNKNOWN SUSPECTS

For the purposes of identification procedures, Code D makes a distinction between a known and unknown suspect.

11.4.1 WHAT CONSTITUTES A KNOWN SUSPECT?

Code D para. 3.4 provides guidance as to when a suspect is 'known' and 'available.' A suspect is known where there is sufficient information known to the police to justify the arrest of a particular person for suspected involvement in an offence. A suspect is available if they are immediately available or will be within a reasonably short period of time and are willing to take an effective part in an identification procedure that is practicable to arrange.

11.4.2 WHAT IF THE SUSPECT IS UNKNOWN?

Where the suspect is not known, the police may take a witness to a particular neighbourhood or place to see if they can identify the suspect. Code D para. 3.2 stipulates the safeguards the police need to be mindful of when taking a witness around an area. A detailed record of all the circumstances must be kept and no attempt must be made to direct a witness's attention to a particular individual.

11.4.3 SHOWING A WITNESS PHOTOGRAPHS OF POSSIBLE SUSPECTS WHERE THE SUSPECT IS UNKNOWN

If the suspect's identity is not known, the witness may be shown photographs subject to safeguards contained in Annex E of Code D. The safeguards include:

- a requirement that the witness should be shown twelve photographs at a time which should be of a similar type;
- a witness must not be prompted or guided in his choice in any way;
- if a witness makes a positive identification from a set of photographs no other witness can be shown the set and each of the witnesses should be asked to attend a parade.

Once the police have a known suspect in mind and have arrested the individual concerned an identification procedure should follow.

Code D para. 3.3 prohibits the police from showing photographs to a witness if the identity of the suspect is known to the police and the suspect is available to stand on an identification parade. Showing photographs in advance of a formal identification procedure would seriously compromise the integrity of the formal identification procedure in that it would effectively render the procedure irrelevant.

11.4.4 OBLIGATION ON THE POLICE WHERE THE SUSPECT IS KNOWN AND AVAILABLE

Once a suspect is known and is available the police should proceed to a formal identification procedure: Code D para. 3.4.

In order to test the ability of a witness to identify a suspect and to safeguard against mistaken identity, the police can use a number of identification procedures, which are governed by Code D and its annexes A–E.

The annexes to Code D deal with the following procedures:

- Annex A: video identification
- Annex B: identification parades

- Annex C: group identification
- Annex D: confrontation by a witness.

11.5 WHEN MUST AN IDENTIFICATION PROCEDURE BE HELD?

The key provision in this respect is Code D para. 3.12:

'Whenever:

(i) a witness has identified a suspect or purported to have identified them prior to any identification procedure set out in paragraphs 3.5 to 3.10 having been held; or

(ii) there is a witness available, who expresses an ability to identify the suspect, or where there is a reasonable chance of the witness being able to do so, and they have not been given an opportunity to identify the suspect in any procedures set out in paragraphs 3.5 to 3.10, and the suspect disputes being the person the witness claims to have seen, an identification procedure shall be held unless it is not practicable or it would serve no useful purpose in proving or disproving whether the suspect was involved in committing the offence. For example, when it is not disputed that the suspect is already well known to the witness who claims to have seen them commit the crime.'

11.5.1 TYPES OF IDENTIFICATION PROCEDURES AND WHO DECIDES ON WHICH TYPE

The hierarchy of identification procedures places the video identification as the preferred first choice. Where an identification procedure must be held in accordance with Code D para. 3.12, para. 3.14 provides the suspect must initially be offered a video identification unless this is not practicable or an identification parade is more practicable and suitable or the officer in charge of the investigation considers that a group identification is more suitable than the other forms of identification and the identification officer believes it is practicable to arrange.

The decision to adopt a particular procedure is taken by the officer in charge of identification procedure in conjunction with the investigating officer. A suspect must be allowed to make representations as to the appropriate procedure. There is no doubt that video parades can be set up much faster than conventional parades and are less intimidating for witnesses. The conduct of the identification procedure is the sole responsibility of an officer of at least the rank of inspector who is independent of the investigation.

11.5.2 EXPLAINING RIGHTS TO A SUSPECT BEFORE CONVENING AN IDENTIFICATION PROCEDURE

Some important rights must be explained to the suspect in advance of convening an identification procedure. They are set out in D 3.17. They include:

- the right of the suspect to have access to free legal advice;
- an explanation that the suspect does not have to consent or co-operate in a video identification, parade or group parade but that if he does not consent his refusal can be given in evidence against him in any subsequent trial and the police may proceed covertly without his consent or make other arrangements to test whether a witness can identify him.

The formal identification procedures that are regarded as being the fairest to the suspect are the video parade and the identification parade. They provide the suspect with the best chance of not being picked out as the suspect has some measure of control in their composition.

A suspect who refuses to co-operate in the conduct of a video procedure can be treated as being unavailable (Code D para. 3.21). In these circumstances, the identification officer may make arrangements for the suspect's image to be captured covertly or for still photographs to be used in the compilation of the video identification procedure. The confrontation procedure is a procedure of last resort and may not be used unless all other options are impracticable.

11.6 IS THE REQUIREMENT TO HOLD A FORMAL IDENTIFICATION PROCEDURE MANDATORY?

What if prior to an arrest, the eyewitness is able to make a full and complete identification at or near the scene of the crime? What if the suspect is someone who the eyewitness recognises? Does Code D give the police discretion whether to hold a parade or, is it a mandatory requirement in all cases where identification of the suspect is disputed?

The issue as to whether the police must convene an identification procedure has given rise to a considerable number of appeals culminating in the House of Lords decision in *R v Forbes* [2001] 1 AC 473 which concerned an earlier version of Code D.

In *Forbes*, the victim was attacked and almost robbed at a cash-dispensing machine. The victim managed to get away and called the police. He was taken on a tour of the area and was able to point out the man who had robbed him. The appellant was arrested. He vigorously protested his innocence. No parade was held, as the police believed it would have been futile. In the opinion of the House of Lords a parade was a mandatory requirement save in exceptional cases where the eyewitness makes it plain that he cannot identify the person responsible, or in a case of pure recognition of someone well known to the eyewitness.

Statutory effect has been given to the decision in *R v Forbes* in the current edition of Code D. However, the question of whether an identification procedure is mandatory in all instances is still open to question. Under Code D para. 3.12 the requirement to convene an identification procedure is rebutted where, in all the circumstances, it would serve no useful purpose in proving or disproving whether the suspect was involved in the offence, including, for example, where the suspect is well known to the witness making the identification.

It will be apparent that the wording gives the police some discretion in ascertaining whether a suspect is well known to the witness and whether an identification procedure would therefore serve any useful purpose. A decision by the police not to convene an identification procedure should always be critically scrutinised. It affords a potential ground for the defence to seek the exclusion of identification evidence on the basis that it would be unfair to admit such evidence (s. 78 PACE) where no formal procedure to test the reliability of that evidence was convened in advance of trial.

The police need only convene a parade in a case where identification is not in dispute. In *R v Lambert* [2004] EWCA Crim 154, the police did not consider identification was in issue as the defendant admitted being at the scene of the crime but denied involvement in an assault that had taken place at that scene. The defendant made no comment in a subsequent interview and did not raise the issue of identification until trial. In this case, the Court of Appeal concluded there had been no obligation on the part of the police to convene a parade as the defendant had not put his identification as a possible assailant in issue at the police station.

The issue of the mandatory requirement to convene a parade was central to the two cases we include below. Both cases concerned earlier versions of Code D but the judgments are relevant to the current version of Code D.

R (on the application of H) v DPP [2003] EWHC 133

The victim (V) was 15. It was alleged that she had been assaulted by the defendant (D), a 16-year-old. The assault lasted some several minutes. V had been assaulted on a previous occasion by D and had reported the matter to the police. D denied the assault and denied being present when the attack took place. No identification parade was held. At her trial before magistrates, D's defence solicitor submitted there had been a breach of Code D para. 2.3 (under the previous Code D), and that consequently there was no evidence of identification.

V had known D for about 18 months and had been a credible witness. Finding D guilty, the magistrates concluded that the police were entitled to refuse to hold an identification parade in this instance, as it would have been futile. Applying the dicta in *Forbes* (highlighted above), the Divisional Court concurred with the decision of the magistrates. The defendant had indicated she knew V and it was not suggested by the defendant or her legal representative at anytime during her interview with the police that the question of recognition was an issue for her. In these circumstances this was a case of pure recognition and an identification parade would have served no useful purpose as V was bound to have identified D.

R v Harris [2003] EWCA 174

Two victims (A and B) were robbed of their mobile phones in the street by a group of youths. Both A and B claimed to recognise the appellant (C). They had previously been at school with C and knew him by his first name of Tristan. C had been in the year above them. A and B purported to recognise C, even though he was wearing a hooded top. A had recognised the boy's voice when he came over to him. It was accepted by A and B that they had not known C well at school and that they had not seen him since he had left. C denied any involvement and put forward an alibi. There was no other evidence to link him to the crime. Evidence was given from the school's headmaster, who confirmed that A and B would have been in attendance from 1998 until 2000 when C had left. There would have been 500 pupils in the school at the time, and only one pupil at that time and since had the name of Tristan. No identification parade had been held and it was submitted at trial that the evidence of identification should have been excluded under s. 78 PACE.

Reviewing the evidence, the Court of Appeal concluded that Code D did require an identification procedure to be held in this particular case. The purpose of an identification procedure is not merely to afford an opportunity to the eyewitness to identify the perpetrator but also to afford the accused to test the reliability of the eye-witness identification.

While this was a case of recognition it did not, on the facts, satisfy the specific example given in D (where it is not in dispute that the suspect is already well known to the witness). Although the defendant had not requested a parade, he had made it clear in his defence statement to the police that he denied any involvement and that he did not know A or B. Was C well known to A and B, within the meaning of Code D? The Court of Appeal concluded he was not: neither A, nor B had seen C for the past two years; C would have been 14 at the time; neither A, B or C had been in the same class; there had not been any direct contact between them. This led the Court of Appeal to the conclusion that there was at least: 'a live possibility that one or both witnesses might not have picked out the appellant on an identification parade. In that event, the defence would have been able to rely at trial on such non-identification as adding weight to the defence of alibi.'

In reaching its conclusion that C's conviction be quashed, the Court of Appeal were not of the view that the evidence of recognition should have excluded under s. 78 PACE, however the failure by the trial judge to properly direct the jury as to the purpose of Code D and the effect of a breach, meant the defendant had not received a fair trial.

From the point of view of the police officer investigating the offence, the decision not to convene an identification procedure requires careful consideration.

11.7 SPECIFIC SAFEGUARDS ASSOCIATED WITH THE VARIOUS IDENTIFICATION PROCEDURES

Whichever identification procedure the police decide to use, the specific safeguards associated with each of the identification procedures are contained in the various annexes supplementing Code D. We include here a summary of the main provisions.

11.7.1 VIDEO IDENTIFICATION (ANNEX A)

- A set of video images including the suspect and at least eight others is shown to the witness;
- where there are two suspects of similar appearance, at least 12 images should be shown to the witness;
- the eight other people should resemble the suspect in age, height, general appearance and position in life and should show the suspect and the other people in the same position or carrying out the same sequence of movementsp;
- steps must be taken to conceal any distinguishing features the suspect may have;
- the suspect's solicitor must be offered the opportunity of attending the identification suite when the compiling of the video parade is made and when the compilation is subsequently shown to the eyewitness;
- a suspect or his solicitor/appropriate adult must be given the opportunity to see the complete set of images before it is shown to any witnesses. If the suspect has reasonable objections to the set of images or any of the participants, steps shall, if practicable, be taken to remove the grounds for objection;
- the witness sees the all the images at least twice;
- the witness is asked whether the suspect is the person seen on a previous occasion;
- a record must be made of procedures and those involved.

11.7.2 IDENTIFICATION PARADE (ANNEX B)

- The parade should consist of at least eight people in addition to the suspect who as far as possible should resemble the suspect in terms of appearance, age etc.;
- the suspect must be told that he may object to the arrangements or to a participant and that he may obtain legal advice;
- witnesses attending the parade must not be allowed to communicate with each other about the case or overhear a witness who has already made an identification;
- witnesses must not be allowed to see any participant in advance of the parade or see or be reminded of any photographs or description of the suspect or be given any indication as to the suspect's identity;
- the suspect may choose his own position in the line;
- each witness should be brought into the identification suite one at a time;
- video recording or colour photograph shall normally be made of the parade;
- where the identification officer is satisfied that the witness has properly looked at each member of the parade, they shall ask the witness whether the person they saw on the earlier relevant occasion is on the identification parade and, if so, indicate the person the number of the person concerned;
- if the witness wishes to hear any identification parade member speak or adopt any specified posture or move, they shall first be asked whether they can identify on the basis of appearance alone and reminded that the participants in the parade have been chosen on the basis of their appearance alone.

11.7.3 GROUP IDENTIFICATION (ANNEX C)

- May be held with or without the suspect's consent;
- the witness sees the suspect amongst a group of other people, e.g. shopping centre, rail station;
- the chosen location should take into account number of people present, general appearance of people;

- a colour photo or video should be taken at scene immediately after identification;
- the suspect's solicitor or friend can be present.

11.7.4 CONFRONTATION BY A WITNESS (ANNEX D)

- The witness is asked: 'Is this the person you saw on the earlier occasion?';
- force may not be used to make the suspect's face visible to the witness;
- the confrontation may either be through a one-way screen or face-to-face with the suspect;
- the confrontation will usually be held at the police station in a normal room or one equipped with a screen permitting a witness to see the suspect without being seen.

11.8 WHAT ARE THE EVIDENTIAL CONSEQUENCES OF A FAILURE TO COMPLY WITH CODE D?

The safeguards contained within Code D are important. If the police obtain identification evidence in breach of the safeguards, the defence advocate can apply to have the evidence excluded under s. 78 PACE. The court's discretion to exclude evidence that has been obtained unlawfully or unfairly is considered in Chapter 9.

Breach of Code D does not inevitably lead to the exclusion of identification evidence. It is a matter for the court to determine whether the probative value of the resulting evidence is outweighed by the prejudicial effect of admitting it, having regard to the breaches of Code D. Decisions in relation to identification evidence largely turn on their own facts. The more blatant the breach, the better the prospects are for exclusion. To illustrate the above we include two cases with differing outcomes, both of which involved breaches of Code D.

R v Finley [1993] Crim LR 50

Evidence of identification was excluded in this case under s. 78 PACE for several breaches of Code D. The defendant was implicated in a robbery at an insurance office. There were several eyewitnesses who all worked together. One witness was shown a set of 12 police photographs from which she selected the defendant. He was a blonde skinhead, whilst most of the photographs were of dark-haired men. The defendant was able to produce an alibi, and nothing had been found to link him to the robbery during a search of his flat. The composition of the parade was criticised, in that most of the volunteers were of heavier build than the defendant and had darker hair. Witnesses had been kept together before the parade and the fact that one of their colleagues had made a prior selection from photographs and had probably discussed this with her colleagues was very prejudicial.

R v Rutherford (1994) 98 Cr App R 191

It had been alleged that the defendant and another had forced their way into the home of an elderly lady. They sprayed a liquid into her eyes, bound and gagged her. It was further alleged that £1,000, some Indian rupees and a piece of paper with a telephone number written on it had been stolen. The defendant was arrested in the vicinity soon after. Found in his possession were a quantity of cash, some Indian rupees and a piece of paper containing a telephone number. The defendant's appearance matched that of descriptions given by a couple of witnesses. The police declined to convene an identification parade, in spite of a request by the defendant, because of what they perceived to be the strength of other evidence against the defendant. The Court of Appeal concluded, notwithstanding the breach of Code D, the prejudice to the defendant had been dealt with in the judge's summing-up and there had been ample circumstantial evidence upon which to convict.

11.8.1 REQUIREMENTS ON THE JUDGE TO DIRECT THE JURY WHERE THERE HAS BEEN A BREACH OF CODE D

The decision of the Court of Appeal in *R. v Allen* [1995] Crim LR 643 makes it clear that a trial judge must explain to the jury why identification evidence is being admitting in breach of Code D. In accordance with several authorities, including *R v Conway* (1990) 91 Cr App R 143 and *R. v Quinn* [1995] 1 Cr App R 480, when summing-up, the judge should make reference to the specific breach or breaches of Code D, leaving it up to the jury to decide how much weight to place on the evidence of identification in the circumstances.

Guidance has also been provided by the House of Lords in *R v Forbes* [2001] 1 AC 473. In cases where there has been a breach of the requirement for the police to convene an identification parade or video parade, a trial judge must explain to a jury that the purpose of such a parade is to enable a suspect to test the reliability of a witness's identification. In cases where an identification/video parade has not been held contrary to Code D, the suspect loses the benefit of the safeguard a parade affords him. The jury must be instructed to take account of this when assessing the case against the defendant. Additionally, even in a case where an informal identification is followed up by a properly conducted parade from which the defendant is chosen, a warning should still be given to the jury. The judge must stipulate that that although the prosecution's case is strengthened by the identification, the jury should be aware of the possible risk that the witness might have identified, not the culprit who committed the crime, but the suspect identified by the witness on the earlier occasion.

11.9 ARE THERE CIRCUMSTANCES IN WHICH CODE D HAS NO APPLICATION?

Code D is not all embracing and there are many instances in which identification is made which fall outside it, as illustrated by *R v Hickin* below. In circumstances where the Code has no application, there can be no breach of it. However, considerations of fairness remain paramount and evidence may still be excluded in the exercise of the court's discretion under s. 78 PACE.

R v Hickin [1996] Crim LR 585

A fight broke out between gangs of rival football supporters on Blackpool seafront, resulting in a serious injury. Three eyewitnesses were taken round the area in a police car to see if they could identify the culprits. Having rounded up those whom the police considered to be involved, the witnesses were asked to identify those they considered responsible for the violent assault. Fourteen men were subsequently arrested and charged. No identification parades were held. There was little doubt that, having arrived on the scene, the police had had to act fast and arrange for the available witnesses to confront the available suspects. In addition it was impracticable to convene 14 identification parades at short notice. The Court of Appeal felt the situation faced by the police was not specifically covered by the Codes and so there was no breach of Code D. However there were serious questions about the reliability of the evidence of identification having regard to the manner in which it had been obtained. In this regard the Court of Appeal noted the lack of any detailed descriptions taken from the eyewitnesses before seeing the suspects. This was coupled with the fact that the eyewitnesses travelled together in the police car and there was no record of what the witnesses had said when viewing the suspects. All in all, the evidence had to be excluded under s. 78 of PACE in the interests of ensuring a fair trial.

11.10 VOICE IDENTIFICATION

The current version of Code D makes no provision for an identification made on the basis of voice alone. Voice identification is fraught with even more danger than visual identification, and requires special caution. For two cases in which selection was based on voice identification, see *R v Hersey* [1998] Crim LR 281 and *R v Roberts* [2000] Crim LR 183. Home Office guidance on the use of voice identification is available.

11.11 DOCK IDENTIFICATIONS

Dock identifications are very rare, and occur where the victim or another witness testifies on oath that the accused standing in the dock is the person he saw at the scene of the crime. Dock identifications are very rarely used as they have little probative value, because the identification of the accused in these circumstances is virtually inevitable and therefore highly prejudicial. In exceptional circumstances, dock identification might be used where the defendant has resisted all other pre-trial methods of identification. Even where this occurs, however, to ensure fairness, the defendant should be asked to take a seat in the courtroom as opposed to standing alone in the dock to be formally identified. The principles governing the use of dock identifications were restated in *Barnes v Chief Constable of Durham* [1997] 2 Cr App R 505 and *Karia v DPP* (2002) 166 JP 753.

11.12 PRACTICAL STEPS THE LEGAL ADVISER CAN TAKE IN RELATION TO IDENTIFICATION EVIDENCE

- Unless you have a thorough working knowledge of Code D and its annexes you will not be in a position to actively defend your client's interests at the police station. Always have a copy of Code D with you.

- It is important that you keep an independent record of all that goes on in relation to identification procedures, including the advice you give to your client.

- Be prepared to make representations where appropriate and ensure that your representations are properly recorded. Every decision taken by the identification officer must be justified. Code D para. 3.12 is important and is set out in full in the early part of this chapter. It leaves room for discretion on the part of the police as to when an identification procedure must be held. A failure by the police to convene a parade may ultimately be open to challenge in court. Be prepared to challenge a decision not to convene an identification procedure if you feel this is appropriate. If your client is indicating that he does not know the eyewitness make the police aware of this.

- You are entitled to make representations as to the most appropriate identification procedure that should be used. But remember a failure by the suspect to consent or to co-operate can lead to a potentially prejudicial identification procedure being adopted and it can lead to adverse evidential inferences being drawn.

- A properly convened video identification will include the suspect's image amongst eight other people who resemble the suspect in age, height, general appearance and position in life. Police forces using the latest VIPER technology have access to an extensive database of volunteer faces. The images used must show the suspect and the other volunteers in the same positions or carrying out the same sequence of movements. You are allowed to see the complete set of images before they are shown to a witness. Indeed you should be present when the compilation is put together. Ensure that your objections are recorded. Unusual features can be disguised using the video technology now available. The compiled video is burned onto a DVD and is usually shown to the eyewitness at a later date. You are entitled to be present when the compilation is shown to the witness.

- If a conventional identification parade is used there are many practical things you can do to ensure it is to be conducted fairly. You should check the layout to ensure witnesses cannot communicate with each other or see members of the parade in advance. You might want to take a photograph of the parade to show its composition. A photograph will be supplied to you on request but it may take some time.

- Where there is time (and where there are varying descriptions of the suspect by different witnesses), make representations as to the composition of the parade.

- If your client has a unique identifying feature perhaps a scar or strange hairstyle, ensure that steps are taken by the police to disguise it. Participants in the parade might be asked to use a plaster on the same part of their face or to wear a hat or adopt a seated position.

- Offer your client advice on where to stand on a conventional parade or where to be placed in a video compilation and, in the case of a conventional parade, how to deal with a) being identified and b) not being identified.

- If dissatisfied with the parade's composition, make sure your representations are noted in the parade record.

- If an inferior form of identification is to be utilised including a group identification or confrontation, it is important to observe all aspects of the procedure and to document them all.

- Always assess and record the degree of confidence with which a witness purports to make a positive identification is made.

11.13 WHAT ARE THE OTHER WAYS IN WHICH EVIDENCE OF IDENTIFICATION CAN BE DERIVED?

11.13.1 FORENSIC EVIDENCE

Forensic evidence found at the crime scene may provide compelling circumstantial evidence linking the defendant to the offence. Forensic evidence can be available in a number of forms. The person responsible for the crime may have left fingerprints, sample of handwriting, footprints, ear prints, a dental impression or DNA. DNA can be extracted from blood, semen stains, saliva, sweat or body hairs found at or near the crime scene or on the victim. Alternatively, specimens from the crime scene, such as fragments of glass, pollen or foliage, may be present on the suspect's clothing or footwear.

The forensic science service has an important role to play in this regard. DNA is extracted from the crime scene sample and a profile is obtained. The profile is forensically compared to DNA profiles kept on the national database or to a suspect's known sample and an opinion is formulated as to the likely source of the DNA. If the expert's opinion is accepted by the court it can provide very strong circumstantial evidence of the defendant's presence at the scene and his consequent involvement in the crime.

The police are able to assist the forensic investigation in that they have powers under the PACE 1984 to obtain intimate and non-intimate body samples from suspects to enable forensic comparison with samples found at the crime scene.

The suspect is a very important source of evidence and as part of the investigation into a crime, the police may well wish to obtain a set of fingerprints or sample from a suspect for forensic comparison with evidence linked with the commission of the crime.

11.13.2 FINGERPRINTS AND FOOTWEAR IMPRESSIONS

The power to obtain fingerprints and footwear impressions is contained in s. 61 PACE (as amended) and s. 61A PACE respectively and can be exercised by a constable. Fingerprint and footwear impressions may be taken at a police station with the written consent of the suspect. They can be taken without consent where a suspect has been arrested and detained in connection with a recordable offence in circumstances where the suspect has not had his fingerprints/footwear impression taken in the course of the investigation, or if he has, a complete set was not taken, or some of the prints/impressions are of insufficient quality. Fingerprint and footwear impressions may also be taken without consent where the suspect has been charged or informed that he will be prosecuted for a recordable offence and he has not had his fingerprints/impressions taken in the course of the investigation, etc.

The Serious Organised Crime and Police Act 2005 (SOCPA) s. 117 has amended PACE, by inserting s. 61(6A) PACE, allowing an officer to take a person's fingerprints without consent prior to an arrest and away from the police station where:

(a) the officer reasonably suspects that the person is committing or attempting to commit an offence or has committed or has attempted to commit an offence; and

(i) the name of the person is unknown and cannot be readily ascertained by the officer; or

(ii) the officer has reasonable grounds for doubting whether a name furnished by the person is his real name.

The development and use of mobile digital fingerprint readers that can be connected to the National Automated Fingerprint Identification System (NAFIS) by mobile communications technology means the police can verify a person's identity at the scene of a crime in accordance with s. 61A PACE.

As with samples of an intimate and non-intimate nature (considered below), fingerprint and footwear impressions may be used for the purpose of a speculative search against forensic databases, and the suspect should be warned of this fact.

11.13.3 PHOTOGRAPHS

Under s. 64A PACE, as amended, photographs (which includes a moving image) may be taken of any person who is detained at the police station with and without consent. If consent is withheld, force may be used. SOCPA 2005 s. 116 has extended the power by enabling the police to take a photograph without consent at a place other than a police station where the suspect has been arrested and in some circumstances prior to arrest.

11.13.4 NON-INTIMATE SAMPLE

The authority to obtain a sample of a non-intimate nature from a suspect is contained in s. 63 PACE (as amended). A non-intimate sample is defined in s. 65 PACE to include a sample of hair other than pubic hair, a scraping from under a nail, a swab taken from the mouth, a footprint, or bodily impression. Non-intimate samples may be taken with the consent of your client. Where consent is withheld, s. 63 PACE permits a non-intimate sample to be taken where a suspect has been arrested and detained in connection with a recordable offence or has been charged or informed he will be reported for an offence and no such sample has yet been taken in the course of the investigation or such sample as may already have been taken has proved insufficient. In addition, a non-intimate sample may be taken without consent from a person upon conviction for a recordable offence.

11.13.5 INTIMATE SAMPLE

An intimate sample (also defined in s. 65 PACE) includes a dental impression or a sample of blood, tissue fluid, urine, pubic hair or swabs taken from a person's genitals or body orifice other than the mouth An intimate sample may only be taken with the consent of the suspect under s. 62 of PACE. A failure to consent to providing an intimate sample, without good reason, can be used in evidence against the defendant (section 62(10) PACE). An intimate sample may only be taken from a suspect if an inspector authorises it, having reasonable grounds for suspecting the person to be involved in a recordable offence and that the sample would confirm or disprove the suspect's involvement. The suspect's written consent must be obtained, and the sample (other than urine) must be taken by a health care professional.

Evidence from samples obtained unlawfully remains admissible, subject to the court's exclusionary discretion at common law and under s. 78 of PACE (see Chapter 9).

11.13.6 RETAINING THE SUSPECT'S FINGERPRINTS/PHOTOGRAPHS/DNA SAMPLES

The retention and use of a suspect's fingerprint/footwear impression and DNA samples is governed by s. 64 PACE (as amended). Such samples may be retained even if the person from whom they were taken is acquitted of the offence or a decision is taken not to prosecute. Retained samples may only be used for a purpose related to the prevention or detection of crime, the investigation of an offence or prosecution of a case. The retention of samples in the case of an acquitted person was challenged in Chief Constable of South Yorkshire, ex parte Marper [2004] 1 WLR 2196 under Article 8 (the right to privacy). The court held that even if the provision was an interference with Article 8, it was proportionate to the aim it sought to achieve.

Samples taken from a person not suspected of an offence (i.e. as part of mass screening) must be destroyed as soon as they have fulfilled their purpose. Where such samples should have been destroyed, they may not be used in evidence or for the purposes of investigation against such a person (s. 64(3) PACE). However, in the case of the Attorney-General's Reference (No 3 of 1999) [2001] 2 AC 91 (a case preceding the change in the law allowing the retention of samples from an acquitted person), the House of Lords ruled that where a DNA sample should have been destroyed, although section 64 of PACE prohibited its use in the investigation of any other offence, it did not make evidence obtained as a result of a failure to comply with that prohibition, inadmissible. It is left to the discretion of the trial judge (s. 78 PACE).

11.14 DNA EVIDENCE

The UK has one of the most comprehensive DNA databases in the world. The forensic techniques involved in extracting an individual DNA profile and comparing it with other DNA samples have attracted considerable attention from scientists, lawyers and the media. The techniques are relatively new having been perfected in the late 1980s. Over the course of time, however, the techniques have grown increasingly sophisticated, such that DNA evidence can yield very compelling evidence. Every human being has a unique DNA make-up (apart from an identical twin). The profiling techniques enable a forensic scientist to compare two biological samples and to determine the likelihood that the two samples originated from the same source. DNA evidence is perceived as being particularly cogent evidence because of the statistical improbabilities that profiling produces. The process of extraction, extrapolation, interpretation and presentation of results is explained by Lord Justice Phillips in *R v Doheny* [1997] 1 Cr App R 369.

R v Doheny establishes the procedure the prosecution should follow in respect of the disclosure and presentation of DNA evidence. The defence may call their own expert witness to challenge the validity of the opinion provided by the prosecution's expert witness. Issues of sample degeneration, cross-contamination and deliberate planting of samples by prosecuting authorities can significantly diminish the probative value of the DNA evidence. Indeed, there may be a perfectly innocent explanation to account for a defendant's DNA being found at the crime scene. The ultimate evaluation of DNA evidence, as with other forensic opinion evidence, is a matter for the jury or magistrates. DNA technology today is approaching individualisation. When odds against a random match of one in 60 billion are quoted, DNA evidence all but positively identifies the person whose profile matches the crime stain as being the source of the evidence.

11.15 FACIAL MAPPING

In addition, evidence of a defendant's involvement can be provided by other expert testimony, this includes experts in facial mapping techniques and voice recognition experts. The admissibility of expert opinion evidence is considered in Chapter 24. Facial mapping might be required in a case where still photographs or a video image have been taken of the suspect and a comparison with the suspect is available. Experts in photographic technologies and anatomical features can enhance picture quality and offer an opinion as to the likelihood of the defendant and the person pictured being one and the same. In *R v Clare and Peach* [1995] 2 Cr App R 333, a police officer who had viewed a video recording some 40 times with lengthy and studious consideration was permitted to give evidence on whether persons shown on the recording committing acts of violent disturbance inside a football ground were the accused.

KEY POINT SUMMARY

- Eye-witness identification is of huge practical importance in an investigation but is notoriously unreliable.

- To effectively advise on police procedures in relation to identification evidence, the legal adviser must have a thorough working knowledge of Code D and its annexes.

- A failure by a suspect to co-operate in the conduct of an identification procedure or to provide an intimate sample can lead to adverse evidential inferences being drawn.

- It is important for the legal adviser to make appropriate representations about the manner in which identification evidence is obtained and to ensure those representations are properly recorded. In doing so not only are you protecting your client's rights at the police station, you are setting up the potential of a s. 78 PACE argument at trial for the exclusion of any identification evidence obtained in breach of Code D.

- Understand that the admissibility of identification evidence obtained in breach of Code D is vulnerable to challenge under s. 78 PACE, but that breach does not mean such exclusion will be automatic.

- Know when the police are justified in obtaining a sample from your client under ss. 61–63 PACE.

SELF-TEST QUESTIONS

Consider our case study *R v Lenny Whyte*.

You will recall Lenny has been charged in connection with a burglary at the home of an old age pensioner. His defence is one of complete denial; however, he is linked to the crime by, *inter alia*, eyewitness identification. In discharging its legal burden of proof beyond reasonable doubt, the prosecution will be relying on evidence of identification in this case.

- Assess the strength of the identification evidence against Lenny.

- Consider how the evidence of identification in this case has actually materialised.

- Can you point to any specific breaches of Code D in relation to the manner in which the evidence has been obtained and which would, in your view, enable the trial advocate to apply to have the evidence excluded under s. 78 PACE in the interests of ensuring a fair trial?

FIGURE 11.1 OBTAINING EVIDENCE OF IDENTIFICATION

Pre-trial safeguards under Code D – their purpose

- To ensure the quality and reliability of eye-witness identification, the detail of which can be found through:
  - video parade Annex A;
  - identification parade Annex B;
  - group parade Annex C;
  - confrontation Annex D;
  - showing photographs Annex E.

↓

When can an eyewitness be shown photographs?

- When there is no known and available suspect in mind (Code D para. 3.3).

↓

When must an identification procedure be convened?

- Where the suspect disputes being the person the witness claims to have seen, an identification procedure should be held unless:
  - it is not practicable; or
  - it would serve no useful purpose in proving or disproving the suspect was involved in the offence, Code D para. 3.12.

CHALLENGING THE ADMISSIBILITY OF EYE-WITNESS IDENTIFICATION

- Use s. 78 PACE on the basis that the admission of such evidence would have an adverse effect on the fairness of the proceedings.

- Relevant factors would be proven breaches of Code D, including:
  - failure to convene an identification procedure;
  - failure to properly record an identification procedure;
  - failure to disguise a prominent feature in the suspect's appearance;
  - allowing eyewitnesses contact with one another before a parade;
  - use of photographs in a case where the suspect was known;
  - a failure to properly conduct an identification procedure – see Annexes to Code D.

12 ADVISING AT THE POLICE STATION – PRACTICAL STEPS

12.1 INTRODUCTION

This chapter may well be of more relevance to those LPC students undertaking an Advanced Criminal Litigation Elective, in that it aims to bring together the matters explored in the previous chapters in Part II with particular emphasis on the practical steps a legal adviser will need to undertake when discharging the onerous responsibility of advising a suspect at the police station.

Most specialised criminal law firms will have members of staff on the Police Station Duty Solicitor Scheme, providing 24-hour assistance to suspects in detention. The task of advising the suspect at the police station is not always fulfilled by a qualified solicitor. The task may be given to an accredited clerk or trainee solicitor who will have completed or be undertaking the Law Society's Police Station Advisor's Accreditation Scheme if their firm wishes to receive payment from the Legal Services Commission for the representation provided.

The legal adviser has a multi-faceted role at the police station, likely to require the following legal skills:

- interviewing;
- analysis;
- advising;
- negotiation;
- advocacy.

Interviewing

The purpose of interviewing is primarily to extract information. You need to be able to effectively extract the salient information not only from your client, but also from the custody officer and investigating officers.

Analysis

You will be required to analyse the information you have gleaned from the custody record and from what the investigating officers and your client have disclosed to you, in order to evaluate the strength or weakness of the evidence against your client and to formulate a strategy.

Advising

The police station adviser will clearly be called upon to give advice. The advice might include:

- whether to answer questions in interview;
- whether to remain silent;
- whether to make a full and frank confession;
- whether to participate in an identification procedure, or perhaps to consent to a search.

Negotiation

Negotiation skills are needed. They are most likely to be deployed in your dealings with the custody officer who must take many of the important decisions under PACE and the Codes of Practice in relation to your client's detention. You may need to negotiate your client's release from custody or persuade the appropriate individual that a conditional caution or simple caution is preferable to your client being charged, or that your client should be granted bail if charged.

Advocacy

Advocacy skills are required because you may need to intervene in an interview in a pro-active way to protect and advance your client's legal rights.

In order to discharge the role effectively, the legal adviser needs to be:

- knowledgeable;
- organised;
- assertive;
- decisive.

All police station advisers need a detailed knowledge of police powers and procedure under PACE and the Codes of Practice. A sound grasp of the substantive criminal law, the Bail Act 1976, rules of evidence and the rules of professional conduct are also necessary. It is impossible to effectively advise a client without such knowledge.

Given the number of tasks the legal adviser is likely to be called upon to fulfil, you need to be organised and assertive. If a legal adviser is to protect his client's best interests, this may require you to challenge the authority of the police.

Legal advisers have to be decisive. You will be required to exercise your powers of critical thinking on the spot. The decisions that your client makes on your advice may have significant repercussions. Do you, for example, advise your client to remain silent, knowing that adverse inferences might be drawn under s. 34 Criminal Justice and Public Order Act 1994? (See Chapter 8.) Do you advise your client to admit the offence? If so, what is the basis for your advice? If your client makes admissions during interview, charges may follow or your client may be offered a caution/reprimand.

The onerous nature of the solicitor's role at the police station was aptly expressed by Court of Appeal in *R v Wahab* [2003] 1 Cr App R 15:

> 'One of the duties of a legal advisor, whether at a police station, or indeed at a pre-trial conference, or during the trial itself, is to give the client realistic advice. That emphatically does not mean that the advice must be directed to 'getting the client off', or simply making life difficult for the prosecution. The advice may, and sometimes ought to be robust, sensibly considering the advantages which the client may derive from evidence of remorse and a realistic acceptance of guilt, or the corresponding disadvantages of participating in a 'no comment' interview. The exercise of the professional judgment in circumstances like these is often very difficult, often dependent on less than precise instructions from the defendant . . . . . .'

It should be added that the working environment within the police station is less than ideal. You may be called out or telephoned after work or in the early hours of the morning. You will be entering a largely male-dominated environment where the police will often want one result and you will want another. You may well be under pressure of time in an urgent investigation. Until you have undertaken some reflective practice and experience, you may well feel isolated and intimidated.

The police station is at the sharp end of the adversarial justice system. In a serious case, where the police have considerable resources at their disposal and a strong suspicion that your client is involved, what does your client have? The answer is: you.

Having worked through the chapters on police powers, the detention process, the rules relating to the admissibility of confession evidence and evidence of identification, as well as the law relating to drawing adverse inferences from silence, you are now better equipped to be able to offer a suspect advice at the police station. Our Online Resource Centre includes a comprehensive set of video clips depicting the role of the solicitor at the police station. The scenario (which can only be accessed via password) explores the process of detention and investigation of a fictional character called Peter West who is under arrest on suspicion of the rape of a 14-year-old girl. The scenario is unscripted and was brought to life by real-life police officers and an accredited police station representative.

How, then, might you undertake this role in practice?

12.2 INITIAL CONTACT

You may be asked to represent a suspect at the police station either because the suspect has requested you or your firm to attend or a third party has sought your help on behalf of someone in detention or at the request of the Duty Solicitor Service.

Make and keep contemporaneous notes from the outset. When you receive the initial telephone call from the station, note the following:

- time;
- station;
- person to whom you are speaking;
- client's name, age, nature of the offence;
- name of investigating officers;
- whether your client has been interviewed or whether the police intend to interview.

Try to speak with your client and check whether your conversation can be overheard. Ascertain if the client wants you to attend and whether he has made any admissions. If you are to attend, your client is best advised to say nothing until you arrive. In all but the most straightforward of road traffic cases, you should attend in person if your client is to be interviewed. Speak to the custody officer and let him know your estimated time of arrival at the station, and ask that your client is not interviewed or asked to undergo any procedures until you get there.

12.3 WHAT SHOULD YOU TAKE WITH YOU TO THE POLICE STATION?

You need to be very organised at the police station, so ensure you have with you a notebook, pen, PACE, the Codes of Practice, proof of ID, legal aid forms, and your checklists. At the end of this chapter you will find a checklist for use at the police station, which is reproduced with the kind permission of Lichfield Reynolds Solicitors in Staffordshire.

12.4 WHAT SHOULD YOU DO ON ARRIVAL?

- Go to reception and make sure your mobile telephone is switched off. Do not use your mobile secretly, as this could compromise your integrity.
- Ask to speak to the Custody Officer, explaining who you are. He may want some proof of your identity.
- Check the custody record. You have the right to consult the custody record (Code C para. 2.4). Take your time to consider it, as it is a very important document in evidential terms and will provide you with a lot of useful information. From the custody record you will be able to check your client's time of arrest, reason for arrest, time of arrival at the police station and the reasons for detention. It should have details of the risk assessment undertaken in relation to your client and any requests made by your client. It will provide a record of any decisions in relation to your client's detention including any searches and their authorisation, reviews of detention at six- and nine-hourly intervals and any complaints by your client. You need to know the rules relating to the process of detention and questioning (see Chapter 7) to be in a position to properly evaluate the content of the

custody record. Having considered the custody record, you should then ask to speak with the investigating officer/s.

12.5 INITIAL CONTACT WITH THE INVESTIGATING OFFICER/S

This is a very important stage in your role as an adviser at the police station. Have you a right to disclosure of the evidence the police purport to have against your client? The legal obligations upon the police to make disclosure of their evidence at this stage are minimal. They are set out in Code C para. 10.3 Note 10B and were considered in *R v Imran and Hussain* (1997) Crim LR 754, in which the Court of Appeal held there is no legal obligation on the police to make disclosure of evidence prior to interview.

R v Imran and Hussain (1997)

In this case, it became apparent during the interview that the police had video evidence of the robbery in which the defendants were alleged to have been involved. Neither the defendants or their legal adviser asked that the interview be suspended so that the content of the video could be viewed. On appeal, it was contended on behalf of the defendants that the police should have disclosed the video, and having failed to do so, that no adverse inference could be drawn under s. 34. Rejecting such a proposition, the Court of Appeal reasoned:

'In support of the application it is submitted that the tenor of sections 34 to 38 of the Criminal Justice and Public Order Act 1994 require the police to give as full a briefing as possible of disclosing all material to a legal representative before the interview with the suspect commences. We do not agree. There is of course a duty on the police not actively to mislead any suspect, but it is in our judgment totally impossible to spell out either expressly or by any permissible implication from those five sections any such requirement on the part of the police . . . .'.

Notwithstanding the minimum legal requirements set out above, you must press the investigating officers for complete disclosure of the evidence they have against your client at this stage. Be assertive if necessary. You are not going to be in a good position to offer your client informed advice as to what strategy to adopt unless you can make an assessment of the strength of the evidence against him. Keep a careful record of what you are told. It is not uncommon (particularly in relation to serious crimes) for the 'disclosure interview' to be recorded.

You should ask what witness statements the officers have and what they contain. If searches have been undertaken, ascertain for what purpose and what evidence they might have yielded. Check if your client has made any incriminating admissions to date.

How much information you extract at this stage may depend on the personalities of the investigating officers and the nature of the investigation being conducted. Your purpose in extracting as much information as you can, is to enable you to evaluate the extent and strength of the evidence before you speak with your client. Press for full disclosure, including a full list of your client's previous convictions. Point out the mutual benefits of such disclosure in that your client will be forced to seek legal advice repeatedly during the interview as new facts emerge. This will require the interview to be repeatedly suspended.

One good way of ascertaining whether you have been told all by the police is to ask: 'Is there any information you have not disclosed?' The police cannot lie to you and you will either be answered with a yes, no, or not prepared to say.

12.6 THE IMPORTANCE OF KEEPING A COMPREHENSIVE RECORD

The importance of keeping detailed notes cannot be over-emphasised. Keep a written record of everything. Checklists are extremely useful in this regard, in that they act as a comprehensive *aide-mémoire*. You may not be taking the matter further than the police station and, as such, you need to ensure your notes are comprehensive. Anyone reviewing the file in the office or at court at a later date, ought to be able to quickly ascertain the key points of what took place at the police station.

Whatever representations you make at the police station, ensure they are recorded on the custody record.

12.7 EVALUATING THE DISCLOSED EVIDENCE

To be in a position to correctly advise your client, you need to constantly evaluate the evidence against him. This is why you must carefully consider the information in the custody record and press the investigating officers for disclosure. Your evaluation of the evidence needs to take account of the rules of evidence.

Generally speaking, the burden of proving your client's guilt rests on the prosecution. This should always be borne in mind. On occasions, a legal burden of proof rests on the defendant where certain defences are to be raised. In discharging its legal burden of proof, the prosecution must rely on admissible evidence. Consequently, if the evidence the police disclose to you is, in your view, likely to be inadmissible at trial, you will no doubt take the view that the evidence at this stage is weak. Similarly, if the principal evidence comes from your client's spouse, or from a co-accused, the prosecution may be unable to compel the witness to give evidence. It is a fact that in relation to many allegations of domestic assaults, after the initial complaint has been made to the police, the victim will often retract her complaint at a later stage. You have to ask yourself – will the prosecution be able to prove my client's guilt?

12.8 INTERVIEWING YOUR CLIENT AT THE POLICE STATION

Your client has the right to be interviewed in private (Code C para. 6.1 and Note 6J). Introduce yourself, as your client may not know you. He may feel suspicious of you, given his current surroundings. Provide proof of identification and assure your client of your total independence and that anything they say will be treated in absolute confidence. You might wish your client to tell his story in an uninterrupted fashion. Iron out the detail by a series of closed questions. You will need to explore the evidence that has been disclosed by the police. You may need to be assertive with your client, stressing how important it is that he is completely honest with you. Take notes and be alert for signs of stress/vulnerability in your client.

You will need to be in a position to answer any questions your client may have about his detention. He might wish to know for how long he can be detained without charge, whether he has to give a sample of his fingerprints or a sample of an intimate or non-intimate nature. Such matters are considered in Chapters 7 and 11.

Does your client understand what he has been arrested for? What are the elements of the offence which the prosecution will ultimately have to prove? Listen carefully to your client. What is he saying? Is he firmly maintaining his innocence? Is he indicating he may have a defence to the allegation against him? Does he have an explanation for the evidence against him? Is he prevaricating or reticent? Re-evaluate the strength of the prosecution's evidence in the light of what your client has had to say. As you observe your client consider how he is likely to come across in interview. If you have reason to doubt your client's state of mind, or general health, make representations to the custody officer and press for the opinion of a health care practitioner. It goes without saying that you should always be wary of your personal safety when interviewing a client in private. Be sure to record the advice given to your client. That advice will of course include assistance to your client in determining what strategy to adopt with the police.

12.9 STRATEGIES OPEN TO YOU

There are a limited number of strategies your client might be advised to adopt, depending on the circumstances. They include:

- making admissions;
- remaining silent;
- putting forward a prepared statement;
- answering all questions/advancing an explanation/denial or defence;
- answer some questions, but not others.

12.10 ADVISING YOUR CLIENT TO MAKE ADMISSIONS

The admissibility of confession evidence is discussed in Chapter 10. Clearly, a defendant is going to have difficulty under s. 76 and/or s. 78 PACE challenging the admissibility of a confession which has been obtained in the presence of a legal adviser. In *R v Dunn* (1990) 91 Cr App R 237, the presence of a legal adviser prevented the defendant from relying on these grounds, as the legal adviser's presence was deemed to have cured the alleged breaches of Code C. It is an entirely different proposition where a solicitor is misled by the police and advises his client to confess as a result (*R v Mason* [1988] 1 WLR 139).

In what circumstances would you advise your client to confess? Generally speaking, you might advise your client to do so where the evidence disclosed by the police is so overwhelming that there is little point in denying it. If it is blatantly obvious that, in the event of charges being made against your client, he will invariably have to plead guilty, credit will be given to your client in mitigation of sentence if the advocate can point to your client's co-operation with the police during the investigation stage. You might be able to persuade the police to caution/reprimand your client as an alternative to prosecuting him, but only in circumstances where your client admits the offence.

Suppose your client confesses his guilt to you, but you are of the opinion that the police do not have a strong case against your client? Are you bound to advise your client to confess in interview? Your client is not obliged to assist the police in any way. The burden of proof rests on the prosecution and it is an onerous one: proof beyond reasonable doubt. If you take the view that the evidence disclosed to you by the police is weak then, by confessing, your client increases the likelihood that he will be charged. You should explain this to your client.

If you have concerns about the reliability of your client's admissions, explore them with him. Does your client understand the ingredients of the offence to which he purports to confess, or does he have a defence in law? Consider whether your client may be confessing to something he has not done for reasons of expediency: a desire to protect someone/or a desire to relieve the pressure of the situation, particularly in the case of a drug addict. You should always explore the possibility that the police may have offered your client an inducement to confess.

If your client has made a voluntary and unambiguous confession to you, you cannot allow your client to go into the interview maintaining his innocence, as this would be a serious breach of professional conduct, but you may properly advice silence in these circumstances.

12.11   ADVISING SILENCE

We looked in detail at the law relating to drawing adverse inferences from silence in Chapter 8. You will recall that the essence of a s. 34 CJPOA 1994 inference is whether your client acted reasonably in the circumstances in remaining silent. Legal advisers at the police station must fully understand the effect of s. 34 if they are to be in a position to properly advise a client at the police station.

Taking account of the case law to date when might you advise silence? In practice this is one of the most difficult questions to answer, requiring a careful and considered exercise of critical judgment. Some instances in which you can properly advise silence may be more clear-cut than others.

12.11.1   STRENGTH OF EVIDENCE

An important consideration is whether the prosecution would ultimately be able to prove a case against your client. This is clearly going to depend on the nature of the allegation and the strength of the evidence. For the most part, the burden of proof is on the prosecution throughout and the suspect is not obliged to assist the prosecution in this respect by answering questions. Arguably, you should advise your client to remain silent in these circumstances. In the absence of any incriminating admissions from your client and in the face of contradictory or uncertain evidence from prosecution witnesses, your client is unlikely to be charged in this situation and if charged, unlikely to be convicted.

12.11.2   ASSESSMENT OF YOUR CLIENT'S ABILITY TO COPE WITH AN INTERVIEW

Your client will hopefully have explained his version of the facts to you. Having interviewed him you will have formed an opinion as to your client's state of mind. If your client is emotional, unwell, in a state of shock or under the influence of an illicit substance or inebriated or heavily medicated, the safest course of action may be to advise silence in interview. Your client is more likely to incriminate himself in these circumstances if he chooses to answer questions. This remains the case even where a police doctor has pronounced your client fit to be interviewed. You should always ask yourself: 'is my client fit enough to be interviewed?'

Does you client need access to further information before he can safely advance a defence? Suppose the circumstances are such that your client is not in a position to fully articulate his defence to the allegations? Perhaps his defence is dependant upon access to documentation not currently in his possession or is one of alibi. There may be a danger in disclosing the details of the alibi too soon as the police will want to talk to the individual before you have an opportunity to do so. Perhaps the safest course would be to remain silent.

12.11.3 CLIENT IS COMPLAINING OF MISTREATMENT

Suppose your client makes a complaint about mistreatment while in custody and feels he cannot trust the investigating officers. Unless, this is resolved to you and your client's satisfaction in advance of an interview, the safest course may be to advise silence.

12.11.4 LACK OF DISCLOSURE BY THE POLICE

What if you have pressed the police for disclosure of their evidence but you feel they are holding information back, such that you feel you are unable to usefully advise? In *R v Roble* [1997] Crim LR 449, CA, this was a factor in assessing the reasonableness of a defendant's decision to remain silent.

We have previously seen that the legal disclosure obligations placed on the police during the investigation stage are minimal. However, this should not stop the legal adviser from pressing the investigating officers for as much disclosure as possible. There are mutual benefits to be derived in that your client will not be forced to repeatedly stop the interview to seek legal advice. It is good practice to ask the interviewing officer, at the commencement of the interview, whether there has been complete disclosure of the evidence to you. The police cannot lie to you. If inadequate disclosure has been made, the safest course of action is to remain silent. As facts emerge in interview, you may wish to reconsider your advice at a later stage, either in a further interview, or upon your client being charged.

Suppose the allegation involves legal complexities or relates to an incident many years before. Would an immediate response by your client be prudent in such circumstances?

12.11.5 FURTHER CONSIDERATION OF *R v HOWELL* [2005] Cr App R1 AND WHAT IT MEANS FOR THE LEGAL ADVISER

You will be aware from Chapter 8 that the Court of Appeal has made some strongly worded statements in relation to the role of the legal adviser at the police station, suggesting that there should be objectively sound reasons for giving a client advice to remain silent. It had previously been the case (*R v Betts and Hall* [2001] 2 Cr App R 16) that a jury had to be instructed that if it concluded that the defendant's reliance upon legal advice had been genuine, it could not draw an adverse inference. Since the decision in *R v Howell*, the position now is that a jury may draw an adverse inference where it is satisfied that although the defendant genuinely relied on legal advice, his reliance was not reasonable in the circumstances.

Some commentators have described the decision in *R v Howell* as being dangerous, while others feel its effect has been overstated. As examples of the type of instance in which a solicitor could justifiably advise silence, the Court of Appeal cites such matters as the suspect's mental condition and his ability to recollect events without reference to documents or some other source. You are already aware that if a defendant is to avoid an adverse inference being drawn under s. 34, he will invariably need to put forward an explanation for his decision. Where the decision was based on legal advice, the defendant is not immune from having an adverse inference drawn. The reasonableness of the defendant's decision to remain silent remains a question of fact for the court. In assessing the true reason for a defendant remaining silent, the adequacy of the explanation advanced by the defendant will help the court decide whether reliance upon legal advice was the true and genuine motive for not mentioning facts. What if a suspect has an explanation to put forward, but you feel there are sound tactical reasons for advising silence?

Suppose the evidence disclosed at the police station does not reveal a particularly strong case against your client? Why should he potentially help the police in this regard by answering their questions and possibly incriminating himself? In essence this is what we must assume the defence solicitor in *R v Howell* had reasoned. At the time of Howell's arrest the police had only an oral as opposed to a signed written statement of complaint from the victim and the suggestion from Mr Howell that his friend, the victim, might not wish to pursue a complaint. There was therefore a distinct possibility that the prosecution might not have been able to prove its case. The solicitor wished to wait to see how matters developed. Is such an approach to be regarded as being unreasonable in an adversarial system of justice where a suspect enjoys the right not to incriminate himself? The Court of Appeal did not find these reasons to be objectively sound. Mr Howell had a defence and could have articulated it. He had been the only person present at the flat when his friend was stabbed. He must have known whether he injured his friend accidentally or in self-defence. Was Mr Howell let down by his solicitor in your view? Was his solicitor's advice ill-conceived? If Mr Howell was not in a fit state to be interviewed because he was no doubt tired and emotional, having regard to the serious injury inflicted on his friend, this might have afforded a more convincing reason (in the eyes of the court) for failing to mention facts which he subsequently relied on.

There is a school of thought that subscribes to the point of view that if the police have evidence against your client and he has an explanation or denial to the allegations and is capable of advancing the explanation in interview, he should answer police questions. If charges follow, the defendant is protected from an adverse inference under s. 34. The statements in *R v Howell* and subsequent cases endorsing it, support this school of thought.

The advice given in *R v Howell* was based on tactical considerations. The tactics might have paid off had the victim not in fact wished to pursue a complaint to trial.

The danger of *R v Howell* is that the legal adviser makes choices without the benefit of hindsight. The decision does not make the role of the legal adviser any easier! You must trust your judgment. Experience and reflection will help to fashion that judgment. If there are (in your view) cogent reasons for advising silence, do not shirk from your responsibilities for so advising, but be careful about advising silence for purely tactical reasons where your client is indicating he is not guilty and is capable of advancing a defence to the allegations. Always keep a full and contemporaneous note of the instructions you receive and the advice that you give as you may be required to give evidence as to why you advised silence.

12.11.6 IMPLICATIONS FOR LEGAL PROFESSIONAL PRIVILEGE WHERE THE DECISION TO REMAIN SILENT IS BASED ON LEGAL ADVICE

Any legal advice given to a client at the police station is protected from disclosure by legal professional privilege. The privilege is that of your client and only your client can expressly or impliedly waive it. If an accused is to persuade a court that his decision to remain silent was reasonable in the circumstances, an explanation for his decision will invariably need to be given. Where an accused chooses to remain silent on legal advice, the legal adviser may be called upon to adduce evidence (in person, or by adducing contemporaneous written notes) as to the reasons for the advice given. In such a case, the accused must waive his legal professional privilege.

12.11.7 WARNING YOUR CLIENT ABOUT EXERCISING HIS RIGHT TO REMAIN SILENT

Your client must be informed of the full effect of s. 34 CJPO 1994, and in particular that the fact that you are advising silence does not automatically prevent your client from having an adverse inference drawn against him at any subsequent trial. The question of whether it was reasonable for your client to have remained silent is a question of fact for the jury or the magistrates. If your client is to avoid an adverse inference, an explanation for his silence will need to be tendered and this may involve a waiver of legal professional privilege (see *R v Condron* [1997] 1 Cr App R 185). It is not easy to advise a lay person as to the operation and effect of s. 34. You should break it down into its three constituent elements and ask your client to explain it back to you in order to be certain your client fully understands what he is consenting to. You should record your advice in writing and get your client to sign and date your written record.

12.11.8 WHAT AMOUNTS TO WAIVER OF LEGAL PROFESSIONAL PRIVILEGE?

If your client or you (his legal adviser) tell the police the reasons for remaining silent, this will amount to a waiver of privilege. The solicitor in *R v Bowden* [1999] 4 All ER 43 unwittingly did this by making an opening statement on the tape-recorded interview. His statement was subsequently adduced in evidence at court. You need to consider whether you want to put the reasons for your advice on tape. The Criminal Law Committee of the Law Society recommends the following form of words to be recited by the legal adviser at the outset of the interview:

'(i) I am . . . . a solicitor/trainee/accredited police station adviser with (firm/PDS)

> I am now required to explain my role. It is to protect my client's basic and legal rights. I shall continue to advise my client throughout the interview.

(ii) I shall intervene in the interview if

– my client requests or requires legal advice; or

– your questioning is inappropriate; or

– you make statements which are not based on matters that have been made known to me.

(iii) After receiving legal advice my client has decided:

(either) to exercise the right to silence because (consider giving reason). Please respect that decision.

(or) to answer questions which you may raise that are relevant to my client's arrest.'

If you are at all concerned about waiving legal professional privilege then, in stating the fact that your client is to remain silent, you must avoid reference to any privileged conversation with your client. As an alternative to (iii) above, you might say: 'I now advise my client not to answer questions [because. . . .]' If the reason for your advice is based on something external to your instructions and consequent advice, e.g. lack of police disclosure or your client's mental condition, then it should be safe to put this forward as a reason since it is without reference to any privileged conversation.

12.11.9 PREPARING YOUR CLIENT FOR THE NO COMMENT INTERVIEW

Your client should be warned about the difficulties of the no comment interview. Is he going to remain silent throughout or is he going to say: 'No comment.'? The latter is easier. The fact that your client is going to remain silent will not of course prevent the police from putting their questions. There will be considerable psychological pressure brought to bear on your client. This might manifest itself in the officers seeking to undermine you and the advice you have given, asking innocuous questions in order to get the interview started and pointing out the tactical advantages to your client if the matter goes to trial. Always advise your client that if he answers easy and innocuous questions, he will find it difficult not to carry on answering questions.

12.12 THE PREPARED STATEMENT

As an alternative to remaining completely silent, your client may choose to read out a prepared statement. The prepared statement is self-serving in nature and admissible in evidence at a subsequent trial where your client relies on the same defence as set out in his prepared statement. The prepared statement is used in conjunction with your client being advised not to answer questions in interview. The statement should be drafted in your client's handwriting with your assistance and is usually read out by the legal adviser. It can be read during the course of the interview or upon your client being charged. The statement protects your client from having an adverse inference being drawn against him, provided his defence advanced at trial is the same. Any material departure from the prepared statement is likely to be the subject of adverse comment and possible inference under s. 34 CJPOA 1994. The adverse inference that might be drawn in these circumstances would be that your client did not wish to have his defence subject to critical questioning by the police. The leading case on prepared statements is *R v Knight* [2004] 1 Cr App R 9, which is considered in Chapter 8. Once again, a prepared statement will not prevent the police from asking questions.

12.12.1 WHEN MIGHT YOU ADVISE A CLIENT TO PUT FORWARD A PREPARED STATEMENT?

Prepared statements are best limited to straightforward cases where you can be clear and confident of your client's defence at the outset. Until you have had full disclosure of all the relevant and critical facts in the investigation which will require an answer, it may be prudent to wait until after the first interview before finalising a prepared statement. This is especially so if the police have been reticent in terms of their disclosure. A prepared statement may be a sensible option for a client who maintains his innocence but who is not best placed to advance his defence or explanation by agreeing to answer all questions.

12.13 ANSWERING ALL QUESTIONS/ADVANCING AN EXPLANATION/DENIAL OR DEFENCE

When might you advise your client to answer questions? If as a result of the interview with your client, you have formed the view that your client is fit to be interviewed and the minimum disclosure requirements under Code C para. 10.3 and Notes for Guidance 10.B have been made, your client might properly be advised to advance his defence or explanation for the evidence against him in answer to the allegations.

It should be carefully explained to the client that if he is advancing a defence such as an alibi, the police are likely to interview that person before you are able to do so. Can you be sure that the defence to be put forward is credible or not? It should be explained to your client that he must be honest with you, since if his defence changes at trial, he will be at risk of an adverse inference being drawn against him. Once again, you should prepare your client for the interview experience. You should not coach your client but make him aware of the tactics and ploys the police may adopt. Anticipate questions likely to form the basis of ss. 36 or 37 CJPOA 1994 inferences (see Chapter 8). If, as is likely, the interview is to be tape recorded, explain the mechanics of this.

It is becoming an increasingly common practise for the police to bail suspects under s. 37(7)(a) PACE 1984 in circumstances where a suspect denies an offence. The purpose of this is to enable the police to seek the advice of the CPS as to whether charges should be brought.

On a purely pragmatic level, if there is a significant risk that your client will be refused bail if charged, a denial at this stage may be a sound tactical option.

12.14 ANSWERING SOME QUESTIONS BUT NOT OTHERS

Your client should never be advised to answer some questions but not others. This would be an evidential disaster. Visualise how it would look to a court if your client did so. It would imply that your client had something to hide.

12.15 HOW DO I DECIDE WHAT ADVICE TO GIVE?

There is no easy answer to the above question. Experience will help. However, a good strategy is to draw up a list of the advantages and disadvantages of your client remaining silent and compare them to a list of the advantages and disadvantages of answering questions or advancing a prepared statement.

12.16 WHAT SHOULD THE LEGAL ADVISER DO DURING THE INTERVIEW?

A lot of behavioural psychology occurs during the police interview. The atmosphere may well be tense. It is the police who are in control. They control time, space and information. It is important that you regain some of the psychological control.

In the interview room you should sit where you feel comfortable and not where you are asked to sit, if you feel this hinders your ability to communicate with your client. Remember you may have an appropriate adult or interpreter in the interview room with you. It is worth reminding such individuals as to the nature of your respective roles.

Code C – Notes for Guidance para. 6D acknowledges the nature of the legal adviser's role in the interview:

> 'A detained person has a right to free legal advice and to be represented by a solicitor. The solicitor's only role in the police station is to protect and advance the legal rights of his client. On occasions this may require the solicitor to give advice which has the effect of his client avoiding giving evidence which strengthens a prosecution case. The solicitor may intervene in order to seek clarification or to challenge an improper question to his client or the manner in which it is put, or to advise his client not to reply to particular questions or if he wishes to give his client further legal advice.'

The extract justifies a *positive* role in the interview. You must interrupt if you feel the questions being put are:

* unclear;
* ambiguous;
* oppressive;
* irrelevant;
* threatening;
* not questions at all.

You may at any time advise your client not to answer a question.

You will recall ss. 76 and 78 PACE (see Chapters 9 and 10). These give you justification to intervene during an interview. So, if an officer is asking leading questions of a vulnerable suspect, or the questions asked are unfair, you have the authority to intervene. Place your objections on the record and set up the argument for the trial advocate should the matter come to court.

If you are taken by surprise by a question (perhaps with reference to evidence against your client not previously revealed), advise your client not to answer the question. If you feel your client is losing control of the situation you should ask your client if he wants further legal advice. Hopefully, he will say yes, resulting in the interview being suspended and allowing you to consult with your client in private. Consider what you would do if, against your advice, your client starts to answer questions? You would ask your client if he wants further legal advice. If the interview is suspended for this purpose, you should make your advice very clear and keep a note to this effect. If your client chooses to ignore your advice, so be it. Most advisers would consider it good practice to get their client to sign a written disclaimer to this effect.

If investigating officers choose to comply with only the minimum disclosure requirements in Code C para. 10.3 Notes for Guidance 10.B, you may need to stop the interview frequently in order to take instructions as new facts emerge. You might wish to ask the investigating officers at the outset of the interview if they have disclosed to you everything of relevance to the allegation made against your client. If they say they have but it later transpires that new evidence emerges you should point out the unfairness to your client and ask whether he wants further legal advice. Indeed, your advice about answering questions may need to be revised.

12.16.1 CAN THE POLICE ASK YOUR CLIENT ABOUT HIS PREVIOUS CONVICTIONS?

The implementation of the bad character provisions (ss. 98–112) under the Criminal Justice Act 2003 (CJA) has implications for advice given to suspects at a police station. The provisions are considered in Chapter 26. The effect of the new law is to increase the situations where evidence of the defendant's bad character may be admitted at trial. For this reason, it will be easier for the police to justify the questioning of suspects on their past record in interview. Under the provisions, there are a series of gateways through which the prosecution are able to adduce evidence of bad character. Three of these gateways can be triggered by your client at the police station if he (a) gives a false impression of himself and/or (b) attacks the character of another person or (c) introduces his own bad character in interview.

Suspects clearly need to be advised about these provisions and the legal adviser may need to reinforce the advice during interview, perhaps by advising a client to make no comment in relation to questions about past offending.

12.16.2 CAN A LEGAL ADVISER BE EXCLUDED FROM AN INTERVIEW?

The relevant provisions are contained in Code D paras. 6.9–6.11. A legal adviser may only be required to leave if his conduct is such that the interviewer is unable properly to put questions to the suspect. Such conduct could include answering questions on behalf of your client. The decision to remove a legal adviser from an interview is a very serious step and as such it requires the interviewing officer to consult with an officer of superintendent rank, who will take the ultimate decision. If the legal adviser is removed, the suspect must be given the opportunity to consult another solicitor and to have that person present in interview.

12.17 IDENTIFICATION PROCEDURES

In many cases the police will wish to take samples from your client, or they may wish your client to participate in an identification procedure. You need to discuss these matters with your client and advise as to what response to give the police. Full consideration is given to these matters in Chapter 11, which also examines the law relating to the admissibility of identification evidence.

12.18 POST INTERVIEW

Your role does not end once the interview is concluded. There are a number of different outcomes that may occur at the police station. A decision might be taken to:

- charge your client and either release on bail (conditional or otherwise – s. 47(1A) PACE) or charge and withhold bail (s. 38 PACE);
- release your client from police custody on bail pending further enquiries (s. 37(7)(b) PACE) or release him unconditionally (s. 37(7)(c) PACE);
- continue to detain your client (subject to custody time-limits and justification under s. 37(2) PACE);
- release your client on bail pending a decision to charge or conditionally caution by the CPS under s. 37(7)(a) PACE. Conditions may be imposed to the grant of police bail in these circumstances.

You must be prepared to make appropriate representations. Knowledge of PACE and Code C is important in this regard.

12.18.1 THE DECISION TO CHARGE

You will recall that s. 37(7) PACE 1984 imposes a statutory duty on the custody officer, in conjunction with the CPS, to either charge or release a detainee where there is sufficient evidence to charge him with an offence and it is in the public interest to so charge.

An individual who has been arrested but not charged may only be detained where the custody officer is satisfied that there are grounds for detaining him. Section 37(2) provides that where a custody officer concludes there is insufficient evidence to charge the detainee, he must be released with or without bail unless the custody officer reasonably believes that detention of the suspect is necessary to secure or preserve evidence relating to the offence for which he has been arrested or to obtain such evidence by questioning him. You will be aware that custody time limits apply (see Chapter 7) and that continued detention is subject to review.

If the investigation has been completed and your client has been interviewed, the police/ CPS ought to be in a position to determine whether to charge or not. Having undertaken an interview of your client and having assessed the overall state of the evidence against him, you should be in a position to make representations in this regard.

If you are of the opinion that there is insufficient evidence you should be pressing for your client's release with or without bail (ss. 34 and 47 PACE 1984). Where an investigation is likely to be ongoing, your client can expect to be released on police bail, pending further enquires or a decision to prosecute by the CPS in accordance with s. 37(7)(a) PACE (see Chapter 7, paragraph 7.4.4).

Where it is being proposed that your client should remain in custody for the time being, you need to ascertain the reasons for this and make appropriate representations. Your client's continued detention must be justified in accordance with the conditions laid down in s. 37(2) PACE where, for example, the police wish to undertake a further interview or conduct further enquiries of witnesses. Press for your client's release on police bail if this is likely to take some time. Custody time limits will of course continue to apply if your client continues to be detained (s. 41 PACE).

A caution (conditional or simple) is an alternative to charging your client. For a caution to be administered however, your client must have accepted his involvement in the crime and consent to a caution. This alternative course of action should be discussed with your client and if it is appropriate you might choose to raise it with the custody officer. The utilisation of a caution as an alternative to a prosecution is considered in Chapter 13.

12.18.2 NEGOTIATING POLICE BAIL

Full consideration is given to police bail in Chapter 7, paragraphs 7.4.4 and 7.14.2.

Ensure that before you leave the police station your client fully understands the state of the investigation and where he stands. If his detention is to continue, you will need to provide him with the necessary reassurances and that if a further interview is to be undertaken you will be informed. It is sensible to advise your client that 'walls have ears' in police stations, and that if he does not wish to incriminate himself, he should be very careful about who he speaks to and what he says.

12.19 PAYMENT FOR POLICE STATION ADVICE

Public funding of criminal defence services is administered by the Legal Services Commission (LSC). Firms of solicitors wishing to undertake publicly funded criminal defence work must hold a contract with the LSC. Advice given at the police station is covered by the Police Station Advice and Assistance Scheme. Under this scheme, any individual under arrest or who is to be questioned under caution is entitled to free legal advice. Suspects are given the choice of their own solicitor or a duty solicitor. Changes were brought about to the scheme on 17 May 2004 in that a solicitor will be paid for telephone advice only in connection with the following categories of case:

- the client is detained in relation to a non-imprisonable offence;
- the client is arrested on a bench warrant for failing to appear in court and is being held for production before a court;
- the client is arrested on suspicion of driving with excess alcohol; failure to provide a specimen; driving while unfit;
- the client is detained in relation to breach of police or bail conditions.

Attendance in connection with these cases may be justified if an interview or identification procedure is going to take place, the client requires an appropriate adult or interpreter or the client is complaining of serious maltreatment.

12.20 THE ETHICS OF POLICE STATION ADVICE

The dynamics of advising the suspect at the police station are all-encompassing, requiring the legal adviser to be constantly on his or her guard. Your foremost duty is to protect the interests of your client, but as with all aspects of legal practice, this has to be done within the rules of professional conduct. Professional conduct issues may well arise at the police station. What would you do in the following situations? The rules we are about to cite are contained in the Law Society's Code of Conduct [2004], expected to come into force in 2006.

A conflict of interest arises between two suspects

It is not unusual to find more than one person arrested in connection with a criminal matter. A legal adviser may advise more than one suspect in an investigation, provided there is no conflict or significant risk of conflict between them. If your duty of confidence to one client conflicts with the duty of openness to another, you must cease to act for either (Rule 3). Having interviewed one client, it may become apparent that a conflict of interest is likely to arise, in which case you should advise the second client to consult an alternative legal adviser. Detailed guidance on conflicts between co-defendants can be found in Rule 3, Guidance Note 23–35.

Your client wants you to pass on a message to a third party

Given your client's confinement, this is not an unusual request. However, be very careful that you are not being used as an innocent conduit to tip-off someone implicated in a criminal enterprise. Clearly a lot will depend on the nature of the crime your client has been arrested for and the nature of the message you are being asked to pass on. Always explain to your client that you will have to discuss his request with the custody officer.

Your instructions come from a third party

It is not unusual to be asked to represent someone in custody by a friend or relative of the detained individual. You should attend the police station and inform the custody officer that you have been asked to attend on behalf of X and that you would like X to be informed of that fact. Clearly X cannot be forced to see you, but if X does speak with you, you must obtain his authority to enable you to act for him (Rule 2).

Your client seeks to give misleading information to the police

You must never put yourself in a position where you allow your client to knowingly mislead the court (Rule 11.01). You run the risk of having criminal proceedings instituted against you for perverting the course of justice. Although the rules are expressed in the context of the court, they should be applied equally in the context of the police station.

A client who admits his guilt to you (in circumstances where you have no reason to doubt his admission) can still plead not guilty and put the prosecution to proof of its case. You cannot, however, allow your client to make a positive assertion of innocence in your presence during the interview (Rule 11.01, paragraphs 9 and 10)). If your client insists, you must cease to act. In these circumstances however, you are still bound by client confidentiality (r. 4.01). A client who has given the police false particulars is likely to be found out, particularly if they have been in trouble with the police before.

Suppose your client is giving you inconsistent instructions?

Rule 11 guidance paragraph 14 provides that a solicitor is not under a duty to enquire in every case whether his client is telling the truth. In some instances the solicitor may be put on enquiry and may need to check the truth of what his client asserts before relying on such assertions in court. The fact that a client has given his solicitor inconsistent instructions is not a ground for refusing to act further. Where it is clear, however, that a client is attempting to put forward false information, the solicitor should cease to act (Rule 11.01, paragraphs 9 and 10).

You must never construct a defence for your client (Rule 11.01). Your role is to offer advice, based on the evidence and the applicable substantive law.

Your client states he is not guilty but is prepared to take the blame and to plead guilty

You can offer your client advice and endeavour to persuade your client to plead not guilty, but you must not assist him in the deception (Rule 11.01, paragraphs 9 and 10). You should point out the difficulties he could later find himself in if he was to change his mind and of course, there is a risk that if the true facts emerge he could be prosecuted for perverting the course of justice. If in doubt, refuse to act.

KEY POINT SUMMARY

- Keep and maintain a contemporaneous written note of all that occurs whilst you are at the police station.

- Extract all the necessary information from the custody record on your arrival.

- Press the investigating officer(s) for as much disclosure of evidence as you can, as this will have a direct bearing on the advice you give your client.

- Carefully evaluate the evidence against your client before deciding on the most appropriate strategy for your client.

- Be prepared to advise silence when you consider it to be the appropriate advice.

- Where silence is to be advised, ensure your client gives his or her informed consent by making him or her fully aware of the consequences.

- Consider whether a prepared statement might be the best option for your client.

- Ensure that any representations you make are recorded on the custody record.

- Be proactive during the interview and intervene where necessary even where your client is exercising his right to remain silent.

- Prepare your client for the interview experience.

- Instruct your client in advance to answer in the affirmative if you ask him during the interview whether he wants further legal advice. This way the interview has to be suspended enabling you to consult in private with your client.

- After the interview has concluded, press the custody officer for a decision and be prepared to make appropriate representations.

SELF-TEST QUESTIONS

Case study 1: *R v Lenny Whyte* – alternative hypothesis

You will be aware that having worked through the Lenny Whyte scenario up to this point, Lenny was not represented at the police station, and made incriminating admissions to his involvement in the burglary. Let's take an alternative course and imagine you had been called to the police station to represent Lenny upon his arrest. Picture yourself walking into the custody suite:

What is the first thing you would do?
You would speak to the custody officer and ask to consult the custody record. By consulting the custody record, you would know the reason for Lenny's arrest (domestic burglary at the home of an old age pensioner). You would be able to ascertain the reasons for his detention (which in Lenny's case would be the need to secure or preserve evidence relating to the offence or to obtain such evidence by questioning). There would be a record of all searches undertaken in connection with the investigation, from which you would be able to ascertain that Lenny's flat has been searched.

Having extracted all the pertinent information from the custody record, what would you do next?
You would ask to speak with the investigating officer and your goal would be to ascertain the precise nature of the evidence against your client. What is revealed to you depends to a large extent on the type of questions that you ask and the personality of the investigating officer.

With the information that you have from the custody record, what questions do you think you would put to the officer/s? Would you ask open ended questions or closed questions?

You would want details of the burglary (time/place/account of what was stolen etc. . . .). You would clearly want to know whether there were any witnesses to the burglary and an account of what they saw. You need to try and ascertain the nature of the evidence that has led to Lenny's arrest. Do the police have a statement of complaint? Has any particular witness identified Lenny? Has an identification procedure been convened or is an identification procedure being contemplated? Is there any forensic evidence? Has Lenny made any admissions? Why was his flat searched and has any material been seized and if so, why? You would need to press for full details of the co-accused. Has this individual implicated Lenny in any way? Does this individual have any previous convictions?

Let's assume you ascertain the following information from the investigating officer:

- Lenny lives in the vicinity of the burgled property and his appearance matches the description of two eyewitnesses;

- the victim has identified Lenny to the police as someone she had spoken to in her street a short while before the burglary;

- there is an eyewitness who saw the burglar who may be able to identify him;

- the suspected burglar was seen to be wearing white trainers;

- entry to the burgled property was through the back door of the property and a scene of crime officer has lifted shoeprints;

- a pair of white trainers were recovered from Lenny's flat and have been sent for forensic comparison with the shoeprint discovered at the scene;

- the police are not prepared to disclose whether or not the co-accused Lloyd Green has made any significant statement;

- Lloyd Green has one previous conviction for a motoring matter;

- Lenny has a string of previous convictions for drug possession, theft and burglary.

What has been the purpose of your exchange with the investigating officer?

Your purpose has been to find out the nature of the evidence against your client and to assess it.

What conclusion have you reached as regards the strength of the evidence?

There is some circumstantial evidence of Lenny's involvement in the burglary and further investigation by the police is merited. The next stage will be for you to interview Lenny.

How will you conduct this interview and what is its purpose?

Having met Lenny and explained your role, you should let him speak. This gives you the opportunity to observe his demeanour. Through a series of closed questions, and preferably with the aid of a questionnaire, you need to ask Lenny for all relevant details and put to him the evidence that has been disclosed to you. Your questioning should have picked up the fact that Lenny is undergoing treatment for a mental disorder and that he is not in possession of his medication. This triggers a number of the safeguards under Code C. With Lenny's permission, you will need to alert the custody officer and you may wish to make representations as to why this fact was not picked up on the booking-in procedure. Make sure your representations are recorded on the custody record. Lenny needs to be medicated by a qualified health professional. It will almost certainly be necessary for a doctor to be called to check and administer the correct dosage and to offer advice as to whether Lenny is fit to be interviewed. This is likely to cause a significant delay. You need to decide whether to stay or to return to the station later. In view of Lenny's mental disorder he must have access to an appropriate adult.

Assume it is a couple of hours later. You continue to interview Lenny, this time in the presence of an appropriate adult (his sister). He states he is not guilty of the burglary and that he probably has an alibi but the details are vague. He knows Lloyd Green who (he says) is a drug dealer. Lenny accepts he possesses a pair of white training shoes but says they were given to him a couple of weeks ago and he has never worn them.

What advice will you give to Lenny, assuming the police doctor has deemed him fit to be interviewed? Should he exercise his right to remain silent or should he put forward his defence and an explanation? What factors have a bearing on this?

- **Are you satisfied with the disclosure of evidence?**
- **Do you feel Lenny's state of mind is such that he could cope in an interview situation?**
- **What assessment have you made as regards the strength of the evidence that has been disclosed?**

On balance, you should advise Lenny to exercise his right to remain silent. The police have little substantive evidence against Lenny at this time. Lenny is likely to incriminate himself if he answers police questions. His alibi is very sketchy and you do not know at this stage whether the co-accused has implicated him. If he has, this is likely to come out in the interview. If the co-accused is a drug dealer, Lenny may wish to proceed with caution out of concern for his own safety. Lenny should be advised about the potential risks of remaining silent. On tape you should state that your client is to remain silent and consider giving your reasons for this advice (without reference to any privileged conversation with Lenny). Your reason might be the fact of Lenny's mental illness. Assuming Lenny follows your advice, the investigation is not advanced through Lenny's interview. Let us assume that it is not apparent that Lloyd Green has implicated Lenny in any way, as no questions are put to Lenny as regards anything Lloyd Green might have said. At the conclusion of the interview, you should be pressing for Lenny's release on police bail.

Should you advise Lenny to participate in an identification procedure?

The issues surrounding the identification of Lenny Whyte are specifically considered in Chapter 11. On balance, Lenny should be advised to consent to either a video parade or an identification parade conducted in your presence. The police are obliged to disclose records of the initial description by an eyewitness (Code D para. 3.1) and it would be important to obtain them in this case.

If Lenny answers police bail at a later date, whereupon he is identified by one of the eyewitnesses at a video parade and a forensic link is established between the training shoes recovered from Lenny's flat and the print by the back door, what then?

The police may charge Lenny without holding a further interview or they may wish to interview further.

Would your advice to Lenny change? Should he now answer questions or continue to remain silent?

The evidence against Lenny is now stronger but Lenny's alibi is no further advanced as he has not been to see you in the meantime. He is however adamant that he did not commit the burglary. It becomes a calculated risk at this point. Which course of action poses the less risk? Arguably it would be remaining silent. If Lenny were to make incriminating admissions during the interview, the prosecution would have a much stronger case against him when combined with the other evidence. If he were to remain silent he would be less likely to incriminate himself. If charged, his defence at trial may be confined to cross-examining prosecution witnesses on the basis that their identification of Lenny is mistaken. This would not trigger s. 34 CJPOA 1994 (*R v Moshaid* [1998] Crim LR 420). If Lenny were to advance a defence of alibi he would of course be at risk of an adverse inference under s. 34. However, if you were to give evidence explaining the reason for your advice, the court may accept it was reasonable for Lenny to have remained silent. In any event, the jury must be satisfied that there is a sufficiently strong case against Lenny before any question of an adverse inference is considered.

All of the above is hypothetical in the light of what did in fact occur in this case scenario. You will recall that Lenny was interviewed without a legal adviser being present. He made a number of incriminating admissions which resulted in him being charged and which will no doubt be used by the prosecution in evidence against him.

One way of deciding whether to advise a client to remain silent or answer questions is to consider:

1. What are the advantages to the client of answering questions?

2. What are the disadvantages to the client in answering questions?

3. What are the advantages to the client remaining silent?

4. What are the disadvantages to the client of remaining silent?

These questions should be constantly asked and re-evaluated. They do not always result in a clear and simple answer, but they should at least guide your thought processes on this difficult and challenging aspect of legal practice.

Attendance at Police Station Record – PS2

Date _____

Name of Member of Staff Who First Spoke to Client _____   Fee Earner _____

Name of Fee Earner First Contacted About Client _____   Time Arrived _____

Time Departed _____

Time informed by police ready for interview or
agreed time when would be ready for interview _____   ☐ Volunteer   ☐ Arrested

Custody Record Details

Police Station _____   Custody Number _____

Surname _____   Telephone _____

Forenames _____   Occupation _____

Address _____   Date of Birth _____

_____   Height _____

Arrested BY _____   Place of Arrest _____

Officer in case _____   Date of Arrest & Time _____

Reason for Arrest _____   Date and Time Arrived at Station _____

Appropriate Adult _____   Custody Sergeant _____

Contact details of adult _____   Time Contacted _____

Unsolicited Comments Noted _____

Condition of client noted _____

Injuries Noted _____

Body Sample

Legal Authority? ☐ Y ☐ N   Reasons for Procedure _____

Consent obtained? ☐ Y ☐ N   Details of Samples _____

Intimate/Non-intimate search

Legal Authority? ☐ Y ☐ N   Reasons for Procedure _____

Consent obtained? ☐ Y ☐ N   Type of Search _____

What evidence obtained _____

_____

Medical Examination

Fit to be detained? ☐ Y ☐ N   Date and Time _____

Fit to be interviewed? ☐ Y ☐ N   Name of Police Surgeon _____

Other relevant comments _____

_____

_____

Attendance at Police Station Record – PS2

Information from Police

Officer Spoken To _____   Date of Offence _____   Time of offence _____

Police Version of Offence

What evidence is there?

Details of any eyewitnesses

Is identification an issue? ☐ Y ☐ N

Details of any relevant object, substance or mark found on client or in place of arrest

If any of the above found note any relevant response made by the client

Was client arrested at a material place at or about the time the offence was committed?

If yes to above note any relevant response made by the client

Has there been any previous interview or questioning?

Obtain record of any significant comments made by client

Names of any co-accused

Are the co-accused in custody?

What have the co-accused said?

Who have the co-accused instructed?

Details of any premises searched

Legal Authority for search? ☐ Y ☐ N

Details of any evidence gathered

Attendance at Police Station Record – PS2

Information from Client

☐ *Check custody record details are correct and note any discrepancies*

National Insurance Number _____

Status   ☐ Married   ☐ Single   ☐ Divorced   ☐ Separated
              ☐ Widowed   ☐ Cohabiting   ☐ Living with Parents

Who owns accommodation? _____

How long has client lived there? _____

Dependants

Number of children _____

Ages of children _____

Do children live with client? _____

Employment

Details of employment _____

How long employed _____

Income and capital

Income and its source _____

Further details

Details of any current criminal proceedings _____

Details of any current bail _____

Any previous convictions?

Particular Needs

Is client mentally disordered/handicapped, or has limited understanding? _____

Has client particular needs ie medication, disability, need for doctor or translator? _____

Is client fit for interview? _____

Instructions from Client

Client told of information obtained from Police? ☐ Y ☐ N

Client response and version of events _____

_____

_____

_____

_____

_____

_____

_____

_____

_____

_____

_____

_____

_____

Attendance at Police Station Record – PS2

Name and address of any factual witnesses ....

....

....

Details of any alibi and names and addresses of any alibi witnesses ....

....

....

Client's response to any significant statements ....

....

....

Medical Problems

Details of any medical condition of client relevant to fitness for interview or safe custody of client ....

....

Client's explanation of the effect of the medical condition ....

....

Is client under or prescribed any medication? ☐ Y ☐ N

Is it appropriate to have an entry made in the custody record? ☐ Y ☐ N

Client's Injuries

Description of any injury suffered by client during alleged offence, arrest or detention ....

....

Client's explanation of the cause ....

....

Details of witnesses to the injury ....

....

Is it appropriate to call the police surgeon? ☐ Y ☐ N

Does the injury affect the client's fitness to be interviewed? ☐ Y ☐ N

Have details of the injury been entered on the custody record? ☐ Y ☐ N

☐ *Advise client to have photographs taken of injury on leaving station*

Co-accused

Is any co-accused known to the client? ....

Details of the client's version of the co-accused's role in the offence ....

....

....

If you have been requested to act for the co-accused, is there any conflict of interest? ....

Attendance at Police Station Record – PS2

Advising the client

NB:Note Advice Given

☐ *If the client is under 17 or mentally handicapped or disordered advise the client of the role of the appropriate adult*

....

☐ *If non-intimate samples are requested advise whether to consent and implications of refusal*

....

☐ *If intimate samples are requested advise whether to consent and implications of refusal*

....

....

☐ *If samples taken or to be taken advise on retention of such samples*

....

....

☐ *Where there is an alibi advise the client of the implications of failing to give details when questioned under caution*

....

....

☐ *When any substances or marks were found on the client or in the place of arrest and their presence is in issue advise the client of the implications of the failure to account for these when questioned*

....

....

☐ *Where on arrest the client was found at a material place at or about the time of the offence and this is in issue advise the client of the implications of the failure to account for this when questioned*

....

....

☐ *Advise the client prior to any interview of whether to answer questions and the implications of any failure to raise any facts when questions or being charged which are later relied on in defence*

....

☐ *Advise client whether to lodge a 'Prepared statement'*

....

....

☐ *Advise client whether to give reasons for making a 'no comment' interview or prepared statement*

....

Interview Procedure

Interview start time .... Interview End Time ....

☐ *Note the details of the interview and attach notes*

Attendance at Police Station Record – PS2

Result of Police Station Attendance

Legal Aid

☐ *Complete CDS 1 and 2 if appropriate and advise what the funding will cover*

☐ *Complete Application for representation order if appropriate*

☐ *Complete DSS Authority if appropriate*

Enquiries on-going

☐ *Advise client of position and to insist police contact us if they require a further interview or the client requires advice about another issue*

☐ *Advise the client we will monitor his detention in the police station*

☐ *Request custody sergeant to contact us if a further interview is required*

Police Bail Back

Date, time and place of return ....

☐ *Advise the client of the consequences of failing to answer bail* ....

Charged and Bailed

Details of the charges ....

....

....

Date, time and venue of the court hearing ....

Bail conditions, security or surety imposed ....

☐ *Advise the client of the consequences of failing to answer bail* ....

Charged and in Custody

Details of the charges ....

....

....

Date, time and venue of hearing ....

☐ *Advise the client of the prospects of success re Bail*

☐ *Advise the client whether bail application will be made*

☐ *Advise the client of the procedure and date of bail application*

Other Action

Was the client released with no further action? ☐ Y ☐ N

Was the client cautioned, warned or reprimanded? ☐ Y ☐ N

was the client reported for summons? ☐ Y ☐ N

Was the file sent to the CPS for advice? ☐ Y ☐ N

Complaint against the Police

Nature of the client's complaint ....

☐ *Advise the client of the procedure for making a complaint **and** whether to make any complaint prior to leaving the police station*

13 THE DECISION TO PROSECUTE

13.1   INTRODUCTION

The conclusion of the police investigation may result in a number of outcomes for the suspect. If there is insufficient evidence to charge, the suspect will be eliminated from the police investigation without further action being taken. In some situations the case may remain on a police file, which means that if further evidence comes to light which implicates the suspect in the offence, he could be charged at a later date. A client should be advised of the potential consequence of his case being left on file. In other cases the case file may be referred to the CPS to decide whether there is sufficient evidence to charge and/or what the appropriate charge should be. In this situation, s. 37A PACE permits your client to be released on conditional police bail.

Where there is sufficient evidence, the suspect may be charged at the police station and given conditional or unconditional police bail or be remanded in custody pending his first court appearance.

As a result of the reforms introduced by the Criminal Justice Act 2003, the responsibility for charging is now shared between the CPS and the police depending on the nature and seriousness of the offence. In a straightforward case, the suspect may be charged within a few hours after the commission of the alleged offence. The investigation of a more serious offence may take a several days or weeks or even months.

In this chapter, we explain the grounds that must be satisfied in deciding whether there is sufficient evidence to charge and later in the chapter, the alternatives to prosecution are considered including cautioning the suspect or administering a conditional caution.

The specific issues dealt with in this chapter include:

- deciding who charges the suspect;
- the procedure on charge;
- applying the Full Code Test under the Code for Crown Prosecutors;
- applying the Threshold Test under the Code for Crown Prosecutors;
- simple cautions;
- conditional cautions;
- reprimands or final warning in the case of a juvenile offender;
- the ways in which the defence solicitor might influence the decision to charge.

13.2 CHARGING THE SUSPECT – THE TRADITIONAL POSITION

The Prosecution of Offences Act 1985 (which created the Crown Prosecution Service) established a division of responsibilities between the police and Crown Prosecution Service. In virtually all cases the police were responsible for investigating crime and deciding whether there was sufficient evidence to charge. Where a charge was justified, the police would formally begin the proceedings by laying an information or by completing the charge sheet.

After charge, the police would pass the crime file to the CPS where the Crown Prosecutor would confirm that the suspect had been charged with the correct offence and decide whether the prosecution should continue.

In deciding whether the prosecution should continue, the Crown Prosecutor would apply the 'evidential test' and the 'public interest test' under the Code for Crown Prosecutors to the facts of the case. Where both tests were satisfied, the prosecution would continue. If the case failed either test, the CPS would issue a notice of discontinuance and the proceedings would be halted.

13.3 THE DECISION TO CHARGE UNDER THE CRIMINAL JUSTICE ACT 2003

As noted in Chapter 7, s. 28 Criminal Justice Act 2003 has reformed the charging procedure by requiring closer cooperation between the police and the CPS. In most cases, the CPS has assumed responsibility for charging the suspect. The police retain the power to charge in a range of minor summary offences, or where the defendant indicates an early admission of guilt in other specified summary offences explained at paragraph 13.3.1 below. Guidance on the operation of the new scheme is contained in the Home Office document entitled *Guidance to Police Officers and Crown Prosecutors* issued by DPP under s. 37A PACE, accessible at and on the web-link section to our Online Resource Centre (http://www.cps.gov.uk/publications).

online resource centre

13.3.1 OFFENCES WHERE THE POLICE CHARGE THE SUSPECT

Under the DPP's Guidance on Charging, the police may charge the suspect in all summary/either-way cases where it appears to the custody officer that a guilty plea is likely and the case is suitable for sentencing in the magistrates' court, except for:

- offences of wounding or grievous bodily harm, s. 20 OAPA 1861;
- assault occasioning actual bodily harm, s. 47 OAPA 1861;
- violent disorder, s. 2 Public Order Act 1986;
- affray, s. 3 Public Order Act 1986;

- offences of deception and handling stolen goods, under the Theft Acts 1968 and 1978.

The police will continue to charge the suspect with the following offences (whether an early plea is made or not):

- offences contrary to the Bail Act 1976;
- offences contrary to s. 5 Public Order Act 1986;
- Town Police Clauses Act 1847 offences;
- Vagrancy Act 1824 offences;
- Street Offences Act 1959;
- all summary offences punishable on conviction with a term of imprisonment of three months or less
- any bye law offence; and
- all motoring offences except:
  - cases involving death;
  - allegations of dangerous driving;
  - aggravated vehicle taking; and
  - allegations of unlawful taking unless suitable for an early disposal as a guilty plea in the magistrates' court.

13.3.2 THE PROCEDURE WHERE THE POLICE CHARGE THE SUSPECT

In deciding whether to charge, the custody officer applies the Full Code Test to the facts of the offence. For a charge to be laid, the Full Test Code, which is found in section 5 of the Code for Crown Prosecutors (see paragraph 13.3.5 below), requires the custody officer to be satisfied that, first, 'there is sufficient evidence to achieve a realistic prospect of a conviction' and second, that 'it is in the public interest for the suspect to be charged'.

If both elements are satisfied the suspect will be charged most probably by the police laying an information at the magistrates' court. The court will then issue a summons to secure the suspect's attendance at his first court hearing.

> **Looking Ahead**
>
> When the provisions of ss. 29–31 CJA 2003 come into force, all public prosecutions will commence with the issue of a written charge, which will be accompanied by a 'requisition' informing the defendant when he is to appear in court to answer the charge against him.

After charge, the police pass the case file to the Crown Prosecutor, who, under section 4 of the Code for Crown Prosecutors is under a duty to review the file to confirm that the defendant has been charged with the correct offence and that the evidential and public interest criteria under the Full Code Test are satisfied.

13.3.3 THE RESPONSIBILITY OF THE CPS TO CHARGE

The Crown Prosecutor must decide the charge in the following offences:

- all offences tried on indictment only;
- any offence triable on indictment due to the seriousness of the offence and/or the defendant's previous convictions;

- offences under the Terrorism Act 2000;
- any other offence linked with terrorist activity;
- offences under any Official Secrets Acts;
- any offence involving any racial, religious or homophobic aggravation;
- any offences under the Sexual Offences Act 2003 committed by or upon any person under the age of 18.

13.3.4 THE PROCEDURE WHERE THE CROWN PROSECUTOR DECIDES THE CHARGE

In many cases where the Crown Prosecutor decides whether to charge, in accordance with s. 37B PACE, the suspect will be released on bail. It was previously the case that conditions could only be imposed on the grant of bail post-charge. In accordance with s. 37(7)(a) CJA 2003, conditions may now be attached to bail pending a decision whether to charge.

After the suspect has been bailed, an officer involved in the investigation of the offence will refer the case file (known as MG3 'Report to Crown Prosecutor for a Charging Decision') to the Crown Prosecutor for a decision.

In deciding whether to charge, the Crown Prosecutor will apply the Full Code Test to ascertain whether the evidence discloses a realistic prospect of a conviction and it is in the public interest for the suspect to be charged.

After applying the Full Code Test, the Crown Prosecutor will give the investigating officer written notice of his decision, s. 37B(4).

Where the Crown Prosecutor decides that:

- the suspect should be charged or cautioned, the suspect should be charged or cautioned accordingly, s. 37B(6) PACE; or
- there is insufficient evidence to charge or caution, or sufficient evidence to charge or caution, but that person shall not be charged or cautioned with an offence, the custody officer must give the person concerned notice in writing that he is not to be prosecuted (s. 37B(5) PACE).

13.3.5 THE FULL CODE TEST – SECTION 5, CODE FOR CROWN PROSECUTORS

As already mentioned, for the suspect to be charged, the two elements of the Full Code Test must be satisfied. The custody officer or the Crown Prosecutor must believe that:

- there is sufficient evidence for there to be a realistic prospect of conviction; and
- that it is in the public interest to prosecute.

online
resource
centre

The Code is the basis for a Crown Prosecutor's work (and now for the police as well) to ensure that fair and consistent decisions are made about a commencing and continuing with a prosecution. The latest version of the Code came into effect in November 2004. As a public document it can be accessed from a number of sources, including our Online Resource Centre website and www.cps.gov.uk/publications/docs/. In deciding whether to charge and what the appropriate charge should be, the Code will also be used in conjunction with other official documents including the DPP's Guidance on Charging (see 13.3 above) and the National Charging Standards. A defence lawyer should have a good working knowledge of the Code and understand the way in which the local Crown Prosecutors and caseworkers apply its provisions. The CPS has an extremely informative website of its own: www.cps.gov.uk.

What is the evidential test?

The evidence in the case should provide a realistic prospect of conviction. The evidential test is determined by applying an objective test – would a jury or bench of magistrates properly directed as to the law more likely than not convict the defendant of the offence charged?

The evidence against the accused must be relevant, admissible and reliable for the prosecution to continue. If the evidence is not sufficient to prove one or more elements of the *actus reus* and *mens rea* of the offence, or if the offender cannot be identified to the exclusion of other suspects, a prosecution should not be started. If the evidential test is satisfied, the Crown Prosecutor will then apply the 'public interest' test.

The 'public interest' test

The Code requires that the prosecution must be in the public interest. In 1951 Lord Shawcross, who was then the Attorney-General, made an important statement about the public interest in prosecuting criminal offences, which has been supported by Attorney-Generals ever since:

> 'It has never been the rule in this country – I hope it never will be – that suspected criminal offences must automatically be the subject of prosecution.'

The public interest factors that can affect the decision to prosecute usually depend on the seriousness of the offence or the circumstances of the suspect. Section 5.9 of the Code for Crown Prosecutors identifies some common public interest factors in favour of the prosecution, including:

- a conviction is likely to result in a significant sentence;
- a weapon was used or violence was threatened during the commission of the offence;
- the offence was committed against a person serving the public (for example, a police officer, a prison officer or a nurse);
- the defendant was in a position of authority or trust;
- the evidence shows that the offender was a ringleader or an organiser of the offence;
- there is evidence that the offence was premeditated;
- there is evidence that the offence was carried out by a group;
- the victim of the offence was vulnerable, had been put in considerable fear, or suffered personal attack, damage or disturbance;
- the offence was motivated by any form of discrimination against the ethnic or national origin, sex, religious beliefs, political views or sexual preference;
- the offence, although not serious in itself, is widespread in the area where it was committed.

Paragraph 5.10 of the Code identifies some common public interest factors against the prosecution continuing.

A prosecution is less likely if:

- the court is likely to impose a very small or nominal penalty;
- the offence was committed as a result of a genuine mistake or misunderstanding (these factors must be balanced against the seriousness of the offence);
- the loss or harm can be described as a minor and was the result of a single incident, particularly if it was caused by a misjudgement;
- there has been a long delay between the offence taking place and the date of the trial, unless:
  - the offence is serious; or
  - the delay has been caused in part by the defendant; or

- the offence has only recently come to light; or

- the complexity of the offence has meant that there has been a long investigation;

• a prosecution is likely to have a very bad effect on the victim's physical or mental health, always bearing in mind the seriousness of the offence.

The test requires the Crown Prosecutor to decide the importance of each factor applied to the specific circumstances of the case and to make an overall assessment of whether it is in the public interest for the prosecution to proceed.

The victim and the public interest test

The interests of the victim should always be taken into account when deciding to prosecute. The victim should always be notified of any developments in the case. The victim's charter is available from the CPS website.

13.4 THE CODE ON DOMESTIC VIOLENCE

While there is no statutory offence of domestic violence, the term is used to describe a range of behaviour often used by one person to control and dominate another, with whom they have or have had a close or family relationship. An offence involving domestic violence may arise out of the physical, sexual, psychological, emotional or financial abuse by one person against another. While most abuse is perpetrated by a male family member on a female, the Code recognises that abuse can also be inflicted on victims in same-sex relationships or the victims of abusive family members. The Code also recognises that members of certain minority ethnic groups, the disabled, lesbians and gay men may be reluctant to report abuse. Other factors which may prevent the reporting of domestic violence are religious, cultural or language barriers.

The Crown Prosecution Service has a detailed policy on prosecuting cases of domestic violence and works closely with other criminal justice agencies such as the police, Victim Support and Refuge. In deciding whether to prosecute, the safety of the victim, any children in the case and any other person involved are given priority – although in more serious cases a prosecution may continue even where the victim has requested that no further action should be taken against the alleged perpetrator. In deciding whether the cases of domestic violence should be prosecuted or continue, the CPS will again apply the 'public interest' and the 'evidential' tests to the facts of the particular case.

13.5 WHAT IS THE POSITION IF THE CUSTODY OFFICER BELIEVES THAT THE SUSPECT SHOULD NOT BE RELEASED ON BAIL PENDING THE DECISION TO PROSECUTE?

As noted at paragraph 13.3.4, in many cases, the suspect may be bailed under s. 37B PACE to allow the Crown Prosecutor to make a decision about whether to charge. However, there will be cases where the suspect presents such a substantial bail risk that he should not be released from custody, and sufficient evidence is not available to allow a charging decision to be made. As some or all of the potential evidence in the case is not available it will not be possible to satisfy the 'realistic prospect of conviction test' under the Full Test Code. In these circumstances, what action can the Crown Prosecutor take?

The Crown Prosecutor is entitled to apply the Threshold Test (section 6, Code for Crown Prosecutors). The test requires the Crown Prosecutor to decide:

• whether there is at least a reasonable suspicion that that the suspect has committed the offence; and if there is:

• whether it is in the public interest to charge the suspect.

In deciding the reasonable suspicion test, the following factors will be applied:

- the evidence available at the time;
- the likelihood and nature of further evidence being obtained;
- the reasonableness for believing that evidence will become available;
- the time it will take to gather the evidence and the steps being taken to do so;
- the impact the expected evidence will have on the case; and
- the charges that the evidence will support.

If the Crown Prosecutor is satisfied that there is at least a reasonable suspicion that the suspect has committed the offence, and it is in the public interest to do so, the suspect may be charged. Following the charge, the suspect must be placed before the court at the next available sitting to decide whether his pre-trial custody should continue or whether he should be released on bail.

After a reasonable period, which will depend on the circumstances of the case, the Crown Prosecutor must review the case and once all the evidence in the case is available, apply the Full Code Test.

13.6 THE SELECTION OF CHARGES – SECTION 7, CODE FOR CROWN PROSECUTORS

The Crown Prosecutor should select charges which:

- reflect the seriousness of the offence and the extent of the offending;
- give the court adequate powers to sentence and impose appropriate post-conviction orders; and
- enable a case to be presented in a clear and simple way.

13.7 ALTERNATIVES TO PROSECUTION

There a number of ways in which a suspect may be diverted from formal criminal proceedings. An adult may be cautioned or receive a conditional caution.

13.7.1 SIMPLE CAUTION

The police retain the discretion to caution a suspect. The decision to caution will most likely be taken in consultation with the CPS. Guidance as to when to administer a caution is contained in Home Office Circulars 30/2005 (see link in the web-links section of our Online Resource Centre). The main points are as follows.

A simple caution will be appropriate where:

- the evidence is sufficient to have warranted a prosecution;
- the offender admits his guilt; and
- the person being cautioned agrees to such a disposal after being made aware that the caution may be cited in court if he offends in the future.

An important pre-condition for a simple caution is that the suspect must admit his guilt. The court may strike down a caution where no admission by the defendant has been obtained (see *Metropolitan Police Commissioner, ex p. P* [1995] TLR 305). A simple caution is normally administered in formal circumstances at a police station by an officer of at least the rank of inspector.

online
resource
centre

The offender will sign a form acknowledging that he agrees to the caution and that he admits his involvement in the offence.

A client should be advised that while a simple caution does not constitute a conviction, records are kept and the caution may be cited in court if he later reoffends. It is also important to advise that a caution does not prevent the possibility of future prosecution. The CPS may still instigate proceedings at a later date even after the detainee has been formally cautioned although the defence could strongly argue that this could amount to abuse of process (see Chapter 9).

While any offender other than a juvenile may be cautioned, in practice a 'vulnerable' detainee is more likely to receive a simple caution than other offenders, depending on the nature of the offence alleged. Included in the category of a vulnerable detainee are:

- the elderly;
- the infirm;
- where the detainee is suffering from a mental condition or impairment;
- where the detainee is suffering from a physical disability;
- where the detainee is under severe emotional distress.

Where the police consider that the Threshold Test is met in a case other than an indictable-only offence and determine that it is in the public interest instead to administer a simple caution or reprimand or final warning in the case of a youth, the police may do so without referring the case to a CPS lawyer. However, the police may wish to consult.

13.7.2 CONDITIONAL CAUTION

A conditional caution is a disposal available under ss. 23–27 Criminal Justice Act 2003 and is appropriate where the Crown Prosecutor considers that there is sufficient evidence for a prosecution but it is in the interests of the suspect, the victim and the community to require the suspect to comply with specified conditions aimed at his rehabilitation. A factor in deciding whether a conditional caution is appropriate, as opposed to a simple caution or prosecution, is whether the specified conditions will be an appropriate and effective way of dealing with an offender's behaviour, or making reparation for the effects of the offence on the victim and on the community.

A conditional caution is available where:

- the suspect is 18 or over;
- the suspect admits the offence to an authorised person; and
- in the opinion of the relevant prosecutor, there is sufficient evidence to charge the suspect with the offence.

The police have no discretion to impose a conditional caution, which may only be given by a prosecutor even in those cases where it would have been open for the police to have charged the suspect.

In deciding whether a conditional caution is appropriate, regard should be had to the suspect's criminal record and the seriousness of the present offence.

The conditional caution will usually be given at the police station but may also be administered at the offender's home or at any other appropriate location. When the conditional caution is administered, the offender is required to sign a document which contains:

- details of the offence;
- an admission by him that he committed the offence;
- his consent to being give the conditional caution; and
- an agreement to comply with the conditions attached to the caution.

13.7.3 THE CONDITIONS ATTACHED TO THE CAUTION

The conditions attached to the caution must be:

- appropriate to the offence;
- achievable; and
- proportionate.

The conditions should be aimed at the offender's rehabilitation and/or reparation. The rehabilitative element may require the offender to attend a drug or alcohol rehabilitation course or an anger management course. The reparative element might include repairing or making good any damage caused to property such as cleaning graffiti or simply apologising to the victim.

13.7.4 TIME LIMITS FOR IMPOSING A CONDITIONAL CAUTION

The time limit for administering a conditional caution must not be excessively long, especially in connection with a summary offence where a prosecution would have to be commenced within six months of the commission date, if the offender fails to comply with the conditions of the caution.

13.7.5 WHAT IS THE PENALTY IF THE OFFENDER FAILS TO COMPLY WITH THE CONDITIONAL CAUTION?

If the suspect fails to comply with the conditions of the caution, he is liable to be prosecuted for the original offence. The conditional caution may be cited in any subsequent criminal proceedings.

For further guidance on conditional cautioning, see www.homeoffice.gov.uk and the CPS website. Conditional cautioning is currently being introduced on a rolling basis throughout the country.

online resource centre

13.8 THE DEFENCE SOLICITOR INFLUENCING THE DECISION TO CHARGE

The greater availability of CPS staff in police stations means that custody officers will usually be acting on the advice of the Crown Prosecutor. It should still be possible, however, for the defence solicitor to influence the decision to charge where the evidence that links the suspect to the offence appears to be weak or unreliable. In this situation, the solicitor should persuade the custody officer to release his client unconditionally or on police bail. Even where the evidence discloses a case to answer, the defence solicitor could persuade the Crown Prosecutor or custody officer to deal with his client by alternative disposal to a formal prosecution. It may be appropriate for a client to be cautioned or to receive a conditional caution or be informally warned about his future behaviour.

In many cases, and especially where the police have made a full disclosure of the evidence against the suspect, it will be clear that the Full Code Test is satisfied and the defence solicitor's latitude for negotiation may be limited. In some situations it might be in a client's interests to be charged as soon as possible where, for example, he has been in police detention for a long time or where the defence solicitor considers that it would not be in his client's interests to be interviewed again by the police.

As with all representations made in connection with a client's detention at the police station, it is vital to ensure that they, and the custody officer's or Crown Prosecutor's responses thereto, are accurately recorded on the custody record and in the defence solicitor's own contemporaneous notes.

online resource centre

Guidance on how adult cases are prosecuted and managed by the CPS is provided by the Criminal Cases Management Framework (CCMF), published in July 2004. The Framework document can be accessed at http://www.cjsonline.gov.uk. The CCMF complements the first draft of the Criminal Procedure Rules (highlighted in Chapter 1).

KEY POINT SUMMARY

- Understand the division of charging responsibilities between the police and the CPS.

- Know the procedures to be followed where the decision to charge is taken by the police or the CPS.

- Have a good working knowledge of the Full Code Test under the Code for Crown Prosecutors and an understanding of the ways in which the evidential and the public interest tests are applied in the decision to charge.

- Know when the Threshold Test applies.

- Understand the alternatives to prosecution and be prepared to negotiate with the police and/or the CPS to divert your client from being prosecuted.

SELF-TEST QUESTIONS

The self-test questions in this chapter are designed to test your understanding and application of the evidential and public interest tests applied by Crown Prosecutors. Before attempting the questions, consider the following example.

Wayne, aged 24, has been arrested on suspicion of assault occasioning actual bodily harm under s. 47 Offences Against the Person Act 1861. The offence occurred during Wayne's wedding reception, when Brian, the bride's brother, made insulting comments about Wayne. There are several witnesses to the offence who would be willing to testify in court. Wayne denies the offence and Brian has indicated to the CPS that he wishes further action to be taken against Wayne. Wayne has two convictions for violent disorder under s. 6 Public Order Act 1986 for separate offences outside a nightclub. Consider whether the evidential and public interest tests are satisfied as required by the Full Code Test under the Code for Crown Prosecutors.

Advice

In applying the Code for Crown Prosecutor's to Wayne's case, it appears that the evidential test is satisfied as there are several witnesses to the offence who would be willing to testify in court. There is nothing to suggest that these witnesses would not give relevant and reliable testimony and that the *actus reus* and *mens rea* of the offence could be proven. In terms of the public interest test, there are factors in favour of continuing the prosecution, not least the use of violence and in his previous criminal conduct – Wayne appears to have a propensity to be violent. On the particular facts of the case, it is likely that Wayne will be charged and prosecuted.

By applying the Code for Crown Prosecutors, consider whether the 'evidential' test and the 'public' interest test are satisfied in the following cases. You might also consider whether there are alternative methods by which the potential defendant may be dealt with.

1. Gerald, aged 75, has been charged with 14 counts of indecent assault arising out of his employment in a residential home for children. The alleged offences occurred between 1968 and 1973. The police have traced four victims of the offences who are willing to testify at Gerald's trial. Gerald has no criminal convictions.

2. Debbie, aged 35, is a single parent with three children. She has been charged with three offences of theft under s. 1. Theft Act 1968 by stealing a pack of disposable nappies, a jar of coffee and a bottle of vodka from Cutcost Supermarket. Debbie denies the offence. The supermarket's policy is always to prosecute shoplifters. In support of the prosecution case, the store detective will testify at trial and there is a security video tape of the alleged offence.

3. Jim, aged 49, is charged with using threatening behaviour under s. 4 Public Order Act 1986 against his neighbour Sally. The offence arises out of a long-standing dispute about Sally's sons playing loud music every night until at least 2 am or 3 am. The only witnesses to the incident are Sally's husband and her sons, aged 19 and 21. The arresting police officer did not witness the actual incident, but did see Sally very distressed and frightened immediately after Jim had allegedly threatened her. Jim has no previous convictions and strongly denies the offence.

4. Kyle, aged 27, is charged with using threatening behaviour under s. 4 Public Order Act 1986. The police allege that Kyle was travelling on a train without a ticket and used verbal abuse when Mohamed, the train manager, challenged him. Kyle has no previous convictions.

5. After Patrick, aged 14, tells his father, Frank, that he (Patrick) is in a gay relationship, Frank hits Patrick, causing him actual bodily harm. Patrick is attacked by his father on two further occasions. Frank also locks Patrick in his room preventing him from leaving the house to keep him away from his boyfriend. After a week Patrick's mother, Mary, tells the police who intervene and arrest Frank. Patrick does not want any action to be taken against Frank.

FIGURE 13.1 THE DECISION TO CHARGE

The decision to charge or to offer an alternative course is for the most part the responsibility of the CPS in conjunction with the custody officer under the CJA 2003 (s. 37B PACE).
The decision to charge is based on two tests contained within the CPS Code for Crown Prosecutors, November 2004. The test comprises:

- evidential test – is there sufficient evidence to provide for a realistic prospect of conviction?

- public interest test – is it in the public interest that the defendant is prosecuted? (This requires the application of various factors listed in the Code.)

ALTERNATIVES TO PROSECUTION

Simple caution (reprimand/final warning for under 18s)

- Defendant may be cautioned where:
  - evidence is sufficient to have warranted prosecution;
  - defendant admits guilt; and
  - defendant agrees to be cautioned (Home Office Circular 1990/59 and 1994/18).

Conditional cautions: ss. 23–27 Criminal Justice Act 2003

- Defendant may receive a conditional caution where:
  - he is over 18;
  - defendant admits the offence to an authorised person; and
  - in the opinion of the prosecutor there is sufficient evidence to charge.

- The condition(s) attached to the caution must be:
  - proportionate to the offence;
  - achievable; and
  - appropriate.

- The condition(s) might require the defendant:
  - to attend drug/alcohol rehabilitation course;
  - to attend anger management course;
  - to make good damage to property.

- It is likely that increasing use will be made of the conditional caution as a means of diverting an offender from the formal prosecution process.

- A conditional caution can be imposed more than once if there has been a five year gap or a different type of offence is involved – see Home Office Code of Practice on Conditional Cautioning.

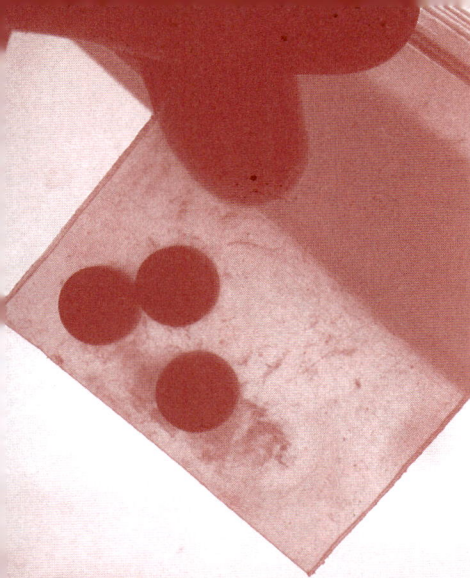

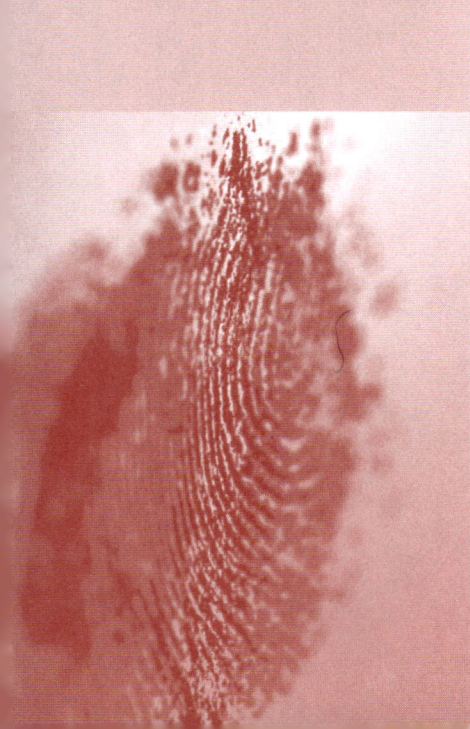

Part III

FROM CHARGE TO TRIAL

Part III considers the procedural stages between charge/summons and the defendant having to appear in court to answer the allegations made against him.

In Chapter 14 we consider public funding of criminal proceedings and the early stages of the criminal litigation process.

In Chapter 15 we consider the court's role in granting and refusing bail.

Chapter 16 considers the special procedure in relation to an either-way offence.

In Chapter 17 we explore the rules relating to the pre-trial disclosure of evidence in criminal proceedings.

In Chapter 18 we consider the conduct of summary trial.

Finally, in Chapters 19 and 20 we consider the conduct of trials on indictment before the Crown Court.

14 PUBLIC FUNDING AND EARLY STAGES OF THE CRIMINAL JUSTICE PROCESS

14.′ INTRODUCTION

In this chapter we consider:

- the public funding of criminal defence work; and
- the early stages of a criminal case, including a defendant's initial appearance before court and the steps a solicitor will need to take in preparation for this.

14.2 PUBLIC FUNDING – A HUMAN RIGHT?

Every individual charged with a criminal offence is entitled to defend himself in person or through legal assistance. Article 6(3)(c) European Convention on Human Rights enshrines this right and further stipulates that the entitlement to legal representation must be given free where an individual has insufficient means to pay and when the interests of justice so requires.

A client faced with a criminal charge may be prepared to pay privately for legal representation. This, however, is very rare! The vast majority of defendants who retain a solicitor in private practice have their legal expenses met by the state under the Access to Justice Act 1999. It is part of a solicitor's professional duty to look into the provision of state funded assistance for his client (Professional Conduct Rules r. 5.01).

14.3 LEGAL SERVICES COMMISSION AND THE CRIMINAL DEFENCE SERVICE

Private practice firms of solicitors can only provide publicly funded criminal defence services if they have a contract with the Legal Services Commission (LSC). The arm of the LSC that has specific responsibility for the provision of criminal defence services is the Criminal Defence Service (CDS). The General Criminal Contract with the LSC requires all client files to be opened and maintained in a quality assured way. Firms 'report' the work they have undertaken on a regular basis and receive monthly block payments based on their average monthly claims report. Firms are subject to random assessment of their files based on a newly introduced system of independent peer review. Trainee solicitors working within franchised firms can expect to be inducted into the procedures for opening and maintaining LSC files in order to comply with LSC requirements.

Publicly funded services are also provided by salaried CDS lawyers. In April 2001, the CDS established a pilot of six Public Defender offices, comprising staff directly employed by the Criminal Defence Service.

A distinction is made in terms of the funding of criminal defence services between work undertaken pre-charge and work undertaken post-charge.

14.4 FUNDING AVAILABLE AT THE POLICE STATION

For an account of funding at the police station see Chapter 12 (12.19).

14.4.1 ADVICE AND ASSISTANCE PRE-CHARGE

Under this scheme, you will need to complete forms CDS1 and CDS2. The scheme is means tested and covers a client who seeks advice in connection with a matter for which he is under investigation but has not been charged. It also covers representation in connection with an investigation by a non-police body such as the Department of Work and Pensions. Clients in receipt of certain welfare benefits (including income-based job seeker's allowance and income support) qualify automatically under the means test.

14.5 ADVICE AND ASSISTANCE POST-CHARGE

This scheme is reserved for those clients who require preparatory advice and assistance from a solicitor having had criminal proceedings instituted against them after having been charged or issued with a summons.

Post-charge advice and assistance will, in most cases, be covered under the terms of representation order, which is dealt with at section 14.8 below. As your client should apply for a representation order on Form A as soon as possible and where one or more of the interest of justice test under Schedule 3, Access to Justice Act 1999 is satisfied, the cost of all such work (save for that undertaken at the police station under the police station representation scheme) through to representing the client in court will be covered by the representation order. The areas of work typically covered under post-charge advice and assistance include:

- assisting the client to complete an application for a representation order on Form A;
- drafting initial correspondence to the police and CPS; and
- taking a proof of evidence.

If the representation order is refused, one hour's work can be claimed for up to the date of the refusal.

14.6 REPRESENTATION IN COURT

A defendant charged with a criminal offence who wishes to be represented by a solicitor in court must either seek representation by the court duty solicitor or apply to the court for a representation order or pay privately.

A public information booklet on the various publicly funded schemes called *A Practical Guide to Criminal Defence Services* is available from the Legal Service Commission's website at: http://www.legalservices.gov.uk.

online
resource
centre

14.7 DUTY SOLICITOR SCHEME

Representation at court by a duty solicitor is completely free and is not subject to the interests of justice test. However, under the Court Duty Solicitor Scheme, there are certain matters that a duty solicitor can undertake and certain matters which the duty solicitor cannot cover.

A duty solicitor can represent:

- anyone in custody;
- anyone charged or summonsed in connection with an imprisonable offence;
- anyone applying for bail (unless they have previously used a duty solicitor for a previous application);
- anyone at risk of imprisonment for failing to pay a fine or failing to obey a court order.

A duty solicitor may not represent someone in connection with:

- a trial;
- a hearing to commit a case to the Crown Court;
- an application for bail (if they have used a duty solicitor for a previous application); and
- a non-imprisonable offence (unless they are in custody).

A duty solicitor is most likely to represent those appearing before a magistrates' court for the first time or those who wish to plead guilty and be sentenced before the magistrates in connection with a summary-only or either-way offence. The duty solicitor cannot conduct a trial on behalf of an individual, who must either represent himself or seek an adjournment to enable him to see a solicitor who can then apply for a representation order.

14.8 REPRESENTATION ORDERS

A representation order is granted by a magistrates' court and is subject to the 'interests of justice' test. An application for a representation can also be granted by the Crown Court, however, as all defendants appear initially before a magistrates' court, it is most likely to be granted by magistrates.

A copy of a blank application for a representation order is included at the end of this chapter. It is known as Form A. The form is completed on behalf of the applicant by the solicitor either at the police station following a decision to charge or at court or in the office before his client makes his initial appearance before magistrates.

Representation orders are currently available regardless of a defendant's means. This is set to change (see 14.14). There is no liability to pay a contribution. However, if the case is to proceed to the Crown Court there is a risk of the court imposing a recovery of defence costs order (RDCO) in the event of conviction.

14.8.1 HOW DO YOU APPLY FOR A REPRESENTATION ORDER?

Application is made to the court in which your client is due to appear. You need to complete Form A and forward it to the relevant court with a covering letter. An application for a representation order is usually processed quickly. When appearing before the court, a solicitor can check with the magistrates' legal adviser if the application has been granted. If there is insufficient time to submit a written application in advance, a solicitor can hand in a completed application at the hearing or can submit a completed form as part of an oral application before the court.

14.8.2 WHAT DOES A REPRESENTATION ORDER COVER?

A representation order covers the entire proceedings in the magistrates' courts. It can be extended to cover an appeal from magistrates in relation to a decision regarding bail or in relation to an appeal against conviction or sentence.

Advocates must be careful to ensure that a representation order is extended to cover proceedings in the Crown Court in relation to an either-way matter where mode of trial has been determined in favour of the Crown Court, if a 'through order' was not made at the outset. For indictable-only cases, the order will cover representation in the Crown Court. A representation order therefore covers the work necessary to prepare a case for trial or plea in mitigation if your client is to plead guilty in either the magistrates' court or in the Crown Court. Representation orders which cover the Crown Court extend to obtaining advice on the making of an appeal against conviction and/or sentence to the Court of Appeal. Costs are subsequently claimed on a standard fee or non-standard fee basis depending on the nature of the case. The claim is submitted on the appropriate form to the Criminal Defence Service.

14.8.3 WHAT IS THE CRITERION FOR GRANTING A REPRESENTATION ORDER?

In order to obtain a representation order, the applicant must convince the court that his case merits representation by a solicitor. The 'merits' test is satisfied if the court concludes that representation is necessary, in the interests of justice.

The Access to Justice Act 1999 Sch. 3, para. 5 provides that if any of the following factors apply, the interests of justice test is met and a defendant is entitled to a representation order:

- The offence is such that if proved the defendant is likely to lose his liberty or livelihood or suffer serious damage to his reputation (the form prompts you to include any subsisting sentences or penalties the applicant might be subject to).
- The case involves a substantial question of law.
- The accused is under a mental or physical disability or has inadequate knowledge of English such that they are unable to follow the proceedings or put their case.
- The defence will involve the tracing and interviewing of witnesses or expert cross-examination of a prosecution witness.
- Legal representation is desirable in the interests of someone other than the accused.

14.9 ARTICULATING THE INTERESTS OF JUSTICE TEST

A trainee solicitor will frequently be asked to complete an application for a representation order on behalf of a client.

How do you articulate the interests of justice test? Form A specifies the factors that are included in the interest of justice test. It is not enough to simply tick the relevant box. Each factor in the interest of justice criteria is listed with a blank box against it for articulation. It is important that you consider the various factors in support of the interests of justice test with care and that you apply them to the individual circumstances of your client's case. You should try to articulate as many of the factors as you can and include as much detail on the application as possible. This maximises your chances of having a representation order granted. The articulation of the various factors is considered below.

14.9.1 LOSS OF LIBERTY

Obviously the more serious the offence, the more likely it is that your client could go to prison if convicted. There must be more than simply a theoretical risk of imprisonment, there must in fact be a real and practical risk. You need to make this clear on the application form. Many offences carry a theoretical risk of imprisonment, such as theft. However, a first time conviction for theft of a modest amount would not result in a sentence of imprisonment.

In *R v Liverpool Magistrates, ex p. McGhee* [1993] Crim LR 609, the Divisional Court confirmed that a community order does not satisfy the loss of liberty ground, but the possibility of such an order may be relevant in satisfying the interests of justice as the factors in Sch. 3, para. 5 were not exhaustive.

Research the relevant sentencing guidelines for the offence charged and consider whether there are any aggravating features in the offence which makes a custodial sentence likely. This might include where your client has previous convictions for an offence of a similar nature or he committed this offence while subject to bail in connection with other criminal matters. Sentencing law and practise is considered in Part VI; however, a good source of information as to the likely sentence your client might receive in the event of conviction are the Magistrates' Court Sentencing Guidelines 2004 (extracts from which are reproduced with the kind permission of the Magistrates' Association at Appendix 4).

The guidelines cover the vast majority of summary-only and either-way offences and indicate the entry point in terms of sentencing for a particular offence. In relation to an offence of burglary for example, the guidelines require the magistrates to ask whether their maximum power of six months imprisonment is sufficient. You should refer to the guidelines where they assist in establishing your client's likely loss of liberty. Similarly, if your client is subject to a suspended sentence, the risk of a prison sentence in the event of conviction for the new offence becomes more likely. It will be self-evident that virtually all indictable-only offences will enable articulation of this particular ground.

14.9.2 LOSS OF LIVELIHOOD

Does your client stand to lose his job in the event of a conviction? If he does, this needs to be carefully and fully articulated. The likely loss of livelihood should be a direct consequence of conviction or sentence. Articulation of this factor depends on your client's job and the nature of the offence he faces. Clearly, if your client is at risk of a custodial sentence, the chances of him losing his employment are likely to be high. The risk of a job being lost would be particularly high where, for example the offence involves an allegation of theft from an employer or the offence is of a sexual or violent nature and your client's job includes contact with children. Loss of livelihood normally refers to current livelihood. Arguably someone training for a profession may be able to bring themselves within the criteria.

Road traffic offences have the potential to result in loss of livelihood in the event of your client being disqualified from driving. However, they are not among the more serious of criminal offences, and magistrates are reluctant to grant representation orders for driving offences. Assertions that mandatory disqualification from driving will result in a loss of livelihood will be examined critically. A right to representation would not normally be justified where a defendant sought to avoid disqualification under the totting-up disqualification procedure having acquired twelve or more penalty points on his driving licence. Where there is a strong argument for advancing special reasons for avoiding disqualification, the interests of justice may apply.

14.9.3 DAMAGE TO REPUTATION

In the event of conviction, is your client likely to suffer damage to his reputation? If he is, articulate this. Examples might include a conviction in relation to a sexual offence, or a first time conviction for dishonesty or an allegation of perverting the course of justice. You need to be imaginative and the guidance in the Access to Justice Act 1999 refers to serious damage. If your client already has previous conviction for a similar offence or has a conviction for a more serious offence, it will be difficult to argue that he is likely to suffer damage to his reputation. A previous conviction of itself however, does not preclude articulation of this ground where for example, your client has a previous conviction for a minor public order offence but is now charged with theft or a sexual offence. Your client's job and the precise nature of the offence will be relevant to the assessment of loss of reputation.

14.9.4 SUBSTANTIAL QUESTION OF LAW

Does your client's case involve a substantial question of law? If it does, explain in detail what the point of law is. This could include arguments about the definitional elements of the offence where, for example, your client is pleading not guilty to theft claiming that he did not have a dishonest intent as required by *R v Ghosh* [1982] 3 WLR 110. A substantial question of law also involves challenging the admissibility of prosecution evidence. This could include:

- argument as to whether it is appropriate to draw an adverse inference from an accused's silence at the police station under s. 34 Criminal Justice and Public Order Act 1994 (see Chapter 8);

- an application to have a confession excluded under ss. 76 and 78 PACE for breach of Code C (see Chapter 10);

- an application to have identification evidence excluded under s. 78 PACE for breach of Code D (see Chapter 11);

- a dispute as to the admissibility of hearsay evidence (see Chapter 25);

- argument as to the admissibility of evidence of bad character under the Criminal Justice Act 2003 (see Chapter 26).

You must explain precisely the point of law your client's case is likely to give rise to.

14.9.5 INADEQUATE KNOWLEDGE OF ENGLISH; PHYSICAL OR MENTAL DISABILITY

This ground is self-explanatory and will be appropriate where your client has inadequate knowledge of English or is unable to communicate (including lack of literacy) or he suffers from a mental or physical disability. Clearly, it is in the interests of justice for him to be represented by a lawyer.

14.9.6 TRACING AND INTERVIEWING OF DEFENCE WITNESSES

The interests of justice test will be satisfied where your client's case requires potential defence witnesses to be traced and/or interviewed. You should explain on Form A in what way a witness might assist your client's case, by, for example, providing him with an alibi. If a prosecution witness is to be interviewed on behalf of the defendant, this should be undertaken by a solicitor. Explain this in the space provided. You are reminded that it would be an unusual step for a defence solicitor to interview a prosecution witness in advance of trial (see professional conduct rule on this point – Chapter 4, paragraph 4.6.8). This ground can also be used in support of a client's case, where the defence require the services of an expert witness.

14.9.7 EXPERT CROSS-EXAMINATION

This ground does not mean that your client's case involves the cross-examination of an expert witness. This factor is capable of being articulated in relation to any client who is to plead not guilty, as this will trigger the necessity of cross-examining witnesses. Once again, it is important that you explain which witnesses will need to be cross-examined. It might be an expert witness, but it could also be a witness with a purpose of his own to serve or cross-examination of the victim, or an eyewitness or a police officer.

14.9.8 THE INTERESTS OF SOMEONE OTHER THAN THE DEFENDANT

Is it in the interests of someone other than the defendant that he is represented by a solicitor?

This factor often seems to cause confusion. The 'someone other' is largely restricted to those who are directly affected by the proceedings most obviously, witnesses. It would not be appropriate for a vulnerable person such as an elderly eyewitness to a burglary or a child witness to be cross-examined by the defendant. In this situation, it is in the interests of justice for the defendant to be legally represented. Note ss. 34–39 Youth Justice and Criminal Evidence Act 1999 prohibit a defendant from personally cross-examining a complainant in a case involving a sexual offence.

14.9.9 ANY OTHER REASON?

As the interests of justice criteria are not exhaustive, you should use your imagination on this catch-all factor. A not guilty plea of itself probably does not satisfy the test, but if your client's case is to be heard in the Crown Court, it is highly unlikely that he would be able to represent himself adequately, and it is in the interests of justice for him to be legally represented. Also relevant would be if your client is deeply anxious, excessively nervous or has limited intelligence or would disrupt the proceedings. In short, is your client adequately able to represent himself?

14.9.10 GRANTING A REPRESENTATION ORDER

Your client will be granted a representation order where his case satisfies one or more of the interests of justice criteria explained above. Obviously, it is more difficult to satisfy the test where your client is charged with a minor, summary offence, and conversely the interests of justice test is more easily satisfied in connection with an either-way or indictable-only offence. In granting or refusing a representation order, the court must give reasons. Defendants jointly charged in circumstances where there is no conflict of interest between them will normally be assigned the same LSC-contracted solicitor.

14.9.11 APPEALS AGAINST THE REFUSAL OF REPRESENTATION ORDER

Where an application for a representation order is refused, there is no formal appeal procedure. The solicitor can renew the application with further details. The solicitor may consider that an oral application direct to the magistrates is more likely to succeed where there has been a previous refusal of a written application.

14.10 DISBURSEMENTS

You may need to incur disbursements in some criminal cases. This might include obtaining the services of an expert witness, an interpreter or enquiry agent or the transcript of an interview. Solicitors should always seek the prior authorisation of the LSC to incur expenditure in excess of £100 using Form CDS4. You will need to show that the course of action you seek to take is in the best interests of your client and that it is reasonable to incur the disbursement and that the amount to be incurred is reasonable. You should ascertain in advance the amount of expenditure that will be needed. In our first case study, *R v Lenny Whyte* (the complete version of which can be accessed on our Online Resource Centre), you will see that as part of case preparation, Lenny's solicitor obtains the prior authorisation of the LSC to obtain an expert report from Lenny's consultant psychiatrist.

14.11 RECOVERY OF DEFENCE COSTS ORDER

Representation orders are currently granted irrespective of a defendant's means. However, in those cases that are ultimately disposed of in the Crown Court (which will obviously include all indictable offences; either-way matters which have been committed to the Crown Court and an appeal against conviction), your client is obliged to complete a statement of means on Form B. In the event of your client being convicted before the Crown Court, the Criminal Defence Service (Recovery of Defence Costs Orders) Regulations 2004 requires a court to impose an order requiring the offender to pay all or some part of his legal costs.

14.12 ACQUITTED DEFENDANTS

Defendants who are acquitted and who have incurred expenditure in their defence are generally entitled to an award of costs from central funds under s. 16 Prosecution of Offences Act 1985. Such orders are at the discretion of the court (magistrates'/Crown/Divisional/ Court of Appeal) but should normally be awarded unless it is felt that the accused brought suspicion on himself by his own conduct and misled the prosecution into thinking the evidence against him was stronger than it in fact was. Guidance can be found in *Practice Direction* (*Costs: Criminal Proceedings*) [2004] 2 All ER 1070. A legally aided acquitted defendant's costs will be met under the representation order.

14.13 WASTED COSTS

In circumstances where a solicitor (defence or CPS) has wasted the court's time by an improper, unreasonable or negligent act or omission, the power exists under s. 19 Prosecution of Offences Act 1985 for a court to make an order for the wasted costs involved.

14.14 FUTURE OF PUBLIC FUNDING

Criminal Defence Service Act 2006

Funding of criminal defence services is set to change in the future. The CDSA 2006 received its Royal Assent in March 2006. The Act will re-introduce means testing for criminal legal aid in the magistrates' court. The projected date for implementation is Autumn 2006. In summary, its effect will be as follows:

- Representation orders will continue to be granted subject to the interest of justice criteria.

- Determination of the merits test will cease to be exercised in a judicial capacity by a legal adviser. In future, it will become an administrative function conducted by court staff under an agreement with the LSC.

- There will be a right of appeal to a magistrates' court where refusal to grant a representation order is based on the interests of justice test.

- There will be a two-tier scheme, under which defendants will apply for legal aid in the form of a non-means-tested advice and assistance scheme which will cover the first hearing. Thereafter the defendant will need a representation order and will have sufficient time to provide evidence of his financial position.

- Representation orders granted in connection with magistrates' court proceedings will be subject to means testing in addition to the interests of justice test. Under the published draft regulations, there will be an initial filter based on annual gross income. Applicants with an annual gross income of £34,000 or above will be ineligible, while those with a lower income threshold of £19,000 will be eligible. The annual gross income figure is subject to a formula which factors in whether the applicant lives alone or has dependant children. Where an applicant's gross annual income, based on the formula, is between £19,000 and £34,000, a full means test will then be carried out to assess their disposable annual income, net of income tax, national insurance and making allowance for dependants, housing costs and the like. If the applicant's disposable income is less than £3,156 per annum, the means test is satisfied. Applicants in receipt of various welfare benefits will qualify automatically in terms of their means.

- The means test will be assessed administratively by court staff. While there is a right of review, there is no right of appeal against refusal based on the means test.

- The position in relation to Crown Court is still unclear. The Government favours a means test in the Crown Court which would see income-based contributions being made by some defendants. Recovery of Defence Costs Orders would remain where the case cost more than the contribution.

- Acquitted legally aided defendants would be entitled to recover any contributions they had made.

We will bring you any significant developments as regards the Criminal Defence Service Act 2006 via the updating pages of our Online Resource Centre. For a detailed consideration of the new scheme, see the Framework documents at http://www.official-documents.co.uk.

online resource centre

The Carter Report

In spite of the changes to the public funding of criminal cases proposed in the Criminal Defence Service Act 2006, the Government is also considering more radical medium to long term reform of publicly funded criminal defence services. In its report *Procurement of Criminal Defence Services: Market Based Reform* published in February 2006 the working group chaired by Lord Carter has advocated a radical departure from the present arrangements which would be phased in over three years. In the first year there would be fixed pricing for all criminal legal aid work, including that provided at the police station, magistrates' courts and Crown Courts. The second year would see the introduction of a managed market awarding contracts to efficient and good quality providers of legal advice and representation in criminal cases. The third year would see managed price competition between firms.

The proposed move to a more market based provision of publicly funded criminal defence services is seen as an attempt to cut back on the £1.2 billion that it spent in England and Wales on criminal legal aid.

LSC Peer review

To ensure that franchised criminal legal aid firms are working in an effective and efficient way, the LSC is introducing a system of peer review to replace the traditional audit of case files. The advice given at all stages of a firm's representation of a criminal client will be peer reviewed against a benchmark of quality issues, including whether a fee earner was appropriately experienced when advising the client and a detailed assessment of the quality of the advice and supporting documentation at all stages of the case, from initial interview through to trial representation.

14.15 EARLY STAGES OF THE CRIMINAL LITIGATION PROCESS AND INITIAL APPEARANCE

Having considered Chapters 2 and 3, you will already have some idea of how a criminal case progresses. Having been charged or summonsed, your client will have a date on which he will make his first appearance before a magistrates' court. You will therefore be working towards this date. Typical steps that need to be undertaken in this regard include:

- opening a file;
- conducting an initial interview (if your firm did not represent the defendant at the police station);
- submitting an application for a representation order;
- requesting advance information from the CPS;
- anticipating any problems in relation to bail.

14.15 OPENING A FILE

Your firm will be required to open a file in relation to each new client and to complete a standard CDS1 form. Every file has to be allocated a Unique File Number (UFN), a requirement under the General Criminal Contract. All fee-earning time spent on the matter must be recorded.

14.17 INITIAL INTERVIEW

You will need to undertake an initial interview with your client. This may already have been done at the police station.

The initial interview is important for obtaining information while events are still fresh in your client's mind. You will need to obtain all of your client's personal details as well as an accurate list of previous convictions and details of his financial circumstances. If your client has been charged and released on police bail or has received a summons, he might bring the summons or charge sheet with him to the initial interview so that you can check the precise nature of the allegations he is facing.

Criminal clients can be somewhat reticent. Many come from deprived backgrounds with limited education and social functioning. You will need to ask probing questions to take a detailed statement from your client about the circumstances of the offence. This statement will subsequently be typed up into your client's proof of evidence. If your client is indicating that he may have witnesses who can support his case, it is important to obtain full details as steps need to be taken promptly to try and locate and interview potential witnesses.

During the first interview, you will need to discuss funding issues with your client. If representation in court is required a representation order will have to be applied for. You will need to assist your client to complete the application. Your client may well be entitled to have this initial interview funded under the post-charge Advice and Assistance Scheme (see paragraph 14.5 above) where he comes to see you at the office having been charged or summonsed.

General advice about the likely progress of the case and possible plea/sentence might be offered to your client at this stage. Unless the matter is very clear cut however, you should wait until you are in possession of the prosecution's evidence before offering any firm advice as to plea.

At the conclusion of your initial interview, you will typically

- submit an application for a representation order;
- write to your client confirming his instructions;
- request disclosure of the prosecution's 'used' material;
- contact any potential defence witnesses with a view to taking a statement.

Each of these is briefly considered below.

14.17.1 SUBMIT APPLICATION FOR A REPRESENTATION ORDER

The application for a representation order should be sent to the magistrates' court at which your client is to appear with an accompanying letter. If time does not permit the submission of a written application (this occurs most frequently where a defendant is charged and remanded into police custody pending first appearance before a magistrates' court), the solicitor may hand to the court a completed Form A and make an oral application.

14.17.2 WRITE TO YOUR CLIENT CONFIRMING HIS INSTRUCTIONS

Having undertaken an initial interview with your client you will need to draft a written statement, or proof of evidence, based on what your client has told you. This draft proof of evidence should be sent to your client for consideration. Your client should be asked to amend where necessary and sign and date it if he agrees with its content. The proof of evidence will be an important source of information to the advocate who represents your client in court. Along with the draft proof of evidence, you will need to write to your client to confirm his instructions and the advice you have given him. Further, in accordance with Rule 2 of the Solicitor's Code of Conduct you will need to send your client a client-care letter.

14.17.3 REQUEST DISCLOSURE OF THE PROSECUTION'S 'USED' MATERIAL

The rules relating to the pre-trial disclosure of evidence against a defendant are of supreme importance. The rules were briefly introduced in Chapter 3 and the entire process of pre-trial disclosure is considered in greater detail in Chapter 17.

Notwithstanding the classification of offence (summary/either-way/indictable), the CPS will be in possession of 'used' material at an early stage in the proceedings. Used material is evidence which the prosecution intends to use against the defendant at trial. In accordance with the Magistrates' Court (Advance Information) Rules (Part 21 Crim PR), the accused is entitled to seek advance information from the CPS. The CPS is required to serve either copies of the statements of the proposed prosecution witnesses or less commonly a summary of the evidence. The defence solicitor can also request a copy of any tape recorded interview and confirmation of his client's previous convictions. Strictly speaking, the advance information rules apply only to either-way offences. However, the CPS also routinely makes disclosure in summary and indictable-only cases, before further comprehensive disclosure is made later in the proceedings.

Advance information is not always available at the defendant's first appearance in connection with an either-way/summary matter. Consequently the defence solicitor is entitled to ask for an adjournment to enable him to be provided with the necessary statements and to give you proper time to consider them. The importance of obtaining advance information in all but the very simple and clearest of cases cannot be overstated. You will be unable to properly advise your client on the appropriateness of his plea or indeed, which mode of trial to choose in connection with an either-way offence in the event of a not guilty plea, unless you are in possession of and have evaluated the advance information.

At an early stage, you will need to write a letter to the CPS confirming you act for a particular defendant and requesting compliance with the rules on disclosure.

On receipt of advance information you will have a clearer idea of the strength of the evidence against your client and whether the prosecution is likely to discharge its burden of proof on the charges laid against your client. Your client will need to be taken through the advance information, and a further statement should be taken from him dealing with any issues arising. You may need to question your client carefully, gauging his reaction to the statements. You will need to have a good understanding of the rules of evidence to be able to properly evaluate the case against your client. If, in your assessment, the strength of the evidence against your client is strong, you might use this interview to discuss with your client the advantages of an early guilty plea.

As a result of your assessment of the evidence in the case and discussions with your client you might approach the CPS to see if they may be willing to reconsider the decision to prosecute or to reduce the charges or to conditionally caution your cilent. A conditional caution as an alternative to a prosecution is considered in Chapter 13.

14.17.4 APPROACHING POSSIBLE DEFENCE WITNESSES

Any potential defence witness should be approached as soon as possible while events are still fresh in their memories. Where a witness's whereabouts is unknown or their identity needs to be confirmed, an enquiry agent may be instructed. Witness statements should be taken in the absence of the defendant and without the witness seeing any prosecution witness statements in advance. It is important that you obtain the witness's honest, unrehearsed account of the events witnessed.

14.18 INITIAL APPEARANCE BEFORE COURT

The procedure at the initial appearance before the magistrates is depends on the classification of the offence(s) charged and the preparedness of the parties.

Having been charged with an offence your client's initial appearance before magistrates will either be before a remand court, an early administrative hearing (EAH) court or an early first hearing (EFH) court.

Unless the case is straightforward, your client's initial appearance will result in an adjournment. It is likely that your client's application for a representation order will be decided at his first appearance, and where the case is adjourned, the court will decide whether to release your client on unconditional or conditional bail or to remand him in custody.

14.18.1 EARLY FIRST HEARING (EFH)

Cases that are likely to be listed for an EFH are straightforward summary-only or either-way offences where the police anticipate a guilty plea will be entered.

Having spoken with his solicitor before coming to court or indeed at court (most probably the duty solicitor), the defendant may not wish to or be advised to enter a guilty plea at this early stage. Consequently, the defendant's initial appearance is likely to be adjourned with a request being made for the disclosure of full advance information.

14.18.2 **EARLY ADMINISTRATIVE HEARINGS (EAH)**

Early administrative hearings will cover indictable-only cases and other offences where the plea at this early stage is uncertain. Having consulted a solicitor, unless the matter is uncomplicated and a guilty plea can be entered on this first appearance, the matter is likely to be adjourned for the service of advance information. Where an adjournment is necessary, your client will either be remanded on bail or in custody.

14.18.3 **REMAND COURT**

Appearance before a remand court will include all defendants who appear before magistrates in custody. This may be because the police have denied the defendant bail having charged him with an offence. The law relating to court bail is considered in Chapter 15. It should be obvious that a defendant appearing before a court in connection with an indictable-only offence is more likely to be making his first appearance in custody because of the seriousness of the offence.

KEY POINT SUMMARY

- Be able to differentiate between the various funding schemes for the different criminal defence services that are available to a client.
- When articulating the interest of justice criteria for a representation order, complete as many of the grounds on Form A as you consider apply to your client's case.
- Appreciate that if a case is to go to the Crown Court, your client will need to provide a statement of his means using Form B.
- Understand the importance of keeping and maintaining accurate file notes and efficient time records on a client's file.
- Use the initial interview with your client to take a detailed statement from him and to apply for appropriate funding.
- Do not be tempted to advise your client as to his plea at this early stage unless the matter is very straightforward and clear-cut. Remember you are entitled to be served with full particulars of the prosecution's evidence to be used against your client. This may necessitate an adjournment of the initial hearing before a magistrates' court.

SELF-TEST QUESTIONS

Case studies:

R v William Hardy
R v Lenny Whyte
R v Roger Martin (web-based only)

You are familiar with the issues in relation to *R v William Hardy* and *R v Lenny Whyte*. Take the information from each of them and try to complete an application for a representation order on behalf of each of them. You will find a completed application for a representation order in Appendix 1 so far as Lenny Whyte is concerned and in Appendix 2 in relation to William Hardy. Roger Martin's application for a representation order can be found in the case study section of our Online Resource Centre.

    The complete version of all the case studies can be accessed on our Online Resource Centre where you can see all the steps described in the second part of this chapter (including initial files notes and early correspondence) illustrated on the solicitor's file.

online resource centre

online resource centre

APPLICATION FOR THE RIGHT TO REPRESENTATION IN CRIMINAL PROCEEDINGS

FORM A

I apply for the right to representation for the purposes of criminal proceedings in accordance with the Access to Justice Act 1999 and the Criminal Defence Service (General) (No.2) Regulations 2001

1. Personal details

1a. Surname

1b. Forenames

1c. Title (Mr,Mrs,Ms,Miss or another)

1d. Date of birth

1e. Home address

1f. Present address (if different from above)

2. Case Details

2a. What charges have been brought against you? Describe briefly what it is that you are accused of doing; e.g. theft of £10 worth of CDs or assault on a neighbour

2b. Are there any co-defendants in this matter?

No/Yes (if yes give their names)

2c. Give reasons why you and your co-defendants cannot be represented by the same solicitors

3. The Court Proceedings

3a. I am due to appear before

The _____ court

Date _____ at _____ am/pm

or

3b. I appeared before

The _____ court

Date _____ at _____ am/pm

Crown Court Form 6131 (also known as Form A) - w3 - (4.02) Application for the Right to Representation in Criminal Proceedings

And

| My case has been sent to the Crown Court for trial under Section 51 of the Crime and Disorder Act 1998 | |

| My case has been transferred to the Crown Court for trial | |

(tick whichever applies)

| I was committed for trial to the Crown Court | |

| I was convicted and/or* sentenced and I wish to appeal against the conviction/sentence* to the Crown Court/Court of Appeal/House of Lords*
(*Delete as appropriate) | |

| I was convicted and committed for sentence to the Crown Court | |

| A retrial has been ordered under Section 7 of the Criminal Appeal Act 1968 | |

| Other (please specify nature of hearing) | |

4. Outstanding matters

If there are any other *outstanding* criminal charges or cases against you, give details including the court where you are due to appear.

5. Reasons for wanting representation

To avoid the possibility of your application being delayed, or publicly funded representation being refused because the court does not have enough information about the case, you must complete the rest of this form. When deciding whether to grant publicly funded representation the court will need to know why it is in the interests of justice for you to be represented. If you need help in completing the form you should speak to a solicitor.

Details	Reasons for grant or refusal (for court use only)
5a. It is likely that I will lose my liberty (*you should consider seeing a solicitor before answering this question*)		
5b. I am currently subject to a sentence that is suspended or non-custodial that if breached may allow the court to deal with me for the original offence. (*Please give details*)		

5c. It is likely that I will lose my livelihood

5d. It is likely that I will suffer serious damage to my reputation

5e. A substantial question of law is involved.
(*You will need the help of a solicitor to answer this question*)

(Please give authorities to be quoted with law reports references)

5f. I shall be unable to understand the court proceedings or state my own case because:
i) My understanding of English is inadequate*
ii) I suffer from a disability*
(**Delete as appropriate*)

Details	Reason for grant or refusal (for court use only)

5g. Witnesses have to be traced and/or interviewed on my behalf (*State circumstances*)

5h. The case involves expert cross examination of a prosecution witness (*give brief details*)

5i. It is in someone else's interests that I am represented

5j. Any other reasons (*Give full particulars*)

6. Legal Representation

a) If you do not give the name of a solicitor, the court will select a solicitor for you.
b) You must tell the solicitor that you have named him.
c) If you have been charged together with another person or persons, the court may assign a solicitor other than the solicitor of your choice.

> The solicitor I wish to act for me is:

> Give the firm's name and address (if known)

Declaration to be completed by the legal representative

[The legal representative may wish to confirm with the Legal Services Commission the status of the above named solicitor should he/she not be sure of the above named solicitor's authorisation to provice publicly funded representation]

I,..., representing the above named applicant, certify that the named solicitor above is authorised to provide representation under a crime franchise contract, or a general criminal contract, or an individual case contract.

I understand that only firms with a general criminal contract or individual case contract may provide representation in the magistrates' court.

or

I,..., representing the above named applicant, certify that the named solicitor above is employed by the Legal Services Commission in a Public Defender Office and is authorised to provide representation.

Signed...Date..

7. Declaration

> If you knowingly make a statement which is false, or knowingly withhold information, you may be prosecuted.
>
> If convicted, you may be sent to prison for up to three months or be fined or both (section 21 Access to Justice Act 1999)

I apply for representation for the proceedings set out in Section 3 of this form.

I understand that should my case proceed to the Crown Court or any higher court, the court may order that I pay for some or all of the costs of representation incurred in the proceedings by way of a Recovery of Defence Costs Order.
I understand that should my case proceed to the Crown Court or any higher court, I will have to furnish details of my means to the court and/or the Legal Services Commission.

Signed..dated.......................................

FOR COURT USE ONLY

> Any additional factors considered when determining the application, including any information given orally.

Decision on Interests of Justice Test

> I have considered all available details of all the charges and it/is not in the interests of justice that representation be granted for the following reasons:

Signed...Appropriate Officer

Date..

To be completed where right to representation extends to Crown Court

Statement of means Form B given to defendant on..........................(date)

Indicate type of case:
Sent case under s. 51 Crime and Disorder Act 1998
Transferred for trial
Committal for trial/sentence*
Appeal against conviction/sentence*
Retrial under s. 7 of the Criminal Appeal Act 1968
Other (specify).....................................
(* Delete as appropriate)

First date of hearing at Crown Court...

FIGURE 14.1

ADVICE AND ASSISTANCE

- Post-charge or summons, client requires preparatory advice, including:
    - completing application for representation order on Form A;
    - taking proof of evidence;
    - writing correspondence to the police, CPS, etc.
- Eligibility under the 'interests of justice' test.

REPRESENTATION ORDER

- Application to magistrates' court on Form A.
- Eligibility under the 'interests of justice' test (Sch. 3, Access to Justice Act 1999) where the defendant:
    - is likely to lose his liberty; or
    - is likely to lose livelihood; or
    - is likely to suffer serious damage to his reputation; or
    - the case involves a substantial question of law; or
    - is under a physical or mental disability; or
    - has inadequate knowledge of English; or
    - the defence case involves the tracing and interviewing of witnesses; or
    - the defence case involves the expert cross-examination of a prosecution witness; or
    - legal representation is desirable in the interests of someone other than the accused.
- Where granted, the order covers:
    - summary offence, the entire proceedings in magistrates' court including an appeal if extended;
    - either-way offence proceedings in magistrates' court and in the Crown Court if a 'through' order is granted;
    - indictable-only offence, entire proceedings in the Crown Court and drafting ground for leave to appeal to the Court of Appeal.
- Defendant will be required to submit a statement of means (Form B) if his case is to be tried on indictment as the Crown Court judge is required to consider making a recovery of defence costs order in the event of conviction.

15 THE LAW AND PRACTICE RELATING TO COURT BAIL

15.1   INTRODUCTION

Whenever a magistrates' court or Crown Court adjourns a case (which it will invariably have to do in criminal proceedings), the court will be required to decide whether the defendant should be remanded on bail or remanded in custody during the period of the adjournment.

The only instance where a court need not remand a defendant is where a defendant appears before the court on a summons and has not previously been remanded.

Bail in criminal proceedings may be granted by the police or by the court. In this chapter, we are concerned with the grant of bail by a court. Bail can be granted of course by the police during an ongoing investigation into an offence and when a suspect is charged with a criminal offence (ss. 38 and 47 PACE 1984). The granting of police bail is addressed in Chapter 7. Many of the principles that govern the grant of bail by a court similarly apply to the grant of bail by the custody officer under s. 38 PACE.

In this chapter we examine:

- the grounds upon which bail might be refused;
- the factors a court can have regard to in determining the question of bail;
- the procedure at a contested application for bail;
- appeals against bail decisions;
- prospective changes to bail under the Criminal Justice Act 2003 (CJA);
- the relationship between bail and Article 5 ECHR.

Rules of court relevant to bail are contained in Parts 18–21 Criminal Procedure Rules.

15.2 WHAT IS BAIL?

Bail is the release of the defendant, subject to a duty to surrender to the court at a specified time and date. Bail may be granted to a defendant unconditionally or with conditions attached.

The provisions governing the granting of bail by the courts are contained within the Bail Act 1976. For some defendants the need to secure bail assumes far greater importance than the final outcome of the proceedings. In most instances a defendant's bail status will be a matter of negotiated agreement between the prosecution and the defence. Where a defendant's desire to enjoy bail conflicts with the prosecution's desire to see a remand in custody, a contested bail hearing will need to take place before a court.

The majority of bail hearings are conducted in magistrates' courts. A decision by the police to withhold bail following a decision to charge in accordance with s. 38 PACE 1984 provides a sound indication that bail may be opposed by the Crown Prosecution Service (CPS) when the defendant makes his initial appearance before a court. For a court, the enquiry into bail requires a speculative exercise. Bail is essentially a question of trust. Can this court trust this defendant if it releases him on bail?

15.3 A RIGHT TO BAIL?

Section 4 of the Bail Act 1976 gives the defendant a *prima facie* right to bail when charged with a criminal offence. There is said to be a presumption in favour of bail. Where the prosecution seeks to rebut this presumption by objecting to the defendant being granted bail, the court will invite both the prosecution and the defence to make submissions on the matter. In deciding whether the accused should be granted bail the court will carefully consider the grounds for objecting to bail articulated by the prosecution and challenged by the defence.

The presumption in favour of bail under s. 4 Bail Act 1976 applies solely to the grant of bail by a court post-charge and prior to conviction during all stages of the proceedings. The presumption continues to apply post-conviction where a court adjourns the case for the preparation of pre-sentencing reports. Strictly speaking, s. 4 Bail Act 1976 has no application where:

- the decision to grant bail taken by a custody officer when the defendant is initially charged at the police station – s. 38 PACE (see Chapter 7);

- upon conviction and sentence of an offender, whether by magistrates or in the Crown Court, where that person intends to appeal against conviction or sentence;

- magistrates have convicted a defendant but have chosen to commit him to the Crown Court for sentence.

Although the presumption in favour of bail does not apply in these instances, the court retains discretion to grant bail. The criteria under the Bail Act 1976 are likely to be followed in these instances. In what circumstances can the right to bail be witheld?

15.4 SECTION 25 CRIMINAL JUSTICE AND PUBLIC ORDER ACT 1994 (CJPOA)

Section 25 CJPOA provides that where the accused is charged with or convicted of murder, attempted murder, manslaughter, rape or attempted rape and has been previously convicted of any of these offences, they should only be granted bail where there are 'exceptional circumstances' for doing so. In the case of an earlier manslaughter conviction, it must have resulted in a sentence of imprisonment. Section 25 effectively creates a presumption against the grant of bail in these circumstances. The question of whether s. 25 can be applied compatibly with Article 5 of the ECHR has been considered by the Law Commission (see paragraph 15.20).

15.5 GROUNDS FOR DENYING BAIL IN CONNECTION WITH IMPRISONABLE OFFENCES

Where the accused is charged with an imprisonable offence, Part 1 of Sch. 1, para. 2 to the 1976 Act provides that the accused need not be granted bail where the court is satisfied that there are *substantial grounds for believing* that if released on bail (conditional or otherwise), the accused would:

1(a) fail to surrender to custody; or

(b) commit an offence while on bail; or

(c) interfere with witnesses or otherwise obstruct the course of justice,
whether in relation to himself or any other person.

Schedule 1, Part 1 further provides:

2A The defendant need not be granted bail if—

(a) the offence is an indictable offence or an offence triable either way; and

(b) it appears to the court that he was on bail in criminal proceedings on the date of the offence.

(3) The defendant need not be granted bail if the court is satisfied that he should be kept in custody for his own protection, or if he is a child or young person, for his own welfare.

(4) The defendant need not be granted bail if he is already serving a custodial sentence.

(5) The defendant need not be granted bail where the court is satisfied that it has not been practicable to obtain sufficient information to take a decision in relation to bail.

(6) Having been released on bail in connection with the same offence, the defendant has been arrested for absconding or breaking conditions of bail.

(7) Where the case has been adjourned for enquiries or a report, it appears to the court that it would be impracticable to complete the enquiries or make a report unless the accused is kept in custody.

In practical terms, the first three substantive grounds set out in para. 2(1)(a)–(c) of Sch. 1 are the most important and account for 95 per cent or more of refusals of bail. Given the frequency with which these grounds are commonly cited, we consider them in detail in paragraph 15.9.

Whilst many of the other grounds contained in para. 2 of Sch. 1 are self-explanatory, we briefly consider some of them.

15.5.1 THE OFFENCE IS AN INDICTABLE OFFENCE OR AN OFFENCE TRIABLE EITHER WAY AND IT APPEARS TO THE COURT THAT THE DEFENDANT WAS ON BAIL IN CRIMINAL PROCEEDINGS ON THE DATE OF THE OFFENCE

Paragraph 2A was inserted into the Bail Act by s. 26 Criminal Justice and Public Order Act 1994. Consider the following example: X is presently on police bail in connection with an allegation of vehicle interference (summary only). He has been arrested and charged with burglary (an either way) and appears before magistrates. At the date of the burglary offence, X was on police bail, therefore, in accordance with s. 26 CJPOA, the court need not grant him bail. Section 26 applies to the grant of bail by a court and by the police. The effect of s. 26 is that whilst a court may still grant X bail in the exercise if its discretion, X cannot claim to have a right to bail in these circumstances. Paragraph 2A of Schedule 1 is prospectively repeated by the CJA 2003 (see paragraph 15.6.1).

15.5.2 REMANDED IN CUSTODY FOR HIS OWN PROTECTION

A defendant is likely to be remanded in custody for his own protection where he poses a danger to himself or is charged with an offence that excites considerable public revulsion, e.g. child sexual abuse/paedophilia.

15.5.3 THE DEFENDANT IS ALREADY SERVING A CUSTODIAL SENTENCE

Clearly a defendant who is already serving a custodial sentence for another crime cannot expect to be granted bail in connection with new matters and should not seek to make a bail application in such circumstances. The court should, however, ascertain the earliest date of release to ensure a defendant is not remanded in custody beyond that date.

15.5.4 INSUFFICIENT DETAILS TO GRANT BAIL

There may be instances where the police have charged a suspect but still have insufficient details as to their identity and address. In these circumstances a court is entitled to refuse bail until such time as the information is available.

15.5.5 POST CONVICTION – ADJOURNMENT FOR REPORTS

The ground for denying bail covers the situation where a defendant has been convicted of an offence or has pleaded guilty, but there are concerns that the defendant may not co-operate with the probation service in the preparation of a pre-sentence report. The obvious instance of this would be in the case of a defendant who is unable to offer a fixed address to which he can be bailed and by means of which contact can be made with him.

15.5.6 POSITIVE DRUG TESTING

A further new ground for refusing bail is provided by s 19(4) CJA 2003, inserting s. 6B into the Bail Act 1976. Bail need not be granted in the circumstances specified under this section unless the court is satisfied there is no significant risk of his committing an offence while on bail (whether subject to conditions or not). The relevant circumstances are as follows:

- the accused must be over 18;
- the accused must have tested positive for the presence of a Class A drug;

- the accused must be charged with a Class A related drug offence or the court must have substantial grounds for believing that the misuse of a Class A drug caused or contributed to the offence with which the accused is charged; and
- the accused refuses to (a) undergo an assessment of his dependency on or propensity to misuse drugs, or (b) having undergone such an assessment, and having had follow-up action proposed to address his dependency/propensity, refuses to undergo such follow-up.

Where bail is granted under s. 6B, it must be subject to a condition that the defendant undergoes an initial assessment or participates in any follow-up treatment. This provision came into force nationally on 31 March 2006. The power of the police to take a drug sample at the police station and to require a defendant to undergo an initial assessment where he has tested positive is considered in Chapter 7 (7.14.3).

15.6 SUBSTANTIATING THE GROUNDS FOR OPPOSING BAIL – THE STATUTORY FACTORS

The Bail Act 1976, para. 9 of Part 1 of Sch. 1, obliges a court to have regard to a number of factors in determining whether the grounds for withholding bail under paras 2 and 2A are made out. These include:

- the nature and the seriousness of the offence;
- the defendant's character, his record, his associates and community ties;
- the defendant's bail record;
- the strength of the evidence against the defendant.

Many of the factors listed in para. 9 of Sch. 1 Part 1 are self-explanatory. It goes without saying that the more serious the offence, the greater the risk of a custodial sentence being imposed thereby increasing the risk of absconding. In completing the file for the CPS, the police will have provided details of the defendant's past criminal record and personal circumstances. The CPS will therefore be aware of the type of person the defendant is and whether he has family, a job, or other commitments in the area. Clearly the defendant's previous bail record will be of considerable importance to the court.

It is the inter-relationship between the grounds for refusing bail and the applicable factors which determine the grant or refusal of bail. We consider the interplay between grounds and factors in paragraph 15.9, where we look at bail in practice.

15.6.1 CRIMINAL JUSTICE ACT 2003 – CHANGES TO THE GROUNDS FOR REFUSING BAIL

Looking Ahead

The changes relating to bail under the CJA 2003 are designed to make it harder for a court to grant bail to defendant who has been arrested and charged in connection with an imprisonable offence and has previously absconded in the proceedings or has committed a further offence whilst on bail.

Sections 14 and 15 of the Act create a presumption against bail in the circumstances provided for in each section. **These sections are not currently in force**.

Section 14 inserts a new s. 2A into Sch. 1 Part 1 of the Bail Act 1976. It provides that bail may not be granted to an individual aged over 18 who is already on bail on the date of the offence unless there is no significant risk of the defendant committing an offence on bail. In assessing the specific risk under s. 14 as to whether the defendant would commit further offences if released on bail (be it conditional bail or otherwise), the court shall give particular weight (inserting a new para. 9AA) to the fact that the defendant was on bail on the date of the offence. There is no requirement for the offence to be either way or indictable-only. The provisions would therefore cover someone arrested in connection with a summary matter who is already on bail in connection with a separate summary matter.

Similarly, under s. 15 (amending sub-paragraph 6 of Sch. 1 Part 1), bail need not be granted to a person over 18 who it appears, having been released on bail in connection with the proceedings, has failed to surrender to custody unless the court is satisfied that there is no significant risk that if released on bail, the defendant would fail to surrender to custody. In assessing the specific risk as to whether the defendant would fail to surrender to custody, the court is required to give particular weight to the fact that the defendant failed to surrender (inserting a new para. 9AB).

15.7 GROUNDS FOR DENYING BAIL IN RELATION TO NON-IMPRISONABLE OFFENCES

Where the accused is charged with a non-imprisonable offence, Part 2 of Sch. 1 to the Bail Act 1976 provides that the accused need not be granted bail where:

- it appears to the court that having been previously granted bail he has failed to surrender to custody or to comply with his obligations under the bail order; or
- the court is satisfied that the accused should be kept in custody for his own welfare or protection; or
- he is already in custody in respect of any sentence; or
- having been released on bail in connection with the present offence, he has been arrested for absconding or breaking bail conditions and there are substantial grounds for believing that the defendant, if released on bail (whether subject to conditions or not) would fail to surrender to custody, commit an offence on bail or interfere with witnesses or otherwise obstruct the course of justice.

15.8 BAIL CONDITIONS

A defendant may be granted conditional or unconditional bail. It is very common for the court to impose conditions on a defendant when granting of bail. The imposition of bail conditions is governed by s. 3 of the Bail Act 1976. Common bail conditions include:

- reporting to a police station (perhaps two or three times a week or even daily);
- living at a specified/alternative address (this might include a bail hostel);
- avoiding contact with prosecution witnesses;
- avoiding a particular area (this could require a defendant not to enter a particular building or area or go within a specified radius of it);
- avoiding a particular activity (this could include a condition that the defendant does not to drive any motor vehicle or visit licensed premises);
- the imposition of a curfew (requiring a defendant to remain at a specified address between certain hours – for example, 8 pm to 7 am – it could also include a 'doorstep' condition or electronic tagging);
- requiring a surety (see below);
- surrendering a passport;
- a requirement that the defendant keep appointments with his solicitor.

It is important to realise that conditions may only be attached to bail where it is necessary to ensure either that a defendant (s. 8 Bail Act 1976);

- will surrender to custody;
- does not commit further offences;

- does not interfere with witnesses or obstruct the course of justice; or

- for the person's own protection (introduced under s. 13 CJA 2003);

- in the case of a convicted offender, to ensure the accused is available to enable inquiries for the purposes of a report to be made to the court.

To reduce the risk of absconding, a court might choose to impose a condition that the defendant reside at a specified address and/ or report to a police station. A condition that the defendant surrenders his passport and/or provides a surety is also designed to alleviate the risk of an accused failing to surrender.

Where a court is concerned that a defendant might commit further offences, it could impose a curfew. This is useful where, for example, an accused has a habit of committing night-time burglaries.

A condition could also be imposed to prevent the accused from entering a certain place; for example, a supermarket chain where the accused habitually steals merchandise. Where there is a risk of an accused committing further offences because of the accused's relationship with a particular victim, a court could impose a condition that the defendant reside at an alternative address and does not attempt to contact the injured party. These latter two conditions might also be used by a court to prevent an accused from interfering with a witness or obstructing the course of justice.

The decision to impose one or more conditions must be a proportionate measure to alleviate the risk/s identified by the court. In negotiating bail with the CPS, the defence solicitor may need to offer or agree the imposition of conditions. Such conditions must not of course be offered without the consent of the defendant. This is something the solicitor is likely to discuss with the defendant either at the police station or in the holding cell at court. Where an alternative address is likely to be needed the defence solicitor may have to take steps to verify the alternative. If a bail hostel place is to be sought, the defence solicitor will need to liaise with the probation service to see if the defendant would be suitable (a mentally unstable or drug-dependant defendant might not be) and that a place is currently available.

15.8.1 SURETY

A court may require a defendant to provide a suitable surety or sureties before granting him bail. A surety is a person who promises to forfeit a sum of money fixed by the court and known as a recognisance if the defendant fails to attend court as directed. It is the solemn duty of the surety to ensure the defendant's future attendance at court. A recognisance may be entered into before the court itself, a justice of the peace or justices' clerk. The amount of recognisance is determined by the court and depends on the surety's financial resources. If the defendant fails to answer his bail, any surety is liable to forfeit whole or part of his recognisance.

A surety must be a suitable surety. Such a person would need to attend court and give evidence on oath, confirming amongst other things, their financial resources, their character and any previous convictions and their relationship and proximity to the defendant. Such a condition can be imposed where the defendant is at risk of failing to surrender, perhaps because they have links to a foreign jurisdiction.

A court can require a defendant to deposit a security before he is released. This is rather like a bail bond. It requires the defendant or someone on his behalf to deposit a sum of money or other valuable security as a guarantee to ensure attendance. The sum can be forfeited if the defendant absconds.

15.8.2 THE CONSEQUENCES OF FAILING TO ABIDE BY BAIL CONDITIONS

If bail is granted subject to conditions, the importance of abiding by the conditions will be explained to the defendant in court. The defence solicitor ought to reiterate their importance. A failure to abide by any condition of bail can lead to a defendant's arrest and reappearance before the court in custody. A power of arrest is available where a police constable has reasonable grounds for believing that a person has broken, or is about to break a condition of bail. Although the defendant does not commit a further offence by breaking a condition of his bail, the court may decide the defendant has had his chance and shall therefore be remanded in custody for the duration of the proceedings (s. 7 Bail Act 1976).

Where a breach of bail conditions is alleged, the Divisional Court has held, in *R. (on the application of the DPP) v Havering Magistrates' Court* [2001] 2 Cr App R 2, that the breach of proceedings fall within Article 5 of the ECHR. Such proceedings do not invoke the right to a fair trial provisions in Article 6. Although the proceedings do not constitute a trial, the need for hearing to be adversarial with each side enjoying equality of arms, means the prosecution has to adduce some evidence of the breach. In turn the defendant must have a full and fair opportunity to contest the allegation if he denies it.

15.9 BAIL IN PRACTICE

The most often cited reasons for opposing bail before a court are those contained within Sch. 1, para. 2(1)(a)–(c), namely that there is a substantial risk that if released on bail the defendant will:

- abscond; or
- commit further offences; or
- interfere with witnesses and obstruct the course of justice.

These grounds will be further strengthened when ss. 14–15 CJA 2003 come into force (see paragraph 15.6.1).

On a daily basis in magistrates' courts up and down the country there will be arguments centred on the above grounds. It is not enough for the prosecution to suggest that the defendant might abscond, or might commit further offences, there must be substantial grounds for the belief.

Below, we provide some common illustrations of typical arguments put forward by the CPS in opposition to bail being granted using the grounds set out in Sch. 1, para. 2. You will see how the statutory factors listed in para. 9 (see paragraph 15.6) are used to substantiate the prosecution's chosen grounds for opposing the grant of bail. We further consider how the defence advocate might counter the prosecution's objections.

Examples

The risk of absconding from the prosecution perspective

Why can this particular defendant not be trusted to remain in the area? What provides the incentive for the defendant to abscond? Perhaps the defendant is charged with a serious offence and risks a substantial sentence of imprisonment if convicted. Perhaps the defendant is currently subject to a suspended sentence of imprisonment. Even if a prison sentence for the new offence is not a certainty, the fact that a conviction would put him in breach of a suspended prison sentence may provide sufficient incentive. Perhaps the defendant has previous convictions for failing to surrender. If he has poor community ties, let us say no job, no immediate family in the area what incentive is there for the defendant to remain in the jurisdiction of the court?

What the prosecuting advocate might say in court in this regard:

'Sir, you and your colleagues will be aware that this defendant has three previous convictions for absconding.'

'Madam, this defendant was granted bail on an earlier occasion and failed to turn up. He appears before you this morning pursuant to a warrant for his arrest.' (See s. 15 CJA 2003 above.)

'Sir, this defendant's community ties are poor. He is unable to offer a stable address in the area. He has no job and no reason to stay here.'

'The accused is a foreign national whose family reside abroad. He poses a flight risk.'

Risk of absconding from the defence perspective

It does no harm to remind the court of the presumption in favour of bail (s. 4 Bail Act 1976). If the defendant has a record for absconding, it is important for the defence solicitor to find out what he can about the absconding offences. Were they deliberate? How long ago were they? Did the defendant ultimately surrender and plead guilty, or was he arrested? If the defendant has a good bail record, this should be stressed! The defence solicitor should examine his client's community ties. Does he have a job, a mortgage, family, anything to keep him in the area?

It is pertinent to ask whether the defendant is going to be convicted of the offence he is charged with. This requires the defence solicitor to examine the strength of the evidence against his client. The defendant may indicate he is pleading not guilty and wishes to challenge the evidence against him. In these circumstances it is legitimate to point out that the defendant will not abscond, because he wishes to clear his name of the charges he faces. If the defendant is likely to plead guilty, the defence solicitor should ask himself whether a custodial sentence is an absolute certainty. If not, he should make the appropriate representations.

Finally, the defence solicitor needs to consider what conditions to offer in order to allay the court's fear of the defendant absconding. Possibilities might include a condition of residence at a fixed address or at a bail hostel. In addition, the court may want the defendant to report to a police station on specified days and at certain times. On occasion, a court will want the defendant to surrender his passport if he poses a flight risk. Less occasionally, the court may only be prepared to grant bail subject to the defendant providing a suitable surety or security.

The commission of further offences from the prosecution perspective

The prosecutor must ask himself why this particular defendant is likely to commit further offences if released on bail. This may be due to the defendant's extensive criminal record indicating that he is a prolific offender. It might be because the defendant has a particular need to commit offences, the most obvious being to feed a drug addiction. Added to this may be the fact that the defendant has no stabilising influence in his life and in some instances no fixed address. In some cases the risk of the commission of further offences may be due to the defendant's close proximity with the victim. An example of the latter would include a domestic assault where the injured party fears reprisals if the defendant remains under the same roof.

What the prosecuting advocate might say in court in this regard:

'Madam, the defendant was already on bail for another similar offence when arrested in connection with these matters.' (See s. 14 CJA 2003 above.)

'The defendant is a man with a substantial criminal record for theft and burglary. . . . '

'The defendant is a substance abuser who steals to fund his habit. . . .'

'Sir, this defendant cannot keep out of trouble – you only have to examine his criminal record. You will also see he is the subject of an anti-social behaviour order made three months ago. . .'

'The defendant has committed offences whilst subject to a sentence of this court – in short, he cannot be trusted.'

Commission of further offences from the defence perspective

The defence solicitor needs to carefully consider the defendant's criminal record. Are the defendant's previous convictions recent? Have circumstances changed such that there is now a stabilising influence in the defendant's life? Does the defendant have responsibilities such as the care of a child who is likely to be taken into care if the defendant is remanded? Once again, what evidence connects the defendant to the offence with which he is charged? Does the defendant admit the charge in respect of which he is already on bail? Looking at the defendant's past criminal record, is it possible to say whether no offences have been committed by the defendant whilst on bail?

Will the imposition of suitable conditions help to allay the magistrates' fears that this defendant will commit further offences? Possibilities might include the imposition of a curfew where a defendant tends to commit offences at night. A condition that excludes the defendant from engaging in particular behaviour or going to a certain place may be effective, i.e. a condition not to visit licensed premises or to go within a certain radius of a particular shop. The availability of an alternative address away from the area where the crime is alleged to have occurred may alleviate the risk.

Interference with witnesses or obstructing the course of justice from the prosecution perspective

This ground might be argued where for example there is more than one co-accused who s still at large. It could also cover the situation where the defendant is implicated in a burglary or robbery and there is stolen property that has yet to be recovered. It also extends to those instances where a defendant may know or be related to a victim or witness and may well wish to contact that person.

What the prosecuting advocate might say to the court in this regard:

'Sir, this defendant has previous convictions for violence.'

'Sir, this defendant has a previous conviction for perverting the course of justice.'

'Sir, there is as you can imagine a lot of ill-feeling in the area where the defendant resides. If released on bail the danger that the defendant might be embroiled in further confrontation cannot be ignored. . . .'

'Madam, there is a large amount of stolen property that has still to be recovered and a co-accused still at large.'

Interference with witnesses or obstructing the course of justice from the defence perspective

Once again, if the defendant is not admitting the offence, assess the strength of the evidence against him. Point out that the defendant would not wish to make matters worse for himself by doing the things suggested. What was the date on which the offence is alleged to have occurred? Stolen property that is not immediately recovered is unlikely ever to be recovered. Consider whether there is any evidence that the defendant will threaten or interfere with a witness. Look at the defendant's record in this respect. Can conditions be suggested to allay the magistrates' fears? Possibilities include a condition that the defendant does not contact a witness or does not go within a certain radius of a particular area. The availability of alternative accommodation away from the witness or the area may greatly assist.

One of the factors a court ought to have regard to when determining bail is the strength of the evidence against a defendant. From the defence perspective, if the defendant has not made damaging admissions and intends to plead not guilty, it is always worth challenging the evidence linking the defendant to the offence. It would be wholly unjust for the bench to remand your client into custody on weak evidence, so consider whether to advance a defence at this stage.

15.10 PROCEDURE AT A CONTESTED BAIL HEARING

Surprisingly, there is no set procedure prescribed for a contested bail hearing. The usual practice after a court has decided to adjourn the case is for the prosecution to make representations as to why bail should not be granted. This will be based on the information contained in the police file that may not be complete at this stage. The defendant is then given his opportunity to put any relevant considerations before the court. This will usually be done through the defendant's solicitor of choice or the duty solicitor in court.

Neither advocate is likely to have had a lot of time in which to prepare for the bail hearing. From the point of view of the defence solicitor, the application for bail is likely to occur early on in the proceedings before the defendant has had the benefit of pre-trial disclosure of prosecution evidence (used material). There is in fact no statutory requirement to make disclosure for the purpose of a bail hearing. The obligations to provide pre-trial disclosure of prosecution evidence arise later in the proceedings. For consideration of the rules relating to the pre-trial disclosure of evidence, see Chapter 17. Case law, in the form of *R. v DPP, ex p. Lee* [1999] Z Cr App R 304 and *Wildman v DPP* [2001] Crim LR 565 has provided that, whilst full pre-trial disclosure of prosecution evidence is not appropriate at this stage, such disclosure as to ensure the defendant enjoys equality of arms at the bail hearing is required. The defence solicitor may have some idea of the evidence against his client if he or a member of his firm attended the defendant at the police station, otherwise the defence solicitor must press the prosecution for disclosure at court and ask for a short adjournment to consider it if necessary.

Contested bail hearing take the form of a mini-trial at which the rules of evidence are relaxed. The Bail Act 1976 gives each side the framework for the representations they are likely to make. The CPS lawyer will refer to the witness statements he has on file and the account the defendant gave at the police station in making the court aware of how the defendant came to be charged in connection with the matter(s) for which he appears. The prosecutor will outline his objections and hand in a copy of the defendant's previous convictions. The defence solicitor will then make his submissions, countering the arguments put by the prosecution. If the defendant has a job or an offer of work that is likely to be lost if he is remanded, the defence solicitor should try and get a letter from the employer to this effect. If residence is likely to be a problem, the defence solicitor needs to make enquiries as to alternative accommodation.

Any available witnesses such as a surety or evidence of an alternative address will be put before the court. Having heard the representations on both sides, the magistrates will decide on the matter and announce their decision. You are able to view a contested bail hearing in the video clip section of our Online Resource Centre. Before you do so, however, you might like to attempt the exercise we have set in conjunction with the case study at the end of this chapter, together with two other short scenarios designed to test your understanding of bail.

15.10.1 THE COURT'S DECISION – GIVING REASONS

Section 5 of the Bail Act 1976 provides that where a court withholds bail or imposes conditions on the grant of bail, the reason(s) for doing so must be announced in open court. Where bail is refused, the defendant must be given a notice setting out both the exception(s) and the reason(s) for the magistrates' decision.

Paragraph 9A of Part 1 of Sch. 1 to the Act requires a court to state its reasons for granting bail to an accused charged with an offence that triggers the application of s. 25 CJPOA 1994 (see above), in circumstances where the prosecution have opposed the application. It is the usual practice in magistrates' courts to give reasons for the grant of bail in all cases where bail has been opposed.

It should be stressed that bail is a decision for the court and it should be considered at every remand hearing, whether it is applied for or not. Magistrates can grant bail, notwithstanding prosecution objections, and may also remand a defendant in custody where there is no objection from the prosecutor.

A defendant who is 21 or over will be remanded to a prison if bail is denied. Between the ages of 17 and 20, remand is normally to a remand centre or an adult prison if no places are available at a remand centre. Defendants under the age of 17 are generally remanded into the care of social services.

It is important to remember that in the event of conviction, the sentencing court will take into account the time served on remand. A tactically aware defendant, who knows he is likely to plead guilty or be convicted of offence and receive a prison sentence will realise that being remanded in custody on full privileges has its benefits! Such defendants may not wish to pursue an application for bail.

15.11 REMAND PERIODS

When magistrates remand a defendant in custody on the occasion of his first appearance, the period on remand must not exceed eight days. It may be a number of weeks before a case is ready for trial or committal to the Crown Court. Provision is made in s. 128A MCA 1980 for an accused to be remanded for up to 28 days without his consent. The power only applies once a magistrates' court has set a date for the next stage of the proceedings to take place and decides the accused should be remanded in custody until that date. The power does not apply on the occasion of a first remand. Thus an accused is allowed two applications for bail before this power can be exercised. If the defendant is to be further remanded after 28 days, he must be produced at the next court hearing. The increasing use of TV video-links from prisons to some magistrates' courts and Crown Courts means prisoners do not have to be physically produced.

Having been convicted, a court may remand a defendant pending sentence where a pre-sentence report or some other report is required before sentence can be properly imposed. Where a court grants a defendant bail after conviction, the maximum period is four weeks. Where a defendant is remanded in custody pending completion of reports, the maximum period is three weeks.

15.11.1 CUSTODY TIME-LIMITS

When your client has been refused bail, s. 22 of the Prosecution of Offenders Act 1985 imposes maximum time-limits during which an accused may be remanded in custody between various stages in the proceedings before trial. These periods are as follows:

(a) 70 days between an accused's first appearance in the magistrates' court and committal proceedings;

(b) 70 days between first appearance and summary trial for an offence triable either way (reduced to 56 days if the decision for summary trial is taken within 56 days);

(c) 56 days between first appearance and trial for a summary-only offence; and

(d) 112 days between committal for trial and arraignment in the Crown Court.

Where an indictable-only offence is sent straight to the Crown Court under s. 51 Crime and Disorder Act 1998 (see Chapter 19), the maximum custody time length is 182 days with time running from the date the case is sent up by the magistrates, less any time already spent in custody.

If the prosecution fails to comply with the custody time-limits, the defendant has an absolute right to bail. A court can impose conditions on the defendant's bail, such as reporting or a condition of residence, but it cannot require the defendant to provide a surety or security as a condition of his release.

The prosecution can apply for an extension of the custody time-limit before its expiry. The criteria for granting an extension is laid down in s. 22 of the Prosecution of Offenders Act 1985. The prosecution's application may be granted where the court is satisfied that the need for extension is due to:

• the illness or absence of the accused, a necessary witness, the judge or magistrate, s. 22(1) POA 1985; or

• a postponement due to the court ordering separate trials in the case of two or more accused or two or more offences, s. 22(2) POA 1985; or

• some other good or sufficient cause, s. 22(3) POA 1985.

In addition to satisfying one of the above grounds, the court has to be satisfied that the prosecution is acting with all due diligence and expedition.

Much of the case law under ss. 22 and 23 POA has developed in relation to the test of good or sufficient cause and where the prosecution seek to extend a defendant's period in custody before trial and you should be aware of the principles developed by the court. An important case on the court's approach to interpreting the good and sufficient cause test is *Manchester Crown Court, ex p. McDonald* [1999] 1 WLR 841, in which Lord Bingham CJ set out the principles to be applied:

• The defendant is entitled to enjoy the presumption of liberty set out in Article 5(3) ECHR that anyone arrested or detained for trial shall be entitled to be tried within a reasonable time or to be released pending trial.

- The legal burden is on the prosecution to prove to the court on the balance of probabilities that the statutory ground for extending the custody time limit applies.

- The necessary standard to apply to the prosecutor's conduct is that of a competent prosecutor, conscious of his duty to bring the case to trial as quickly and as reasonably as possible.

- In judging whether the standard has been met, the court should take into account the nature and complexity of the case, the preparation necessary for trial, the conduct of the defence, the extent to which the prosecutor was dependant on factors outside his control and other relevant factors.

- What amounts to a good and sufficient cause should be decided on the particular facts of the case – but prosecution staff shortage and sickness is not an acceptable reason for the delay.

- The court should state the reasons for its decision.

A considerable body of case law has developed in relation to applications to extend custody time-limits. For further consideration, see *Blackstone's Criminal Practice* 2006.

15.12 NUMBER OF BAIL APPLICATIONS THAT CAN BE MADE

While a court is under a duty to consider the grant of bail at each hearing after it has been refused, the defendant is prevented from making repeated applications for bail. The position is governed by Part IIA of Sch. 1 to the Bail Act 1976 (as amended by s. 154(2) Criminal Justice Act 1988). This provides:

> 'At the first hearing after that at which the court decided not to grant the defendant bail he may support an application for bail with any further argument as to law or fact that he desires. . . . At subsequent hearings the court need not hear arguments as to fact or law which it has heard previously . . . .'

Where an accused has been refused bail at a previous hearing, he may make one further application only. Thereafter, unless there has been a change of circumstances, the court need not hear argument at a subsequent hearing.

Consider the following examples of the operation of Part IIA:

X makes an unsuccessful application for bail on his first appearance. He makes a further unsuccessful application for bail on his second appearance. Thereafter Part IIA bites and the court need not entertain a further application on his appearance unless there has been a change in circumstances.

X chooses not to make an application for bail on his first appearance. He makes an unsuccessful application for bail on his second appearance. Part IIA bites and the court need not entertain a further application on X's next appearance unless there has been a change in circumstances.

X makes an unsuccessful application for bail on his first appearance. He chooses not to make a further application on his second appearance. Part IIA bites and the court need not entertain a further application on X's next appearance unless there has been a change in circumstances. A change of circumstances need not be a major change either in the defendant's personal circumstances or in the proceedings connected with the case. So, for example, where an accused has been charged with an indictable offence and has been refused bail at two previous hearings, the fact that the case against him appears less strong when full pre-trial disclosure is made during the course of the proceedings, may amount to a change of circumstances.

15.13 WHAT IF BAIL IS REFUSED?

Where magistrates have heard a full application for bail, the court must issue a full argument certificate. A copy must be given to the accused. Armed with this an accused refused bail by the magistrates can apply to a Crown Court judge under s. 81 Supreme Court Act 1981. The procedure for applying to the Crown Court is contained in Part 19.18 Crim PR. Applications are usually dealt with within 48 hours of the initial refusal, although the defence must give 24 hours' notice of their intention appeal to the Crown Prosecution Service. The 'appeal' will be conducted before a Crown Court judge in chambers and will take the form of a complete rehearing. Trainee solicitors and unqualified clerks have full rights of audience. The application to the Crown Court will be covered by an existing representation order.

15.14 APPEAL BY THE PROSECUTION

If bail is opposed by the prosecution but is granted to a person charged with or convicted of an offence carrying imprisonment or an offence of taking a vehicle without consent or aggravated vehicle-taking, the prosecution may, under s. 1 Bail (Amendment) Act 1993 (as amended by s. 18 CJA), appeal to a judge of the Crown Court against the grant of bail. There are strict procedural requirements governing the prosecution's right to appeal. The prosecution must give oral notice of appeal at the conclusion of the proceedings in which bail was granted and before the defendant is released from custody. The oral notice must be confirmed in writing within two hours after proceedings end. Pending the appeal, the magistrates must remand the defendant in custody. The Crown Court must hear the appeal within 48 hours. The form of the appeal will be a complete rehearing.

15.15 RECONSIDERATION OF BAIL

There is power under s. 5B of the Bail Act 1976 (inserted by the Criminal Justice and Public Order Act 1994) for a court to reconsider the grant of bail on application by the prosecution. The power only applies if the offence with which the defendant is charged is indictable only or triable either way. The application must be based on information that was not available to the court or the police at the last hearing. In other words, new information must have come to light since the last occasion, which puts the question of bail in a new light. Under this power, the court can vary the bail conditions it imposed last time, impose new ones or remand in custody.

15.16 VARYING BAIL CONDITIONS

Either side can apply to have bail conditions varied or, in the prosecution's case to have conditions imposed on the grant of unconditional bail. The position is governed by s. 8(a) and (b) of the Bail Act 1976. It is not uncommon for a defendant to seek to have bail conditions varied. This requires an application to the court that imposed the conditions or to the Crown Court if a matter has already been sent there for trial or sentence.

Circumstances may have changed since the defendant was conditionally bailed that make the conditions impracticable or unworkable, i.e. securing a job outside the immediate area or the need to change address. The CPS may or may not wish to make submissions in relation to the application. In the domestic violence example we give below, the CPS opposes the application. If the application is to succeed the alleged victim will need to give evidence in support. This may include the need for an individual to give evidence oath.

Example: *R v Brown*

Raymond Brown (aged 26) is accused of two counts of assault occasioning actual bodily harm against his partner Donna Andrews (aged 22). The couple have two young children. Mr Brown is further charged with resisting a constable in the execution of his duty. On the last occasion the matter was adjourned Raymond Brown was granted conditional bail to reside at an alternative address to his partner's home and not to contact Ms Andrews or the other prosecuting witness, the couple's babysitter. Ms Andrews has now retracted her statement of complaint to the police and wishes Mr Brown to be able to reside with her and their two children. The CPS lawyer does not have the retraction statement on file and in any event, in accordance with the CPS code of practice on domestic violence, can still continue to pursue the prosecution even though the complaint has been retracted. The defence solicitor for Raymond Brown calls Ms Andrews to the stand.

Question: 'Is it true you made a statement to the police on the 2nd of this month alleging your partner Raymond Brown assaulted you?'

Answer: 'Yes I did.'

Question: 'Is it true you have since retracted that statement?'

Answer: 'Yes I have.'

Question: 'Can you recall where and when you retracted your original statement?'

Answer: 'I think it was five days ago. I went to the police station.'

Question: 'What has made you retract your statement?'

Answer: 'Things have changed – we have sorted things out.'

Question: 'What would you like this court to do this morning?'

Answer: 'I'd like Raymond to be able to come back home.'

Question: 'Are you under any pressure whatsoever to come to court today?'

Answer: 'No – I am not under any pressure.'

Question: 'Do you have any reason to fear Mr Brown?'

Answer: 'No I do not.'

Under cross-examination by the prosecutor

Question: 'Ms Andrews, what date did you make your retraction?'

Answer: 'I can't remember – it was about five days ago.'

Question: 'You made it less than a week after your original complaint?'

Answer: 'Yes.'

Question: 'Do you recall that when you made your original complaint you told the police about an assault that had occurred that day and one that had occurred ten days earlier?'

Answer: 'Yes.'

Question: 'Do you recall the police having to break into your house to apprehend Mr Brown?'

Answer: 'Yes I do.'

Question: 'And am I correct in saying the assault alleged to have occurred on the 2nd was witnessed by your babysitter, who made a statement to the police?'

Answer: 'It was.'

Question: 'Do you recall telling the police that it wasn't the first time you had been assaulted by Mr Brown?'

Answer: 'I don't recall.'

Question: 'And you say today you have nothing to fear from Raymond Brown?'

Answer: 'I do.'

Question: 'What has changed in ten days?'

Answer: 'It's not all his fault. We have talked. I won't happen again.'

Question: 'You understand that it is not your decision as to whether this case proceeds?'

Answer: 'Yes.'

Question: 'You understand that these conditions have been imposed for your protection and not to inconvenience Mr Brown?'

Answer: 'I understand.'

Question: 'Are you saying you no longer have anything to fear?'

Answer: 'That is what I am saying.'

The prosecutor concludes, stating it is a matter for the magistrates.

Magistrates' decision

The bail conditions are removed, save for the condition that the defendant does not contact the baby-sitter.

Section 16 of the Criminal Justice Act 2003 has amended the Bail Act 1976 to allow a defendant to appeal to the Crown Court against the imposition of any of the following conditions:

- residence away from a particular place;

- surety;

- curfew.

Such an appeal may not be brought if the defendant or the prosecution has already applied to a magistrates' court to have bail conditions varied and the matter has been dealt with or, in the case of the prosecution, it has applied for bail to be reconsidered in accordance with s. 5B of the Bail Act 1976 and the matter has been determined. Section 16 came in to force on 5 April 2004.

15.17 WHAT IF AN ACCUSED FAILS TO SURRENDER, HAVING BEEN GRANTED BAIL?

Section 6(1) of the Bail Act 1976 creates the offence of absconding where the accused has been released on bail (whether by the police or by a court) and fails, without reasonable excuse, to surrender to custody at the time and date specified in the bail notice. Section 6(2) makes it an offence for a defendant who has a reasonable excuse for failing his bail, not to have then surrendered himself as soon as was thereafter reasonably practicable. Where the accused fails to surrender, the burden will be on the accused to prove that he had reasonable cause for failing to surrender.

Where the defendant is found guilty, absconding is punishable by up to three months' imprisonment and/or a maximum fine of £5,000 in the magistrates' court. Where bail was imposed by the Crown Court, the offence of absconding is punishable by a maximum sentence of 12 months' imprisonment and/or an unlimited fine. Guidance has recently been issued by the Lord Chief Justice on the matter of failure to surrender: *Practice Direction (Bail: Failure to Surrender)* [2004] 1 WLR 589. In the Direction, Lord Woolf states that sentence for breach of bail should usually be custodial and consecutive to any other custodial sentence unless there are circumstances that make this inappropriate. A Bail Act offence should be regarded as a 'significant factor weighing against the re-grant of bail' and in the case of a defendant who cannot or is unlikely to receive a custodial sentence, the court might consider trial in the defendant's absence.

Where an accused fails to surrender or, having surrendered, then disappears before his case is called on, the court must decide what to do. Where there is no explanation for the accused's failure to appear the court is likely to issue a warrant without bail for the accused's immediate arrest. Where some explanation is forthcoming to account for a defendant's absence, e.g. the defendant manages to contact his solicitor alerting him of a family emergency, the court is likely to grant bail in absence or issue a warrant backed with bail. The court may require proof for the absence, such as a medical certificate, to be produced on the next occasion.

15.18 BAIL GRANTED BY THE CROWN COURT

The Crown Court has its own inherent jurisdiction to grant bail. The Crown Court can exercise that jurisdiction when:

* The defendant has been remanded in custody by magistrates prior to committal or summary trial and appeals to the Crown Court.
* The defendant has been sent or committed to the Crown Court for trial or has been committed for sentence.
* The defendant has been summarily convicted, imprisoned and denied bail pending an appeal to the Crown Court.
* The defendant has been convicted and sentenced before a Crown Court and now wishes to appeal to the Court of Appeal.

15.19 BAIL AND THE HIGH COURT

The High Court's jurisdiction to hear an appeal against a refusal or bail or a refusal to vary conditions of bail in connection with criminal proceedings being conducted before a magistrate's court or Crown Court was abolished by s. 17 of the Criminal Justice Act 2003. Section 17 is already in force. The High Court retains jurisdiction to grant bail in the limited instance of a convicted and imprisoned offender appealing against conviction or sentence by way of case stated or by judicial review.

The decision in *R (Shergill) v Harrow Crown Court* [2005] EWHC 648 confirms that where a Crown Court judge's decision to refuse bail is 'Wednesbury' unreasonable, the High Court has an inherent jurisdiction to judicially review the decision of the Crown Court. Such an application, however, should only be made in 'exceptional cases'.

15.20 HUMAN RIGHTS AND BAIL

The Law Commission in its Report No. 269: *Bail and the Human Rights Act 1998* concluded that the existing law in relation to bail was broadly compliant with the European Convention on Human Rights. It did, however, identify some areas for concern, most of which have been addressed by amendments to the Bail Act 1976 introduced by the Criminal Justice Act 2003 (see paragraph 15.6.1).

What is clear is that it is Article 5 and not Article 6 that is invoked in relation to decisions about bail. Article 5 guarantees an individual's right to liberty and security. It therefore has clear relevance to bail decisions. Article 5(1) allows the right to be abrogated in defined instances and in accordance with a procedure prescribed by law. The prescribed instances include the lawful detention of a person after conviction by a competent court (Article 5(1)(a)) and the lawful arrest or detention of a person effected for the purpose of bringing him before a court on reasonable suspicion of having committed an offence or when it is reasonably necessary to prevent his committing an offence or fleeing after having done so (Article 5(1)(c)).

Article 5(1)(c) should be read in conjunction with Article 5(3), which provides:

> 'Everyone arrested or detained in accordance with paragraph (1)(c) shall be brought before a judge or other officer authorised by law to exercise judicial power and shall be entitled to trial within a reasonable time or to release pending trial. Release may be conditioned by guarantees to appear for trial.'

In its analysis of the jurisprudence of the European Court of Human Rights (ECtHR), the Law Commission Report concluded that Article 5 permits the detention of an individual pending trial where there is a real risk that the defendant would:

(a) fail to attend trial;

(b) interfere with evidence or witnesses, or otherwise obstruct the course of justice;

(c) commit an offence while on bail; and

(d) be at risk of harm against which he or she would be inadequately protected.

These grounds broadly correspond to the grounds contained within the Bail Act 1976 as amended by the CJA 2003.

The Law Commission expressed some concern that s. 25 CJPOA 1994 (see paragraph 15.4) could be applied in a way that is not compliant with Article 5. Article 5 provides there is a presumption in favour of an individual's liberty. In relation to s. 25, it is possible to interpret the section as creating a presumption against the grant of bail in the serious offences specified within the section. In *CC v United Kingdom* [1999] Crim LR 228, the European Commission of Human Rights emphasised the need for a court to closely examine all the facts in an individual's case, having due regard to the presumption of innocence. To ensure compliance in the application of s. 25, the Law Commission advises courts to go through the usual balance of factors for and against bail, discussed above, giving special weight to the fact that this is a case falling within s. 25. The Law Commission advises that if the imposition of bail conditions would adequately address the risks identified by a court, the defendant should be granted conditional bail in preference to being remanded into custody.

KEY POINT SUMMARY

- Remember defendants tend to think of the short-term – for them, gaining bail may be of considerable importance – more important than the final outcome.

- Make sure you distinguish between the grounds for opposing bail and the factors used to substantiate the grounds.

- Anticipate the likely objections to bail with your client and see what conditions you and your client can agree in an attempt to surmount the likely objections.

- Find out in advance on what grounds the prosecution is going to oppose bail.

- Press the prosecution for disclosure of its evidence at this early stage together with confirmation of your client's criminal record.

- Be prepared to challenge the evidence against your client at this early stage.

- Present a structured submission to the court, dealing with each of the prosecution's objections in turn.

- Take a note of the court's decision and explain what it means to your client.

- Remember you have more than one opportunity to apply for bail, and the option of applying to a Crown Court judge in chambers where bail is refused by a magistrates' court.

SELF-TEST QUESTIONS

To test your knowledge and understanding of the substantive law of bail, consider the following scenarios. Formulate what you consider would be your objections to bail being granted having regard to the grounds for opposing bail and the factors the court is likely to have regard to. What submissions would you put forward to counter these objections to try and ensure bail is granted? An analysis of the scenarios is provided in Appendix 5.

1. *R v Karl Green*

Karl Green is charged with wounding with intent, contrary to s. 18 of the Offences Against the Person Act 1861 (OAPA). He appears before magistrates. The prosecution seeks the usual eight-day adjournment to enable the case to be sent to the Crown Court. It is alleged that Karl assaulted David Murphy outside a public house on the housing estate where both the men live. The offence occured two days ago. The injured party is presently in a coma. One witness, who is a friend of the injured party, has provided the police with a statement in which he identifies Karl Green as the person who punched his friend. In his statement he refers to the two men exchanging words. In one swift movement, he alleges, Green punched his friend with such force as to cause him to fall unconscious to the around. An independent witness has provided a statement giving a similar account of the incident and a description of the man responsible being consistent with Green's appearance. The witness also states he observed the man who threw the punch flee the scene.

Karl Green is presently on conditional bail for a serious s. 18 OAPA 1861 assault on a police constable, alleged to have occurred six weeks earlier. He was seriously drunk at the time and one of the conditions of his bail, which includes him reporting to his local police station, prohibits him from visiting licensed premises. He appeared before magistrates last week admitting a breach of his bail condition not to visit licensed premises. The magistrates were prepared to renew his bail, having regard to the explanation offered by Green which had been to fetch his sister who works at a public house as her baby was sick. According to his list of antecedents, Karl Green lives apart from his wife and is out of work. He has six previous convictions. The most recent relates to an assault occasioning actual bodily harm (s. 47 OAPA) last year, for which Green received a six-month prison sentence suspended for 18 months. He has further convictions for assault dating some three and four years ago, two previous convictions for theft and a conviction for a public order offence. He was convicted of absconding three years ago.

In interview with his solicitor, Karl Green admits to throwing the punch. He maintains, however, that he acted in self-defence. He claims the injured party was the aggressor and went for him. In self-defence, Green took one punch. When the injured party did not get up, Green panicked. His brother was with him when the incident occurred and will testify on his behalf. Green lives with his mother. He and his ex-wife are attempting a reconciliation. She had been dating the injured party but had terminated the relationship in recent weeks, believing she could salvage her marriage. She and Green have a son, Stephen, who is four years old. Karl says he is currently in work – he works for his cousin's skip-hire company. If remanded in custody he is likely to lose his job. His previous failure to surrender was due to sickness; however, no medical evidence was ever obtained. Green voluntarily surrendered himself and was fined for the offence of failing to answer his bail. So far as the assault on the policeman is concerned, he will be pleading guilty to a less serious charge of assault. He was seriously intoxicated at the time and does not recall much of what happened. He has expressed his deep remorse. Green tells his solicitor that he has a sister who may be prepared to offer him accommodation ten miles outside the area of the estate where he and his victim live.

2. *R v Daniel Phillips*

Daniel Phillips has been charged with arson contrary to s. 1(1) of the Criminal Damage Act 1971 and with resisting a constable in the execution of his duty. The allegation is that he deliberately set fire to his former partner's house, causing extensive damage. He has been remanded into police custody pending his initial appearance before magistrates. The prosecution requests an adjournment of three weeks in order to prepare a full file for disclosure to the defence.

Daniel is 26. His former partner, Rachel Hughes, is 22. She has made a statement to the police. The couple have a child aged three who Rachel cares for. The relationship ended two years ago but Daniel has been reluctant to accept it. Rachel refused Daniel access to their son but this was resolved 18 months ago by court order. In recent weeks Rachel has formed a new relationship.

The police were called to Rachel Hughes's home at 6 am three days ago (a Saturday). Her property was on fire. Initial forensic tests have revealed the fire was started deliberately by someone pouring an accelerant through the front door letterbox and igniting it with a match. The finger of suspicion points to Daniel.

Daniel collected his son from Rachel for an access visit on the Saturday afternoon. She asked him to deliver their son back to her mother – the child was going to spend the night with his grandmother. She told Daniel Phillips that she would be staying with a friend of hers overnight. Her friend received a telephone call at 5.30 am. A male voice, which she thinks she recognised as Daniel, requested her to inform Rachel that her house was on fire.

Daniel was arrested three days later as the police were unable to locate him immediately – he was no longer living at his mother's address. There is no forensic evidence to link him to the crime scene as yet, but tests are continuing. Daniel made no comment in interview on the advice of his solicitor.

Rachel maintains she is absolutely terrified of Daniel, who has four previous convictions recorded against him. He was convicted of criminal damage two years ago. Following an argument with Rachel he damaged her car. He was conditionally discharged for this offence for a period of one year. Six months later he was convicted of assault occasioning actual bodily harm and breach of a conditional discharge. The incident followed the breakdown of his relationship with Rachel. She started to date another man. When Daniel found out, he assaulted the man. He denied involvement but was found guilty by magistrates. He was given a community supervision order for two years. Last year Daniel was convicted of an offence under s. 2 of the Harassment Act 1997. He pleaded guilty before a Crown Court judge and was sentenced to six months' imprisonment, suspended for 18 months to run alongside his existing community supervision order of some two years. Daniel was also subject to a restraining order of five years forbidding him to contact or communicate with Rachel except when and for the sole purpose of collecting his son for an access visit. The harassment had taken the form of obscene text messages. Rachel was also bombarded with dozens of pictures taken of her, some of which were cut up. She started to receive menacing telephone calls in the early hours of the morning, which were eventually traced to a mobile telephone registered to Daniel.

In interview with his solicitor, Daniel steadfastly denies setting fire to the property. He maintains he has no axe to grind so far as Rachel is concerned. In fact he has formed a new relationship in recent months. His new girlfriend, Anna, aged 19, is pregnant with his baby. He was with her at the time of this alleged incident, at her mother's house. She and her mother will verify this. He left his mother's home several weeks ago, as he could not cope with her alcoholic mood swings. Daniel maintains the access visit with his son went off without problem and that he would not do anything to jeopardise his relationship with his son. Furthermore he is complying with the requirements of the community supervision order which is helping him to address the reason for his earlier offending. He is residing on a permanent basis with his new girlfriend and has a job as a mechanic. He denies resisting the police constable in the course of his arrest, maintaining the officer was much too heavy-handed.

Case Study: *R v Lenny Whyte*

Consider the advance information in relation to this case study, together with Lenny Whyte's list of previous convictions (located in Appendix 1, Documents 18 A–P and Document 12). Assume you are the CPS lawyer and that this is Lenny's second appearance before magistrates. He has been remanded in custody since being charged. Upon what grounds will you oppose bail, and what factors will you have regard to in substantiating your objections? The prosecution's submission in this case can be viewed on the video section of our Online Resource Centre. A transcript of the prosecuting solicitor's submission can be located on our Online Resource Centre in the case study section. For general consideration of the skills of advocacy, see Chapter 4.

Now look at this file from the perspective of the defence. Having regard to both the advance information and Lenny's statement (Documents 1 and 18, located within Appendix 1), construct a defence submission in this case countering the prosecution's objections. How are you going to convince the court to grant bail in this case? The defence submission in this case can be viewed on the video section of our Online Resource Centre. A transcript of the defence solicitor's submission can be located on our Online Resource Centre in the case study section.

An account of the magistrates' decision in relation to bail is contained in Document 13. You will see that Lenny appeals the refusal of bail to a judge in chambers in the Crown Court and is subsequently grated conditional bail' (Document 17). Documents 14–16 can be found in the case study section of our Online Resource Centre, which contains a complete set of the documentation forming the *R v Lenny Whyte* case study.

Case study: *R v William Hardy*

Case study: *R v Roger Martin* (web-based only)

With regards to *R v William Hardy* and *R v Martin*, although there have been adjournments in each of these cases, there is no contentious issue as regards bail and each defendant is remanded on conditional bail during the proceedings.

FIGURE 15.1 COURT BAIL

EXCEPTIONS TO THE RIGHT TO BAIL

The Bail Act 1976 (s. 4) generally presumes the defendant should be granted bail. However,

- bail should only be granted exceptionally where a defendant is charged with murder, manslaughter, rape (or attempts) and he has previous convictions for one of these offences (s. 25 CJPOA 1994);

- the defendant need not be granted bail if he is over 18 and is already on bail unless there is no significant risk of him committing an offence on bail (s. 14 CJA 2003);

- the defendant need not be granted bail if he is over 18 and has previously been granted bail in the proceedings and has failed to surrender unless the court is satisfied there is no significant risk of the defendant failing to surrender if released on bail (s. 15 CJA 2003);

- the defendant need not be granted bail if he has tested positive to a Class A drug and is charged with offence involving a specified Class A drug under Misuse of Drugs Act 1971, or court is satisfied that his offending is due to his drug dependency and the defendant refuses to undergo an assessment or fo low-up treatment for his dependency (s. 19 CJA 2003).

REBUTTING THE PRESUMPTION TO BAIL

- the presumption to bail may be rebutted where defendant is charged with imprisonable offence; and

- the court is satisfied (Part 1, Sch. 1, Bail Act 1976) there are **substantial grounds** for believing the defendant will:

  - fail to surrender to custody; or

  - commit an offence while on bail; or

  - interfere with witnesses or obstruct the course of justice; or

- the court is satisfied that the defendant should be kept in custody for his protection (or welfare where a juvenile); or

- the defendant is already serving a custodial sentence; or

- the court is satisfied it has not been practicable to obtain sufficient information to take a decision under the Bail Act 1976; or

- where the case has been adjourned for preparation of a report, it appears impracticable to complete the enquiries or report unless the defendant is in custody.

PARAGRAPH 9 FACTORS

- In deciding whether the ground/s for refusing bail are made out, the court takes into account paragraph 9 Bail Act 1976 factors:

  - the nature and seriousness of the offence;

  - defendant's character, antecedents, community ties;

  - bail record;

  - strength of the evidence; and

  - any other relevant matter.

BAIL CONDITIONS

- bail can be unconditional or conditional;

- conditions ensure that the defendant:

  - will surrender to custody; or

  - does not commit further offences; or

  - does not interfere with witnesses or obstruct the course of justice; or

  - to ensure defendant available to assist with preparation of a pre-sentence report.

FIGURE 15.1 (CONTINUED)

- conditions include:
  - reporting to a police station;
  - living at a specified address (possibly bail hostel);
  - curfew;
  - surety;
  - the defendant should not contact a specific individual;
  - exclusion from specified locality or place.

APPEALING BAIL DECISIONS

- defence can 'appeal' against refusal of bail or bail conditions to Crown Court judge in chambers;

- prosecution can appeal to Crown Court against allowing bail where offence is punishable with imprisonment.

16 PROSECUTING AN EITHER-WAY OFFENCE

16.1 INTRODUCTION

There are a considerable number of either-way offences. They include assault occasioning actual bodily harm, unlawful sexual activity, theft and burglary. The procedure that determines where an either-way offence shall be tried is known as the mode of trial enquiry.

Either-way offences can be committed with varying degrees of seriousness. The seriousness of an either-way offence depends on the presence of aggravating features in the particular case. The more aggravating features there are, the more serious the offence will be regarded. A magistrates' court powers of sentence are limited compared to those of the Crown Court. We will see that if a magistrates' court considers its maximum sentencing powers in relation to one or more either-way offences to be insufficient, the case will be sent to the Crown Court. Theft offences provide a good illustration. Theft can range from simple shoplifting to the appropriation of property worth tens of thousands of pounds. Clearly, the trial of the offender charged with shoplifting would be most appropriately dealt with summarily while the more serious, high-value theft should be dealt with in the Crown Court.

Looking Ahead

The Criminal Justice Act 2003 is set to make some significant changes to the way in which either-way cases are allocated. These changes are tied to an increase in the maximum sentencing powers of the magistrates' court under the CJA 2003. The detailed provisions relating to the allocation of an either-way offence are contained in Schedule 3 CJA 2003. The predicted date for implementation of these provisions at the time of going to press is November 2006. Given that there is always a risk that this date could be put back and given the need for transitional provisions in relation to cases that will have already commenced at the date of implementation, we have decided to consider the existing framework under which decisions relating to either-way cases are made, but have highlighted the changes that are set to be implemented in the near future. It is our intention to bring you a comprehensive update on the changes once they have been implemented later in the year through the updated pages of our Online Resource Centre.

online
resource
centre

In this chapter we examine:

* the procedure for deciding where an either-way offence should be tried;
* the relative merits of summary trial and trial on indictment; and
* for those either-way offences that are to be tried in the Crown Court, the next stage of the proceedings – the committal hearing conducted under MCA 1980, s. 6(1) or s. 6(2).

16.2 THE DEFENDANT'S FIRST APPEARANCE FOR AN OFFENCE TRIABLE EITHER WAY

An account of the very early stages of an either-way case is provided in the latter part of Chapter 14.

You are reminded that a defendant charged with an either-way offence is entitled to pre-trial disclosure of the prosecution's evidence against him in accordance with Part 21 Crim PR. As you will see, a defendant charged with an either-way offence is required to indicate his plea at an early stage in the proceedings. Unless the matter is clear-cut, disclosure of the prosecution's evidence under the Advance Information Rules should be sought before offering appropriate advice as to plea. A full prosecution file is unlikely to be available in time for a defendant's initial appearance and therefore an adjournment is most likely. At the conclusion of the first hearing matters relating to the grant of a representation order (Chapter 14) and the defendant's bail status (Chapter 15) will have been determined.

16.3 MODE OF TRIAL PROCEEDINGS

Once the defendant is in possession of full advance information and his solicitor has had sufficient time to consider the same, the defendant's next court appearance should determine where the either-way matter shall be tried.

MCA 1980 s. 17(A) provides that where a defendant aged 18 or over is charged with an either-way offence, mode of trial proceedings must be held to determine whether the defendant should be tried summarily or on indictment before any evidence is called. The procedure at the mode of trial hearing is governed by ss. 17–21 Magistrates' Courts Act 1980.

16.4 PLEA BEFORE VENUE

All defendants charged with an either-way offence are subject to the plea before venue procedure. The procedure provides the defendant with an opportunity to indicate to the court how he intends to plead to the charges laid against him. The plea before venue procedure is illustrated in the video section of our Online Resource Centre in relation to the *R v William Hardy* case study.

16.4.1 PROCEDURE AT PLEA BEFORE VENUE

The legal adviser to the court will check with the parties whether a plea can be indicated. If it can, the legal adviser will then explain to the accused in ordinary language that he will be asked to indicate to the court whether he intends to plead guilty or not guilty. The legal adviser will go on to explain that if the defendant indicates a guilty plea, the magistrates will proceed to sentence him and deal with him as if he had been found guilty and therefore there will be no trial and no evidence will be called. The defendant will also be warned that notwithstanding an indication of a guilty plea, the magistrates may still commit him for sentence to the Crown Court under PCC(S)A 2000, s. 3, if they consider their sentencing powers to be insufficient. The legal adviser will then read the charge to the accused who is asked to indicate how he intends to plead. A defendant has four possible responses. He can indicate a guilty plea, a not guilty plea, give no indication of plea or enter an equivocal plea.

16.4.2 WHAT HAPPENS IF THE DEFENDANT INDICATES A GUILTY PLEA?

If the defendant indicates that he would plead guilty, the case will be dealt with summarily on the basis of a guilty plea, and sentence will follow. Sentencing may be adjourned to a later date if the court considers a pre-sentence report is required.

If the case continues on the day, the CPS advocate will outline the facts of the case and give details of the defendant's previous convictions. The defence advocate will make a plea in mitigation during which he will seek to put the defendant's actions in the best light in the hope that the magistrates will be persuaded to impose a less severe sentence than might otherwise be the case. A detailed examination of the practice and procedure in making a plea in mitigation is dealt with in Part V.

If on hearing the full facts of the offence and the defendant's antecedents, the magistrates consider their powers of sentence to be inadequate, the defendant can be committed to the Crown Court for sentence under the Powers of Criminal Court (Sentencing) Act 2000, s. 3. The defendant can then be sentenced on the same basis as if he had been convicted on indictment. Further consideration is given to the power under s. 3 in Chapter 28. **Indeed, the whole basis of magistrates declining jurisdiction to sentence on conviction for one or more either-way offences is best understood when you have completed your consideration of sentencing law and practice.**

16.4.3 ### WHAT HAPPENS IF THE DEFENDANT INDICATES A NOT GUILTY PLEA OR MAKES AN EQUIVOCAL PLEA?

If, at the plea before venue, the defendant indicates that he would plead not guilty, the court will proceed to the mode of trial enquiry. The case will also proceed to the mode of trial where the defendant makes an equivocal plea. An equivocal plea is where the defendant's response to the charge is ambiguous or the defendant indicates no plea at all. Where the court is uncertain as to the defendant's plea, a not guilty plea will be entered on his behalf.

16.5 ## THE MODE OF TRIAL ENQUIRY – SS. 18–20 MCA 1980

In some cases the CPS lawyer and the defence may agree about the appropriate place of trial. The only time there is likely to be disagreement between the two parties is where the prosecution seeks to persuade the magistrates to decline jurisdiction but the defendant seeks to persuade the magistrates to accept jurisdiction. In outlining the bare facts of the case, the prosecution will either represent that the case is suitable for summary trial or it will make representations as to why the case would be more appropriately dealt with in the Crown Court. The magistrates will then listen to any representations from the defence advocate before coming to a decision as to where the case should be dealt with.

It is important to remember that in the first instance the decision as to where the case will be tried lies with the magistrates. In reaching their decision, the magistrates will take into account the submissions made by the parties, the statutory factors contained in MCA 1980, s. 19 and the National Mode of Trial Guidelines reproduced in Appendix 3.

16.5.1 ### THE STATUTORY FACTORS

The statutory factors under MCA 1980, s. 19 require magistrates to have regard to the following in deciding whether the offence is more suitable for summary trial or trial on indictment:

(1) the nature of the case;

(2) whether the circumstances make the offence one of a serious character;

(3) whether the powers of punishment in the magistrates' court would be adequate if the defendant was found guilty;

(4) any other circumstances which appear to the court to make it more suitable for the offence to be tried summarily or on indictment.

Of central importance to the mode of trial enquiry is the extent of the magistrates' powers of sentence in the event of conviction. Again, the importance of this will be more fully appreciated and understood after you have covered the sentencing law and practice in Part V. Currently the maximum sentence a magistrates' court can impose on conviction for an either-way offence is six months' imprisonment. This increases to a maximum of 12 months where the defendant is convicted of two or more either-way offences.

> **Looking Ahead**
>
> When s. 154 Criminal Justice Act 2003 comes into force, magistrates' court powers of sentence on conviction for a single offence will significantly increase to a maximum custodial term of 51 weeks, and up to 65 weeks where consecutive sentences are imposed for two or more offences. When these changes are implemented it is anticipated that fewer either-way cases will need to be committed to the Crown Court for trial or for sentence. It should also be noted that when Sch. 3 CJA is brought into force, save for specified offences (of a violent or sexual nature under s. 224 CJA 2003), where a magistrates' court has accepted jurisdiction to try an accused for an either-way offence and has found the defendant guilty, there will be no power to commit a convicted offender to the Crown Court for sentence.

In applying the statutory factors to the facts of your client's case, the magistrates will consider any aggravating factors which may justify the case being tried in the Crown Court.

Commonly applied aggravating factors include instances where a defendant has acted in a premeditated way; where the victim of the crime was vulnerable; or where the property damaged or stolen was of high value. The decision in *R v Colchester Justices, ex p. North East Essex Building Co.* [1977] 1 WLR 1109 suggests that, as a matter of practice, in assessing the nature and seriousness of the case the defendant's previous convictions should not be taken into account in deciding mode of trial. This is something of an anomaly which has never been satisfactorily resolved, since it is accepted that previous convictions are an aggravating factor that must be taken into account on sentencing (s. 143(2) CJA 2003).

> **Looking Ahead**
>
> When the relevant provisions under Sch. 3 to the Criminal Justice Act 2003 come into force, the CPS will be invited to give details of the defendant's previous convictions at the mode of trial enquiry.

Where the magistrates determine that trial on indictment is more appropriate, the defendant has no right of election and the magistrates' decision is communicated to him. The mode of trial enquiry then stands adjourned and a date is set for a committal hearing to be held. Pending the adjournment the CPS will prepare and serve the committal bundle on the defence. The practice and procedure at committal is considered in paragraphs 16.11–16.17 below.

16.5.2 SPECIAL RULES RELATING TO CERTAIN EITHER-WAY OFFENCES

In the context of a third burglary offence, any previous convictions for burglary are important. If a defendant is charged with a third offence of domestic burglary the court will apply PCC(S)A 2000 s. 111. This provision requires a person convicted of a third offence of domestic burglary (where all three of the offences were committed after 30 November 1999) to be given a custodial sentence of three years unless there are circumstances that do not justify imposing such a sentence. As this sentence is clearly in excess of the magistrates' sentencing powers, magistrates have no choice but to treat the offence as triable only on indictment, with the result that it must be sent to the Crown Court (s. 51 Crime and Disorder Act 1998) (see Chapter 19).

In addition to the statutory factors in s. 19 MCA 1980, the magistrates will have regard to the National Mode of Trial Guidelines.

16.5.3 **THE NATIONAL MODE OF TRIAL GUIDELINES**

In determining whether the case is suitable for summary trial or trial on indictment, the court will take into account the National Mode of Trial Guidelines (reproduced in Appendix 3). As their name implies, the object of the guidelines is to provide guidance only. Magistrates should apply the guidelines but are required to consider each case individually on its own facts.

The guidelines provide that:

(a) the court should never make its decision on the grounds of convenience or expedition;

(b) the court should assume for the purposes of deciding mode of trial that the prosecution version of the facts is correct;

(c) the fact that offences are alleged to be specimens is a relevant consideration; the fact that the defendant will be asking for offences to be taken into consideration, if convicted, is not;

(d) where cases involve complex questions of fact or difficult questions of law, the court should consider committal for trial;

(e) where two or more defendants are jointly charged with an offence each has an individual right to elect his mode of trial;

(f) in general, except where otherwise stated, either-way offences should be tried summarily unless the court considers that the particular case has one or more features set out in the guidelines and that its sentencing powers are insufficient;

(g) the court should also consider its power to commit an offender for sentence under s. 3 PCC(S)A 2000, if information emerges during the course of the hearing which leads them to conclude that the offence is so serious, or the offender is such a risk to the public, that their powers to sentence him are inadequate.

The guidelines suggest that a case should not be committed to the Crown Court because it appears to be the easier option. It may be that the defendant is already committed to stand trial in the Crown Court on similar or unrelated earlier charges. It makes sense to have all matters tried and resolved at the same time but a committal should not be ordered on this basis alone.

For the purposes of the mode of trial enquiry, magistrates must take the prosecution's case at its highest and must assume that the prosecution's version of the facts is correct. The guidelines further suggest that either-way cases should be tried summarily unless there are aggravating factors, which make trial on indictment more likely. The National Mode of Trial Guidelines specify the aggravating features of a number of common either-way offences which can have the effect of increasing the seriousness of the either-way offence.

In relation to burglary of a dwelling house, for example, aggravating factors include:

• entry to the house during daytime when the occupier or another is present;

• entry to the house at night, which is normally occupied, whether or not the occupier or another is present;

• the offence is alleged to be one of a series of offences;

• when in the house, soiling, ransacking, damage or vandalism occurs;

• the offence has professional hallmarks;

• The unrecovered property is of high value.

National Mode of Trial Guidelines – theft and fraud

Cases of theft and fraud should normally be tried summarily unless the court considers that one or more of the following aggravating factors are present and that its sentencing powers are insufficient:

• breach of trust by a person in a position of substantial authority, or in whom a high degree of trust is placed;

• theft or fraud which has been committed or disguised in a sophisticated manner;

- theft or fraud committed by an organised gang;
- the victim is particularly vulnerable to theft or fraud, e.g. the victim is elderly or infirm;
- the unrecovered property is of high value.

The practice and procedure at a mode of trial enquiry is illustrated in the video section of our Online Resource Centre in relation to the *R v Lenny Whyte* case study.

online resource centre

16.6 CRIMINAL JUSTICE ACT 2003 – CHANGES TO MODE OF TRIAL PROCEDURE

Looking Ahead

Criminal Justice Act 2003 – changes to mode of trial procedure

The changes to mode of trial proceedings under Schedule 3 CJA 2003 are coupled with an extension in the sentencing powers of magistrates, highlighted above. They are designed to try to ensure a greater number of cases remain in the magistrates' courts. A defendant retains a right to elect trial by jury when given the choice. Prosecution and defence will still make representations; however, the prosecution will be allowed to refer to a defendant's previous convictions in order to allow the court to consider whether it feels its sentencing powers to be sufficient. New 'allocation guidelines' will be issued by the Sentencing Guidelines Council, and these will replace the current National Mode of Trial Guidelines.

In cases where magistrates are prepared to accept jurisdiction, it will be explained to the defendant that he has a choice. He should be told that he will not be committed for sentence to the Crown Court unless he falls to be sentenced under the 'dangerousness' provisions in s. 224 CJA 2003. Under the amended s. 20 MCA 1980, the defendant is entitled to ask for a broad indication of sentence i.e. 'In the event of conviction, am I likely to receive a custodial or non-custodial sentence?' The answer to such a question may well influence a defendant as to the appropriate venue and as to his possible plea. However, a court is not be bound to give an indication. Where it does give an indication, and the defendant pleads guilty, the indication will be binding on any subsequent sentencing court. Having received an indication, the defendant can, if he wishes, reconsider any indication he gave or declined to give at his plea before venue. The SCG has issued draft allocation guidelines which can be accessed at http://www.sentencing–guidelines.gov.uk.

Summary of the changes under the CJA 2003

- If a not-guilty plea is indicated, a mode of trial enquiry will still be necessary.
- Prosecution and defence will make representations.
- The defendant's previous convictions will be adduced as part of the mode of trial enquiry.
- Magistrates will apply new allocation guidelines set to be finalised and issued by the Sentencing Guidelines Council.
- The decision to accept jurisdiction will be based, for the most part, on the adequacy of the court's sentencing powers (taking into account the seriousness of the offence/s charged and any relevant discount for a timely guilty plea).
- Having accepted jurisdiction to try a case summarily, magistrates will be unable to commit for sentence in the event of conviction save where the offence triggers the 'dangerous' offender provisions under s. 224 CJA 2003).
- Where jurisdiction is accepted, the defendant may seek an indication as to likely sentence in the event of conviction.
- The court need not give an indication.
- Where an indication of sentence is given and the defendant pleads guilty, the court may not impose a custodial sentence, unless such a sentence was indicated.

16.7 DECIDING ON TRIAL BY JURY OR TRIAL BEFORE A MAGISTRATES' COURT WHERE THE DEFENDANT IS GIVEN THE CHOICE

Where the magistrates believe the case is suitable for summary trial, the defendant has the absolute right to elect trial by jury before the Crown Court or to consent to being tried summarily before magistrates.

At an early stage in the proceedings after receiving advance information from the CPS, the defendant's solicitor should make an assessment of the nature of the prosecution evidence against his client and be prepared to advise his client about the relative advantages of summary trial or trial on indictment if a plea of not guilty is to be entered. Part of this advice will be based on a number of practical factors including how the defendant's case is funded and the defendant's personal circumstances. Clearly, if a defendant is a privately paying client, summary trial will be much cheaper than trial on indictment. If your client is of a particularly nervous disposition, he may not be capable of dealing with the considerable pressures of a Crown Court trial.

In addition to any practical considerations, you should also consider the relative advantages and disadvantages of both types of proceedings having regard to the particular facts of your client's case. While it is part of the defence solicitor's professional duty to advise his client where his case should be tried, the decision is ultimately that of your client.

16.7.1 RELATIVE MERITS OF TRIAL ON INDICTMENT

Higher acquittal rate

In spite of inconclusive evidence, most defence lawyers believe that trial by jury provides a better chance of their client being acquitted. There is a commonly held perception that magistrates tend to be case-hardened because they sit on a regular basis and tend to hear the same defence on a regular basis. This point is especially significant in cases involving disputed police evidence, as magistrates may be more prepared to accept the evidence of the police in preference to that of the defendant. There is a widely held perception that jurors come to a case with a more open mind. For a client charged with theft who pleads not guilty on the basis that he lacked the necessary dishonest intent, a jury of 12 people hearing this defence for the first time may be more likely to give him the benefit of the doubt.

Disputed evidence

Where your client's case involves disputed evidence, the judge, as a legally qualified professional, is clearly much better placed to deal with points of law. The separation of function in the *voir dire* between judge and jury makes defence challenges to the admissibility of prosecution evidence during the trial itself much more effective. The jury is excluded from the *voir dire* hearing. Where your client's case involves disputing the admissibility of the prosecution's identification evidence for example, or challenging the admissibility of a confession, trial on indictment should be advised. Apart from the problems that some lay magistrates may experience in fully appreciating the advocate's legal submissions about the admissibility of prosecution evidence, if the defence submission is upheld, lay magistrates are required to put the excluded evidence to the back of their minds and continue trying the case. The increasing use of pre-trial hearings in the magistrates' court at which binding rulings on disputed evidence can be made means this problem should arise less frequently.

Delay

It can take months before a case finally comes to trial in the Crown Court. Delay can be both an advantage and a disadvantage. You might use the inevitable delay of trial in the Crown Court to prepare your client's case and to test the prosecution case.

Cost

Representation orders are currently granted irrespective of the defendant's means. There is provision, however, for the recovery of defence costs (RDCO) under reg. 11 of the Criminal Defence Service (Recovery of Defence Costs Orders) (Amendment) Regulations 2004. The regulations apply to those defendants who are convicted of offences before a Crown Court. Under the regulations, a judge is required to make a RDCO, taking into account the offender's means. Prosecution costs in the event of conviction, are likely to be much higher in the Crown Court, in the event of conviction, than they are in the magistrates' court.

Powers of sentence

The Crown Court's powers of punishment are far greater than those of the magistrates' court. The Crown Court can impose a sentence up to the statutory maximum for that offence. Fines are likely to be considerably higher in the Crown Court. This may be an important factor for your client.

16.7.2 THE RELATIVE MERITS OF SUMMARY TRIAL

Powers of sentence

If convicted in summary proceedings, your client is likely to receive a less severe sentence, as the magistrates' sentencing powers are much more limited compared to the Crown Court. The maximum custodial sentence that can be imposed is currently limited to six months for an either-way offence or 12 months for two of more either-way offences. The maximum fine magistrates can impose is £5,000 per offence. However, it is always good professional practice to remind your client about the magistrates' power to commit to the Crown Court for sentence under PCC(S)A 2000 s. 3, where the magistrates believe their sentencing powers to be insufficient.

Delay

The delay in Crown Court proceedings may have a detrimental effect on your client, especially if he is anxious or has been in custody after being refused bail. The time between the date of the alleged offence and your client's trial is often much shorter in summary cases enabling the case to be completed sooner.

Publicity

Trial in the Crown Court will usually involve your client being exposed to greater publicity. Representatives of the local press and sometimes the national media will often take a greater interest in Crown Court proceedings. This is an important factor where your client is a public figure, or the case is of particular public interest, for example, where your client is a teacher charged with an offence of a sexual nature.

Stress

The relative informality of summary proceedings makes the magistrates' court more appropriate for a nervous client. By contrast, the atmosphere of the Crown Court is considerably more formal.

Defence pre-trial disclosure of evidence

Under the Criminal Procedure and Investigations Act 1996 (CPIA), there is no obligation on the accused to serve a defence statement in summary proceedings. In trials on indictment, after the prosecution has served 'initial' disclosure of 'unused' evidence, the accused is required to serve a defence statement. In summary proceedings, the service of a defence statement is voluntary (see Chapter 17).

Presenting advocate

If the defendant's trial is in the magistrates' court, he is likely to have met his advocate on a number of occasions prior to trial. It is more likely that the advocate will be fully conversant with the facts, whereas at the Crown Court, briefs delivered to counsel are sometimes delivered at a very late stage and often there is no guarantee that the barrister instructed by the solicitor will be the person who actually appears to represent your client at trial.

16.8 THE SPECIAL PROCEDURE WHERE THE ACCUSED IS CHARGED WITH CRIMINAL DAMAGE

Where a defendant is charged with criminal damage contrary to the Criminal Damage Act 1971 s. 1, then unless the offence involves damage by fire, there are special rules regarding mode of trial. If the value of the damaged property is £5,000 or less, the magistrates should proceed to try the case summarily. The defendant has no right of election to the Crown Court. The maximum sentence a magistrates' court can impose for such an offence is three months' imprisonment and/or a £2,500 fine. If the damage to the property is over £5,000, the court is required to hold a mode of trial hearing in the normal way.

The procedure described above deals with situations where a solicitor is representing one adult defendant at the mode of trial hearing. In some cases two or more defendants may be charged in the same proceedings or the defendant may be charged with a co-accused who is a young person (under the age of 18). Below, we consider the procedure where there are two or more co-accused. The procedure in relation to defendants under the age of 18 is considered in Chapter 35, which deals with youth justice.

16.9 MODE OF TRIAL WHERE THERE IS MORE THAN ONE ACCUSED

In a case where there is more than one defendant charged with the same offence and the magistrates are prepared to accept jurisdiction of the matter, each accused enjoys a separate right of election. The decision of one co-accused to elect summary trial or trial on indictment does not bind the other(s). This point was confirmed by the House of Lords in *R v Brentwood Justices, ex p. Nicholls* [1992] 1 AC 1.

Where a defendant facing an either-way offence is charged jointly with another adult defendant who faces an indictable only offence which is related to the either-way matter, the either-way matter must be sent to the Crown Court in accordance with the requirements of s. 51 Crime and Disorder Act 1998 (see Chapter 19). In these circumstances, the defendant facing the either-way offence has no individual right of election.

> **Example**
>
> A is charged with causing grievous bodily harm with intent contrary to s. 18 Offences Against the Person Act 1861 (indictable only). A and B are jointly charged with affray (triable either way). The affray allegation arises out of the assault. A will be sent for trial in the Crown Court. If B appears before magistrates at the same time as A, B's case will also be sent to the Crown Court.

16.10 CHANGING THE ORIGINAL DECISION IN RELATION TO MODE OF TRIAL

The decision at the mode of trial to try the case in either the magistrates' court or the Crown Court is not irrevocable. Section 25(2) MCA 1980 provides that where a decision to try the defendant summarily has been taken and the defendant pleads not guilty, the magistrates may, at any stage before the close of the prosecution case, discontinue the trial and proceed to hold committal proceedings. Such a procedure should be adopted where the prosecution case discloses that the circumstances of the offence are more serious than the magistrates at first realised, with the result that they no longer consider their sentencing powers adequate in the event of conviction.

The power under s. 25(2) only arises once the magistrates have begun to try the case. If an accused has consented to summary trial and then enters a guilty plea, there is no power under s. 25(2) to change their decision from summary trial to trial on indictment. A similar power applies under MCA, s. 25(3), where the original decision at mode of trial was to decline jurisdiction in favour of trial on indictment. At any time before the close of the prosecution case at the committal hearing, the defendant may be offered the right to elect summary trial.

16.11 COMMITTAL PROCEEDINGS – INTRODUCTION

Once a mode of trial enquiry has been held and the defendant has either chosen to elect trial by jury in the Crown Court or the magistrates have declined jurisdiction in favour of the Crown Court, a date will be fixed for the next stage of the proceedings which is the committal hearing. It is usual to have an adjournment of between six and eight weeks from the conclusion of the mode of trial enquiry until the date set for committal. In a case where an accused has been remanded into custody the committal hearing must be held within 28 days. Rules of court relating to committal hearings are contained within Part 10 of the Crim PR.

During the period of the adjournment, the defence solicitor will receive what is commonly referred to as being the 'committal bundle'. This comprises all the 'used' material the prosecution intends to call or rely on against the defendant at trial, together with a list of exhibits and a copy of the draft indictment. The defence solicitor must be satisfied that a prima facie case is disclosed in the 'committal bundle'. An example of a typical committal bundle is contained in our *R v Lenny Whyte* case study (Appendix 1).

Where the advocate feels a *prima facie* case is not disclosed he can request a long style committal at which he will make oral submissions that the case be dismissed at this stage. Otherwise, the matter will be committed to the Crown Court at a short style committal hearing.

16.12 THE PURPOSE OF COMMITTAL PROCEEDINGS

The Crown Court's time is both precious and expensive. The criminal justice system has long required that a defendant should not be sent for trial by jury unless there has been a detailed consideration of whether the evidence discloses a case for the defendant to answer. This filtering role has been fulfilled by the holding of a committal hearing before a panel of magistrates, known as examining justices.

Committal hearings are now held only where the accused is charged with an offence triable either way where the court has decided that the case should be tried in the Crown Court for trial or the defendant has elected trial on indictment. At the committal hearing the CPS is required to establish a prima facie against the accused. This standard is considerably lower than beyond reasonable doubt which the prosecution will have to satisfy at trial in order to secure a conviction.

There are two types of committal proceedings – a committal with consideration of the evidence under MCA, s. 6(1) and a committal without consideration of the evidence under MCA, s. 6(2). The vast majority of committal hearings will fall within s. 6(2) – the short-style committal, as it is commonly known.

16.13 EVIDENCE AT THE COMMITTAL HEARING

It is only the prosecution that is required to present evidence to the court at the committal. For the evidence to be admissible it must be in written form, as oral evidence is not heard, and it must be in the correct form prescribed by ss. 5B, 5C, 5D and 5E MCA 1980. The most common form of evidence tendered at the committal is tendered under s. 5B.

- The statement should be signed by the maker; and
- contain a declaration by the maker that it is true to the best of his knowledge and belief, and that he made knowing it that if he tendered it in evidence he could be prosecuted for wilfully stating in it anything he knew to be false or did not believe to be true; and
- a copy of the statement should be given to each of the parties at the committal before being tendered to the court.

Some documents, such as certificates of convictions or documents from the DVLA will prove themselves and are made admissible at the committal by s. 5E MCA.

16.14 A COMMITTAL WITH CONSIDERATION OF THE EVIDENCE – S. 6(1) MCA

A committal under s. 6(1) will be held in two circumstances. First, where the defendant is not legally represented and secondly, where the defendant's solicitor has requested a s. 6(1) committal in order to make a submission of no case to answer. In this situation the examining justices are required to hear the substance of the prosecution's case against the accused. The key point to remember about this type of committal is that the magistrates will consider the prosecution evidence before deciding whether to commit the case to the Crown Court for trial. The enquiry is limited however in that the magistrates do not hear from live witness, relying instead on the prosecution reading from its witness statements. Furthermore, magistrates have no power at this stage to determine the admissibility of any disputed evidence arising under ss. 78 or 76 PACE 1984 (see Chapters 9 and 10).

16.14.1 PROCEDURE AT A SECTION 6(1) COMMITTAL

A committal under s. 6(1) begins with the charge being read to the defendant. The defendant is not required to enter his plea at this stage. Reporting restrictions apply and any application to have them lifted is dealt with.

The CPS lawyer opens the case by outlining the facts and explaining any relevant points of law. The prosecutor will then formally tender the prosecution evidence to the court. The prosecution needs to present sufficient evidence to establish a prima facie case. Consequently the prosecution does not have to tender all of its evidence at the committal hearing. The prosecution evidence will be written and will consist of the witness statements and exhibits that have been served on the defence in the 'committal bundle'. The prosecution evidence may be read by the magistrates or summarised by the prosecutor to the court. The defence is not required to tender evidence to the court.

After the magistrates have considered the prosecution case, the defence may make a submission of no case to answer. The defence submission will succeed where the prosecution evidence does not disclose a prima facie case to be committed to the Crown

Court. This may be because the prosecution's evidence fails to prove an essential element in the alleged offence or because the evidence is hopelessly weak or seriously contradictory.

Where a submission of no case to answer is upheld, the defendant is discharged. This is not the same thing as being acquitted. In theory the prosecution can re-charge the accused at a later stage and start the criminal litigation process all over again. Alternatively, the CPS could apply to the High Court to prefer a voluntary bill of indictment. It would be open to the defendant to level an abuse of process accusation in support of an application to stay proceedings were the CPS to adopt this course of action.

Where the circumstances and the evidence permit it, magistrates may decide to commit a defendant for trial on a less serious or alternative charge.

If the magistrates decide to commit the defendant to the Crown Court, it is likely to be to the Crown Court that is most geographically convenient, unless there are special features about the case making it desirable for it to be tried elsewhere at a Crown Court outside the area.

16.15 PROCEDURE AT COMMITTAL WITHOUT CONSIDERATION OF THE EVIDENCE – S. 6(2) MCA

By far the vast majority of committals take the form of the short-style committal. Most defendants will choose this form of committal as in most cases there is very little point in choosing a s. 6(1) committal as the threshold the prosecution is required to satisfy is so low that a submission of no case to answer is difficult to sustain. The practical effect of a committal without consideration of the evidence under s. 6(2) (sometimes referred to as a 'paper' committal) is that the accused agrees to be committed to the Crown Court for trial. A s. 6(2) committal will be appropriate where all the evidence tendered by the prosecution consists of written statements in compliance with s. 5 MCA 1980, the defendant is legally represented; and this is not case where you intend to make a submission of 'no case to answer' at this stage.

A s. 6(2) committal is largely an administrative exercise. The charge will be read to the defendant although he will not be expected to plead. The clerk will then check that all the evidence in the committal bundle is in the correct form and that it has been served on the defence. The prosecution evidence disclosed in the committal bundle is not considered and the case is formally committed by the magistrates to the Crown Court for trial.

Once a case has been committed to the Crown Court a date will be fixed in the Crown Court for the defendant's plea and case management hearing (PCMH). The steps to be undertaken in preparation for this hearing are considered in Chapter 19.

16.16 CHANGING FROM TRIAL ON INDICTMENT TO SUMMARY TRIAL

Section 25(3) MCA 1980 provides that where, at the mode of trial enquiry the magistrates considered the case was suitable for trial on indictment, at any time before the close of the prosecution evidence at the committal, the magistrates on hearing the prosecution evidence, conclude that the case is less serious than they originally thought, they should ask the prosecutor and the defence advocate for their views on whether to change to summary trial. If the advocates are in agreement, the legal adviser should then explain to the accused the possibility of committal for sentence and ask him whether he consents to be tried summarily.

16.17 ANCILLARY ISSUES TO BE DEALT WITH UPON COMMITTAL

16.17.1 CRIMINAL PROCEDURE RULE DIRECTIONS

Once a case has been committed for trial under s. 6 MCA 1980, a date will be set for a Plea and Case Management Hearing (PCMH) (see Chapter 19) in the Crown Court. The Criminal Procedure Rules (Crim PR) require a PCMH to be held within seven weeks after committal. In accordance with the Crim PR, the magistrates' court will issue directions to enable the PCMH to be an effective hearing. The standard directions contained in the case management form can be accessed at: http://www.dca.gov.uk. Much of the defence solicitor's post-committal preparation will be to ensure compliance with the directions in preparation for the PCMH. The standard directions make provisions for the service of initial disclosure and defence statement and notification of which prosecution witnesses the defence wishes to attend trial. Once the prosecution has been given notice of witness requirements, the onus is placed on the police to ascertain witness availability. This information will be required at the PCMH. Provision is also made in the standard directions for the service of:

- any application for a special measures direction (see Chapter 22);
- notice to admit hearsay or evidence of bad character, (see Chapters 25 and 26);
- defence notice objecting to the admission of hearsay or bad character.

16.17.2 BAIL

When the case is adjourned after the committal, the issue of a defendant's bail might arise. Where the defendant has previously been refused bail, a fresh application for bail might be made depending on how many previous applications for bail have already been made. Generally the committal of a defendant to stand trial at the Crown Court does not amount to a change in circumstances supporting a third application for a bail (see Chapter 15). You should ensure bail is extended to cover the Crown Court proceedings where your client is currently subject to bail (conditional or otherwise).

16.17.3 REPRESENTATION ORDER

If the defendant's representation order is not a 'through order', i.e. it covers the costs of his legal representation both in the magistrates' court and in the Crown Court, the defence solicitor must make an oral application to have the order extended to cover the proceedings in the Crown Court.

16.17.4 DISCLOSURE

By the time of the committal, the prosecution will have disclosed to you the substance of the case against the defendant under the Advance Information Rules and in the 'committal bundle'. The provisions of the Criminal Procedure and Investigations Act 1996 (CPIA) regulating the disclosure of unused material, apply on committal or as soon as reasonably practicable thereafter. The matter of the pre-trial disclosure of used and 'unused' material is considered in detail in Chapter 17. The first stage of disclosure of unused material under the CPIA 1996 requires the prosecution to serve on the defence any initial prosecution disclosure together with a schedule of any 'unused' material. The prosecution may well have included any initial disclosure in the 'committal bundle'. The defendant has 14 days after the prosecution has served or has purported to serve initial disclosure, to serve a defence statement which is mandatory in all cases to be tried on indictment.

16.17.5 **OBJECTING TO STATEMENTS BEING READ AT TRIAL**

Schedule 2 CPIA 1996 is of particular importance. The usual way of placing evidence before a Crown Court is for the prosecution to call witnesses to give oral evidence and to be cross-examined. Schedule 2 however, provides that any committal statements tendered at the committal hearing 'may without further proof be read as evidence on the trial of the accused'. The CPS is obliged to serve notice of the defendant's right to object to evidence being read at trial at the same time as service of the committal bundle (Part 27.2 Crim PR). An example of such a notice is contained in the Lenny Whyte case study, the complete documentation to which can be accessed via the student resource section of our Online Resource Centre. If a defendant objects to a witness statement simply being read out at trial he must give written notice of his objection to the prosecution within 14 days of his committal. It is therefore important for the defence solicitor to remember the 14-day time-limit. As a matter of good practice and to be on the safe side, the defence solicitor ought to automatically send out a letter to the CPS objecting to any witness statements being read out at trial. If the defence solicitor's view on this changes as he prepares for trial, the CPS can be notified at a later date that the defence is now prepared to agree the witness's statement being read to the court.

online resource centre

16.18 CRIMINAL JUSTICE ACT 2003 – ABOLITION OF COMMITTAL PROCEEDINGS

Looking Ahead

Committal proceedings in relation to either-way offences will be abolished in accordance with Sch. 3 of the CJA 2003. The provisions are not expected to be implemented until November 2006. When they are, and once a decision has been taken by magistrates to decline jurisdiction or the accused has been given the choice and has elected trial by jury, the matter will be sent to the Crown Court, under a procedure (s. 51 Crime and Disorder Act 1998) which very similar to that which applies to indictable-only offences (see Chapter 19).

16.19 COMMITTING A LINKED SUMMARY OFFENCE TO THE CROWN COURT FOR TRIAL – S. 40 CJA 1988

What happens where a defendant is committed for trial in the Crown Court but is also accused of a related summary offence? A linked summary offence for the purpose of CJA 1988, s. 40 means a summary offence that is founded on the same facts as the indictable offence or is part of a series of offences of the same or similar character as the indictable offence and the summary offence comes within the category of offences that can be committed to the Crown Court for trial under CJA 1988, s. 40. These offences are:

- common assault;
- assaulting a prison warder;
- taking a motor vehicle without consent;
- driving while disqualified;
- criminal damage of £5,000 or less.

Where a defendant is charged with an either-way offence and a specified linked summary offence, the court may commit both offences to the Crown Court for trial with both the summary and the either-way offence included in the indictment. The 'committal bundle' must disclose evidence of the summary offence.

The effect of s. 40 is that where the defendant is arraigned in the Crown Court, the count in respect of the summary offence and the offence to be tried on indictment will be put to the accused. If he pleads not guilty, a jury will be sworn and evidence will be heard in respect of both offences. If the defendant is found guilty of the summary offence, the Crown Court's sentencing powers will be limited to those of the magistrates – a maximum custodial sentence of six months and/or a £5,000 fine or less if the statute creating the offence so dictates.

Example

Brian has been charged with the burglary of a dwelling house (either way) and to escape from the crime scene, he took a car without the owner's consent (summary only). At the mode of trial enquiry, after hearing the submissions of the prosecutor and the defence advocate and by applying the statutory factors and the mode of trial guidelines, the magistrates believe that the offence of burglary should be tried on indictment. At the s. 6(2) committal the prosecution will seek to have both offences committed to the Crown Court for trial. At Brian's trial, the taking without consent will be included on the indictment along with the count relating to the burglary. Brian will be asked to plead to each count. If he pleads not guilty the jury will be sworn and the prosecution will present evidence to the court in respect of both offences.

16.20 COMMITTING A LINKED SUMMARY OFFENCE FOR PLEA TO THE CROWN COURT – S. 41 CJA 1988

Where a defendant is committed for trial on an either-way offence, s. 41 CJA 1988 permits the magistrates to commit a linked summary offence to the Crown Court for sentence. For s. 41 to apply, the summary offence must:

- be punishable with either imprisonment or disqualification from driving; and
- must arise out of the same set of circumstances that are similar to or are connected with the either-way offence.

It is important to be aware of a number of points about s. 41:

- The section applies to either-way offences only that have been committed to the Crown Court for trial.
- The Crown Court will not try the summary case under s. 41. It is committed only for a plea to be taken. If the defendant is found guilty of the either-way offence and pleads guilty to the summary offence, he can be sentenced by the Crown Court for both offences. The Crown Court's sentencing powers in respect to the summary offence are limited to those of the magistrates.
- If the defendant pleads not guilty to the summary offence or is acquitted of the either-way offence, the Crown Court will not deal with the summary offence and will have to remit the summary offence back to the magistrates to be tried. When the Courts Act 2003, s. 66 comes into force (empowering Crown Court judges to exercise the powers of magistrates), a Crown Court judge (sitting without a jury) will be able to try the summary offence.

Example

Donald is charged with dangerous driving (an either-way offence) following a police pursuit. He is also charged with driving without insurance (a summary-only offence). Having committed the offence of dangerous driving to the Crown Court for trial, the magistrates can include the insurance offence for a plea to be taken under s. 41 CJA 1988 as the offence can result in disqualification and it arises out of circumstances connected to the either-way matter.

In the Crown Court, if Donald is found guilty of dangerous driving, he will be asked plead to the offence of driving without insurance. If he pleads guilty to this offence he may be sentenced for both the either-way offence and the summary offence. If he pleads not guilty to the summary offence or is found not guilty of dangerous driving, the driving without insurance offence will be remitted to the magistrates for trial.

Looking Ahead

Section 41 is prospectively repealed by Sch. 3 CJA 2003. This is linked to the abolition of committal proceedings highlighted at paragraph 16.18 above. In future, either-way matters that are to be tried in the Crown Court, will be sent there under an amended s. 51 Crime and Disorder Act 1998 (see Chapter 19). Under the notice procedure, the magistrates will also be able to send the defendant to be tried on any related summary offence punishable with imprisonment or disqualification from driving.

16.21 ALTERNATIVES TO COMMITTAL

We make brief mention of the other methods by which a person charged with an either- way offence may lawfully be required to stand trial before a Crown Court without having been committed for trial by a magistrate's court. Further consideration is given to these methods in *Blackstone's Criminal Practice*. They include:

- voluntary bill of indictment;
- notice of transfer in relation to serious or complex frauds – s. 4 CJA 1987;
- notice of transfer in relation to an offence of a violent or sexual nature where there is a child witness – s. 53 CJA 1991.

In relation to the latter two, the defendant will still make an initial appearance before magistrates at which ancillary matters relating to bail and legal aid will be determined. Provision is made for an accused to apply to the Crown Court to have the charges specified in the notice dismissed.

KEY POINT SUMMARY IN RELATION TO EITHER-WAY OFFENCES

- In relation to all either-way offences, a defendant will be required to give an indication of his plea – this is known as the plea before venue.
- If the defendant indicates a guilty plea, the magistrates must accept jurisdiction but can commit the defendant to the Crown Court for sentence.
- Where a not guilty plea or no plea is indicated, a mode of trial enquiry must be held and the initial decision as to where the case shall be tried lies with the magistrates.
- In reaching a decision as regards mode of trial, the magistrates will apply the statutory factors in s. 19, MCA 1980 and the National Mode of Trial Guidelines and will consider, in particular, whether their maximum sentencing powers are likely to be sufficient.
- When advising your client about mode of trial not only consider the legal merits of advising in favour of summary trial or trial on indictment but consider also your client's personal circumstances and whether he could cope with the considerable demands of a Crown Court trial.
- Find out in advance the prosecution's views on mode of trial and if necessary be prepared to argue against the CPS.
- The CPS can indirectly control the mode of trial in that it enjoys a largely unfettered discretion as regards charging a suspect and adjusting those charges at a later date. Thus a defendant charged

with common assault as opposed to assault occasioning actual bodily harm (s. 47 OAPA 1861) can only be tried summarily. Representations may be appropriate. Reference should be made to the Code for Crown Prosecutors – see Chapter 13.

KEY POINT SUMMARY IN RELATION TO COMMITTAL HEARINGS

- On receipt of the committal bundle the defence solicitor must set aside some time to go through the documentation in order to see if a *prima facie* case is disclosed.

- The circumstances in which a s. 6(1) committal is sought will be rare.

- Reporting restrictions apply at committal proceedings but an application can be made by the defence to have them lifted.

- Where the matter is committed to the Crown Court, the defence solicitor must ensure he deals with post committal matters (legal aid/bail/writing to the CPS objecting to committal witness statements being read at trial).

SELF-TEST QUESTIONS

Consider the following short scenarios.

- What representations do you consider the prosecution might make as regards mode of trial in each case?

- Applying s.19 MCA 1980 factors and the National Mode of Trial Guidelines, do you consider the magistrates will accept or decline jurisdiction?

- Outline the procedure in relation to each possibility and consider, if the accused in each of the following exercises were given the choice as to election, what advice you would give in this regard.

Exercise 1

Gordon Davey is 45 years old. He is charged with unlawful sexual activity with his 14-year-old niece, contrary to s. 9(1) Sexual Offences Act 2003. It is alleged that he committed the indecent assault by touching her through her clothes. He is pleading not guilty and has no previous convictions.

Exercise 2

Simon Hayley is a 36-year-old pharmacist. He is charged with 16 offences of false accounting (s. 17 Theft Act 1968) and obtaining money transfers worth £15,830 by deception (s. 15A Theft Act 1968) from the Prescription Pricing Authority. It is alleged that over a period of eight months he claimed expenditure for dispensing ordinary purpose syringes when his records show that he in fact dispensed a cheaper plastic disposable syringe. Simon is a man of impeccable character and denies the allegation.

Exercise 3

Wayne Mason faces three charges, including dangerous driving (s. 2 Road Traffic Act 1988 – triable either way), taking a vehicle without the owner's consent (s.12 Theft Act 1968 – summary-only) and driving without insurance (s. 143 Road Traffic Act 1988). It is alleged he stole a VW Golf vehicle. When pursued by an unmarked police car, it is alleged that the driver of the vehicle drove at speeds in excess of 60 miles an hour for a short period of time in a built-up area while permitting his passenger to throw beer cans out of the passenger side window into the path of the police car giving chase. The car was driven to the end of a cul-de-sac before being abandoned. Two youths were seen running off in the direction of Wayne Mason's home.

Wayne Mason denies the charge, maintaining he has an alibi for the relevant time. The main witness against him is the police officer who gave chase, who claims to recognise Wayne as being the driver of the car. Wayne has several previous convictions, including several driving-related convictions. He was not offered an identification parade at the police station and denies knowing the officer who purports to have recognised him. There would appear to be no forensic evidence linking him to the scene.

Case Studies: *R v Lenny Whyte; R v William Hardy*

Plea before venue in practice

The offences in each of these case studies are triable either way. In each case, we have requested and received advance information. Having reviewed the advance information in relation to *R v Lenny Whyte* (see relevant documents in Appendix 1), a not guilty plea is entered and the matter proceeds to the mode of trial enquiry. Having reviewed the advance information in relation *R v William Hardy* (see relevant documents in Appendix 2) you will see his solicitor advises him to plead guilty (see Documents 11 and 12).

For an illustration of the plea before venue procedure, you need to access the video section of our Online Resource Centre in relation to *R v Hardy*. You will see William Hardy taken through the plea before venue before confirming an intention to plead guilty. In this case the court decides to accept jurisdiction to sentence William Hardy. The court could have just as easily decided to commit Mr Hardy to sentence in the Crown Court. The court passes sentence on William Hardy following an adjournment for a pre-sentence report. We invite you to defer consideration of the plea in mitigation in this case until you have considered Part V on sentencing practice.

Mode of Trial – *R v Lenny Whyte*

Take a look at *R v Lenny Whyte* in the video section of our Online Resource Centre. You will recall that Lenny is charged with domestic burglary. His initial appearance ended in an adjournment to enable the CPS to provide advance information. Lenny was remanded in custody. Since his first appearance, advance information has now been provided and considered. Lenny's solicitor takes him through the prosecution witness statements and gives him advice as regards mode of trial. The advice of Lenny's solicitor is contained in a file note (see Document 20 in Appendix 1).

You will see that Lenny's solicitor does not feel the magistrates will accept jurisdiction to try Lenny's matter, as domestic burglary offences are invariably regarded as being serious by magistrates' courts. Lenny's solicitor nevertheless goes on to consider what Lenny should do in the event of the magistrates accepting jurisdiction. On the video you can see Lenny's second appearance before magistrates at which he indicates a not guilty plea followed by his mode of trial enquiry. You will also see the outline by the CPS lawyer inviting the bench to decline jurisdiction to try the matter. At the conclusion of the mode of trial enquiry the magistrates decline jurisdiction and adjourn the matter for committal to the Crown Court. The reason for their decision is that they do not believe their sentencing powers would be sufficient in the event of conviction having regard to a number of aggravating factors.

R v Lenny Whyte – committal to the Crown Court

In relation to *R v Lenny Whyte*, the magistrates declined jurisdiction. His case is therefore adjourned and a date has been set for his committal hearing. The CPS serves the 'committal bundle' on Lenny's solicitor (see Document 23 located in Appendix 1). Lenny's solicitor accepts the committal bundle discloses a case to answer and she agrees a short-style committal in accordance with s. 6(2) MCA 1980 (see Document 24).

Lenny's solicitor attends the short-style committal and Lenny's case is committed to the Crown Court with a date being fixed for his PCMH (see Document 24). This is confirmed in a letter to Lenny (see Document 28). Lenny's solicitor is in possession of a through representation order. You will see that she subsequently writes to the CPS inter alia, objecting to witness statements being read out at Lenny's trial (see Documents 32 and 33.) Any documents referred to that are not included in Appendix 1 can be located in the complete *R v Lenny Whyte* case study contained in our Online Resource Centre.

FIGURE 16.1 EITHER-WAY OFFENCE – GENERAL SEQUENCE OF EVENTS

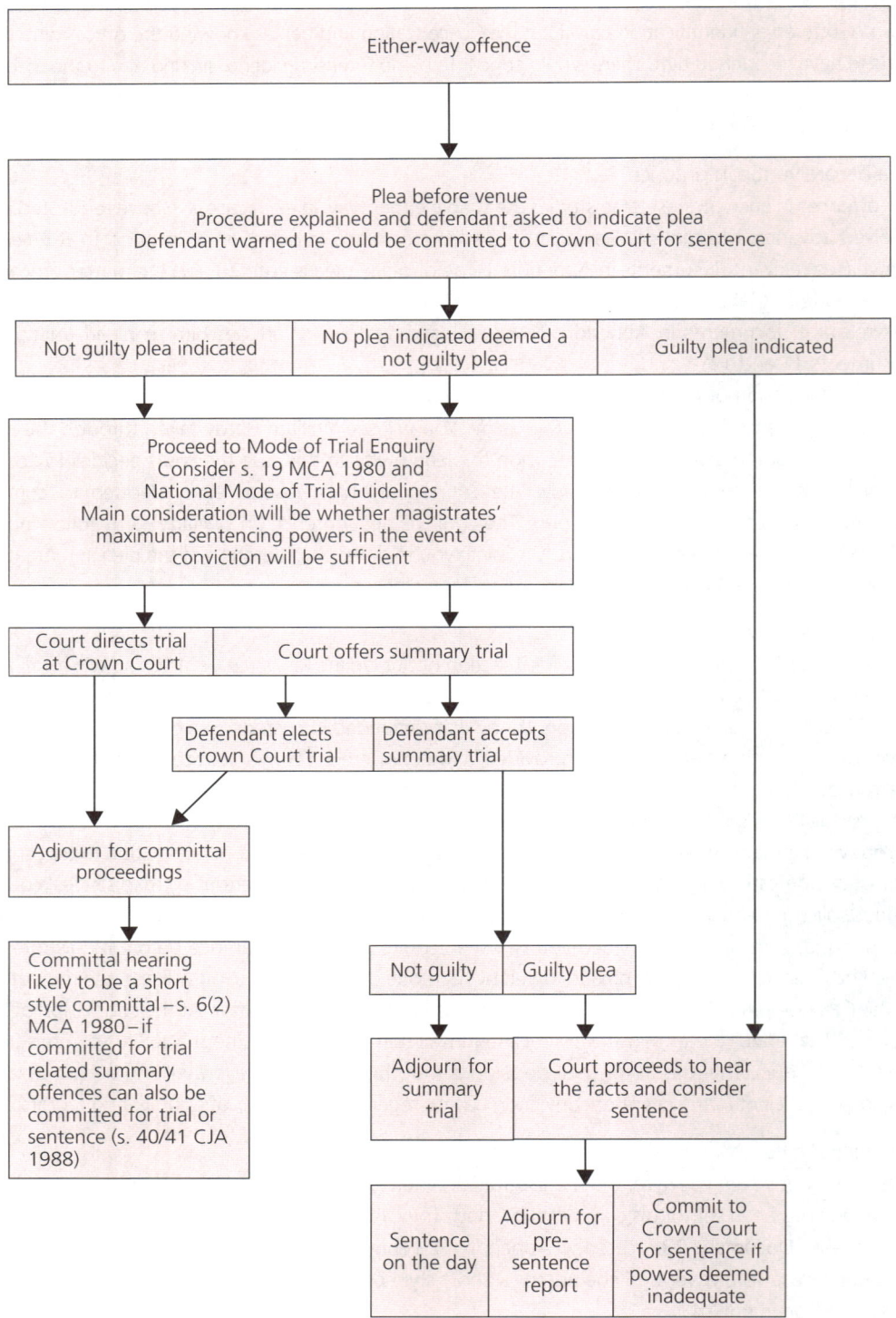

17 PRE-TRIAL DISCLOSURE OF EVIDENCE

17.1 INTRODUCTION

At a number of stages in a criminal case the rules governing the pre-trial disclosure of evidence impose extensive obligations on the prosecution. The precise operation of the rules depends on the classification of the offence that is being tried. For this reason, we have decided to include the rules in a separate chapter to provide a coherent overview of them. You will therefore need to cross-reference this chapter to earlier and later chapters where issues of pre-trial disclosure of evidence arise.

The rules relating to the pre-trial disclosure of evidence apply for the most part to the prosecution and are critical to a defendant's right to a fair trial. Clearly a defendant cannot be expected to defend allegations made against him unless he is aware of the precise evidence in support of those allegations. It would be wholly wrong for the prosecution (with the resources it has available) to withhold evidence that weakens the prosecution's case. Although the aim in the adversarial system of trial is to win, there are wider obligations on the prosecution to assist the search for the truth and to ensure that a miscarriage of justice does not occur.

The right to the pre-trial disclosure of evidence is enshrined in the European Convention on Human Rights (ECHR) as being fundamental to the right to a fair trial under Article 6(1). Article 6(3)(b) provides:

> 'Everyone charged with a criminal offence has the right to be informed promptly, in a language which he understands and in detail of the nature and cause of the accusation against him.'

As well as supporting the defendant's right to a fair trial, the pre-trial disclosure of evidence greatly assists the administration of justice by enabling the court and the parties to identify the issues that are likely to be in dispute at trial. The parties' pre-trial preparations are therefore focused on these issues and the trial is less likely to be diverted by having to deal with unexpected, subsidiary matters. There are also time-saving advantages in requiring pre-trial disclosure. On the basis of the disclosed evidence, a client can be advised on whether, for example, to elect trial on indictment for an either-way offence or whether to plead guilty at an early stage to attract the full sentencing discount. A timely guilty plea also saves considerable time and expense for the parties and the court. Pre-trial disclosure may lead to the evidence of some prosecution witnesses being agreed in written form without the requirement for them to attend court, thereby saving time and expense.

17.2 WITHHOLDING RELEVANT EVIDENCE

Occasionally, the prosecution or a third party will resist the disclosure of otherwise relevant and admissible evidence on the basis that that it is 'sensitive' and it is not in the wider public interest for it to be heard in the public domain of a criminal trial. The defence, however, may wish to see such evidence in order to evaluate and challenge it. Where disclosure is opposed on this basis, the prosecution raises an issue of public interest immunity (PII). While many aspects of disclosure are regulated by statute, the principles relating to PII remain governed by the common law. We briefly consider the law relating to PII towards the end of this chapter.

17.3 WHERE CAN YOU FIND THE RULES ON THE PRE-TRIAL DISCLOSURE OF EVIDENCE?

The entire process of disclosure has become unnecessarily complicated, for the following reasons:

- The rules are not contained in one place and have developed piecemeal.
- Some of the rules are embodied in statute while others have developed as a result of the common law.
- Guidance on the application of the rules is found in the non-statutory source of the Attorney-General's Guidelines on Disclosure. The importance of these guidelines cannot be underestimated. They can be accessed from our Online Resource Centre, and at http://www.lslo.gov.uk/pdf/disclosure.doc.
- The disclosure regime applies differently depending on the classification of the offence.

online resource centre

- The Criminal Justice Act 2003 has introduced important changes to the rules governing the pre-trial disclosure obligations of both the prosecution and the defence.

17.4 USED AND UNUSED MATERIAL

Central to an understanding of the rules relating to disclosure is the distinction between 'used' and 'unused' material. These words are not defined formally but are adopted by us as convenient labels to assist understanding.

'Used' material refers to evidence the prosecution intends to rely on at trial and is usually disclosed during the early stages of the case. Our case studies (*R v William Hardy*, *R v Lenny Whyte*, *R v Roger Martin* (web-based only)) include examples of 'used material'.

'Unused' material comprises evidence which the prosecution is aware of but which will not form part of the prosecution's case against the accused at trial.

online
resource
centre

17.5 EITHER-WAY OFFENCES AND THE DISCLOSURE OF USED MATERIAL

The prosecution has a duty to disclose 'used' material at an early stage in connection with an offence triable either way. It is known as advance information.

Prior to the plea before venue/mode of trial hearing, Part 21 Crim PR requires the Crown Prosecution Service to have served on the defence either a summary of the prosecution case or more usually copies of the prosecution witness statements. Disclosure at this early stage will also include a summary or copy of any tape-recorded interview.

We have already considered in Chapter 16 the importance of obtaining advance information of the prosecution case in all but the most clear-cut of cases. You will not be able to advise your client properly on whether to plead guilty or not guilty or whether to elect trial by jury if he is pleading not guilty unless the prosecution has disclosed the substance of its case against your client and you have evaluated the strengths and weaknesses.

17.5.1 FURTHER PRE-TRIAL DISCLOSURE OF 'USED MATERIAL' IN EITHER-WAY CASES POST MODE OF TRIAL

The rules on the further disclosure of 'used' material for either-way offences will depend on whether the case is to be tried summarily or on indictment at the Crown Court. Where the mode of trial enquiry has been adjourned for a committal hearing, the prosecution is required to serve on the defendant a 'committal bundle' prior to the committal hearing (see Chapter 16). The 'committal bundle' will be similar to advance information, but will be more detailed. It should contain the draft indictment, prosecution witness statements and other evidence, including lists of all exhibits. All prosecution witness statements will be typed. There is no obligation on the prosecution to disclose all the evidence it intends to rely on at trial at this stage, although in practice it usually will.

The primary purpose of the committal hearing is to determine whether there is a case to answer before it is committed to the Crown Court. The 'committal bundle' must be served before the committal hearing in order to give the defence time to consider whether a *prima facie* case is in fact made out and to ascertain which prosecution witnesses the defence requires to attend trial. Once the case is committed to the Crown Court, the disclosure provisions relating to 'unused material' are triggered. These provisions are contained in the CPIA 1996 and are considered in detail below.

If the either-way case is to remain in the magistrates' court, then once a not guilty plea is entered, provision is made for the disclosure of 'unused material' under the CPIA at this stage.

17.6 SUMMARY OFFENCES AND THE DISCLOSURE OF USED MATERIAL

In summary proceedings, there is no statutory requirement for the prosecution to disclose the evidence that it intends to use at the trial (*R v Stratford Justices, ex p. Imbert* [1999] 2 Cr App R 276). Since this decision, the Attorney-General's Guidelines on Disclosure (para. 57) provide it is good practice for the CPS to disclose 'used' material to the defence in summary-only cases. As such, advance information is routinely made available for summary-only offences on request. Where an accused indicates an intention to plead not guilty to a summary-only offence, the provisions relating to 'unused material' under the CPIA 1996 are triggered.

17.7 INDICTABLE-ONLY OFFENCES AND THE DISCLOSURE OF USED MATERIAL

In accordance with s. 51 of the Crime and Disorder Act 1998, indictable-only offences must be sent forthwith to the Crown Court for trial following the defendant's initial appearance before magistrates. The procedural course of an indictable-only offence is explored in Chapter 19. The Rules of Court (Crime and Disorder Act 1998 (Service of Prosecution Evidence) Regulations 2005 SI 2005/902) provide for the disclosure of 'used' material (in the form of a 'case sent bundle'). The 'case sent bundle' is similar to the 'committal bundle' and should be served within 70 or 50 days (the shorter time applying to a defendant remanded in custody) of the case being sent to the Crown Court. The provisions relating to notice of additional evidence apply to any evidence not adduced in the case sent bundle which the prosecution proposes to rely on at trial.

Although the Advance Information Rules have no application to indictable-only offences, the CPS will normally serve available advance information at an early stage in indictable-only cases where a request is made and where fairness requires such disclosure. This is particularly important as bail is more likely to be contested in indictable-only offences and in relation to an application for bail, one factor the court will have regard to, is the strength of evidence against the accused (see Chapter 15). The requirement is endorsed in para. 55 of the Attorney-General's Guidelines on Disclosure.

17.8 DISCLOSURE PROVISIONS RELATING TO 'UNUSED' MATERIAL AND THE CRIMINAL PROCEDURE AND INVESTIGATIONS ACT (CPIA) 1996

The disclosure of 'unused' material is regulated by the Criminal Procedure and Investigations Act 1996 (CPIA). Some of the changes to the disclosure of unused material under the CJA 2003 came into force in April 2005; others have not. Before April 2005, disclosure involved a three-stage process:

- primary prosecution disclosure;
- service of a defence statement;
- secondary prosecution disclosure.

Under the CJA 2003, the disclosure process is replaced with initial disclosure (embracing what was previously primary and secondary disclosure) and an on-going duty on the CPS to keep disclosure under review throughout the proceedings.

The defence solicitor will need to consider the application of the CPIA 1996 in relation to all contested summary proceedings and all contested cases to be tried on indictment. Our case study *R v Lenny Whyte* is an example of an either-way offence which is to be tried on indictment. The requirements of the CPIA 1996 are illustrated in the context of this case as part of preparation for trial on indictment (see Chapters 19 and 20).

online resource centre

The substantive provisions of the CPIA 1996 are supplemented by a detailed Code of Practice in Part II of the CPIA 1996 (s. 23) and by the Attorney-General's Guidelines on Disclosure. The Code of Practice has been revised to take account of the CJA 2003 changes. The code can be accessed via the web-links section of the Online Resource Centre and at http://police.homeoffice.gov.uk.

17.8.1 KEEPING TRACK OF INVESTIGATIVE MATERIAL

The Code of Practice (para. 5) requires the recording and retention of all relevant information and material gathered or generated during an investigation. A disclosure officer has to be appointed to each investigation, who may be a member of the investigative team. The requirement to record extends to all types of information, including evidence obtained during the investigation (searches of the person or his property), evidence generated by the investigation (incriminating admissions and no comment interviews, etc.) and information received orally. Paragraph 5 of the Code specifies the types of relevant material which should be routinely retained in a criminal case. It includes:

- crime reports;
- custody records;
- records of telephone calls, e.g. 999 calls;
- final versions of witness statements (and draft versions, where their content differs from the final version);
- interview records;
- communications between the police and experts such as forensic scientists, reports of work carried out by experts, and schedules of scientific material prepared by the expert for the investigator, for the purposes of criminal proceedings;
- information provided by a accused person which indicates an explanation for the offence with which he has been charged;
- any material casting doubt on the reliability of a confession;
- any material casting doubt on the reliability of a witness;
- records of first description of a suspect by each potential witness who purports to identify or describe the suspect, whether or not the description differs from that of subsequent descriptions by that or other witness.

Where there is any doubt about the relevance of material gathered or generated, the investigator must retain it.

17.8.2 DISCLOSURE SCHEDULES

Paragraph 6 of the Code requires material which is relevant to the investigation and which the disclosure officer thinks will not form part of the prosecution's case to be listed in a schedule of non-sensitive material. If the disclosure officer believes the material to be sensitive it must be listed on a separate sensitive schedule.

Sensitive material is material which the investigating officer believes would not be in the public interest to disclose, including evidence relating to national security or police informants, location of surveillance positions and material relating to children.

The schedules are then passed to the Crown Prosecution Service. The schedules must be prepared in the following instances:

- where the offence is indictable only; or
- it is an either-way offence likely to be tried in the Crown; or
- where the defendant is likely to plead not guilty to a matter which is to be tried summarily.

The material must be listed in the schedule with sufficient detail to enable the prosecutor to decide whether he needs to inspect it before a decision is made to disclose it to the defence. In addition to the listing of material, the disclosure officer must provide the prosecutor with a copy of any material which undermines the prosecution's case, including records of first description of a suspect and information relating to any explanation by the defendant for the offence charged (para. 7). The schedules may need to be amended in the light of consideration of the evidence by a CPS lawyer.

By virtue of s. 26 CPIA 1996, the Code is admissible in evidence where breach of its provisions is relevant to a question arising in the proceedings. Section 26 further provides that a failure by the police to observe the Code will not result in civil or criminal liability. A failure by the prosecution to comply with its disclosure obligations clearly affects the fairness of the proceedings however and could well be the subject of an application by the defence to stay the proceedings for abuse of process.

17.8.3 SECTION 3 CPIA 1996 (AS AMENDED BY S. 32 CJA 2003) – INITIAL DISCLOSURE

'The prosecutor must

(a) disclose to the accused any prosecution material which has not previously been disclosed to the accused and which might reasonably be considered capable of undermining the case for the prosecution against the accused or of assisting the case for the accused.'

In *R v Vasilou* [2000] 4 Archbold News 1, the Court of Appeal held this would include the disclosure of a prosecution witness's previous convictions.

The test the prosecutor must apply under s. 3 CPIA is objective. The prosecutor must decide which evidence might reasonably undermine the prosecution's case. In the Attorney-General's Guidelines on Disclosure (paras. 10–14), material that can reasonably be considered capable of undermining the prosecution case against the accused or assisting the defence case will include:

'10. . . . . . . anything that tends to show a fact inconsistent with the elements of the case that must be proved by the prosecution. Material can fulfil the disclosure test:

(a) by the use to be made of it in cross-examination; or

(b) by its capacity to support submissions that could lead to:
    (i) the exclusion of evidence; or
    (ii) a stay of proceedings; or
    (iii) a court or tribunal finding that any public authority had acted incompatibly with the accused 's rights under the ECHR, or

(c) by its capacity to suggest an explanation or partial explanation of the accused's actions.

11. In deciding whether material may fall to be disclosed under paragraph 10, especially (b)(ii), prosecutors must consider whether disclosure is required in order for a proper application to be made. The purpose of this paragraph is not to allow enquiries to support speculative arguments or for the manufacture of defences.

12. Examples of material that might reasonably be considered capable of undermining the prosecution case or of assisting the case for the accused are:

- any material casting doubt upon the accuracy of any prosecution evidence;
- any material which may point to another person, whether charged or not (including a co-accused) having involvement in the commission of the offence;
- any material which may cast doubt upon the reliability of a confession;
- any material that might go to the credibility of a prosecution witness;
- any material that might support a defence that is either raised by the defence or apparent from the prosecution papers;
- any material which may have a bearing on the admissibility of any prosecution evidence.

13. It should also be borne in mind that while items of material viewed in isolation may not be reasonably considered to be capable of undermining the prosecution case or assisting the accused, several items together can have that effect.

14. Material relating to the accused's mental or physical health, intellectual capacity, or to any ill treatment which the accused may have suffered when in the investigator's custody is likely to fall within the test for disclosure set out in paragraph 8 above.'

Disclosure under s. 3 CPIA is limited to information in the prosecutor's possession or which the prosecutor has inspected. The prosecutor's disclosure duty is thus entirely dependent on the efficiency and honesty of the disclosure officer who prepares the schedule. Disclosure can be made by either giving a copy of the material to the defence or allowing the defence to inspect it at a reasonable time and place.

If no initial disclosure is available, the CPS must provide a written statement to the defendant confirming this is the case. Along with initial disclosure, the CPS must also disclose a copy of the schedule of non-sensitive material prepared by the disclosure officer in the case.

17.9 DEFENCE DISCLOSURE UNDER THE CPIA 1996 (AS AMENDED BY CJA 2003)

The biggest and most controversial change under the CJA 2003 relates to defence disclosure. The provisions are contained in ss. 33–36 CPIA and will amend the current s. 6 CPIA to include ss. 6A, 6B, 6C, 6D and 6E. Submitting a defence statement is a compulsory requirement in all cases to be tried on indictment (s. 5 CPIA). It is voluntary for cases to be tried in the magistrates' court (s. 6 CPIA). A failure by the defendant to comply with any of the obligations imposed by the CPIA 1996 may result in an adverse inference being drawn under s. 11 CPIA 1996.

17.9.1 TIME IN WHICH TO SERVE DEFENCE STATEMENT

The accused has 14 days in which to file a defence statement in compliance with s. 5 CPIA 1996. Time runs from the date on which the prosecution complies or purports to comply with its obligations under s. 3. The inclusion of the words 'purporting to comply' is worth highlighting. It implies partial disclosure is enough to trigger the defence disclosure obligation under s. 5. The defence can apply for an extension of the time limit before it expires but the decision to extend lies at the discretion of the court.

17.9.2 WHAT MUST A DEFENCE STATEMENT CONTAIN?

Section 6A requires that a defence statement must be in writing and must:

(a) set out the nature of the accused's defence including any particular defences on which he intends to rely;

(b) indicate the matters of fact on which he takes issue with the prosecution;

(c) set out, in the case of each matter, why he takes issue with the prosecution; and

(d) indicate any point of law (including any point as to the admissibility of evidence) which he wishes to take, and any authority on which he intends to rely for that purpose.

A defence statement that discloses an alibi must give particulars including the name, address and date of birth of the witness, or as many of those details as are known to the accused when the statement is given, including any information in the accused's possession which might be of material assistance in identifying or finding any such witness. There is a continuing duty on the accused to provide this information if it comes to light after service of the defence statement.

As a result of s. 6A, defence statements have to contain a greater degree of specificity than was previously the case. The level of detailed required will no doubt cause considerable practical difficulties for defence solicitors who struggle sometimes to obtain clear instructions from a client with little recollection of the events and within a very tight timeframe.

17.9.3 SERVICE OF AN UPDATED DEFENCE STATEMENT

There is now a requirement on the accused to serve an updated defence statement nearer the start of the trial (s. 6B CPIA, inserted by s. 33 CJA 2003). Instead of an updated defence statement, the defendant may give a witness statement stating that he has no changes to make to the defence statement which he has already given.

Provision is made in s. 33 (amending s. 5 CPIA 1996) for defence statements to be served on co-accused upon the application of any party or by the court of its own motion fairness to each co-defendant would normally require disclosure to be mutual. These two provisions are not currently in force.

17.9.4 NOTIFYING THE PROSECUTION OF INTENDED WITNESSES

Section 34 CJA inserts s. 6C into the CPIA and will require a defendant to indicate whether he intends to call any persons as witnesses. If defence witnesses are to be called, the defendant must provide details which include the names, address and date of birth of each witness, if known. This will enable the prosecution to run checks on the character of such witnesses before trial. The possibility of the prosecution interviewing such witnesses before trial is a distinct one. A Code of Practice in relation to this is currently being drafted.

Section 6C has the potential to cause considerable practical difficulties for defence lawyers, as the decision about whether to call a particular witness is a tactical one that is subject to constant review. There is nothing in s. 6C that permits the prosecution to comment on a failure by the defendant to call a specified witness. The only comment that is permitted is in relation to a decision to call a witness who has not previously been specified. Where this results in a case being adjourned the defence can expect a wasted costs order to be made against it. This would be entirely consistent with the duty imposed on the courts under Crim PR, Part 3 to actively manage cases. Section 6C is not currently in force.

17.9.5 NOTIFICATION OF THE DECISION TO INSTRUCT AN EXPERT WITNESS

Section 6D has also been added to the CPIA. It provides that if an accused instructs an expert witness with a view to providing an opinion as evidence at trial, he must give to the court and the prosecutor a notice specifying the person's name and address unless specified in the defence statement. The implementation of s. 6D CPIA is another controversial measure. Section 81 PACE and the Crown Court (Advance Notice of Expert Evidence) Rules 1987 already requires both the prosecution and the defence to disclose any expert evidence to be called at trial. The prosecution would also come under a duty to disclose an expert's report that has been obtained but will not be used at trial, if it falls within the ambit of s. 3 CPIA 1996.

Section 6D will redress the balance in favour of the prosecution by preventing the defence from instructing several experts until a report is obtained which supports its case. It will also allow an unused defence expert to be contacted by the prosecution.

Having obtained a report, the defence might choose not to rely on the expert's report for any number of reasons. There is of course no property in a witness. However, experts will normally have been sent legally privileged information before being asked to provide a report. If the prosecution were to seek access to such a witness in advance of trial the potential for inadvertent disclosure of legally privileged material is high. Section 6D is not currently in force.

17.9.6 SANCTIONS FOR FAILURE TO COMPLY

Section 39 CJA 2003 extends the sanctions for non-compliance under s. 11 CPIA to the extended obligations under the CJA 2003 including a failure to file an updated statement or calling a witness not previously notified.

A defence statement will be deemed to have been made on the instructions of an accused, making it more difficult for an accused to distance himself from it and blame any omission or mistakes on his solicitor. At the discretion of the trial judge, the statement or an edited version may be made available to the jury and in some instances it may be admitted into evidence (s. 6E CPIA 1996, inserted by s. 36 CJA 2003).

17.10 DRAFTING A DEFENCE STATEMENT TO AVOID AN ADVERSE INFERENCE FROM BEING DRAWN

Section 11 CPIA 1996 states that where the accused:

- fails to give a defence statement (where this is compulsory);
- fails to serve a defence statement within the time limit;
- fails to serve an updated defence statement or witness statement;
- fails to serve an updated defence statement or witness statement in time;
- sets out inconsistent defences in the defence statement;
- puts forward at his trial a different defence than that set out in the statement;
- adduces evidence in support of alibi without having given the necessary particulars of the alibi;
- gives a witness notice but fails to do so within the relevant time; or
- at his trial calls a witness not included, or not adequately identified, in a witness notice,

the court, or any other party (with the court's leave) may make such comment as appears appropriate and the court or jury may draw such inferences as appear proper in determining the defendant's guilt in connection with the offence for which he is being tried.

In practical terms, s. 11 of CPIA 1996 is very important. Whether a defence statement is compulsory (indictable cases) or voluntary (summary cases), careful drafting is needed to avoid comment and hence an adverse inference being drawn.

Section 11(5) gives the trial judge and magistrates discretion as to whether comment is permissible and as a consequence whether an inference might be drawn. Importantly, under s. 11(10), a person cannot be convicted solely on an adverse inference drawn under s. 11 alone.

In excercising discretion under s. 11(5) what must the court take into account? The defendant is entitled to put forward an explanation as to why an adverse inference should not be drawn. Section 11(8) specifically requires a court to have regard to the defendant's justification where the defendant has set out inconsistent defences before making or permitting comment. The nature of the inference drawn will therefore depend on the nature of the omission under s. 11 and the reasons for it. It may be that a different defence is put forward at trial because of a change in the prosecution's case from that indicated in the service of committal papers. It must be assumed that in such an instance no adverse comment would be made.

R v Wheeler [2001] 1 Cr App R 10

The defendant gave evidence at his trial inconsistent with his defence statement. At his trial he explained there had been a mistake in his defence statement for which his solicitors accepted responsibility. This was referred to in passing by the judge in his summing-up. The Court of Appeal held the judge should have directed the jury to accept the mistake as a fact in this case. As the defendant's credibility had been at the centre of the case the conviction had to be quashed. The Court of Appeal strongly suggested it should be standard practice for defence statements to be signed by the defendant personally and should not be served on the prosecution until defence solicitors are sure as to their accuracy.

The problem identified in this case is now overcome by s. 6E (see above).

The probable effect of an adverse inference drawn under s. 11 will be to cast doubt on the defence an accused has raised. An inference drawn under s. 11 cannot of itself prove the defendant's guilt. Its evidential effect is similar to the adverse inference that may be drawn from a suspect's silence under the Criminal Justice and Public Order Act 1994, which was considered in Chapter 8.

Can the defence statement be put in evidence as part of the prosecution's case? The Attorney-General's Guidelines provide at paragraph 37:

> 'Prosecutors cannot comment upon, or invite inferences to be drawn from, failures in defence disclosure otherwise than in accordance with section 11 of the Act. Prosecutors may cross-examine the accused on differences between the defence case put at trial and that set out in his or her defence statement. In doing so, it may be appropriate to apply to the judge under section 6E of the Act for copies of the statement to be given to a jury, edited if necessary to remove inadmissible material. Prosecutors should examine the defence statement to see whether it points to other lines of enquiry. If the defence statement does point to other reasonable lines of inquiry, further investigation is required and evidence obtained as a result of these enquiries may be used as part of the prosecution case or to rebut the defence.'

It would therefore seem that a defence statement can be put in evidence for the limited evidential purpose of proving inconsistencies in the nature of the defence or the particulars of an alibi and may be used for the purpose of pursuing further enquiries.

Once a defence statement has been served the prosecution is required by s. 7A CPIA 1996 to look again at the retained 'unused' material to see what might reasonably be said to assist the accused in putting forward the defence he has indicated in his defence statement.

17.11 PROSECUTOR'S CONTINUING DUTY

Section 7A CPIA 1996 (as amended by the CJA 2003) provides that after the prosecutor has complied with initial disclosure under s. 3, and before the accused is acquitted or convicted or the prosecutor decides not to proceed with the case, the prosecutor must keep under review the question whether at any given time (and in particular, following the service of a defence statement), there is prosecution material that might reasonably be considered capable of undermining the case for the prosecution against the accused or of assisting the case for the accused. If, after service of a defence statement, the prosecution concludes no further obligation to make disclosure arises, this fact should be communicated to the defendant.

17.12 APPLYING FOR FURTHER DISCLOSURE

The accused will be able to apply to the court for further disclosure if he has grounds to believe there may be material which satisfies the objective test for disclosure.

The defendant can only make an application under s. 8 where he has filed a defence statement in accordance with the requirements under ss. 5 or 6 of the Act. The defendant must prove to the court that he reasonably believes there is prosecution material which may assist his defence. The defendant must be clear in his articulation and may not use a s. 8 application as a 'fishing expedition'.

You should be aware of disclosure issues at all stages and vigorously pursue legitimate requests for disclosure. A failure by the prosecution to disclose material falling within the definition of initial disclosure will give grounds for an appeal against conviction based on a material irregularity at trial. A failure to disclose does not however absolutely guarantee a conviction being quashed (*R v Craven* [2001] 2 Cr App R 181).

17.13 DRAFTING A DEFENCE STATEMENT

In the light of s. 11 CPIA, great care needs to be taken when drafting a defence statement if an adverse inference is to be avoided. You must avoid putting forward inconsistent defences so there is a need to ensure your client's instructions will not change, or that the trial advocate will not adopt a different approach. Disclosing your client's defence has implications for legal professional privilege which should be discussed with your client. You should try to ensure your client's instructions are completely accurate, that full advice has been given to your client regarding the statement and its implications and that your client checks, signs and dates the statement.

A tactical judgment has to be made as to how much information the defence statement should contain. The more detail it contains the easier it is to facilitate further disclosure and the less risk of an adverse inference being drawn from non-disclosure. Conversely, a more detailed defence statement will assist the prosecution in identifying the potential lines of cross-examination that may be raised against prosecution witnesses at trial. It is doubtful (especially in the light of the changes brought about by the CJA 2003 requiring a greater degree of specificity) that simply stating 'self defence'; 'no dishonest intent' or 'mistaken identity' would be sufficient to avoid an adverse inference under s. 11 (*R v Tibbs* [2001] 2 Cr App R 309).

Assistance is given to defence practitioners in the Attorney-General's Guidelines:

> 'A defence statement must comply with the requirements of section 6A of the Act. A comprehensive defence statement assists the participants in the trial to ensure that it is fair. The trial process is not well served if the defence make general and unspecified allegations and then seek far-reaching disclosure in the hope that material may turn up to make them good. The more detail a defence statement contains the more likely it is that the prosecutor will make an informed decision about whether any remaining undisclosed material might reasonably be considered capable of undermining the prosecution case or of assisting the case for the accused, or whether to advise the investigator to undertake further enquiries. It also helps in the management of the trial by narrowing down and focussing on the issues in dispute. It may result in the prosecution discontinuing the case. Defence practitioners should be aware of these considerations when advising their clients.
>
> Whenever a defence solicitor provides a defence statement on behalf of the accused it will be deemed to be given with the authority of the solicitor's client.' (paragraphs 15 and 16)

17.13.1 DEFENCE STATEMENTS AND SUMMARY TRIALS

In summary trials, the submission of a defence statement is voluntary. Why would a defendant choose to reveal the nature of his defence? The answer comes down to tactical considerations. The legal adviser knows that service of a defence statement will force the prosecutor to look again at the 'unused' material (s. 7A CPIA) to see whether there is any previously undisclosed material that might assist the case for the defendant. You therefore need to carefully consider the disclosure schedule when served with initial disclosure of unused material under s. 3, and determine whether service of a defence statement might unearth further useful disclosure.

It is not entirely clear, on the face of it, whether the obligations under ss. 6C CPIA 1996 (to give notification of intention to call defence witnesses) and 6D (to give notification of having instructed an expert witness) apply to summary trials where a defence statement has not been served (defence statements being optional in summary cases). There is an argument for saying that the obligations under ss. 6C and 6D should be confined to those cases where a defence statement has been served. Such a view would not perhaps be consistent with the aims of the newly published Criminal Procedure Rules. In due, it is anticipated that any revision of the Crim PR will address the issues of disclosure under the CJA 2003.

The practical aspects of disclosure under the CPIA 1996 are considered further in the context of our case study, *R v Lenny Whyte*, in Chapter 19, which considers the preparation of cases that are to be tried on indictment. Our other case studies, *R v William Hardy* and *R v Roger Martin* (web-based only), do not raise CPIA 1996 disclosure issues, as the defendants in each case choose to plead guilty.

online resource centre

17.14 SEEKING DISCLOSURE OF INFORMATION HELD BY THIRD PARTIES

The CPIA 1996 has no application to material in the possession of third parties. Clearly, if the information has come into the hands of the police, it will fall within the disclosure regime. The Attorney-General's Guidelines (paragraphs 51–54) provide as follows:

'51. There may be cases where the investigator, disclosure officer or prosecutor believes that a third party (for example, a local authority, a social services department, a hospital, a doctor, a school, a provider of forensic services) has material or information which might be relevant to the prosecution case. In such cases, if the material or information might reasonably be considered capable of undermining the prosecution case or of assisting the case for the accused prosecutors should take what steps they regard as appropriate in the particular case to obtain it.

52. If the investigator, disclosure officer or prosecutor seeks access to the material or information but the third party declines or refuses to allow access to it, the matter should not be left. If despite any reasons offered by the third party it is still believed that it is reasonable to seek production of the material or information, and the requirements of section 2 of the Criminal Procedure (Attendance of Witnesses) Act 1965 or as appropriate section 97 of the Magistrates Courts Act 1980 are satisfied, then the prosecutor or investigator should apply for a witness summons causing a representative of the third party to produce the material to the Court.

53. Relevant information which comes to the knowledge of investigators or prosecutors as a result of liaison with third parties should be recorded by the investigator or prosecutor in a durable or retrievable form (for example potentially relevant information revealed in discussions at a child protection conference attended by police officers).

54. Where information comes into the possession of the prosecution in the circumstances set out in paragraphs 51–53 above, consultation with the other agency should take place before disclosure is made: there may be public interest reasons which justify withholding disclosure and which would require the issue of disclosure of the information to be placed before the court.'

If a third party will not voluntarily disclose information, either side may issue a witness summons. In the crown Court, a summons can be applied for under the Criminal Procedure (Attendance of Witnesses) Act 1965 and s. 97 Magistrates Court Act 1980. The procedure is somewhat restrictive, however, in that a summons cannot be served outside the jurisdiction and the witness must be able to give 'material evidence'. The principles which govern a court's decision to issue a summons were developed in *R v Reading Justices, ex p. Berkshire County Council* [1996] 1 Cr App R 239. Whether the prosecution or the defence makes the request for disclosure, the third party may resist the request on the basis of public interest immunity in accordance with the procedure set out in s. 16 CPIA (*R v Brushett* [2001] Crim LR 471). The principles relating to PII are discussed below.

17.15 SUMMARY OF DISCLOSURE OBLIGATIONS ON THE DEFENDANT

Compared to the prosecution, the disclosure obligations on the defence are limited. However, the changes brought about by the CJA 2003 have increased the obligations on the defence.

Currently, the defendant is obliged to:

- submit a defence statement in all cases to be tried on indictment in accordance with the requirements of s. 11 CPIA 1996;
- submit an updating defence (not yet in force);
- give notice of intention to call defence witnesses (not yet in force);
- give notification of names of expert instructed by the defence (not yet in force);
- if the defendant is to place reliance on the evidence of an expert witness, then like the prosecution, the defendant is required to give notice under s. 81 PACE 1984, as supplemented by Part 24 Crim PR which apply to trials on indictment. They provide that a party seeking to rely on expert evidence must provide the other party with a statement in writing on any findings or opinion on which he proposes to rely at trial. A failure to disclose means the evidence cannot be adduced without leave of the court. Similar rules apply in relation to summary trials (Part 24 Crim PR). The prosecution will already have complied with the requirements under s. 81 PACE, as expert evidence will normally have been disclosed in accordance as 'used' or 'unused' material. The rules do not require a defendant to disclose expert reports that have been commissioned but have proved to be unhelpful although, as noted above, the defence will be required to give notification of having instructed an expert under s. 6D CPIA when the provision comes into force.

17.16 PUBLIC INTEREST IMMUNITY

The public interest in the proper administration of justice which demands the disclosure of all relevant information for a court's consideration sometimes conflicts with the need to withhold information in the public interest. Where disclosure would be damaging to the public interest, the issue of public interest immunity arises. Where a claim for PII is upheld, a witness may not be asked and the prosecution (or possibly a third party) will not be ordered to disclose the relevant information.

Under s. 21(2) of the CPIA 1996, the prosecution's duty of disclosure at both the initial and the further disclosure stage is subject to the rules of public interest immunity.

The CPIA does not change the common law rules which determine both the procedure by which public interest claims are conducted and the principles by which they are determined. At common law, where the prosecutor believes that relevant evidence ('used' or 'unused') should be withheld on the basis of public interest immunity, an application must be made to the court. Only a court can sanction the prosecutor's view that it would not be in the public interest for the material to be disclosed to the defendant. Where an accused applies for disclosure under s. 8 CPIA, s. 8(5) provides the court with the power not to order disclosure where it would be contrary to the public interest.

17.16.1 WHAT MATERIAL MIGHT DAMAGE PUBLIC INTEREST IF IT WERE TO BE DISCLOSED?

Evidence covered by the phrase 'public interest' will include: documents and other material relating to national security; confidential information; the identity of police informants and undercover police officers; details of premises used for police surveillance; and information pertaining to the welfare of children.

The Code of Practice issued under the CPIA 1996 requires the disclosure officer to list sensitive information on a separate 'sensitive schedule', which is disclosed to the prosecution only.

The Act creates procedures (s. 14 in relation to indictable trials and s. 15 in relation to summary trials) for reviewing court orders to withhold material in the public interest and provides a means (s. 16), by which a third party can intervene where there has been a request for material held by a third party which the third party considers it would not be in the public interest to disclose. A court is required to keep the decision to withhold material from the defence under constant review. The relevant rules of court relating to public interest immunity applications are contained in Part 25 Crim PR.

In a criminal case, the overriding principle which governs a judge's or magistrates' decision about whether to order disclosure is based on ensuring an innocent defendant is not convicted. This principle is derived from the judgment of Lord Taylor CJ in *R v Keane* [1994] 1 WLR 746:

> 'If the disputed material may prove the accused's innocence or avoid a miscarriage of justice, then the balance comes down resoundingly in favour of disclosing it.'

In essence, if disclosure would avoid a miscarriage of justice, there is no balancing act to be undertaken: disclosure must be ordered. If the prosecution refuses to disclose the evidence having been ordered to do so by the court, its only option will be to abandon the prosecution. On the facts in *R v Keane*, the Court of Appeal did not consider the disclosure that had been sought would prove the defendant's innocence or avoid a miscarriage of justice. It called upon trial judges to scrutinise applications for the disclosure of sensitive information with 'great care' and 'adopt a robust approach in declining to order disclosure.' The Court of Appeal went on to observe that the fuller and more specific the indications given by the defence of an issue likely to be raised, the more accurately the judge and the prosecution are able to assess the value of the material to the accused.

17.16.2 THE PROCEDURE FOR ASSERTING PUBLIC INTEREST IMMUNITY

The procedure governing the resolution of PII claims is set out in Part 25 Crim PR. The rules give effect to those devised at common law, in the Court of Appeal's decision in *R v Davis, Johnson and Rowe* [1993] 1 WLR 613.

In most cases the prosecution is required to notify the defence that they are applying to the court for a ruling and to indicate the type of material over which the immunity is claimed. This is known as an *inter partes* application. The defence will be given an opportunity to make representations to the court that the material should be disclosed as it is relevant and important to the accused's defence. On the basis of each party's submissions, the nature of the case and the nature and significance of the evidence over which public interest immunity is being claimed, the judge will decide the issue.

In some cases it may not be in the public interest for the prosecution to reveal the category of the material to be disclosed. In these circumstances, the prosecution will notify the defence that an application has been made but will not reveal the category of the material that is the subject of the application. The application will then be made to the court and the initial hearing will be made on an *ex parte* basis without the defence attending. The judge will first consider whether the defence should be informed and have the opportunity of making representations. Where this decision is reached, an *inter partes* hearing will be held. Exceptionally, due to the highly sensitive nature of the material and the need to preserve secrecy, the prosecution will not inform the defence of its application at all.

In *Edwards v UK* (1992) 15 EHRR 417, the European Court of Human Rights (ECtHR) concluded that fairness necessitated disclosure to the defendant of all material evidence for or against the accused. However, in *Rowe and Davis v UK* (2002) 30 EHRR 1, the ECtHR concluded that the right to full disclosure is not an absolute right and can be restricted for the purpose of protecting national security, vulnerable witnesses and sources of information. Crucially, however, it held that any restriction to a defendant's rights had to be proportional and counterbalanced by procedural safeguards. The principal safeguard, the ECtHR observed, was the adoption of an adversarial procedure by which the defence is given an equal opportunity to make representations as regards the withheld material as that afforded to the prosecution. This has led to the argument that the *ex parte* procedure is incompatible with Article 6. For further consideration of this point we refer you to *Blackstone's Criminal Practice* and to the recent decision of the House of Lords (reviewing all the relevant authorities) in *R v C; R v H* [2004] 2 WLR 335.

For further detailed consideration of pre-trial disclosure of evidence, take a look at the Disclosure Manual of the CPS http://www.cps.gov.uk/legal/section20. It should also be noted that the Crown Court has recently issued a protocol on the disclosure of unsued to be followed in all cases to be tried in the Crown Court. The protocol can be accessed at: http://www.hmcourts-service.gov.uk. Both these documents can be accessed via the web-links section of our Online Resource Centre.

online resource centre

KEY POINT SUMMARY

- Your client is entitled to disclosure of the evidence the prosecution intends to rely on in discharging its burden of proof.

- Unless there is a clear indication of guilt to a relatively straightforward summary-only or either-way matter, disclosure of 'used' material should always be sought as it is only on this basis that a thorough evaluation of the case against your client can be made.

- Entitlement to initial prosecution disclosure of unusued material under s. 3 CPIA 1996 only arises in a case to be tried summarily where a not guilty plea is indicated.

- The submission of a defence statement is voluntary in summary cases but mandatory in indictable cases.

- Great care needs to be taken when drafting a defence statement in order to avoid an adverse inference from being drawn under s.11 CPIA.

- The prosecution is obliged to keep disclosure of unused material under constant review, particularly in the light of service of a defence statement.

- Where the prosecution seeks to withhold relevant/material evidence on the ground that it is sensitive, application must be made to a court to sanction the withholding of such material.

- Important detail as regards the operation and effect of the CPIA 1996 is contained in its accompanying Code of Practice and in the Attorney-General's Guidelines on Disclosure.

- Currently, the disclosure obligation on the defence are limited compared to those on the prosecution but will become more onerous under the CJA 2003 when all the relevant provisions are fully implemented.

SELF-TEST QUESTION

Consider the following scenario and attempt to answer the questions posed at the conclusion.

Barry (aged 28) is charged with rape contrary to s. 1 Sexual Offences Act 2003. His victim is Tina, aged 15. The attack is alleged to have occurred in some public toilets inside a park where Barry is employed as a park attendant. Tina reported the rape to staff at the care home where she resides some two days after it was alleged to have occurred. Tina is subjected to a full forensic examination which reveals visible bruising around the vaginal area.

Having identified Barry as being the man responsible, he is arrested. He too is subject to a full forensic examination. In interview Barry denies the offence, stating Tina did approach him outside the public toilets in the park offering him sex in return for money. He refused her advances. She called him a paedophile and walked off.

The attack is said to have been witnessed by Leroy aged 15. He has given a statement to the police stating he witnessed a girl matching Tina's description emerge from some public toilets in the park in a state of distress claiming she had been raped. Kelly, a friend of Tina, has given a statement to the police claiming that Barry has asked Tina for sex on a number of occasions and become aggressive when Tina refused. Barry informs you that he has observed Tina in the company of males on numerous occasions, while in the park and believes her to be sexually promiscuous. The allegations against him are a complete fabrication.

A defence witness has come forward who wishes to remain anonymous claiming that Tina is an attention seeker and that she has previously made a false accusation of rape against a male care-worker several months ago, having allegedly offered him sex. She later withdrew the allegation. Leroy is also a resident of the care-home at which Tina resides and is very much under Tina's 'control'.

Chart the various stages of disclosure in this case by answering the following:

- What is the classification of the offence with which Barry is charged?

- Can you expect advance information in this case, and if so, what do you anticipate you are likely to receive? (Think in terms of what the investigative process is likely to yield.)

- At what stage will the prosecution come under an obligation to disclose 'unused' material?

- Will you need to serve a defence statement in this case, and if so, what will the content of that statement comprise?

- Do you anticipate there may be material that the prosecution might not wish to disclose? If so, on what basis and how would the situation be resolved in procedural terms?

Analysis of these questions is provided in Appendix 5, where the scenario is further developed.

Postscript:

For the sake of completeness, we refer you to two very recent publications on disclosure:
Protocol for the Provision of Advance Information and Prosecution Evidence and Disclosure of Unused Material in the Magistrates' Courts;
Disclosure: A Protocol for the Control and Management of Unused Material in the Crown Court
See also http://www.judiciary.gov.uk/judgment_guidance/protocols.

online resource centre

Each of these protocols, issued by the Judicial Communications Office, provides a comprehensive explanation of the law relating to pre-trial disclosure and important guidance therein. A link on the web-links section of our Online Resource Centre will take you to them.

FIGURE 17.1 PRE-TRIAL DISCLOSURE OF EVIDENCE

SUMMARY OFFENCES

- Prosecution will disclose used material in the form of advance information as a result of the Attorney-General Guidelines.

- If defendant pleads not guilty, any 'unused' material (initial disclosure) which might reasonably be considered capable of undermining the case for the prosecution or of assisting the case for the accused must be disclosed, s. 3 CPIA 1996.

- Within 14 days of initial disclosure, defence may voluntarily serve a defence statement, s. 6 CPIA 1996;

- Prosecution must serve any further 'unused' evidence which might reasonably be expected to assist the defence as disclosed in the defence statement under its continuing duty to review unused material, s. 7A CPIA 1996.

OFFENCES TRIABLE EITHER WAY

- Prosecution will disclose the substance of its case against the accused under the Advance Information Rules (Crim PR Part 21).

- The disclosure obligations on each party will then depend on whether the case is to be tried summarily or on indictment.

- If committed for trial to the Crown Court, initial disclosure of prosecution unused material will be made 14 days after committal.

- If being tried before a magistrates' court as per summary offences, above.

- If being tried on indictment, as per indictable offences below.

INDICTABLE-ONLY OFFENCES AND CASES TO BE TRIED ON INDICTMENT

- Evidence and other material which the prosecution intends to use at trial will be disclosed to the defence under reg. 2 Crime and Disorder Act 1998 (Service of Prosecution Evidence) Regulations 2005 within 70 or 50 days of the case being sent to the Crown Court for trial under s. 51 Crime and Disorder Act 1998.

- Any 'unused' material (initial disclosure), which might reasonably be considered capable of undermining the case for the prosecution or of assisting the case for the accused must be disclosed, s. 3 CPIA 1996.

- Within 14 days of initial disclosure, defence must serve a defence statement, s. 5 CPIA 1996 (note the possible drawing of adverse inferences under s. 11 CPIA 1996).

- Prosecution must serve any further 'unused' evidence which might reasonably be expected to assist the defence as disclosed in the defence statement under its continuing duty to review unused material, s. 7A CPIA 1996.

18 SUMMARY PROCEEDINGS

18.1 INTRODUCTION

In this chapter we consider the steps involved in preparing for a summary trial. A summary trial will be held where a defendant enters a not guilty plea to a summary-offence or pleads not guilty to an either-way offence which is to be tried summarily with the defendant's consent having undergone the mode of trial enquiry.

Some summary-only matters can be tried in the Crown Court where they are linked to a related indictable-only offence under s. 51 Crime and Disorder Act 1988 (see Chapter 19) or they are committed for trial alongside an either-way offence under s. 40 Criminal Justice Act 1988 (see Chapter 15).

This chapter should be read in conjunction with the latter part of Chapter 14 which provides an account of the early stages of a summary and either-way offence and Chapter 3 which provides an overview of a typical summary-only and either-way case.

In this chapter we specifically consider:

- pleading guilty by post;
- the circumstances in which a defendant can be summarily tried in his absence;

- the rules governing the drafting of the information;
- the pre-trial disclosure of evidence in a summary case;
- the pre-trial review;
- typical preparatory steps undertaken by a solicitor in preparation for trial;
- the procedure at a summary trial on a not guilty plea;
- the procedure on pleading guilty to a matter to be tried summarily.

18.2 COMMENCING A PROSECUTION FOR A SUMMARY-ONLY MATTER

As we have already seen (Chapter 3, paragraph 3.4) criminal proceedings are commenced either by the police charging an individual at the police station, or by the court issuing a summons. The written charge against a defendant is referred to as 'the information'. Currently, the prosecution must lay an information before a court before a summons or warrant for arrest can be issued and served on the person named in the information. The terminology is set to change under s. 29 CJA 2003. When implemented, all public prosecutions will be commenced by the prosecutor issuing a written charge (previously the information) and a requisition (previously a summons) requiring the person to appear before a magistrates' court. Laying an information, followed by the issue of a summons, will continue to be available for private prosecutions.

18.2.1 TIME-LIMITS FOR THE PROSECUTION OF SUMMARY-ONLY OFFENCES

A magistrates' court may not try a defendant for a summary offence unless the information was laid within six months of when the offence was allegedly committed (s. 127(1) MCA 1980).

18.3 PLEADING GUILTY BY POST

Under s. 12 MCA 1980, a defendant may plead guilty by sending a letter to court in the following circumstances where:

(a) the offence is summary only;

(b) there is a specified offence; and

(c) the proceedings have been started by summons.

Until the implementation of s. 308 CJA 2003, pleading guilty by post was only permitted in connection with an offence for which the maximum penalty was three months' imprisonment, but this restriction has now been lifted.

Where the defendant pleads guilty by post, the prosecution must serve on the defendant:

(i) the summons;

(ii) a brief statement of the facts upon which the prosecution is to rely, or a copy of any statements written in compliance with s. 9 CJA 1967; and

(iii) any information relating to the defendant that will be put before the court; and

(iv) a notice explaining the procedure.

If the defendant wishes to plead guilty, he must notify the court and may submit to the court a statement in mitigation. The court proceeds on the basis of the written statements submitted by both sides which must be read to the court. The magistrates may refuse to accept a guilty plea if the statement in mitigation reveals a defence or the plea is unclear. If the guilty plea is accepted, the magistrates can sentence immediately, depending on the type of sentence or following an adjournment requiring the attendance of the defendant.

18.4 SUMMARY TRIAL IN THE ABSENCE OF THE DEFENDANT

There are a number of situations in which a defendant can be tied summarily in his absence.

Where a defendant fails to answer a summons to appear and it is established that the summons was served on the defendant within a reasonable time before the hearing, s. 11 MCA 1980 permits the court to enter a not guilty plea and for the case to be proved in absence. If the offence alleged in the summons is summary only, it is sufficient to prove the summons was sent to the defendant's last known address or usual address by registered post or recorded delivery. Where the summons alleges an either-way offence, the prosecution must establish the defendant was aware of the proceedings.

Subject to proof of service, the burden of proving a case in the absence of the defendant falls on the prosecution. It may discharge its burden either by calling witnesses or, if s. 9 CJA 1967 statements were served alongside the summons, by reading the statements to the court. Where it is necessary to adjourn for proof, the court must send the defendant an adjournment notice. If the adjournment notice is not served, the prosecution will not be able to prove in the defendant's absence even though there is proof of service of the summons itself.

Where the defendant was present in court on the last occasion, he is deemed to be aware of the next stage of the proceedings. This will normally be the case in an either-way offence since the defendant needs to be present for the mode of trial proceedings. Where it is clear that the defendant knows of the date set for his trial and there is no explanation for the defendant's absence, the court can either chose to adjourn the trial and issue a warrant for the defendant's arrest without bail (s. 13 MCA 1980) or proceed to try the defendant in his absence. In the latter case, if the defendant is represented, his solicitor can still put the prosecution to prove of its case and make submissions and a closing speech. If the defendant is merely on summons to attend, the court might consider an adjournment and issue of a warrant backed for bail to ensure the defendant's attendance at the adjourned hearing. If there is an explanation for the defendant's absence, the court is more likely to accede to a request that the trial be adjourned to a later date.

A trial in the absence of a defendant, particularly an unrepresented defendant is most likely to result in a conviction as the evidence against the defendant is not contradicted. Having convicted an absent defendant, a court may choose to sentence in absence or adjourn sentence and issue a warrant for the defendant's arrest.

18.4.1 DEFENDANT UNAWARE OF COURT PROCEEDINGS

If the defendant was unaware of the proceedings, s.14 MCA 1980 permits him to make a statutory declaration that he knew nothing of the proceedings within 21 days of finding out. The declaration may be made before the court or a defence solicitor. The effect of the declaration is that the summons and all the proceedings are void. The information, however, remains valid.

18.5 JOINDER OF OFFENCES AND DEFENDANTS IN THE INFORMATION

At the commencement of a summary trial, the defendant is asked to plead guilty or not guilty to the information containing the charge/s. The information will either be contained in the charge sheet or in a summons issued by the court following the laying of an information by the police.

The general rule is that an information may only charge one defendant with a single offence unless the prosecution allege that the offence was committed jointly by more than one defendant.

> **Example**
>
> Ben and Chris are both charged with common assault arising out of a fight outside a nightclub on 23 January, when the prosecution allege both defendants assaulted the victim. As both defendants committed the offence jointly, each will be tried on the same information.

The information should only charge one offence, (Part 7.3 Crim PR). An information which charges more than one offence is bad for duplicity and the prosecutor will have to decide which charge he wishes to proceed with.

In some situations, where the defendant faces more than one charge, the court may try a defendant on the same occasion with both charges. Informations may be tried together where:

- the defence agree to the informations being tried together; or
- the court orders the offences to be tried together because it is in the interests of justice to so and the offences form part of a series of offences of the same or similar characters.

If the defence do not agree to the informations being tried together, for the alternative ground to apply, the court has to be satisfied that the offences are part of a series of offences of the same or similar character. This requires firstly that there should be some connection between them in time and place and the nature of the offences. The second factor the court will take into account is whether it is in 'the interests of justice' for the informations to be tried together. Guidance on the application of the interest of justice test is provided by the House of Lords in *Chief Constable of Norfolk v Clayton* [1983] 2 AC 473. When applying the interests of justice test, the court must consider the convenience to the prosecution of having the informations tried together against any injustice that might arise to the defendant. In most cases the defence will resist having the informations tried together. A common submission is that it is not in the interests of justice as the evidence from one offence might unfairly prejudice the magistrates in deciding a defendant's guilt in respect to the other offence.

> **Example**
>
> (i) Over the course of three days Lee commits four offences of theft and obtaining property by deception by going from shop-to-shop and obtaining goods from each of them using a false credit card.
>
> (ii) In a domestic dispute over the course of two weeks, Neil commits common assault against his ex-girlfriend, her new boyfriend and his ex-girlfriend's mother.
>
> (iii) Julie steals two books from the library. The following day she committed an offence of careless driving.
>
> In examples (i) and (ii) the two conditions for the informations to be tried together appear to be satisfied. First, the offences are part of a series of offences of the same or similar nature. There is also proximity between them in terms of time. Second, the court would rule that it is in the interests of justice for the informations to be tried together after considering the balance of convenience to the prosecution and the potential prejudice to Lee and Neil.
>
> In example (iii) the grounds for trying the informations together are not satisfied. As the defence will not agree and the offences are not the same or of a similar nature, Julie will be tried separately on each information.

18.5.1 AMENDING THE INFORMATION

What is the position if details contained in the information are incorrect or inconsistent with the evidence called by the prosecution? Section 123 MCA 1980 permits the information to be amended at any stage of the proceedings provided the error has not caused injustice to the defendant. Examples of minor errors which would not cause injustice are where the defendant's name or the location of the offence is misspelt in the information. Where the error is regarded as 'substantial', the court may allow the amendment but will also grant an adjournment to allow the defence to deal with any issues arising out of the amendment, s. 123 MCA.

> ### 💡 Example
>
> Rashid is charged with driving a motor vehicle with a defective tyre. The information specifies the defective tyre to be 'on the rear offside of the vehicle'. In fact, the defective tyre was on the rear nearside of the vehicle. In this situation, amending the information will be permitted and it is unlikely that the error would be regarded as substantial.
>
> Majinder is charged with common assault, which is wrongly specified in the information as having been committed on 23 March. In fact the alleged offence occurred on 26 March. As Majinder has an alibi for his whereabouts on 23 March, it is likely that the proposed amendment is 'substantial' and the court will adjourn the proceedings to enable the defence to deal with the amendment.

18.6 THE EARLY STAGES OF A SUMMARY-ONLY/EITHER-WAY OFFENCE

As we saw in the latter part of Chapter 14, in the early stages of a summary-only or either-way offence the defence solicitor will be called upon to offer his client advice as to plea. Before a solicitor can undertake such a task, he will typically need to:

* interview his client;
* contact the CPS in order to request advance information;
* obtain a representation order on behalf of his client;
* interview any potential defence witnesses;
* evaluate the evidence against his client.

online resource centre

These important early steps are covered in Chapter 14 and will invariably necessitate one or more adjournments in the early stages of the case. The steps are also illustrated by our case studies *R v William Hardy* (Appendix 2) and *R v Roger Martin* (web-based only).

18.7 TAKING A PLEA

If the decision is taken to plead guilty, this can be done in the early stages of a summary-only offence or at the plea before venue in relation to an either-way offence. A guilty plea will require the court to pass sentence either on the day or following an adjournment for a pre-sentence report.

Where the defendant indicates a not guilty plea to a case which is to be tried summarily, the matter will usually be listed for a pre-trial review.

18.8 THE PRE-TRIAL REVIEW

In those cases where the defendant enters a not guilty plea to an offence that is to be tried summarily, the court will fix a date for a pre-trial review to be conducted before a justice's legal adviser. The purpose of the hearing is to make directions to ensure the parties are clear as to what steps must be undertaken in preparation for trial.

Allied to the Criminal Procedure Rules, and the active case management powers that they give to the court, is s. 45 (schedule 3) of the Courts Act 2003, which permits binding rulings to be made at pre-trial hearings in criminal cases heard in the magistrates' court. It places the pre-trial review, outlined above, on a formal footing, bringing the procedure in magistrates'courts into line with that in the Crown Court. The power to make pre-trial binding rulings is available following a not guilty plea up to the commencement of the trial and will extend to issues of law and the admissibility of evidence. The rulings made by one bench of magistrates will bind the trial court.

Under the Criminal Procedure Rules, provision is made for standard directions to apply in all cases to be tried in the magistrates' court. The directions allow the parties eight weeks in which to prepare for trial, or 14 weeks where there is to be expert evidence. The standard case management directions form can be accessed via the web-links section of our Online Resource Centre. The parties must come to the pre-trial review hearing prepared to provide the information set out in the case management form. The court will make orders in relation to the following:

online resource centre

- the identification of a case progression officer for each side and the court;
- date by which a prosecution application for special measures in relation to a witness needs to be served;
- date on which any further prosecution disclosure is to be served;
- date for service of any notice to adduce hearsay evidence or evidence of bad character;
- date on which defence must serve notice of objection to the above;
- date on which a defence statement must be served if a defence statement is to be given;
- date on which the defence must notify the prosecution of which of its witnesses if wishes to cross-examine;
- date on which the defence must serve any s. 9 CJA 1967 statements on the prosecution;
- date on which any skeleton arguments might be served;
- date for submission of a certificate of readiness for trial;
- directions will also be made in relation to expert evidence, including the date on which a party relying on expert evidence must serve the expert's report and the date by which the opposing party must indicate whether the expert is required to attend at trial.

18.9 PREPARING FOR TRIAL

Where the case is listed for trial (and having regard to the Part 3 Crim PR outlined above), the defence solicitor should begin preparing for a summary trial as soon as possible. This may include some or all of the following.

18.9.1 VISITING THE CRIME SCENE

Visiting the crime scene can give the defence solicitor a better understanding of the circumstances in which the alleged offence occurred. It is often useful to prepare a plan or take photographs, especially in road traffic collision cases where there is a dispute between the prosecution and your client about the position of the vehicle on the road.

18.9.2 INSTRUCTING EXPERTS

Many summary offences do not require expert evidence. In those summary cases where expert evidence is required, you should instruct your expert witness at the earliest opportunity. If your client is the subject of a representation order, you should obtain the written authority of the Legal Services Commission using form CDS 4, before formally instructing the expert. It is common practice to support your application by explaining the reason why an expert is required and what their fee will be.

Where either the prosecution or the defence intends to call expert evidence at trial, Part 24 Crim PR and the Magistrates' Court (Advance Notice of Expert Evidence) Rules 1987 require the pre-trial disclosure of the expert's report.

18.9.3 THE PRE-TRIAL DISCLOSURE OF EVIDENCE

The pre-trial disclosure of evidence in relation to all types of offences is considered in Chapter 17. In cases that are to be tried summarily we simply remind you of the key provisions.

The rules governing the pre-trial disclosure of 'used material' are contained in Part 21 Crim PR and the Attorney-Gerneral's Guidance on Disclosure. Strictly speaking they apply to either-way offences, but are invoked in relation to summary-only offences. They require the Crown Prosecution Service to serve on the defence either a summary of the prosecution case or more commonly copies of prosecution witness statements. Entitlement also extends to a summary of any tape recorded interview and records held under PACE 1984.

Where an accused indicates an intention to plead not guilty to a case that is to be tried summarily, the provisions relating to 'unused material' under the CPIA 1996 are triggered.

18.9.4 'UNUSED' MATERIAL

Section 3 of the CPIA requires the prosecution to provide the defendant with initial disclosure (any evidence not previously disclosed, which might reasonably be considered capable of undermining the case for the prosecution or of assisting the case for the accused). This obligation arises in cases to be tried summarily where the defendant pleads not guilty. After service of initial prosecution disclosure the defendant may choose to file a defence statement in compliance with s. 6 CPIA, indicating on what matters he takes issue with the prosecution case and for what reasons and giving particulars of any defence or alibi he intends to rely on at trial. The filing of a defence statement is voluntary for cases to be tried summarily.

On the occasions when a defence statement is served in cases being tried summarily, the prosecution must fulfil its ongoing obligation to keep disclosure under review in accordance with s. 7A CPIA. In particular the CPS must now disclose material which it has not previously been disclosed and which might reasonably be expected to assist the accused's case as disclosed in the defence statement.

Where a defence statement is filed, the court may comment or draw adverse inferences from disclosure which is late, defective or inconsistent with the defence case at trial. In view of these potential sanctions, it might be asked why a defence solicitor would choose to serve a defence statement in a summary trial. The mechanics of disclosure under the CPIA 1996 and the tactical considerations involved in drafting a defence statement are explored in much greater detail in Chapter 17.

18.9.5 AN EVALUATION OF THE EVIDENCE

Having obtained full disclosure of the prosecution's case and an updated proof of evidence from the defendant and any defence witnesses, the defence solicitor should now be in a position to evaluate the strength of the prosecution's case and to formulate a strategy for defending the case in court. In preparing for trial it may be necessary to research the elements of the offence so the advocate knows the facts in issue which the prosecution must prove to secure the defendant's conviction. Research may also be necessary where the defence intends to challenge prosecution evidence at trial. The defence advocate should come to court prepared to cite relevant statutory sections and case law in support of his submission to have the evidence excluded.

18.9.6 SECURING THE ATTENDANCE OF WITNESSES AT TRIAL

As the trial approaches, you will have formed a clear idea of how you intend to defend your client in court. An important part of your preparation will be to decide which of the witnesses from whom you have taken a proof of evidence, will be called to give evidence for the defence. Initially, you will write to a prospective witness giving full details of the time and location of the court hearing asking him to attend voluntarily or to produce a document. If the witness does not reply or indicates that he is not willing to appear voluntarily it will be necessary to apply to the court for a witness summons to be issued. A summons will be granted where the court considers it is in the interests of justice to secure the attendance of the person concerned to give evidence or produce a document or thing.

Some witnesses will be reluctant to attend even where they have been served with a witness summons. In this situation, s. 97(2) MCA 1980 authorises an arrest warrant to be issued against the witness to ensure his attendance.

18.9.7 STATEMENTS ADMISSIBLE UNDER S. 9 CRIMINAL JUSTICE ACT 1967

Where either the prosecution or the defence consider it is unnecessary for a particular witness to attend the trial to give oral evidence, an application can be made to the opposing side for consent to allow the witness's evidence to be read to the court in the witness's absence under s. 9 Criminal Justice Act 1967. For s. 9 statements to be admissible, the following conditions must be met:

- it is in the proper form, i.e. it complies with the requirements of s. 9 CJA; and
- before the trial a copy of the statement has been served on the other parties in the case; and
- none of the parties object to the witness's statement being tendered in evidence in the witness's absence; and
- the statement's contents would have been admissible if the witness had given oral evidence.

The key point to remember about s. 9 statements is that the opposing side must consent to the statement being admitted in evidence in this way. If objection is taken, the statement will not be admissible under s. 9 and the witness will have to attend court to give oral evidence unless the statement falls within another provision permitting the reception of hearsay evidence. A s. 9 CJA statement is appropriate for a witness whose evidence is not in dispute and has been agreed by the other side and whom is therefore not required to attend court to be cross-examined.

18.9.8 CORRESPONDENCE WITH THE CPS

When preparing a case for trial, you will often correspond with the CPS to see if evidence can be agreed and where appropriate to make representations about the nature of the charge(s) and whether the disclosed evidence supports the charge(s). In some circumstances the Crown Prosecutor might agree to amend the charge(s) to which your client could plead guilty, thereby avoiding a trial.

18.9.9 DISPUTED EVIDENCE

Disputes about the admissibility of evidence do not arise as frequently in the magistrates' courts as at trials in the Crown Court. However, where evidence is disputed, the matter will be decided by the magistrates during the course of the trial or at the beginning of the trial. In some circumstances a *voir dire*, or trial within a trial, will need to be held (*R v Liverpool Juvenile Court, ex p. R* [1987] 2 All ER 668). At a *voir dire*, evidence may be called and legal submissions are made as to why the disputed evidence should be excluded. If the magistrates determine that the evidence is inadmissible, no further mention will be made of it and no reliance placed on it. A *voir dire* will commonly be held are where the defendant disputes the admissibility of a confession, or seeks to have identification evidence excluded for breach of Code D. The *voir dire* works much better in the Crown Court, where there is a strict division of function between the judge and the jury. *Voir dire* issues in the Crown Court are determined in the absence of the jury. This is not possible in the magistrates' court as magistrates are arbiters of both fact and law. The use of pre-trial binding rulings under the Courts Act 2003 (highlighted at paragraph 18.8 above) overcomes this difficulty as the trial bench will be differently composed.

18.9.10   **APPLICATION OF THE RULES OF CRIMINAL EVIDENCE**

Much of the preparatory work in connection with a summary offence is a fact finding exercise to enable you to assess the respective strengths of the prosecution and defence case, and then to properly advise your client as to his plea. Your knowledge of criminal evidence and your ability to apply the law to the facts of your client's case is also highly significant at this stage. How can you assess the strength of each party's case unless you have a clear understanding of the rules relating to the legal burden of proof and the admissibility of evidence? Also, irrespective of whether your client pleads guilty or not guilty, it should not be forgotten that successful advocacy in court comes from a thorough preparation at the pre-trial stage.

18.10   **RIGHTS OF AUDIENCE BEFORE MAGISTRATES' COURT AND TERMS OF ADDRESS**

Trainee solicitors do not have rights of audience before magistrates' courts. Solicitors and barristers have rights of audience to conduct summary trials. You might recall that a trial can be conducted before a lay bench of three magistrates or before a district judge or deputy district judge. Although you do not have rights of audience at this stage, the magistrates' court is an invaluable learning resource – take full advantage to watch and learn.

When addressing the bench, in the case of a district judge, the address is 'Sir' or 'Madam'. A lay bench can be addressed collectively as 'Your Worships . . .' Alternatively an advocate may choose to address the chairperson of the bench and say 'Madam and your colleagues' or 'Sir and your colleagues'. When referring to the clerk, it is customary to state 'Your learned clerk' and when referring to your opposing advocate, you might say 'My friend for the prosecution' or, in the case of a barrister, 'My learned friend'.

18.11   **THE PROCEDURE AT A SUMMARY TRIAL ON A NOT GUILTY PLEA**

Where the defendant pleads not guilty, the whole prosecution case is put in issue. The relevant rules of court relating to the conduct of summary trials are contained in Part 36 (Crim PR).

(1)   The hearing begins with the defendant's full name, address and date of birth and the name of his solicitor being given to the court.

(2)   The charge(s) will be put to the defendant by the justice's legal adviser and the defendant confirms that he pleads not guilty to the charge(s).

(3) The prosecutor may make an opening speech by addressing the court with regard to:
- the prosecution's version of the facts;
- the witnesses to be called in support of the prosecution case; and
- any legal issues that will arise.

(4) The first prosecution witness is questioned by the prosecutor in examination-in-chief, the purpose of which is to obtain answers from the witness which supports the prosecution case. All factual witnesses must remain outside the courtroom until they have given their evidence. Each witness called will firstly take the oath or affirmation and state their name. It is customary to point out to the witness that they should speak clearly and at a slow pace, addressing their answers to the bench. Certain witness may give their evidence with the benefit of special measures. The rules relating to witness testimony are explained in Chapter 22.

(5) The witness may then be cross-examined by the defence with a view to undermining the accuracy or truthfulness of what the witness said during examination-in-chief and/or to undermine the witness's credibility.

(6) The prosecution may re-examine the witness to repair any damage that may have been inflicted on the witness during cross-examination.

(7) The magistrates may ask the witness questions at any time but in most courts the convention applies that the witness will be questioned after the parties have finished asking questions.

The process of witness testimony of examination-in-chief, cross-examination and re-examination continues until all the prosecution witnesses have testified.

(8) As well as calling witnesses to give oral evidence, the prosecution may also put its case to the court by presenting evidence in other forms including statements of witnesses who are not in court under s. 9 Criminal Justice Act 1967, or under the hearsay provisions, video recordings, tape recordings or real evidence such as an exhibit presented in court.

(9) At the conclusion of the prosecution's case, the defence may submit that there is no case to answer where the prosecution has failed to establish an essential element of the alleged offence; or the prosecution evidence has been so discredited in cross-examination or is so manifestly unreliable that no reasonable tribunal could safely convict on it (Practice Direction (Submission of No Case) [1962] 1 WLR 227).

(10) Where a submission of no case to answer is not made or is unsuccessful, the defence may put its case to the court. The defence advocate may make an opening speech, but, as he is normally allowed only one speech, it is usual practice to reserve this to the end of the defence case so that he may have the advantage of the 'last word'.

(11) The defence calls its first witness, subjecting the witness to an examination-in-chief. Where the accused exercises his right to testify, he must be the first defence witness and has the right to leave the dock and give evidence from the witness box (*R v Farnham Justices, ex p. Andrew Gibson* [1991] Crim LR 642).

(12) The defence witness may then be cross-examined by the prosecution and any co-accused.

(13) The defence advocate may re-examine the witness to repair any damage that may have been inflicted on the witness during cross-examination.

(14) The witness may be questioned by the justices.

The process of witness testimony of examination-in-chief, cross-examination and re-examination continues until all the defence witnesses have testified.

(15) The defence will usually close the proceedings by making a closing speech.

(16) The court will then announce its decision of guilty or not guilty after retiring to consider the evidence. On finding the defendant guilty, the court will consider whether it is necessary to obtain a pre-sentence report. Where a pre-sentence report is ordered the case will be adjourned to enable the report to be prepared. Before proceeding to sentence, the prosecution will disclose to the court the defendant's previous convictions (if any). The defence advocate will make a plea in mitigation. The court then passes sentence. In relation to an either-way offence, the court can commit the defendant for sentence to the Crown Court under s. 3 PCC(S)A 2000 where it is of the view that its powers of sentence are insufficient. Section 6 of the same Act enables the court to also commit any summary offence for which the defendant has been convicted alongside the either-way offence. The practice and procedure of sentencing, including the power to commit for sentence are considered in Part V.

(17) Where the defendant is found not guilty, he is free to leave. If the defendant is non-legally aided he may make an application to have his costs met out of central funds under s. 16 Prosecution of Offences Act 1985. Such orders are at the discretion of the court but should normally be awarded unless it is felt that the accused brought suspicion on himself by his conduct misled the prosecution into thinking the evidence against him was stronger than it in fact was. Guidance can be found in *Practice Direction (Crime: Costs)* [1991] 1 WLR 498. A legally aided acquitted defendant's costs will be met under the representation order.

We further consider trial advocacy in the context of trials before the Crown Court in Chapter 20.

In conducting a summary trial you are reminded of the various rules of professional conduct that could arise, which are considered in Chapter 4.

KEY POINT SUMMARY

- Be aware of the circumstances in which a defendant can be tried in his absence.

- Know the law which permits two or more informations to be tried together and how you might challenge the 'interests of justice' test.

- Know the responsibilities of each side in the pre-trial disclosure of evidence.

- Know the procedure for securing the attendance of witnesses at trial.

- Know the practice for admitting a witness's written statement in hearsay form under s. 9 Criminal Justice Act 1967.

- Be aware of the purpose of and the issues that will be covered at the pre-trial review and what will be the increasing importance of the new active case management powers given to the criminal courts under Part 3 of the Criminal Procedure Rules.

- Know the sequence of events where the defendant pleads not guilty.

- Know the test to support a submission of no case to answer.

SELF-TEST QUESTIONS

1. What is the test to determine whether a defendant can be tried for two or more informations at the same time where a defendant does not consent?

2. Explain how the defence solicitor will find out what the prosecution's evidence comprises in advance of trial.

3. How can the solicitor ensure the attendance of witnesses?

4. What is the role of the legal adviser in a summary case?

5. At what point might a submission of no case to answer be made and what is the test to support such a submission.

FIGURE 18.1 THE PROSECUTION OF A SUMMARY OFFENCE AND SUMMARY TRIAL

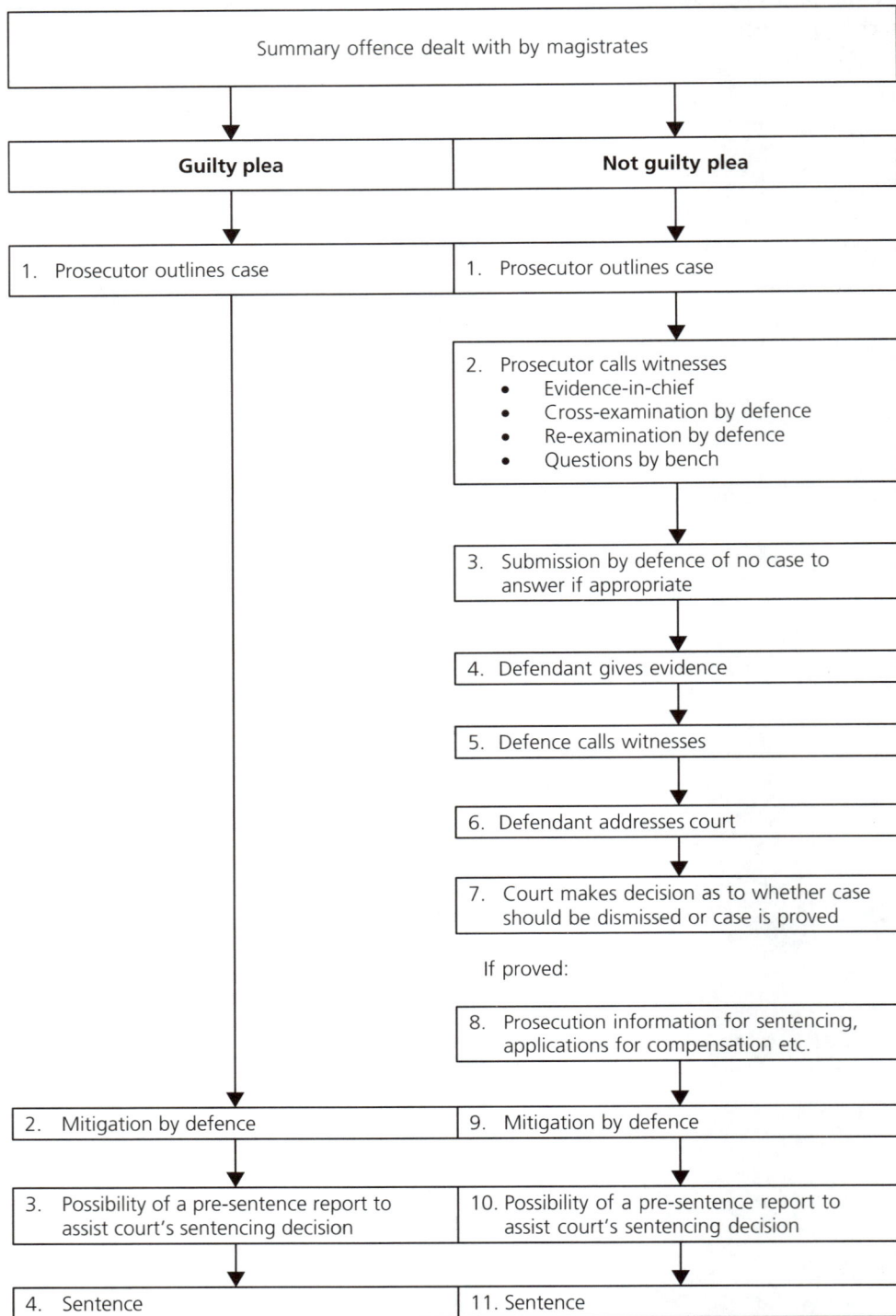

Summary offence dealt with by magistrates

Guilty plea

Not guilty plea

1. Prosecutor outlines case

1. Prosecutor outlines case

2. Prosecutor calls witnesses
   - Evidence-in-chief
   - Cross-examination by defence
   - Re-examination by defence
   - Questions by bench

3. Submission by defence of no case to answer if appropriate

4. Defendant gives evidence

5. Defence calls witnesses

6. Defendant addresses court

7. Court makes decision as to whether case should be dismissed or case is proved

If proved:

8. Prosecution information for sentencing, applications for compensation etc.

2. Mitigation by defence

9. Mitigation by defence

3. Possibility of a pre-sentence report to assist court's sentencing decision

10. Possibility of a pre-sentence report to assist court's sentencing decision

4. Sentence

11. Sentence

19.1   INTRODUCTION

As a trainee solicitor you will be involved in assisting defendants charged with indictable-only offences. Much of the preparatory work will be the same as for a summary trial, although indictable offences by their nature usually involve more complex issues of law, evidence and fact. Also, with much greater powers of punishment available to the Crown Court, the potential consequences for a defendant are much more serious if his case is not properly prepared.

You may wish to read this chapter in conjunction with Chapter 3 which provides an overview of the procedural course of an indictable-only offence, and the latter part of Chapter 14 which addresses the early stages of an indictable offence and the initial preparatory steps that will occupy the defence solicitor.

This chapter deals with pre-trial practices and procedures that are followed when dealing with a client charged with an indictable offence. It covers:

1. the sending of indictable-only cases to the Crown Court under s. 51 Crime and Disorder Act 1998 (CDA);

2. preparing for the preliminary hearing in the Crown Court;

3. preparing for trial on indictment;

4. instructing counsel;

5. pre-trial hearings including the plea and case management hearing (PCMH).

You will be aware that either-way offences can also be tried on indictment in the Crown Court. The procedure by which an either-way matter can be sent to the Crown Court for trial is explained in Chapter 16. Our case study concerning *R v Lenny Whyte* is an example of such a case. Once an either-way offence is committed to the Crown Court, a date is set for the defendant's plea and case management hearing (PCMH) in the Crown Court. Steps 3–5 listed above apply to all cases to be tried on indictment, not just indictable-only offences, and are illustrated by the documentation supporting the Lenny Whyte case study which is analysed further at the end of this chapter.

Before considering the general preparatory steps in relation to all cases to be tried on indictment, we will consider some specific provisions in relation to indictable-only offences (steps 1–2).

19.2 THE DEFENDANT'S FIRST COURT APPEARANCE FOR AN INDICTABLE OFFENCE – S. 51 CRIME AND DISORDER ACT 1998

Despite being charged with an indictable-only offence, the defendant will make his first appearance in connection with the matter before a magistrates' court. At this preliminary hearing, matters relating to the grant of representation orders and bail will be decided. These matters have been fully considered in Chapters 14 and 15 and we do not propose to repeat them here. Bail is more likely to be opposed by the prosecution in connection with an indictable-only offence because of the seriousness of such offences and the consequent risk of absconding.

Although the rules relating to the pre-trial disclosure of advance information do not strictly apply to indictable only offences, the CPS will normally provide this information before the defendant's initial appearance.

Having made an initial appearance before a magistrates' court, s. 51(1) Crime and Disorder Act 1998 requires that the case should be sent immediately to the Crown Court. The Criminal Procedure Rules provide that a preliminary hearing is not required in every case. Where a preliminary hearing is ordered, it should be held about 14 days after the case is sent. Whether or not a magistrates' court orders a preliminary hearing, a Plea and Case Management Hearing (PCMH) must be ordered within about 14 weeks after sending where a defendant is in custody and within about 17 weeks after sending where a defendant is on bail. In sending the case, the magistrates' court is required (as part of its active case management powers) to complete a case progression form which imposes standard directions on the parties relating to the service of prosecution evidence, defence disclosure. The directions form can be accessed via the weblinks section of our Online Resource Centre.

19.2.1 SENDING 'RELATED' OFFENCES TO THE CROWN COURT FOR TRIAL

What is the position where a defendant is charged with an indictable-only offence and a further offence(s) which is an either-way or summary offence? Section 51(3) CDA 1998 provides that where an adult defendant is sent for trial under s. 51, the magistrates must also send any related either-way offence for which the defendant appears at the same time. An either-way offence is 'related' where it can be joined in the same indictment because it is founded on the same facts or form part of a series of offences of the same or similar character, s. 51E CDA 1998. The magistrates' court must also send any related summary offence for which the defendant appears at the same time, s. 51(3)(b) CDA 1998. A related summary offence must arise out of circumstances which are the same as or connected with the indictable-only offence and be punishable with imprisonment or disqualification (s. 51(11)).

Consider the following examples of how linked summary or either-way offences may also be sent to the Crown Court for trial.

Example 1

Gordon is charged with grievous bodily harm with intent, contrary to s. 18 Offences Against the Person Act 1861 (an indictable-only offence). He also faces an allegation of affray, contrary to s. 3 Public Order Act 1986 (either-way offence). Both incidents arise out of a brawl in the centre of town involving football supporters from rival clubs. The either-way offence is founded on the same facts as the indictable only offence (s. 51E) and must therefore be sent to the Crown Court along with the indictable-only offence under s. 51(3)(a) CDA 1998.

Example 2

Denis is charged with driving while disqualified (a summary offence). In the course of the investigation into the offence he gives false particulars to the police leading to the arrest of someone other than himself. He is therefore charged with perverting the course of justice (an indictable-only offence). As the summary-only offence arises out of circumstances connected with the indictable-only offence and is punishable with imprisonment, both offences must be sent for trial to the Crown Court under s. 51(3)(b) CDA 1998.

Where a defendant appears before magistrates on a separate occasion having been charged with a related either-way or summary offence, the magistrates have discretion to send the matter(s) up to the Crown Court so that they may be joined with the indictable-only matter(s) (s. 51(4)).

19.2.2 SENDING A LINKED CO-DEFENDANT TO THE CROWN COURT

Example

What is the position where a co-accused is charged with an either-way offence which is related to the indictable-only offence? To take the example of Gordon above, let us assume that Tom is also charged with affray arising out of the brawl. In these circumstances, s. 51(5) CDA 1998 requires the magistrates to send Tom's matter to the Crown Court along with Gordon's indictable-only offence if Tom appears at the same time as Gordon. Co-defendants facing an either-way offence which is related to an indictable-only offence therefore have no right of election in these circumstances. If Tom were to appear on an occasion subsequent to Gordon's initial appearance, charged with affray, the magistrates would have discretion to send Tom's either-way offence to the Crown Court.

19.2.3 SENDING YOUNG OFFENDERS TO THE CROWN COURT

What is the position in relation to a young offender (aged under 18) who is jointly charged with an indictable-only offence? Section 51(7) CDA 1998 provides that the magistrates shall send the young person for trial in the Crown Court along with the adult if it is in the interests of justice. If this power is exercised, the magistrates can also send any 'related' either-way or summary matter which the young person faces. (For an explanation of the interests of justice test and for full consideration of the young person in the criminal justice system, see Chapters 34 and 35.)

> **Looking Ahead**
>
> When Sch. 3 CJA 2003 comes into force and committal proceedings are abolished, s. 51 CDA 1998 will apply where the defendant is charged with one or more either-way offence in circumstances where the magistrates' court has either declined jurisdiction to try the offence or the defendant has elected trial on indictment. The notice of transfer under what will be s. 50A CDA 1998 will also include any summary offences that could previously have been committed to the Crown Court under s. 41 Criminal Justice Act 1988 (see Chapter 16, paragraph 16.19).

19.3 PRELIMINARY HEARING BEFORE THE CROWN COURT

The principal purpose of the preliminary hearing is to enable the judge to devise a timetable within which disclosure of the prosecution's case must be served and a defence case statement served. Disclosure of evidence is further considered below. The judge will also set a date for a Plea and Case Management Hearing (PCMH) to be held some weeks later.

A substantial amount of preparatory work will be undertaken in preparation for the PCMH; this is explained below. Some judges ask for an indication of plea at the preliminary hearing, although there is no obligation to give an indication of plea at this stage. If an indication of guilt is given, a pre-sentence report can be ordered in time for the PCMH and the defendant will of course be given maximum credit for a timely guilty plea.

19.3.1 CROWN COURT BAIL

As the preliminary appearance before the Crown Court will invariably end in an adjournment, the question of the defendant's bail may arise once more. The defendant can of course make two contested bail applications, after which the provisions of Part 2A Sch. 1 Bail Act 1976 apply. Under this provision a court need not hear argument on the question of bail unless there has been a change in circumstances. The defendant may already have made an unsuccessful application for bail at a previous appearance before the magistrates. A second application is permitted before the Crown Court. If this is unsuccessful and the defendant is remanded in custody, the trial judge and the prosecution should be aware of the defendant's custody time limits when setting the timetable for the PCMH (see Chapter 15).

19.4 PREPARATORY STEPS IN THE EARLY STAGES OF AN INDICTABLE-ONLY OFFENCE

The preparatory work undertaken in the early stages of all criminal cases, including indictable cases are considered in Chapter 14. Typically, the early stages of an indictable-only matter will include:

- interviewing your client;
- preparing your client's proof of evidence;
- contact with the CPS to:
  — confirm that you are acting for your client;
  — request a copy of your client's criminal record;

— obtain a record of any police interviews with your client;

— obtain a copy of your client's custody record;

— enquire whether advance disclosure of the prosecution case is available;

• interviewing witnesses;

• visit the crime scene;

• instructing expert witnesses if necessary;

— where the prosecution or the defence intends to call expert evidence at trial, Part 24 Crim PR requires the pre-trial disclosure of the expert's report.

For an illustration of many of the above steps, you are reminded of the stage we have reached in our case study *R v Lenny Whyte*.

19.5 DISCLOSURE OF 'USED' MATERIAL AND TRIALS ON INDICTMENT

In indictable-only cases, a defence solicitor will not generally be in a position to properly advise his client until the prosecution has made a full disclosure of the case against him. The standard directions which apply to a case sent for trial by magistrates under s. 51 CDA 1998, require the service of prosecution case papers to be made within 50 days where the defendant is in custody and within 70 days in other cases.

The 'case sent bundle' will be very similar to the 'committal bundle' currently served in committal proceedings (you are referred to the *R v Lenny Whyte* case study which comprises a committal bundle). The 'case sent bundle' will comprise 'used' material, which will include:

• the charge(s);

• witness statements;

• the draft indictment;

• schedule of unused material; and

• initial prosecution disclosure in accordance with s. 3 CPIA 1996.

Once the prosecution has served the 'case sent bundle', an important part of the defence solicitor's case preparation will be to carefully scrutinise the prosecution witness statements and other evidence to assess the strength of the case against his client. This assessment will be very important when advising a client whether to plead guilty or not guilty.

19.6 DISCLOSURE OF 'UNUSED' MATERIAL – CRIMINAL PROCEDURE AND INVESTIGATION ACT 1996 (CPIA)

In addition to the obligation on the prosecution to disclose evidence it intends to rely on at trial, the Criminal Procedure and Investigations Act 1996 (CPIA) imposes obligations on the prosecution to disclose evidence in its possession which it will not use at trial. This is known as 'unused' material.

You will recall that we have included a dedicated chapter on the pre-trial disclosure of evidence (Chapter 17) which covers the provisions relating to used and unused material. We do not intend to repeat the substantive detail contained in Chapter 17. In the context of cases to be tried on indictment, we simply remind you of the key provisions and alert you to the fact that the CJA 2003 has brought about a number of changes to the disclosure regime.

19.6.1 INITIAL PROSECUTION DISCLOSURE IN CROWN COURT TRIALS

Section 3 CPIA requires the prosecution to provide the defendant with initial disclosure (any evidence not previously disclosed, which might reasonably be considered capable of undermining the case for the prosecution or of assisting the case for the accused). At the initial disclosure stage, the defence will receive a schedule detailing non-sensitive material in the prosecutor's possession. In indictable-only cases initial disclosure should be included in the 'case sent bundle.' In either-way cases that have been committed to the Crown Court, initial disclosure is made post-committal.

19.6.2 DEFENCE DISCLOSURE UNDER THE CPIA

After initial disclosure, s. 5 CPIA requires that a defence statement should be served on the court and the CPS. The defence statement must be served within 14 days of the prosecution's initial disclosure. A defence statement is a mandatory requirement in cases to be tried on indictment. Failure to comply with the requirement to serve the defence statement can lead to adverse comment and inferences being drawn by the court under s. 11 CPIA. The importance of correctly drafting a defence statement cannot be overstated. We invite you to consider once more Chapter 17, paragraphs 17.9–17.10 and 17.13 to illustrate the point.

19.6.3 FURTHER PROSECUTION DISCLOSURE

After service of the defence statement, s. 7A CPIA requires the prosecutor to look again at the schedule of unused material and disclose any material that falls within s. 3 CPIA which has not previously been disclosed by the prosecution. This is likely to apply to material which might reasonably be expected to assist the accused's defence as disclosed in the defence statement.

19.7 WHAT IF THE PRE-TRIAL DISCLOSURE OF EVIDENCE REVEALS THE PROSECUTION TO HAVE A WEAK CASE?

Where the 'case sent bundle' indicates a weak prosecution case, the defence may make an application to the Crown Court to dismiss the charge(s).

19.7.1 AN APPLICATION TO DISMISS THE CHARGE

Under Sch. 3 CDA 1998, the defence may make an oral or a written application to the Crown Court to dismiss the charge(s) against the defendant. In most cases, the application will be decided on the basis of written submissions unless the defendant requests that oral evidence should be heard at the hearing and the judge considers that it is in the interests of justice that oral evidence should be heard. In this situation, prosecution witnesses may be required to attend the hearing and be cross-examined. This option to call oral evidence is prospectively repealed by Sch. 3 CJA 2003. The defence may also make submissions to have disputed evidence excluded under s. 76 or s. 78 PACE. The detailed rules relating to an application to dismiss charges sent or transferred to the Crown Court are contained in Part 13 Crim PR. On hearing the representations from each side, the judge will dismiss the charge(s) against the defendant where there is insufficient evidence for a jury to properly convict the accused. Where the application to dismiss is unsuccessful, the date will be confirmed for the Plea and Case Management Hearing (PCMH). Reporting restrictions will apply at a hearing to dismiss. A defendant may apply to have reporting restrictions lifted (Sch. 3, para. 3 CDA 1998).

19.7.2 WHAT HAPPENS TO ANY RELATED CHARGES IF THE INDICTABLE-ONLY OFFENCE IS DISMISSED LEAVING ONLY AN EITHER-WAY OR SUMMARY OFFENCE?

The procedure under Sch. 3, paras 7 to 15 of the CDA 1998, requires the Crown Court to carry out the plea before venue procedure in relation to an either-way offence. If the defendant indicates a not guilty plea or makes no indication at all, the mode of trial procedure must be conducted. If it is decided to deal with the either-way offence summarily, the case will be remitted to the magistrates' court. A summary-only offence would also be remitted to the magistrates where the linked indictable offence has been dismissed.

19.8 PRE-TRIAL HEARINGS IN THE CROWN COURT

Before the case proceeds to trial, both the prosecution and the defence will be required to attend one or more pre-trial hearings. The hearing enables the trial judge to play an influential role in the pre-trial management of cases so that when the case is finally tried in the Crown Court, all the preliminary issues will have been dealt with. Pre-trial hearings are designed to prevent ineffective trials. The current system of case management in the Crown Court is likely to become even more robust in the light of Crim PR, Part 3.

19.8.1 PLEA AND CASE MANAGEMENT HEARING (PCMH) – SS. 39–43 CPIA 1996

All cases to be tried on indictment will have a plea and case management hearing (PCMH).

The initial purpose of the PCMH is to arraign the accused, i.e. to hear whether he intends to plead guilty or not guilty. The PCMH then proceeds on the basis of whether the defendant pleaded guilty or not guilty.

19.8.2 PLEADING NOT GUILTY AT THE PCMH

Where the defendant pleads not guilty, the PCMH ensures that any steps necessary for trial will be taken and that the court is provided with sufficient information to fix a trial date. At this hearing the judge will expect the parties to be able to provide the necessary answers/information to enable the judge to complete the Plea and Case Management Form. The form can be accessed via the web-links section of our Online Resource Centre. A slightly expedited version of the form can be found at the conclusion of this chapter. Amongst other things, the judge will want to have details of:

online resource centre

- how many witnesses will give oral evidence;
- how many witnesses will give written evidence;
- any facts formally admitted;
- any exhibits or schedules;
- any expert evidence to be relied on;
- any point of law or evidential issues that will be put before the court together with the authorities relied upon;
- details of any alibi evidence which has been disclosed to the prosecution;
- the estimated length of the trial; and
- the dates on which the witnesses and the advocates are available.

One very important step that the defence solicitor will need to undertake is to provide the CPS with a full list of all the prosecution witnesses the defence requires to attend trial. The standard 'case sent' directions stipulate this should be done within seven days of receiving disclosure of the prosecution's case. This gives the police the chance to check witness availability in advance of the PCMH. At the conclusion of the PCMH, the judge will either fix the trial date or place the case on the warned list. The warned list contains those cases for which a trial date has yet to be fixed. Once the case enters the warned list it could be listed for hearing in a very short space of time. Alternatively the case may need to be listed for a further pre-trial hearing.

19.8.3 PLEADING GUILTY AT THE PCMH

If it is your client's intention to plead guilty at the PCMH, you should notify the court and the prosecution as soon as possible and not less than 14 days before the hearing. Notification enables the court to order a pre-sentence report in time for the PCMH. Where the defendant does plead guilty at the PCMH, the judge may proceed to sentence. Alternatively, the sentencing hearing may be adjourned to enable the preparation of a pre-sentence report if such a report has yet to be prepared.

19.8.4 PREPARATORY HEARINGS

A preparatory hearing in accordance with ss. 28–38 Criminal Procedure and Investigations Act 1996 is appropriate in long and complex cases to be heard in the Crown Court. The relevant rules of court are contained in Part 15 Crim PR. It is for the judge to decide whether there should be a preparatory hearing either on the application of the parties or by the court's own motion. In practice, the decision whether to hold a preparatory hearing is likely to be made at the PCMH.

Where a preparatory hearing is held, it will take place before the jury is sworn, and may clarify any difficult or contentious issue which will assist the jury's comprehension of the issues; identify issues which are likely to be material to the jury's verdict; and expedite the proceedings or assist the judge's management of the trial. The preparatory hearing is part of the trial process.

19.8.5 PRE-TRIAL RULINGS

Sections 31–39 Criminal Proceedings and Investigation Act 1996 (CPIA) provides that a judge may make a binding ruling at any pre-trial hearing (including the PCMH) on matters relating to the admissibility of evidence and/or a question of law.

Where a pre-trial ruling has been made, it may only be varied or discharged where it is in the 'interests of justice' to so do. An application to vary a binding ruling will not be heard, unless there has been a 'material change of circumstances' since the making of the original ruling. The CPIA provides a right of appeal to the Court of Appeal against a pre-trial ruling.

Matters of law and evidence likely to be determined at a pre-trial hearing could include:

* determining the competency of a witness;
* ruling on a special measures direction for a vulnerable or intimidated witness;
* deciding whether to hold a joint trial for two or more accused or whether to sever an indictment in a case where an accused faces more than one charge;
* resolving disputes as to the admissibility of bad character evidence or hearsay evidence;
* determining a public interest immunity (PII) application to withhold evidence;
* making a ruling as to the admissibility of disputed confession evidence or evidence of identification.

The above list is not exhaustive. The benefit of making such rulings is that any subsequent trial should proceed on the day. Pre-trial rulings will also have a bearing on whether an accused might choose to change his plea to one of guilty.

19.9 PREPARATION FOR TRIAL

Much of the defence solicitor's preparation for trial will have been undertaken in preparation for the PCMH. Typical preparatory matters are considered below.

19.9.1 WITNESSES

If the case is to proceed to trial, it is the responsibility of the defence to ensure the attendance of its witnesses. Where the defence is not satisfied that a witness will attend voluntarily, an application to summons the witness to attend can be made under ss. 2–4 Criminal Procedure (Attendance of Witnesses) Act 1965. The Crown Court (Part 28 Crim PR) will issue a witness summons if it is in the interests of justice to do so.

19.9.2 ADDITIONAL OBLIGATIONS UNDER THE CPIA 1996 PRIOR TO TRIAL

You are reminded of the additional obligations imposed on the defence under the CPIA 1996 (as amended by the CJA 2003). They are covered in Chapter 17 and include:

- the need to serve an updated defence statement (s. 6B) not yet in force;
- the need to notify the court and the CPS of intention to call defence witnesses. If defence witnesses are to be called full particulars need to be given (s. 6C) not yet in force;
- the need to give notification of names of experts instructed by the accused (s. 6D) not yet in force.

Rules of court will stipulate the time at which these obligations must be discharged. They are not currently available.

19.9.3 BRIEFING COUNSEL

Your client will need to be represented at the PCMH by a barrister or a solicitor-advocate with a higher right of audience. The advocate will need to be briefed. The task of briefing counsel is commonly given to a trainee solicitor. A properly drafted brief is a disciplined exercise requiring you to organise the materials in a file and to think very carefully about the issues in the case.

When to brief

The Law Society provides the following guidelines for when counsel should be instructed. In an either-way offence committed to the Crown Court, the guidelines suggest the brief should be sent to counsel within 21 days of committal under s. 6(1) or s. 6(2) Magistrates' Courts Act 1980, or within seven days of the committal if the defendant is in custody. For an indictable-only offence the date set for the PCMH will dictate the time by which the brief should be delivered.

If the defence solicitor requires assistance in completing the defence statement, counsel should be instructed at an even earlier stage. It will obviously be easier to organise a conference with counsel in advance of the PCMH if the brief is sent in plenty of time.

It is preferable that the advocate who represents the defendant at the PCMH will also represent him at trial. Unless your firm employs a solicitor-advocate with higher rights of audience, your firm will have a preferred choice of barrister. A barrister's services are booked through the clerk at his or her chambers. All the papers in the case and the instructions will be sent to the barrister in a brief to counsel.

What should a brief to counsel contain?

Whilst there is an etiquette to briefing counsel, the precise practice may vary from firm to firm and your firm may have a preferred style of briefing counsel. The brief to counsel we have drafted in conjunction with the *R v Lenny Whyte* case study is written in the third person.

The brief should contain a back sheet with details of the case, the date and type of hearing with the instructing solicitors details typed down the right-hand side of the page. The left-hand side of the back page is left blank to enable counsel to handwrite endorsements onto it. If the case is legally aided, the back page of the brief should make this clear.

Where appropriate the brief may cover counsel's representation at both the PCMH and at trial. In other cases separate briefs will be sent.

The front page of the brief should contain the case heading and a numbered list of enclosures. The list of enclosures depends entirely on the particular case you are dealing with, but would typically include:

- defendant's proof of evidence;
- draft indictment;
- committal papers/case sent bundle;
- relevant correspondence with CPS;
- expert report(s).

The brief should begin with an introduction which deals with the defendant's personal details, the charge(s), the history of the case and any bail arrangements.

The brief should provide an analysis of the prosecution case by cross-referencing to the prosecution witness statements and other evidence that has been disclosed under the pre-trial disclosure rules and will be included with the brief as enclosures. Any strengths or weaknesses in the prosecution case should be identified as should the admissibility of any items of prosecution evidence which may be challenged at trial.

The brief should also contain a summary of the defence case and identify any strengths or weaknesses.

Counsel should also be clearly directed on what advice is sought. This might relate to witness requirements, points of evidence, advice on plea or assistance with drafting a defence statement. Counsel's attention should also be directed to the factors that might be raised in mitigation in the event of your client being convicted.

Commonly, the brief will ask whether counsel believes a conference with instructing solicitors will assist in the case preparation.

The brief will be sent to counsel who should respond within the return date. At this stage, the solicitor needs to be mindful of key dates, particularly in relation to filing a defence statement or to indicating to the CPS which prosecution witnesses are required to attend trial to be cross-examined. A failure to notify the CPS of which prosecution witnesses are required to attend by the defence will result in their evidence being read at trial without them being present in court. Counsel may well send written advice in advance of the PCMH. It is important that counsel's advice is followed up. This may involve further interviews with the defendant or witnesses or further correspondence with the CPS. If counsel suggests a conference is needed, you might be asked to organise one. This involves contacting counsel's clerk for available dates as well as contacting your client. The conference usually takes place at counsel's chambers.

19.10 RECOVERY OF DEFENCE COSTS ORDER

You will recall that a representation order is granted on the basis of the interests of justice test. In cases that are to be tried on indictment, the defendant must complete and file Form B which comprises a statement of his means. The information about his financial circumstances will allow the judge at the end of the trial in the Crown Court to make a recovery of defence costs order (RDCO) if it is considered appropriate. Form B will need to be served before the PCMH.

KEY POINT SUMMARY

- Understand that all indictable-only offences must be sent to the Crown Court along with related (either-way/summary) offences in accordance with s. 51 CDA 1998 following an initial appearance before magistrates.

- Trials on indictment cover not just indictable-only offences but either-way offences which have been sent for trial by magistrates.

- Be aware of the rules dealing with the pre-trial disclosure of evidence by both the prosecution and the defence under the CPIA 1996.

- Know the conventions about instructing counsel.

- Understand the purpose of the PCMH and the procedures where the defendant pleads guilty or not guilty at the arraignment.

SELF-ASSESSMENT QUESTIONS

1. What is the purpose of the initial hearing in the magistrates' court where the defendant is charged with an indictable-only offence?

2. What obligations do the prosecution have in relation to the pre-trial disclosure of evidence in an indictable-only offence?

3. Explain the procedure at the application to dismiss the charge in the Crown Court.

4. Explain the purpose of the PCMH.

5. In which type of case will it normally be appropriate to hold a preparatory hearing?

Case study: *R v Lenny Whyte*, Appendix 1

You will recall that Lenny Whyte has been committed to stand trial on the burglary allegation and a date has been set for his Plea and Case Management Hearing before Lyme Crown Court. Initial prosecution disclosure of unused material, in compliance with s. 3 CPIA 1996, is made (see Document 31). Before you look at the defence statement in relation to Lenny Whyte, you may wish to attempt a draft of your own. The defence statement submitted in this case is at Document 34A. Further disclosure, in compliance with the CPS's duties under s. 7A CPIA 1996 are contained in Documents 35, 36 and 37. Subject to the prosecution's duty to keep disclosure under review, the pre-trial disclosure of evidence in relation to *R v Lenny Whyte* is complete. You will see that Lenny's solicitor has obtained a psychiatric report from Lenny's consultant (see Document 38). The requirement under s. 81 PACE for the disclosure of expert report to be adduced in court has been complied with.

You now have all the necessary information to undertake a brief to counsel. Our suggested brief to counsel in this case is included at Document 39.

You will see on Lenny Whyte's file an account of his PCMH before Lyme Crown Court (Document 41). In correspondence between Lenny's solicitors and the CPS leading up to the PCMH (see Document 33), the defence suggests a further pre-trial hearing will be needed to address the issues surrounding the admissibility of Lenny's confession and the admissibility of Lenny's record of past criminal convictions. At the PCMH, counsel for the CPS concede that Lenny Whyte's confession had been obtained in breach of PACE and Code C and that the CPS will not be relying on it. The matter is then listed for trial. A further, very short brief to counsel to represent Lenny Whyte at trial is subsequently sent (see Document 44).

online resource centre

FIGURE 19.1 THE PROSECUTION OF INDICTABLE-ONLY OFFENCES AND TRIAL ON INDICTMENT

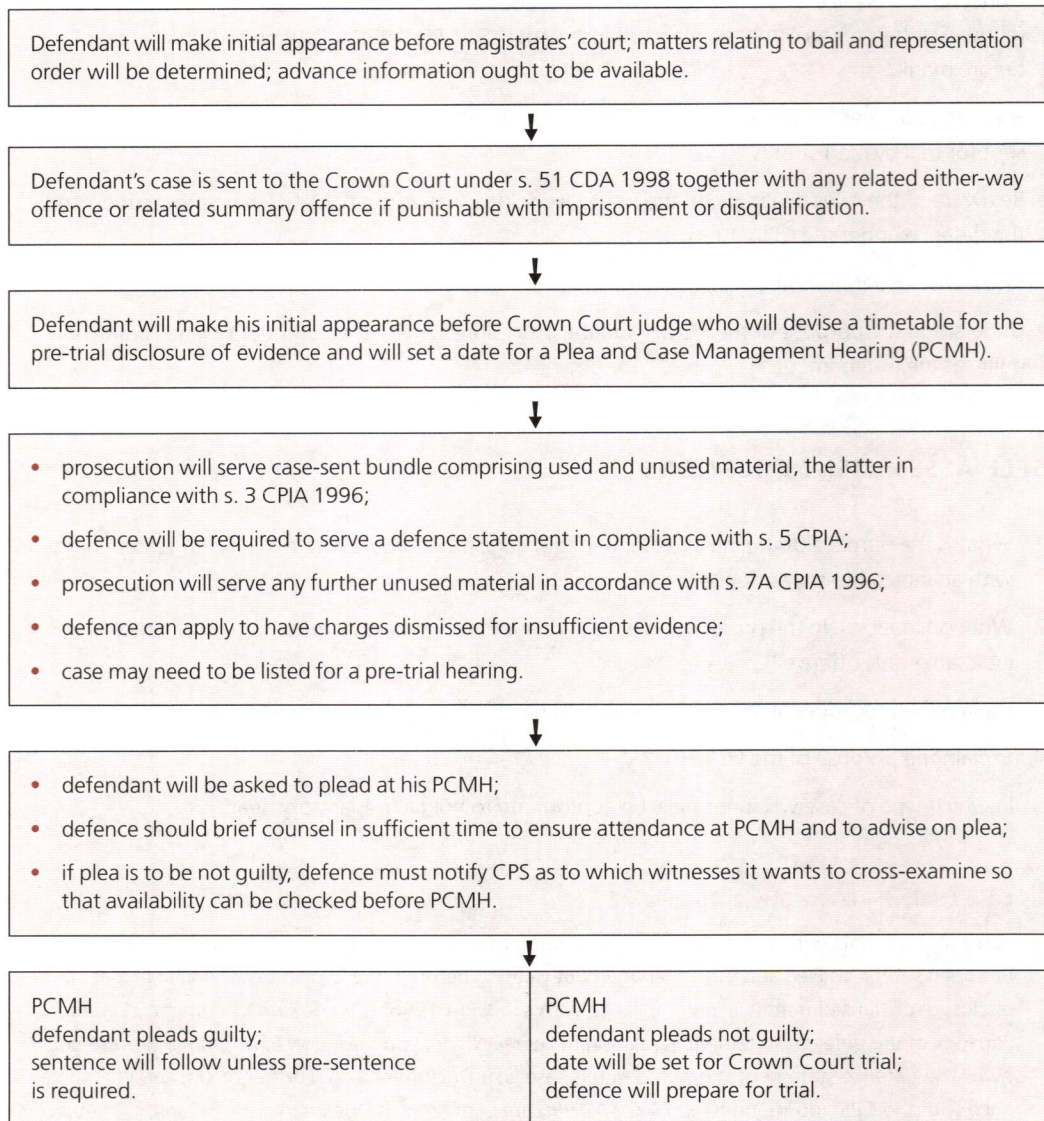

Defendant will make initial appearance before magistrates' court; matters relating to bail and representation order will be determined; advance information ought to be available.

↓

Defendant's case is sent to the Crown Court under s. 51 CDA 1998 together with any related either-way offence or related summary offence if punishable with imprisonment or disqualification.

↓

Defendant will make his initial appearance before Crown Court judge who will devise a timetable for the pre-trial disclosure of evidence and will set a date for a Plea and Case Management Hearing (PCMH).

↓

- prosecution will serve case-sent bundle comprising used and unused material, the latter in compliance with s. 3 CPIA 1996;
- defence will be required to serve a defence statement in compliance with s. 5 CPIA;
- prosecution will serve any further unused material in accordance with s. 7A CPIA 1996;
- defence can apply to have charges dismissed for insufficient evidence;
- case may need to be listed for a pre-trial hearing.

↓

- defendant will be asked to plead at his PCMH;
- defence should brief counsel in sufficient time to ensure attendance at PCMH and to advise on plea;
- if plea is to be not guilty, defence must notify CPS as to which witnesses it wants to cross-examine so that availability can be checked before PCMH.

↓

| PCMH
defendant pleads guilty;
sentence will follow unless pre-sentence
is required. | PCMH
defendant pleads not guilty;
date will be set for Crown Court trial;
defence will prepare for trial. |

PLEA AND CASE MANAGEMENT HEARING IN THE CROWN COURT

Date of hearing: Judge:

P			represented by:		☐
D1		in custody/on bail	represented by:		☐
D2		in custody/on bail	represented by:		☐
D3		in custody/on bail	represented by:		☐
D4		in custody/on bail	represented by:		☐
D5		in custody/on bail	represented by:		☐

Tick right hand column if the advocate is instructed for trial

No. of case in Crown Court: URN:

Has the defendant been advised about credit for pleading guilty?   D1 ☐ D2 ☐ D3 ☐ D4 ☐ D5 ☐

Has the defendant been warned that if he is on bail and fails to attend, the proceedings may continue in his absence?   ☐ ☐ ☐ ☐ ☐

Is the Crown Court Case Details form up-to-date?   P ☐ ☐ ☐ ☐ ☐ ☐

Matters likely to be applicable to all trials

1) TRIAL JUDGE
Should the future management of the case be under the supervision of the trial or a nominated judge?   **YES/NO**

2) RESOLVING THE CASE WITHOUT A TRIAL   **Not applicable ☐**
a. **Might the case against a defendant be resolved by a plea of guilty to some counts on the indictment or to a lesser offence?** D1 ☐ D2 ☐ D3 ☐ D4 ☐ D5 ☐
b. **If so, how?**

c. **Is the prosecution prepared to resolve the case in this way?** ☐ ☐ ☐ ☐ ☐
d. **If no, does the court take the provisional view that the case should be resolved in this way?** ☐ ☐ ☐ ☐ ☐
e. *If yes, the court orders:*

3) GUILTY PLEA   **Not applicable ☐**
a. **Is there a written basis of plea?** D1 ☐ D2 ☐ D3 ☐ D4 ☐ D5 ☐

b. **Is the basis of plea acceptable to the prosecution?** ☐ ☐ ☐ ☐ ☐
a. **Is the basis of plea acceptable to the court?** ☐ ☐ ☐ ☐ ☐
b. **If not acceptable, section 25 (Newton Hearing) will also apply.**
c. *The defendant(s) will be sentenced on:*
d. *The prosecution to serve any further material relevant to sentence by:*
e. *The pre-sentence report, if required, to be received by the Crown Court and made available to the defence and the prosecution by:*
f. *The defence to serve any material which it wishes the court to consider when sentencing the defendant by:*
g. **Will "derogatory assertions" be made in mitigation?** ☐ ☐ ☐ ☐ ☐

h. *If yes, the court orders:*

i. **Are there any other matters which should be dealt with at the same time as these proceedings (other offences/TICs)?** ☐ ☐ ☐ ☐ ☐
j. **If yes, give brief details:**

k. *If there are other matters, the court orders:*

l. *Further orders (e.g. orders re medical or psychiatric reports or confiscation proceedings):*

4) NOT GUILTY - TRIAL DATE   **Not applicable ☐**
a. **If the defendant is in custody and if the provisions regarding custody time limits apply, when does the custody time limit (or any extension thereof) expire?**
D1:   **; D2:**   **; D3:**   **; D4:**   **; D5:**
b. **Set out other reasons why the trial should take place earlier or later than it might otherwise?**

1

c. *If the defendant is in custody and the date of the trial is outside the custody time limit period, the court makes the following orders:*

d. **What is the estimated length of the prosecution, defence cases?**
Prosecution   Defence

e. *The trial will take place on: and the length of it will be:*

5) READINESS FOR TRIAL
The parties' case progression officers to inform the Crown Court case progression officer in writing that the case is ready for trial, that it will proceed as a trial on the date in 4e and will take no more/less time than the period in 4e, by:

6) EVIDENCE - WITNESSES
a. **Have the parties completed Annex A?**   **YES/NO**
b. *If yes, does the court approve Annex A?*   **YES/NO**
c. *If the list of witnesses to be called orally is not agreed or approved, agreement (which is subject to the court's approval) must be reached and notified to the court by:*
d. *Absent agreement, the prosecution shall seek further directions by:*

7) EVIDENCE - DEFENDANTS' INTERVIEWS   Not applicable ☐
a. **Should the interviews be edited before the trial?**

P	D1	D2	D3	D4	D5
☐	☐	☐	☐	☐	☐

b. *Proposals for the editing of interviews shall be drafted by: and served by:*
c. *The other parties shall respond by:*
d. *The agreed interviews shall be filed with the Court by:*
e. *Absent agreement, the party(ies) named in b) shall seek further directions by:*

8) DEFENCE STATEMENT

	D1	D2	D3	D4	D5
a. **Has a defence statement been served?**	☐	☐	☐	☐	☐
b. **Is there an issue as to its adequacy?**	☐	☐	☐	☐	☐
c. *The court gives a warning to:*	☐	☐	☐	☐	☐

d. *The court orders:*

9) PROSECUTION ADDITIONAL EVIDENCE   Not applicable ☐
a. *Any additional evidence to be served by:*

b. **Which topic/issue will the additional evidence relate to?**

10) FURTHER PROSECUTION DISCLOSURE   Not applicable ☐
a. *The prosecution to complete any further disclosure by:*

	D1	D2	D3	D4	D5
b. **Is the defence alleging that the prosecution has not complied with its obligation to disclose material?**	☐	☐	☐	☐	☐

c. *If yes, the court orders:*

11) EVIDENCE - ADMISSIONS/SCHEDULES
a. **Have the parties considered which admissions/schedules can be agreed:**   **YES/NO**
b. *If yes and if the court agrees that the proposed admissions/schedules are sufficient, they shall be drafted by:*
c. *and sent to the other parties by:*
d. *The other parties shall respond by:*
e. *The agreed admissions/schedules shall be filed with the court by:*
f. *Absent agreement, the named party in b) shall seek further directions by:*
g. *If the answer to question a. is no or if the court does not approve the proposed admissions/schedules, the court orders:*

Matters which may apply to any trial

12) EVIDENCE - EXHIBITS
a. **Have the parties completed and agreed Annex B?**   **YES/NO**
b. *If Annex B is not agreed, agreement must be reached and notified to the court by:*
c. *In the absence of agreement, the prosecution shall seek further directions by:*
d. *If, in the view of the court, any exhibits should be presented in a particular way in order to be more easily understood by the jury, the court orders:*

e. *Further orders:*

13) EVIDENCE - VIDEO EVIDENCE   Not applicable ☐

	D1	D2	D3	D4	D5
a. **Has the prosecution delivered to the defence the transcript of video witness evidence upon which it proposes to rely?**	☐	☐	☐	☐	☐

b. *If no, the prosecution to do so by:*

c. *The defence shall submit any editing proposals by:*
d. *The prosecution shall respond by:*
e. *The agreed transcripts and edited video shall be filed with the court by:*
f. *Absent agreement, the prosecution shall seek further directions by:*

14) EVIDENCE - CCTV EVIDENCE   Not applicable ☐

	P	D1	D2	D3	D4	D5
a. **Has any unedited CCTV evidence been made available in full to the other parties?**   ☐ ☐ ☐ ☐ ☐ ☐

b. *If yes, copy of proposed composite/edited film/stills to be served by:*
c. *The other parties to respond by:*
d. *Absent agreement, the party seeking to rely on the evidence shall seek directions by:*

15) EVIDENCE - EXPERT EVIDENCE   Not applicable ☐

	P	D1	D2	D3	D4	D5
a. **Expert evidence is likely to be called by:**   ☐ ☐ ☐ ☐ ☐ ☐

b. **To prove/disprove:** P:
D1/2/3/4/5:

c. Does the court approve of the need for the identified expert evidence?   ☐ ☐ ☐ ☐ ☐ ☐
d. If no, why?

e. *In any event the evidence to be served by:*

f. **Should the expert evidence be presented in a particular way in order to be more easily understood by the jury?**   ☐ ☐ ☐ ☐ ☐ ☐
g. *If yes, the court orders:*

h. **Would it be helpful if the experts consulted together and if possible agreed a written note of points of agreement or disagreement with a summary of reasons?**   ☐ ☐ ☐ ☐ ☐ ☐
i. *If yes, and if the parties agree, the court orders:*

16) ELECTRONIC EQUIPMENT – COMPATIBILITY   Not applicable ☐

	P	D1	D2	D3	D4	D5
a. **Does the trial courtroom have the appropriate equipment to allow the presentation of electronic evidence (CCTV, live link, audio recordings, DVD etc)?**   ☐ ☐ ☐ ☐ ☐ ☐

b. *If no, the court orders:*

17) EVIDENCE - SPECIAL MEASURES AND LIVE LINK   Not applicable ☐

	D1	D2	D3	D4	D5
a. **Any outstanding issues about special measures or live links?**   ☐ ☐ ☐ ☐ ☐

b. If yes, the court orders:

18) MISCELLANEOUS ORDERS RE. WITNESSES AND DEFENDANT   Not applicable ☐

	P	D1	D2	D3	D4	D5
a. **Does any witness or defendant need an interpreter or have special needs for which arrangements should be made?**   ☐ ☐ ☐ ☐ ☐ ☐

b. *If yes, the court orders:*

c. **Are any special arrangements needed for a child defendant?**   ☐ ☐ ☐ ☐ ☐ ☐
d. *If yes, the court orders:*

e. **Will a defendant be unrepresented at trial?**   ☐ ☐ ☐ ☐ ☐ ☐
f. *If yes, the court orders:*

19) HEARSAY / BAD CHARACTER EVIDENCE   Not applicable ☐

	P	D1	D2	D3	D4	D5
a. **Further applications regarding hearsay evidence or bad character evidence are to be made by:**   ☐ ☐ ☐ ☐ ☐ ☐

b. *The court orders:*

20) PRODUCTION OF MATERIAL FROM THIRD PARTIES   Not applicable ☐

	P	D1	D2	D3	D4	D5
a. **Applications for production of material (e.g. social services, hospital, banking records) from third parties to be made by:**   ☐ ☐ ☐ ☐ ☐ ☐

b. *The court orders:*

21) PRE-TRIAL RESOLUTION OF ISSUES   Not applicable ☐

a.   **What are the legal or factual issues which should be resolved before the trial:**

b.   *If the issues are not capable of being resolved at the plea and case management hearing, the necessary hearing will take place on*   *and will last:*

	P	D1	D2	D3	D4	D5

c.   **Do the parties wish to call witnesses to give evidence orally to enable the court to resolve the issues?**

d.   *If yes, and if the court approves, the court makes the following orders:*

e.   *Skeleton arguments to be submitted by:* P by: D1/2/3/4/5 by:

22) PUBLIC INTEREST IMMUNITY: ON NOTICE APPLICATIONS   **Not applicable** ☐

a.   **What is the nature of the prosecution's application on notice for public interest immunity?**

b.   *The court orders:*

23) FURTHER ORDERS CONCERNING THE CONDUCT OF THE TRIAL

a.   *Prosecution case summary/opening, if necessary, to be served by:*

b.   *To ensure that the trial does not take more time than the period in 4e., the court orders:*

24) ANY FURTHER MISCELLANEOUS ORDERS - INCLUDING ORDERS RE. LITIGATION SUPPORT

25) NEWTON HEARING   **Not applicable** ☐

a.   *The Newton hearing will take place on:*   *and the length of it will be:*

b.   *The issues to be resolved are:*

c.   *The prosecution to serve any further material by:*   *and the defence by:*

d.   *The following witnesses will be called to give evidence orally:*

e.   *Further orders (including any orders re. hearsay/bad character):*

Judge's signature:

4

20.1 INTRODUCTION

Where the defendant pleads not guilty when arraigned at the Plea and Case Management Hearing (PCMH), the judge will set the date for the trial in the Crown Court. This chapter considers the procedural and practical steps at a trial on indictment by examining the following:

- the rules dealing with the indictment;
- supporting counsel at trial;

- empanelling the jury;
- the presentation of the prosecution and defence cases;
- the judge's summing-up; and
- the jury's verdict.

20.2 THE INDICTMENT

Where the accused has been sent for trial in the Crown Court, the prosecution is required to draw up the indictment. The indictment is the formal document that contains the charge(s) the accused will plead to at trial, and is included in the committal or case sent bundle. Each charge on the indictment is known as a count, and the defendant will plead guilty or not guilty to each count at the PCMH.

The prosecution is required to draw up the indictment within prescribed time limits (Criminal PR). A bill of indictment, which is the draft indictment, should be preferred (i.e. delivered) to an officer of the appropriate Crown Court.

After being signed by an officer of the court the bill of indictment, then becomes the indictment on which the defendant is tried. An example of a draft bill of indictment can be located in our case study *R v Lenny Whyte* (see Appendix 1, Committal bundle). There are complicated rules relating to the drafting of indictments that are outside the scope of this Handbook. However, more than one count may be joined on the same indictment where the offences are either:

(a) founded on the same facts; or

(b) form or are part of a series of offences of the same or similar nature, r. 9, Indictment Rules 1971;

As regards (b), the courts have given a wide interpretation to the phrase 'series of offences of the same or similar character'. In *Ludlow v MPC* (1970) 54 Cr App R 233, the House of Lords determined that for offences to be similar, there must be some nexus between them both in terms of law and fact. An indictment can, of course, charge two or more defendants jointly either as principal offenders or as secondary parties and an indictment can charge defendants in separate counts but in the same indictment, providing there is a linking factor between the counts.

Consider the following example of the joinder of counts and defendants on a single indictment.

> ### Example
>
> Arif is charged with Count 1, affray. William is charged with wounding, Count 2. Both charges arise out of a disturbance when both defendants were refused entry to a night club. All courts may be joined in the same indictment under r. 9 Indictment Rules 1971, as they are founded on the same facts.

20.3 SUPPORTING THE DEFENCE COUNSEL AT TRIAL

Supporting the defence counsel at trial is a task that has commonly been allocated to a trainee solicitor. It is quite common for a trainee solicitor to be handed a file at short notice and to be told to act as a 'watching brief' in the Crown Court. This will require the trainee solicitor to quickly assimilate the information contained in the file.

As a result of changes introduced to the funding of criminal cases, a representative will now only be paid for attending counsel at trial where the proceedings come within one of the following categories:

- very serious indictable offences;
- serious fraud cases;
- where the defendant is a child or a young person;
- where the defendant will not be able to follow the proceedings because of illness, disability or inadequate command of English; or
- on the day that your client is likely to be given a custodial sentence.

If your client's case does not come within one of the above categories, your presence at the Crown Court may be paid for where the judge issues an attendance certificate. An attendance certificate is likely to be issued where:

- there are a significant number of defence witnesses to be marshalled on any given day; or
- there are a significant number of defence documents; or
- the defence advocate is representing more than one accused; or
- the accused is likely to be disruptive if the advocate appeared alone; or
- the advocate will need notes taken for the proper conduct of the defence; or
- there are any other exceptional circumstances.

20.4 LAST-MINUTE CHECKLIST

Where you are to attend the trial, in the period leading up to the trial date you should ensure that:

- any matters arising out of counsel's written advice or given in conference have been complied with;
- there are sufficient copies of the defence and prosecution documentation;
- your client's previous convictions have been checked;
- the prosecution and defence witnesses have been checked for previous convictions;
- each defence witness has been warned to attend trial or summonsed if necessary;
- any domestic arrangements for the defence witnesses have been made, for example, that hotel accommodation has been booked.

20.5 FIRST DAY OF TRIAL

On the first day of the trial you should aim to arrive at court as early as possible. Ensure that you have all the relevant documentation and contact numbers for your barrister and defence witnesses in case something does not go according to plan. Confirm with the court staff in which court your client's case is being heard. If you have any immediate concerns, the court usher is usually an invaluable source of information. You will look out for the defendant and the defence witnesses. This is a time where you will need good interpersonnel skills to allay any of your side's nervousness. The prosecution witnesses will normally have been met by Witness Support staff.

Contact counsel and confirm and that he has everything he needs. It is common immediately before the start of the trial to be given last-minute tasks such as:

- photocopying;
- providing the defence witness's with copies of their statement to enable each witness to refresh their memory before testifying;

- liaising with the defence witnesses as counsel cannot talk directly to the witnesses who are to be called;
- familiarising the witnesses with the layout of the courtroom; or
- undertaking legal research.

20.5.1 CONFERENCE WITH COUNSEL

Invariably, counsel will wish to speak with the defendant. This may be the first time your client has met his barrister. You will be required to make the introductions and to keep a careful note of the matters covered in the conference. You will also act as a contact between counsel and any defence witnesses. Professional conduct rules prevent counsel from having direct contact with witnesses, so any points of evidence that need clarifying with the witnesses will be done through you.

Counsel may give advice that your client does not wish to hear – most commonly that that he should consider pleading guilty to some or all of the charges. Negotiations between opposing counsel on plea bargaining are not uncommon on the first day of a trial. You may also be involved in these discussions which may influence the outcome of the proceedings.

20.6 PLEA BARGAINING

There is no formal system of plea bargaining in England and Wales, and it remains of central importance that a defendant has a genuine choice whether to plead guilty or not guilty. It is common for the prosecution and the defence to negotiate about the gravity of the charge and the defendant's plea. Where a guilty plea to a lesser alternative charge is acceptable to all sides, the prosecution will offer no evidence on the more serious charge or ask for the charge to lie on the court file. Where a defendant faces multiple counts and indicates guilty pleas to some of those counts which are acceptable to the prosecution, the remaining counts can either be withdrawn or allowed to lie on file.

In deciding whether to accept the defendant's guilty plea to a lesser charge, the prosecutor may seek the advice of the trial judge in chambers. Equally, before entering a guilty plea, defence counsel may wish to see if the trial judge is prepared to give an indication of likely sentence on the basis of a guilty plea. In *R v Goodyear* [2005] 2 Cr App R 20, the Court of Appeal acknowledged the right of defence counsel to seek an indication from the judge of the maximum sentence that would be passed in the event of a guilty plea but also indicated that the judge is not required to do so if he considers it be inappropriate.

20.7 DURING THE TRIAL

You will also make an important contribution during the trial. You will sit behind counsel taking a careful note of the proceedings and be available to give any assistance, particularly if your client wishes to communicate with his barrister. It is especially important to keep an accurate note of the answers given by the prosecution witnesses during cross-examination and by the defence witnesses during examination-in-chief, as counsel may not be able to make a written record of the witness's answers whilst asking questions.

There may be times during the trial when counsel has missed an important point or you have an idea that might be useful to the defence case. Write a legible note to counsel summarising the point and slide it forward to bring it to counsel's attention. If a more serious issue arises, it may be necessary to hold a conference with counsel at the end of the day or even at an adjournment during the main proceedings.

At the conclusion of the case you should write a full note of the court's decision and ensure that the brief is properly endorsed and that all the accompanying papers are received back from counsel.

Depending on the jury's verdict, this may be a time to congratulate your client on his acquittal or to provide further advice and support to the defendant and his family about the outcome and any avenues of appeal.

20.7.1 THE ARRAIGNMENT IN COURT

The trial formally begins with the defendant's arraignment. While he has already been arraigned at the PCMH and indicated a not guilty plea, the count(s) in the indictment will be put to the defendant again. After the count, the defendant is asked whether he pleads guilty or not guilty. Where the defendant enters a not guilty plea, the jury is empanelled.

20.7.2 EMPANELLING THE JURY

The jury will be empanelled or selected from a jury in waiting of 20 or more people who have been summonsed to do jury service at the Crown Court. The clerk of the court calls out the potential juror's names from a recently shuffled pack of cards, each card bearing a juror's name. This fulfils the requirement under s. 11 Juries Act 1974 that jurors should be selected randomly.

Once 12 names have been selected, the individuals are called forward to take the jury oath. Before being sworn, each juror may be asked to 'stand by' by the prosecution or challenged 'for cause' by either the prosecution or the defence.

20.7.3 ASKING A JUROR TO 'STAND BY'

The prosecutor can ask a juror to 'stand by' as he is about the take the oath. Whilst the prosecutor does not have to give a reason to ask a juror to 'stand by', most commonly it will be the result of the vetting of the jury panel by the police. The practice of asking a juror to 'stand by' has been severely curtailed by the Attorney-General's Guidelines on Exercise by the Crown Court of its Right of Stand-by (1989).

20.7.4 CHALLENGE FOR CAUSE

Both the prosecution and the defence may challenge a juror for cause, s. 12(3) Juries Act 1974. This is done orally immediately before the juror is sworn. The party making the challenge has the burden of proving that:

- the juror is not qualified to serve;
- the juror is biased; or
- the juror may reasonably be suspected of being biased.

20.7.5 JUDICIAL CHALLENGES

The judge has a residual power to remove a juror where, for example, the juror is illiterate or otherwise is deemed unsuitable or incapable of sitting as a juror. A juror may be discharged by the judge during the trial where, for example, he is ill or for 'any other good reason'.

20.7.6 THE COMPOSITION OF THE JURY

An empanelled jury should consist of 12 jurors, although cases are regularly heard with 11 or even only 10 jurors.

20.8 THE PROSECUTION CASE

After the jury has been empanelled, the formal part of the trial begins by the prosecution advocate making an opening speech.

20.8.1 THE OPENING SPEECH

The purpose of the prosecutor's opening speech is to outline the case in a simple, narrative form by explaining the facts that are alleged and the evidence the prosecution intends to rely on. The opening speech affords the advocate the opportunity to advance a theory of the case.

In his opening speech, the prosecutor will:

- outline the facts of the case;
- instruct the jury that it is the prosecution which brings the case and it is the prosecution which has the burden of proving to the jury of the defendant's guilt for the offence and that if they are unsure the defendant is entitled to the benefit of the doubt to be found not guilty;
- explain relevant points of law, although always indicating that the judge is the sole arbiter when matters of law are raised;
- identify the witnesses he intends to call, and in general terms outline what he expects them to tell the court.

Most disputes about the admissibility of evidence will have been dealt with at a pre-trial hearing and be the subject of a binding ruling by the trial judge. Where items of disputed evidence remain to be decided, the prosecutor must not refer to the disputed evidence during the opening speech. Any outstanding evidential issues will be decided in a *voir dire*, i.e. at a trial within the main trial conducted in the absence of the jury.

20.9 THE COURSE OF TRIAL – PRESENTING EVIDENCE

Having been sworn or affirmed, each prosecution witness gives evidence in the following order:

- examination-in-chief by the prosecution advocate;
- cross-examination by the defence advocate;
- re-examination (where appropriate) by the prosecution advocate.

Evidence may also be presented in written form, through formal admissions and by adducing exhibits.

Questioning of witnesses through examination-in-chief or cross-examination must be conducted in accordance with the rules of evidence and in compliance with the advocate's professional conduct responsibilities.

- The advocate should always be in control of the witness.
- The advocate should have clear objectives when examining the witness and an awareness of how those objectives can be achieved.
- The advocate should know what the witness is going to say and how the witness is going to say it – the examination of a witness at trial is not about ascertaining the truth – it is about getting the witness to say something that supports the advocate's case. Whether in a summary trial or a trial on indictment, pre-trial preparation, based on the disclosure of evidence will have alerted the advocate to the questions that should be put to witnesses in examination-in-chief or in cross-examination.

It should not be forgotten that a witness may be giving evidence with the benefit of special measures (see Chapter 22).

20.9.1 EXAMINATION-IN-CHIEF

The purpose of examination-in-chief is to elicit evidence in support of the party calling the witness.

The rules of evidence associated with examination-in-chief are explained in Chapter 23. One of the most important rules of examination-in-chief is not to ask your witness leading questions unless this is with the express agreement of the opposing advocate.

20.9.2 CROSS-EXAMINATION

Cross-examination has a number of purposes, which include the opportunity to:

- elicit helpful replies or concessions from a witness;
- expose errors, weaknesses or inconsistencies in the witness's account;
- undermine the witness's personal credibility – subject to the permissible limits allowed by the rules of evidence.

The rules relating to cross-examination are explained in Chapter 23. A great deal of importance is attached to cross-examination in the adversarial system of justice. It may seem an obvious point to make, but witnesses are far from infallible. Witnesses may be biased. They may not come to court to tell the truth, the whole truth and nothing but the truth. Memory fades over time. The witness's actual perception of the event may not have been made in ideal circumstances. All of these fallibilities can be exposed and explored in cross-examination. Cross-examination gives the advocate a chance to put his case to the opponent's witness.

20.9.3 RE-EXAMINATION

In asking questions of his witness in re-examination, the advocate is restricted to matters that have arisen in cross-examination. The advocate cannot introduce new matters which he omitted to ask the witness in examination-in-chief. Re-examination is generally regarded as a damage limitation exercise. It can be used to rehabilitate the witness in the eyes of the court where this is necessary.

We briefly illustrate the process of examination-in-chief and cross-examination in the context of our case study of *R v Lenny Whyte*. At Document 45, located on our Online Resource Centre in the case study section, we have included an extract from the examination of the eyewitness Shirley Lewis.

online
resource
centre

20.10 DEFENCE SUBMISSION OF NO CASE TO ANSWER

At the close of the prosecution case, the defence may make a submission of 'no case to answer'. The decision is made by the judge in the absence of the jury. The basis of a submission of no case to answer in the Crown Court was explained by Lord Lane in *R v Galbraith* [1981] 2 All ER 1060, in the following terms:

'How then should the judge approach a submission of 'no case'? (1) If there is no evidence that the crime alleged has been committed by the defendant, there is no difficulty. The judge of course will stop the case. (2) The difficulty arises where there is some evidence but it is of a tenuous character, for example because of the inherent weakness or vagueness or because it is inconsistent with other evidence. (a) Where the judge comes to the conclusion that the Crown's evidence, taken at its highest, is such that a jury properly directed could not properly convict on it, it is his duty, on a submission being made, to stop the case. (b) Where however the Crown's evidence is such that its strength or weakness depends on the view to be taken of a witness's reliability, or other matters which are generally speaking within the province of the jury and where on one possible view of the facts there is evidence on which a jury could properly come to the conclusion that the defendant is guilty, then the judge should allow the matter to be tried by the jury.'

Where the submission of no case to answer is rejected by the court, or a submission is not made, it is likely that the defence will call evidence to support the accused's plea of not guilty.

online
resource
centre

Our case study based on *R v Lenny Whyte* concludes with a successful submission of no case to answer, which is made at the close of the prosecution's case (see Document 46 located on our Online Resource Centre in the case study section).

20.11 THE DEFENCE CASE

- The defence advocate may make an opening speech in which he may outline his own case and/or seek to undermine the prosecution evidence.
- The defence will then call evidence in support of its case – beginning with the accused where he elects to testify.

Each defence witness gives evidence in the following order:

- examination-in-chief by the defence advocate;
- cross-examination by the prosecution advocate;
- re-examination (where appropriate) by the defence advocate.

If the defendant chooses to give evidence on oath, he will be the first defence witness to give evidence (s. 79 PACE 1984). The evidential consequences of the defendant choosing not to give evidence on oath are considered in Chapter 26.

20.12 THE CLOSING SPEECHES

At the close of the defence case, the prosecution advocate and then the defence advocate make a closing speech to the judge and jury. The closing speech is the advocate's final opportunity to persuade the jury of the merits of his party's case. The advocate will attempt to present his case in the most favourable light by identifying any evidence which supports his party's case and will try to explain away evidence that undermines it. The defence advocate will usually remind the jurors that if they are left in any doubt about the defendant's guilt, they must acquit.

20.13 THE SUMMING-UP

Following the defence advocate's closing speech, the judge will sum up the case to the jury. The judge directs the jurors on points of law and evidence, and helps them to consider the facts. The following issues are commonly referred to in the summing-up:

- an explanation that the jury are the sole arbiters of the facts in the case, but they must accept judge's direction on points of law and evidence;
- an explanation of the offence(s) charged including an examination of each of the elements;
- a clear direction on the burden and standard of proof;
- an assessment of the evidence put before the court. The judge may comment on the evidence presented by each party as counsel might have done in their closing speeches. The judge may direct the jurors' attention to any answers from a witness which might appear to be implausible or to examine why a particular witness might have a motive to lie;
- Depending on the issues in the case, the trial judge may be required to direct the jury on the following evidential issues:
  — the dangers of relying on identification evidence;
  — the dangers of relying on certain types of uncorroborated evidence;

— the use that can be made of evidence of a defendant's bad character;

— the use that can be made of the defendant's good character;

— the precise circumstances in which an adverse inference from the defendant's silence might be drawn under ss 34, 35, 36 and 37 Criminal Justice and Public Order Act 1994;

— the special circumstances that apply to expert evidence;

— the need to consider the evidence in relation to each count separately unless the rules of evidence dictate otherwise;

— the rules relating to confession evidence;

— the dangers of relying on hearsay evidence;

— The significance of lies told by the defendant.

Many of the directions the judge is required to give can be found in the Judicial Studies Board specimen directions, available at www.jsboard.co.uk. Quite often the trial judge will discuss his directions with counsel before directing the jury.

When attending counsel or a solicitor advocate in the Crown Court, it is very important that you take a verbatim record of the trial judge's directions. An error in the summing-up can provide a defendant with grounds for appeal in the event of a conviction.

At the end of the summing-up the judge advises the jury to appoint a foreman and instructs the jury to retire to seek a unanimous verdict.

20.14 THE VERDICT

If the jury reaches a unanimous verdict the jurors return to the courtroom and the judge asks whether they have reached such a verdict. If the answer is 'Yes', the jury foreman reads out the verdict on each count on the indictment. Where the indictment contains alternative counts, for example, counts of burglary or theft, the jury will only return a verdict on one count. An indictment may expressly, or impliedly, include a lesser alternative office such as manslaughter in place of murder. The decision to leave alternative counts to the jury is a matter for discussion between the advocates and the trial judge.

20.14.1 A UNANIMOUS OR A MAJORITY VERDICT?

In his summing-up the judge will direct the jury to try to reach a unanimous verdict. However, where it is not possible for all the jurors to agree, s. 17 Juries Act 1974 allows for majority verdicts of 11:1 or 10:2 or, if the jury is reduced below 12, a majority 10:1 or 9:1. The defendant may either be convicted or acquitted by a majority verdict.

Before a majority verdict can be considered, the jury must have retired for at least two hours or such longer period as is reasonable, having regard to the nature and complexity of the case. If at the end of that time the jury indicates there is no possibility of reaching a unanimous verdict, the judge may send them out for a further period. If the judge decides that he is willing to accept a majority verdict, the jurors are directed they should continue to reach a unanimous verdict but if they cannot, a majority verdict will be accepted.

20.15 THE PROCEDURE AFTER THE JURY'S DECISION

Where the accused is found guilty, the court will proceed to sentence, either on the day or, more likely, the proceedings will be adjourned, for pre-sentence reports to enable the court to enquire into the accused's background. Part V of this handbook covers sentencing. Where your client is remanded in custody pending sentence, it will be necessary for you and counsel to see your client in the cells to discuss the verdict and any possible grounds for appeal.

In the event of your client being convicted before the Crown Court, the Criminal Defence Service (Recovery of Defence Costs Orders) (Amendment) Regulations 2004 require a court to impose an order requiring the offender to pay all or some part of his legal costs. A defendant's means (the details of which are contained in Form B) will clearly be a relevant consideration in the making of such an order. Given the high incidence of custodial sentences in the Crown Court, and the fact that the vast majority of defendants have limited means, recovery of defence cost orders are limited, unless the offender has significant assets.

20.16 ACQUITTED DEFENDANTS

Defendants who are acquitted, and who have incurred expenditure in their defence, are generally entitled to an award of costs from central funds under s. 16 Prosecution of Offences Act 1985. Such orders are at the discretion of the trial judge, but should normally be awarded unless it is felt that the accused brought suspicion on himself by his own conduct or misled the prosecution into thinking the evidence against him was stronger than it in fact was. Guidance can be found in *Practice Direction (Costs: Criminal Proceedings)* [2004] 2 All ER 1070. A legally aided acquitted defendant's costs will be met under the representation order.

20.17 THE PROSECUTION'S RIGHT OF APPEAL

Although dealt with in more detail in paragraph 33.12 below, this is an appropriate place to explain that the prosecution enjoys a right of appeal over limited range of matters arising out of a Crown Court trial.

First, under ss. 35 and 36 Criminal Procedure and Investigations Act 1996, the prosecution may make an interlocutory appeal against a binding ruling made by the trial judge at a preparatory hearing.

Second, ss. 57–61 CJA 2003 allows the prosecution to appeal to the Court of Appeal against a terminating ruling made by the judge in relation to an issue at a trial on indictment and which cannot otherwise be the subject of an appeal to the Court of Appeal. The appeal can be against any judicial ruling made during the trial until the beginning of the summing-up to the jury. The procedure is described as appealing against a terminating ruling, as the prosecution must agree that in the event of failing to obtain leave to appeal or the appeal is abandoned, the defendant will be automatically acquitted. The appeal can follow an expedited or non-expedited route.

Third, section 62 gives the prosecution a right of appeal against an evidentiary ruling which has the effect of significantly weakening the prosecution's case but which is not fatal to it. Section 62 is not currently in force.

Fourth, the CJA 2003 has radically revised the traditional operation of *autrefois acquit*. Section 76 CJA 2003 allows the prosecutor to apply to the Court of Appeal for an order to quash the defendant's acquittal for a qualifying offence and to order a new trial. Generally a qualifying offence is any offence which carries a sentence of life imprisonment. The Court of Appeal must order a retrial if there is new and compelling evidence in the case and it is in the interests of justice for the order to be made.

20.18 TRIAL WITHOUT JURY

Looking Ahead

Sections 43–50 CJA 2003 make provision for the prosecution to apply for a serious or complex fraud case to be tried in the absence of the jury. The judge may so order if he is satisfied that the length and complexity of the case is likely to make the trial burdensome for the jury, and the interests of justice require serious consideration to be given to trial by judge alone.

A trial may also be conducted in the absence of a jury where there is a real and present danger of jury tampering, or where the jury has been discharged because of jury tampering. The judge must be satisfied that the risk of jury tampering is substantial, notwithstanding any steps, including police protection, which could be taken to prevent it, as to make it necessary in the interests of justice. These provisions are not yet in force, and there is some doubt as to whether they ever will be.

KEY POINT SUMMARY

- Have some understanding of the circumstances in which a defendant can be tried for more than one offence and can be tried jointly with others.

- Having reached the day of trial your role becomes one of supporting both your firm's client and the trial advocate.

- Be aware that although there is no formal system of plea bargaining, counsel may, with your client's express consent negotiate or take up an offer to plead guilty to a less serious alternative offence.

- Keep clear written notes of the conduct of the proceedings including what is said by counsel in conference and what is said during the course of the evidence.

- Understand the various stages of the trial on indictment and the verdicts which a jury can return.

SELF-TEST QUESTIONS

1. What is a bill of indictment?

2. What is the test for joining more than one count in an indictment?

3. What grounds do the defence have to satisfy to successfully make a submission of no case to answer at a trial in the Crown Court?

4. What procedure should be adopted in the Crown Court if a point of law arises?

5. Why is the trial judge's summing-up so important?

6. What is an attendance certificate?

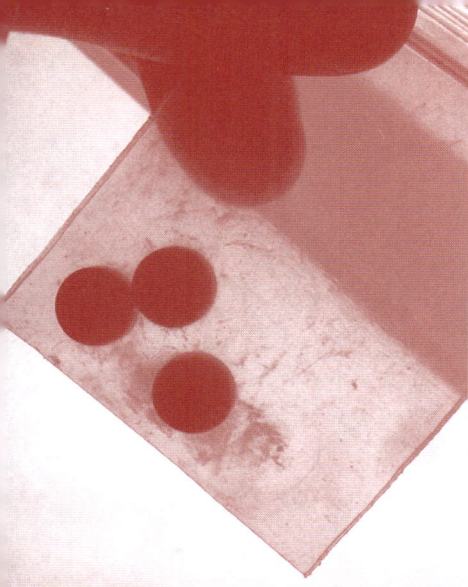

Part IV

PROVING THE CASE – THE RULES OF CRIMINAL EVIDENCE

In Part IV we are concerned with the way in which a criminal case is proved in court. Consequently, Part IV covers the rules of criminal evidence which regulate the process of proof. You are reminded that some of the rules of criminal evidence are covered in Part II and that the rules relating to the pre-trial disclosure of evidence are explained in Chapter 17 (Part III).

In Chapter 21 we consider the rules relating to burdens and standards of proof.

In Chapters 22–23 we consider the rules relating to witness testimony.

In Chapter 24 we consider a number of miscellaneous evidence provisions relating to opinion evidence, eye-witness identification and corroboration.

Chapter 25 examines the rules relating to the admission of hearsay evidence in criminal cases.

Chapter 26 considers the special position of the defendant as a witness in the case and in particular the rules relating to the admissibility of a defendant's past bad character.

Finally, in Chapter 27 we consider the rules of evidence which raise aspects of private privilege.

THE BURDEN OF PROOF

21.1   INTRODUCTION

In most criminal offences where the defendant pleads not guilty, the prosecution has the responsibility of proving the defendant's guilt. This principle is known as the legal burden of proof. The general rule about the legal burden reflects the presumption that the defendant is innocent until proven guilty and that in the interests of ensuring a fair trial it is appropriate that, as the prosecution is alleging criminal conduct against the defendant, the prosecution has the responsibility of proving the defendant's guilt.

In this chapter we consider:

- the general rule about the incidence of the legal burden of proof;
- the exceptional situations where a legal burden is imposed on the defence (known as reverse burden clauses);
- how a party discharges an evidential burden;
- the meaning of the standards of proof;
- the compatibility of reverse burden clauses with the presumption of innocence under Article 6(2) ECHR; and
- proof without evidence.

21.2 THE LEGAL BURDEN OF PROOF – THE GENERAL RULE

The principle that the prosecution has the responsibility for proving the defendant's guilt is known as the legal burden of proof. This fundamental rule is found in the leading case of *Woolmington v DPP* [1935] AC 463.

Woolmington v DPP [1935] AC 463

The accused was charged with the murder of his wife. He admitted that he had shot her, but claimed that the gun had gone off by accident. The trial judge, in directing the jury, stated that if the jury were satisfied that the accused had killed his wife, then it was for him to satisfy the jury that it was an accident. The accused was convicted and appealed. The case went to the House of Lords where the direction was overruled and the conviction quashed. The House of Lords reaffirmed the principle that it was for the prosecution to prove every element of the offence charged, including disproving any proper defence, such as self-defence.

In Chapter 5 which introduces the law of criminal evidence, we explained that the legal burden of proof is determined by the facts in issue in the case which are the actus reus and mens rea of the offence with which the defendant is charged. To remind you, on a charge of theft under s. 1 Theft Act 1968, the facts in issue are:

Actus reus	*Mens rea*
Appropriates	Dishonestly
Property	Intention to permanently deprive
Belonging to another	

Under the '*Woolmington* principle', the prosecution has the legal burden of proving the defendant dishonestly appropriated property belonging to another with the intention to permanently deprive.

Where the prosecution fails to discharge its legal burden in relation to one or more of the facts in issue, the defence may make a submission of no case to answer as outlined in *R v Galbraith* [1981] 2 All ER 1060 for trials in the Crown Court (see Chapter 20 paragraph 20.10) and *Practice Direction (Submission of No Case)* [1962] 1 WLR 227 at trials in the magistrates' court (see Chapter 18, paragraph 18.11). Where the submission of no case to answer is successful, the defendant will be acquitted.

21.3 EXCEPTIONS TO *WOOLMINGTON* – REVERSE BURDEN CLAUSES

Whilst the *Woolmington* principle applies in most criminal cases, including the most serious offences such as murder and rape, there are a number of exceptional situations where at common law or under statute the defendant has the legal burden of proof on one or more of the facts in issue. These have become known as reverse burden clauses. Whenever a legal burden of proof is cast on a defendant, the presumption of innocence is effectively reversed. Consequently the imposition of a reverse burden of proof raises human right considerations, which are explored in further detail at paragraph 21.7 below.

21.3.1 THE REVERSE BURDEN CLAUSE AT COMMON LAW

At common law where the accused submits that at the time of the offence he was insane within the meaning of *McNaghten's Rules* (1843) 10 Cl & F 200, he has the legal burden of proving insanity.

21.3.2 EXPRESS STATUTORY REVERSE BURDEN CLAUSES

In a number of statutes, Parliament has expressly passed the legal burden to the accused to prove one or more facts in issue. An example of where Parliament has expressly placed the legal burden on the accused to prove a fact in issue is s. 139 Criminal Justice Act 1988, which prohibits a person from possessing a knife in a public place. Under s. 139(4) CJA 1988, the accused has a defence where he can show 'good reason or lawful authority' for possessing the knife in a public place.

After the prosecution has discharged the legal burden of proving that the accused was found in possession of a knife in a public place, the accused then has the legal burden of proving that he had good reason or lawful authority for possessing the knife.

A similar approach is taken with ss. 2 and 4 of the Homicide Act 1957 (HA). Parliament has expressly provided the accused has the legal burden of proving the defence of diminished responsibility under s. 2 HA 1957 or acting in pursuance of a suicide pact under s. 4 HA 1957. After the prosecution has discharged the legal burden of proving the mens rea and actus reus of murder, the defendant has the legal burden of proving that at the time of the victim's death he was suffering from diminished responsibility or was acting in pursuance of a suicide pact.

21.3.3 IMPLIED STATUTORY REVERSE BURDEN CLAUSES

In other statutes, Parliament has, by implication, placed the legal burden on the accused to prove a fact in issue. An example that you will commonly encounter in summary trials is provided by s. 101 Magistrates' Courts Act 1980, which states:

> 'Where the defendant to an information or complaint relies for his defence on any exception, exemption, proviso, excuse or qualification, whether or not it accompanies the description of the offence or matter of complaint in the enactment creating the offence or on which the complaint is founded, the burden of proving the exception, exemption, proviso, excuse or qualification shall be on him; and this notwithstanding that the information or complaint contains an allegation negating the exception, exemption, proviso, excuse or qualification.'

An example of the operation of s. 101 MCA 1980 is provided by s. 143 Road Traffic Act 1988 which makes it an offence to drive a motor vehicle without insurance. Once the prosecution has discharged its legal burden by proving that on the date specified in the information the defendant drove a motor vehicle on the public highway, the legal burden passes to the accused to prove that at the time he was driving he was insured to do so. If the defendant successfully discharges the legal burden on this issue, he will be acquitted. The application of s. 101 MCA 1980 is a question of statutory interpretation and construction to be decided by the court on the words used by Parliament when creating the offence. The section applies most commonly to regulatory offences which prohibit or restrict the certain activities such as selling alcohol unless the defendant has a licence to do so or is permitted to engage in a specified activity that is otherwise illegal.

The rationale behind the common law and statutory exceptions to the Woolmington principle is that the facts in issue which are covered by reverse burden clause are within the defendant's exclusive knowledge or control and it is therefore easier for the defendant to prove the fact(s) in issue rather than for the prosecution to disprove.

However, the imposition of a legal burden of proof on a defendant which effectively requires the defendant to prove his innocence is, on the face of it, incompatible with Article 6(2) ECHR which explicitly provides that everybody charged with a criminal offence shall be presumed innocent until proven guilty. We consider the compatibility of reverse burden clauses with the presumption of innocence under Article 6(2) ECHR at paragraph 21.7.

21.4 THE STANDARD OF PROOF REQUIRED TO DISCHARGE THE LEGAL BURDEN

Whenever the legal burden of proof falls on a party, not only is the prosecution, or exceptionally the defence, required to prove the facts in issue, the evidence presented in support must have the necessary degree of persuasiveness to convince the court. This is known as the standard of proof. Where the prosecution has the legal burden of proving a fact in issue, it must convince the court to the standard of 'beyond a reasonable doubt'. Whilst the courts are reluctant to provide a detailed formulation of the phrase, preferring to give the words their ordinary, natural meaning, judicial guidance has been given in a number of cases.

In *Miller v Minister of Pensions* [1947] 2 All ER 372, beyond reasonable doubt was explained in this way:

> 'It not need reach certainty but it must carry a high degree of probability. Proof beyond a reasonable doubt does not mean proof beyond a shadow of a doubt . . . . . . If the evidence is so strong against a man as to leave only a remote possibility in his favour . . . the case is proved beyond reasonable doubt.'

In *Kritz* [1950] 1 KB 82 it was suggested that the jurors or magistrates 'should be sure' of the defendant's guilt, whilst in *R v Summers* [1952] 1 All ER 1059 the phrase that the jurors or magistrates 'should be satisfied so they feel sure' was approved.

The standard of beyond reasonable doubt only applies where the prosecution has the legal burden. Where the defence has a legal burden of proof, the appropriate standard is on the balance of probabilities. In *Re H (Minors) (Sexual Abuse: Standard of Proof)* [1996] 1 All ER 1, Lord Justice Nicholls suggested the phrase meant the following:

> 'The balance of probability standard means that the court is satisfied an event occurred if the court considers that, on the evidence, the occurrence of the event was more likely than not.'

21.5 THE EVIDENTIAL BURDEN

A party will prove its case or discharge its legal burden by putting evidence before the court to support its version of the facts and interpretation of the law. This is known as discharging the evidential burden. The party which bears a legal burden of proof usually also bears an evidential burden. The legal burden of proof cannot be discharged unless sufficient evidence is adduced.

The evidential burden will be discharged by:

* calling witnesses to give oral evidence to the court to prove a fact in issue;
* putting documentary evidence before the court to prove a fact in issue;
* putting photographic or video evidence before the court to prove a fact in issue;
* presenting real evidence before the court to prove a fact in issue – for example the alleged weapon at a murder trial; or
* presenting expert opinion evidence before the court for example the presence of the defendant's DNA at the crime scene.

Where a submission of no case to answer is successfully made at the close of the prosecution's case, the prosecution has failed to discharge its evidential burden of proof. Such a submission is determined by the judge in the absence of the jury. An unsuccessful submission of no case to answer does not of course mean that the prosecution has discharged its legal burden of proof, since this is determined by the jury/magistrates at the conclusion of the case and on the totality of the evidence presented on both sides.

Where the defendant simply pleads not guilty but does not put forward an affirmative defence, he may rely on the cross-examination of the prosecution witnesses to instigate reasonable doubt in the mind of the magistrates or jurors about his guilt. In this sense the defendant does not bear an evidential burden. However, in other cases it will be appropriate for the defendant to testify or to call defence evidence.

If the defendant goes further than merely denying the allegation and puts forward an affirmative defence such as self-defence, duress or provocation or non-insane automatism, he has an evidential burden to put some evidence in support of the defence before the court. The defendant will discharge the evidential burden where, if believed and left uncontradicted, his evidence would induce a reasonable doubt in the mind of the magistrates or the jury as to whether his version might be true or not. Where the defendant has discharged his evidential burden, the prosecution then has legal burden to disprove the accused's defence. If the defendant fails to adduce any evidence of his defence, the trial judge is not obliged to leave the defence to the jury.

21.6 DISCHARGING THE LEGAL AND EVIDENTIAL BURDENS OF PROOF – AN EXAMPLE

Example 1

Consider this example of how the prosecution and the defence would discharge its legal or evidential burdens of proof.

Ali is charged with robbery. He denies the offence and pleads not guilty. The Crown Prosecutor is aware that to discharge the legal burden of proof, the prosecution will have to prove in accordance with s. 8(1) Theft Act 1968, that Ali dishonestly appropriated property belonging to another with the intention to permanently deprive and that before or at the time of doing so and in order to do so, Ali used force on any person or put any person in fear of force being used.

To discharge the legal burden of proof, the prosecution must adduce evidence (i.e. discharge its evidential burden) by calling, for example, the investigating officers to testify. The officers will give evidence in examination in chief about the investigation including whether incriminating items were found in Ali's possession linking him to the robbery. The officers will also be able to tell the court if Ali had made incriminating admissions to the police during the investigation or at the police station. Other prosecution witnesses might be called to testify in examination in chief that immediately before the robbery they saw Ali at the crime scene. The victim is likely to be an important prosecution witness. She may give evidence in examination in chief about the property that was stolen from her and the force that was used against her.

Other types of evidence may also be used by the prosecution including real evidence; footage of CCTV recordings and documentary evidence and quite possibly forensic evidence in the form of expert opinion evidence.

The defence will seek to undermine the prosecution case by cross-examining each defence witness by challenging the witness's factual evidence and/or trying to undermine the witness's personal credibility as a witness. The defence may also put evidence before the court in support of Ali's defence. If, for example, Ali is pleading not guilty because he has an alibi, evidence should be put before the court to prove Ali's alleged whereabouts at the time of the offence. However, in this case there is no legal burden of proof on Ali and, as he is not advancing an affirmative defence, there is no evidential burden on him either. His only burden is a tactical one which is to adduce some evidence to raise a reasonable doubt in the mind of the jury.

Where the prosecution fail to adduce evidence in support of an element of the actus reus or the mens rea of robbery, at the close of the prosecution case, the defence may make a submission of no case to answer, as outlined in *R v Galbraith* [1981] 2 All ER 1060.

Assuming a submission of no case to answer is not made in this case or, if it is made, it is unsuccessful following a direction from the judge, the jury will decide whether Ali is guilty on the basis of the evidence presented.

21.7 CHALLENGES TO REVERSE BURDEN CLAUSES UNDER ARTICLE 6 EUROPEAN CONVENTION ON HUMAN RIGHTS 1950

In a number of recent cases, defence lawyers have submitted that imposing a legal burden on the defendant infringes the presumption of innocence under Article 6(2) ECHR. The principles developed so far suggest the courts are dealing with the issue on case-by-case basis. Where the imposition of a legal burden of proof on the defendant does infringe Article 6(2), the court must either apply the purposive statutory interpretation as provided by s. 3 Human Rights Act 1998, and read the wording of the statute down to impose an evidential burden of proof only on the defendant or make a declaration of incompatibility, in which case the matter is referred back to Parliament (see Chapter 4).

The starting point for considering the compatibility of a reverse burden clause European with the presumption of innocence is *Salabiaku v France* (1988) 13 EHHR 370. In this case the Court of Human Rights held that reverse burden clauses are not automatically incompatible with the presumption of innocence under Article 6(2) provided the legal burden imposed on the defence is not unreasonable and is proportionate to the aim of the provision.

An authoritative decision in domestic law on the relationship between a reverse burden clause and Article 6(2) is *R v Johnstone* [2003] 2 Cr App R 33.

R v Johnstone [2003] 2 Cr App R 33

In *Johnstone*, the defendant was prosecuted for an offence under s. 92 Trade Marks Act 1994 which provides that it is an offence where the accused 'with a view to gain for himself or another or with intent to cause loss to another and without the consent of the proprietor (a) applies to goods or their packaging a sign identical to or likely to be mistaken for a registered trade mark . . . '. It is a defence under s. 92(5) Trade Marks Act 1994 for a person to show 'that he believed on reasonable grounds that the use of the sign in the manner in which it was used or was to be used, was not an infringement of the registered trade mark'.

The Court of Appeal concluded that the defence under s. 92(5) TMA 1994 imposed an evidential burden only on the accused. It would therefore be sufficient for the accused to adduce some evidence in support of the defence before the court. The prosecution would then have the legal burden of disproving the defence.

In overruling the Court of Appeal, the House of Lords appeared to adopt a two-stage approach in deciding whether the section imposed a legal or an evidential burden on the accused. First, the House concluded that under the normal rules of statutory interpretation the defendant had a legal burden to prove the 'reasonable grounds' defence as any other interpretation would appear to be incompatible with Parliament's intention when passing the legislation. Second, to ensure compliance with the ECHR and the courts' interpretive obligation under s. 3 Human Rights Act 1998, the House was satisfied that imposing a legal burden on the accused was compatible with the presumption of innocence under Article 6(2) and that the measure was proportionate to the aim of the legislation.

21.7.1 REVERSE BURDEN CLAUSES – THE GUIDING PRINCIPLES

If a defendant is charged with an offence containing a reverse burden clause, what guidelines have developed to assist lawyers in determining whether the defendant has to discharge a legal or an evidential burden of proof? The following points are relevant to the advice a lawyer might give and include the guidance that was issued by the Court of Appeal in the case of *Attorney-General's Reference (No. 1 of 2004)* [2004] 1 WLR 2111.

- Reverse burden clauses are more easily justified where the overall burden to prove the essential ingredients of the offence remain on the prosecution.

- If only an evidential burden is cast on the defendant, there will be no risk of contravention of Article 6(2).

- A legal burden is more easily justified where the defendant is required to prove something within his own knowledge. In other words, it is easier for the defendant to prove than for the prosecution to disprove.

- Conversely, where the prosecution would face considerable practical difficulty in establishing the facts the imposition of a legal burden of proof on a defendant is more easily justified.

- Where the court construes a statute as imposing a legal burden of proof on the defendant compatibility depends on whether the imposition of a legal burden is proportionate with the aims of the legislation.

- The stronger the public interest in preventing the type of harm covered by the legislation, the more likely that a legal burden will be placed on the accused:

  - the counterfeiting of goods prohibited by s. 92 Trade Marks Act 1994 was a proportionate response to the adverse economic effects of counterfeiting on free and fair trade (*R v Johnstone* [2003] 2 Cr App R 33);

  - s. 139 CJA 1988 was a proportionate response to the social problem of people carrying knives in public (*R v Matthews* [2004] QB 690 and *L v DPP* [2002] 1 Cr App R 32);

  - s. 11(1) Terrorism Act 2000 was not proportionate, given the extraordinary breadth of the particular provision and the practical difficulty a defendant would have in establishing a defence.

- The more severe the penalty available to the court on a finding of guilt the more reasonable it would be to impose an evidential burden only on the accused.

- It is easier to justify the imposition of a legal burden of proof on a defendant where the offence is of a regulatory nature (*R (on the application of Grundy and Co. Excavations Ltd and the Forestry Commission) v Halton Division Magistrates Court* (2003) 167 JP 387).

For further judicial guidance on reverse burden clauses and the presumption of innocence, see the following cases: *R v Lambert* [2002] 2 AC 545; *R v Mathews* [2004] QB 690; *R v Drummond* [2002] 2 Cr App R 352; *Attorney-General's Reference (No. 1 of 2004)* [2004] 1 WLR 2111; and most authoritatively the House of Lords decision in *Attorney-General's Reference (No. 4 of 2002); Sheldrake v DPP* [2005] 1 AC 264.

21.8 BURDENS OF PROOF – PRACTICAL CONSIDERATIONS

In practical terms, it is important to research the elements of the offence with which your client is charged so that you can be sure what elements the prosecution must prove and whether there is a legal burden on your client to prove a fact(s) in issue. The same considerations apply when advising clients at the police station. Where a defence is advanced at the earliest opportunity and is maintained at trial, the defendant's credibility is considerably enhanced. You can research the particulars of any offence in *Blackstone's Criminal Practice*.

21.9 PROOF WITHOUT EVIDENCE

As you now understand the general rule is that where the prosecution or the defence has a legal or an evidential burden of proof, the facts in issue have to be proven by relevant and admissible evidence. Exceptionally, in a number of situations explained below, the court may accept a fact as proven without direct evidence being presented in respect to that fact. These situations are:

- irrebuttable presumptions of law;
- judicial notice; and
- formal admissions.

21.9.1 IRREBUTTABLE PRESUMPTIONS OF LAW

Where a presumption applies, the court is entitled to presume certain facts without having those facts directly proven. Whilst presumptions are more significant in civil cases, s. 50 Children and Young Persons Act 1933 creates the irrebutable presumption of law that no child under ten years of age can be guilty of a criminal offence. Where the defence offer evidence that the accused is a child under ten years of age, the court will presume that the child is incapable of committing a criminal offence.

21.9.2 JUDICIAL NOTICE

In some situations a criminal court will accept the existence of an issue without any proof in support of that fact. There are two types of judicial notice: judicial notice without inquiry, and judicial notice after inquiry.

Judicial notice without inquiry is taken in respect to those facts which are so much part of common knowledge that they require no proof at all. Facts which fall into this category include that a fortnight is too short a period for human gestation and that the normal duration of human gestation is nine months.

Judicial notice after inquiry applies to those facts which are not so part of common knowledge of which judicial notice may be taken after the judge or magistrates have made appropriate inquiries.

21.9.3 FORMAL ADMISSIONS IN A CRIMINAL CASE – S. 10 CRIMINAL JUSTICE ACT 1967

The effect of s. 10 Criminal Justice Act 1967 is that an admission can be made by either the prosecution or the defence before or at the trial. If made before the trial, the admission must be in writing and where the defendant is legally represented, the admission must be made by his solicitor or barrister. Formal admissions help save a considerable amount of court time and are actively encouraged.

KEY POINT SUMMARY

- The rules relating to the incidence of legal and evidential burdens of proof are of considerable practical importance.
- Know the general rule about the incidence of the legal burden of proof in a criminal case.
- Know the exceptions to the 'Woolmington principle'.
- Know the relationship between the legal burden and the evidential burden and the exception to this general rule.
- Be aware of the standard of proof that a party has to satisfy in order to discharge the legal burden.
- Understand that where a legal burden of proof is imposed on a defendant an issue of compatibility with Article 6(2) ECHR might arise.
- Know the evidential effect of a formal admission in a criminal case.
- Be able to apply these basic evidential rules to your client's case.

SELF-TEST QUESTIONS

1. What is the general rule about the incidence of the legal burden of proof in a criminal case?

2. Explain the meaning of the phrase 'reverse burden clause'.

3. What factors do the courts take into account in deciding the compatibility of a reverse burden clause with Article 6(2) European Convention on Human Rights 1950?

4. Consider the following short scenarios and answer the question that follows each of them.

(4a) Robert and Pete have been charged with rape contrary to s. 1 Sexual Offences Act 2003. The victims are two women who were at a nightclub on the evening of Saturday 4 April. The women claim that a man came over to them and proceeded to buy them drinks. They say that a man fitting Robert's description offered to give them a lift home. They got into his car, which they describe as an old saloon car, black in colour with a large spoiler mounted on the boot. The vehicle was also very noisy when driven, as if the exhaust were blowing. The women allege that there was a second man in the car. Instead of taking them home, however, the men took them to a house or flat in the area. The women claim that while at the flat they were given more alcoholic drinks and that the drinks were spiked. Both women recall waking up later in a state of undress. They maintain the men had sex with them without their consent. Their complaint is not made until a week after the event.

Robert states he was at Valentino's night club on the Saturday night in question. He was with his friend, Pete. They did pick up two young women, both of whom were pretty drunk. At the club the women were trying to seduce both men. Robert offered to take them back to his flat for a drink. They accepted the lift. All four travelled in Robert's car to his flat. The evening quickly became quite raunchy, with further drink being consumed. Robert says that both he and Pete ended up having consensual sex with the women. Afterwards, one of the women said that she felt sick. Robert did not want either woman being sick in his flat and so he took them from the flat in his car to the area where they said that they lived. It was about a four-mile journey. He dropped them on a corner as they requested.

Having regard to the likely facts in issue in this case, explain which party bears a legal/evidential burden.

(b) Lee is seen by police throwing a knife behind a low wall and is charged with possessing a knife in a public place under s. 139 Criminal Justice Act 1988. Lee maintains he has a good reason for carrying the knife in a public place.

Having regard to the likely facts in issue in this case, explain which party bears a legal/evidential burden.

FIGURE 21.1 THE LEGAL AND EVIDENTIAL BURDENS OF PROOF

THE LEGAL BURDEN OF PROOF

- as a general rule and as a fundamental component of Article 6 the prosecution has the legal burden of proving the defendant's guilt (*Woolmington v DPP*);

- the prosecution will not know whether it has succeeded in discharging its overall burden of proof until the jury/magistrates return a verdict.

↓

EXCEPTIONS TO THE *WOOLMINGTON* PRINCIPLE WHERE THE DEFENDANT HAS A LEGAL BURDEN OF PROOF (REVERSE BURDEN CLAUSES)

- at common law where the defendant pleads insanity under the *McNaghten Rules* 1843;

- express or implied statutory exceptions (e.g. s. 2 Homicide Act 1957, s. 101 Magistrates' Courts Act 1980 in summary proceedings);

- reverse burden clauses give rise to a potential Article 6 argument.

↓

THE STANDARD OF PROOF

- the legal burden of proof must be discharged 'beyond reasonable doubt' i.e. it not need reach certainty but it must carry a high degree of probability, (*Miller v Minister of Pensions*);

- 'on the balance of probabilities' wherever legal burden falls on the defence i.e. the court considers that, on the evidence, the occurrence of the event was more likely than not, (*Re H (Minors) (Sexual Abuse: Standard of Proof)*).

↓

THE EVIDENTIAL BURDEN OF PROOF

- the general rule is that the party with the legal burden also has an evidential burden;
- it is a burden to adduce some evidence;
- a failure by the prosecution to discharge its evidential burden at the close of the prosecution's case will result in a successful submission of no case to answer by the defence (*R v Galbraith* for Crown Court trials; *Practice Direction (Submission of No Case)* in summary cases);
- there is always a tactical burden on the defendant to exploit the 'reasonable doubt';
- where the defendant raises an affirmative defence, there is an obligation to adduce some evidence of it.

22 WITNESSES EVIDENCE – THE PRELIMINARY ISSUES

22.1 INTRODUCTION

This is the first of two chapters on the practice and procedures of a witness giving evidence at trial. The rules relating to witness testimony apply in a case where the defendant pleads not guilty, by requiring witnesses to give evidence at trial.

Chapter 23 explains the course of witness testimony at the defendant's trial through examination-in-chief, cross-examination and re-examination. This chapter considers the preliminary issues of witness testimony which apply to both summary proceedings and at trials on indictment, including:

- dealing with witnesses before testifying;
- the use of out-of-court memory-refreshing documents;
- the tests to decide a witness's competence to give evidence;

- the compellability of a witness;
- the assistance available to 'vulnerable' or 'intimidated' witnesses to give evidence under a special measures direction;
- a witness taking the oath or affirming.

22.2 DEALING WITH WITNESSES BEFORE TESTIFYING

On the day of the trial, it is the responsibility of the prosecution and defence to ensure that its witnesses are present in the precincts of the court and available to give evidence. The marshalling of witnesses is often the responsibility of a trainee solicitor or a paralegal or a CPS caseworker.

A witness remains out of court until called to give evidence. This ensures that his testimony is not influenced by having heard other evidence. This practice is subject to two exceptions. First, an expert witness will usually be permitted to sit in court before testifying as it is unlikely that his evidence will be influenced by hearing other witnesses. Second, the police officer in charge of the case may also be in court where the defence gives consent. The investigating officer's presence recognises his position as the prosecution client and he will be available to advise the prosecutor on any issues that arise during the trial.

22.3 REFRESHING THE WITNESS'S MEMORY OUT OF COURT

As a witness is likely to have written or dictated his statement some months earlier to the police or a member of the defence team, while waiting to give evidence the witness should read over his statement to remind himself of the matters about which he is going to testify (*R v Richardson* [1971] 2 QB 484). A witness should not compare or discuss his evidence with other witnesses.

22.4 THE ORDER OF CALLING WITNESSES

Both the prosecution and the defence have discretion in which order to call its witnesses, subject to s. 79 PACE, which requires that the defendant be called before any other defence witness.

22.5 THE COMPETENT WITNESS – S. 53 YOUTH JUSTICE AND CRIMINAL EVIDENCE ACT 1999 (YJCEA)

Before a witness can testify, the court must be satisfied he is competent to give evidence. A witness is competent where, as a matter of law, the court can receive his evidence. Section 53(1) YJCEA presumes that all witnesses are competent to testify. It provides:

> 'At every stage in criminal proceedings all persons are (whatever their age) competent to give evidence.'

Where there is reason to doubt the competency of a witness, the test to be satisfied is set out in s. 53(3). A person will be competent if it appears to the court that the person is able to understand questions put to him and give answers to them which can be understood. This satisfies the test of 'intelligible testimony'.

A witness aged 14 years and over will be presumed competent to give sworn (s. 55) evidence. A witness under 14 years is presumed competent to give unsworn evidence (s. 56).

22.6 CHALLENGING THE COMPETENCE OF A WITNESS – S. 54 YJCEA

In modern cases it is rare for a party (or the court) to challenge a witness's competence and is only likely to be made in respect to a child witness, a young person or a mentally impaired witness. The challenge may be made at the pre-trial review in summary proceedings or at the plea and case management hearing in the Crown Court. The issue may also be raised at trial either immediately before or just after the witness has begun to testify. An objection to a witness testifying may relate to his competence *per se* or his competence to give sworn evidence.

In deciding the witness's competence, the court may hear expert evidence and take into account whether the witness will be subject to a 'special measures direction' under s. 19 YJCEA (see paragraph 22.7 onwards).

Issues of competency are determined in the Crown Court in the absence of the jury and the burden of proving the witness's competence rests on the party calling the witness. Proof is on the balance of probabilities.

22.6.1 THE COMPETENCE OF A CHILD

For the purposes of giving evidence, a 'child' is a person under 14 years of age and must give unsworn evidence. Where the presumption in favour of competence is challenged, the court must be satisfied that the child satisfies the test under s. 53(3) YJCEA (that is the child is able to give 'intelligible testimony'). This situation is only likely to apply to very young children.

22.6.2 THE COMPETENCE OF A YOUNG PERSON

A young person, aged between 14 and 17 years, who is able to give 'intelligible testimony' within the definition of s. 53(3) YJCEA is presumed to be competent to give sworn evidence (s. 55(3)). If there is a question as to the witness's ability to give sworn evidence, the test that must be satisfied is set out in s. 55(2) YJCEA. A witness is capable of giving sworn evidence if, having attained the age of 14, the witness has sufficient appreciation of the solemnity of the occasion and the particular responsibility to tell the truth which is involved in taking an oath.

Whether a young person is competent to give sworn evidence depends on his emotional maturity and understanding. If he fails the test for giving sworn evidence under s. 55(2), but satisfies the test of intelligible testimony as defined by s. 53(3), he may give unsworn evidence under s. 56(2) YJCEA and will be in the same position as a witness aged under 14 years.

22.6.3 THE COMPETENCE OF A MENTALLY IMPAIRED WITNESS

Provided the witness is aged 14 years and over, he will be presumed competent to give sworn evidence under s. 53(1) and s. 55(3) YJCEA. If he fails the sworn evidence test (s. 55(2)), he may give unsworn evidence under s. 56(2) YJCEA. In making these decisions, the court will also take into account that a mentally impaired witness will be the subject of a special measures direction if he comes within the meaning of a 'vulnerable' witness under s. 16 YJCEA.

22.6.4 DEALING WITH ISSUES OF COMPETENCE

Good case preparation will have identified and anticipated any problems that might arise in relation to the competence of a witness. On the same basis, before trial the defence solicitor should have identified any witnesses to be called by the other side whose competence may be challenged.

The difficulties encountered with the competence and credibility of the main prosecution witness during the first Damilola Taylor murder trial is a good illustration of what might happen when these matters are not properly addressed during case preparation. Damilola Taylor was a ten-year-old schoolboy who bled to death in November 2000 on the stairwell of a block of flats on the North Peckham Estate in south London. Two 16-year-old brothers were charged with murder. In pleading not guilty, the defence claimed the boy had injured himself accidentally.

A key prosecution witness was a 14-year-old girl, known only as witness Bromley, who claimed that she had witnessed the attack. However, the reliability of her testimony was tainted after it was suggested in cross-examination that she was only giving evidence to claim a £50,000 reward offered by the *Daily Mail* in connection with the conviction of Damilola's murderers. As a result of the attacks on the witness's credibility, the prosecution case collapsed and the brothers were acquitted.

22.7 A SPECIAL MEASURES DIRECTION UNDER S. 19 YJCEA

An application for a special measures direction may be made by the prosecution or the defence or by the court. The rules of court relating to such application are contained in Part 29 Crim PR. The application will usually be made at the pre-trial review in summary proceedings or at the plea and case management hearing in indictable offences.

Special measures will be ordered where the witness is either 'vulnerable' under s. 16 YJCEA or 'intimidated' under s. 17 YJCEA and the court is satisfied that it will improve the quality of the witness's evidence (s. 19(2) YJCEA).

22.7.1 A 'VULNERABLE' WITNESS – S. 16 YJCEA

A vulnerable witness is:

* a witness under 17 at the time of the court hearing; or
* a witness who has a significant impairment of intelligence and social functioning, mental disability, mental or physical disorder or a physical disability.

A vulnerable witness will automatically attract a special measures direction entitling him to a range of facilities to assist him to give oral evidence. Section 21 YJCEA provides additional safeguards for a child witness in need of special protection who gives evidence about sexual and other specified offences including kidnapping and assault.

22.7.2 AN 'INTIMIDATED' WITNESS – S. 17 YJCEA

A special measures direction can be made in relation to an 'intimidated' witness where the court is satisfied the quality of the witness's evidence would be diminished by his fear or distress connected with testifying in the proceedings.

The intimidation may result from the witness's personal and/or social circumstances. Under s. 17(2) YJCEA, the court will take into account the following:

* the nature of and the alleged circumstances of the offence to which the proceedings relate;
* the age of the witness;
* the social and cultural background and ethnic origin of the witness;
* the domestic and employment circumstances of the witness;
* any religious and political beliefs, the behaviour of the accused towards the witness, members of accused's family or associates and the views of the witness.

A complainant in a sexual offence automatically falls within this section. The range facilities that are available under a special measures direction depends on whether the witness is a child, a vulnerable adult or an intimidated witness and whether the witness testifies at the Crown Court or in the magistrates' court.

22.7.3 THE USE OF A SCREEN – S. 23 YJCEA

Under s. 23(1) YJCEA a special measures permits a screen to be used which prevents the witness from being seen by the accused while testifying. The screen should not prevent the witness from being seen and seeing:

- the judge and jury;
- the justices;
- the advocates; and
- any person who has been appointed to assist the witness, for example an interpreter appointed under s. 29 YJCEA.

Giving evidence from behind a screen is available for a child, a vulnerable adult or an intimidated witness in both the Crown Court and in the magistrates' court.

22.7.4 GIVING EVIDENCE BY A LIVE TELEVISION LINK – S. 24 YJCEA

A special measures direction may permit the witness to give evidence by a live television link. In *Camberwell Green Youth Court, ex p. D and Others* [2003] 2 Cr App R, the defence submitted that permitting a witness to testify through a live TV link infringed the defendant's right to a fair trial under Article 6 ECHR. This argument was rejected: the proceedings were not unfair simply because the child witness and the accused were not in the same room. The decision has subsequently been confirmed by the House of Lords [2005] 2 Cr APP R 1.

Giving evidence by a live television link is available for a child, a vulnerable adult or an intimidated witness in both the Crown Court and in the magistrates' court.

⚖ Looking Ahead

When s. 51 CJA 2003 comes into force, the court may make much greater use of evidence through live TV link. The court will be permitted to authorise a witness, other than the defendant, to give evidence via live link in any case where it is satisfied that it is in the interests of efficient or effective administration of justice and where suitable facilities are available. The section has a potentially general application and there are no guidelines currently available on how the power under s. 51 should be exercised. It is thought that it will be used in those instances where a witness may be in a different part of the country and it is impractical to ensure their physical attendance in court.

22.7.5 GIVING EVIDENCE IN PRIVATE – S. 25 YJCEA

A special measures direction excludes from the court certain people specified in the direction. The direction may only be made where:

- the proceedings relate to a sexual offence; or
- it appears to the court that there are reasonable grounds for believing that any other person than the accused has sought or will seek to intimidate the witness in connection with testifying in the proceedings.

The following participants in the trial may not be excluded:

- the defendant;
- the defendant's legal representatives;
- an interpreter appointed to assist the witness;
- a court reporter representing a news-gathering organisation.

Giving evidence in private is available for a child, a vulnerable adult or an intimidated witness in both the Crown Court and in the magistrates' court.

22.7.6 REMOVING THE LAWYERS' WIGS – S. 26 YJCEA

A special measures direction may provide that the wearing of wigs or gowns to be dispensed with during the giving of a witness's evidence. A special measures direction requiring the advocates to remove their wigs is available for a child, a vulnerable adult or an intimidated witness in the Crown Court only.

22.7.7 VIDEO-RECORDED EVIDENCE-IN-CHIEF – S. 27 YJCEA

A special measures direction may provide for the video-recording of an interview with the witness which may be admitted as his evidence-in-chief, unless it would not be in 'the interests of justice' to allow the recording to be admitted.

Giving video-recorded evidence-in-chief evidence is available to a child or vulnerable adult witness in the Crown Court and a child witness in need of special protection in the magistrates' court. The facility has limited availability to an intimidated witness appearing in the Crown Court which is subject to a pilot scheme. Video-recorded evidence-in-chief evidence is not available to an intimidated witness in the magistrates' court.

> **Looking Ahead**
>
> When s. 137 CJA 2003 comes into force, wider use may be made of video-recorded evidence in cases involving serious crimes. The section will enable a court to authorise a video-recording of an interview with a witness (other than the accused) to be admitted as the evidence-in-chief provided that:
>
> (a) the person claims to be a witness to the offence, or part of it, or to events closely connected with it; and
>
> (b) the video recording of the statement was made at a time when the events were fresh in the witness's memory; and
>
> (c) the offence is indictable-only, or is a prescribed either-way offence.
>
> Where the recording is admitted under this provision, it is treated as the final statement of the matters it deals with (s. 138 CJA 2003) that is, it will constitute the witness's evidence-in-chief.

22.7.8 VIDEO-RECORDED CROSS-EXAMINATION OR RE-EXAMINATION – S. 28 YJCEA (NOT YET IN FORCE)

Where a special measures direction provides for the video recording to be admitted under s. 27 YJCEA as the witness's evidence-in-chief, the direction may also provide that any cross-examination or re-examination be video recorded. The recording must be made in the presence of the judge or justices and the legal representatives acting in the proceedings. The recording may be made in the absence of the accused.

22.7.9 EXAMINATION OF A WITNESS THROUGH AN INTERMEDIARY – S. 29 YJCEA

A special measures direction may provide for the witness to be examined through an interpreter or through any other person as the court may direct. The intermediary is required to communicate questions to the witness and may give to the person asking the questions the witness's reply.

A special measures direction requiring the witness to be examined through an intermediary is only available to a child or a vulnerable adult in a Crown Court or a magistrates' court that is part of the pilot scheme. The facility is not available to an intimidated witness in either the Crown Court or the magistrates' court.

22.7.10 AIDS TO COMMUNICATION – S. 30 YJCEA

A special measures direction may provide for the witness while giving evidence (whether in court or otherwise) to be provided with such device as the court considers appropriate with a view to enabling questions or answers to be communicated to or by the witness despite any disorder or disability or other impairment which the witness has or suffers from.

This facility is available is to child or a vulnerable adult in the Crown Court and a magistrates' court. It is not available to an intimidated witness in either the Crown Court or the magistrates' court.

22.7.11 CAN THE DEFENDANT GIVE EVIDENCE UNDER A SPECIAL MEASURES DIRECTION?

The defendant is not entitled to give evidence under a special measures direction. *R (On the application of S) v Waltham Forest Youth Court and (1) Crown Prosecution Service and (2) Secretary of State for the Home Department* [2004] 2 Cr App R 21 explained the rationale for this prohibition, on the basis that in deciding the defendant's guilt, the jurors or the magistrates will assess the defendant's demeanour and body language as well as the probative force and the persuasiveness of his evidence. If the defendant gave evidence from behind a screen or through a live television link or by a video recording, it would not be possible for the fact-finder to effectively assess the defendant's demeanour.

22.8 THE COMPELLABILITY OF A WITNESS

Where a person is competent to testify, he will also generally be a compellable witness. A witness is compellable if, as a matter of law, he can be made to give evidence, and a failure to give evidence may result in that person being committed to prison for contempt of court.

There are two main exceptions to the general rule about a witness's compellability to give evidence – the defendant and the defendant's spouse. The position of the defendant as a witness is considered in Chapter 26.

22.8.1 THE SPOUSE AS A COMPELLABLE WITNESS

The second exception to the general rule about the compellability of a witness is the defendant's spouse. The position is governed by s. 80 PACE and establishes the following principles:

- the defendant's spouse is competent and compellable to give evidence on behalf of the defendant unless the spouse is jointly charged in the proceedings, s. 80(4) PACE;

- the spouse of one defendant is competent and compellable to give evidence on behalf of any other co-defendant charged in the proceedings subject to the restriction in s. 80(4) PACE;

- the general rule is that the spouse of the defendant is a competent but not a compellable witness for the prosecution except where s. 80(3) PACE applies by making the spouse a compellable witness where the defendant is charged with an assault on, or injury or a threat of injury to, the wife or husband or a person who was at the material time under the age of 16 or is charged with a sexual offence alleged to have been committed in respect of a person who was at the material time under that age.

> **Example**
>
> Gordon is pleading not guilty to separate offences of theft and sexual assault on Lucy, who is eight years old.
>
> Moira, who is Gordon's wife, is a competent and a compellable defence witness for both offences. If the prosecution wish to call Moira to give evidence against Gordon, she will be a competent but not a compellable witness at Gordon's trial for theft. If the prosecution wish to call Moira to give evidence against Gordon at his trial for sexual assault, Moira will be both competent and compellable. She is compellable, as the offence of sexual assault falls within s. 80(3) PACE.

22.9 TAKING THE OATH OR AFFIRMING

After the preliminary issues of witness testimony have been dealt with before testifying, the witness has to take the oath or affirm.

Where the witness is a religious observer, s. 1 Oaths Act 1978 allows the oath to be taken on the New Testament or, in the case of a Jewish witness, on the Old Testament. The witness will be required to state: 'I swear by Almighty God . . .' and then the appropriate form of words as prescribed by law.

Where the witness follows another faith, an appropriate form of oath will be taken. For example, a Muslim witness is sworn on the Koran 'I swear by Allah . . .', while a Sikh will swear on the Sunder Gutka 'I swear by Waheguru . . .'

If the witness refuses to take an oath or the oath is contrary to his religion, s. 5 Oaths Act 1978 allows the witness to make a solemn affirmation in the following form: 'I [name] do solemnly, sincerely and truly declare and affirm. . . '

KEY POINT SUMMARY

- All witnesses are presumed to be competent to give evidence.

- A witness aged 14 and over is presumed competent to give sworn evidence.

- Anticipate and be prepared to argue against any challenges to the competence of your witnesses and to raise argument as to the competency of an opposing party's witness.

- Know the tests that a witness has to satisfy to be competent and to be able to give sworn evidence.

- Know the rules governing the compellability for competent witnesses for both the prosecution and the defence.

- Special measures directions are available to assist vulnerable or intimidated witnesses to give evidence.

- Know the practice and procedure for applying for a special measures direction and the facilities that are available.

SELF-TEST QUESTIONS

To test your understanding of the preliminary issues of witness testimony, consider the following scenario and answer the questions that follow.

David is charged with sexual assault on his stepdaughter, Florence, aged 14. Florence has learning difficulties. David is pleading not guilty. The prosecution have witness statements from Susie, David's wife and their son, Aaron aged seven.

(a) Is Susie a competent and compellable witness for the prosecution?

(b) Which type of evidence will Florence be presumed competent to give?

(c) Consider why there may be doubts about Florence's competence to give this type or any other type of evidence.

(d) Which type of evidence will Aaron be presumed competent to give?

(e) What provisions are there to assist Florence and Aaron to give evidence?

(f) In view of the public disquiet over the case, during the week before his trial, David has received several telephone calls during which his life was threatened unless he admitted his guilt for the offences. What facilities are available to assist David to testify at his trial?

Case Study: *R v Lenny Whyte*

With reference to the *R v Lenny Whyte* case study, consider whether any of the potential witnesses in this case might qualify in terms of a special measures direction.
Analysis can be found in Appendix 5.

FIGURE 22.1 WITNESS COMPETENCE AND COMPELLABILITY

COMPETENCY

- a witness is competent where as a matter of law his evidence can be received by the court;

- all witnesses are presumed competent to give evidence (s. 53(1) YJCEA);

- a witnesses aged 14 years and above will be presumed competent to give sworn evidence;

- a witness aged under 14 years will be presumed competent to give unsworn evidence;

- where a witness's competence is challenged, s. 54 YJCEA lays down the procedure for the court to decide the issue;

- the court must be satisfied that the witness is able to understand questions put to him and give answers to them which can be understood (s. 53(3) YJCEA).

- a witness may be granted the benefit of a special measures direction before a determination as to competency is made (s. 54(3) YJCEA).

COMPELLABILITY

- a witness is compellable where he can be made to give evidence and a failure to testify may result in him suffering a penalty;

- generally, all witnesses are competent and compellable for the prosecution, except
  - the defendant and co-defendant; and
  - the defendant's spouse BUT see s. 80(3) PACE.

SPECIAL MEASURES DIRECTION, S. 19 YJCEA

- a special measures direction seeks to reduce the trauma of a 'vulnerable' or an 'intimidated' witness to give evidence;

- s. 16 YJCEA defines a 'vulnerable' witness as:
  - a witness under 17 years; or
  - a witness who suffers from significant impairment of intelligence and social functioning;

- s. 17 YJCEA defines an intimidated witness as:
  - a witness whose quality of evidence is diminished by fear or distress associated with testifying;

- where a special measures direction is made under s. 19 YJCEA, the court may order the following, subject to availability:
  - witness may give evidence from behind a screen, s. 23 YJCEA
  - witness may give evidence through a live TV link, s. 24 YJCEA;
  - witness may give evidence in private, s. 25 YJCEA;
  - removal of lawyers' wigs, s. 26 YJCEA;
  - witness may video-record his evidence-in-chief, s. 27 YJCEA;
  - witness may video-record his cross-examination and re-examination, s. 28 YJCEA;
  - witness may give evidence through an intermediary, s. 29 YJCEA;
  - witness may give evidence with the benefit of a communication aid, s. 30 YJCEA.

23 THE RULES RELATING TO WITNESS TESTIMONY

23.1 INTRODUCTION

Once the preliminary issues of witness testimony have been dealt with, the witness's evidence will usually be presented to the court in three stages. The first stage is examination-in-chief, where the witness is questioned by the advocate calling him. The second stage involves the witness being cross-examined by the other side's advocate. The third stage is re-examination, where the advocate calling the witness has an opportunity to repair any damage done to the witness's factual evidence or personal credibility during cross-examination.

In this chapter we provide an overview of the evidential and procedural issues that may arise during each stage of witness testimony, including:

- the purposes of examination-in-chief, cross-examination and re-examination;
- the law governing leading questions and the use of memory-refreshing documents;
- the practice and procedure where a witness is ruled as 'hostile';
- the evidential effect of a witness's previous consistent and inconsistent statements;
- cross-examining the witness on his factual evidence;
- attacking the witness's credibility in cross-examination.

Changes introduced under the Criminal Justice Act 2003 are highlighted.

23.2 EXAMINATION-IN-CHIEF

This is the process by which the party calling the witness elicits the witness's testimony. The examination-in-chief of a party's own witness has the following purposes:

- to obtain answers from the witness about his factual evidence which supports the party's case;
- to put questions to the witness which enhance his personal credibility;
- to raise any matters which the advocate anticipates might be raised in cross-examination.

Having previously taken the witness's statement when events were fresh in the witness's mind, the trial advocate will know which questions he needs to ask in examination-in-chief.

23.3 LEADING QUESTIONS

A leading question either suggests to the witness the answer desired, or assumes the existence of disputed facts that have not yet been satisfactorily proven.

💡 Example 1

The advocate questions the witness in the following way:

'The car you saw the defendant drive away from the crime was a blue Ford Escort, wasn't it?'

'Is it correct to suggest that when you saw the defendant he was acting suspiciously?'

These questions clearly offend the rule against leading questions, as the witness is led into giving the answer the advocate desires.

The general rule is that leading questions are not allowed during examination-in-chief. Where a leading question is asked, the judge or the magistrates' adviser will suggest to the advocate that the question should be put differently.

23.3.1 ARE LEADING QUESTIONS EVER PERMITTED DURING EXAMINATION-IN-CHIEF?

As exceptions to the general rule, leading questions are permitted during examination-in-chief in two situations:

- at the start of a witness's testimony for purely formal or introductory matter, such as the witness's name, address and occupation; or
- where a fact is not in dispute between the parties.

23.4 THE USE OF DOCUMENTS TO REFRESH MEMORY WHILE GIVING EVIDENCE

A witness is permitted to refresh his memory not only before testifying but also while giving evidence. The law governing the use of memory-refreshing documents is now contained in s. 139 Criminal Justice Act 2003.

Under s. 139 Criminal Justice Act 2003, a witness is entitled to refresh his memory from a document or transcript of a sound recording at any stage while testifying, provided:

- the document was made or verified by the witness on an earlier occasion; and

- the witness states in his oral evidence that the document records his recollection of the matter at the earlier time; and

- his recollection of the matters about which he is testifying is likely to have been significantly better at that time than it is at the time of his oral evidence.

Before the witness can use the document, it must be produced for inspection by the court and by the opposing advocate. Where the witness is cross-examined on those parts of the document which the witness used to refresh his memory, the document does not form part of the evidence in the case.

Where the cross-examiner strays outside those parts of the document that the witness used to refresh his memory, the whole document may be put in evidence to be considered by the jury/magistrates as evidence of the truth of what it states (s. 120(3) CJA 2003).

Example

The most commonly encountered memory-refreshing document is a police officer's notebook. Where the officer wishes to refresh his memory during examination-in-chief, it is customary for the following exchange to take place between the advocate and the officer.

Police officer:	'May I refer to my pocket book?'
Advocate:	'When did you make up your pocket book, officer?'
Police officer:	'When I returned to the police station.'
Advocate:	'Were the events still fresh in your mind when you made up your pocket book?'
Police officer:	'Yes they were'.

The court usher will then pass the notebook to be inspected by the court and the defence advocate. The defence advocate should carefully note the parts used by the officer to refresh his memory and should restrict cross-examination to those parts to avoid the entire document becoming part of the evidence in the case.

A 'lay' witness may also refer to a memory-refreshing document, for example, a piece of paper on which he noted the description and registration number of a car he saw at the crime scene.

23.5 THE ADMISSIBILITY OF PREVIOUS CONSISTENT (SELF-SERVING STATEMENTS) AT COMMON LAW

The position in relation to the admissibility of a witness's previous consistent statement has, at common law, always been clear. Save with regard to a small number of exceptions, such statements were inadmissible, lacking any significant probative value. The common law placed great reliance on the witness's evidence in the witness box, not what the witness said on an earlier out-of-court occasion. Consequently, at common law, a witness could not be asked about a previous consistent statement. The exceptions to the rule included:

- evidence that a victim of a sexual offence voluntarily made a recent complaint *R v Osbourne* [1905] 1 KB 551; *R v Birks* [2003] 2 Cr App R 122;

- self-serving exculpatory statements made by an accused upon being accused of a criminal offence consistent with the defence being advanced at trial (*R v Pearce* (1979) 69 Cr App R 365);

- statements admitted to rebut a suggestion of recent fabrication (*R v Oyesiku* (1971) 56 Cr App R 240);

- previous consistent identification – where a witness who has previously identified the defendant at an identification procedure but has forgotten the defendant's number in the line-up or is unable to confirm the defendant's identity at trial, evidence may be given of the witness's earlier identification (*R v Osbourne* [1973] QB 678);

- documents admitted under the memory-refreshing rule on which the witness is cross-examined (see paragraph 23.4 above).

Where such statements were admitted under the common law exceptions to the previous consistent statement rule, their evidential value was limited. The earlier statements could not be taken as evidence of the truth of what they stated (this would offend the rule against admitting hearsay evidence). Such previous statement were admissible only as evidence of the witness's consistency.

23.5.1 THE ADMISSIBILITY OF PREVIOUS CONSISTENT STATEMENTS UNDER THE CRIMINAL JUSTICE ACT 2003

Section 120 CJA 2003 has extended the situations where a witness's previous consistent statement can be admitted in evidence. The statement can be admitted in the following situations:

- to rebut the allegation that the witness's evidence has been recently fabricated s. 120(2) CJA (this is dealt with at paragraph 23.13 below in the context of re-examination);

- where a memory-refreshing document has been referred to by the witness, the document is admissible as evidence of any matter of which oral evidence by him would have been admissible, s. 120(3) CJA 2003. This provision applies where the witness has been cross-examined on issues contained in the document that were not used to refresh the witness's memory during examination-in-chief;

- where the witness has made the statement, which to the best of the witness's knowledge is true, and where one of the following conditions is satisfied:

  - the statement identifies or describes a person, object or place, s. 120(5) CJA 2003; or

  - the statement was made when the matters were fresh in the witness's memory but he does not remember them and cannot reasonably be expected to remember them well enough to give oral evidence about them in the proceedings, s. 120(6) CJA 2003; or

  - the witness as the victim of the alleged crime had made a complaint to another person about what had happened to him, and the complaint was made by the victim as soon as could reasonably be expected after the alleged conduct by the defendant and was not made as a result of a threat or promise, s.120 (7) CJA 2003.

The recent complaint exception is extended to all offences, not just sexual offences. The application of a s. 120 CJA 2003 statement is designed to add to the witness's testimony, not to supplant it.

Importantly, where a previous consistent statement is admitted under s. 120, the statement is admissible as evidence of any matter stated of which oral evidence by the witness would be admissible. This important change in the evidential use that can be made of such previous consistent statements is part of the general reforms to the hearsay rule, considered in Chapter 25.

Example 1

Section 120(5) CJA 2003 now permits a previous consistent statement to be admitted by the court where the statement identifies or describes a person, object or place. This provision will now make the following exchange between the advocate and the witness admissible:

Advocate:	'Tell the court about the car you saw at the scene of the crime on the day in question.'
Witness:	'It was a red Ford Fiesta, but I do not think I can recall the registration number off the top of my head.'
Advocate:	'Did you confirm the car's description and registration number verbally to the police officer and in your written statement?'
Witness:	'Yes. I did.'
Advocate:	'Is this a copy of your earlier written statement?'
Witness:	'Yes it is.'
Advocate:	'Whose signature appears at the bottom of each page on the statement?'
Witness:	'It is my signature.'
Advocate:	'When you made that statement to the police were the events that it recalls fresh in your mind?'
Witness:	'Yes they were. . . .'
Advocate:	'Can I ask you to look at your earlier statement. What did you say the Ford Fiesta's registration was in that statement?'
Witness:	'I said it was DH 05 FRJ.'
Advocate:	'To the best of your knowledge was that earlier statement you made based on your honest recollection of events?'
Witness:	'Yes it was. . . .'

Where the witness's previous consistent statement is admitted under s. 120(5) CJA 2003, it is admissible as evidence of the truth of the statement's contents – i.e. that the witness did see the car of that description and registration number at the crime scene.

Example 2

Gill is the victim of a street robbery. Heavily traumatised by the incident, she goes home and tells her brother Chris about the robbery and describes the assailant.

Under s.120(7) CJA 2003, provided the court is satisfied that Gill told her brother about the robbery at the first reasonable opportunity, evidence of the conversation may be admitted in evidence at the trial of the person accused of robbing Gill, providing Gill gives a first-hand account of what occurred. As with example 1, where Gill's previous consistent statement is admitted under s.120(7) CJA 2003, it is admissible as evidence of the truth of the statement's contents – i.e. that Gill was the victim of a street robbery committed by the person Gill described to her brother.

23.6 UNFAVOURABLE AND HOSTILE WITNESSES

At an early stage in the proceedings the prosecution and the defence will have taken a proof of evidence from each witness it intends to call to give evidence and support its case at trial. In most cases, a witness will give the answers expected of him and his oral evidence will be consistent with his earlier statement. In this situation, a witness is said to 'come up to proof'. Sometimes a witness does not give the answers expected of him during examination-in-chief. This may be because the witness is either an unfavourable witness or is hostile.

23.6.1 UNFAVOURABLE WITNESS

A witness is unfavourable where he cannot recall some a fact(s) about his testimony even after refreshing his memory. The advocate cannot assist his witness by putting leading questions or by prompting him – even though the witness's inability to answer his questions may damage his side's case. In this situation, it is good practice to get the witness out of the witness box as soon as possible – subject, of course, to the other party's right to cross-examine him.

23.6.2 HOSTILE WITNESS

While an unfavourable witness may be potentially damaging to your case, a more serious situation arises where your witness appears to be hostile. A witness is hostile where he shows no desire to tell the truth in support of the case of the party calling him.

The clearest example is where a witness has deliberately changed his evidence since making his written statement, whether from a desire not to be involved in the case or through fear or through malice.

23.6.3 WHAT ACTION CAN BE TAKEN IF THE WITNESS APPEARS HOSTILE?

The advocate will ask the judge to send the jury out and in their absence apply for leave to treat the witness as hostile. In summary proceedings the advocate will make a submission to the justices, who will seek the advice of their legal adviser.

The judge or magistrates will then be shown the witness's previous written statement as evidence in support of the application to have the witness ruled as hostile. The court will decide whether the witness is hostile or merely unfavourable by considering the witness's demeanour, attitude and any other relevant factor.

If your witness is ruled hostile, there are a number of options available to the advocate:

- the advocate may ask his witness leading questions by way of cross-examination; and/or
- s. 3 Criminal Procedure Act 1865 permits the advocate to ask his witness whether or not he has made an earlier statement which is inconsistent with his present oral testimony.

Where the witness adopts his earlier written statement as his evidence or the written statement is proven against him, s. 119(1) Criminal Justice Act 2003 provides that the statement becomes evidence of any matter stated in it of which oral evidence would have been admissible.

> **Example**
>
> Brian is pleading not guilty to assault occasioning actual bodily harm against Gordon. In her statement to the police, Emma states that she saw Brian hit Gordon in the face. At Brian's trial, Emma is called by the prosecution and in examination-in-chief, she states that Brian did not hit Gordon. The prosecutor may ask Emma to refresh her memory from her written statement. The prosecutor will put the question to Emma again. If she continues to deny that Brian hit Gordon, the prosecutor may apply to the court for Emma to be treated as a hostile witness. If the court grants leave to treat Emma as a hostile witness, the prosecutor may ask Emma leading questions and/or ask her whether she made a previous written statement that is inconsistent with her present oral evidence. If Emma adopts her earlier written statement as her evidence, or her earlier written statement is proven against her, the effect of s.119(1) CJA 2003 is that her statement that she saw Brian hit Gordon in the face may be admitted in evidence. It will be a matter for the jury/magistrates to determine where the truth lies.

23.7 CROSS-EXAMINATION

Cross-examination of a witness has a number of purposes:

- to obtain factual evidence from the witness which supports the case of the cross-examiner;
- to test the truthfulness of the evidence the witness has given in examination-in-chief or to cast doubt on the witness's evidence;
- to undermine the witness's credibility.

23.7.1 CHALLENGING THE WITNESS'S FACTUAL EVIDENCE

Where the advocate, in cross-examination, contradicts the witness's factual evidence, the cross-examiner should put his client's version of the facts to the witness in order to give the witness the opportunity to explain the contradiction. A failure to cross-examine a witness on his factual evidence will be taken by the court as acceptance of the witness's evidence-in-chief on that issue.

Questions asked in cross-examination are not only restricted to the issues that arose during examination-in-chief but may be directed to any fact in issue or to attacking the witness's credibility. Leading questions are allowed and are essential for effective cross-examination.

Consider the following examples of questions that you would put to a witness in cross-examination to challenge his factual evidence.

> **Example**
>
> Advocate: 'You have told the court that on the 5th May you saw the defendant driving the complainant's car.'
>
> Witness: 'Yes, that is right.'
>
> Advocate: 'I suggest that you are mistaken. The defendant did not drive the complainant's car on the 5th May. In fact he was 30 miles away in Leeds. Will you admit to the court that you were mistaken?'
>
> Witness: 'No. I was not mistaken. It was definitely him I saw driving the complainant's car.'

online resource centre

An example of the way in which witness testimony is obtained in court is provided in the *R v Lenny Whyte* case study in relation to the eyewitness, Shirley Lewis. The complete version can be accessed on our Online Resource Centre.

23.8 ATTACKING THE WITNESS'S CREDIBILITY

The cross-examiner may also attack the witness's credibility to persuade the jury or the magistrates to give little or no weight to the witness's oral evidence. Matters affecting the credibility of a witness's evidence are said to be collateral issues in the case and subject to the finality rule. There are various ways in which a witness's credibility may be undermined, including accusing the witness of bias; of having made a previous statement inconsistent with the evidence he now gives or generally being unworthy of belief because of past bad character.

23.8.1 THE FINALITY RULE

Generally, questions asked in cross-examination to undermine the witness's general credibility are subject to the finality rule. This means that evidence cannot be called to rebut the witness's answer – even if the cross-examiner does not accept the answer given by the witness. This is because the witness's credibility is a collateral or secondary issue that runs alongside the central issue at trial – the determination of the defendant's guilt or innocence.

23.8.2 EXCEPTIONS TO THE FINALITY RULE

The common law provides a number of exceptions to the finality rule, where the cross-examining advocate is allowed to adduce evidence to contradict the answer given by the witness. The exceptional situations include establishing that the witness:

- is biased; or
- is a person with previous convictions, s. 100 CJA; or

- has a reputation for untruthfulness; or
- suffers from a physical or mental disability.

23.8.3 SUGGESTING THE WITNESS IS BIASED

Where a witness appears to be biased to the party calling him, the issue of his bias can be raised in cross-examination. Where the witness denies the allegation, his denial may be rebutted by evidence and independently proved. While there are many examples of conduct that may amount to bias, the allegation often relates to where a witness has taken a bribe or has a close relationship with the party calling him, or holds a particular grudge against the cross-examining party.

23.8.4 IDENTIFYING INCONSISTENCIES BETWEEN THE WITNESS'S ORAL EVIDENCE AT TRIAL AND AN EARLIER STATEMENT

In cross-examination, the advocate will have a copy of the witness's written statement disclosed under the pre-trial disclosure of evidence rules (see Chapter 17) and will expect answers that are consistent with the witness's written statement. However, where the witness gives answers that are inconsistent with his earlier written statement, s. 5 Criminal Procedure Act 1865 permits the witness to be cross-examined about those parts of his written statement that are inconsistent with his oral evidence.

If the witness denies that he made a written statement that is inconsistent with his present oral testimony and the advocate wishes to contradict the witness, the advocate must draw the witness's attention to those parts of his statement that are inconsistent with his oral testimony. The witness will then be asked whether he wishes the court to adopt the version of his evidence contained in the written statement or his oral evidence.

Section 4 Criminal Procedure Act 1865 provides a similar provision in relation to an inconsistency between a witness's previous oral statement and his oral testimony in court. The cross-examiner can point out the inconsistencies to the witness and ask him which version he wishes the court to adopt as his evidence.

At common law, admission of a witness's previous inconsistent written or oral statement was only relevant in assessing the witness's credibility. Section 119(1) Criminal Justice Act 2003 now provides that where a previous inconsistent statement is proved, the statement becomes evidence of any matter stated in it of which oral evidence would have been admissible.

> **Example**
>
> Mandy (on trial for the attempted murder of her husband) insists in cross-examination that she was unaware that her husband had a life assurance policy, until the police investigation began. She denies even having had a conversation with her neighbour in which she stated that (a few weeks before the attempt on her husband's life) she had found her husband's life policy. The prosecution can call the neighbour to prove the earlier statement under s. 4 CPA 1865 which can now be admitted as evidence of fact (s. 119(1) CJA 2003).

23.8.5 CROSS-EXAMINING THE WITNESS ABOUT HIS PREVIOUS CONVICTIONS

Traditionally, a witness called to give evidence in a criminal trial has not enjoyed the same immunity as the defendant about being cross-examined on his character and convictions. Some witnesses, it would be fair to say, have been embarrassed by the dredging up of past misdemeanours designed to undermine their credibility in the eyes of the jury/magistrates. The questions put to a witness in cross-examination must satisfy the requirement of relevance. In the context of cross-examination on previous convictions, the courts have tended to adopt a wide definition of relevance.

23.9 CRIMINAL JUSTICE ACT 2003 – ADMISSIBILITY OF A NON-DEFENDANT'S BAD CHARACTER

The admission of a non-defendant's bad character is governed by s. 100 CJA 2003. Section 100 provides:

'(1) In criminal proceedings evidence of the bad character of a person other than the defendant is admissible if and only if:

(a) it is important explanatory evidence;

(b) it has substantial probative value in relation to a matter which –

(i) is a matter in issue in the proceedings, and

(ii) is of substantial importance in the context of the case as a whole;

or

(c) all parties to the proceedings agree to the evidence being admissible.

(2) For the purposes of subsection (1)(a), evidence is important explanatory evidence if:

(a) without it, the court or jury would find it impossible or difficult properly to understand other evidence in the case, and

(b) its value for understanding the case as a whole is substantial.

(3) In assessing the probative value of evidence for the purposes of subsection (1)(b), the court must have regard to the following factors (and to any others it considers relevant):

(a) the nature and number of the events, or other things, to which the evidence relates;

(b) when those events or things are alleged to have happened or existed;

(c) where:

(i) the evidence is evidence of a person's misconduct, and

(ii) it is suggested that the evidence has probative value by reason of similarity between that misconduct and other alleged misconduct,

the nature and extent of the similarities and the dissimilarities between each of the alleged instances of misconduct;

(d) where:

(i) the evidence is evidence of a person's misconduct,

(ii) it is suggested that that person is also responsible for the misconduct charged, and

(iii) the identity of the person responsible for the misconduct charged is disputed,

the extent to which the evidence shows or tends to show that the same person was responsible each time.'

Section 100 is part of the controversial reforms to the law relating to the admissibility of bad character under the CJA 2003. While the rules relating to the admissibility of a defendant's past bad character have been relaxed (see Chapter 26), the rules permitting the admission of a witness's bad character have been tightened. The aim of s. 100 CJA is to protect witnesses from embarrassment and irrelevant questioning. It remains to be seen how s. 100 is interpreted by the courts, particularly as regards the defendant's right to a fair trial which may well require questions to be put to a witness, thereby exposing the witness's bad character.

23.9.1 THE AMBIT OF S. 100 CJA 2003

Section 100 applies not only to witnesses in the case but to any person other than the defendant. Furthermore the effect of s. 100 is not limited to evidence adduced in cross-examination. Its ambit stretches to any attempt by either side to adduce evidence of a non-defendant's past bad character.

23.9.2 WHAT CONSTITUTES EVIDENCE OF A NON-DEFENDANT'S BAD CHARACTER?

The application of s. 100 depends on whether the evidence sought to be adduced falls within the definition of bad character under the Act. Bad character is defined in s. 98 CJA 2003 as evidence of or a disposition towards misconduct other than evidence which has nothing to do with the alleged facts of the offence for which the defendant is charged, or is evidence of misconduct in connection with the investigation or prosecution of that offence. If the circumstances fall within the definition of bad character, leave of the court must be granted before evidence of a non-defendant's bad character may be adduced. Where leave is granted, the defendant may find his own previous convictions are exposed under s. 101(g) CJA 2003 (see Chapter 26).

Having regard to s. 98, the defence would not require leave to put it to the investigating officer that he planted the evidence on the defendant or that he fabricated the defendant's confession. This is evidence of misconduct during the investigation. Arguably, no leave is required where a defendant seeks to accuse a witness of being responsible for committing the crime as this would be questioning to do with the alleged facts of the offence.

23.10 CIRCUMSTANCES IN WHICH LEAVE TO ADDUCE EVIDENCE OF A NON-DEFENDANT'S BAD CHARACTER UNDER S. 100 CJA IS REQUIRED

In deciding whether to grant leave, the court must be satisfied that the evidence of the witness's bad character either:

- is important as explanatory evidence, s. 100(1)(a) CJA 2003; or
- has substantial probative value in relation to a matter raised in the proceedings and is of substantial importance in the context of the case as a whole, s. 100(1)(b) CJA 2003.

Alternatively, the parties can agree for the evidence of bad character to be disclosed (s. 100(1)(c) CJA 2003). Leave is not required in this instance.

Where the witness denies a conviction(s), the cross-examiner can prove the conviction under s. 6 Criminal Procedure Act 1865.

A party seeking leave will be required to give notice to the court in accordance with Part 35.2 Crim PR. The party who receives the notice may oppose the application by giving notice in writing. Such matters can be dealt with at trial or, more likely, at a pre-trial hearing.

23.10.1 IMPORTANT AS EXPLANATORY EVIDENCE – S. 100(1)(a) CJA 2003

The witness's bad character will only be admitted as explanatory evidence where, without it, the court would find it impossible or difficult to properly understand the other evidence in the case and its value for understanding the case as a whole is substantial. In some situations it will be necessary for a party to give explanatory background information to the offence, which may result in part or the whole of the witness's bad character being disclosed.

> :bulb: **Example**
>
> Nigel is charged with arson by starting a fire in the hostel for resettling young offenders in which he was living at the time of the alleged offence. Nigel has previous convictions for dishonesty and drug-related offences. He denies the offence.
>
> Wayne gives evidence for the prosecution that on the day of the fire, he saw Nigel storing five large containers of barbeque fuel and fire lighters under his bed. In providing the court with the background facts of the arson offence, the prosecutor will have to refer to the fact that Wayne was residing at the hostel. This will obviously imply that Wayne has a criminal record. It will be unnecessary for the prosecution to disclose the substance of that criminal record in this context.

23.10.2 THE WITNESS'S BAD CHARACTER HAS SUBSTANTIAL PROBATIVE VALUE IN THE CASE – S. 100(1)(b) CJA 2003

Section 100(1)(b) subjects the admission of a non-defendant's bad character into evidence to a test of enhanced relevance. Evidence that has only marginal value or no real significance or goes to a trivial or minor issue in the case will not be admissible. In deciding whether evidence of the witness's bad character has 'substantial probative value' in the case, s. 101(3) (a), (b) and (c) CJA 2003 set out a non-exhaustive list of factors for the court to consider, including:

- the nature and number of the events or other things to which the evidence relates;
- when those events or things are alleged to have happened or existed;
- it is evidence of the person's misconduct and it is suggested that the evidence has probative value by reason of the similarity between that misconduct and other misconduct.

A witness's bad character may have substantial probative value in the case, where for example, the defendant wishes to use similar fact evidence as part of his defence.

To highlight some of the potential difficulties in the operation of s. 100, we include some worked examples for you to consider.

Example 1

Consider the earlier example of Nigel, accused of starting a fire in a hostel for young offenders. Nigel denies the offence and states Wayne is responsible. Wayne has previous convictions for arson. Nigel wishes to adduce evidence of Wayne's previous convictions. Arguably, Nigel does not require leave to accuse Wayne of having committed the offence, since it has to do with the alleged facts (s. 98 CJA 2003). In substantiating that allegation, however, Nigel would want to adduce evidence of Wayne's propensity to cause damage by fire as Wayne's propensity is clearly relevant to Nigel's defence. If the parties cannot agree that the evidence be adduced, leave of the court will be required. Arguably, the evidence has substantial probative value in this case.

Alternatively Nigel might deny the offence and simply accuse Wayne of lying when he states he saw Nigel storing lighter fuel under his bed. If Wayne's previous convictions relate only to arson, it is difficult to see how these can be said have substantial relevance in relation to the issues in this case. If Wayne's previous convictions, however, related to theft and burglary, they would arguably assume the necessary substantial probative value as they cast Wayne's credibility as a witness in a different light.

Example 2

Suni is on trial for rape. He says his victim (V) consented and that she is lying when she says she was raped. V has two previous convictions for theft and benefits fraud, committed two and four years ago respectively. Will the defence be allowed to put these convictions to V under s. 100 in order to undermine her credibility?

If the prosecution do not agree, the defence advocate will have to seek leave and the court would need to be satisfied that V's previous convictions have substantial probative value in relation to a matter in issue which is of substantial importance in the context of the case as a whole. In the absence of forensic evidence of injury, this is a case which comes down to which of the parties the jury will believe. That is clearly a matter of substantial importance in the overall context of the case. Do these convictions carry substantial probative weight? They might. Arguably they suggest that V has a propensity for being dishonest although this does not necessarily mean that she would falsely accuse someone of rape!

If the above facts are varied somewhat, such that V previously made a knowingly false accusation of indecent assault against someone five years ago, should Suni be allowed to adduce evidence of this? Under s. 100 there would be little argument about this since the fact (if it can be proved) carries significant probative value in relation to an important matter in issue.

Example 3

Danny is on trial for burglary. He calls Andrew to give evidence of alibi. Andrew has two recent convictions for dishonesty. Will the prosecution be able to put these questions to Andrew? If the defence does not agree, the prosecution will need to seek leave under s. 100. Arguably the previous convictions cast doubt on the credibility of Andrew, who is obviously an important witness for the defence.

23.10.3 WHAT DOES S. 100 CJA 2003 MEAN IN PRACTICE?

Unless both parties agree to the admission of a non-defendant's bad character, s. 100 CJA 2003 is triggered. Where the defence make an application, the judge will no doubt be mindful of the risk of appeal in the event of conviction. It should be remembered that there is no burden of proof on the defendant. All the defendant has to do is raise a reasonable doubt. For this reason it ought to be easier for the defence to demonstrate that the line of questioning has substantial probative value, at least in the context of the defence case.

The defence advocate will have to ask himself whether the evidence he wishes to adduce which raises aspect of a person's bad character is important to his client's case. Would his client's trial be unfair if he did not put this question to the witness/or adduce the evidence in some other form?

The provisions of the CJA 2003 have no application to the restrictions on asking or adducing evidence of a victim's past sexual history under s. 41 Youth Justice and Criminal Evidence Act 1999, nor the provisions which allow a party to impeach his own witness in accordance with s. 3 Criminal Procedure Act 1865 (see paragraph 23.6.3).

23.11 PROVING THAT A WITNESS HAS A REPUTATION FOR UNTRUTHFULNESS

An advocate can cross-examine a witness or call another person to prove to the court that the witness has a reputation for untruthfulness (*R v Richardson* [1961] 1 QB 299). The evidence is usually put in this way by the cross-examining advocate suggesting to another witness: 'From your knowledge of Gordon, would you believe him on his oath?' The rule is rarely used in practice.

23.12 CROSS-EXAMINING THE WITNESS ON HIS PHYSICAL OR MENTAL DISABILITY

Medical evidence may be introduced during cross-examination to prove that the witness suffers from a physical or mental disability that may undermine the accuracy of his testimony (*Toohey v Metropolitan Police Commissioner* [1965] AC 595). The law requires the evidence of unreliability to come from a recognised medical specialist so that if you intend to challenge an aspect of a witness's physical or psychiatric fitness to give evidence, you will have to instruct an expert witness to testify.

Example

The witness states that he saw the defendant at a distance of 100 metres breaking into a car. There is evidence to suggest the witness was not wearing his glasses at the time. To rebut this identification, evidence could be introduced to prove that the witness is short-sighted and cannot see any further than 40 metres without corrective lenses.

23.13   **RE-EXAMINATION**

The third stage of witness testimony is re-examination, where the party calling the witness is entitled to ask further questions of his witness following cross-examination. Re-examination enables the advocate to repair the damage done to his witness's credibility during cross-examination and to explain any confusion or ambiguities in the witness's evidence. Leading questions are not permitted because, as with examination-in-chief, the advocate is dealing with his own witness. Re-examination is confined to matters arising out of cross-examination. The re-examining advocate cannot take the opportunity to ask the witness about a matter he omitted to cover in examination-in-chief.

As noted in paragraph 23.5.1 above, an issue that may arise during re-examination is where the opposing advocate, in cross-examination, has suggested that the witness has recently made up or fabricated his evidence. This is a potentially serious attack on the witness's credibility and re-examination provides an opportunity to rebut this allegation of recent fabrication. Section 120(2) CJA 2003 permits the witness's previous statement to be admitted in evidence to show that his evidence has not been recently made up. Where the previous consistent statement is admitted, it becomes evidence of the truth of the matters stated in it. In *R v Oyesiku* (1971) 56 Cr App R 240, the wife of the defendant, charged with assaulting a police officer, had given a statement to the defendant's solicitor in which she accused the police officer of being the aggressor before she had had the opportunity of speaking to her husband following his arrest arrest. When it was put to her in cross-examination by the prosecution, that she was making up her evidence to help her husband, the defence was allowed to adduce evidence of her earlier statement.

23.14   **CROSS-EXAMINATION OF VICTIMS OF SEXUAL OFFENCES**

Special rules apply to cross-examination of a complainant in cases involving a sexual offence. The rules contained in ss. 41–43 Youth Justice and Criminal Evidence Act 1999 prohibit a defendant from asking a complainant about any past sexual behaviour or experiences the complainant might have involving the defendant or any other person save with leave of the court in certain defined circumstances. The rules were challenged as being incompatible with a defendant's right to a fair trial in the leading authority of *A (No. 2)* [2002] 1 AC 45. The rules, which are not without complexity, are outside the scope of this work but may be researched in the current edition of *Blackstone's Criminal Practice.*

KEY POINT SUMMARY

- Be aware of the purposes of examination-in-chief and prepare your questions to your witnesses to elicit answers that are favourable to your client's case.

- Know the general rule against asking leading questions and the limited circumstances in which leading questions are permitted.

- Have a good understanding of the practice and procedure for your witness to refer to a memory-refreshing document during examination-in-chief.

- Be aware of the limited situations in which your witness's previous consistent statement can be put in evidence.

- Know the distinction between an unfavourable and a hostile witness and be aware of the practice and procedure for dealing with your witness who falls into one of these categories.

- Be aware of the purpose of cross-examination and the purpose of the advocate being permitted to ask leading questions.

- Know the distinction between questions going to an issue in the case, collateral issues and the finality rule.

- Know the exceptions to the finality rule.

- Be aware of the practice and procedure dealing with a witness's previous inconsistent statement.

- Understand that s. 100 CJA 2003 now regulates the admissibility of evidence of a non-defendant's bad character and that, in the absence of agreement between the parties, leave of the court in accordance with s. 100 is required.

- Be aware of the purpose of re-examination and the use that can be raised during this stage of witness testimony.

SELF-TEST QUESTIONS

1. Are leading questions permitted during examination-in-chief?

2. What conditions are required by s.139 CJA 2003 for a document to be used by a witness to refresh his memory during examination-in-chief?

3. What is a hostile witness?

4. Explain the purposes of cross-examination.

5. What is a collateral issue during cross-examination?

6. What allegation can be rebutted during re-examination?

7(a) Kyle is on trial for grievous bodily harm. The incident occurred in a nightclub. The victim is Ben. Chris, a key witness for the prosecution, is a good friend of Ben. Kyle states he acted in self-defence when he was attacked by Ben and Chris. Ben has a recent previous conviction for affray committed during a disturbance in a town centre. Chris has recent previous convictions for public order offences and assault. Should Kyle be allowed to adduce evidence of these previous convictions?

7(b) If the facts in the above scenario are changed such that Chris has a previous conviction for perverting the course of justice (he gave false particulars to the police in order to avoid a driving related prosecution), would leave be granted to put this conviction to the witness?

FIGURE 23.1 WITNESS TESTIMONY

EXAMINATION-IN-CHIEF

- Purpose of questions in examination-in-chief is to:
  - elicit factual evidence which supports the party's case;
  - enhance the witness's personal credibility;
  - anticipate issues to be raised in cross-examination.
- Leading questions are generally not permitted.

Memory refreshing by a witness

- s. 139 CJA 2003 permits that a witness may refresh his memory from a document made or verrified by him if he states:
  - the document records his recollection at an earlier time; and
  - his recollection of the matter is likely to have been significantly better at that time.

Admissibility of previous consistent statements by a witness

- s. 120 CJA 2003 permits evidence of the witness's previous consistent statement to be admitted as evidence of its truth, including where the victim of the crime made a recent complaint to another person, s. 120(7) CJA 2003.

Unfavourable witness

- is a witness who cannot recall some facts about his testimony and simply does not come up to proof.

Hostile witness

- is a witness who shows no desire to tell the truth at the behest of the party calling him:
  - where the witness is ruled hostile, the advocate can cross-examine his own witness and under s. 3 Criminal Procedure Act 1865 put his previous statement to the witness;
  - where the previous statement is proven against the witness; or
  - where the witness adopts his previous statement; s. 119(1) CJA 2003 makes his statement evidence of the truth of any matter stated in it.

THE RULES RELATING TO WITNESS TESTIMONY | 339

FIGURE 23.1 (CONTINUED)

CROSS-EXAMINATION

- **The purpose of cross-examination is to:**
  - elicit factual evidence which supports the cross-examiner's case;
  - test the truthfulness of the witness's evidence in examination-in-chief; and
  - undermine the witness's credibility.

  Leading questions are permitted.

- **Proving the witness has made a previous inconsistent statement,** s. 4 Criminal Procedure Act 1865
  - where the previous statement is proven against the witness; or
  - the witness adopts his previous statement,
  - s. 119(1) CJA 2003 makes his statement evidence of the truth of any matter stated in it.

- **Undermining the witness's general credibility**
  Such questioning is subject to the finality rule in that the cross-examiner must take the witness's answer as being final unless the cross-examiner submits the witness:
  - is biased;
  - has previous convictions;
  - has a physical or mental disability which undermines the reliability of his evidence.

- **Adducing evidence of a witness's bad character**
  - usually raised in cross-examination;
  - under s. 100(a) CJA 2003, the court may only grant leave to admit evidence of the bad character of someone other than the accused if:
    - it is important explanatory evidence;
    - it has substantial probative value in relation to a matter which is a matter in issue in the proceedings *and* is of substantial importance in the context of the case as a whole; or
    - all parties agree;
  - s.100 CJA 2003 has no application if the witness's misconduct is connected with the investigation or prosecution of the present offence, see s.98 CJA 2003;
  - adducing evidence of another person's bad character can result in the accused's bad character revealed to the court (s. 101(1)(g) CJA 2003).

RE-EXAMINATION

- **The purpose of re-examination is to:**
  - repair any damage inflicted during cross-examination.

- Leading questions are not permitted.

- A witness may rebut an allegation of recent fabrication the evidence of rebuttal is admitted as a previous consistent statement and as evidence of its truth (see s. 120(2) CJA 2003).

---

24 1 INTRODUCTION

There is a common link between the first two evidential rules explained in this chapter. Both the law governing the use of corroborative or supporting evidence and the application of the 'Turnbull guidelines' in cases involving disputed evidence of eye-witness identification ensure that the court reaches its verdict on the basis of 'reliable' evidence, thereby avoiding miscarriages of justice or convictions being overturned on appeal as 'unsafe'.

In this chapter we will also explain the rules relating to opinion evidence and to expert opinion evidence in particular.

We will consider:

- the nature of corroborative evidence;

- the situations where corroborative evidence is required as a matter of law;

- the situations where a corroboration warning might be given as a matter of judicial discretion;

- the application of the 'Turnbull guidelines' in cases where eye-witness identification is disputed;

- the general rule excluding opinion evidence
- the admissibility of expert evidence.

24.2 WHAT IS CORROBORATIVE EVIDENCE?

Corroborative evidence is independent evidence which supports or confirms other evidence in the case.

Evidence that needs to be corroborated is said to be unreliable or deficient or tainted in some way. A common example is where a witness may have a purpose of his own to serve by testifying.

In evaluating the evidence in a criminal case, the lawyer should always make an assessment of his witness's credibility. How will the witness appear to the jury/magistrates? Is the witness likely to be believed? Does the witness have a motive for giving false evidence? These all involve considerations of weight. Where a witness's evidence is questionable in some respect, a corroboration warning might be called for. Such a warning alerts the jury/magistrates of the dangers of relying solely on the evidence of the particular witness, and the need for independent evidence which is capable of supporting what the witness has to say.

24.2.1 WHEN IS CORROBORATIVE EVIDENCE REQUIRED?

While corroboration has assumed less formal significance in criminal trials in recent years, corroborative evidence may still be encountered in two situations:

- where the offence charged requires corroborative or supporting evidence as a matter of law before the accused can be convicted; and
- where the court deems it necessary, in the exercise of judicial discretion to give a warning in relation to the evidence of an 'unreliable' witness.

24.3 CORROBORATIVE EVIDENCE REQUIRED AS A MATTER OF LAW

A limited number of statutes require prosecution evidence to be corroborated as a matter of law before the defendant can be convicted of the offence, including perjury (s. 13 Perjury Act 1911) and treason (s. 1 Treason Act 1795).

The only offence in this category which you might encounter is where a defendant is charged with speeding. Section 89(2) Road Traffic Regulation Act 1984 requires that the defendant cannot be convicted of speeding on the opinion evidence of one witness. The vehicle's speed has to be corroborated by the opinion evidence of another witness. In practice, s. 89 RTRA 1984 has been superseded by modern technology, as in most prosecutions, the vehicle's speed is proved by an electronic device such as a radar gun or the police vehicle's speedometer reading which does not need to supported by independent evidence.

24.4 CORROBORATION AND THE EXERCISE OF JUDICIAL DISCRETION

Traditionally, the evidence of certain witnesses such as children, the complainant in a sexual offence and an accomplice (a co-accused who gives evidence against another person charged in the offence) was regarded as less reliable than the testimony of other witnesses. When directing the jury about the evidence of these witnesses, the judge was required, as a matter of law, to give a mandatory warning about the dangers of convicting the accused on the unsupported evidence of these witnesses. The requirement for mandatory warnings was abolished by s. 34 Criminal Justice Act 1988 in respect to the unsworn evidence of children and s. 32 Criminal Justice and Public Order Act 1994 in connection with the unsupported evidence of an accomplice or the victim of a sexual offence. A failure to give a mandatory corroboration warning under the old law invariably afforded a convicted defendant with grounds for appeal against conviction. As the mandatory warning has long since been abolished, what is the current position?

The present position is that a corroboration warning is entirely discretionary and will depend on the particulars facts and circumstance of each case. There are no longer categories of witnesses whose evidence should automatically be accompanied by a warning.

The modern case on corroboration is *R v Makanjuola; R v Easton* [1995] 3 All ER 730, where the Court of Appeal laid down the following general guidelines:

- A corroboration warning is not a mandatory requirement because the witness is a child giving unsworn evidence or an accomplice or the complainant of a sexual offence.

- It is matter for the judge's discretion what, if any warning, is considered appropriate in relation to the evidence of a particular witness.

- In some cases, it may be appropriate for the judge to warn the jury to exercise caution before acting on the unsupported evidence of a witness. There will need to be an evidential basis for suggesting that the evidence of the witness may be unreliable.

- If any question arises whether a special warning should be given in respect of a witness, it is desirable that the question be resolved with counsel in the absence of the jury before final speeches.

- Where the judge decides to give a warning in respect of a witness, it will be appropriate to do so as part of the judge's review of the evidence and the manner in which the judge gives a direction is a matter for his discretion.

- The Court of Appeal will not interfere with the trial judge's discretion except where the judge acted in an 'unreasonable' way as explained in *Associated Picture Houses Ltd v Wednesbury Corporation* [1948] 1 KB 223.

24.4.1 WHAT WARNING IS REQUIRED TO BE GIVEN UNDER *MAKANJUOLA*?

Where a warning is considered appropriate, the guidelines enunciated in *R v Makanjuola* gives the court discretion to tailor the warning to the specific facts of the case. For example, if the witness has been shown to be unreliable, it may be appropriate for the judge to urge caution. In a more serious situation where the witness is shown to have lied or is shown to bear a grudge against the defendant or in a sexual offence, the complainant is shown to have made previous false complaints, a stronger warning may be appropriate. The judge may suggest to the jury that it would be wise to look for some supporting material before acting on the impugned witness's evidence.

The defence advocate must always be alert to the need for a corroboration warning in a particular case. From the defence advocate's perspective, whenever there is some concern about the reliability of a witness's evidence, he should press the judge to give a corroboration warning to the jury, or if it is a summary trial, he should raise the issue with the magistrates in his closing speech.

There are many witnesses whose evidence might be said to be unreliable or tainted in some way. This would include any witness with a proven propensity to be untruthful or with a motive to lie. Where a particular witness has an axe to grind against the defendant or stands to profit from the defendant's conviction, the defence advocate might seek a corroboration warning. This will include an accomplice, who though initially charged, chooses to plead guilty and give evidence for the prosecution implicating a fellow co-accused (*R v Cheema* [1994] 1 WLR 147). It could also extend to co-defendants who are running cut-throat defences (*R v Jones* [2004] 1 Cr App R 5. Where there is evidence to suggest collusion between witnesses or some ulterior motive for the evidence that has been given, a corroboration warning might be called for. The same considerations apply to a mentally unbalanced witness whose evidence might be said to be inherently unreliable. In essence, a corroboration warning has the potential to be given in relation to any witness who might be regarded as having a purpose of his own to serve in giving false evidence in the particular case.

A trial judge cannot be made to give a corroboration warning. As we have already stated, it is a matter of discretion. However, in a case where the trial judge fails or refuses to give a warning and a conviction results, there may be grounds for an appeal against conviction. The case highlighted below illustrates the post-*Makanjoula* position.

R v L [1999] Crim LR 489

L had separated from the complainant's mother after each claimed to have been attacked by the other at a public house. Shortly after, the complainant, J, who was then nine years old, complained to her mother that L had indecently assaulted her. L maintained that the complaint arose because of the mother's grievance against him about the incident in the public house. The complainant knew about the incident. The indictment against L contained allegations of indecent assault in counts 1–4; attempted rape in count 5 and indecent assault in preparation for rape in count 6.

When she gave evidence at trial, J could not be sure how many times she had been indecently assaulted by L. The judge directed the jury that L should be acquitted on counts 2, 3, and 4. The jury also acquitted him on counts 1 and 5, but found him guilty on count 6. L appealed against the conviction on the ground that the judge had not directed the jury about how to approach the child's evidence and in particular that no warning had been given about the dangers of convicting on the evidence unsupported by other external evidence.

In dismissing the appeal, the Court of Appeal stated that following the decision of *R v Makanjuola*, in exercising his discretion, the judge should first consider whether any warning is desirable, and if it is, the appropriate direction will depend on the circumstances of the particular case, the issues raised and the content and quality of the witness's evidence. L had come nowhere near to persuading the court that the exercise of discretion not to give a corroboration warning, in accordance with *R v Makanjuola* was '*Wednesbury* unreasonable'.

24.5 THE REQUIREMENTS FOR EVIDENCE TO BE CORROBORATIVE

In *R v Baskerville* [1916] 2 KB 658, the essential requirements for evidence to be corroborative were stated as:

- the evidence should be admissible in its own right;
- it must be independent of the evidence to be corroborated;
- it must implicate the accused in a material way with the crime charged in not only suggesting that the offence was committed, but also that it was committed by the accused.

24.5.1 WHERE IS CORROBORATIVE EVIDENCE TO BE FOUND?

Corroborative evidence may come from any other evidence in the case, including:

- the oral testimony of another witness;
- confession by a defendant;
- documentary evidence;
- real evidence;
- circumstantial evidence (see *R v McInnes* (1990) 90 Cr App R 99);
- lies told by the defendant can support the prosecution, where:
  —the lie is deliberate and is material to an issue in the case;

—the lie is motivated by a realisation of guilt and fear of the truth; and

—the lie can be proved to be a lie by other evidence;

—the jury should be reminded that some people may lie for reasons other than perhaps hiding their guilt for the present offence including where the accused lied out of shame or to bolster a defence or out of a wish to conceal their disgraceful behaviour from their family (see *R v Lucas* [1981] QB 720).

- forensic evidence such as DNA linking the defendant to the crime scene;

- the defendant's refusal, without good cause, to consent to give an intimate sample under s. 62 PACE;

- inferences from a defendant's silence under CJPOA 1994, ss. 34–37 (see Chapter 8);

- a defendant's previous convictions where they show a propensity for the defendant to behave in a way that is relevant to proving the facts of the present offence (see Chapter 26.).

24.6 THE 'TURNBULL GUIDELINES'

The Turnbull guidelines are of considerable practical importance in trials where the defendant claims he is the victim of mistaken identity.

In Chapter 11 we explained the pre-trial safeguards contained in Code D of the Codes of Practice in dealing with identification procedures used by the police during the investigation to confirm or exclude the defendant's involvement in an offence. Identification evidence obtained in breach of these procedures is vulnerable to challenge under s. 78 PACE 1984.

Disputed evidence of eye-witness identification is treated with caution, as extensive psychological research has highlighted the errors eyewitnesses make when they observe, interpret and recall information. An honest witness may be a very convincing witness but may still be mistaken in identifying the defendant at the crime scene. In order to minimise the risk of a miscarriage of justice based on mistaken identification, the Court of Appeal has developed guidelines as how the courts should approach evidence of disputed eye-witness identification. The guidelines were formulated in *R v Turnbull* [1977] QB 224.

The Turnbull guidelines apply in a case where the defendant disputes the accuracy of eye-witness identification and are fundamental to ensuring the defendant enjoys a fair trial.

A slightly abridged version of the Turnbull guidelines appears below. The trial judge must adapt the guidelines when directing the jury in accordance with the case under consideration. The guidelines provide:

'First, whenever the case against an accused depends wholly or substantially on the correctness of one or more identifications of the accused which the defence alleges to be mistaken, the judge must warn the jury of the special need for caution before convicting the accused in reliance on the correctness of the identification . . . In addition he should instruct them as to the reason for the need for such a warning and should make some reference to the possibility that a mistaken witness can be a convincing one and that a number of such witnesses can all be mistaken.

Secondly, the judge should direct the jury to examine closely the circumstances in which the identification by each witness came to be made. How long did the witness have the accused under observation? At what distance? In what light? Was the observation impeded in any way, as for example by passing traffic or a press of people? Had the witness ever seen the accused before? How often? If only occasionally, had he any special reason for remembering the accused? How long elapsed between the original observation and the subsequent identification to the police. Was there any material discrepancy between the description of the accused given to the police by the witness when first seen by them and his actual appearance? . . . Finally, he should remind the jury of any specific weaknesses which had appeared in the identification evidence.

Recognition may be more reliable than identification of a stranger; but even when a witness is purporting to recognise someone whom he knows, the jury should be reminded that mistakes in recognition of close relatives and friends are sometimes made.

All these matters go to the quality of the identification. If the quality is good at the close of the accused's case, the danger of a mistaken identification is lessened; but the poorer the quality, the greater the danger.

. . . when the quality is good, as for example when the identification is made over a long period of observation, or in satisfactory conditions by a relative or neighbour, a close friend, a workmate and the like, the jury can safely be left to assess the value of the identifying evidence even where there is no other evidence to support it; provided always, however that an adequate warning has been given about the special need for caution.

When, in the judgment of the trial judge, the quality of the identifying evidence is poor, as for example a fleeting glimpse of a witness or a longer observation made in difficult conditions, the situation is very different. The judge should then withdraw the case from the jury and direct an acquittal unless there is other evidence which goes to support the correctness of the identification. This may be corroboration in the sense lawyers use that word; but it need not be so if its effect is to make the jury sure that there has been no mistaken identification . . .

The judge should identify to the jury the evidence capable of supporting the identification. If there is any evidence or circumstances which the jury might think was supporting when it did not have this quality, the judge should say so . . .

Care should be taken by the judge when directing the jury about the support for an identification which may be derived from the fact that they have rejected an alibi. False alibis may be put forward for many reasons: an accused, for example, who has only his own truthful evidence to rely on may stupidly fabricate an alibi and get lying witnesses to support it out of fear that his own evidence may not be enough. Further, alibi witnesses can make genuine mistakes about dates and occasions like any other witnesses can. It is only when the jury is satisfied that the sole reason for the fabrication was to deceive them and there is no explanation for its being put forward can fabrication provide any sort for identification evidence. The jury should be reminded that providing the accused has told lies about where he was at the material time does not of itself prove that he was where the identifying witness says he was.'

The Turnbull guidelines require the judge to make an initial qualitative assessment of the evidence of identification. If the trial judge concludes the evidence of identification is poor and is unsupported by any other evidence in the case, he must withdraw the case from the jury and direct an acquittal. If the trial judge concludes the evidence is poor but is supported by other evidence in the case, or the evidence of identification is good, he can leave the case to the jury but he must direct the jury in accordance with the Turnbull guidelines and stress the special need for caution. In a case where the evidence of identification is poor but supported, the judge must point out the evidence that is capable of providing the support. Supporting evidence will be similar to corroborative evidence as outlined in paragraph 24.5.1 above.

In accordance with the guidelines, the judge must explain why there is a special need for caution associated with such evidence, and direct that while an honest witness may be a very convincing witness, the witness may nevertheless be mistaken. He should invite them to consider the circumstances in which the identification of the defendant was made and point out to them any specific weaknesses in the identification. Specific weakness would include:

- a failure by a witness to make a positive identification;
- a breach of Code D, such as a failure to convene a formal identification procedure;
- inconsistencies between witnesses' original descriptions.

24.6.1 EYE-WITNESS IDENTIFICATION IN 'GOOD' CONDITIONS

The Turnbull guidelines give examples of identification in 'good' conditions including where:

- the identification is made over a long period of observation; or
- the identification is made by a relative or neighbour or a close friend or a workmate etc.

24.6.2 EYE-WITNESS IDENTIFICATION IN 'POOR' CONDITIONS

The Turnbull guidelines give examples of identification in 'poor' conditions including where:

- the witness has a fleeting glimpse of the crime scene; or
- the observation is made in difficult lighting or weather conditions; or
- the witness gets a distant view of the crime scene.

24.6.3 THE TURNBULL GUIDELINES IN SUMMARY PROCEEDINGS

The Turnbull guidelines apply with identical effect to trials in magistrates' courts. In a summary case involving disputed evidence of identification of the accused, the legal adviser will remind the magistrates of the guidelines in open court and the special need for caution.

24.6.4 WHAT ARE THE CONSEQUENCES WHEN A TURNBULL WARNING IS NOT GIVEN?

The failure to give a Turnbull warning in cases of disputed eye-witness identification will invariably provide a convicted defendant with a good ground for appeal against conviction, on the basis that his conviction is 'unsafe'.

24.6.5 WHEN DO THE TURNBULL GUIDELINES NOT APPLY?

The Turnbull guidelines should be followed in all cases where the possible mistaken identification of the accused is in issue. The guidelines will not apply to:

- cases involving the identification of motor vehicles;
- the evidence of police officers who base their identification on long periods of observation or surveillance;
- cases in which there has been no formal identification of the defendant, only evidence of a description;
- most cases where the accused admits his presence at the crime scene.

With regard to the last listed matter, a Turnbull direction may still be appropriate in a case where a defendant admits to being at the scene but denies involvement in the crime. An example is afforded by the facts in *R v Thornton* [1995] 1 Cr App R 578.

R v Thornton [1995] 1 Cr App R 578

An altercation developed between guests at a wedding reception. The appellant, a guest at the wedding and as such appropriately attired, had been identified by a neighbour and her son as being the assailant. He admitted being at the scene but said he had been trying to shield the victim. There were others in the vicinity all dressed the same. The Court of Appeal concluded it did not automatically follow that where the accused admitted his presence at or near the scene but denied involvement, the Turnbull direction had to be given. It would depend on all the circumstances. In this case, a direction was appropriate given the risk of error.

> ### ⚗ Example
>
> Frank is 21 and has been arrested on suspicion of burglary of commercial premises. He is white, of medium build, 6' tall with bleached white hair. The break-in occurred at 3.30 am. A description of the alleged assailant is provided by a security guard. He explains that when the alarm bell was activated, he chased the assailant across the yard of the factory for approximately 40–50 seconds before the assailant climbed over a wall. The yard was partially illuminated and he saw the person from a distance of approximately 30 yards. The security guard describes the youth as white, average height (about 5' 10') and build, aged in his early twenties. The youth had fair hair and was wearing denims and a black short jacket. The assailant ripped his clothing on wire meshing covering the top of the wall.
>
> At 3.45 on the night in question, two officers in a police patrol vehicle arrested Frank. At the time of the arrest, Frank was wearing dark trousers and blue tee-shirt. No jacket was found.
>
> Frank chose not to be represented by a solicitor at the police station and proceeded to deny any involvement in the burglary. He agreed to participate in a video identification procedure. In interview he refused to answer questions and failed to account for a large tear in his jeans. Frank was released on police bail. Four days after witnessing the incident, the security guard attended the identification suite to view the video parade. After some hesitation he selected Frank's image. Frank was subsequently charged with burglary. Frank denies the offence and calls evidence of alibi at his trial.
>
> At Frank's trial, a Turnbull direction would be given about the evidence of the security guard's eye-witness identification. The judge or magistrates would be required to assess the quality of the security guard's identification evidence. If the judge concludes the evidence is poor quality and is unsupported by other evidence, the case will be withdrawn from the court. If the identification evidence is supported by other independent evidence, it can be left to the jury or the magistrates to assess the reliability of the evidence by examining the circumstances in which the identification was made.
>
> In this case the judge may conclude that the evidence is weak but is supported by the fact that Frank refused to answer questions at the police station and failed to give an account of the tear in his jeans. If the case is left to the jury, the judge will invite them to consider the fact that the initial observation of the assailant was in less than ideal circumstances. The security guard had the person under observation for only a short period of time, and at a distance. The lighting was good, however, although it does not appear that Frank is known to the security guard. Although an honest witness, the security guard may nevertheless be mistaken. The judge should remind the jury that the security guard was hesitant before making a formal identification of Frank.

24.7 OPINION EVIDENCE

A witness is called to court to give factual evidence based on what the witness perceived with his own senses. The general rule in criminal proceedings is that opinion evidence is inadmissible. A witness will not be permitted to state orally or to write that the 'defendant is obviously guilty' or the 'defendant was up to no good'. In addition to being inadmissible, a witness's opinion is irrelevant and offends the 'ultimate issue' rule. The 'ultimate issue' relates to the defendant's guilt or innocence, which must be decided by the magistrates or the jury on the basis of all the evidence in the case.

There are two important exceptions to the general rule where opinion evidence is admissible: facts personally perceived by the witness, and opinion evidence given by expert witnesses.

24.8 FACTS PERSONALLY PERCEIVED BY THE WITNESS

A lay witness may give an opinion on a fact that he has personally perceived but which does not require expertise. For example, it would be admissible for the witness to state that 'the defendant was drunk, or 'the defendant's car was speeding as it approached the road junction'.

In each example, the witness is giving his opinion on a matter within his personal knowledge and experience that does not require expertise or training. In effect such statements are statements of fact and are necessary to communicate to the court an accurate impression of the events the witness is seeking to describe.

24.9 EXPERT WITNESSES

An expert witness may give his opinion on an issue that goes beyond the ordinary competence of the court. The list of matters upon which expert evidence is required in criminal proceedings continues to grow and includes:

- accident investigation;
- ballistics;
- blood tests;
- breath tests;
- blood-alcohol levels;
- fingerprints;
- handwriting;
- computer technologies;
- facial mapping and facial identification;
- medical, psychological, scientific and forensic investigations.

These are highly technical matters of which the court has no knowledge or experience. The expert's duty is to provide impartial, objective information in his field of expertise to assist the court to reach a verdict on the evidence presented.

The value of expert forensic evidence in establishing the identity of a suspect is explored in Chapter 11. Expert evidence is like any other evidence in the case and is subject to an assessment of the weight to be accorded to it by the jury/magistrates.

24.9.1 WHO IS AN EXPERT?

Whether a witness is competent to give 'expert' evidence is a matter of law to be decided by the court. In deciding this issue, reference will be made to the witness's education; academic qualifications and professional experience. One of the first questions to be asked of an expert witness in examination-in-chief will be directed at establishing the witness's credentials as an expert in his particular field. The following cases serve to illustrate those witnesses who qualified as an expert in terms of their practical experience.

R v Clare and Peach **[1995] 2 Cr App R 333**

In this case, the police officer did not know the accused but had viewed a video-recording of the incident in which the defendant was alleged to have been involved, 40 times. He had examined it in slow motion, rewinding it and replaying it, and so was permitted to give evidence of identification based on a comparison between the video image and a known photograph of the defendant.

R v Hodges and Walker **[2003] 2 Cr App R 247**

The appellants were convicted of supplying heroin. They had been observed by undercover officers for several days in the street meeting numerous people for brief periods. The meetings involved short physical contact. There was no evidence from the officers that they saw drugs actually being passed in this way. When arrested, W was in possession of a 14 g bag of heroin, which he claimed was for his personal use. He was also carrying £350. Scales with traces of heroin and other material were found in

W's house. The prosecution relied on statements made by H in interview. To prove an intention to supply, the prosecution needed to establish that drugs had been transferred via the contact between the defendants and passers-by on the street and that the quantity of heroin in H's possession was inconsistent with personnel use.

Expert evidence was admitted from a detective constable (DC), a drugs officer of 17 years' experience, as to the method of supply of heroin on the streets, the local purchase price, and that 14g was more than would have been held for personal use.

The defendants appealed on the basis that the evidence of the DC had been wrongly admitted as expert evidence.

In dismissing the appeal, the Court of Appeal held that the DC's evidence had been rightly admitted as expert evidence. While the officer did not have medical or toxicological qualifications, he was entitled to refer to his expertise obtained as a result of talking to drug dealers and drug users.

Sounding a note of caution in this case, the Court of Appeal made some observations about the degree of weight to be attached to the DC's evidence. As a serving police officer it was necessary for the trial judge to give a direction to the jury about the weight to be given to the officer's opinion, as clearly it would be very difficult for him to provide the necessary objectivity normally required of an expert witness.

24.9.2 EXPERT EVIDENCE AND THE RULE AGAINST HEARSAY

The application of the hearsay rule (considered in Chapter 25) is relaxed in relation to expert witnesses because an expert is allowed to refer to works of authority, research papers, etc. as part of the process of forming an opinion. In *R v Abadom* [1983] 1 WLR 126, the defendant was charged with robbery. It was the opinion of the expert witness for the prosecution that fragments of glass found in the defendant's shoes matched glass from the broken window at the crime scene. According to the prosecution's expert, the refractive index of the glass taken from the crime scene matched the refractive index of the glass found under the defendant's shoes. The expert gave evidence that he had consulted Home Office statistics and had found that the index occurred in only four per cent of all glass samples. The defendant appealed on the basis that the expert's evidence was hearsay, as the expert had no personal knowledge of the statistics. The Court of Appeal confirmed that an expert's opinion must always be based on primary facts and those primary facts must be proved by admissible evidence. However, once the primary facts upon which an opinion is based have been proved by admissible evidence, the expert is entitled to draw on works of others as part of the process of arriving at his conclusion.

24.9.3 THE PROCEDURE FOR ADMITTING EXPERT EVIDENCE

There are special rules that require the pre-trial disclosure of expert evidence which apply to both the prosecution and the defence. They are contained in s. 81 PACE 1984 and in Part 24 Crim PR.

In accordance with Part 24, where either party proposes to rely on expert evidence (at a summary or an indictable trial), it must, as soon as is practicable, furnish the otherside with a statement in writing of any finding or opinion which it is proposed to adduce and a copy of any observation, test, calculation or other procedure on which the expert's opinion is based. A failure to give notice results in the expert evidence not being admitted unless leave of the court is granted.

The rules do not detract from the prosecutor's general duty of disclosure in relation to used material and under the CPIA 1996 in relation to unused material (see Chapter 17). Specific duties were imposed on forensic scientists following the decision in *R v Ward* [1993] 1 WLR 619. If an expert has carried out experiments or tests which tend to prove or cast doubt on the opinion the expert is expressing (or knows that such experiments have been carried out in his laboratory), he is under a clear obligation to bring such knowledge to the attention of the party instructing him.

Section 30 Criminal Justice Act 1988 permits an expert's report to be admitted in evidence whether or not the author of the report attends to give oral evidence.

24.9.4 EXPERT EVIDENCE AND DEFENCE DISCLOSURE

As stated in the preceding paragraph, wherever a party intends to rely on expert evidence, he must disclose the expert's report to the opposing side. If the defendant obtains an unfavourable expert report, the defence is under no obligation to disclose the report since it is protected by legal professional privilege (see Chapter 27).

Note however that when s. 6(D) CPIA 1996 (as amended by the CJA 2003) comes into force, an accused who instructs an expert witness with a view to providing an opinion for use as evidence at trial, must give to the court and the prosecutor a notice specifying the person's name and address unless specified in the defence statement (see Chapter 17, paragraph 17.9.5).

KEY POINT SUMMARY

- Understand and be able to recognise the circumstances in which a corroboration warning might be called for.

- Understand and be able to recognise the circumstances in which the Turnbull guidelines are applicable.

- The decision to give a corroboration warning lies with the judge/magistrates, with the relevant guidance provided by the decision in *R v Makanjuola*.

- A failure to give a Turnbull warning in a case where it must be given, affords a convicted defendant strong grounds for appeal against conviction.

- Expert opinion evidence is admissible in relation to an issue which is outside the competency of the court.

- An expert witness's competency is determined by his qualification and or relevant experience.

- Wherever a party seeks to rely on expert evidence, rules of court require that party to give notice.

SELF-TEST QUESTIONS

Consider the factual scenario below and answer the questions which follow.

You act for Stefan who has been charged with causing grievous bodily harm with intent, contrary to s.18 Offences Against the Person Act 1861 (OAPA). The assault is alleged to have been racially motivated. He pleads not guilty at his trial, giving evidence on oath that he was not involved in the crime. He calls his girlfriend to substantiate his defence of alibi.

The assault occurred outside a public house at 11.30 pm in a busy city centre street. Witnesses describe two white youths attacking an Asian youth. Eyewitnesses provided varying descriptions of the attackers. An anonymous witness told the police that Stefan and Andrew (also charged in connection with the proceedings) were involved. Upon his arrest and having been confronted with positive identification evidence, Andrew admitted his limited involvement and implicated Stefan as being the principal instigator of the attack and of being completely out of control.

Stefan was subsequently arrested. His solicitor advised him not to answer police questions as he considered the evidence against Stefan to be very weak. Stefan followed his advice. In the interview, Stefan was cautioned and asked to account for visible bruising to his nose. He offered no explanation. Stefan consented to participating in a video identification procedure.

It was several days before the victim was able to assist the police. Shortly after being hospitalised, the victim was shown several sets of photographs of convicted offenders (which included a photograph of Stefan) to see if he could spot his attacker. He selected Stefan's photograph. Three weeks later the victim was well enough to view the video parade and selected Stefan's image.

At trial, the prosecution accepts Andrew's guilty plea to a much less serious offence of assault occasioning actual bodily harm (s. 47 OAPA 1861) and agrees to withdraw the s. 18 charge. Andrew gives evidence for the prosecution, putting the blame on Stefan as being the person responsible for kicking the youth while he was on the ground.

Stefan maintains Andrew is lying in order to coverup his own involvement in a serious offence. Stefan denies being at the scene. Andrew is to be married in a few weeks time to a woman whose brother is a member of the investigative team.

In evidence, Stefan states that, while he and his girlfriend were in the city centre on the evening in question and had a drink with Andrew and some of his friends, they left before any trouble occurred.

CCTV footage is available of the incident. Sergeant Peter Taylor is called for the prosecution to give evidence of the fact that the blurred image on one of the stills is that of Stefan. The sergeant has studied the stills for a number of hours using video enhancing equipment.

Questions:

- Do you have any concerns as regards the manner in which the evidence of identification has been obtained in this case? If so, is there anything you can do about this?

- On what basis will Sergeant Taylor's evidence be admitted?

- Is this a case which calls for a Turnbull direction? If so, explain why. What will the requirements of that warning be?

- Is this is a case which calls for a corroboration warning? If so, explain why.

Case Study: *R v Lenny Whyte*

Consider whether a Turnbull warning would need to be given in *R v Lenny Whyte*, and whether any issues in relation to expert opinion evidence arise in this case.

FIGURE 24.1 CORROBORATION

- **What is it?**

  Corroborative evidence is independent evidence which supports or confirms other evidence in the case (see *R v Baskerville*).

- **What type of witness might it apply to?**

  Where there is reason to doubt the reliability/truthfulness of a prosecution witness (perhaps because the witness has a purpose of his own to serve in giving false/unreliable evidence), a corroboration warning about the dangers of relying upon the unsupported evidence of the witness may be required.

- **Where might supporting evidence come from?**

  - another witness's oral testimony; or

  - documentary or real evidence; or

  - forensic evidence; or

  - the defendant's lies or admissions (*R v Lucas*).

- **Corroborative evidence required as a matter of law**

  s. 89(2) Road Traffic Act 1984 stipulates that a defendant cannot be convicted of speeding on the opinion evidence of one witness.

- **Corroboration as a matter of judicial discretion**

  A judge may choose to give a corroboration warning to a jury (or magistrates can warn themselves) about the dangers of relying on the uncorroborated evidence of a suspect witness where 'it is in the interests of justice' (see *R v Makanjuola and Easton*).

THE 'TURNBULL GUIDELINES'

- Guidelines laid down by the decision in *R v Turnbull*;

- 'Turnbull' applies to evidence of eye-witness identification where the defendant disputes his presence at the crime scene;

- Turnbull guidelines require:

  - the court to proceed with caution as an honest witness may be a mistaken witness;

  - the jury or magistrates' court should consider the circumstances of the eye-witness identification, including:

    - the length of time the witness allegedly observed the defendant;

    - the light and distance etc. in which the identification occurred;

    - did the witness have a special reason for remembering/recognising the defendant etc.

- Where the identification took place in 'good' conditions, the jury or magistrates may assess the value of the identifying evidence;

- Where the identification take place in poor conditions, the evidence should be withdrawn unless there is supporting evidence about the correctness of the identification;

- Jury/magistrates should be reminded of any specific weakness in the evidence of identification, including breaches of Code D (under PACE 1984).

OPINION EVIDENCE

- Generally inadmissible in a criminal case, except:

  - facts personally perceived by the witness which does not require expertise; or

  - expert evidence on an issue beyond the ordinary competence of the court, including:

    - forensic science;

    - facial mapping;

    - accident investigation.

- Expert's role is to provide impartial information to assist the court reach a decision in the case;

- Pre-trial disclosure of expert evidence required under Part 24 Criminal Procedure Rules.

25 HEARSAY EVIDENCE

25.1   INTRODUCTION

Hearsay evidence is often described as 'second-hand' evidence and offends the preferred way in which evidence is presented at a criminal trial. This requires the witness to attend court to give oral evidence about facts of which the witness has personal knowledge. This is the most reliable evidence on which the court decides the defendant's guilt or innocence. In comparison, hearsay evidence is inferior to the direct oral testimony of the original witness of fact.

Hearsay evidence in criminal cases most often arises in two situations: first, where a witness seeks to adduce evidence of facts of which he has no personal knowledge because the facts have been passed to the witness by another person who is not in court; and second, where a party seeks to adduce as evidence a witness's written statement because the witness is unable to attend court for some reason to give oral evidence.

Consider the following example of hearsay evidence.

☀ Example 1

Mandy witnesses a robbery in which a pensioner's handbag is stolen. She tells her friend John that the person responsible was a white male of average height, wearing a black jogging top and baggy black trousers with a tattoo on the left-hand side of his face. If Mandy cannot attend court to give a first-hand account of what she witnessed, can John be called to repeat what Mandy had told him about the circumstances of the robbery? In a criminal case, the answer is no because John's evidence infringes the rule against admitting hearsay evidence. John has no personal knowledge of the facts about which he is testifying, as he did not see the man alleged to be responsible at the scene of the crime. As John is relying on what Maggie has told him, he cannot be effectively cross-examined.

Alternatively, if Mandy had made a written witness statement to the police but was unable to attend trial to give oral evidence, could the prosecution adduce Mandy's written statement? The written statement constitutes hearsay evidence. As in the first instance, it will not be possible to cross-examine the absent witness to test the reliability and truthfulness of the witness's evidence, and once again, the court would be relying on 'second-hand' evidence.

Hearsay evidence can be first-hand hearsay or multi-hand hearsay (the latter will have gone through more than one stage of reporting).

25.2 HEARSAY EVIDENCE – THE GENERAL RULE

The general rule in criminal cases is that hearsay evidence is inadmissible for the reasons explained in the introduction. Unless the hearsay evidence can be brought within a recognised common law or statutory exception, it remains inadmissible. The Criminal Justice Act 2003 (CJA) has, however, *considerably* widened the basis for admitting hearsay evidence in criminal cases.

25.3 IDENTIFYING HEARSAY EVIDENCE

Hearsay has been defined as:

'Any statement other than one made by a person while giving oral evidence in the proceedings is inadmissible to prove the truth of any fact stated in it.' (*R v Kearley* [1992] 2 AC 228)

To come within the definition of hearsay evidence, the statement sought to be adduced must have the following three elements:

(1) The hearsay evidence must be contained in a 'statement'. All forms of communication come within the meaning of a 'statement', including:

- a written witness statement;
- a document compiled in the course of a business or by a public authority;
- a witness's oral evidence;

- a witness's evidence recorded on an audio or video tape;
- evidence contained on a computer disc;
- a gesture by a witness (*R v Gibson* [1887] LR 18 QBD).

(2) The hearsay statement must have been made by the witness other than while giving evidence in the present proceedings.

The 'statement' will come within the hearsay rule where the oral or written statement was made, or the document was compiled, or the gesture was made on any occasion other than while the witness was giving evidence to the court in the present proceedings.

(3) To come within the hearsay rule, the statement must be put in evidence to prove the truth of the statement's content and not for any other reason, for example, to prove the statement was made or to show the witness's state of mind at the time the statement was made.

A confession is a good illustration of evidence that contains the constituent elements of a hearsay statement.

- a defendant's confession will be contained in a 'statement' i.e. a written transcript of the interview with the police and/or a tape-recording of the interview;
- the confession will be made on an occasion other than while the defendant gives evidence in the present proceedings – i.e. the defendant will make his confession at the police station during the investigation of the alleged crime; and
- the purpose of putting the statement before the court is to prove its truth – i.e. that the accused admits his involvement in the offence charged.

For the reasons explained in Chapter 10, confession evidence is admissible by virtue of a common law exception to the rule against hearsay evidence. A confession in itself, however, can only be used in evidence against its maker. As against any other person the confession might implicate, it constitutes inadmissible hearsay evidence.

25.3.1 DEFINITIONAL DIFFICULTIES WITH HEARSAY EVIDENCE

Not every out-of-court statement made by a witness will come within the hearsay rule. If the earlier out-of-court statement is being adduced for a reason other than proving the truth of facts asserted on that earlier occasion, the statement will not amount to hearsay. A good example of this point is provided by *Subramanian v Public Prosecutor of Malaya* [1956] 1 WLR 965 where the defendant was charged with possession of ammunition at a time when this was a capital offence in Malaya under emergency regulations. His defence was that he had been forced to act as a courier for Chinese terrorists under duress, that is, by threats to himself and his family. At his trial, the judge refused to allow him to repeat the words of the threats, ruling that this would be hearsay. It was held on appeal to the Privy Council that the judge was wrong. The words were not hearsay because they were put in evidence not to prove the truth of their contents but merely to show that they were said and to show the likely effect on the defendant's mind.

In *R v Davis* [1998] Crim LR 659, the defendant sought to prevent the jury from drawing an adverse inference under section 34 of the Criminal Justice and Public Order Act 1994 (see Chapter 8). He had remained silent at the police station based on advice given to him by his solicitor. On oath he sought to repeat the advice his solicitor had given him but was prevented from doing so by the trial judge who ruled it would infringe the rule against admitting hearsay. The Court of Appeal concluded that the trial judge had been in error. Where a defendant simply wanted to give an account of his solicitor's advice to show the jury the effect it had on him and therefore his reasons for remaining silent, the evidence was not hearsay, as the defendant was not seeking to prove the truth of anything his solicitor said to him.

25.3.2 IMPLIED ASSERTIONS AND THE 'NEW' STATUTORY DEFINITION OF HEARSAY

An implied assertion is a statement which is not intended by its maker to explicitly assert a fact but which does so by implication. This distinction is not always easy to make. In *R v Kearley* [1992] 2 AC 228, in order to prove K was dealing in drugs, police officers were allowed to repeat in court the content of conversations they had had with anonymous callers to K's house during the period shortly after his arrest, requesting K to supply them with their 'usual'. No explicit assertion of K being a drug dealer was made by these callers, but an implicit assertion to this effect arguably was. The House of Lords concluded that an implied assertion is hearsay. The problem of the implied assertion is now dealt with by s. 115(3) of the Criminal Justice Act 2003 (CJA). The hearsay provisions under the CJA will only apply to a statement that appears to have been made in order

> 'to cause another person to believe the matter, or to cause another person to act or a machine to operate on the basis that the matter is as stated. . . .'

In short, unless the maker of the statement was intending to assert a fact, the hearsay rule, as redefined under CJA 2003, does not apply and the evidence may be admitted as direct evidence of a fact providing it has relevance to the particular case.

25.3.3 DOCUMENTS CREATED BY A COMPUTER

Does a document created by a computer constitute hearsay? Where the computer performs an entirely automated process which does not involve any human input of information, the printout reading will be classed as real evidence. This means that readings from a speedometer, police radar gun and Intoximeter would not amount to hearsay evidence. Similarly, the automated telephone exchange records which log the date, times and numbers of telephone calls made and received are frequently admitted in evidence as items of real evidence.

Where the evidence has been created by a computer as a consequence of information inputted by a human being, the evidence is likely to come within the hearsay rule if it is sought to use the computer printout to prove the truth of some fact asserted by the person who entered the information. However, section 115(2) CJA 2003 confines the hearsay provisions to statements made by a person. It therefore excludes statements produced or created by a mechanical device. The latter are admissible under s. 129(1) CJA 2003, which provides that:

> 'where a representation of fact:
>
> (a) is made otherwise than by a person, but
>
> (b) depends for its accuracy on information supplied (directly or indirectly) by a person,
>
> the representation is not admissible in criminal proceedings as evidence of the fact unless it is proved that the information was accurate.'

For other types of information stored on computers such as e-mail correspondence, business records, invoices etc., which constitute statements made by a person, their admissibility is subject to s. 116 or s. 117 Criminal Justice Act 2003 (see below).

25.3.4 PHOTOGRAPHS/TAPE-RECORDINGS AND VIDEOS

These forms of communication are commonly admitted in evidence. Photographs, CCTV footage, audio and video etc. are regarded as real evidence and do not fall within the hearsay rule. The provenance of the evidence will still need to be proved, therefore it is necessary to adduce evidence of when the video was shot and by whom.

Now that you have an understanding of the constituent elements of a hearsay statement, we will examine the exceptions to the general exclusionary rule which allow hearsay evidence to be admitted in criminal cases. The exceptions are defined by the common law and by statute. The Criminal Justice Act 2003 now regulates the admissibility of hearsay evidence in criminal cases.

25.4 THE STATUTORY EXCEPTIONS TO THE HEARSAY RULE

There are a number of important statutory exceptions to the hearsay rule in criminal cases. Until recently, the main statutory provisions were contained in sections 23–26 Criminal Justice Act 1988. These provisions have been replaced by the Criminal Justice Act 2003, which has codified the most important exceptions to the rule. Much of the case law that built up around the previous statutory provisions will continue to be relevant. Before we consider the new provisions, we will highlight two other important statutory exceptions to the exclusionary hearsay rule.

25.4.1 SECTION 9 CRIMINAL JUSTICE ACT 1967

In practice section 9 CJA 1967 is the most important exception to the hearsay rule, and is in daily use in all Crown Courts and magistrates' courts. Section 9 CJA 1967 permits a witness's written statement to be read to the court without the witness attending the trial where:

- the statement is signed by the maker; and
- contains a declaration in specified words as to the statement's truth; and
- the statement has been served on the opposing party; and
- within seven days the opposing party has not objected to the statement being admitted as hearsay.

The key point to note about a 'section 9 statement' is that the consent of the opposing side must be obtained before the statement may be admitted as hearsay. If objection is taken (for whatever reason), the court has no power to overrule the objection and admit the statement in evidence. Section 9 statements are therefore used only for non-controversial matters where the evidence contained in the statement is effectively agreed by the opposing side, as there will be no opportunity to cross-examine or challenge the witness's evidence.

When preparing a case for trial, the defence solicitor should consider whether there are any prosecution witnesses whose evidence could be read to the court under s. 9 CJA 1967. With reference to our case study *R v Lenny Whyte*, you will see that in preparing Lenny Whyte's case for trial a number of prosecution's witness statements have been agreed.

25.4.2 STATEMENTS ADDUCED AT COMMITTAL HEARINGS

As previously noted in Chapter 16, Schedule 2 of the Criminal Procedure and Investigations Act 1996 requires the defendant to notify the prosecution, within 14 days of the service of evidence in an either-way case that has been sent to the Crown Court, of any objections the defence may have to the written statements of those witnesses tendered in evidence from being read out at trial.

Both s. 9 CJA 1967 and Sch. 2 CPIA 1996 are expressly preserved by the CJA 2003.

25.5 HEARSAY EVIDENCE UNDER THE CRIMINAL JUSTICE ACT 2003

Section 114 of the Criminal Justice Act 2003 regulates the admissibility of hearsay evidence in criminal cases. The section provides:

'a statement not made in oral evidence in the proceedings is admissible as evidence of any matter stated if it comes within one of the four exceptions.'

Section 114(1)(a)–(d) then identifies the following four situations where hearsay will be admissible under the Act:

- s. 114(1)(a) – hearsay will be admissible where it comes within one of the categories of admissible hearsay evidence under the Act (chiefly where a witness is unavailable to give evidence – ss. 116 and 117 CJA 2003) and any other preserved statutory section (s. 9 CJA 1967 and Schedule 2 CPIA 1996, see above);
- s. 114(1)(b) – hearsay will be admissible where it comes within one of the preserved common law rules (s. 11);
- s. 114(1)(c) – hearsay will be admissible where the parties agree to the evidence being admitted;
- s. 114(1)(d) – hearsay will be admissible where the court is satisfied that it is in the 'interests of justice' for the hearsay statement to be admitted (the so-called safety-valve).

The main statutory gateways for admitting hearsay are provided by ss. 116 and 117 CJA 2003.

25.5.1 THE UNAVAILABLE WITNESS – S. 116 (FIRST-HAND HEARSAY)

A statement will only be admissible under s. 116(1) CJA 2003 where:

- the person could have given oral evidence if he had attended court;
- the person who made the statement is identified to the court's satisfaction;
- the person who made the statement had the requisite capability (s. 123 CJA 2003) at the time he made the statement. Capability is defined in the same terms as the test for competency to give oral evidence under s. 53 Youth Justice and Criminal Evidence Act 1999 (can the witness understand questions put to him, and give answers that can be understood).

Section 116 CJA 2003 mirrors the old s. 23 CJA 1988 in that (subject to the requirements above) it permits a statement to be admitted where the witness is unable to attend court for one of the following reasons:

- the witness is dead or is unfit because of his bodily or mental condition (116(2)(a) and (b));
- the witness is outside the UK and it is not reasonably practicable for him to attend (s. 116 (2)(c));
- the witness cannot be found although such steps as it is reasonably practical to take to find him have been taken (s. 116(2)(d));
- that through fear the witness does not give evidence (or does not continue to give evidence) (s. 116(2)(e)).

Under s. 116 CJA it is immaterial whether the hearsay statement is contained in a document or was made orally. Once the condition for admitting the hearsay statement is proved under s. 116, the evidence can be admitted.

The burden of proving the relevant condition rests on the party seeking to adduce the hearsay evidence. Rules of court (Part 34 Crim PR) determine the procedure that must be followed where a party seeks to admit evidence under the provisions of the 2003 Act. Disputes as regards admissibility are likely to be determined at a pre-trial hearing.

25.5.2 THE REASONS FOR A WITNESS'S UNAVAILABILITY

Reason 1 – the witness is dead or unfit.
R v Setz-Dempsey [1993] 92 CR App R 98 confirms that an assessment of the witness's 'unfitness to attend' can include mental or physical capacity. A death certificate or medical report should discharge the burden of proving this ground.

Reason 2 – the witness is (a) outside the UK and (b) it is not reasonably practicable to secure his attendance.

If the witness's statement is to be given as hearsay, both conditions have to be satisfied by the party seeking to rely on s. 116(2)(d) CJA 2003. In *R v Castillo* [1996] 1 Cr App R 438, the Court of Appeal identified a number of factors that need to be considered in determining whether it is practicable for the witness to attend, including:

- the importance of the evidence the witness could give;
- the expense and inconvenience of securing the attendance of the witness;
- the seriousness of the offence;
- whether the witness's evidence could be given via live television link; and
- the prejudice likely to be caused to the defendant given he would have no opportunity to cross-examine.

Reason 3 – all reasonable steps have been taken to find the witness, but he cannot be found.

The party seeking to put the hearsay statement in evidence must prove that all reasonable steps have been taken to find the witness. This would include adducing evidence of what steps were in fact undertaken to trace the witness and with what result.

Reason 4 – the witness does not give evidence through fear.

Fear is widely defined in s. 116(3) to include fear of death or injury of another person or financial loss. In *R v Martin* [1996] Crim LR 589 (a case under the previous statutory regime), the Court of Appeal stated that the word 'fear' should be given its natural meaning, and would include not only threats made through witness intimidation arising out of the crime, but also to factors unconnected with the commission of the crime. The witness's fear does not need to have a rational basis.

The witness's fear must be proved by admissible evidence. The existing case law on this ground will continue to apply. In *Neill v North Antrim Magistrates' Court*[1992] 4 All ER 846, the court held that fear was not proved in a case where the investigating police officer told the court that the witness's mother had told him of her son's fear. The evidence of the police officer was based on hearsay. Had the police officer witnessed first-hand the witness's fear, he could have given evidence of this either under the *res gestae* exception or as circumstantial evidence of fact from which the appropriate inference could have been drawn. Fear can be proved by the witness giving sworn evidence at a *voir dire* as to why he does not wish to give evidence. In *R v Rutherford* [1998] Crim LR 490, fear was proved by a signed written statement from the witness.

Where a party seeks to rely on the fear ground within the meaning of 116(2)(e), the leave of the court must be sought under s. 116(4). Leave will only be granted if the court considers that it would be in the interests of justice to admit the statement having regard to:

(a) the statement's contents;

(b) to any risk that its admission or exclusion will result in unfairness to any party (with particular reference to how difficult it will be to challenge the statement if the relevant person does not give evidence);

(c) in appropriate cases to the fact that a special measures direction could be made in relation to the relevant person (see Chapter 22);

(d) any other relevant circumstance.

The requirement to seek leave in respect of this ground is an important safeguard in protecting the defendant's right to a fair trial under Article 6. The relationship between hearsay evidence and Article 6 is considered at paragraph 25.13 below.

Consider the following examples of admitting hearsay under s. 116 CJA 2003

Example 1

Ethel, aged 84, is the victim of a burglary. She describes the burglar to her daughter Dianna. Ethel suffers a stroke soon after and is unable to provide a formal written statement to the police or indeed to attend trial. Can the prosecution call Dianna so that she may repeat in court what her mother told her about the burglar? This would clearly constitute hearsay evidence. Hearsay evidence is generally inadmissible unless it comes within the exceptions under the CJA 2003. Assume Ethel was capable at the time she spoke with her daughter. On the face of it, the conditions for admissibility under s. 116 CJA 2003 would appear to be satisfied. The identity of the maker of the statement is not in dispute and Ethel is unable to attend trial for a prescribed reason under s. 116(2)(b).

Example 2

Simon is the victim of a homophobic assault. He gives the police a detailed description of his attackers in a written witness statement. Simon refuses to give evidence in court as he fears for his personal safety. Can the prosecution adduce Simon's written statement as hearsay evidence? Simon's statement would appear to be admissible under s. 116(2)(e) CJA 2003. Simon is clearly identifiable as the maker of the statement and is unavailable to give oral evidence out of fear. In choosing to admit Simon's statement the court must have regard to the factors set out in s. 116(4) CJA 2003, including the availability of special measures to assist witnesses like Simon to give evidence.

25.6 BUSINESS DOCUMENTS – S. 117

Business documents are readily admissible under s.117 Criminal Justice Act 2003 and take into account the modern business practice where millions of documents are created on a daily basis. As it would be impossible to require every person who had personal knowledge of the document's contents to testify in court, s. 117(2) makes business documents admissible as hearsay in criminal proceedings where the following conditions are satisfied:

- the document was created or received in the course of a trade, business, profession or other occupation, or as the holder of a paid or unpaid office (s. 117(2)(a)); and
- the person who supplied the information contained in the statement (defined as the relevant person) had or might reasonably be expected to have had personal knowledge of the matters dealt with in the statement (s. 117(2)(b)); and
- each person (if any) through whom the information was supplied from the relevant person received the information in the course of a trade, business, profession or other occupation or as the holder of a paid or unpaid office (s. 117(2)(c)).

As with its predecessor under s. 24 CJA 1988, s. 117 permits the reception into evidence of multi-hand hearsay which satisfies the requirements of the section. In each case the person creating or receiving the document must be acting as part of a trade, business, profession, or as the holder of a paid or unpaid office. The person who supplied the information contained in the statement must reasonably be supposed to have personal knowledge of the matters dealt with. If the information came through an intermediary, the information must have been received by a person in the course of a trade, business, profession, or as the holder of a paid or unpaid office.

Business records, ledgers, invoices and hospital records etc will all be admissible under s. 117(2).

25.6.1 DOCUMENTS PREPARED FOR THE PURPOSE OF A CRIMINAL INVESTIGATION OR PROCEEDINGS – SPECIAL RULES

Section 117(4) provides that documents, be they business or other records, which have been prepared for the purposes of pending or contemplated criminal proceedings which are sought to be adduced as hearsay must satisfy the conditions laid down in s. 117(5). Such statements are admissible providing any one of the five conditions set out in s. 116(2) relating to the absence of the relevant person is satisfied (see paragraph 25.5.1 above), or as an additional reason, the relevant person (the person who supplied the information contained in the document) cannot reasonably be expected to have any recollection of the matters dealt with in the statement having regard to the length of time since he supplied the information and all other circumstances (s. 117(5)(b)).

Section 117(7) CJA 2003 incorporates an important safeguard in relation to all documents that are sought to be admitted under s. 117. It provides that a court may make a direction to exclude a statement if the statement's reliability as evidence for the purpose for which it is tendered is doubtful in view of:

(a) its contents;

(b) the source of the information contained in it;

(c) the way in which or the circumstances in which the information was supplied or received; or

(d) the way in which or the circumstances in which the document concerned was created or received.

Consider the following examples of admitting hearsay under 117(4) CJA 2003.

Example 1

Take the example of Ethel which we considered earlier in the context of s 116. Assume Ethel has been able to provide the police with a written statement, but thereafter is unable to attend trial. Her written statement would be admissible under s. 117(4)–(5) CJA 2003. It comprises a document prepared for the purposes of criminal proceedings and a prescribed reason for not calling Ethel is made out, namely she is not well enough to attend trial. There would appear to be no obvious reason for doubting the reliability of her statement (s. 117(7)).

Example 2

Ingrid gives an oral statement to a police officer having witnessed a serious road traffic accident. The officer records her statement in his notebook. The police have since been unable to trace Ingrid in order to take a formal statement from her. Can the police officer's notebook recording the conversation be admitted under s. 117 CJA 2003? The document (which comprises second-hand hearsay) was created in the course of the police officer's job. Ingrid is the 'relevant person' for the purposes of s. 117(4) in that she is the person who supplied the information contained in the statement and can be assumed to have personal knowledge of the facts. However, the police officer's notebook is a document prepared for the purposes of a police investigation and so a s. 116 reason must be proved. Assuming that all reasonable steps have been taken to trace Ingrid (and there is no reason to doubt Ingrid's capability at the time she gave her oral statement), the conditions for admitting the notebook under s. 117 CJA 2003 would appear to be made out.

25.7 HEARSAY ADMISSIBLE UNDER THE PRESERVED COMMON LAW RULES (S. 118 CJA 2003)

The CJA specifically preserves many of the common law exceptions to the hearsay rule, of which the most important are *res gestae* and confessions. The other common law provisions that are preserved include public documents, evidence regarding a family's reputation or tradition, expert opinion drawing on published works and of course confession evidence.

25.7.1 *RES GESTAE* STATEMENTS (S. 118(4)(A)–(C) CJA 2003)

Res gestae means transaction, or series of events. There are various situations which cover the admission of evidence under the *res gestae* rule under s. 118(4). One such instance is under what is commonly referred to as the 'spontaneous utterance rule'. The leading common law authority on such statements is *R v Andrews* [1987] AC 281. In this case, the House of Lords held that a statement made by a fatally stabbed man soon after he was attacked which named his two attackers, was properly admitted under the *res gestae* rule.

Section 118(4)(a) CJA 2003 preserves the 'spontaneous utterance rule' and allows an earlier out-of-court statement to be adduced in evidence providing the statement was made by a person 'so emotionally overpowered by an event that the possibility of concoction or distortion can be disregarded.'

A *res gestae* statement can also be admitted where the witness is available to give evidence. The admissibility of hearsay evidence under the *res gestae* principle remains subject to the courts discretion to refuse to admit the statement under s. 78 PACE on the grounds of fairness (s. 126(2) CJA 2003).

In *R v W* (Reference under s. 36 CJA 1972) [2003] 2 Cr App R 29 the defendant was accused of a very serious assault on his mother. She had been pushed down the stairs and had her hair set on fire. There were several witnesses who witnessed the aftermath of the attack during which the victim told each of these witnesses that her son had gone berserk and attacked her. At a later stage, however, the victim refused to give a formal statement to the police and later went on to give a deposition before magistrates in which she completely retracted her oral allegation maintaining she had accidentally fallen downstairs. She declined to comment on how her hair had been burned.

Realising that there would little point in calling the victim to give evidence, the prosecution sought to call the witnesses to whom the victim had spoken in the immediate aftermath to give evidence under the *res gestae* principle. The Court of Appeal held there was nothing in *R v Andrews* which prohibited a *res gestae* statement being admitted, even though the witness was available to give evidence. There was no doubt that what the victim had been heard to say in this case fell within the definition of *res gestae* and was therefore *prima facie* admissible. However, as with every other type of evidence, this particular piece of hearsay evidence was subject to the court's exclusionary discretion under section 78 PACE. It was not suggested that the prosecution were seeking to rely on a *res gestae* statement as a device to avoid calling the victim. However, given the importance of this witness to the prosecution's case and the inability of the defendant to cross-examine the hearsay witness, the defendant could not have enjoyed a fair trial in accordance with Article 6 of the European Convention on Human Rights.

25.7.2 STATEMENTS IN PUBLIC DOCUMENTS (S. 118(1) CJA 2003)

Statements contained in a public document or certified true copies of them are admissible at common law as evidence of the truth of their contents. This exception to the hearsay rule has long been recognised because such evidence was considered to be reliable and very often the public official who compiled the document would have no recollection of the facts, or be dead, or be unfit to testify. Many statutes now make provision for the admissibility of certain specific classes of documents, such as certified true copies of entries in a register of deaths compiled by the Registrar of Births, Deaths and Marriages, as evidence of the date of a person's death where this is a relevant fact in issue in any proceedings.

In addition to such specific provisions, most statements in public documents will be admissible in criminal cases by virtue of s. 117 Criminal Justice Act 2003.

25.7.3 CONFESSION EVIDENCE (S. 118(5) CJA 2003)

Confession evidence has always been admissible as a common law exception to the rule against hearsay. The admissibility of confession evidence is considered in Chapter 10.

25.8 HEARSAY WILL BE ADMISSIBLE WHERE THE PARTIES AGREE TO THE EVIDENCE BEING ADMITTED (S. 114(1)(C) CJA 2003)

This ground is self-explanatory.

25.9 THE 'SAFETY-VALVE' (S. 114(1)(D) AND S. 121 CJA 2003)

Section 114(1)(d) gives a court discretion to admit hearsay evidence which does not come within one of the specified categories for admitting hearsay evidence under CJA 2003. A court may only chose to admit such hearsay evidence if it considers it is in the interests of justice.

In applying the discretion to decide whether it is in the 'interests of justice' for the hearsay statement to be admitted, the court will take into account a number of factors laid down in s. 114(2)(a)–(i). They are:

(a) how much probative value the statement has (assuming it to be true) in relation to a matter in issue in the proceedings, or how valuable it is for the understanding of other evidence in the case;

(b) what other evidence has been, or can be, given on the matter or evidence mentioned in paragraph (a);

(c) how important the matter or evidence mentioned in paragraph (a) is in the context of the case as a whole;

(d) the circumstances in which the statement was made;

(e) how reliable the maker of the statement appears to be;

(f) how reliable the evidence of the making of the statement appears to be;

(g) whether oral evidence of the matter stated can be given and, if not, why it cannot;

(h) the amount of difficulty involved in challenging the statement;

(i) the extent to which that difficulty would be likely to prejudice the party facing it.

The 'safety-valve' represents a new departure and gives the court an inclusionary discretion to admit hearsay evidence. In theory, this provision should be used exceptionally where hearsay evidence cannot be admitted under any other provision, although it should be noted that there is nothing in the CJA 2003 which dictates this should be so. It remains to be seen how frequently the safety-valve is invoked and how it will be interpreted by the courts.

Where multiple hearsay is sought to be admitted, it is subject to a specific safety-valve in s. 121(1)(c) CJA 2003. This section requires the court to consider whether the value of the statement is so high (taking into account how reliable the statement appears to be) that the interests of justice require it to be admitted. In assessing whether the value of the statement is 'so high', it is anticipated that the court will additionally consider the factors set out in s. 114(2)(a)–(i).

The following are examples of how the 'safety-valve' might apply.

Example 1

Take the example of Ethel above and vary the facts further. Assume Ethel gives a description of the perpetrator to her neighbour Arthur. Arthur relays the information to his son Tom. Assume that both Ethel and Arthur are unable to give oral evidence at trial. Will the prosecution be able to call Tom to give evidence of what Ethel said to Arthur which in turn was said to him?

This example raises the issue of multiple hearsay evidence. The original statement has gone through more than one stage of reporting. It cannot therefore be admissible within the terms of s. 116 CJA 2003 and it is not admissible under s. 117 CJA 2003 as that section is restricted to documentary hearsay. The only possibility in this instance is the safety-valve (s. 121). Assume there is no reason to doubt the credit-worthiness of any of the witnesses. The statement is of importance to the prosecution. There is a good reason for Ethel's inability to give oral evidence and the defence can still challenge the evidence. On balance, the court might chose to admit the evidence given its reliability and probative value.

Example 2

An anonymous telephone to call to Crime Stoppers provides the registration number of a 'getaway car' involved in a fatal drive-by shooting. As a result of the information, the car is located and subject to forensic analysis linking a number of the suspects to the vehicle. Can a transcript of the telephone call be admitted? It cannot be admitted under s. 117(4). Although it is a document prepared for the purposes of a criminal investigation, the requirements under s. 116 are not made out as the relevant person (the person who supplied the information) cannot be identified. The only means by which the transcript could be admitted is if the court exercises its discretion under s. 114. It is not possible to comment on the reliability of the maker of the statement. However, the statement is arguably important in explaining how the car came to be recovered. In this instance, it would be entirely within the court's discretion to either admit or reject the evidence having regard to the factors laid down in s. 114(2)(a)–(i).

25.10 MISCELLANEOUS PROVISIONS RELATING TO THE USE THAT CAN BE MADE OF STATEMENTS ADMITTED AS PREVIOUS INCONSISTENT STATEMENTS/PREVIOUS CONSISTENT STATEMENTS AND UNDER THE WITNESS MEMORY REFRESHING RULES

- Section 119 CJA provides that where a witness admits making a previous inconsistent statement or it has been proved that he has made such a statement, the statement can now be admitted as evidence of the truth of what it asserts. (For the rules on proving a previous inconsistent statement, see Chapter 23.)

- Section 120 CJA extends the evidential effect of a witness's previous consistent statement so that it may be admitted as evidence of the truth of what it asserts. This includes previous consistent statements used to rebut a suggestion of recent fabrication; recent complaints and statements used to refresh a witness's memory upon which the witness is cross-examined, resulting in the statement being put in evidence (see Chapter 23).

- Section 120(4) CJA provides that a witness's previous statement may be admissible as evidence of the facts stated, if while giving evidence the witness indicates that to the best of his belief he made the statement; that it states the truth and the statement falls within one of the prescribed categories under s. 120(5), (6) and (7) (see Chapter 23).

25.11 **ADDITIONAL SAFEGUARDS WHEN ADMITTING HEARSAY EVIDENCE**

Although the CJA 2003 introduces a more liberal regime in admitting hearsay, even where the conditions for admissibility are satisfied, the Act introduces a number of safeguards to limit multiple hearsay and provisions for challenging the capability and credibility of a hearsay witness. The availability of these safeguards will be a relevant consideration in determining the arguments that are bound to arise regarding these new provisions and their compatibility with Article 6 and the defendant's right to a fair trial.

25.11.1 **RESTRICTING MULTIPLE HEARSAY – S. 121 CJA 2003**

Multiple hearsay occurs when a statement passes through more than one intermediary. Section 121 provides that a hearsay statement is not admissible to prove the fact that an earlier hearsay statement was made unless:

- either of the statements is admissible under s. 117 CJA; or under s. 119 as a previous inconsistent statement; or under s. 120 as a previous consistent statement; or
- the parties agree to it being admitted (s. 121(1)(b)); or
- the court is satisfied that the value of the evidence, taking into account how reliable the statement appears to be, is so high, that the interests of justice require it to be admitted (s. 121(1)(c) – see para. 25.9 above and the examples, plus example 2 at para.25.6.1).

25.11.2 **CAPABILITY OF THE WITNESS TO MAKE THE STATEMENT – S. 123**

Nothing in section 116, 119 or 120 makes a statement admissible as evidence if it was made by a person who did not have the requisite capability at the time when he made the statement. The same requirement applies to statements admitted under s. 117(2) in relation to the person who supplied or received the information or created or received the document.

25.11.3 **CHALLENGING THE HEARSAY WITNESS'S CREDIBILITY – S. 124 CJA 2003**

Section 124 CJA 2003 permits the opposing party to challenge the hearsay witness's credibility in the same way as if the witness had given oral evidence.

25.11.4 **STOPPING THE CASE WHERE EVIDENCE IS UNCONVINCING – S. 125 CJA**

Section 125 requires the court to stop the case and to acquit the defendant where the case against him is based wholly or partly on an out of court statement which is so unconvincing that considering its importance to the case, a conviction would be unsafe. This power applies only to trials on indictment.

25.11.5 **EXCLUDING UNNECESSARY HEARSAY – S. 126 CJA 2003**

Section 126(1) CJA gives the court discretion to exclude hearsay evidence where the court is satisfied that the value of the evidence is substantially outweighed by the undue waste of time which its admission would cause.

25.11.6 **DISCRETION TO EXCLUDE HEARSAY – S. 126 CJA 2003**

Section 126(2) CJA 2003 preserves the discretion under s. 78 PACE (unfairness) and at common law s. 82(3) (probative value outweighed by prejudicial effect) to exclude hearsay evidence. This is a very important safeguard to ensure that a defendant continues to enjoy a fair trial under the CJA 2003 hearsay provisions.

25.11.7 **DIRECTING THE JURY**

In accordance with the Judicial Studies Board specimen directions, in determining the weight to be given to hearsay evidence, the judge should point out to the jury the limitations of hearsay evidence, namely, the jury has not had the benefit of seeing or hearing the witness, nor has the witness been subject to cross-examination.

25.12 **PROCEDURE FOR ADMITTING HEARSAY EVIDENCE**

A party seeking to introduce hearsay evidence must give notice to the court and all other parties. The rules of court relating to the procedure to be adopted are contained in Part 34 Crim PR. Having received notice of hearsay evidence, a party may oppose its admission by giving notice within 14 days on a prescribed form. Any dispute between the parties is likely to result in a pre-trial ruling on the matter.

25.13 **HEARSAY EVIDENCE AND THE EUROPEAN CONVENTION ON HUMAN RIGHTS 1950**

Article 6(3)(d) (under the fair trial provisions of Article 6) confers on a defendant the right to examine or have examined witnesses against him and to obtain the attendance and examination of witnesses on his behalf under the same conditions as witnesses against him. Where evidence is admitted as hearsay, the defendant is unable to cross-examine the witness. Is the admission of hearsay evidence intrinsically unfair? The case law of the European Convention of Human Rights suggests not, providing the defendant is able to challenge effectively the evidence (*Kostovoi v Netherlands* [1990] 12 EHHR 434). There have in fact been numerous decisions by the ECtHR on the use of hearsay evidence. Distilling clear, guiding principles is difficult.

In *Luca v Italy* [2003] 36 EHHR 46, the European Court of Human Rights suggested that Article 6 might be breached where the hearsay is the sole or decisive evidence against the defendant. This proposition was rejected by the Court of Appeal in *R v Sellick and Sellick* [2005] 1 WLR 3257 and earlier in *R v M* [2003] 2 Cr App R 21, in a case where the defendant had been found unfit to plead and the only witness to the crime refused to give evidence due to fear, which the trial judge found to have been orchestrated by the defendant.

Under the previous law contained in ss. 23–26 Criminal Justice Act 1988, the admissibility of hearsay evidence was subject not only to proof of the preconditions for admissibility but also to an additional interests of justice test under either s. 25 or 26 CJA 1988. This requirement has now ceased to apply. The hearsay provisions under the new Act are intended, and believed to be, complaint with the European Convention on Human Rights. Challenges to the new law, based on Article 6, however, are to be expected. It is likely that the adequacy of the safeguards identified in relation to the admission of hearsay evidence in a case where a witness is in fear (s. 116(4); the specific safeguards to be applied in relation to the safety-valve exceptions (s. 114 (2)(a)–(i) and s. 121(1)(c); and the general safeguards applicable throughout contained in sections 123–126, will be the key to determining whether the new law is ECHR-compliant. Section 126 CJA 2003 is particularly important in this regard in its specific preservation of the court's general discretion to exclude any prosecution evidence, the admission of which would prejudice a fair trial (s. 78 PACE).

We include a handful of cases illustrate the factors a court is likely to regard in determining Article 6 considerations. They are all concerned with the pre-2003 Act provisions.

R v Radak [1999] Crim LR 223

In this case the Court of Appeal took the view that Article 6(3)(d) had been infringed. The witness was in the USA. He refused to attend trial. The witness's evidence was of some importance to the prosecution and had the prosecution chosen to do so, the evidence of the absent witness could have been elicited in the USA under s. 3 Crime (International Co-operation) Act 1990 (now 2003). Given the importance of the evidence and the inability to cross-examine or contradict with other evidence, the Court of Appeal concluded the trial judge had been wrong to admit the evidence in the exercise of his discretion.

R v Sellick and Sellick [2005] 1 WLR 325

In this case the chief prosecution witnesses, who were in a witness protection programme, disappeared. There was evidence to suggest that the defendant was implicated in the r decision to disappear. However, they were important witnesses for the prosecution, and for this reason it was important for the defendant to be able to cross-examine. Their witness statements were admitted as hearsay evidence in the exercise of the trial judge's discretion under s. 23 CJA 1988. What were the counter-balancing safeguards available to the defence? In deciding whether to admit the evidence as hearsay, the trial judge had carefully considered the interests of justice and the following factors were felt to be important:

- The evidence of each witness had been credible.
- The credibility of the witnesses had been challenged.
- The trial judge gave a clear direction as regards the witness's credibility and the shortcomings of hearsay evidence compared to oral evidence.
- Regard should be had to the fact that the defendant was to a large extent the author of his own inability to cross-examine witnesses against him.
- Regard should also be had to the rights of victims and their families.
- If there was a rule that a defendant could not be said to enjoy a fair trial because the main evidence against him constituted hearsay evidence, it would lead to greater intimidation of witnesses. Such an absolute rule cannot have bee been intended by the ECtHR.

R v Imad Al Khawaja [2006] 1 Cr App R 9

The defendant, a doctor, had been convicted of indecent assault on two female patients. His treatments included hypnotherapy. Prosecution witness one (W1) and witness two (W2) did not know each other. W1 committed suicide shortly before the trial. Her witness statement was admitted as hearsay evidence in the exercise of the trial judge's discretion under s. 23 CJA 1988. On appeal, the defence cited *Luca* and *Kostovski* in that the defendant had not been given and could not now be given any effective opportunity to challenge the written evidence and given its importance to the prosecution's case, the defendant could not be said to have enjoyed a fair trial. Affirming the conviction and citing *Sellick* with approval, the Court of Appeal observed:

'Where a witness who is the sole witness of a crime has made a statement to be used in its prosecution and has since died, there may be a strong public interest in the admission of the statement in evidence so that the prosecution may proceed. That was the case here. That public interest must not be allowed to override the requirement that the defendant have a fair trial. Like the court in *Sellick* we do not consider that the case law of the European Court of Human Rights requires the conclusion that in such circumstances the trial will be unfair. The provision in Art.6(3)(d) that a person charged shall be able to have the witnesses against him examined is one specific aspect of a fair trial: but if the opportunity is not provided, the question s 'whether the proceedings as a whole, including the way the evidence was taken, were fair . . . .' This was not a case where the witness had absented himself, whether through fear or otherwise, or had required anonymity, or had exercised a right to keep silent. The reason was death, which has a finality which brings in considerations of its own . . . .'

The safeguards identified in this case included:

- the fact that the judge had carefully weighed up the arguments for and against;
- the defendant had been afforded the opportunity of having the evidence excluded;
- the prosecution would have to have abandoned its case had the evidence been excluded;
- the defendant could still challenge the witness's credibility by adducing expert evidence of altered perceptions under hypnosis;
- there was no evidence to suggest collusion between the two principal witnesses;
- the jury had been appropriately directed.

KEY POINT SUMMARY

- Understand what hearsay evidence is. It is any out of court statement which is repeated in court for the purpose of proving the truth of a fact or facts asserted in the earlier out-of-court statement.
- Understand that as a general rule, hearsay evidence is inadmissible in criminal cases unless it happens to fall within a recognised common law or statutory exception. (Note: the categories for admission have been significantly broadened by the CJA 2003.)
- Recognised common law exceptions admitting hearsay evidence include statements admitted as part of the spontaneous utterance rule (*res gestae*) and confession evidence.
- Hearsay evidence can be admitted with the agreement of the parties under s. 9 Criminal Justice Act 1967 (agreement will be confined to those written statements that do not contain contentious facts requiring the witness to be cross-examined).
- The other main statutory basis for admitting hearsay is contained within ss. 114–126 Criminal Justice Act 2003.
- The statutory requirements of sections 116 CJA 2003 (unavailable witness) and s. 117 CJA 2003 (business documents) must be proved before hearsay evidence can be admitted.
- Understand the categories for admission of hearsay under the CJA 2003, including the safety-valve s. 114(1)(d), which covers hearsay that is not capable of being admitted under any other provision in the Act providing it is in the interests of justice.
- Be aware of the statutory safeguards that will apply in the context of the CJA 2003 and the need to ensure the admission of hearsay evidence does not prejudice a defendant's right to a fair trial.

SELF-TEST QUESTION

The CPS is prosecuting an armed robbery involving several defendants. Duane (who has provided the police with a detailed statement during the investigation) is a key prosecution witness. He has received a number of menacing telephone calls warning him against testifying. He has a young family and tells the police he will not testify in court. What evidential problem does this development give rise to and how can the prosecution get around it?

FIGURE 25.1 HEARSAY EVIDENCE

THE GENERAL RULE

- Hearsay is any statement made on an earlier out-of-court occasion which is being adduced in court to prove the truth of facts asserted in that earlier out-of-court statement.

- Section 114 CJA 2003 provides that hearsay evidence being: 'a statement not made in oral evidence in the proceedings, is admissible as evidence of any matter stated in it, if it comes within one of the four exceptions', s.114 CJA 2003.

- The exceptions which permit the reception of hearsay evidence in criminal cases are set out in section 114(1)(a)–(d) Criminal Justice Act 2003.

- The exceptions include:
  - s.116 CJA 2003 (unavailable witness providing the witness is identified);
  - s.117 CJA 2003 (business documents);
  - s.114(1)(b) CJA 2003 (it comes within one of the preserved common law exceptions);
  - s.114(1)(c) CJA 2003 (the parties agree to the hearsay being admitted); or
  - s.114 (1)(d) CJA 2003 (the court decides that it is 'in the interests of justice' for the hearsay to be admitted).
  - s.9 CJA 1967 (agreed witness statements);
  - sch. 2, CPIA 1996; (witness statements adduced at committal);

- The CJA 2003 contains a number of safeguards, including the application of s. 78 PACE to ensure use of hearsay evidence is compatible with Article 6 and special provisions as regard multiple hearsay.

REASONS FOR WITNESS UNAVAILABILITY (S. 116 CJA 2003)

- witness is ill, s.116(2)(a) CJA 2003; or

- is dead, s.116(2)(b) CJA 2003; or

- cannot be found, s.116(2)(c) CJA 2003; or

- is outside the UK and it is not reasonably practicable for him to attend, s.116(2)(d) CJA 2003; or

- through fear, ss.116(2)(e) CJA 2003 (leave required),

ADMITTING A BUSINESS DOCUMENT AS HEARSAY

- under s.117 CJA 2003, a business document may be admitted as hearsay where:
  - the document was created or received in the course of a business or trade or profession etc; and
  - the person who supplied the information contained in the statement had or might reasonably be expected to have had personal knowledge of the matters dealt with in the statement; and
  - if the document passed through an intermediary, each intermediary was acting in the course of a trade, profession etc.

PRESERVED COMMON LAW EXCEPTIONS TO THE HEARSAY RULE

- Hearsay is admissible under s.118 CJA 2003 where the statement falls within one of the preserved common law exceptions, including:
  - the *res gestae* rule;
  - public documents.

FIGURE 25.1 (CONTINUED)

ADMITTING HEARSAY WHERE IT IS 'IN THE INTERESTS OF JUSTICE'

- Where a hearsay statement does not come within one of the recognised exceptions under s. 114(1)(a)–(c) CJA 2003, the court may admit the statement under s. 114(1)(d) CJA 2003 where 'it is in the interests of justice'.

- The following factors under s. 114(2) must be taken into account when exercising discretion, including:
  - the credibility of the statement's maker;
  - the statement's probative value;
  - the reason why oral evidence cannot be given;
  - the statement's importance to the party's case;
  - the difficulty to the other side in challenging the hearsay.

---

26 THE RULES OF EVIDENCE AND THE ACCUSED AT TRIAL

26.1 INTRODUCTION

In this chapter we examine the evidential rules that apply to the defendant at his trial, including:

- the defendant's competence and compellability;
- the course of the defendant's evidence;
- drawing an adverse inference under s. 35 Criminal Justice and Public Order Act 1994, from the defendant's decision not to give evidence in his defence;
- the disclosure of a defendant's past character (with particular emphasis on the defendant's past bad character);
- the factors that have a bearing on whether or not the defendant should give evidence in his defence.

26.2 THE ACCUSED AS A COMPETENT WITNESS FOR THE DEFENCE

Under s. 53(1) Youth Justice and Criminal Evidence Act 1999 (YJCEA), the defendant is a competent witness in his defence at every stage of the criminal proceedings. This means that, as a matter of law, the defendant may have his evidence heard by the court.

While the defendant is a competent defence witness, he is not a compellable witness – i.e. he has the right not to give evidence, which is recognised in s. 1(1) Criminal Evidence Act 1898 (CEA). The effect of s. 1(1) CEA 1898 is that if the defendant elects not to testify, he will not suffer a penalty like any other competent witness – apart from the possibility of adverse inferences being drawn from his silence under s. 35 Criminal Justice and Public Order Act 1994, which is considered in paragraph 26.4. An accused is a competent but non-compellable witness for a co-accused by virtue of s. 53 YJCEA 1999.

26.2.1 THE DEFENDANT AS A PROSECUTION WITNESS

The defendant is not a competent witness for the prosecution whether he is charged alone or jointly with another defendant (section 53(4) YJCEA 1999). In practice, s. 53(4) YJCEA is only relevant where one accused is jointly charged with another. A co-accused cannot give evidence for the prosecution while he remains a party to the proceedings. Under s. 53(5) YJCEA, however, where a co-accused ceases to be a party in the proceedings, he becomes a competent and compellable prosecution witness against any other person who has been charged in the same proceedings. This occurs where:

- the co-accused has been acquitted or has pleaded guilty at an earlier hearing and has been sentenced by the court; or
- the co-accused makes a successful submission of no case to answer at the close of the prosecution's case; or
- proceedings against the co-accused are discontinued; or
- the co-accused is tried separately as a result of a successful application to sever a joint trial.

In any of these circumstances the co-accused may be called by the prosecution to give evidence at a later hearing provided his testimony will support the prosecution case against his former co-accused. If this occurs, the co-accused is said to become an accomplice. Accomplice evidence may call for the jury/magistrates to be given a corroboration warning in accordance with the principles laid down in *R v Makanjuola* [1995] 1 WLR 1348 (see Chapter 24).

26.3 THE COURSE OF THE DEFENDANT'S EVIDENCE

Section 79 PACE 1984 stipulates that if a defendant is to give evidence in his defence, he must normally give his evidence before any other defence witness evidence is called. The course of the defendant's evidence will be the same as for any other witness. Before he testifies the defendant must swear an oath or affirm. He will give evidence from the witness box like any other witness. The accused will be asked questions by the defence advocate in examination-in-chief, cross-examined by the prosecutor and any co-accused and where appropriate, re-examined by the defence. You are reminded that unlike other witnesses in the case, the defendant is not eligible for a special measures direction to assist him in giving evidence.

26.4 THE DRAWING OF ADVERSE INFERENCES FROM THE DEFENDANT'S SILENCE AT TRIAL – S. 35 CRIMINAL JUSTICE AND PUBLIC ORDER ACT 1994

Where the defendant is not called to give evidence on his own behalf, under s. 35 CJPOA 1994, the prosecution may comment on the defendant's failure to testify and, where appropriate, call for inferences to be drawn by the court.

Section 35 CJPOA provides:

'(1) At the trial of any person for an offence, subsections (2) and (3) below apply unless–

   (a) the accused's guilt is not in issue; or

   (b) it appears to the court that the physical or mental condition of the accused makes it undesirable for him to give evidence; . . .

(2) Where this subsection applies, the court shall, at the conclusion of the evidence for the prosecution, satisfy itself (in the case of proceedings on indictment, in the presence of the jury) that the accused is aware that the stage has been reached at which evidence can be given for the defence and that he can, if he wishes, give evidence and that, if he chooses not to give evidence, or having been sworn, without good cause refuses to answer any question, it will be permissible for the court or jury to draw such inference as appears proper from his failure to give evidence or his refusal, without good cause, to answer any question.

(3) Where this subsection applies, the court or jury, in determining whether the accused is guilty of the offence charged, may draw such inferences as appear proper from the failure of the accused to give evidence, or his refusal without good cause to answer any question.

(4) This section does not render the accused compellable to give evidence on his own behalf, and he shall accordingly not be guilty of contempt of court by reason of a failure to do so.'

Before adverse inferences can be drawn under s. 35 CJPOA 1994, the following conditions must be satisfied if the defendant is to enjoy a fair trial:

(1) At the close of the prosecution's case, the judge is required to put the following question to the defence advocate:

'Have you advised your client that the stage has now been reached at which he may give evidence and, if he chooses not to do so, or having been sworn without good cause refuses to answer any question, the jury may draw such inferences as appear proper from his failure to do so?' (Practice Direction (Criminal: Consolidated) [2002] 3 All ER 904).

(2) If the defendant remains silent, the jury (or the magistrates) should be directed in the following terms in accordance with the guidance laid down by the Court of Appeal in *R v Cowan, Gayle and Riccardi* [1995] 4 All ER 939:

   • the legal burden of proof remains on the prosecution;

   • the defendant is entitled to remain silent;

- before drawing an adverse inference from the defendant's silence, the jury/magistrates have to be satisfied that there is a case to answer on the prosecution evidence;

- an adverse inference drawn from the accused's failure to give evidence cannot on its own prove the accused's guilt, s. 38(3) CJPOA;

- only if the jury or magistrates conclude that the only sensible explanation for the accused's silence is that he has no answer to the prosecution's case, or none that would stand up to cross-examination, may adverse inferences be drawn.

Where a defendant asserts he has a physical or mental condition preventing him from giving evidence within the meaning of s. 35(1)(b) the decision in *R v A* [1997] Crim LR 883 confirms an evidential burden is cast upon the defendant to prove his assertion. In *R v Friend* [1997] 2 Cr App R 231 Otton LJ observed:

> 'A physical condition might include an epileptic attack, a mental condition, latent schizophrenia where the experience of giving evidence might trigger a florid state. If it appears to the judge on the *voire dire* that such a physical or mental condition of the defendant makes it undesirable for him to give evidence, he will so rule. The inference cannot thereafter be drawn and he will so direct the jury.'

Where s. 35 has no application, the trial judge in a Crown Court trial must direct the jury not to draw any inference from the defendant's failure to give evidence which is in accordance with the position at common law (*R v Martinez-Tobon* [1994] 1 WLR 388).

26.5 DISCLOSING EVIDENCE OF THE DEFENDANT'S CHARACTER

While most judicial attention is directed towards the admission of a defendant's past bad character, it should not be forgotten that your client's good character, usually though not entirely meaning the absence of a criminal record, also has important evidential value.

26.5.1 THE DEFENDANT'S GOOD CHARACTER

Evidence of good character is always admissible on behalf of an accused to show the court that he is not the type of person who would commit the offence with which he is charged. In some instances, the absence of a 'past track record' is also relevant to an assessment of the defendant's credibility (i.e. whether he is likely to be telling the truth).

'Good character' will usually mean the absence of a criminal record, but particularly praiseworthy activities such as his military service record, or public service, or charitable acts may also be used to enhance your client's character.

The approach to be taken by the courts when dealing with a defendant of good character was laid down by the Court of Appeal in *R v Vye and Others* [1993] 97 Cr App R 134:

- A defendant with no convictions is entitled *per se* to a good character direction as to his propensity (i.e. the defendant is less likely to have committed this offence because he is a person of past good character). This direction must be given irrespective of whether or not the defendant gives evidence in the case.

- A defendant with no convictions is additionally entitled to a good character direction as to his credibility where, before trial, he has asserted his innocence either at the police station and/or has given evidence on oath at his trial.

In the Crown Court, the trial judge is required to direct the jury in accordance with the principles in *R v Vye*. A failure to give a good character direction will afford a convicted offender grounds to appeal against conviction. The same is of course true of summary trials, where it will be incumbent upon the defence advocate to remind the magistrates of the relevance of good character evidence.

The court retains discretion as to whether to give a direction in a case where an accused has no previous convictions, but admits acts of disreputable conduct in the course of the proceedings (*R v Aziz* [1995] 3 WLR 53). In *R v Hickmet* [1996] Crim LR 588, the Court of Appeal confirmed that a good character direction may still be given, albeit in a qualified form, in situations where any previous convictions of the defendant are spent within the definition of the Rehabilitation Act 1974 or are still current but are of a trivial or unrelated nature.

26.5.2 OBTAINING EVIDENCE OF GOOD CHARACTER

When engaging in pre-trial preparation it is extremely useful to obtain character evidence in support of a client who might qualify for a good character direction. Character evidence can be presented orally by calling a character witness or in a written witness statement where the prosecution is prepared to have the statement admitted under s. 9 CJA 1967 as hearsay (see Chapter 25). You will of course have had disclosure of your client's previous convictions (as part of the prosecution's obligations to provide pre-trial disclosure of evidence) if he has any, and you will therefore be in a position to assess whether your client is likely to be entitled to a good character direction.

26.6 ADDUCING EVIDENCE OF THE DEFENDANT'S BAD CHARACTER UNDER THE CRIMINAL JUSTICE ACT 2003

Part 11 of the CJA 2003 has introduced a comprehensive statutory framework for admitting evidence of bad character in criminal cases, covering both the defendant and non-defendant. The new law undermines many of the traditional immunities which generally gave the defendant a shield protecting him from having evidence of his bad character being disclosed to the court.

The previous law relating to the admissibility of a defendant's bad character has been abolished (s. 99 CJA 2003). The previous law, developed over many years, was reasonably clear. It was based on an exclusionary principle. Evidence of a defendant's past bad character was inadmissible for the purpose of showing that by reason of past offending, the defendant was likely to have acted in conformity and was therefore guilty of the current offence.

The justification for an exclusionary rule was based, for the most part, on protecting the defendant from the prejudice that such knowledge would engender in the minds of the jury or magistrates. On a charge of burglary, for example, where the defendant pleaded not guilty and the jury were told that the defendant had several previous convictions for offences of dishonesty, the jury might conclude that the defendant is guilty because he is the sort of person who would commit such acts. In other words the jury would attach too much significance to the fact of the defendant's past bad character and not enough to the evidence said to link the defendant to the actual offence. The position at common law was well summed-up by Lord Sumner in *Thompson v The King* [1918] AC 221:

> 'There is all the difference in the world between evidence proving the accused is a bad man and evidence proving that he is *the* man.'

The exclusionary common law rule did permit the admission of bad character evidence in certain, strictly defined circumstances. However, the exclusionary rule was seen, for the most part, as a key component to the defendant's right to a fair trial. The simple fact remains: the revelation of evidence of a defendant's past bad character is prejudicial and increases the defendant's chance of being convicted.

The CJA 2003 considerably extends the boundaries for admitting evidence of a defendant's bad character while seemingly providing few safeguards.

26.6. STATUTORY DEFINITION OF BAD CHARACTER

Section 98 CJA 2003 defines evidence of a person's bad character as 'evidence of, or of a disposition towards, misconduct on his part . . .'

The term 'misconduct' is further defined by s. 112 CJA 2003, as the commission of an offence or other 'reprehensible' behaviour.

The definition of bad character under the Act is wide and includes:

* evidence of the defendant's previous convictions;
* evidence of charges on which the defendant is being concurrently tried;
* evidence relating to an offence(s) with which the defendant has been charged but was not prosecuted; and
* evidence relating to an offence(s) with which the defendant has been charged but acquitted;
* evidence not amounting to criminal conduct but which nevertheless constitutes 'reprehensible' behaviour.

Section 98 goes onto say that the provisions of the Act *do not* apply to evidence of, or of a disposition towards, misconduct on his part which:

'(a) has to do with the alleged facts of the offence with which the defendant is charged, or

(b) is evidence of misconduct in connection with the investigation or prosecution of that offence.'

Evidence of misconduct going directly to the central facts in the case is not subject to the statutory regime governing the admission of bad character evidence under the CJA 2003. The admissibility of such evidence is governed simply by its relevance to the issues in the case. Consider the following examples:

Example 1

Nigel is charged with arson by starting a fire in a hostel for resettling young offenders in which he was living at the time of the alleged offence. The fire occurred shortly after a dispute between Nigel and a member of the hostel staff who accused Nigel of breaking the hostel's curfew rules. In proving the facts, the prosecutor will have to refer to the fact that Nigel was residing at a hostel for the resettling of young offenders. It has to do with the facts of the offence and therefore does not trigger the character provisions under the Act (s. 98(a)).

Example 2

Gary is accused of a serious offence of assault. The prosecution wishes to adduce evidence that Gary has tried to intimidate a prosecution witness in the case. Such evidence as the prosecution might have would be freely admissible as it is evidence connected with the prosecution of the offence (s. 98(b)).

26.6.2 GATEWAYS TO ADMISSION

Section 101(1) CJA 2003 is very significant. It is reproduced below in full. It provides a number of gateways through which evidence of a defendant's bad character can be admitted.

'Section 101 Defendant's bad character

(1) In criminal proceedings evidence of the defendant's bad character is admissible if, but only if—

(a) all parties to the proceedings agree to the evidence being admissible,

(b)   the evidence is adduced by the defendant himself or is given in answer to a question asked by him in cross-examination and intended to elicit it,

(c)   it is important explanatory evidence,

(d)   it is relevant to an important matter in issue between the defendant and the prosecution,

(e)   it has substantial probative value in relation to an important matter in issue between the defendant and a co-defendant,

(f)   it is evidence to correct a false impression given by the defendant, or

(g)   the defendant has made an attack on another person's character.

(2)   Sections 102 to 106 contain provisions supplementing subsection (1)

(3)   The court must not admit evidence under subsection (1)(d) or (g) if, on an application by the defendant to exclude it, it appears to the court that the admission of the evidence would have such an adverse effect on the fairness of the proceedings that the court ought not to admit it.

(4)   On an application to exclude evidence under subsection (3) the court must have regard, in particular, to the length of time between the matters to which that evidence relates and the matters which form the subject of the offence charged.'

Provided the evidence of bad character falls within one of the gateways, it is not necessary for a party to seek the permission of the court to adduce evidence of bad character. Is there any judicial discretion to exclude such evidence?

26.6.3   DISCRETION TO EXCLUDE EVIDENCE OF BAD CHARACTER

The answer to the above question is yes, but only in relation to gateways (d) and (g) and only upon application by the defence to have the evidence excluded. Section 101(3) permits the court to exclude evidence of bad character under either gateway (d) or (g), if the admission of the evidence would have an adverse effect on the fairness of the proceedings. The test for the exercise of this judicial discretion is the same as that exercised under s. 78 PACE (see Chapter 9). In exercising discretion the court is specifically required to have regard to the length of time that has passed since the bad character sought to be admitted was in fact committed (s. 101(4) CJA 2003).

   The discretion to exclude evidence of bad character contained in section 101(3) is specific to gateways (d) and (g). Does the discretion to exclude evidence also apply to the other gateways for admitting bad character? There is nothing in the 2003 Act which indicates a clear parliamentary intention to limit the operation of s. 78 PACE or the common law discretion to exclude any prosecution evidence, the prejudicial effect of which outweighs its probative value (s. 82(3) PACE). In the absence of an express provision excluding the operation of s. 78 PACE, it must be assumed that s. 78 discretion, as well as the common law discretion, apply to the admission of all bad character under the 2003 Act. This is supported by dicta in the Court of Appeal's decision in *R v Highton; R v Van Nguyen; R v Carp* [2005] 1 WLR 3472:

'However, it is right that we should say that, without having heard full argument, our inclination is to say that section 78 provides an additional protection to a defendant. In light of this preliminary view as to the effect of section 78, judges may consider that it is a sensible precaution, when making rulings as to the use of evidence of bad character, to apply the provisions of section 78 and exclude evidence where it would be appropriate to do so under section 78, pending a definitive ruling to the contrary. Adopting this course will avoid any risk of injustice to the defendant . . . and any risk of a court failing to comply with Article 6.'

26.6.4 PROCEDURE FOR SEEKING ADMISSION OF EVIDENCE OF A DEFENDANT'S PAST BAD CHARACTER

Where the prosecution seeks to admit evidence of the defendant's bad character under gateways (c)–(g), it is required to give notice in accordance with Crim PR, Part 35. The party seeking to adduce evidence of bad character must serve notice in the prescribed form in accordance within time limits laid down in Part 35. For indictable offences the notice should be not more than 14 days after service of the 'case sent bundle.' The defendant has 14 days in which to give notice in the prescribed form if he opposes the application to have the evidence admitted. In the magistrates' court, the notice of application to have evidence of bad character admitted must be given at the same time as the prosecutor complies or purports to comply with his initial disclosure obligations under s. 3 Criminal Procedure and Investigations Act 1996. Provision is made to enable an application to be made orally and out of time where the interests of justice require it.

Where a dispute arises about the admissibility of evidence of past bad character in a case to be tried on indictment, the matter will be determined by the judge in the absence of the jury. The matter will be raised and possibly resolved at the Plea and Case Management Hearing (PCMH). (See Chapter 19, paragraph 19.8.) A judge is able to give a binding ruling on a point of law at the PCMH. A binding ruling in favour of admitting evidence of a defendant's bad character may persuade a defendant to plead guilty. The position is the same in magistrates' courts, in that s. 45 (Sch. 3) of the Courts Act 2003 allows a magistrates' court to make binding rulings of law at a pre-trial hearing.

When making a ruling on the admissibility of bad character evidence, the court must give reasons (s. 110 CJA 2003).

Our case study *R v Lenny Whyte* includes an application by the prosecution to admit evidence of Lenny Whyte's criminal convictions under s. 101(1) CJA 2003. The relevant documentation can be accessed from our Online Resource Centre.

Below we look in detail at the gateways for admission of the defendant's bad character under s. 101.

26.6.5 SECTION 101(1)(a) CJA 2003

All parties to the proceedings agree to the evidence of the defendant's bad character being admitted.

26.6.6 SECTION 101(1)(b) CJA 2003

Evidence of the defendant's bad character is adduced by the defendant himself or is given in answer to a question asked by him in cross-examination and intended to elicit it.

Sections 101(1)(a) and(b) are largely self-explanatory. In relation to s. 101(b), there may be tactical advantages in a defendant choosing to adduce evidence of his bad character in a case where the prosecution has chosen not to adduce it as part of its case.

26.6.7 SECTION 101(1)(c) CJA 2003 – EVIDENCE OF THE DEFENDANT'S BAD CHARACTER AS IMPORTANT EXPLANATORY EVIDENCE

This gateway is further defined in s. 102, and is available only to the prosecution.

'Section 102 "Important explanatory evidence"

For the purposes of section 101(1)(c) evidence is important explanatory evidence if–

(a) without it, the court or jury would find it impossible or difficult properly to understand other evidence in the case, and

(b) its value for understanding the case as a whole is substantial.'

In some cases it will be necessary for the prosecution to give explanatory background information about the offence, which may result in part or the whole of the defendant's bad character being disclosed. Section 101(1)(c) CJA 2003 gives statutory effect to the previous position at common law. Background evidence was admitted in the pre-2003 CJA case of *R v Stuart Campbell* [2005] EWCA Crim 248. C was convicted of the murder of Danielle Jones, his 15-year-old niece. Her body has never been found. There was circumstantial evidence implicating C in the well-publicised disappearance of Danielle. Items of underwear and stockings containing Danielle and C's DNA were found in C's loft. C had denied any inappropriate relationship with his niece in interview but had kept a diary containing numerous references to Danielle. The prosecution maintained that C was sexually infatuated with Danielle and had a constant need to photograph her. When she grew tired of C's advances, this gave him the motive to murder her. A selection of photographs and downloaded images of teenage girls in provocative poses, some very similar in appearance to Danielle, were admitted as background evidence in this case. The admissibility of the evidence was disputed as being more prejudicial than probative on the critical issue of who murdered Danielle. The Court of Appeal held the evidence was rightly admitted as background evidence as it put the other evidence in the case (the diary, the stockings and the defendant's lies in interview) into context. It constituted, in other words, necessary background evidence, without which the jury would be receiving an incomplete picture.

The Court of Appeal's decision in *R v Edwards; Fysh; Duggan and Chohan* [2006] 1 Cr App R 3 (specifically the appeal of Chohan) affords a useful illustration of the gateway 101(1)(c). Chohan was charged with burglary. He denied the offence. The main evidence against him came from an eyewitness who formally identified him at an identification parade. In fact, the parade was not convened for some considerable time as Chohan left the country during the investigation. The identification of Chohan was based on recognition. The female eyewitness claimed Chohan had been her drug dealer. Chohan denied involvement in the burglary and accused the eyewitness of fabricating her evidence because he had terminated a sexual relationship with her, some time previously. Chohan denied ever having supplied drugs to her. The supply of drugs clearly constituted reprehensible behaviour. The trial judge permitted the evidence to be adduced under gateway 101(1)(c) as it comprised important explanatory evidence. It explained the basis of the eye-witness's identification and why she was so confident that her identification of Chohan was accurate.

Evidence of misconduct which has to do with the alleged facts of the offence with which the defendant is charged (see s. 98(a) above) will often be difficult to distinguish from background evidence sought to be admitted under s. 101(1)(c), Example 1 (above) affords a good illustration of this point.

26.7 SECTION 101(1)(d)

Evidence of the defendant's bad character is relevant to an important matter in issue between the defendant and the prosecution.

This very important gateway is further defined in s. 103 and is available only to the prosecution.

'Section 103 "Matter in issue between the defendant and the prosecution"

(1) For the purposes of section 101(1)(d) the matters in issue between the defendant and the prosecution include—

(a) the question whether the defendant has a propensity to commit offences of the kind with which he is charged, except where his having such a propensity makes it no more likely that he is guilty of the offence;

(b) the question whether the defendant has a propensity to be untruthful, except where it is not suggested that the defendant's case is untruthful in any respect.

(2) Where subsection (1)(a) applies, a defendant's propensity to commit offences of the kind with which he is charged may (without prejudice to any other way of doing so) be established by evidence that he has been convicted of–

    (a) an offence of the same description as the one with which he is charged, or

    (b) an offence of the same category as the one with which he is charged.

(3) Subsection (2) does not apply in the case of a particular defendant if the court is satisfied, by reason of the length of time since the conviction or for any other reason, that it would be unjust for it to apply in his case.

(4) For the purposes of subsection (2)–

    (a) two offences are of the same description as each other if the statement of the offence in a written charge or indictment would, in each case, be in the same terms;

    (b) two offences are of the same category as each other if they belong to the same category of offences prescribed for the purposes of this section by an order made by the Secretary of State.

(5) A category prescribed by an order under subsection (4)(b) must consist of offences of the same type.

(6) Only prosecution evidence is admissible under section 101(1)(d).

An important matter in issue between the prosecution and the defence is defined in s. 103 to include:

- the question whether the defendant has a propensity to commit offences of the kind with which he is currently charged (unless the propensity makes him no more likely to be guilty of the offence with which he is charged); and/or

- the question whether the defendant has a propensity to be untruthful (unless it is not suggested that the defendant's case is untruthful).

This gateway for admission is very significant because it makes it considerably easier for a defendant's bad character to be admitted than was previously the case under the common law. Section 103 sweeps away the old provisions relating to the admissibility of similar fact evidence. The new test (the evidence must be relevant to an important matter in issue) implies a much lower threshold of relevance than was the case under the similar fact evidence rule where the probative value of the bad character evidence had to be sufficiently high to overcome its prejudicial effect. Previous convictions which fall within s. 103(2) may now be admitted against the defendant, irrespective of whether they have probative force on the basis that they are simply relevant to an important matter in issue between the prosecution and the defence, subject to the discretion to exclude under s. 101(3).

In *R v Hanson*; *R v Gilmore*; *R v Pickstone* [2005] 2 Cr App R 21, the Court of Appeal sent out a message of restraint to prosecutors in the following terms:

> 'The starting point should be for judges and practitioners to bear in mind that Parliament's purpose in the legislation, as we divine it from the terms of the Act, was to assist in the evidence based conviction of the guilty, without putting those who are not guilty at risk of conviction by prejudice. It is accordingly to be hoped that prosecution applications to adduce such evidence will not be made routinely, simply because a defendant has previous convictions, but will be based on the particular circumstances of each case.'

26.7.1 **PROPENSITY TO COMMIT OFFENCES OF THE KIND WITH WHICH HE IS CHARGED**

By virtue of s. 103(2) CJA 2003, propensity may be established by evidence that the defendant has been convicted of an offence of the same description as that with which he is charged or has been convicted of an offence of the same category as that with which he is charged. Section 103(2) does not apply if a court concludes that by reason of length of time since conviction or for any other reason, it would be unjust to apply this method to inferring propensity from the defendant's criminal record.

26.7.2 **WHAT IS AN OFFENCE OF THE SAME DESCRIPTION/CATEGORY?**

An offence will be of the same description if the statement of offence would in each case be the same (s. 103(4)(a)). Thus for example, if X is facing a charge of assault occasioning actual bodily harm contrary to s. 47 Offences Against the Person Act 1861 and has a previous conviction for a s. 47 assault, this would constitute an offence of the same description and would therefore be admissible to show X's propensity to commit violent assault.

Offences of the same category have to be prescribed by the Secretary of State (s. 103 (4)(b)). Currently there are two categories of offences that fall within the same category. They are theft and child sex offences:

> 'The purpose of the Order . . . is to ensure that when a defendant being tried for either a theft or child sex offence has a previous conviction for an offence which falls within the same category, the strong presumption should be that the conviction should be revealed to the jury.'

Theft offences of the same category will include theft, robbery, burglary, aggravated burglary, taking a motor car without consent, aggravated vehicle taking, handling stolen goods, going equipped to steal, making off without payment and inchoate offences of the same description. In relation to sexual offences against persons under the age of 16, the Order includes a full list of all such offences in Part 2. They include rape, indecent assault, unlawful sexual intercourse and incest, together with the new offences involving children under the Sexual Offences Act 2003.

26.7.3 **PROVING PROPENSITY IN OTHER WAYS**

Proof of propensity to commit an offence of the kind with which the defendant is charged is not confined to previous convictions for offences of the same description or category. For example, Tina is charged with a serious assault arising out of an incident in a nightclub. She claims to have acted in self-defence. She has previous convictions for affray and for a public order offence under s. 5 Public Order Act 1986. Although Tina's previous convictions are not of the same description or category as the current charge, the prosecution could legitimately argue that they indicate a propensity on Tina's part to engage in acts of violence and public disturbance, making her defence less credible. Her previous convictions are therefore relevant to an important matter in issue between the prosecution and the defence.

In fact, evidence of a defendant's propensity is not restricted to proof of previous convictions *per se*. Section 103(2) specifically stipulates that a defendant's propensity to commit offences of the kind with which he is charged can be proved in other ways. Propensity could be established by proof of conduct that is not criminal (provided it is reprehensible), and indeed it could stem from a previous acquittal if the evidence is relevant. Two pre-2003 Act cases afford good illustrations.

- *R v Butler* (1987) 84 Cr App R 12. In this case, the defendant denied indecently assaulting a woman in a very degrading manner in the back of the woman's car, maintaining the woman's identification of him was mistaken. The prosecution was allowed to adduce evidence from the defendant's former girlfriend of the degrading and very similar sexual acts she had allowed him to perform on her. Although the evidence disclosed no criminal acts on the defendant's part (they being consensual), it provided significant probative value on the issue of the accuracy of the victim's identification of her attacker.

- In *R v Z* [2000] 3 WLR 117, the defendant denied a charge of rape, maintaining his victim had consented. Evidence was adduced of the fact that he had previously been tried and acquitted of rape in three separate trials, having used the same defence in each.

In *R v Weir* [2005] EWCA Crim 2866, the Court of Appeal held that propensity could be established by proof of a caution in relation to a particular matter and in *R v Smith* [2005] EWCA

3244, from an allegation made by an alleged victim in respect of which the defendant had never been tried. In this case the Court of Appeal stipulated that it is for the judge to police the gateway, i.e. to determine admissibility and the relevance of the evidence, it is the job of the jury to evaluate the evidence once it is admitted.

26.7.4 CHALLENGING PROPENSITY EVIDENCE

The effect of s. 103(2) is that previous convictions of the same description/category are taken to show the defendant's propensity. This assumption should not go unchallenged by the defence. The defence should require the court to ask itself: 'Is the defendant's propensity (as identified by the prosecution) truly relevant to the facts in issue?' Another way to express this might be: 'Does the defendant's propensity make it more likely that he committed the offence?' Even if the answer to either of these questions is yes, the defence should still apply to have the evidence excluded on the basis that it would have an adverse effect on the fairness of the proceedings. The nature of the defence relied on will be significant in determining the relevance and therefore the admissibility of bad character evidence.

Issues of propensity to commit offences of the kind with which the defendant is charged will involve difficult questions of fact for the judge/magistrates. It may be insufficient for the prosecution to simply rely on the defendant's criminal record of conviction as the court may need to hear the facts behind the conviction in order to determine its true relevance and whether it is indicative of a propensity on the defendant's part. Suppose a defendant is facing a disputed allegation of common assault but happens to have a previous conviction for assault contrary to s. 47 Offences Against the Person Act 1861. This is clearly an offence of the same description. However, an assault can be committed in different ways and for many different reasons.

26.7.5 CASE LAW GUIDANCE ON S. 101(1)(d) AND THE ISSUE OF PROPENSITY

In one of the first key decisions on the bad character provisions under the 2003 CJA, the Court of Appeal has provided the following guidance in *R v Hanson; R v Gilmore; R v Pickstone* [2005] 2 Cr App R 21:

1. Where the prosecution relies on the defendant's propensity to commit offences, there are three questions to be answered:

    (i)   Does the history of conviction(s) establish a propensity to commit offences of the kind charged?

    (ii) Does that propensity make it more likely that the defendant committed the offence charged?

    (iii) Is it unjust to rely on the conviction(s) of the same description or category; and, in any event, will the proceedings be unfair if they are admitted?

2. Propensity is not confined to offences of the same description or category. As such s. 103(2) is not exhaustive of the types of convictions which might be relied on to show evidence of propensity to commit offences of the same kind. Equally, simply because an offence falls within the same description or category is not necessarily sufficient to show a propensity.

3. There is no minimum number of events that are required to show propensity. The fewer the number of convictions, the weaker the evidence of propensity is likely to be. A single previous conviction may show evidence of propensity where the offence discloses unusual tendencies or the modus operandi discloses significant features such as to give the previous misconduct probative force.

'Child sexual abuse, or fire setting, are comparatively clear examples of such unusual behaviour but we attempt no exhaustive list. Circumstances demonstrating probative force are not confined to those sharing striking similarity. So, a single conviction for shoplifting will not, without more, be admissible to show propensity to steal. But if the modus operandi has significant features shared by the offence charged, it may show propensity.'

4. Having regard to the exercise of judicial discretion under s. 101(3), and under s. 103 (3), the court should take into consideration:

   (i) the degree of similarity between the previous conviction and the offence charged, albeit they are both within the same description or prescribed category. For example, theft and assault occasioning actual bodily harm may each embrace a wide spectrum of conduct. This does not, however, mean that what used to be referred as striking similarity must be shown before convictions become admissible;

   (ii) the respective gravity of the past and present offences;

   (iii) a key factor will be an assessment of the strength of the prosecution's case. If there is little or no evidence, it is unlikely to be just to admit a defendant's previous convictions.

5. The date of the commission of an offence is often going to be more significant than the date of conviction. Old convictions, with no special features shared with the offence charged, are likely to have an adverse effect on the fairness of the proceedings.

6. It will often be necessary, before determining admissibility and even when considering offences of the same description or category, to examine each individual conviction rather than merely to look at the name of the offence or at the defendant's record as a whole.

7. The sentence passed will not normally be probative or admissible at the behest of the Crown, though it may be at the behest of the defence.

8. Where past events are disputed, the judge should be careful not to permit the trial to drift into satellite litigation by a prolonged investigation into the circumstances of the past misconduct:

'. . . the Crown needs to decide, at the time of giving notice of the application, whether it proposes to rely simply upon the fact of conviction or also upon the circumstances of it. The former may be enough when the circumstances of the conviction are sufficiently apparent from its description, to justify a finding that it can establish propensity, either to commit an offence of the kind charged or to be untruthful and that the requirements of s. 103(3) and 101(3) can, subject to any particular matter raised on behalf of the defendant, be satisfied. For example, a succession of convictions for dwelling-house burglary, where the same is now charged, may well call for no further evidence than proof of the fact of the convictions. But where, as will often be the case, the Crown needs and proposes to rely on the circumstances of the previous convictions, those circumstances and the manner in which they are to be proved must be set out in the application. There is a similar obligation of frankness upon the defendant, which will be reinforced by the general obligation contained in the new Criminal Procedure Rules to give active assistance to the court in its case management (see r.3.3). Routine applications by defendants for disclosure of the circumstances of previous convictions are likely to be met by a requirement that the request be justified by identification of the reason why it is said that those circumstances may show the convictions to be inadmissible. We would expect the relevant circumstances of previous convictions generally to be capable of agreement, and that, subject to the trial judge's ruling as to admissibility, they will be put before the jury by way of admission. Even where the circumstances are genuinely in dispute, we would expect the minimum indisputable facts to be thus admitted. It will be very rare indeed for it to be necessary for the judge to hear evidence before ruling on admissibility under this Act.

9. The importance of correctly directing the jury is also stressed. In any case where bad character is admitted, the jury should be instructed not to place undue reliance on bad character evidence:

'Evidence of bad character cannot be used simply to bolster a weak case, or to prejudice the minds of a jury against a defendant. In particular, the jury should be directed; that they should not conclude that the defendant is guilty or untruthful merely because he has these convictions. That, although the convictions may show a propensity, this does not mean that he has committed this offence or been untruthful in this case; that whether they in fact show a propensity is for them to decide; that they must take into account what the defendant has said about his previous convictions; and that, although they are entitled, if they find propensity as shown, to take this into account when determining guilt, propensity is only one relevant factor and they must assess its significance in the light of all the other evidence in the case.'

10.   If a judge has directed himself or herself correctly, the Court of Appeal will be very slow to interfere with a ruling either as to admissibility.

What of the specific appeals in *Hanson?*
In *Hanson*, the charge was theft of money from the living accommodation above a public house. The circumstantial evidence linking Hanson to the crime clearly indicated he had a case to answer, although it was not overwhelming. He denied the offence. He had a string of previous convictions for dishonesty, including dwelling-house burglary, theft from premises, a previous conviction for robbery and aggravated vehicle taking. On the facts in this case, the Court of Appeal observed:

'Convictions for handling and aggravated vehicle taking, although within the theft category, do not, in our judgment, show, without more pertinent information, propensity to burgle as indicted or to steal, to which the applicant pleaded guilty. The applicant's robbery conviction, albeit also within the theft category, might, had it been analysed, have been regarded as being so prejudicial as to adversely affect the fairness of the proceedings in relation to the offence charged. But the applicant had a considerable number of convictions for burglary and theft from private property that were plainly properly admissible to show propensity to commit an offence of the kind here charged.'

In *Gilmore*, an offence of theft was denied. Gilmore was arrested in the early hours of the morning. He had in his possession a bag containing very recently stolen items. Gilmore claimed to have come across the items innocently, believing them to be rubbish. The evidence linking him to the theft was strong. Three recent previous convictions for theft were properly admitted. They were indicative of a recent propensity to steal.

In *Pickstone*, the charges included the rape and indecent assault of P's step-daughter. P denied the offences. There was medical evidence to support the fact of sexual interference. P stated the girl was making up the allegation against him. The respective credibility of the complainant and the defendant was very much in issue. Nine years previous to the current allegation, P had been convicted of the indecent assault of an 11-year-old girl. The trial judge admitted the previous conviction under gateways (d) and (g). He expressly took into account the length of time since the previous conviction, concluding the 'defendant's sexual mores and motivations are not necessarily affected by the passage of time'. In this context, the admission of the evidence under gateways (d) and (g) would not adversely affect the fairness of the proceedings.

26.7.6   A MATTER IN ISSUE CAN INCLUDE THE QUESTION WHETHER THE DEFENDANT HAS A PROPENSITY TO BE UNTRUTHFUL

Section 101(1)(d) CJA 2003 further permits the prosecution to adduce evidence of a defendant's bad character where the defendant's propensity to be untruthful is deemed an important matter in issue between the prosecution and the defence. What is meant by a propensity to be untruthful?

By pleading not guilty, the defendant cannot be regarded as being untruthful! Will evidence of a defendant's previous convictions for shoplifting and theft become routinely admissible to show a propensity on the defendant's part to be untruthful? The Explanatory Notes to the

2003 Act suggest it should be confined to previous convictions for such offences as fraud and perjury. The exclusionary discretion that can be triggered by the defence under s. 101(3) will be a key safeguard in protecting the defendant from the prejudice that could result.

In *R v Hanson* [2005] 2 Cr App R 21, the Court of Appeal has answered some of the points raised above. A propensity to be untruthful is not the same as a propensity to dishonesty (s. 103(1)(b)). Consequently, the prosecution ought not simply to adduce evidence of previous convictions for dishonesty for the explicit purpose of showing the accused has a propensity for untruthfulness:

> 'Thus previous convictions, whether for offences of dishonesty or otherwise, are therefore only likely to be capable of showing a propensity to be untruthful where, in the present case, truthfulness is an issue and, in the earlier case, either there was a plea of not guilty and the defendant gave an account, on arrest, in interview, or in evidence, which the jury must have disbelieved, or the way in which the offence was committed shows a propensity for untruthfulness, for example, by the making of false representations.'

In considering a defendant's criminal record, it is important to check whether the defendant was actually found guilty or pleaded guilty. If he was found guilty, did he actually give evidence on oath?

The following factual examples are designed to illustrate the application of gateway 101(1)(d), based on the guidance available to date.

Example 1

Andrew is charged with assault occasioning actual bodily harm on his neighbour. He pleads not guilty, maintaining he acted in self defence. Andrew has three previous convictions for theft. Could these convictions be admitted as evidence of Andrew's propensity to be untruthful?

In the light of the statements in *Hanson*, the answer is arguably no. A propensity towards dishonesty is not the same thing as a propensity to be untruthful. It would be important to ascertain whether Andrew pleaded guilty to any or all of his previous offences or was found guilty after having given evidence on oath.

In the above example assume instead that Andrew has a previous conviction for s. 20 violent assault six years earlier. He was involved in a fracas in a public house following a football match and pleaded guilty. The prosecution would say that he has a previous conviction for an offence of the same description/type which shows Andrew has a propensity to use violence. The defence should oppose the application to have this previous conviction admitted. Applying the dicta in *Hanson* (this being one previous conviction only with no special feature), can this one previous conviction amount to propensity? It should also be noted that the manner in which the earlier assault came to be committed is somewhat different to the present alleged assault. In addition, regard should be had to s. 103(3) – this previous conviction is six years old. Aside from challenging propensity, the defence should make an application under s. 101(3) to have it excluded on the basis that its admission would have an adverse effect on the fairness of the proceedings. In exercising discretion regard should be had to the guidance in *Hanson*. In particular, the previous offence was more serious than that currently alleged and that the circumstances were different. A pertinent factor will be an assessment of how strong the prosecution's case is, as bad character evidence should not be adduced to bolster an evidentially weak case.

If the evidence was admitted, the judge would need to carefully direct the jury not to place too much reliance on the fact of previous convictions.

Example 2

Ethan is charged with burglary. He denies the offence, maintaining a defence of mistaken identity. He intends to call his girlfriend as an alibi. Ethan has an extensive criminal record which includes a conviction for a violent robbery four years before, and several previous convictions for theft, burglary and possession of drugs over the past 12 years. Will the fact of these previous convictions be admissible?

The prosecution will want to adduce Ethan's previous convictions for dishonesty related offences under s. 101(1)(d), both as evidence of Ethan's propensity to commit offences of the kind with which he is charged and as evidence of his propensity to be untruthful. The previous convictions for robbery, theft and burglary are all offences of the same description/category as the current offence. The assumption will therefore be that they show Ethan's propensity to commit offences of dishonesty.

What can the defence argue in this situation? How relevant is Ethan's propensity to the issue of whether the witness's identification is correct or not, especially as Ethan denies being at the scene? Would it not adversely affect the fairness of the proceedings if they were to be admitted? Wouldn't the jury inevitably disregard the evidence of identification and conclude Ethan is guilty because of his track record? If Ethan's defence is simply one of mistaken identity, in what sense is he putting forward an untruthful defence? Applying the dicta in *Hanson*, previous convictions for offences of dishonesty do not necessarily indicate a propensity to be untruthful. While the previous convictions for theft and burglary may well be admitted on the issue of his propensity, the admission of the robbery conviction might be regarded as being particularly prejudicial. *Hanson* suggests the court should have regard to the respective gravity of past and present offences and the strength of the prosecution's case.

Once again, if the evidence was admitted, the judge would need to carefully direct the jury not to place too much reliance on the fact of previous convictions.

🔆 Example 3

Frank is charged with sexually assaulting his nine-year-old nephew. He denies the offence, maintaining that the child is lying. Frank received a caution 18 months earlier for possession of indecent photographs of young boys which were found on his computer. He only accepted the caution because he felt under pressure and wanted to avoid unwanted publicity as he was teaching at that time. He does not know how the images appeared on his computer. Can the prosecution use this fact in evidence against him at his trial for sexual assault?

The prosecution would argue that the caution suggests Frank has a paedophilic disposition, making it less likely that the nephew is making up the allegation. Although he has only a caution recorded against his name, *Hanson* suggests that sex offences involving children are indicative of unusual behaviour.

The defence advocate might argue that the earlier offence is very different to that currently alleged, and for this reason its relevance in the context of the current case must be doubted. Furthermore, there is doubt as to the safety and reliability of the previous caution. Consequently, the admission of such evidence would prejudice Frank's right to a fair trial on the basis that its prejudicial value exceeds its probative effect. Does it make it more likely that the boy is telling the truth?

26.8 SECTION 101(1)(e)

Evidence of a defendant's bad character has substantial probative value in relation to an important issue between the defendant and a co-defendant.

Section 101(1)(e) CJA 2003 is defined further in s. 104, and applies only to a co-defendant.

'Section 104 "Matter in issue between the defendant and a co-defendant"

(1) Evidence which is relevant to the question whether the defendant has a propensity to be untruthful is admissible on that basis under section 101(1)(e) only if the nature or conduct of his defence is such as to undermine the co-defendant's defence.

(2) Only evidence—

(a) which is to be (or has been) adduced by the co-defendant, or

(b) which a witness is to be invited to give (or has given) in cross-examination by the co-defendant

is admissible under section 101(1)(e).'

This subsection may be invoked where co-accused (A) wishes to lead evidence of his fellow co-accused (B's) propensity to commit offences of a certain kind for the express purpose of showing that it was more likely that B committed the offence in question. A good example of the application of this principle is provided by the decision in *R v Randall* [2004] 1 Cr App R 26. In *Randall*, it was not entirely clear which of the co-accused had inflicted the final, fatal injury. Each blamed the other. Co-accused A sought to introduce B's previous convictions for serious violence to suggest that B was more likely to have inflicted the fatal injury. By contrast, A's previous convictions were for minor offences. The House of Lords quashed A's conviction, maintaining the trial judge should have directed the jury that B's criminal past was relevant to A's defence, and that they could consider B's past when determining the involvement of each in the offence. The key determinate is whether the evidence has substantial probative value on an important matter in issue between co-defendants.

Where one co-accused wishes to adduce evidence of the other's propensity to be untruthful, s. 104(1) specifically stipulates that this will only be allowed where the nature and conduct of the co-accused's defence undermines the defence of his fellow co-accused.

It is assumed that this provision will be invoked on the same basis as the previous law, under s. 1(3)(iii) Criminal Evidence Act 1898. Under the 1898 Act, (B) would lose his shield against the revelation of his past bad character, where, during examination-in-chief or in cross-examination, B's evidence strengthened the prosecution's case against (A) or undermined A's defence. A good illustration is provided by the pre-2003 Act case of *Murdoch v Taylor* [1965] AC 574. In this case, the accused B was charged, together with another A, with handling stolen goods. B testified that he had no knowledge as to what was in a box he had received, because the contents of the box were nothing to do with him but were the sole responsibility of A. The trial judge ruled that B had lost his shield under s. 1(3)(iii) CEA 1898, and that therefore A had the right to cross-examine B on his previous convictions. B appealed against his conviction, contending he had not given evidence against A and that he had not intended to shift the blame from himself onto A. Affirming the conviction, the House of Lords held that, notwithstanding B's lack of motive, his evidence had strengthened the prosecution case against A and had by implication alleged that it was A alone who was the handler of the stolen goods.

The following guidelines are taken from the pre-2003 Act case of *R v Varley* [1982] 2 All ER 519 which, it is submitted, will continue to apply to gateway (e).

- It has to be decided objectively whether the evidence either supports the prosecution case in a material respect or undermines the defence of the co-accused.

- As regards undermining a co-accused's defence, care must be taken to see that the evidence clearly undermines the defence. Inconvenience to or inconsistency with the other's defence is not of itself sufficient.

- Mere denial of participation in a joint venture is not of itself sufficient to rank as evidence against the co-defendant. For the proviso to apply, such denial must lead to the conclusion that if the witness did not participate then it must have been the other who did.

- Where the one defendant asserts or in due course would assert one view of the joint venture, which is directly contradicted, such evidence may be evidence against the co-defendant.

The following should be noted about s. 101(1)(e) CJA 2003:

- Where the grounds for admitting evidence of a co-accused's bad character are satisfied, there is no discretion to disallow cross-examination (the safeguard in this respect is that the evidence must have substantial probative value in relation to an important matter in issue between the co-accused).

• Evidence of a bad character disclosed under this gateway is not limited to simply undermining a co-accused's credibility as a witness, and may therefore (subject to how the judge chooses to direct the jury) be used as evidence going towards the co-accused's guilt.

Consider the following example of the potential operation of s.101(1)(e) CJA 2003.

Example

Wayne and Jordan are jointly charged with murder. The prosecution allege that the victim was fatally wounded as a result of being knifed by one or both of the defendants. Wayne and Jordan are pleading not guilty and are running cut-throat defences by blaming each other. Wayne has several previous convictions. Last year he was convicted of possession of an offensive weapon, namely a knuckle-duster. Five years previously, following a trial at which he gave evidence on oath, he was convicted of robbery, during which an iron-bar was used to inflict a serious injury on a security guard. Wayne has several previous convictions for theft, deception and burglary over a ten-year period. In his examination-in-chief, Wayne states that it was Jordan who knifed the victim. Jordan has one recent previous conviction for theft and a conviction for affray four years previously in respect of which he pleaded guilty.

Jordan's counsel may seek to cross-examine Wayne about his previous convictions on the basis that:

• Wayne's previous convictions have substantial probative value in relation to an important issue between the co-accused – i.e. the identity of the person who inflicted the fatal knife injury on the deceased; and

• in giving evidence, Wayne has undermined Jordan's defence.

Provided these conditions are satisfied, the court has no discretion to prevent Jordan from adducing evidence of Wayne's previous convictions. The bad character evidence is arguably relevant both to undermining Wayne's credibility as a witness (as his previous convictions show that he has a propensity to be dishonest) and to the likelihood that it was more likely to have been Wayne who inflicted the fatal stab wound as his previous recent conviction for possession of an offensive weapon and his conviction for a violent robbery indicate a propensity to commit violent assaults.

For a case that illustrates the application of gateway (e), see *R v Edwards; Rowlands; McClean; Gray and Smith* [2005] EWCA Crim 3244.

26.9 SECTION 101(1)(f)

Evidence of the defendant's bad character is admissible to correct a false impression given by the defendant.

Section 101(1)(f) CJA 2003 is further defined by s. 105 and is available only to the prosecution:

'Section 105 "Evidence to correct a false impression"

(1) For the purposes of section 101(1)(f)–

    (a) the defendant gives a false impression if he is responsible for the making of an express or implied assertion which is apt to give the court or jury a false or misleading impression about the defendant;

     (b) evidence to correct such an impression is evidence which has probative value in correcting it.

  (2) A defendant is treated as being responsible for the making of an assertion if—

     (a) the assertion is made by the defendant in the proceedings (whether or not in evidence given by him),

     (b) the assertion was made by the defendant—

        (i)   on being questioned under caution, before charge, about the offence with which he is charged, or

        (ii) on being charged with the offence or officially informed that he might be prosecuted for it, and evidence of the assertion is given in the proceedings,

     (c) the assertion is made by a witness called by the defendant,

     (d) the assertion is made by any witness in cross-examination in response to a question asked by the defendant that is intended to elicit it, or is likely to do so, or

     (e) the assertion was made by any person out of court, and the defendant adduces evidence of it in the proceedings.

  (3) A defendant who would otherwise be treated as responsible for the making of an assertion shall not be so treated if, or to the extent that, he withdraws it or disassociates himself from it.

  (4) Where it appears to the court that a defendant, by means of his conduct (other than the giving of evidence) in the proceedings, is seeking to give the court or jury an impression about himself that is false or misleading, the court may if it appears just to do so treat the defendant as being responsible for the making of an assertion which is apt to give that impression.

  (5) In subsection (4) 'conduct' includes appearance or dress.

  (6) Evidence is admissible under section 101(1)(f) only if it goes no further than is necessary to correct the false impression.

  (7) Only prosecution evidence is admissible under section 101(1)(f).'

A defendant gives a false impression if he is responsible for the making of an express or implied assertion which is apt to give the court a false or misleading impression about him. A defendant can create a false impression not only by what he says on oath but also through his conduct in the proceedings (s. 105(4)). As with all the gateways, it applies irrespective of whether the defendant gives evidence in his defence. An assertion extends to any false assertion that forms part of the defence case whether asserted at trial or even before trial (s. 105(2)(b)). An assertion made at the police station can therefore trigger the opening of this gateway. A defendant is given the opportunity to avoid this gateway for admission if he withdraws or disassociates himself from the assertion (s. 105(3)). In *Renda* [2005] EWCA Crim 2826, gateway (f) was triggered at the police station when R made false statements regarding his work history. The Court of Appeal held that a concession extracted from a defendant in cross-examination will not amount to a withdrawal or disassociation from a previously made misleading statement.

Evidence is admissible only to the extent necessary to correct the false impression (s. 105(6)). The prosecution may only introduce evidence of the defendant's bad character sufficient to rebut the false impression that was made about the defendant's character. In many cases it will not be necessary for the whole of the defendant's bad character to be disclosed.

There is nothing in the Act which suggests that, having adduced evidence of the defendant's bad character under this gateway, the court cannot use the information to infer guilt. Equally, there is nothing to prevent the judge from directing the jury to make limited evidential use of such evidence. The availability of judicial discretion under s. 101(3) does not apply to this gateway, although there is nothing in the Act which restricts the application of s. 78 PACE and the common law exercise of discretion under s. 82(3) PACE.

🔆 Example

Saeeda is charged with handling a consignment of stolen designer clothes. Both during the police investigation and at trial, Saeeda asserts that she would never do anything dishonest where her business interests are concerned. To rebut this false assertion about her unimpeachable business ethics, the prosecution wish to put in evidence Saeeda's conviction for a VAT fraud committed while she was a director of an unrelated business venture six years ago. The prosecution would be able to put Saeeda's conviction into evidence in order to rebut the misleading impression she has created as regards her business affairs. Had Saeeda made her assertion solely in the course of the interview, the gateway could still be triggered by the investigating officer giving evidence of the assertion in interview. In either instance, Saeeda should be advised to withdraw the statement she made in interview before trial. In these circumstances the gateway under s. 101(1)(f) would not be triggered.

26.10 SECTION 101(1)(g)

Evidence of the defendant's bad character is admissible after the defendant has made an attack on another person's character.

This is another significant gateway for the prosecution. The gateway is further defined in s. 106:

'Section 106 "Attack on another person's character"

(1) For the purposes of section 101(1)(g) a defendant makes an attack on another person's character if—

    (a) he adduces evidence attacking the other person's character, or

    (b) he (or any legal representative appointed under section 38(4) of the Youth Justice and Criminal Evidence Act 1999 (c. 23) to cross-examine a witness in his interests) asks questions in cross-examination that are intended to elicit such evidence, or are likely to do so, or

    (c) evidence is given of an imputation about the other person made by the defendant-

        (i) on being questioned under caution, before charge, about the offence with which he is charged, or

        (ii) on being charged with the offence or officially informed that he might be prosecuted for it.

(2) In subsection (1) "evidence attacking the other person's character" means evidence to the effect that the other person—

    (a) has committed an offence (whether a different offence from the one with which the defendant is charged or the same one), or

    (b) has behaved, or is disposed to behave, in a reprehensible way; and "imputation about the other person" means an assertion to that effect.

(3) Only prosecution evidence is admissible under section 101(1)(g).'

26.10.1 WHAT AMOUNTS TO AN ATTACK?

Gateway (g) effectively replaces the second limb of s. 1(3)(ii) CEA 1898, which stipulated that a defendant choosing to give evidence on oath would lose his shield (protecting him from the revelation of any past bad character), where the nature or conduct of his defence involved casting an imputation against the character of a prosecution witness or the prosecutor or the deceased victim of the crime for which the defendant was on trial. Under the 1898 Act, however, such previous convictions were relevant only to the court's assessment of the defendant's credibility as a witness in his defence and could not be used to infer the defendant was guilty.

In *R v Hanson* [2005] 2 Cr App R 21, the Court of Appeal observed:

'As to s. 101(1)(g), the pre-2003 Act authorities will continue to apply when assessing whether an attack has been made on another person's character, to the extent that they are compatible with s. 106.'

This means that authorities such as *Selvey v DPP* [1970] AC 304 and *R v Britzman* [1983] 1 WLR 350 on what constitutes an 'attack' continue to apply. In *Selvey* it was held that a defendant still loses his shield notwithstanding that attacking the character of another is a necessary part of his defence. Some latitude was given to defendants under the 1898 Act in that a denial of guilt, however emphatic, would not amount to an attack. The cases at common law went so far as to suggest that even calling a witness a liar would not amount to an attack, but a suggestion that the witness had a motive for lying would. Based on the decisions at common law, we can confidently say that the following situations would all amount to an 'attack' on another:

- an allegation that a prosecution witness is biased;
- an allegation that the police have fabricated evidence;
- cross-examining a prosecution witness on any previous convictions they might have;
- accusing a prosecution witness of perjury;
- accusing the investigating officers of deliberately flouting PACE and the Codes of Practice.

It will probably not amount to an 'attack' to put it to a prosecution witness:

- that they are mistaken, confused or simply wrong;
- that the police have got some aspect of the Codes of Practice wrong;
- that a prosecution witness is lying, though this depends on what latitude the court gives to an accused in accordance with the decision in *R v Britzman*.

Gateway (g) is wider than its CEA 1898 predecessor. The section refers to attacking another person's character and is therefore not limited to witnesses in the case. It is irrelevant whether or not the defendant testifies.

'Attack' is defined by s. 106(2) CJA 2003 as suggesting that the person has committed an offence or has behaved in a reprehensible way or is inclined to behave in a reprehensible way. Of particular concern with regard to this provision is that fact that it can be triggered at the police station. In *R v Ball* [2005] EWCA Crim 2826, the use of the epithet 'slag' by B during a police interview when seeking to defend an allegation of rape was enough to trigger gateway (g). Suppose the investigating officer says to the suspect '. . . so are you saying that witness X is lying . . .'. If the suspect answers this affirmatively, he might be regarded as attacking another person's character, triggering the admission of his previous convictions at any subsequent trial. This provision makes the already difficult role of the legal adviser at the police station (considered in Chapter 12) considerably more challenging.

You will recall that as a consequence of s. 100 CJA 2003, the defendant will only be able to 'attack' the character of a witness if he is granted leave under s. 100 CJA 2003. The section is considered in more detail in Chapter 23, paragraphs 23.9–23.10. Leave need not be sought if the conduct in question '*is evidence of misconduct in connection with the investigation or prosecution of that offence*'.

Notwithstanding that a defendant is granted leave to adduce evidence attacking the character of another under s.100 CJA 2003, gateway (g) will still be triggered.

26.10.2 **RELEVANCE OF BAD CHARACTER ADDUCED UNDER GATEWAY (g)**

The CJA 2003 makes no stipulation as to the use that can be made of bad character under the Act. In *R v Highton; R v Van Nguyen; R v Carp* [2005] 1 WLR 3472 the Court of Appeal stated:

> 'In the case of gateway (g), for example, admissibility depends on the defendant having made an attack on another person's character, but once the evidence is admitted, it may, depending on the particular facts, be relevant not only to credibility but also to propensity to commit offences of the kind with which the defendant is charged.'

The importance of correctly directing the jury as to the relevance of the evidence and the need not to place undue reliance upon it as per the *Hanson* judgment is once more stressed in *Highton*.

26.10.3 **THE EXERCISE OF DISCRETION IN RELATION TO GATEWAY (g)**

As with s. 101(1)(d), the defence can make an application under to have the evidence excluded under s. 101(3). The application triggers the exercise of discretion based on the fairness of admitting the evidence. The guidance provided by the *Hanson* judgment (above) should be referred to. Under the previous law, the discretion to exclude evidence of a defendant's previous convictions following the loss of his shield, even where his previous convictions happened to be similar to the offence for which he being tried, was exercised restrictively. In *R v Burke* (1986) 82 Cr App R 156, while acknowledging that 'cases must occur in which it would be unjust to admit evidence of a character gravely prejudicial to the accused, even though there may be some tenuous grounds for holding it technically admissible', the Court of Appeal nevertheless went on to say that:

> 'In the ordinary and normal case the trial judge may feel that if the credit of the prosecutor or his witnesses has been attacked, it is only fair that the jury should have before them material on which they can form their judgment whether the accused person is any more worthy to be believed than those he has attacked. It is obviously unfair that the jury should be left in the dark about an accused person's character if the conduct of his defence has attacked the character of the prosecutor or the witnesses for the prosecution.'

> **Example**
>
> Consider the following example of s. 101(1)(g) CJA 2003. Lim is charged with assaulting his cohabitee on two separate occasions. The couple have had a volatile relationship for some time. Lim denies the allegation and claims he acted in self-defence, maintaining the injured party flew at him in a drunken rage. Lim has previously obtained a civil injunction against his partner. Lim seeks leave under s. 100 CJA 2003 to adduce evidence of his partner's violent acts against him. This is clearly an attack on her character. As a consequence, the prosecution serves notice under s. 101(1)(g) to admit Lim's previous convictions for wounding with intent, assault occasioning actual bodily harm and assault on a police officer, (the most recent committed 8 years ago); offences of theft, handling and deception committed 12 years ago and two drink-related driving offences (failing to provide a specimen and driving with excess alcohol) committed in the last five years. None of his assaults was perpetrated on females.

If leave is granted under s. 100 CJA, it is inevitable that gateway (g) will be opened. The defence could apply to have the evidence excluded on the basis that to admit them would be unduly prejudicial. Lim will say that his previous convictions for violence are considerably dated and that none of them involved him using violence against women. If admitted, Lim might persuade the court to confine their relevance to an assessment of his credibility only. However, given the statements in *Highton*, there is nothing to prevent the court from using the previous convictions on the issue of Lim's propensity if they are relevant and not unduly prejudicial. Previous convictions for deception may well be used as evidence indicating a propensity to be untruthful.

26.11 SAFEGUARDS RELATING TO THE ADMISSION OF EVIDENCE OF BAD CHARACTER

Under s. 107 power is given to a trial judge to stop a trial on indictment at any time before the close of the prosecution's case where evidence has been admitted under s. 101(1)(c)–(g) and the court is satisfied that the evidence is contaminated, with the result that any conviction would be regarded as being unsafe.

26.12 SPECIAL RULES RELATING TO CHILDHOOD CONVICTION

Section 108 CJA 2003 provides that where a person (aged 21 or over) is being tried, evidence of any previous convictions committed by him under the age of 14 shall not be admissible unless both of the offences are triable on indictment and the court is satisfied that the interests of justice require the evidence to be admitted.

26.13 'SPENT' CONVICTIONS UNDER THE REHABILITATION OF OFFENDERS ACT 1974

Generally, where a person has a spent conviction under the 1974 Act, he should be treated as though he was never charged or convicted of the offence, s. 4(1) Rehabilitation of Offenders Act 1974. While the 1974 Act has no application to criminal proceedings, the Practice Direction (Criminal: Consolidated) [2002] 3 All ER 904, states that reference should not be made by the prosecution to a 'spent' conviction without leave of the judge, to be granted only if the interests of justice so require.

26.14 STATUTORY ADMISSION OF SIMILAR FACT EVIDENCE

There are two instances in which Parliament has expressly authorised the use of similar fact evidence. One is under section 1(2) of the Official Secrets Act 1911. The other, more commonly used, is under section 27(3) of the Theft Act 1968. This particular section aids the proof of *mens rea* in relation to the charge of handling stolen goods. Where a defendant denies knowledge or belief that the goods which were found in his possession were stolen, the prosecution may adduce evidence of the defendant's criminal disposition by proving the defendant has previously been in possession of stolen goods, or that the defendant has a previous conviction for handling stolen goods or theft in the preceding five years. Such evidence is capable of casting serious doubt on the defendant's assertion that he did not know the goods were stolen, or that he did not believe them to be so. These provisions remain in force notwithstanding the enactment of the Criminal Justice Act 2003.

26.15 ADVISING YOUR CLIENT WHETHER OR NOT TO GIVE EVIDENCE AT HIS TRIAL

As stated earlier in this chapter, the defendant is a competent but not a compellable witness at his trial and enjoys the right to silence. As the trial date approaches an important part of the defence advocate's case preparation is to advise his client whether to give evidence in his defence. The advice given will be based on both practical considerations and the potential legal implications.

The practical considerations include:

(1) The nature of the prosecution and defence case

Some offences, including, for example, a sexual offence, may involve only two participants – the victim and the defendant. In this situation it is almost inevitable that the defendant will have to testify, as there is no other way in which the defence evidence can be put to the court. Similarly in a case where one co-accused blames the other, your client (as the other) may need to refute the evidence given by his co-accused. In other situations, where there are credible and reliable defence witnesses who can give evidence in support of the defendant's case, it might not be necessary to call the defendant.

(2) Whether a legal burden if proof is placed on the defendant

In a case where a legal burden of proof is placed on a defendant to effectively establish his innocence (see Chapter 21), sometimes the person best-placed to provide evidence in support of that defence will be the defendant.

(3) Will the defendant be a credible witness?

It may be a truism, but it is frequently said that the best prosecution witness is often the defendant! The defence advocate will need to make an assessment of how his client will come across in the witness box. Will he appear to be believable and credible? How will he withstand cross-examination? Appearing as a witness in a criminal trial is a stressful experience. Is the defendant articulate? Does he have the mental wherewithall to cope with the experience?

(4) Strength of the prosecution's case

In a case where the prosecution's evidence is, in your view, unlikely to persuade a jury of the defendant's guilt beyond reasonable doubt, the defence advocate may not wish to tip the scales in favour of the prosecution by calling his client to give evidence if he has some doubt as to his client's ability to cope with cross-examination as discussed above. The advocate's assessment of the prosecution's case may have to wait until he has cross-examined the witnesses for the prosecution. It goes without saying that in a case where a submission of no case to answer at the close of the prosecution's case has been upheld by the court (see Chapter 20, paragraph 20.10), no question of the defendant needing to testify arises!

(5) The legal considerations

As well as the practical factors, the decision whether the defendant should testify also involves an important legal consideration in that if the defendant does not give evidence, adverse inferences may be drawn under s. 35 Criminal Justice and Public Order Act 1994 (see paragraph 26.4 above).

KEY POINT SUMMARY

- Be aware of the evidential value of your client's good character. Evidence of a defendant's past good character should always be advanced.

- The admissibility of evidence of a defendant's past bad character is regulated by the provisions of the Criminal Justice Act 2003.

- Bad character is very widely defined to include any reprehensible behaviour and is not confined to previous convictions.

- Understand that there are seven gateways in s. 101 through which evidence of a defendant's bad character may be adduced, and that each gateway is further defined in ss. 102–106.

- The application of judicial discretion under s. 101(3) may well prove to be a crucial safeguard in ensuring the defendant can enjoy a fair trial as it gives the court discretion (at least in the context of the most frequently engaged gateways (d) and (g)) to exclude bad character evidence if it would have an adverse effect on the fairness of the proceedings.

- Guidance on what constitutes propensity to commit offences of the kind charged and how judicial discretion to exclude evidence of propensity might be exercised has been provided by the decision in the Court of Appeal decisions in *Hanson* and *Highton*.

- The defence must oppose the application of bad character if it is to be excluded – the decision to admit or exclude such evidence may well depend on the quality of the arguments put forward by opposing advocates!

- The defendant is not a compellable witness in a criminal case, but a failure to give evidence without good cause is subject to the risk of having an adverse inference drawn under s. 35 Criminal Justice and Public Order Act 1994.

- Understand the factors that may be taken into consideration when advising your client about whether or not to testify at his trial.

SELF-TEST QUESTIONS

1. Ben is arrested at Dover, along with two others in an undercover drug operation. He was arrested standing near to a car in which a large quantity of heroin is found. Ben is charged with conspiracy to import drugs. He denies the offence and claims he had no idea that the car contained drugs. A search of Ben's house results in the police finding £2,800 in a wardrobe. In his defence, Ben states that he had befriended one of the men and had simply accompanied him on the journey to Dover to collect some contraband cigarettes. Ben's fingerprints were not found on the package containing the drugs. He accounts for the cash stating he buys and sells cars. He has a caution for possession of cannabis five years previously and a conviction for handling stolen goods some two years previously. Three years ago, he stood trial for possession of Ecstasy tablets with intent to supply. He was convicted of possession of the Ecstasy tablets, but was acquitted of possession with intent to supply. Upon what basis do you feel the prosecution would seek admission of Ben's criminal record? If you were the defence advocate, what arguments would you advance in opposition?

2(a) Brian is charged with the rape of a 15-year-old girl. His defence is that the girl consented. He was convicted five years ago of an offence of unlawful sexual intercourse with a 14-year-old girl following a guilty plea. Will the prosecution be able to rely on this earlier conviction? What representations would the defence make as regards an attempt by the prosecution to adduce his previous conviction?

2(b) Vary the facts slightly. Brian is still charged with the rape of a 15-year-old. His defence is that his victim consented. Brian has a previous conviction for raping his former 26-year-old partner, eight years ago. On that occasion, he ran the same defence. Would this previous conviction be admissible? If so, on what basis?

3. Barry and Tina are accused of the murder of Sean, aged three. Barry was Sean's stepfather and Tina was his natural mother. The child died as a result of head injuries. Barry denies murder and states that the child died while in his mother's care and that she has a vicious temper and punched the child while in a drunken stupor. Tina denies murder and claims Barry struck Sean about the head while high on drugs. She maintains she is terrified of Barry and was powerless to do anything. The pathologist's report discloses the fact that the child was malnourished and that his body was covered in bruises and cigarette burns. Barry has several previous convictions for drug-related offences and theft, a previous conviction for criminal damage and one previous conviction for assault occasioning actual bodily harm. Tina has a previous conviction for theft. She

will give evidence in support of her defence. Should Barry give evidence? Does the conduct of his defence give you cause for concern? If so, why?

4. Danielle is charged with causing grievous bodily harm with intent. It is alleged she 'glassed' a man in the face causing facial injuries. She denies the offence. She has no previous convictions. What evidential use can be derived from the last-mentioned fact?

Case scenario: *R v Lenny Whyte*

You are reminded that the complete documentation in relation to this case study can be accessed from our Online Resource Centre.

You will be aware of the issues in this case. The prosecution have served notice to admit Lenny Whyte's previous convictions under s. 101(1)(d) CJA 2003. The defence have served notice opposing their admission.

Do you consider that Lenny's previous convictions would be admissible?

Consider whether it would be advisable for Lenny to give evidence in his defence. What factors would have a bearing on your advice?

FIGURE 26.1 EVIDENTIAL RULES RELEVANT TO THE ACCUSED

COMPETENCE AND COMPELLABILITY OF THE ACCUSED

- The accused is:
  - a competent but non-compellable witness for the defence, s 53 YJCEA 1999;
  - neither a competent or compellable witness for the prosecution, s. 53(4) YJCEA 1999.
- A co-accused is also not a competent or compellable witness for the prosecution unless he ceases to be a party to the proceedings (s. 53(5) YJCEA 1999).

THE COURSE OF THE ACCUSED'S EVIDENCE

- Section 79 PACE requires the accused to testify as the first defence witness.
- Where the accused does not give evidence at his trial, adverse inferences may be drawn against his silence under s. 35 CJPOA 1994, providing:
  - the accused is made aware of his right to testify and the possible consequences of remaining silent, Practice Direction (Criminal Consolidated) [2002]; and the jury or magistrates are reminded that:
    - the legal burden of proving the accused's guilt lies with the prosecution; and
    - the defendant is entitled to remain silent; and
    - the prosecution must have established a *prima facie* case against the accused; and
    - adverse inferences cannot be the sole reason for finding the accused guilty, s. 38(3) CJPOA 1994; and
    - adverse inferences may only be drawn where the only explanation for the accused's silence is that he has no answer to the prosecution case; or none that would stand up to cross-examination (see *R v Cowan, Gayle and Riccardi* [1995]).

GOOD CHARACTER

- A defendant with good character is entitled to a good character direction, see *R v Vye and Others* [1993] as to:
  - propensity (a defendant of good character is less likely to have committed the offence); and
  - credibility as a witness (where the defendant before trial asserts his innocence and/or gives evidence at trial).

ADDUCING THE DEFENDANT'S BAD CHARACTER

- Bad character is defined by s. 98 CJA 2003 as evidence of or a disposition towards misconduct or other reprehensible behaviour.
- S. 101(a)–(g) CJA 2003 provides seven gateways through which evidence of a defendant's bad character can be admitted:

  (a) all parties agree to the evidence being admitted;

  (b) the evidence is adduced by the defendant or is given in answer during the defendant's cross-examination;

  (c) it is important explanatory evidence;

  (d) it is relevant to an important matter in issue between D and P;

  (e) it has substantial probative value in relation to an important matter in issue between a defendant and co-defendant;

  (f) it is evidence to correct a false impression given by a defendant, or

  (g) the defendant has made an attack on another person's character.

- Evidence of bad character sought to be admitted under s. 101(1)(d) and 101(1)(g) is subject to exclusionary discretion in s. 101(3) CJA 2003 based on the fairness of admitting the evidence which is triggered by the defence.
- *R v Hanson* [2005] provides important guidance on what constitutes propensity to commit offences of the kind and propensity to be untruthful.
- In exercising discretion in terms of what is just under s. 103(3) and the fairness of the proceedings under s. 101(3), *Hanson* says the following factors are important:
  - the similarity between past and present offences;
  - the respective gravity of past and present offending;
  - the age of any previous convictions;
  - the strength of the prosecution's case.

27.1   INTRODUCTION

The term 'private privilege' relates to separate privileges that prevent evidence from being disclosed in litigation, or witnesses from being compelled to answer questions at trial. In a criminal case, privilege may be claimed in two situations:

- legal professional privilege;

- the privilege against self-incrimination.

While it is generally regarded as a matter of public policy for cases to be decided on the basis of all available admissible and relevant evidence, private privilege recognises that in certain situations it is in the wider public interest to maintain the confidentiality of communications between a lawyer and his client, or to encourage a witness in his testimony to make a full and frank disclosure of the matters within his knowledge – even where the court is denied the benefit of otherwise admissible and relevant evidence.

In this chapter we consider:

- legal professional privilege in criminal cases;

- legal professional privilege and the courts;

- waiving legal professional privilege;

- the privilege against self-incrimination;

- the privilege against self-incrimination and the European Convention on Human Rights 1950.

While the evidential effect of claiming private privilege is the same as claiming public interest immunity (see Chapter 17), an important difference between them is that private privilege is a personal right that belongs to the client or to a witness and cannot be claimed by any other person, whereas public interest immunity seeks to protect the 'confidentiality' of the work of organisations that operate in the 'public' domain, such as the Police and HM Revenue and Customs.

27.2 LEGAL PROFESSIONAL PRIVILEGE IN CRIMINAL CASES

Legal professional privilege in criminal cases is defined by s. 10 PACE 1984, to include:

'(1) Subject to subsection (2) below, in this Act "items subject to legal professional privilege" means—

    (a) communications between a professional legal adviser and his client or any person representing his client made in connection with the giving of legal advice to the client;

    (b) communications between a professional legal adviser and his client or any person representing his client or between such an adviser or his client or any such representative and any other person made in connection with or in contemplation of legal proceedings and for the purpose of such proceedings and

    (c) items enclosed with or referred to in such communications and made—

        (i) in connection with the giving of legal advice; or

        (ii) in connection with or in the contemplation of legal proceedings and for the purposes of such proceedings;

when they are in the possession of a person who is entitled to possession of them.'

Legal professional privilege applies in the following two situations.

27.2.1 COMMUNICATIONS BETWEEN THE LAWYER AND CLIENT — S.10(1)(a) PACE 1984

All communications passing between the lawyer and client in 'the giving or obtaining of legal advice', and within the proper scope of the lawyer's professional work, will be privileged from disclosure. According to the Court of Appeal in *Balabel v Air-India* [1988] 2 All ER 246, the term 'the giving of legal advice' is not restricted to communications that specifically request or give legal advice, but also includes communications and correspondence that are part of the on-going relationship between the lawyer and the client.

Therefore, legal professional privilege will attach to;

- all communications between a solicitor and his client; and
- communications with counsel,
- communications to salaried legal advisers whether or not they hold a formal legal qualification; and
- communications to foreign lawyers.

The most obvious example of the privilege is that a client cannot be compelled to disclose any oral or written advice given to him by his solicitor or counsel in connection with the case.

While the phrase 'the giving of legal advice' is broadly interpreted, the courts are not prepared to apply the principle to all client-solicitor communications.

Legal professional privilege does not apply to:

- a record of a conveyancing transaction (*R v Crown Court at Inner London Sessions, ex p. Baines and Baines* [1987] 3 All ER 1025);
- a solicitor's documentary records of time spent with a client;
- time sheets;
- fee records;
- the record of a client's appointment in a solicitor's appointment diary, (see *R v Manchester Crown Court, ex p. R (Legal Professional Privilege)* [1999] 1 WLR 832).

These documents are not covered by legal professional privilege as they are not concerned with the giving of legal advice.

27.2.2 COMMUNICATIONS WITH THIRD PARTIES – S. 10(1)(b) PACE 1984

Legal professional privilege will attach to communications between the client, the legal adviser and a third party where the sole or dominant purpose of the communication was in connection with actual or pending litigation.

In deciding the 'dominant purpose test', the court will take an objective view of all the evidence, taking into account the intention of the document's author and the purpose of preparing the document. The key requirement in maintaining the privileged status of communications with third parties is that the communication must relate to pending or contemplated litigation.

> **Example**
>
> Gavin is charged with conspiracy to cause an explosion. As part of the defence lawyer's preparation an expert's report is obtained which proves to be unhelpful to Gavin. In cross-examination the advocate for another co-accused asks Gavin whether his solicitor has commissioned an expert's report.
>
> Gavin cannot be compelled to answer this question as the decision to obtain a report was taken in the course of the solicitor-client relationship. The report itself is protected from disclosure as it is a communication between a lawyer and a third party in connection with actual litigation.

27.3 WHAT IS THE RATIONALE FOR LEGAL PROFESSIONAL PRIVILEGE?

The rationale behind the privilege is that it is in the public interest that when seeking the advice of his lawyer, a client should be able to openly discuss his case, and to make a full disclosure of all relevant information to his lawyer in the knowledge that he cannot be compelled to disclose the content of those discussions, nor will he be compelled to give evidence about them in court.

27.4 LEGAL PROFESSIONAL PRIVILEGE AND THE COURTS

As legal professional privilege underpins the administration of criminal justice, the courts adopt a strict approach to enforcing its application. The position is illustrated by the House of Lords in *R v Derby Magistrates' Court, ex p. B* [1996] AC 487.

> **_R v Derby Magistrates' Court, ex p. B_ [1996] AC 487**
>
> A 16-year-old girl was murdered. The appellant was arrested and made a statement to the police that he alone was responsible for the murder. He later retracted the statement and alleged that although he had been present at the scene of the crime, it was his step-father who had killed the girl. Relying on this second statement, the appellant was acquitted in the Crown Court.
>
> Later, the appellant's step-father was charged with the murder. At the step-father's committal, the appellant was called as a witness for the prosecution and repeated the statement that his step-father had killed the girl. He was cross-examined by the defence about the instructions he had given to his solicitor concerning the murder. The appellant claimed legal professional privilege but the magistrates issued a summons (s. 97 Magistrates' Courts Act 1980) directing the appellant and his solicitor to produce the relevant proofs of evidence as they would be 'likely to be material evidence'.

On appeal, the House of Lords held that a summons could not be issued under s. 97 MCA 1980 to compel the production of documents protected by legal professional privilege unless the privilege had been waived, which in the present case, it had not. In reaffirming its status, the House of Lords stated that legal professional privilege is much more than an ordinary rule of evidence; it is a fundamental condition on which the administration of justice rests.

27.5 WAIVING LEGAL PROFESSIONAL PRIVILEGE

Legal professional privilege vests in the client and may only be waived by the client, either at the pre-trial stage or during the trial. If the client expressly or impliedly waives the privilege a lawyer can be compelled to reveal the contents of the communications between himself and the client, or between himself and a third party. As explained in Chapters 8 and 12, the question of waiver commonly arises where the accused is required to explain his silence in response to questions at the police station, by disclosing the reasons that he was given by his lawyer for refusing to answer. In this situation both the accused and the legal adviser may be cross-examined about the content of the advice given at the police station.

27.6 WHERE LEGAL PROFESSIONAL PRIVILEGE IS LOST

While the sanctity of legal professional privilege is recognised, the privilege is not entirely absolute and will not apply in the following situations.

27.6.1 COMMUNICATION IN THE FURTHERANCE OF A CRIME OR FRAUD

The privilege will be lost where it is used as a vehicle for the furtherance of a criminal offence. It is immaterial whether the lawyer was aware of the illicit purpose of the communication and the 'crime' may relate to an offence under United Kingdom law or an offence in a foreign jurisdiction, see *R v Cox and Railton* [1884] 14 QBD 153. The rule is now contained in s. 10(2) of PACE, which provides: 'Items held with the intention of furthering a criminal purpose are not items subject to legal professional privilege.'

27.6.2 THE PRIVILEGE MAY BE LOST ACCIDENTALLY

Legal professional privilege may be lost accidentally. In *R v Tompkins* (1977) 67 Cr App R 181, the defendant was charged with handling stolen hi-fi equipment. The victim of the theft stated that he could identify his stolen equipment as it had a loose button. The defendant said in examination-in-chief that the button had never been loose, and demonstrated this to the court. During an adjournment, an employee of the prosecution solicitor found a piece of paper on which the defendant had written to his barrister that the button had been loose but that he had stuck it down with glue. Prosecution counsel then showed Tompkins the note and cross-examined him on it. As a result, Tompkins changed his answer and was convicted. On appeal, the Court of Appeal stated there had not been a breach of legal professional privilege because the privileged document had been obtained independently of the privileged relationship and there had not been any improper conduct.

27.7 LEGAL PROFESSIONAL PRIVILEGE AND THE DISCLOSURE OF EXPERT EVIDENCE

The rules on legal professional privilege attaching to communications where the 'third party' is an expert witness should be read in conjunction with the obligation on both the prosecution and the defence to disclose the content of their expert's reports, as required by the Crown Court (Advance Notice of Expert Evidence) Rules 1987; the Magistrates' Courts (Advance Notice of Expert Evidence) Rules 1997 and Part 34 Crim PR.

So far as the obligation to disclose an unfavourable report is concerned, the position in relation to the prosecution is governed by the rules on the pre-trial disclosure of evidence (see Chapter 17.) No such obligation falls on the defendant as the report is protected by legal professional privilege, providing it has been obtained for the purposes of actual or contemplated litigation. When s. 60 CPIA, (as amended by s. 35 CJA 2003) comes into force, an accused who instructs an expert witness with a view to providing an opinion for use as evidence at trial, is required to give the court and the prosecutor a notice specifying the person's name and address unless specified in the defence statement (see Chapter 17, paragraph 17.9.5).

27.8 THE PRIVILEGE AGAINST SELF-INCRIMINATION IN CRIMINAL PROCEEDINGS

The privilege against self-incrimination allows a witness to refuse to answer a question, which in the opinion of the judge, would expose the witness to the possibility of any criminal charge under United Kingdom law.

27.8.1 THE PRIVILEGE BELONGS TO THE WITNESS

The privilege belongs to the witness and must therefore be claimed by the witness during his testimony. While according to *R v Coote* [1873] LR 4 PC 599, a witness is presumed to know the law sufficiently to appreciate that he is not compelled to answer a particular question or to produce a document, the preferred modern practice is for the judge or the magistrates' legal adviser to warn the witness that he does not have to answer the question. Once the court is satisfied that the privilege applies, the witness will not be compelled to answer even if his motive for remaining silent is based in bad faith or he has a motive of his own to serve.

27.8.2 WAIVING THE PRIVILEGE

Only the witness may waive the privilege. Where the witness does not waive the privilege his self-incriminating answers will be admissible as evidence in any proceedings against him.

27.8.3 THE PRIVILEGE AGAINST SELF-INCRIMINATION AND THE EUROPEAN CONVENTION ON HUMAN RIGHTS 1950

As a witness in his defence, the defendant cannot refuse to answer questions in cross-examination on the ground that it would incriminate him as to the offence charged! However, various statutes compel an individual to answer questions and provide information in an investigation on pain of a penalty. Where the answers given or the information supplied is subsequently used in evidence against the defendant at a subsequent trial, the defendant can argue that the process has infringed his right not to incriminate himself. Indeed the use of such evidence may well contravene the defendant's right to a fair trial under Article 6. In *Saunders v United Kingdom* (1997) 23 EHRR 313, in which the defendant had been compelled to answer questions about his business dealings during an investigation by the Department of Trade and Industry, which were then used against him in a prosecution under the Companies Act 1985, the ECtHR held:

> 'While not specifically referred to, the privilege against self-incrimination along with the right to silence are fundamental aspects of an accused's right to a fair trial under Article 6(1) of the European Convention on Human Rights. In *Funke v France* (1993) 16 EHRR 297, the Court of Human Rights held that anyone charged with a criminal offence "has the right to remain silent and not contribute to incriminating himself". The privilege against self-incrimination, which is a common feature in the legal systems of all the Contracting Parties, recognises the right of the accused to remain silent to questions put to

him and not to be compelled to break his silence. The privilege also embodies the principle that the prosecution in a criminal trial is required to prove its case without resorting to evidence that has been obtained through coercion or oppression in defiance of the will of the accused. The privilege also operates in close conjunction with the presumption of innocence under Article 6(2) ECHR. The Court recalls that, although not specifically mentioned in Article 6 of the Convention (art. 6), the right to silence and the right not to incriminate oneself are generally recognised international standards which lie at the heart of the notion of a fair procedure under Article 6 (art. 6). Their rationale lies, *inter alia*, in the protection of the accused against improper compulsion by the authorities thereby contributing to the avoidance of miscarriages of justice and to the fulfilment of the aims of Article 6 . . . The right not to incriminate oneself, in particular, presupposes that the prosecution in a criminal case seek to prove their case against the accused without resort to evidence obtained through methods of coercion or oppression in defiance of the will of the accused. In this sense the right is closely linked to the presumption of innocence contained.'

In domestic law, various statutes require specified persons to answer questions, to produce documents or to disclose certain information even though such disclosure may infringe the person's privilege against self-incrimination. Examples of these provisions include s. 31 Theft Act 1968 which provides that a witness may not refuse to answer any questions in proceedings for the recovery or administration of property or the execution of a trust on the ground that to do so might incriminate him or his spouse of an offence under the Act. A similar provision is contained in s. 2(2) Criminal Justice Act 1987, where the Director of the Serious Fraud Office can compel a person to make a statement in a serious fraud investigation. In relation to each of these offences, provision is made preventing any answers given from being used in evidence against the individuals concerned, in the event of a prosecution for the specified offence.

The most significant challenge to a statutory provision of this type has been in relation s. 172 Road Traffic Act 1988. Section 172(2)(a) RTA 1988 requires the keeper of a motor vehicle to answer questions as to the identity of the driver of the vehicle where the diver is suspected of being involved in a road traffic offence. Failure to provide such information is an offence under s. 172(3) RTA 1988, punishable with a fine and endorsement. The point was considered by the Privy Council in *Brown v Stott*.

Brown v Stott [2001] 2 WLR 817

The police were called to an all-night superstore, where B was suspected of having stolen a bottle of gin. The officers thought that B had been drinking and asked her how she had got to the store. She replied that she had driven there and pointed to a car that she said was hers. At the police station, car keys were found in her handbag, and pursuant to s. 172(2) Road Traffic Act 1988, the police required her to say who had driven the car to the store. B replied that she had driven the car. A breath test was administered that proved positive. B was charged with driving after consuming excess alcohol under s. 5(1)(a) Road Traffic Act 1988.

On appeal, the Privy Council held that evidence of B's admission that she had driven the vehicle to the all-night store did not infringe her privilege against self-incrimination or her right to a fair hearing under Article 6 for the following reasons:

- the rights under Article 6 are not absolute and may be qualified in respect to a proper clear public objective such as road safety;

- there was a clear public interest in enforcement of road traffic legislation and that properly applied, s. 172 RTA 1988, did not represent a disproportionate response to this serious social problem:

  - s. 172 RTA 1988 permitted the police to ask a suspect a simple question, the answer to which does not incriminate the accused *per se*;

  - the penalty for refusing to answer the question is moderate and non-custodial;

  - if there was evidence of coercion by the police, the court had discretion to exclude the suspect's answer.

KEY POINT SUMMARY

- Know the situations where legal professional privilege can be claimed and be prepared to advise your client accordingly.

- Be aware of the circumstances in which legal professional privilege may be lost.

- Understand the privilege against self-incrimination and be prepared to advise your client accordingly.

SELF-TEST QUESTIONS

1. Are all communications passing between a solicitor and his client privileged from disclosure?

2. What is the dominant purpose test for legal privilege to attach to communications between the client, solicitor and a third party?

3. In whom does legal privilege vest?

4. Explain the privilege against self-incrimination.

Analysis of these questions can be found in Appendix 5.

FIGURE 27.1 PRIVATE PRIVILEGE

LEGAL PROFESSIONAL PRIVILEGE

- Prevents the disclosure of all communications between the lawyer/client in connection with the giving or obtaining of legal advice, including (s. 10(1)(a) PACE);
    - letters, memoranda containing legal advice; and
    - communications with counsel.

- Prevents the disclosure of all communications between the client, lawyer and a third party where the sole or dominant purpose is in connection with actual or pending litigation including communications in connection with advice sought from an expert witness (s. 10(1)(b) PACE);

- The courts take a strict approach to enforcing the privilege, see *R v Derby Magistrates' Court, ex p. B.*

- The privilege will be lifted where:
    - it is waived the client; or
    - it used to further a crime; or
    - it is lost accidentally.

PRIVILEGE AGAINST SELF-INCRIMINATION

- Permits a witness to refuse to answer a question on oath where the answer would expose to the possibility of a criminal charge being laid against him.

- The privilege applies to individuals who are compelled to answer questions by investigating bodies, the answers to which are then sought to be used in evidence against that individual in criminal proceedings.

- The privilege belongs to the witness.

- The witness may waive the privilege.

- The privilege is not an absolute right under Article 6 ECHR and may be qualified where:
    - there is a clear public interest in the privilege not applying; and
    - it is proportionate to the aim of the legislation, see *Brown v Stott.*

Part V

POST-CONVICTION: SENTENCING AND APPEALS

Part V covers all aspects of sentencing in the Crown Court and magistrates' court.

In Chapter 28 we consider the general principles that inform the process of sentencing.

In Chapter 29 we consider the decision to impose a custodial term on a convicted offender.

Chapter 30 considers the range of non-custodial penalties available to the courts, including ancillary orders. In particular, it explores community based sentences and fines.

In Chapter 31 we consider the special considerations that apply to the sentencing of road traffic offences.

Chapter 32 considers the procedure on sentencing and the way in which a defence solicitor might prepare and deliver a plea in mitigation.

Finally, in Chapter 33 we consider the process of appeal against sentence and conviction.

28 GENERAL PRINCIPLES OF SENTENCING

28.1 INTRODUCTION

The sentencing of an individual before the Crown Court or magistrates' court will occur upon conviction, either because the individual has pleaded guilty to an offence, or because he has been found guilty after a trial. As the vast majority of criminal clients plead guilty to some or all of the charges against them, it is unsurprising that a considerable amount of a defence lawyer's time will be taken up with the question of sentence.

Criminal defence practitioners will invariably be called upon to:

1. Advise a client on the likely sentence he will face in the event of a successful prosecution;

2. Represent a client at a sentencing hearing requiring the submission of a plea in mitigation;

3. Advise a client on the prospects of a successful appeal against sentence.

In executing any of the above tasks, the well-prepared defence practitioner will need to have a thorough knowledge of sentencing principles and practice.

Sentencing law and practice is complex. We have divided the subject into five separate chapters in order to assist understanding. In this chapter we examine the theoretical basis for sentencing and the factors that underpin, inform and in some instances constrain a court when passing sentence. In Chapters 29 and 30 we explore specific types of sentence, looking at the requisite criteria for each of them. In Chapter 31 we consider the special considerations that apply to sentencing in road traffic matters and in Chapter 32 we consider the process of sentencing and the mechanics of an effective plea in mitigation. Sentencing in relation to youths (offenders under the age of 18) is considered in Chapter 35.

28.2 NEW DEVELOPMENTS – WARNING

Sentencing law is governed by the provisions of the Criminal Justice Act 2003 (CJA) and the Powers of the Criminal Courts (Sentencing) Act 2000 (PCC(S)A). The 2000 Act was a consolidating Act, enshrining the sentencing philosophy of the earlier Criminal Justice Acts of 1991 and 1993. The CJA 2003 has repealed some, although not all of the provisions of the 2000 Act. The fundamental basis of sentencing remains very similar to that under the 2000 Act, although the CJA 2003 has created a number of new sentencing options.

Sentencing law and practice will continue to be in a state of flux for some time as the full impact of the CJA 2003 is gradually absorbed. Important changes to the sentencing powers of the magistrates' court are expected to come into force in November 2006. Our Online Resource Centre will keep you updated on new developments relating to further implementation.

online resource centre

28.3 HIERARCHY OF SENTENCES

The magistrates' court and the Crown Court can pass a range of sentences under the Criminal Justice Act 2003. At this juncture, we simply list the range of sentences in decreasing order of severity. We consider the specifics of each sentence in Chapters 29 and 30:

- custody – immediate/intermittent/suspended;
- community sentence (combining requirements such as unpaid work/curfew/programme requirement/drug treatment and testing requirement/residence requirement);
- fine/compensation order;
- discharge (conditional or absolute).

A court might also consider deferring sentence in appropriate circumstances.

In addition, upon conviction for certain offences, a court may and in some cases must also order endorsement of a driving licence or disqualification from driving, destruction or confiscation of criminal property or the seizure of criminal assets. In other instances, a court may be required to subject the offender to notification requirements under the Sex Offences Act 2003, or to impose a restraining order or banning order.

28.4 SENTENCING AIMS

In passing a particular sentence a court will have in mind one or more sentencing objectives.

In some instances, particularly where the offence is serious because of the presence of aggravating features, a defendant can expect a sentence of a punitive nature to be imposed.

Section 142 of the Criminal Justice Act 2003 stipulates that when a court sentences an offender over the age of 18, it must have regard to one or more of the following purposes of sentencing. They include:

(a) the punishment of offenders,

(b) reduction in crime (including its reduction by deterrence),

(c) the reform and rehabilitation of the offender,

(d) the protection of the public;

(e) the making of reparation by the offender to persons affected by their offences.

The CJA 2003 does not indicate that any one purpose is more important than any other.

Sentences of a punitive nature include custody and certain types of community sentence, including those which require the offender to undertake unpaid work or to abide by a curfew. Such sentences deprive the offender of his liberty. In some cases a sufficiently high fine can be punitive in nature. In particularly serious cases where an offender has used violence, perhaps not for the first time, or has committed a serious sexual offence, there will be a need to ensure protection of the public. Such an offender can expect a lengthy custodial sentence.

Where the offence is less serious and there are underlying reasons for an offender's behaviour, a sentence of a rehabilitative nature might be appropriate which may result in a reduction in further offending. The most obvious example of this is a community sentence with a supervision requirement, or a community sentence that includes a drug rehabilitation requirement. For first-time offender whose offence is not particularly serious, a conditional discharge might be considered.

In terms of reparation as a sentencing objective, the imposition of a court order requiring an offender to pay compensation to his victim for injury, loss or damage is a good example.

28.5 THE BASIS OF SENTENCING UNDER THE CRIMINAL JUSTICE ACT 2003

The Criminal Justice Act 1991 introduced a structured approach to sentencing, adopting the fundamental principle that a sentence should not be more severe than the seriousness of the offence warrants. The type of sentence a court chooses to impose should reflect the seriousness of the offence. This philosophy continues to prevail under the CJA 2003.

28.5.1 WHAT FACTORS HAVE A BEARING ON THE CONCEPT OF THE SERIOUSNESS OF AN OFFENCE?

Section 143(1) CJA 2003 provides that in considering the seriousness of any offence, the court must consider:

• the offender's culpability in committing the offence; and

• any harm which the offence has caused or was intended to cause or might forseeably have caused.

Culpability embraces such matters as the defendant's intention when committing an offence, whether he acted recklessly or had knowledge of the risk he was taking. Harm can include harm to the individual victim but also the wider community.

Statutory aggravating factors affecting seriousness under the Criminal Justice Act 2003 are set out in s. 143(2). The section requires a court to treat an offender's previous convictions as an aggravating factor if the court considers it can reasonably be so treated, having regard to the nature of the offence and the time that has elapsed since conviction. Recent and relevant previous convictions will therefore be regarded as aggravating the seriousness of the current offence before the court.

Section 143(3) requires the court to treat any offence committed while on bail as being an aggravating factor in determining the seriousness of the offence.

Sections 145 and 146 provide that where an offence is either racially or religiously motivated or is motivated out of hostility towards a person's sexual or presumed sexual orientation or disability or presumed disability, this shall be regarded as an aggravating feature in determining the seriousness of the offence.

In addition to any statutory aggravating factors, the court will have regard to any aggravating and mitigating features of the offence itself and any applicable sentencing guidelines.

In its *Overarching Principles: Seriousness* publication, the SCG (see below) provides guidance as to the assessment of an offender's culpability for the purposes of s. 143 CJA 2003. Culpability is determined by such matters as the offender's motivation in committing the offence; whether it was planned or spontaneous and whether the offender was in a position of trust. A further relevant factor would include the deliberate targeting of a vulnerable victim by reference to their age, disability or by virtue of their job. The guidance offers an extensive though by no means exhaustive list of typical aggravating and mitigating features to an offence.

To reiterate, the starting point in tems of sentencing an offender is an assessment by the court of the seriousness of the offence.

28.6 SENTENCING GUIDELINES COUNCIL (SGC)

The Criminal Justice Act 2003 established the Sentencing Guidelines Council (SGC). Its remit has been to take over the Court of Appeal's responsibility for issuing sentencing guidelines. In due course, it will produce sentencing guidelines for all criminal courts and guidelines on the allocation of cases between courts. Sentencing guidelines enable courts to approach sentence in any case from a common starting point. The Sentencing Advisory Panel (which is an independent public body) provides advice to the SGC, based on legal research and consultation. Those guidelines that have already been issued by the Sentencing Advisory Panel (SAP) can be accessed at http://www.sentencing-guidelines.gov.uk.

The SGC has already issued important guidelines on the sentencing framework introduced by the CJA 2003 in relation to the new sentences and the overarching principles that inform the process of sentencing under the 2003 Act. It has also produced guidelines on the appropriate reduction in sentence for a guilty plea.

In due course the SGC is expected to issue guidelines specific to individual offences. At present this function is fulfilled in the Crown Court by Court of Appeal judgments (informed in some instances by the Sentencing Advisory Panel) and in the magistrates' court by the Magistrates' Court Sentencing Guidelines, last revised in January 2004 by the Magistrates' Association. Under the Criminal Justice Act 2003, a court is obliged have regard to the sentencing guidelines produced by the SGC when sentencing an offender and to give reasons where it departs from a SGC guideline sentence (s. 174 CJA 2003).

28.7 HOW DOES THE DEFENCE SOLICITOR BEGIN TO ASSESS THE SERIOUSNESS OF AN OFFENCE?

Defence solicitors must consider their client's role in the particular offence and consider what factors aggravate the seriousness of the offence and what factors mitigate its seriousness. Those factors will include the statutory factors contained in ss. 143 and in the SGC's publication on seriousness (and for now) the factors identified in the Magistrates' Court Sentencing Guidelines 2004 (MCSG 2004) for specific offences. The latter are reproduced in full at our Online Resource Centre with the kind permission of the Magistrates' Association, and can be accessed via password. At Appendix 4 in this Handbook we include a small number of specific sentencing guidelines taken from the guidelines.

28.7.1 **USING THE SENTENCING GUIDELINES TO ASSESS THE SERIOUSNESS OF AN OFFENCE**

To illustrate the concept of seriousness by reference to the MCSG (2004), consider a typical offence of assault occasioning actual bodily harm, contrary to s. 47 Offences Against the Person Act 1861. If you examine the Magistrates' Court Sentencing Guidelines on this particular offence located within Appendix 4, you will see that the suggested guideline starting point in terms of sentence for a first time offence following a not guilty plea is a custodial sentence. Given that this is the suggested starting point in terms of sentence, assaults of this nature are always regarded as being serious. Aggravating features of a s. 47 assault include:

- extensive injury;
- headbutting;
- premeditation;
- vulnerable victim;
- use of a weapon;
- commission of offence on a hospital or school, abuse of trust.

Mitigating factors include:

- minor injury;
- provocation; or
- the use of a single blow.

In further assessing the seriousness of the offence, the court would have regard to the offender's culpability and any harm which the offence caused or was intended to cause or might forseeably have caused (s. 143(1) CJA 2003).

By contrast, take a look at the Magistrates' Court Sentencing Guidelines on theft contrary to the Theft Act 1968 s. 1 (included in Appendix 4). The starting point in terms of sentence for this offence is a community order. Aggravating features of a typical theft offence include:

- high value of the goods stolen;
- planned operation;
- sophisticated;
- organised team;
- adult involving a child.

Mitigating features capable of reducing the seriousness of the offence include:

- impulsive action.

Although the starting point in terms of sentence for theft would seem to indicate that it is not regarded as a serious offence in comparison to other offences, this does not mean that a particular offence of theft might not warrant a custodial sentence if the aggravating factors in the offence substantially outweigh the mitigating factors. There is no offence of theft in breach of trust, but if you consider the guideline on this type of theft (also reproduced at Appendix 4) the starting point in sentencing terms is a custodial sentence.

Additionally, the court would consider the offender's culpability in committing the offence.

Looking Ahead

It is anticipated that the Magistrates Court Sentencing Guidelines will be replaced in due course by guidelines developed by the Sentencing Guidelines Council which will take into account the changes to sentencing contained within the CJA 2003.

Section 174 CJA 2003 requires a court to give reasons for the sentence it is imposing and to specify any aggravating or mitigating factors which the court has regarded as being of particular importance. Moreover, where sentence is passed outside the guidelines for sentence of the particular offence, there must be a specific explanation of the court's reasons.

A defence solicitor must take a realistic view of the offence his client has committed and assess its seriousness. This will help determine the starting point in terms of the type of sentence likely to be imposed.

28.8 TIMELY GUILTY PLEAS

Section 144 Criminal Justice Act 2003 provides as follows:

'(1) In determining what sentence to pass on an offender who has pleaded guilty to an offence in proceedings before that or another court, a court shall take into account—

(a) the stage in the proceedings for the offence at which the offender indicated his intention to plead guilty, and

(b) the circumstances in which this indication was given.'

Section 174(2)(b) provides that in passing sentence on an offender, the court must state in open court in ordinary language that it has given the offender the benefit of a discount under s. 144.

Timely guilty pleas save cost, court time and most importantly spare victims and witnesses from having to give evidence. Section 144 does not specify the amount of discount a court might award. In practice, the average discount which the courts apply is one-third off the sentence passed. A defendant who leaves his guilty plea to the morning of trial can expect only a minimal discount. Sentencing discounts do not apply to compensation orders or to the minimum periods of disqualification and the mandatory imposition of penalty points.

In its guidelines on the effect of pleading guilty (http://www.sentencing-guidelines.gov.uk) the Sentencing Guidelines Council recommends a sliding scale, ranging from a maximum of one-third (where the guilty plea was entered at the first reasonable opportunity), reducing to a maximum of up to one quarter (where a trial date has been set) and up to a maximum of one tenth (for a guilty plea entered at the 'door of the court').

28.9 WHAT CONSTRAINS SENTENCING?

There are a number of factors that constrain sentencing, including:

- the statute creating the offence (statutes creating an offence will specify a maximum penalty for the particular offence);
- whether the sentence is being imposed in the Crown Court or in the magistrates' court (magistrates' courts' powers of sentence are limited);
- statutory requirements laid down by Parliament (in some instances Parliament has removed judicial discretion and requires the imposition of a mandatory sentence of imprisonment or other ancillary penalty);

- the age of the defendant (sentencing in relation to young offenders under the age of 18 is considered in Chapter 35);
- whether the defendant pleaded guilty or was found guilty (timely guilty pleas attract a reduction in the length of sentence).

28.9.1 THE SENTENCING JURISDICTION OF MAGISTRATES' COURTS

The sentencing jurisdiction of magistrates is closely related to mode of trial enquiry for either-way offences. Having considered Chapter 16 you will be aware that one of the principal reasons for magistrates declining jurisdiction to try an either-way matter where the defendant has pleaded not guilty or has given no indication of plea, is the fact that the magistrates feel their maximum sentencing powers to be insufficient. In circumstances where magistrates are prepared to accept jurisdiction to try the accused, he must be warned of the risk that he can still be committed for sentence under s. 3 PCC(S)A 2000 in the event of conviction. As we have seen previously, where a defendant indicates a guilty plea to an either-way offence, magistrates must accept jurisdiction over the case but retain the power to commit the defendant for sentence to the Crown Court under s. 3 PCC(S)A 2000 if they conclude their maximum powers of sentence to be insufficient.

The maximum custodial sentence that a magistrates' court can currently pass is six months upon conviction of a summary matter (s. 78 PCC(S)A 2000 and s. 133 MCA 1980). It matters not that a defendant is convicted of two or more summary matters on the same occasion: the maximum prescribed by statute is six months. The six months maximum can rise to a maximum custodial sentence of 12 months where consecutive prison sentences of six months are imposed on a defendant convicted of two or more either-way matters (proviso to s. 133(1) and s. 133(2) MCA 1980). Magistrates' courts' sentencing powers are set to increase under the CJA 2003.

Even in magistrates' courts however, the statute creating the offence may prescribe a custodial sentence of less than six months. An example of this is conviction for criminal damage of less than £5,000 under s. 4(2) Criminal Damage Act 1971. The current maximum custodial sentence in this regard is three months. Some offences do not carry a custodial penalty, such as careless driving, contrary to s. 3 Road Traffic Act 1988.

Magistrates are further constrained in terms of the size of any fine they may wish to impose. The maximum fine for the majority of offences is £5,000 for each offence. Some offences do, however, specify a maximum fine of less than £5,000. A fine must not exceed the upper statutory limit, often expressed in terms of a level. Level 5 offences carry a maximum fine of £5,000. For an offence of being drunk and disorderly contrary to s. 91 Criminal Justice Act 1967, the maximum fine is £1,000 or level 3.

28.9.2 POWER TO COMMIT FOR SENTENCE UNDER S. 3 PCC(S)A 2000

Upon summary conviction for an either-way offence, magistrates have the power to commit a defendant to the Crown Court for sentence under s. 3 PCC(S)A 2000 where they consider their maximum powers of punishment to be insufficient, having regard to the seriousness of the offence. Committal for sentence may be in custody or on bail. Where this power is exercised, magistrates can also commit the offender for sentence on any other offences for which the defendant has been convicted s. 6 PCC(S)A 2000. This enables the Crown Court to deal with all outstanding matters including any other less serious either-way or summary matters upon which the defendant has been convicted and any suspended sentence or breach of a community penalty or conditional discharge imposed by a magistrates' court for which the accused now stands to be dealt with. However, the Crown Court's powers of sentence in this respect are limited to those of the magistrates and the summary offence/s must be punishable with imprisonment or disqualification.

The power under s. 3 might be exercised in circumstances where it has been revealed that the accused has a record of previous convictions or is asking for other offences to be taken into consideration. If the defendant is committed for sentence under s. 3, the Crown Court will proceed to deal with the defendant as if he had been convicted on indictment.

Although the point has not been definitively determined by case law, the Divisional Court in *North Sefton Magistrates' Court, ex p. Marsh* (1994) 16 Cr App R (S) 401 held that s. 3 discretion is unfettered and that simply because magistrates had decided to accept jurisdiction to try a case does not constrain the court from subsequently coming to the decision to commit the defendant for sentence upon conviction. However, if nothing comes to light in the way of previous convictions or other offences to be taken into consideration, the accused may consider he had a legitimate expectation to be sentenced summarily.

28.9.3 COMMITTAL FOR SENTENCE UNDER S. 4 PCC(S)A 2000

Where an accused has indicated a guilty plea to an either-way offence but has been committed for trial in the Crown Court on a related either-way offence, the magistrates can commit the defendant to the Crown Court for sentence on the matter to which he has indicated a guilty plea under s. 4 PCC(S)A. If the Crown Court convicts the defendant on the related either-way matter, or if the magistrates' court, on committal for sentence under s. 4, state that it also had the power to do so under s. 3, the Crown Court can proceed to sentence on the offence as if the defendant had been convicted on indictment, otherwise its powers are limited to those upon summary conviction.

28.9.4 CRIMINAL JUSTICE ACT 2003 – POWER TO COMMIT FOR SENTENCE UPON SUMMARY CONVICTION

One of the reasons for extending the sentencing powers of magistrates under the CJA 2003 is to try to ensure that fewer cases are committed to the Crown Court either for trial or for sentence. Consequently, the increased powers of sentence available to magistrates under s. 154 CJA 2003 are aligned with the changes relating to the allocation of either-way cases which are contained in s. 41 and Sch. 3 CJA 2003.

When s. 154 of the Act is brought fully into force (latest date for implementation being November 2006), the maximum custodial sentence that a magistrates' court will be able to pass will increase from six months to 12 months for any one offence and to 65 weeks' imprisonment in respect of two or more offences for which terms are to be served consecutively. The Act confers on the Home Secretary the power to amend these limits to a maximum of 18 months and 24 months respectively.

The power to commit for sentence following an indication of a guilty plea remains and a new s. 3 and s. 4 is inserted into the 2000 Act by s. 41 Sch. 3, para. 22 to the 2003 Act. There will be no power to commit for sentence in a case where jurisdiction to try the either-way offence was accepted by magistrates and a conviction has resulted. This is subject to one exception which applies to 'dangerous offenders' only. The decision about whether to accept jurisdiction to deal with an either-way matter will in future be informed by the fact that the court will be able to have regard to a defendant's previous convictions (Sch. 3).

The combined effect of s. 154 (magistrates' increased sentencing powers) and s. 41 (Sch. 3) (preventing magistrates from committing a case for sentence to the Crown Court where the magistrates' court have accepted jurisdiction to try an either-way matter and have found the defendant guilty) should result in considerably fewer cases being committed to the Crown Court for trial or sentence in the future.

28.10 CROWN COURT'S POWERS OF SENTENCE

The Crown Court's powers of sentence are considerably greater than those of the magistrates' court. We offer the offence of theft as an example. Conviction for a single offence of theft under the Theft Act 1968 in a magistrates' court currently carries a maximum six months custodial sentence (this will increase under the prospective changes in s. 154 CJA 2003 highlighted above). Conviction on indictment in the Crown Court carries a maximum custodial sentence of seven years and an unlimited fine.

The increased powers of sentence available to the Crown Court are of course an important factor in an accused's decision to elect trial in the Crown Court where he is given the choice pursuant to the mode of trial enquiry (see Chapter 16).

Where a Crown Court is required to pass sentence on a defendant who has been convicted of or has pleaded guilty to a summary offence which has been committed to the Crown Court alongside an either-way offence under either ss. 40 or 41 Magistrates' Court Act 1980 (see Chapter 16, paragraphs 16.19 and 16.20), the powers of the Crown Court are limited to those of a magistrates' court.

28.10.1 MANDATORY SENTENCES IN THE CROWN COURT

A number of reforms in recent years have removed the discretionary element in sentencing in favour of mandatory sentences. They tend to affect the Crown Court for the most part. Sections 110 and 111 PCC(S)A 2000 require a minimum sentence of seven years for a third conviction of Class A drug trafficking and a minimum three years for a third conviction of domestic burglary. In relation to domestic burglary the defendant must have committed his second burglary after being convicted of his first and in addition, both burglary convictions must post-date 1 December 1999. The court need not impose the minimum term if it is of the opinion that it would be unjust to do so. A court may go below the minimum sentence in order to grant a discount for a timely guilty plea.

Life imprisonment is mandatory for murder. It is up to the court to fix the minimum term in accordance with s. 269 CJA 2003 and *R v Jones* [2005] EWCA Crim 3115.

Sections 224–229 CJA 2003 make special provision for 'dangerous' offenders. These are considered in more detail in Chapter 29 (29.9.5).

28.11 THE IMPORTANCE OF LEGAL RESEARCH IN RELATION TO SENTENCING

Sentencing law is complex and before any advice can be given in relation to likely sentence you will need to engage in some basic legal research. You need to be certain of the range of possible penalties that may be imposed and the maximum sentence your client could be facing (which for an either-way offence depends where the case is ultimately concluded). The maximum sentence for all offences is specified in *Blackstone's Criminal Practice*.

28.12 WHAT INFORMS THE PROCESS OF SENTENCING?

In short, sentencing guidelines and pre-sentence reports inform the sentencing process. We will deal with each in turn.

It is essential to realise that before advice is offered to a client regarding possible sentence, and indeed before any plea in mitigation is attempted, relevant sentencing guidelines for the offence under consideration must be carefully researched. In serious cases, a defence solicitor may wish to take the advice of counsel or a solicitor-advocate on the question of sentence.

28.12.1 SENTENCING GUIDELINES IN THE CROWN COURT

Most Court of Appeal decisions on appropriate levels of sentencing are reported in the Criminal Appeal Sentencing Reports and summarised in *Blackstone's Criminal Practice*, making it an excellent basis upon which to build research into relevant sentencing guidelines.

The Court of Appeal has established sentencing guidelines for a number of offences dealt with in the Crown Court. Some of the guidelines have been influenced by the advice given by the Sentencing Advisory Panel. We include a list of the offences which have been the subject of Court of Appeal sentencing guidelines and a brief summary of two of these decisions.

- Street robbery – *R v Lobban* [2002] 2 Cr App R (S) 77.
- Making and storing indecent photographs of children – *R v Oliver, Hartrey and Baldwin* [2003] 2 Cr App R (S) 151.
- Death by dangerous driving – *R v Cooksley* [2003] 3 All ER 40.
- Rape offences – *R v Billam* (1986) 8 Cr App R (S) 48 and *R v Millberry, Morgan and Larkenby* [2003] 2 Cr App (S) R 31.

In *Billam* (1986) 8 Cr App R (S) 48, the Lord Chief Justice stated that the variable factors in cases of rape are so numerous that it is difficult to lay down guidelines as to the proper length of sentence in terms of years. The court went on to review the aggravating features, including whether violence is used over and above the force necessary to commit the rape; a weapon is used to frighten or wound the victim; the rape is repeated; the rape has been carefully planned; the defendant has previous convictions for rape or other serious offences of a violent or sexual kind.

In *Millberry* [2003] 2 Cr App (S) R 31, the Court of Appeal revised its guidelines, stating that in assessing the gravity of an individual offence of rape it was necessary to consider the degree of harm to the victim, the culpability of the offender and the risk posed by the offender to society. The guidelines applying to relationship or acquaintance rape and stranger rape should in principle be the same. Similarly, there should be no distinction between male and female rape, with additional factors such as pregnancy following female rape being dealt with on a case-by-case basis. There should also be no distinction between anal rape and vaginal rape, with instances where both types of rape were perpetrated on the victim being treated as repeated rape. The effect of the victim's behaviour on the offender's culpability and the position with regard to historical cases was considered.

The starting points for rape, in the absence of aggravating features, were: (1) five years for a single offence on an adult victim by a single offender; (2) eight years following a contested trial where the rape (a) was committed by two or more offenders; (b) was committed by someone who was in a position of responsibility towards the victim; (c) involved abduction or false imprisonment; (d) involved a child or a vulnerable mentally defective victim, or (e) was racially aggravated, repeated, or committed by a man knowingly suffering from a life threatening sexually transmissible disease; (3) 15 years for a campaign of rape either on the same victim or on multiple victims, and (4) an automatic life sentence for an offender with a previous conviction for a serious offence pursuant to s. 109 Powers of Criminal Courts (Sentencing) Act 2000.

- Burglary of a dwelling – *R v McInerney and Keating* [2003] 1 All ER 1089.

Following detailed consideration by the Sentencing Advisory Panel, the Court of Appeal issued fresh guidelines for sentencing in domestic dwelling burglary cases. The guidelines are extremely comprehensive and identify a number of aggravating and mitigating factors. The guidelines specify that a non-custodial sentence may be appropriate in some instances, although the usual sentence will be custody.

online resource centre

The SGC has recently published a compendium of all Court of Appeal sentencing guidelines cases. It can be accessed at http://www.sentencing-guidelines.gov.uk.

28.12.2 SENTENCING GUIDELINES IN MAGISTRATES' COURTS

Sentencing practice in magistrates' courts is informed by the Magistrates' Court Sentencing Guidelines 2004. They cover offences which magistrates deal with on a frequent basis. The aim of the guidelines is to promote consistency in magistrates' court decisions. The guidelines do not constitute a tariff. They provide a starting point for discussion and a structured way in which to approach sentence based on the seriousness of the offence.

A selection of the guidelines relating to certain offences are included at Appendix 4. Each offence indicates a guideline starting point for sentencing. The guideline starting point is based on a first-time offender pleading not guilty. Consider once more the offences of theft and assault occasioning actual bodily harm highlighted earlier. You will recall that the guideline sentence for a s. 47 assault is a custodial sentence. For a first time offence of theft, the guideline starting point in terms of sentence is a community penalty.

In assessing the seriousness of an offence, magistrates will have regard to all aggravating and mitigating factors. The aggravating and mitigating factors in relation to a s. 47 assault and theft are contained within the sentencing guidelines for each offence (see Appendix 4).

Having made an assessment of seriousness, magistrates then proceed to consider any personal offender mitigation. They then arrive at a sentence and apply any relevant discount for a timely guilty plea. A complete copy of the guidelines can be accessed via password from our Online Resource Centre.

28.12.3 PERSONAL OFFENDER MITIGATION

The seriousness of an offence may well point to a particular type of sentence. However each offender who comes before a court must be sentenced on an individual basis. With this in mind, a court must have regard to any personal offender mitigation that might apply in the particular case before it. It is the combination of the seriousness of the offence, and any personal offender mitigation that will determine the appropriate sentence in an individual case. Thus the seriousness of the offence may well point to a custodial sentence. However, there may be strong personal mitigating factors which point to a community based sentence as being the most appropriate sentence in the particular case. Personal offender mitigation will clearly be highlighted in your plea in mitigation (the specifics of which we consider in Chapter 32). Personal offender mitigation may also be highlighted in any pre-sentence report. A pre-sentence report therefore informs the process of sentencing.

28.12.4 PRE-SENTENCE REPORTS – S. 156 CJA 2003

Pre-sentence reports (PSRs), as defined by s. 158 CJA 2003, are prepared by probation officers after consultation with the offender and any other relevant source, including advance information. They are designed to assist the court in finding the most appropriate sentence for the individual concerned. The report should analyse the offence and the offender's culpability. It should assess the offender's attitude to the offence and his awareness of the consequences of his actions. The report will highlight the offender's personal history, previous convictions, education, employment position and state of health. Importantly the report will assess the offender's risk of re-offending based on the current offence and his attitude to it. It will consider appropriate sentences and address such matters as the defendant's suitability for certain types of sentence. A pre-sentence report will not normally contain a recommendation as to sentence but it will contain a proposal, which can often be highly influential, including, where appropriate, the need for a medical/psychiatric report.

In accordance with s. 156 CJA 2003, a court must order a pre-sentence report before:

(a) imposing a sentence of imprisonment;

(b) making a community order with requirements (e.g. supervision, unpaid work, drug rehabilitation requirement, mental health requirement, activity requirement);

Section 156 CJA 2003 provides that the court need not obtain a PSR in the case of an offender over 18 where a report would be unnecessary. An example might include a case where custody is an inevitable sentence although it may be argued that a report could still be useful to address the question of the duration of the term. Unless the sentence in a particular case is clear and a report would make little difference, it is always good sentencing practice to obtain a report where custody or a community sentence is being considered.

A failure to obtain a pre-sentence report does not invalidate a sentence, although it would be a relevant factor to consider in any subsequent appeal.

Sometimes magistrates will indicate the type of sentence they are considering when requesting a pre-sentence report. More often, however, so as not to bind the ultimate sentencing bench, the court will announce that it is requesting a PSR and that it is 'keeping all of its sentencing options open'. This means the court is not ruling out custody. If a court wishes to retain the option of committing the offender to the Crown Court for sentence, it should specifically make mention of this when ordering the PSR. A failure to do so can give rise to a legitimate expectation on the part of the defendant that commital for sentence as an option has been ruled out (*Feltham Justices, ex p. Rees* [2001] 2 Cr App R (S) 1).

Where an offender is on bail, it takes on average four weeks to prepare a full or standard delivery pre-sentence report. Where the offender has been remanded in custody pending sentence, it takes three weeks to prepare a full report.

28.12.5 FAST DELIVERY REPORTS (FDR)

The Fast Delivery Report (FDR) is an expedited pre-sentence report. FDRs are designed to speed up the provision of information to courts to allow sentencing without delay. The FDR is prepared by a probation officer in court on the day or within 24 hours. It will be handwritten by the probation officer. If s/he considers a full report is required, an adjournment will be necessary. FDRs are intended for the more straightforward cases. Magistrates must have a specific sentence in mind when requesting an FDR. Typically this includes a community order of 12 months with a supervision requirements or unpaid work requirement of no more than 100 hours. Where a court requests an FDR, it is effectively tying its hands. If sentence cannot proceed on the particular occasion because the probation service feels a full standard delivery pre-sentence report is needed, it will be difficult for the subsequent sentencing court to pass a more severe sentence than that which was contemplated by the earlier bench.

28.13 VICTIM IMPACT STATEMENTS

There has been a significant move to acknowledge victims' rights within the criminal justice system in recent years. Since October 2001, it has been possible for a victim to make a 'victim impact statement' detailing the effect that the offence has had on him or her. Guidance on the use of such statements was provided in *Practice Direction (Victim Personal Statements)* [2002] 1 Cr App R 69.

28.14 NEWTON HEARINGS

A decision to plead guilty does not necessarily signify acceptance of everything the prosecutor says about the circumstances of the offence in outline to the sentencing court. For example, a defendant may accept he is guilty of assault occasioning actual bodily harm in that he admits having punched his victim. However, he may go on to deny, as alleged by the prosecution, that he used a weapon in the attack. Should the court sentence on the basis of the prosecution's version of the facts or the defendant's version? The answer depends upon whether the facts in dispute would significantly affect the sentence the court is likely to pass. In the above example, the use of a weapon considerably aggravates the seriousness of an assault and would make a material difference when it comes to passing sentence.

Where sentence would not be significantly affected, the court will sentence on the basis of the defendant's version of the facts. It is important for the defence lawyer to notify the Crown Prosecution Service if there is a significant dispute as to the facts upon which the defendant is entering his guilty plea. Having heard any representations from the CPS based on paragraph 9.3 of the Code for Crown Prosecutors, the court may decide to hold a Newton hearing (*R v Newton* (1982) 77 Cr App R 13) in order to determine where the truth lies in relation to the disputed facts. If such a hearing is held, the normal rules of evidence will apply. Witnesses will be called, examined and cross-examined in the same way as they would be at trial. A verdict is then reached based on the evidence.

Notwithstanding that the court finds against the defendant on the disputed fact, the defendant is still entitled to a sentencing discount based on his earlier plea although it may not be as great as it would have been had he pleaded guilty on the basis of the prosecution's version of the facts at the outset. A body of case law on Newton hearings has developed which is covered in *Blackstone's Criminal Practice*. Recently the Court of Appeal has produced guidelines on the use of Newton hearings in *R v Underwood* [2004] All ER (D) 575 (Jul).

Where magistrates or a jury have made a finding of guilt following a trial based on charges brought by the CPS, it is obviously much more difficult for the defendant to contend that he should be sentenced on a factual basis different from that basis upon which the facts in the case were proved. Once again a body of case law has developed on this aspect which is outside the scope of this work but which may be considered further in *Blackstone's Criminal Practice*.

28.15 TAKING OTHER OFFENCES INTO CONSIDERATION

> 'The defendant pleads guilty to the offence of theft charged against him and asks that you take a further 26 offences of a like nature into consideration . . .'

For the most part a defendant is sentenced on those offences for which he has been convicted or for which he pleads guilty. The one exception to this is in relation to those offences which the defendant asks to be 'TIC'd' – taken into consideration. The defendant is not convicted of the offences but admits the offences in court and asks for them to be taken into consideration upon passing sentence.

When interviewing an accused, the police may believe the accused is responsible for other similar offences in the vicinity, for which they have no proof. In an attempt to wipe the slate clean, the accused might admit such offences. Any offences to be taken into consideration should be listed on a schedule which is signed by the defendant. In court, the defendant will be asked to confirm he is admitting the offences listed on the schedule and that he wishes for them to be taken into consideration when the court passes sentence.

There are mutual benefits to such an arrangement. For the prosecution, it assists in the clear-up rate for crimes. For the defendant, although he receives a higher sentence because of the increased number of offences, he knows he cannot be made the subject of a separate prosecution for each of the offences at some later date. The procedure can be initiated by the police during the defendant's detention. It can also be utilised by the prosecutor in court after a finding of guilt by a jury or magistrates. The procedure does not apply to driving matters which carry endorsement and/or disqualification. Courts should not allow offences of a different nature to be taken into consideration, and magistrates should not take into consideration indictable-only offences.

Important guidance on sentencing in relation to offences taken into consideration is provided in the Divisional Court's decision in *R v Miles* [2006] EWCA 256.

28.16 KEEPING UP-TO-DATE

Sentencing law changes frequently as cases are taken to appeal and determined by the Court of Appeal and the Divisional Court. It is important to keep up to date with appellant decisions, the majority of which are published in the *Criminal Appeals Reports (Sentencing)*. Case law is also featured in the *Criminal Law Review*, *Justice of the Peace* and *Archbold's Criminal Digest*. With an eye to the near future, we can expect case law on sentencing arising out of the Sexual Offences Act 2003 and the new offences it has created. Reference might also be made to *Current Sentencing Practice* and the Sentencing Guidelines Council, which publishes its guidance on-line.

KEY POINT SUMMARY

- Know the range of penalties available for the offences you are dealing with.

- Do not necessarily assume that just because your client has pleaded guilty to an either-way offence before a magistrates' court or has been found guilty of such an offence that he will be sentenced summarily – be aware of the power to commit for sentence under s. 3 PCC (S)A 2000.

- Sentencing practice requires courts to sentence on the basis of the seriousness of the offence. Always make an attempt to assess the seriousness of the offence by balancing the aggravating features of the offence against any mitigating features.

- Use available guidelines (including Court of Appeal decisions and the Magistrates' Court Sentencing Guidelines) in order to assess seriousness and to give you a starting point as to likely sentence.

- Although an offence might be regarded as serious and warrant a particular sentence, a court will have regard to personal offender mitigation in arriving at the most appropriate sentence.

- Anticipate the need for a pre-sentence report and understand why such a report is often influential in informing the sentencing process.

- If your client accepts he is guilty but disputes a material aspect of the prosecution's version of events, anticipate the need for a Newton hearing.

- Timely guilty pleas always attract a sentencing discount.

- Significant changes to the sentencing powers of the magistrates' court which are aligned to changes to the mode of trial enquiry for either-way offences are due to come into force in November 2006. Our Online Resource Centre will cover the changes when they come into force.

SELF-TEST QUESTIONS

Consider the following scenario and then try to answer the questions that follow. Apply the provisions of the Criminal Justice Act 2003 in answering these questions.

Scott is charged with assault occasioning actual bodily harm contrary to s. 47 Offences Against the Person Act 1861. It is alleged that Scott, aged 23, was drunk and while at a kebab take-away he and a group of other youths started shouting racial abuse at a group of Asian youths. A disturbance broke out and it is alleged Scott pushed one of the Asian youths to the ground and kicked him about the arms and legs, causing extensive bruising to the young man's body.

Scott pleads not guilty, raising identification as a defence. He is convicted.

At the time of this offence Scott was on bail for an alleged offence of theft but was later acquitted. Scott's previous convictions include:

- 15 months ago: assault occasioning actual bodily harm – s. 47 Offences against the Person Act 1861 (Community Order, 12 months);

- 24 months ago: public order – threatening behaviour – s. 5 Public Order Act 1968 (fine);

- 36 months ago: Theft – s. 1 Theft Act 1968 (conditional discharge).

What is the starting point in terms of sentencing for an assault contrary to s. 47 according to the Magistrates' Court Sentencing Guidelines?
Try to gauge the seriousness of this offence – what factors aggravate the seriousness of this assault?
Is this a case where a pre-sentence report is likely to be requested?
Is Scott entitled to a sentencing discount?

Case Studies *R v William Hardy*; *R v Roger Martin* (web-based only); *R v Lenny Whyte*

In relation to *R v Hardy* and *R v Martin*, you will be able to see the plea in mitigation and the sentencing process on the video clips contained within our Online Resource Centre. Before you view these however, it is important that you engage in the process which culminates in the plea in mitigation. This can only be done by considering this chapter and Chapters 29–31 and engaging in the tasks we have set in relation to the case studies throughout these chapters.

R v William Hardy

It will be recalled that William Hardy has been advised to plead guilty to an offence of engaging in sexual activity with a child contrary to s. 9(2) Sexual offences Act 2003. Prior to 1 May 2004, this offence would have been charged as unlawful sexual intercourse with a girl under the age of 16, contrary to s. 6 Sexual Offences Act 1956. What is the maximum sentence he faces if he is tried before magistrates? What is the maximum sentence he faces if he is sentenced before a Crown Court judge? You should of course note that because William Hardy will be indicating a guilty plea to the either-way offence, jurisdiction to deal with the matter remains in the magistrates' court. However, under s. 3 PCC(S)A 2000, the magistrates can commit the matter to sentence in the Crown Court if they consider their powers of punishment to be insufficient. William would obviously prefer to have the matter dealt with before magistrates.

- Research the relevant sentencing guidelines for this offence in an attempt to assess the level of seriousness.

- Try to ascertain what you consider will be the worst outcome for William Hardy in terms of sentence.

- Do you consider a pre-sentence report should be obtained in this case?

All of the above matters are considered in Appendix 5 when the decision is reached as to where this matter should be sentenced.

R v Roger Martin

If you have considered the documentation in relation to this web-based only case study, you will be aware that Roger Martin has been advised to plead guilty to the offences of common assault, careless driving and failing to stop and report after an accident. All these matters are summary only and Roger Martin must therefore be sentenced before magistrates. You will note that the solicitor's ability to negotiate a reduced charge of dangerous driving down to careless driving has been of enormous benefit to Roger Martin. He no longer faces the risk of a committal to the Crown Court and of course, dangerous driving carries with it a mandatory disqualification period of 12 months.

- Ignoring the driving penalties for the time being, assess the level of seriousness of the common assault. Research any relevant sentencing guidelines.

- Try to ascertain what you consider will be the worst outcome for Roger Martin in terms of sentence.
- Do you consider a pre-sentence report should be obtained in these circumstances?

The questions posed in relation to *R v Roger Martin* are considered further in Appendix 5.

R v Lenny Whyte

You will be aware that Lenny Whyte was acquitted of the offence of domestic dwelling burglary. Had Lenny Whyte been convicted before the Crown Court, what would have been the maximum sentence the judge could have passed? Research the relevant sentencing guidelines for burglary offences tried on indictment. In your view, and being realistic, what sentence do you consider Lenny would have received? Would it have been necessary for a pre-sentence report to have been ordered?

FIGURE 28.1 STRUCTURED APPROACH TO SENTENCING UNDER CJA 2003

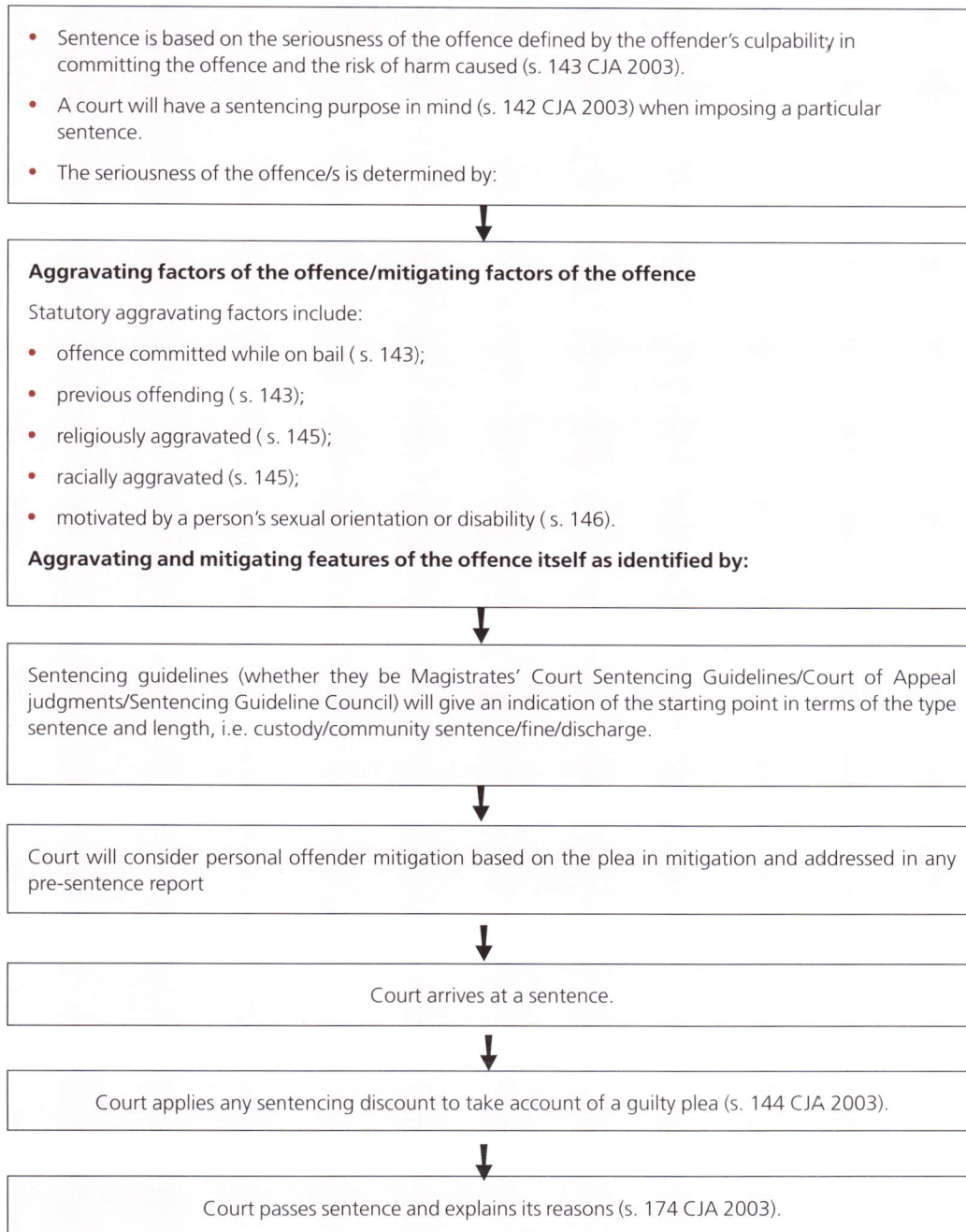

- Sentence is based on the seriousness of the offence defined by the offender's culpability in committing the offence and the risk of harm caused (s. 143 CJA 2003).

- A court will have a sentencing purpose in mind (s. 142 CJA 2003) when imposing a particular sentence.

- The seriousness of the offence/s is determined by:

⬇

Aggravating factors of the offence/mitigating factors of the offence

Statutory aggravating factors include:

- offence committed while on bail (s. 143);

- previous offending (s. 143);

- religiously aggravated (s. 145);

- racially aggravated (s. 145);

- motivated by a person's sexual orientation or disability (s. 146).

Aggravating and mitigating features of the offence itself as identified by:

⬇

Sentencing guidelines (whether they be Magistrates' Court Sentencing Guidelines/Court of Appeal judgments/Sentencing Guideline Council) will give an indication of the starting point in terms of the type sentence and length, i.e. custody/community sentence/fine/discharge.

⬇

Court will consider personal offender mitigation based on the plea in mitigation and addressed in any pre-sentence report

⬇

Court arrives at a sentence.

⬇

Court applies any sentencing discount to take account of a guilty plea (s. 144 CJA 2003).

⬇

Court passes sentence and explains its reasons (s. 174 CJA 2003).

29 CUSTODIAL SENTENCES

29.1 INTRODUCTION

In this and the following chapter, we consider the criteria for imposing a range of sentences available to adult (over 18) criminal courts in England and Wales. The primary focus in this chapter is on custodial sentences.

The Criminal Justice Act 2003 has introduced a new range of custodial sentences available to the courts. As with other aspects of sentencing, the law is likely to be in a transitional state for some time. The provisions in relation to custodial sentences will be phased in over 2006/2007. Some areas are piloting the new custodial sentences. In this chapter, we cover both the existing law and the prospective law.

Before we consider custodial sentences in detail, you are reminded that in passing sentence of any kind, a court will have regard to one or more sentencing objectives specified in s. 142 CJA 2003, which include:

(a) the punishment of offenders;

(b) reduction in crime (including its reduction by deterrence);

(c) the reform and rehabilitation of the offender;

(d) the protection of the public; and

(e) the making of reparation by the offender to persons affected by their offences.

A custodial sentence is clearly punitive in nature. It also provides protection to the public and seeks to deter offenders from committing further crimes. As you will see, some of the changes introduced under the CJA 2003 seek to incorporate an element of reform and rehabilitation upon release.

In this chapter we consider:

* the basis on which a custodial sentence can be passed under the CJA 2003;
* the factors relevant to determining the length of a custodial sentence;
* the types of custodial sentence a court can impose; and
* whether the custodial term has to be served in full.

29.2 WHEN CAN A CUSTODIAL SENTENCE BE IMPOSED?

The fact that an offence carries the possibility of a custodial sentence does not automatically mean that a custodial sentence will be imposed. There is a statutory criterion that must be met before a custodial sentence can be imposed. Section 152(2) CJA 2003 states that:

'. . . the court must not pass a custodial sentence on the offender unless it is of the opinion – that the offence, or combination of the offence and one or more offences associated with it, was so serious that neither a fine alone or a community sentence can be justified for the offence . . .

(3) . . . Nothing in subsection (2) prevents the court from passing a custodial sentence on the offender if (a) he fails to express his willingness to comply with a requirement which is proposed by the court to be included in a community order and which requires an expression of willingness; or (b) he fails to comply with an order under s. 161(2) (pre-sentence drug testing).'

The wording of this section seeks to reinforce the fact that custody should be a sentence of last resort.

29.2.1 THE CUSTODY THRESHOLD TEST – S. 152(2) CJA 2003

Section 152(2) provides what is known as the 'custody threshold test': 'Is the offence so serious that neither a community sentence nor fine can be imposed?' Only if this question can be answered in the affirmative can a custodial sentence be imposed. As we saw in the previous chapter, the seriousness of an offence is assessed according to the presence of aggravating and/or mitigating factors, of which the offender's culpability in committing the offence will be an important consideration. When an initial determination is made that the offence is so serious that it merits a custodial sentence, there may be personal offender mitigation which dictates that a less draconian sentence than custody should be imposed.

It will be self-evident that, in many instances where an offender is convicted of a serious indictable offence, a custodial sentence is inevitable. In the preceding chapter, we highlighted a number of Court of Appeal decisions which have provided sentencing guidelines to the Crown Court in relation to a number of offences. For some offences, such as rape, the Court of Appeal has indicated a custodial sentence is inevitable. You were also introduced to the Magistrates' Court Sentencing Guidelines (2004), which suggest a custodial sentence as being the starting point for a number of different offences, including assault occasioning actual bodily harm and theft in breach of trust.

29.2.2 WHAT IF THE THRESHOLD TEST IS FINELY BALANCED?

Where the custody threshold test is finely balanced, the defence advocate has everything to play for in his plea in mitigation. Case law under the previous threshold test laid down by s. 79(2) of the 2000 Act, has provided some valuable assistance in this regard. The most important case is *R v Howells* [1999] 1 WLR 307. The general guidance of the Court of Appeal is reproduced below.

'It would be dangerous and wrong for this Court to lay down prescriptive rules governing the exercise of that judgment, and any guidance we give, however general, will be subject to exceptions and qualifications in some cases. We do, however, think that in approaching cases which are on or near the custody threshold courts will usually find it helpful to begin by considering the nature and extent of the defendant's criminal intention and the nature and extent of any injury or damage caused to the victim. Other things being equal, an offence which is deliberate and premeditated or which involves an excessive response to provocation; an offence which inflicts personal injury or mental trauma, particularly if permanent, will usually be more serious than one which inflicts financial loss only. In considering the seriousness of any offence the Court may take into account any previous convictions of the offender of any failure to respond to previous sentences (2000 Act, section 151(1)) and must treat it as an aggravating factor if the offence was committed while the offender was on bail (2000 Act, section 151(2)).

In deciding whether to impose a custodial sentence in borderline cases the sentencing court will ordinarily take account of matters relating to the offender:

(a) The Court will have regard to an offender's admission of responsibility for the offence, particularly if reflected in a plea of guilty tendered at the earliest opportunity and accompanied by hard evidence of genuine remorse, as shown (for example) by an expression of regret to the victim and an offer of compensation. Attention is drawn to section 152 of the PCC(S)A 2000.

(b) Where offending has been fuelled by addiction to drink or drugs, the Court will be inclined to look more favourably on an offender who has already demonstrated (by taking practical steps to that end) a genuine, self-motivated determination to address his addiction.

(c) Youth and immaturity, while affording no defence, will often justify a less rigorous penalty than would be appropriate for an adult.

(d) Some measures of leniency will ordinarily be extended to offenders of previous good character, the more so if there is evidence of positive good character (such as solid employment record or faithful discharge of family duties) as opposed to a mere absence of previous convictions. It will sometimes be appropriate to take account of family responsibilities, or physical or mental disability.

(e) While the Court will never impose a custodial sentence unless satisfied that it is necessary to do so, there will be even greater reluctance to impose a custodial sentence on an offender who has never before served such a sentence.

Courts should always bear in mind that criminal sentences are in almost every case intended to protect the public, whether by punishing the offender or reforming him, or deterring him and others, or all of these things. Courts cannot and should not be unmindful of the important public dimension of criminal sentencing and the importance of maintaining public confidence in the sentencing system.

Where the Court is of the opinion that an offence, or the combination of an offence and one or more offences associated with it, is so serious that only a custodial sentence can be justified and that such a sentence should be passed, the sentence imposed should be no longer than is necessary to meet the penal purpose which the Court has in mind . . .'

Sentencing law develops at a fast pace. It is therefore important for the busy defence practitioner to keep up-to-date with new case law. We cite two relatively recent decisions of the Court of Appeal which might assist a defence advocate in trying to avoid a custodial sentence for his client: overcrowding in prisons (*R v Kefford* [2002] 2 Cr App (S) R 106) and sentencing of women with young children (*R v Mills* [2002] 2 Cr App R (S) 229). In *Kefford* Lord Woolf CJ stated:

'The overcrowding of the prison system is not only a matter for grave concern for the prison service, is also a matter of grave concern for the criminal justice system as a whole. Prison sentences are imposed by the courts normally for three purposes: to punish the offender concerned, to deter other offenders and to stop the offender committing further offences in the future. The ability of the prison service to tackle a prisoner's offending behaviour and so reduce reoffending is adversely affected if a prison is overcrowded. The ability of the prison service to service the courts is impeded if prisons are overcrowded, since the prison service is unable to ensure that prisoners arrive at courts at the appropriate time. In the past attempts have been made to relieve overcrowding by using police cells but this is a wholly unsatisfactory remedy. Apart from being extremely expensive, it prevents the police performing their duties in tackling crime.

Those who are responsible for imposing sentences have to take into account the impact on the prison system of the number of prisoners the prison estate is being required to accommodate at the present time. The courts are not responsible for providing prison places. That is the responsibility of the government. However, the courts must accept the realities of the situation. Providing a new prison takes a substantial period of time and in the present situation it is of the greatest importance to the criminal justice system as a whole and the public who depend upon the criminal justice system for their protection against crime, that only those who need to be sent to prison are sent to prison and that they are not sent to prison for any longer than is necessary.

Nothing that we say in this judgment is intended to deter courts from sending to prison for the appropriate period those who commit offences involving violence or intimidation or other grave crimes . . . There are, however, other categories of offences where a community punishment or a fine can be sometimes a more appropriate form of sentence than imprisonment.

What we have said here is of particular importance to magistrates because they deal with a great many cases where the decision as to whether a prison sentence is necessary is frequently made . . .

In the case of economic crimes, for example obtaining undue credit by fraud, prison is not necessarily the only appropriate form of punishment. Particularly in the case of those who have no record of previous offending, the very fact of having to appear before a court can be a significant punishment. Certainly, having to perform a form of community punishment can be a very salutary way of making it clear that crime does not pay, particularly if a community punishment order is combined with a curfew order. In the appropriate cases, it can be better that an offender repays his debt to society by performing some useful task for the public than spending a short time in prison. The recent Halliday Report makes clear the limits of what can be achieved during a short period of custody. It is preferable that the prison service is in a position to deal effectively, uninhibited by the corrosive effects of overcrowding, with those cases for whom imprisonment is necessary.'

In *R v Kefford* the original sentence of 12 months imposed on a building society employee for several dishonesty-related offence totaling £11,120 was reduced to four months.

R v Mills was a case involving a woman of previous good character with the sole care of young children who was convicted of the fraudulent use of a credit card. On appeal against sentence, Lord Woolf CJ observed:

'The first factor that he has to take into account in doing so is that it is now clear that apart from 'the clang of the prison door' type of sentence, which gives a prisoner the opportunity of knowing what is involved in imprisonment, the ability of the prison service to achieve anything positive in the case of a short prison sentence is very limited. Secondly, with a mother who is the sole support of two young children, as is the case here, the judge has to bear in mind the consequences to those children if the sole carer is sent to prison. Finally, he should take into account the current situation in relation to the female prison population . . .

But in a borderline case, in a case where the offence does not in particular involve violence but is one with financial consequences to a commercial concern, it is very important that those who have responsibilities for sentencing take into account the facts to which we have referred with regard to the prison population as well as the other matters. In a case of a person such as this appellant who is of previous good character, who has been performing useful acts in the community, where there is every reason to think that she will not offend again, and where the offending behaviour is out of character with her normal behaviour, the courts should strive to avoid sending her to prison and instead use punishments in the community which enable offenders to repay the harm they have done. It is true that obtaining credit, as this appellant did, is easy for those who resort to dishonesty. The courts should deter those sort of offences, albeit some would say that the credit companies should do more to check references which are given by those who attempt to commit offences of this nature. Be that as it may, commercial concerns are entitled to the protection of the courts. What we have said merely indicates the course which where possible the courts should take to impose a punishment which is fitting and appropriate for that nature of offence.'

In *Mills*, an eight-month prison sentence was reduced to one month.

In formulating a plea in mitigation in a case where there is a risk of custody, defence advocates should not shy away from citing relevant case law and any authorities containing sentencing guidelines that are specific to the particular offence being considered.

29.3 CUSTODY BETWEEN AGES 18 AND 21

Section 89(1) PCC(S)A 2000 provides that an offender under the age of 21 cannot be sentenced to a term of imprisonment in an adult prison. Offenders under the age of 21 but over 18, who are subject to a custodial sentence, will serve their time at a young offenders' institution. This will change when s. 61 Criminal Justice and Courts Service Act 2000 is eventually brought into force, as the sentence will become one of imprisonment to be served in an adult prison.

29.4 GIVING REASONS FOR IMPOSING A CUSTODIAL SENTENCE

In passing a custodial sentence, s. 174(2)(b) CJA 2003 requires a court to state in open court why it is of the opinion that the offence is so serious that no other sentence apart from custody is justified.

29.5 PROHIBITION ON PASSING A CUSTODIAL SENTENCE

Section 83(1) Powers of the Criminal Court (Sentencing) Act 2000 prohibits a court from imposing a sentence of imprisonment on an offender who is not legally represented and who has not previously received a custodial sentence. The prohibition does not apply if the offender has been granted legal representation but the right has been withdrawn because of his conduct or if, having been informed of his right to apply and having had the opportunity to do so, he has failed or refused to apply for such representation. This remains unchanged under the CJA 2003.

29.6 THE NEED FOR A PRE-SENTENCE REPORT

In accordance with the provisions in s. 156 CJA 2003 and subject to s. 156(4), it will normally be necessary to obtain a pre-sentence report before passing a sentence of imprisonment. Additionally, where consideration is being given to sentencing a mentally disordered offender to prison, save for custodial sentences fixed by law, the court should request a medical report. Under s. 157(3) CJA 2003, the court must consider any information before it as regards an offender's mental condition and the likely effect a custodial sentence would have on the condition and on any treatment which may be available.

29.7 LENGTH OF CUSTODIAL SENTENCE

Section 153(2) CJA 2003 requires that a custodial sentence must be for the shortest term that is commensurate with the seriousness of the offence, or the combination of the offence and one or more offences associated with it.

Consequently, a court should not impose a sentence of greater length than the seriousness of the offence merits for the specific purpose of making a special example of the defendant, although it can reflect the need to deter others (*R v Cunningham* (1993) 14 Cr App R (S) 444). The proportionality principle in terms of the length of sentence does not apply to a sentence fixed by law, indeterminate and extended sentences for certain violent and sexual offences (s. 224–229, CJA 2003).

Decisions of the Court of Appeal, including *R v Ollerenshaw* [1999] 1 Cr App R (S) 65 and *R v Howells* (cited earlier in the context of the 2000 Sentencing Act) have encouraged courts to keep custodial sentences as short as possible, consistent with their duty to protect the public interest and to punish and deter the criminal. The well-publicised concern about prison overcrowding reinforces the point, as do the decisions in *Kefford* [2002] Crim LR 432 and *Mills* [2002] 2 Cr App R (S) 229, referred to earlier.

29.7.1 **CONSECUTIVE AND CONCURRENT CUSTODIAL TERMS**

In sentencing an offender for more than one offence, a court must have regard to the totality principle, in that the overall sentence passed must not be disproportionate to the overall seriousness of the offending behaviour. Statutory effect is given to the principle in s. 153(2) CJA 2003 and the principle applies as much to community orders and fines as it does to custodial sentences. The problem most often arises in deciding whether two or more custodial sentences should be served concurrently or consecutively.

Assume a sentence of three months' imprisonment is imposed for an offence of possession of an offensive weapon and a further custodial sentence of three months for driving while disqualified. The sentences are expressed to run consecutively. This means that the offender is required to serve a total of six months' imprisonment. Had the two sentences been expressed to run concurrently, the offender would be required to serve a total of three months in custody. In deciding to impose consecutive custodial sentences, the court must have regard to the totality of the defendant's actions and the need to sentence proportionately.

29.7.2 **CREDIT FOR GUILTY PLEA**

Section 144 CJA 2003 should not be forgotten (see Chapter 28, paragraph 28.8). Credit should be given for a timely guilty plea. Where a custodial sentence is to be imposed the court should reduce the term to take account of the provision in s. 144 CJA 2003.

In its definitive guidelines on s. 144 CJA 2003, the Sentencing Guidelines Council suggests that where an offence crosses the threshold for imposition of a custodial sentence, the application of the reduction principle may properly form the basis for imposing a non-custodial sentence option. The reduction principle has no application to the extended sentences and indeterminate sentence, passed on 'dangerous' offenders.

Section 174 CJA 2003 imposes a duty on the court to state in open court that in consequence of the guilty plea, the court has imposed a less severe sentence than it otherwise would have done.

29.7.3 **TIME SPENT REMANDED IN CUSTODY**

Time spent on remand in prison must also be taken into account in determining the overall length of a custodial sentence. The current rules are contained in s. 240 CJA 2003.

29.7.4 **MAGISTRATES' COURT MAXIMUM SENTENCE**

The length of any custodial sentence passed by a magistrates' court is subject to the statutory maximum of six months in respect of any one offence, unless the statute creating the offence prescribes a shorter period (s. 78 PCC(S)A 2000 and s. 133 MCA 1980). Magistrates can pass an aggregate sentence of 12 months upon conviction for two or more either-way offences (s. 133 MCA 1980). The minimum sentence of imprisonment a magistrates' court can impose is five days (s. 132 MCA 1980). Where, at the mode of trial enquiry or upon sentencing a defendant convicted of an either-way offence, the magistrates conclude their maximum custodial term of six months is insufficient, the court can of course commit the defendant to be sentenced in the Crown Court (ss. 3–4 PCC(S)A 2000).

> ### Looking Ahead
>
> You are reminded that under s. 154 CJA 2003, magistrates' powers of sentence are set to increase significantly (see Chapter 28, paragraph 28.9.4 onwards) and that this should reduce the number of occasions on which a defendant is committed to the Crown Court for sentence. These provisions are not expected to come into force until November 2006.

29.8 FIXED LENGTH SENTENCES

In some instances, the length of a custodial sentence is fixed by law. This applies to conviction for murder and mandatory minimum sentences (under ss. 110 and 111 PCC(S) A 2000) for a third conviction in connection with Class A drug trafficking and burglary. Mandatory minimum periods also apply in relation to certain firearms offences. In relation to each of these, a court is required to impose the minimum statutory term unless it would be unjust to do so. Where an assessment of 'dangerous' has been made in accordance with s. 226 CJA, 2003 (see below), a mandatory sentence of life or an indeterminate sentence for public protection must be passed.

The requirement to give credit for a timely guilty plea under s. 144 CJA 2003 applies to the minimum custodial terms that have to be imposed under ss. 110 and 111 PCC(S) A 2000. Section 144 (2) CJA 2003 stipulates that the maximum reduction for a guilty plea shall be 20 per cent of the determinate sentence of at least three years which would otherwise have been imposed.

29.9 NEW CUSTODIAL SENTENCES UNDER THE CJA 2003

The CJA 2003 has introduced a number of new custodial sentences including custody plus, intermittent custody and custody minus.

29.9.1 CUSTODY PLUS (S. 181) – NOT EXPECTED TO BE IMPLEMENTED UNTIL 2006/2007

Custody plus is the label given to all custodial sentences imposed for a term of less than 12 months.

This new sentence seeks to address a common criticism of short custodial sentences (less than 12 months), which is that there is no supervision of such offenders once they are released from prison. Thus there is no opportunity for the Probation Service to work with the offender to try and ascertain the reason for the offending behaviour.

The custody plus sentence must be passed where a court sentences an offender to a custodial sentence of less than 12 months. The custody plus provision applies to magistrates' courts and the Crown Court.

The term of the sentence must be expressed in weeks and must be for a minimum of 28 weeks, and not more than 51 weeks, in respect of any one offence. If two or more periods of imprisonment are imposed to run consecutively, the maximum aggregate term is 65 weeks.

The court must specify jail time of between two weeks and 13 weeks (26 weeks, if two or more terms of imprisonment are to run consecutively). The court must specify a licence period (which is the remainder of the total term less the maximum permitted cumulative custodial period), which must be for at least 26 weeks. During the period of the licence the offender will be expected to work with his probation officer. During the licence term the court will impose conditions with which the offender must comply. These will be recommended by the probation service in its pre-sentence report.

Conditions could include an unpaid work requirement (s. 199), an activity requirement (s. 201), a programme requirement (s. 202), a prohibited activity requirement (s. 203), a curfew requirement (s. 204), an exclusion requirement (s. 205), a supervision requirement (s. 213) and, in the case of an offender under 25, an attendance centre requirement (s. 214). Some of these conditions must be supported by an electronic tagging requirement. A failure to comply with licence conditions may lead to the licence conditions being revoked and the offender being recalled to prison.

The SGC has recently issued draft guidance on the custody plus provisions. The guidance is available at: http://www.sentencing-guidelines.gov.uk.

> **Example**
>
> Damian is given a 32-week sentence. He must serve at least 26 weeks on licence. In terms of the custodial element, the court can impose a term of between two and six weeks. Therefore it could require Damian to serve six weeks in custody and 26 weeks on licence, making a total of 32 weeks.

The custody plus provisions in relation to custodial terms of less than 12 months are significant. Once they are fully operational, we will bring you a comprehensive update via the updating pages of our Online Resource Centre.

online resource centre

29.9.2 INTERMITTENT CUSTODY – S. 183 CJA (SUBJECT TO PILOT EVALUATION)

Under intermittent custody the offender serves his jail time in blocks, i.e. Friday to Sunday/Monday to Friday, enabling the offender to maintain contact with his community, family, educational course or employment. The sentence is currently being piloted in two prisons. It is widely believed that such a sentence reduces the risk of re-offending.

The court must impose a term of at least 28 weeks but not exceeding 51 weeks, to be served during intermittent periods. Consecutive orders must not exceed 65 weeks. The order must specify the number of days to be served in prison, which can range from at least 14 days but no more than 90 days in total (this increases to 180 if consecutive terms of imprisonment are imposed.) In between prison time, the offender is released on licence and conditions can be attached to that licence. If the terms of the offender's licence are breached, he will be recalled to prison and the privilege of intermittent custody will be lost.

29.9.3 SENTENCES OF 12 MONTHS OR MORE (IMPLEMENTED APRIL 2005)

The CJA 2003 draws a distinction between custodial terms of less than 12 months and custodial terms of more than 12 months. In relation to custodial terms of 12 months or more, relevant provisions are contained in ss. 237–268.

A prison sentence of 12 months or more is served in full, although half the sentence is served on licence in the community. In passing sentence, the court will be able to recommend certain licence requirements, although they will not be binding on the Probation Service. The Probation Service will be able to attach specific requirements to the second half of the custodial sentence to prevent re-offending and to protect the public. A failure to abide by the requirements will result in the offender being recalled to custody. The provisions do not apply to those serving an intermittent custody order or to 'dangerous' offenders or to those offenders subject to extended sentences.

29.9.4 DRUG-TESTING REQUIREMENTS ON RELEASE

> **Looking Ahead**
>
> Section 266 amends s. 64 Criminal Justice and Courts Service Act 2000 by allowing a court to impose a drug testing requirement for any specified Class A drug, for the purpose of determining whether an offender released on licence is complying with the terms of his licence.

29.9.5 SENTENCING DANGEROUS OFFENDERS

Sections 224–230 CJA 2003 introduced significant changes with regard to 'dangerous' offenders.

The provisions apply to adults as well as youth offenders (those under the age of 18). The application of the dangerousness provisions in relation to youth offenders is considered in Chapter 35. The provisions apply to 'specified' and 'serious' offences.

A 'specified offence' is an offence of violence or a sexual offence specified in Schedule 15 of the Act and which carries a sentence of between two and ten years imprisonment. A 'serious offence' is a violent or sexual offence specified in Schedule 15 which carries a sentence of at least ten or more years imprisonment in the case of an adult.

A surprising number of offences are listed in Schedule 15. Some of the offences are triable either way. In deciding whether to accept jurisdiction to try a defendant charged with an either-way offence or to sentence such an offender in the event of conviction, magistrates may need to have regard to the dangerous offender provisions under the CJA 2003. A sentence under the 'dangerousness' provisions can only be passed in the Crown Court.

A court is required to pass a life sentence or an indeterminate sentence for public protection for the most serious sexual and violent offenders who are considered to be dangerous and pose a risk to the public (s. 225 CJA 2003).

A life sentence, with a specified minimum term to be served in custody, is self-explanatory. A sentence for public protection is an indeterminate sentence. In relation to either sentence, a court is required to specify a minimum term which the offender must serve based on the seriousness of the offence (s. 143 CJA 2003). After this point, the offender must remain in custody until such time as the Parole Board decides it is safe for him to be released. Once released, the offender remains on licence indefinitely.

An extended sentence comprises two parts: a custodial sentence for the offence for such length as the seriousness of the offence demands (which must be at least 12 months), and an extended period on licence for such length as the court considers necessary to protect the public from serious harm. The licence period for a specified violent offence must not exceed five years. The licence period for a specified sexual offence must not exceed eight years. The total term must not exceed the maximum for the offence. Therefore, a court might consider the appropriate custodial term for a 'specified' offence to be two years. Providing an assessment of dangerous has been established, it could, for example, impose an extended licence period of three years in addition to the two-year custodial element, making it an extended sentence of five years in total.

Who qualifies for a life sentence or sentence for public protection? Section 225 applies where an offender is aged 18 or over and is convicted of a 'serious offence' AND the court considers that there is a significant risk to members of the public of serious harm (which includes death or serious personal/psychological injury) occasioned by the commission of further 'specified offences.'

Section 225(2) requires the court to impose a sentence of life imprisonment where the offence attracts a life sentence in any event AND the court is of the opinion that there is a significant risk to members of the public of serious harm occasioned by the commission of further 'specified offences.' If s. 225(2) does not apply, a sentence of imprisonment for public protection *must* be passed.

A court may give credit for a timely guilty plea and credit periods on remand, but only in relation to the specified minimum term. Provision for the early release of life prisoners is made in s. 82A PCC(S) A 2000. Early release (but not home detention curfew release) does apply to an extended sentence but release is not automatic at the half-way point. Release depends upon a decision being taken by the Parole Board that it is no longer necessary for the protection of the public that the offender be confined (s. 247 CJA).

Who qualifies for an extended sentence? Section 228 provides that where an offender is aged over 18 and is convicted of a 'specified offence' AND the court considers that there is a significant risk to members of the public of serious harm (which includes death or serious personal/psychological injury) occasioned by the commission of further 'specified offences', the court *must* impose an extended sentence of detention.

How is an offender assessed as being dangerous? Section 229 is all important. It provides that where an offender has not previously been convicted of a 'specified offence', the court:

- must take into account all such information as is available as to the nature and circumstances of the offence;

- may take into account any information it has about any pattern of behaviour of which any of the offences form part;

- may take into account any information it has before it about the offender.

Section 229(3) provides that where an offender has previously been convicted of a 'specified offence', the court MUST ASSUME that there is a risk of serious harm to the public, UNLESS, after taking into account the factors listed above, the court considers that it would be unreasonable to conclude there is such a risk.

It is the responsibility of the CPS to draw the court's attention to the possible application of the 'dangerousness' provisions. The pre-sentence report and any psychiatric report, as well as an offender's previous convictions and mental condition, will be pivotal in helping the court to determine whether someone is 'dangerous' within the meaning of s. 229.

The provisions are draconian and controversial. Important guidance on their application has been provided by the Court of Appeal in *R v Lang and Others* [2005] EWCA Crim 2864. Thirteen appeals were heard based on the 'dangerousness provisions'. In all but three cases the Court of Appeal varied the sentence either because it felt 'dangerousness' was not established on the facts, or the presumption in favour of a life sentence should have been rebutted or a sentence of public protection was more appropriate than a life sentence. The judgment contains the following guidance on the assessment of dangerous and consequential provisions:

'(i) The risk identified must be significant. This is a higher threshold than mere possibility of occurrence and in our view can be taken to mean (as in the Oxford Dictionary) "noteworthy, of considerable amount or importance."

(ii) In assessing the risk of further offences being committed, the sentencer should take into account the nature and circumstances of the current offence; the offender's history of offending including not just the kind of offence but its circumstances and the sentence passed, details of which the prosecution must have available, and, whether the offending demonstrates any pattern; social and economic factors in relation to the offender including accommodation, employability, education, associates, relationships and drug or alcohol abuse; and the offender's thinking, attitude towards offending and supervision and emotional state. Information in relation to these matters will most readily, though not exclusively, come from antecedents and pre-sentence probation and medical reports . . . . The sentencer will be guided, but not bound by, the assessment of risk in such reports . . .

(iii) If the foreseen specified offence is serious, there will clearly be some cases, though not by any means all, in which there may be a significant risk of serious harm. For example, robbery is a serious offence. But it can be committed in a wide variety of ways many of which do not give rise to a significant risk of serious harm. Sentencers must therefore guard against assuming there is a significant risk of serious harm merely because the foreseen specified offence is serious. A pre-sentence report should usually be obtained before any sentence is passed which is based on significant risk of serious harm. In a small number of cases, where the circumstances of the current offence or the history of the offender suggest mental abnormality on his part, a medical report may be necessary before risk can properly be assessed.

(iv) If the foreseen specified offence is not serious, there will be comparatively few cases in which a risk of serious harm will properly be regarded as significant. The huge variety of offences in Schedule 15 includes many which, in themselves, are not suggestive of serious harm. Repetitive violent or sexual offending at a relatively low level without serious harm does not of itself give rise to a significant risk of serious harm in the future. There may, in such cases, be some risk of future victims being more adversely affected than past victims but this, of itself, does not give rise to significant risk of serious harm.

(v) In relation to the rebuttable assumption to which section 229(3) gives rise, the court is accorded a discretion if, in the light of information about the current offence, the offender and his previous offences, it would be unreasonable to conclude that there is a significant risk. The exercise of such a discretion is, historically, at the very heart of judicial sentencing and the language of the statute indicates that judges are expected, albeit starting from the assumption, to exercise their ability to reach a reasonable conclusion in the light of the information before them. It is to be noted that the assumption will be rebutted, if at all, as an exercise of judgment: the statute includes no reference to the burden or standard of proof. As we have indicated above, it will usually be unreasonable to conclude that the assumption applies unless information about the offences, pattern of behaviour and offender show a significant risk of serious harm from further offences.

(vi) In relation to offenders under 18 and adults with no relevant previous convictions at the time the specified offence was committed, the court's discretion under section 229(2) is not constrained by any initial assumption such as, under section 229(3), applies to adults with previous convictions. It is still necessary, when sentencing young offenders, to bear in mind that, within a shorter time than adults, they may change and develop. This and their level of maturity may be highly pertinent when assessing what their future conduct may be and whether it may give rise to significant risk of serious harm.

(vii) In relation to a particularly young offender, an indeterminate sentence may be inappropriate even where a serious offence has been committed and there is a significant risk of serious harm from further offences (see for example, *R v D* [2005] EWCA Crim 2282).

(viii) It cannot have been Parliament's intention, in a statute dealing with the liberty of the subject, to require the imposition of indeterminate sentences for the commission of relatively minor offences.

(ix) Sentencers should usually, and in accordance with section 174(1)(a) of the Criminal Justice Act 2003, give reasons for all their conclusions: in particular, that there is or is not a significant risk of further offences or serious harm; where the assumption under section 229(3) arises for making or not making the assumption which the statute requires unless this would be unreasonable; and for not imposing an extended sentence under sections 227 and 228. Sentencers should, in giving reasons, briefly identify the information which they have taken into account.

29.9.6 **EARLY RELEASE – HOME DETENTION CURFEW**

Due to the recent well-publicised problems of overcrowding, the Government has encouraged the earlier release of short-term prisoners on home detention curfew arrangements. The power to so order is re-enacted in s. 246 Criminal Justice Act 2003 and is exercised at the discretion of the prison governor. Where a prisoner is released early under this scheme, licence conditions must include a curfew arrangement supported by electronic tagging (s. 253 CJA 2003). In *R v Al-Buhairi* (*Abdullah*) [2004] 1 Cr App R (S) 83, the Court of Appeal stated that the home detention scheme provisions should not be taken into account by a court determining the length of a custodial sentence, as the procedure is an administrative one which depends entirely on the prison governor's discretion.

The provisions for the release of offenders subject to a sentence of life imprisonment are outside the scope of this work but are considered in *Blackstone's Criminal Practice*.

29.10 SUSPENDED SENTENCE OF IMPRISONMENT – OR CUSTODY MINUS – S. 189 CJA 2003

The power of a court to impose a suspended sentence of imprisonment changed in April 2005, with s. 189 CJA 2003. Prior to the change, a court could only suspend a sentence of imprisonment if there were 'exceptional circumstances' for doing so. This requirement has been removed, which means the suspended sentence may well become more frequent in the future.

Before a court can impose a suspended sentence the custody threshold test (so serious) must be met. The offender must be aged 18 or over.

A court will be able to pass a suspended sentence where it imposes a term of imprisonment of at least 28 weeks but not more than 51 weeks (subject to the statutory maximum for a magistrates' court). Transitional provisions are currently in place to allow for the operation of s. 189 CJA, until the 'new' custodial sentences under the CJA 2003 are fully operational. The period of suspension can be between 6 months and two years. This new 'custody minus' sentence is designed to be a much more demanding sentence than the old suspended sentence, as the court can order the offender to undertake requirements in the community during the supervision period. The list of requirements is the same as that for a community order (see Chapter 30). Any requirements must be commensurate with the seriousness of the offence. If the offender fails to comply with the requirements, or commits a further offence (whether or not punishable with imprisonment), the presumption will be that the suspended sentence will be activated. A system for review by the sentencing court will be included.

29.11 CONCLUSION

We end this chapter by reference to the guidance issued on seriousness issued by the Sentencing Guidelines Council and its relationship with the imposition of custodial sentence. The guidance can be accessed at http://www.sentencing-guidelines.gov.uk. The SGC suggests at paragraph 1.33 that under the new sentencing framework contained in the CJA 2003, the court should adopt the following approach:

(a) Has the custody threshold been passed?

(b) If so, is it unavoidable that a custodial sentence be imposed?

(c) If so, can that sentence be suspended?

(d) If not, can that sentence be served intermittently?

(e) If not, impose a sentence which takes immediate effect for the term commensurate with the seriousness of the offence.

KEY POINT SUMMARY

• A custodial sentence is the most draconian sentence a court can pass.

• For a custodial sentence to be imposed, the custody threshold test defined in s. 152 CJA 2003 must be met.

- The threshold test under the CJA 2003 requires the offence to be so serious that neither a fine alone, nor a community order, can be justified.
- The duration of a custodial sentence must be commensurate with the seriousness of the offence.
- A custodial sentence can be immediate, suspended and, under the CJA 2003, intermittent.
- Under the CJA 2003, a distinction is drawn between sentences of less than 12 months and more than 12 months. Sentences of 12 months or more will now be served in full with the second half of the sentence served in the community. Sentences of less than 12 months (other than an intermittent sentence) will include post-release supervision in the community.
- A suspended sentence may only be imposed where the custody threshold test is met. The offender can have requirements imposed upon him to complete during the period of suspension.

SELF-TEST QUESTIONS

1. Explain the basis upon which a court can sentence a convicted prisoner to a term of imprisonment.
2. What principles determine the length of a custodial sentence?
3. What types of custodial terms may be imposed?

Further self-test questions based on short factual sentencing scenarios are included at the end of Chapter 30.

FIGURE 29.1 THE CONDITIONS FOR IMPOSING A CUSTODIAL SENTENCE ON AN ADULT

- A custodial sentence may only be imposed if the threshold test is satisfied where:
  - the offence, or combination of offences; or associated offences
  - is so 'serious' that neither a fine alone nor a community sentence can be justified, s. 152(2) CJA 2003; or
  - where the offender fails to consent to a requirement to be included in a community order.
- See *R v Howells* for a judicial interpretation of the 'seriousness' test.
- Discount for pleading guilty will be applied (s. 144 CJA 2003).
- The length of custody should be commensurate with the seriousness of the offence, s. 153(2) CJA 2003.
- The length of custodial sentences passed by magistrates are restricted compared to the Crown Court.
- The court should give reasons in open court for imposing the sentence passed, s. 174(2) CJA 2003.
- Before deciding to suspend a prison sentence, the custody threshold test must be met.
- Time spent on remand shall count as time served when imposing a custodial sentence, s. 240 CJA 2003.

TYPES OF CUSTODIAL PENALTIES UNDER CJA 2003

Custodial sentences up to 12 months when in force will be passed as:

- custody plus, s.181 CJA 2003 or intermittent custody;
- custody plus will be for a specified term after which the offender will be released on licence for at least 26 weeks – the licence may be subject to conditions;
- intermittent custody requires the offender to serve jail time in blocks to maintain contact with family/employment/educational courses:
  - court must impose a custodial period of between 28 weeks (minimum) and 51 weeks (maximum) to be served during intermittent periods;
  - the order must specify the number of days in custody between 14 days (minimum) and 90 days (maximum);
  - between period in custody, offender is released on licence;
  - conditions can be attached to the licence.

Custodial sentences of more than 12 months under the CJA 2003

- Half custodial term spent in custody and half spent on licence.
- Probation service may attach conditions to the licence period.
- Where released on licence, offender can be drug tested to ensure compliance with licence conditions, s. 266 CJA 2003.

30 NON-CUSTODIAL SENTENCES AND ANCILLARY ORDERS

30.1 **INTRODUCTION**

In this chapter we consider the wide range of non-custodial sentences that are available to the courts. These sentences include:

- community sentences;
- fines; and
- discharges.

We also consider a number of ancillary orders a court can, and in some cases must, impose.

30.2 **COMMUNITY SENTENCES**

A community sentence is served in the community. Courts are frequently encouraged to use community-based sentences as an alternative to imposing a custodial sentence. They are commonly proposed by the Probation Service in pre-sentence reports.

The Criminal Justice Act 2003 has introduced significant changes to the structure and enforcement of community-based sentences. These changes were implemented in April 2005. Prior to the Criminal Justice Act 2003, community-based sentences comprised either a:

- community rehabilitation order (CRO);
- community punishment order (CPO);
- community punishment and rehabilitation order (combination order);
- curfew order; or
- drug treatment and testing order (DTTO)

Contrary to popular perception, community-based sentences are very demanding and are rigorously enforced. In choosing to impose a community-based sentence the court will have regard to one or more sentencing objectives (see Chapter 28, paragraph 28.4). Under the Criminal Justice Act 2003, courts now pass a generic community order with one or more specified requirements.

30.2.1 **THE THRESHOLD FOR IMPOSING A COMMUNITY SENTENCE**

As with custodial sentences, there is a threshold test for the imposition of a community order which must be met before a court can impose a community sentence. In accordance with s. 148 Criminal Justice Act 2003.

> 'A court shall not pass a community sentence on an offender unless it is of the opinion that the offence, or the combination of the offence and one or more associated offences with it, is serious enough to warrant such a sentence.'

In short, a community-based sentence can only be imposed for an offence which is considered to be 'serious enough' to warrant it.

Under s. 151 of the 2003 Act, provision is made for a court to impose a community sentence on an offender aged 16 or over who has been convicted by a court on three previous occasions after attaining the age of 16 and has had a fine imposed on him on each of those occasions but whose current offence does not fall within the community sentence threshold. This provision is aimed at persistent petty offenders.

30.2.2 IS THE OFFENCE SERIOUS ENOUGH?

In assessing whether an offence is serious enough to warrant a community sentence, the Magistrates' Court Sentencing Guidelines (2004) provide some assistance. If you consult the guidelines, you will see there are a number of offences, including theft and handling stolen goods which suggest the starting point in terms of sentence should be a community sentence. As previously indicated however, the balance of aggravating and mitigating features in the particular case may tilt the sentence towards a fine or beyond the comunity penalty threshold. The sentencing guidelines indicate the basic starting point.

30.3 COMMUNITY SENTENCES UNDER THE CJA 2003

Section 177 of the Act creates a single, generic community order which will impose one or more requirements on the offender. The community order is available for all offenders aged 16 or over and can last for up to three years.

The requirements that can be imposed under a community order include:

- unpaid work (defined s. 199);
- an activity requirement (defined s. 201);
- a programme requirement (defined s. 202);
- a prohibited activity requirement (defined s. 203);
- a curfew requirement(defined s. 204);
- an exclusion requirement (defined s. 205);
- a residence requirement (defined s. 206);
- a mental health requirement (defined s. 207);
- a drug rehabilitation requirement (defined s. 209);
- an alcohol treatment requirement (defined s. 221);
- a supervision requirement (defined s. 213); and/or
- in the case of an offender under 25, an attendance centre requirement (defined s. 214).

Where a court makes a community order imposing a curfew requirement or an exclusion requirement, the court must also impose an electronic monitoring requirement (s. 177(3)).

30.3.1 HOW WILL THE APPROPRIATE TYPE OF ORDER BE DETERMINED?

Section 148(3) CJA 2003 provides that where the court passes a community sentence:

'(a) the particular requirement or requirements forming part of the order must be such as, in the opinion of the court is, or taken together are, the most suitable for the offenders; and

(b) the restrictions on liberty imposed by the order . . . are commensurate with the seriousness of the offence, or the combination of the offence and one or more associated with it.'

In determining the requirements of a community order, the court will have regard to one or more of the sentencing objectives contained in s. 142(1) CJA 2003. The seriousness of the offence and the risk of harm posed by the offender will determine the nature and combination of requirements and the intensity of those requirements.

Useful guidance on the potential operation of the new style community order is provided by the Sentencing Guideline Council (SGC) in its guidelines on the new sentences under the CJA 2003 (http://www.sentencing-guidelines.gov.uk). The 'seriousness' of the offence will be an important factor in deciding whether the court chooses a low, medium or high range of

online resource centre

requirements. If a court needs to reflect the seriousness of an offence, the requirements a court imposes under the new generic community sentence order need to be demanding. Equally, however, a court should not set up an offender to fail. Proportionality and suitability will be the guiding principles.

In general, the guidelines suggest the lowest range of community sentence should be reserved for those whose offences are relatively minor. Such an order might contain just one requirement of a short duration. The top range would be reserved for those offenders whose offences fall just short of the custodial threshold. The nature and severity of the requirements to be imposed should be guided by:

   (i) the assessment of the offence's seriousness (low/medium/high);

  (ii) the purpose(s) of sentencing the court wishes to achieve;

 (iii) the risk of reoffending;

 (iv) the ability of the offender to comply; and

  (v) the availability of requirements in the local area.

The SGC includes a number of examples of the type of requirements that might be imposed based on an offence of low/medium/high seriousness.

The guidelines stress the importance of obtaining a pre-sentence report to help determine the particular requirements or combination of requirements in a specific case.

30.4   THE REQUIREMENTS

30.4.1   UNPAID WORK (S. 199 CJA 2003)

This is similar to the old community punishment order in that, as the name suggests, the offender is required to perform unpaid work in the community under the supervision of a responsible officer. A court cannot impose an unpaid work requirement unless the court is satisfied that the offender is a suitable person to perform such work. For this reason, a court will invariably require a pre-sentence report to assess the offender's suitability.

The aim of a court in making a community order with an unpaid work requirement is to give the offender the chance to make amends to the community in which the offence has been committed. It is punitive in nature. A supervising officer oversees the community work placement. The work might involve painting, decorating or gardening for organisations or individuals.

The aggregate number of hours of unpaid work must not be less than 40 and not more than 300 hours. The number of hours imposed should be proportional to the level of seriousness of the offence/s committed. An unpaid work requirement may of course be combined with any further requirement/s as the court deems fit.

30.4.2   ACTIVITY REQUIREMENT (S. 201 CJA 2003)

This requires the offender to present himself at a specified place and participate in specified activities. A pre-sentence report will normally be required if the court is considering this as a requirement. The aggregate number of days of an activity order must not exceed 60.

The activities can include day centre attendance, education and basic skills training and reparation to victims with their consent.

30.4.3   PROGRAMME REQUIREMENT (S. 202 CJA 2003)

An offender would be required to participate in a programme of activity which has been accredited by a body established by the Secretary of State. A pre-sentence report would be required in order to check the offender's suitability and the availability of such accredited programme.

Under the old community rehabilitation order, the Probation Service regularly specified offending behaviour programmes as part of the order. The aims of such programmes include to:

- make offenders accept responsibility for their offences;
- avoid further offending;
- attempt to resolve any difficulties linked to offending behaviour, e.g. homelessness, marital or relationship breakdown, unemployment, illiteracy, addiction.

Such programmes have traditionally included:

- Enhanced Thinking Skills Programme. This requires the offender to participate in group work with a view to enabling poorly educated offenders to attain basic literacy and numeracy skills.
- Sex Offender Programme. This is aimed at offenders convicted of sexual offences who have been assessed as suitable for the programme.
- Drink Impaired Drivers Programme. This is aimed primarily at offenders convicted of drink-driving offences.

A programme requirement will invariably be combined with a supervision requirement (undertaken by a probation officer) under the community order.

30.4.4 PROHIBITED ACTIVITY REQUIREMENT (S. 203 CJA 2003)

This requires the offender to refrain from participating in specified activities named in the order on any day or days specified during the requirement period. The requirements that may be included in a prohibited activity requirement are not limited and may include the prohibition of activities that would otherwise be lawful. Possibilities include prohibiting the defendant from visiting a particular place, for example nightclubs, or undertaking a particular activity such as driving, drinking alcohol, attending football matches.

30.4.5 CURFEW REQUIREMENT (S. 204 CJA 2003)

A curfew requires a convicted offender to stay at an agreed address for a specified time of between two and 12 hours, e.g. between 7 pm and 7 am for a period of between one and seven days. A curfew can be imposed for a total of six months.

Curfew orders are enforced by electronic 'tagging', and are a different way of restricting an offender's liberty in a way that is rather like being put under 'house arrest'. Being tagged can make it harder for an offender to commit further crimes and can help to break patterns of offending behaviour by forcing the offender to stay at the specified address.

A tag is attached to the offender's wrist or ankle and is linked to a monitoring machine installed in the place where the offender is living. The machine is linked via a telephone line to a monitoring centre. Staff at the monitoring centre can immediately tell if the curfew is broken.

In imposing a curfew requirement, the court will take account of the offender's religious beliefs, employment, or attendance at an educational establishment and its compatibility with any other requirements imposed as part of the community order. A pre-sentence report may well be required in order for the court to be satisfied that suitable accommodation is available to the offender.

30.4.6 EXCLUSION REQUIREMENT (S. 205 CJA 2003)

This directs the offender not to enter a place or an area specified in the order. An exclusion requirement must not exceed two years and will be monitored electronically. The order can provide for the prohibition to operate only during specified periods and may specify different periods or days during the order.

30.4.7 RESIDENCE REQUIREMENT (S. 206 CJA 2003)

This requires the offender to reside at a place specified in the order. It could include a hostel or institution recommended by a probation officer.

30.4.8 MENTAL HEALTH TREATMENT REQUIREMENT (S. 207 CJA 2003)

Rehabilitative in nature, a mental health requirement requires the offender to submit to treatment by a medical practitioner or psychologist. The treatment may be as a resident patient. Before a court can impose such requirement it must be satisfied that the offender is susceptible to treatment. The offender must express a willingness to comply.

30.4.9 DRUG REHABILITATION REQUIREMENT (S. 208 CJA 2003)

The treatment and testing period must be a minimum of six months and a maximum of three years. Before a court can impose a drug treatment requirement, it must be satisfied the defendant is dependent on drugs and is susceptible to treatment. The defendant must consent to the order. The pre-sentence report must include an assessment from a treatment provider and a place must be available to the defendant. The defendant is subject to regular review by the court and the court may impose a testing requirement on the defendant.

Prior to April 2005, the DTTO (drug testing and treatment order) was a community-based sentence in its own right. It was, and we assume as a requirement it will still be, a high-intensity community order designed to get the offender to look at and change his or her drug use thereby reducing his or her offending. Such an order would involve frequent drug testing and a high level of contact and supervision coupled with a regular monthly review by the courts.

Guidance on the use of DTTOs was recently provided by the Court of Appeal in *Attorney-General's Reference No. 64 of 2003* [2004] 2 Cr App R(S) 106. We assume that the guidance will apply to the imposition of such a requirement under the CJA 2003. The judgment provides:

> 'In the light of the authorities, it is possible to identify, without purporting to be exhaustive, some of the factors relevant when considering whether it is in the public interest that a DTTO should be made:
>
> (i) judges should be alert to pass sentences which have a realistic prospect of reducing drug addiction whenever it is possible sensibly to do so;
>
> (ii) many offences are committed by an offender under the influence of drugs. The fact that a defendant was so acting is not in itself a reason for making a DTTO;
>
> (iii) a necessary prerequisite to the making of such an order is clear evidence that a defendant is determined to free himself or herself from drugs;
>
> (iv) a DTTO is likely to have a better prospect of success early rather than late in a criminal career, though there will be exceptional cases in which an order may be justified for an older defendant;
>
> (v) it will be very rare for a DTTO to be appropriate for an offence involving serious violence or threat of violence with a lethal weapon;
>
> (vi) the type of offence for which a DTTO will generally be appropriate is an acquisitive offence carried out to obtain money for drugs, though the fact that the motive was to feed drug addiction does not compel the conclusion that a DTTO should be made;
>
> (vii) a DTTO may be appropriate even when a substantial number of offences have been committed;
>
> (viii) a DTTO is unlikely to be appropriate for a substantial number of serious offences which either involve minor violence, or have a particularly damaging effect on the victim or victims. There must be a degree of proportionality between offence and sentence, so that excessive weight is not given to the prospect of rehabilitation at the expense of proper regard for the criminality of the offender;

(ix) material about the offender, which becomes available between sentencing and appeal to this Court, may be of particular significance as to the propriety of a DTTO. The Single Judge of this Court may therefore order a further up-to-date assessment in an appropriate case;'

30.4.10 ALCOHOL TREATMENT REQUIREMENT (S. 212 CJA 2003)

Such a requirement provides a means by which courts can specifically respond to those offenders who are dependant on alcohol and whose dependency requires and may be susceptible to treatment. The offender must express a willingness to comply. The treatment can be given as a resident or non-resident of an appropriate institution. The period of treatment cannot be for less than six months.

30.4.11 SUPERVISION REQUIREMENT (S. 213 CJA 2003)

This requirement is similar to the old community rehabilitation order. Under the terms of a supervision requirement the offender must, during the relevant period, attend appointments with the responsible probation officer at times and places determined by the officer. The purpose of the supervision requirement is to promote the offender's rehabilitation.

30.4.12 ATTENDANCE CENTRE REQUIREMENT (WHERE OFFENDER IS AGED UNDER 25) (S. 214 CJA 2003)

An attendance centre requirement obliges the offender to attend at a centre for between 12 and 36 hours. Attendance is limited to one occasion a day and for not more than three hours at any one time. The attendance centre must be reasonably accessible to the offender.

30.5 CREDIT TO BE GIVEN FOR GUILTY PLEA

Section 144 CJA 2003 should not be forgotten (see Chapter 28 paragraph 28. 8). Credit should be given for a timely guilty plea. Where a community sentence is to be imposed, the court should take account of the provision in s. 144 CJA 2003. This may well be reflected in the number of requirements or duration of requirements under a community order. In its definitive guidelines on s. 144, the Sentencing Guidelines Council suggests that, where an offence crosses the threshold for imposition of a community sentence, the application of the reduction principle may properly form the basis for imposing a fine or discharge instead.

30.6 ENFORCEMENT OF COMMUNITY ORDERS UNDER THE CJA 2003 – SCH. 8

The court will explain the consequence of failure to comply with a community order to the offender. An offender can breach a community order by failing to comply with its requirements or by committing further offences while subject to a community order.

More stringent measures have been put in place to deal with breaches of community orders. The Probation Service will issue a single warning about a failure to comply. Thereafter any further failure will result in breach proceedings being commenced against the offender. The Probation Service can apply to have the order revoked. This will require the offender to be brought back before the court. In dealing with an offender for breach of requirements the court must take into account the extent to which the offender has complied with the order.

The courts' powers will include the option to impose more onerous requirements on the existing order; revoke the order if it is in the interest of justice to do so and re-sentence the offender for the original offence and in the case of an offender aged over 18, (who was convicted of an imprisonable offence in the first instance and has willfully and persistently failed to comply with the requirements of the order), the court may impose a prison sentence not exceeding 51 weeks.

In its guidelines, the SGC cautions that, in dealing with a breach of a community sentence, the primary objective should be to ensure that the requirements of the sentence are finished. In other words, custody should be the last resort, reserved for those who deliberately and repeatedly breach the requirements of their order.

30.7 DEFERMENT OF SENTENCE – SS. 1 AND 2 PCC(S)A 2000

Section 1:

> 'The Crown Court or magistrates' court may defer passing sentence on an offender for the purposes of enabling the court, or any court to which it falls to deal with him, to have regard in dealing with him to . . .
>
> > (a) his conduct after conviction (including, where appropriate, the making by him of reparation for his offence) or;
> >
> > (b) any change in his circumstances . . .'

Deferment can only be imposed with the offender's consent and if it is in the interests of justice to do so, having regard to the nature of the offence and the character and circumstances of the defendant.

Deferment may be for up to six months and results in an adjournment of the proceedings.

The power to defer sentence is most appropriately exercised where there has been an offer by the offender to make reparation to his victim or there is expected to be a change in the offender's life which may produce a stabilising influence, e.g. a job/marriage.

The power to defer should be exercised sparingly. In accordance with Sch. 23 to the CJA 2003 (which came into force in April 2005) courts will be able to impose requirements on the offender (similar to those imposed on a community order) during the period of deferment, including, if appropriate, supervision by a probation officer. If the court is satisfied that the offender has failed to comply with one or more requirements, the offender can be brought back to court and the court can proceed to sentence. The expectation is that, if the offender stays out of trouble and does what is required of him by the court, he will not then receive a custodial sentence for the offence for which he has been convicted.

30.8 FINES

A fine is very frequently imposed, particularly in magistrates' courts. The power to impose a financial penalty is contained in ss. 126–129 PCC(S)A 2000. Fines are suitable punishment for offences which are not serious enough to merit a community sentence, nor so serious that a custodial sentence must be considered. A high fine can be regarded as a sentence of a punitive nature and may, in certain circumstances, deter an offender from repeating a course of conduct.

Magistrates' courts can impose a maximum fine of £5,000 per offence (subject to the statutory maximum for the offence, if it is less) and subject to the principle of totality, discussed in Chapter 28 in the context of consecutive custodial sentences. The Crown Court's power to impose a fine is unlimited.

Section 164 CJA 2003) is important.

It provides:

> '(1) Before fixing the amount of any fine to be imposed on an offender who is an individual, a court shall inquire into his financial circumstances,
>
> (2) The amount of any fine fixed by the court shall be such as, in the opinion of the court, reflects the seriousness of the offence.

(3) In fixing the amount of any fine to be imposed on an offender (whether an individual or other person), a court shall take into account the circumstances of the case including, among other things, the financial circumstances of the offender so far as they are known, or appear, to the court . . .'

Power exists under s. 162 CJA 2003 for a court to make a financial circumstances order requiring the offender to make disclosure of his means. It is not a power that is exercised frequently.

It is good practice to obtain a written statement of your client's means which can be handed to the court. Alternatively, the defence advocate should at least have in his possession a full breakdown of his client's income and outgoings.

Some magistrates' courts have their own guideline fines for certain offences. The Magistrates' Court Sentencing Guidelines (2004) also offer assistance. Some offences include a guideline starting point for the imposition of a fine. The magistrates must first decide that a fine is appropriate. On the basis of aggravating and mitigating factors, they must then determine the level of fine (A, B or C).

- Level A fine is assessed on the basis of 50 per cent of weekly take-home pay.
- Level B fine is assessed on the basis of 100 per cent of weekly take-home pay.
- Level C fine is assessed on the basis of 150 per cent of weekly take-home pay.

The magistrates must then set the fine taking into account the offender's individual circumstances. The fine may be reduced if the defendant would suffer hardship. Credit will be given for a timely guilty plea. A final figure is then arrived at and imposed.

Example

Consider the Magistrates' Court Sentencing Guidelines for careless driving (Appendix 4). The starting point in terms of a fine is level B. For the offence of careless driving contrary to s. 3 Road Traffic Act 1988, the magistrates must assess the degree of carelessness involved. Let us assume it is a particularly serious example of careless driving. Although the guideline starting point for a fine is level B, the magistrates might decide to apply level C. Thus an offender in receipt of a weekly income of £200 can expect the starting point for his fine to be £300. Consideration will, however, be given to the offender's means and a deduction of around one third will be made where the defendant has entered a timely guilty plea. Day-to-day experience of your local magistrates' court will give you some idea of the usual level of fines imposed for common offences.

Priority is always given to the payment of compensation orders as against fines. Therefore, if an offender would struggle to pay both compensation and a fine, a compensation order will be awarded in preference to a fine.

Financial penalties (including fines/compensation orders/prosecution costs) may be paid in instalments. The Courts Act 2003, Sch. 5 has introduced a new regime for the collection and enforcement of fines in relation to offenders over the age of 18. Where a financial penalty cannot be discharged immediately, a fines collection order will be made. The means and rate of payment is determined by a fines collection officer. Such officers are empowered under the Fines Collection Regulations 2004 to take enforcement proceedings in the event of default. Enforcement measures include making an attachment or earnings order or deduction from benefits, an increase in the overall fine and even the clamping and sale of vehicles. In due course, fines may be discharged by means of unpaid work. Fine defaulters have a right to seek variation of the order and right of appeal to the magistrates' court. A fine's officer may refer enforcement back to the magistrates' court where all previous enforcement attempts have failed. A magistrates' court can remit whole or part of the fine, though not compensation, and/or order detention in the precincts of the court as a means of discharging the debt. Where all other methods of enforcement have been tried or are inappropriate, a court can order custody in default, but only in the circumstances outlined below:

- the defendant is already serving a custodial sentence;
- the defaulter appears to have sufficient means to pay forthwith; or
- the court is satisfied that the defaulter has willfully refused or culpably neglected to pay. The period of imprisonment may be suspended pending regular payments.

Many convicted offenders have outstanding fine accounts. When sentence is imposed on an offender the court will usually make enquiry to see if any outstanding fine account is up-to-date. If it is, the court may consolidate any new financial penalties with an existing account. Where the fine account is in arrears, the defendant can expect to be called upon to offer some explanation.

A fine can be imposed (and usually is imposed) as a sentence in its own right. It can, however, be combined with a community order, a compensation order and with disqualification from driving. It cannot be combined with a discharge as a means of sentence for a single offence. In theory, a fine can be combined with a sentence of imprisonment. In practice, however, this would be rare, as imprisonment is likely to deprive the offender of his ability to pay.

30.9 COMPENSATION ORDERS

It is a legitimate expectation for a victim of a criminal offence to receive compensation for any injury, loss or damage suffered as a result of a convicted individual's actions. The governing section is s. 130 PCC(S)A 2000. The section imposes a duty on the court to order compensation unless it gives reasons for not doing so. It is immaterial whether the victim has made an application for compensation.

Magistrates can award compensation of up to £5,000 per offence (subject to a lower statutory prescribed maximum). In the Crown Court, the amounts are unlimited. The Magistrates' Court Sentencing Guidelines contain a table of guideline compensation awards for personal injury. In fixing the level of compensation, the offender's means must be taken into account. Priority is given to compensation orders over fines and prosecution costs.

Example 1

X is convicted of assault. The victim sustains a broken nose requiring some manipulation. Based on the guidelines, X can expect to be ordered to pay compensation in the region of £1,000–£1,500. Clearly, if X is in receipt of welfare benefits this sum will be vastly reduced.

Example 2

X is convicted of resisting a police constable in the execution of his duty. The officer falls to the floor during the arrest, sustaining bruising to both knees. The court is considering a fine for the offence. Compensation in the region of £50–£100 may well be ordered. If X is in receipt of welfare benefits and cannot afford to pay a fine as well as compensation, the court will give priority to the compensation element.

Example 3

X is convicted of criminal damage. He pleads guilty to breaking a door. The cost of replacing the door is estimated at £500. X can expect to be asked to pay some or all of this sum by way of compensation, depending on his means.

Compensation can be awarded for psychological injury. It does not matter whether the injured party is an individual or a company.

Where injury or damage has occurred through a road traffic offence, compensation is not awarded by the courts. Such compensation is left to compulsory driving insurance schemes. If the offender is uninsured and the Motor Insurance Bureau will not cover the loss, an award can be made in these circumstances.

The prosecution should normally have compensation details to hand at the point of sentencing. Where personal injury has resulted, the CPS should have the necessary details, including photographic evidence in some instances. Where damage has occurred the court will expect to see an invoice for repairs or an estimate for replacement.

Where a defendant disputes the amount of compensation requested, the court will hear representations. If the matter is incapable of being resolved, the question of compensation may have to be adjourned for further enquiries to be made.

Where there is more than one individual responsible for an offence giving rise to the injury, loss or damage, the court has discretion as to how apportionment should be made. Each offender's culpability will be taken into account, as will their individual ability to pay.

Can the court order compensation when it sends the offender to prison? It is not the usual practice in magistrates' courts to require a defendant to pay compensation where he or she is sentenced to a period in custody for the offence. Having said this, there is no written rule to this effect. Indeed on occasions, the Court of Appeal has stated that such an order is not wrong in principle providing the court is satisfied the offender has the means to pay or will have sufficient earning capacity when released from prison (*R v Jonge* [1999] 2 Cr App R (S) 1).

30.10 CONDITIONAL DISCHARGE

A conditional discharge may be imposed in accordance with the requirements under s. 12 PCC(S)A 2000. Such a sentence is common in magistrates' courts but can also be imposed by a Crown Court. The offender can be conditionally discharged for a period of up to three years. There is no minimum period specified.

It must be explained to the defendant that, if he does not reoffend during the period of the conditional discharge, he will not be punished for the offence for which he has been convicted. However, if he is convicted of a further offence, especially if it is of a like nature, the conditional discharge can be revoked. If this were to happen, the defendant would be sentenced not only in connection with the new matter, but could also be resentenced for the offence for which he received the conditional discharge.

A conditional discharge therefore has a deterrent element to it. It would not be imposed for a serious offence, but it is particularly suitable for first-time offenders, and those who may not have offended in the recent past whose offence is not serious enough to warrant a community sentence. To all intents and purposes, a conditional discharge is passed as a sentence in its own right. It can be combined with an award of compensation and/or costs.

30.11 ABSOLUTE DISCHARGE

Absolute discharges may be imposed in accordance with s. 12 PCC(S)A 2000. In fact, such a sentence is very rare. In effect, the defendant is not being punished at all, although the conviction will be recorded against him. It might be imposed on a defendant who, though technically guilty, is morally blameless, or in connection with a very trivial offence. In respect of the latter, questions might be asked of the Crown Prosecution Service as to why a prosecution was brought in the first place.

30.12 BIND OVER

The bind over is an ancient power possessed by the criminal courts. It is not, in fact, a sentence, in the sense that a conviction is not recorded against the individual concerned. The power to bind over can arise either on complaint or of the court's own motion under common law powers. The power was restated in s. 1(7) Justices of the Peace Act 1968. It enables a magistrates' court to bind over an individual to keep the Queen's peace for a defined period of time and in a sum of money. It can be imposed in a situation where the court considers there might be a breach of the peace in the future. The individual concerned must consent to be bound over. No money is actually taken from the individual, but it must be explained to him that, if he fails to keep the peace and be of good behaviour, he will be required to forfeit all or part of the sum specified. In court, it would be expressed in the following way:

> Chair: 'Stand up – You will be bound over in the sum of £100 for a period of 12 months to keep the peace. . . . This means that you do not have to pay any money now. But if you break the order, you can be ordered to pay all or part of that sum. Do you agree to be bound over?'
> Defendant: 'Yes. . . .'

In practice, a bind over is a matter of negotiation between the defence and the prosecution. They are most commonly imposed in relation to less serious matters involving domestic disputes or disputes between neighbours which have resulted in court proceedings. In such cases, the defendant may feel aggrieved that he is the one being prosecuted when others might be regarded as being equally culpable. The offer of a bind over may therefore be the most pragmatic way of resolving the proceedings. The substantive offence which led the defendant to appear before magistrates in the first place is then withdrawn once a bind over is imposed.

A bind over might also be offered to an offender of previous good character who has engaged in a one-off act of stupidity of a public order nature. An example might be where several accused men cause a disturbance at a hotel through their drunken antics.

The defendant may not, of course, wish to consent to the bind over. If a not guilty plea to the substantive matter is maintained, a trial date will be fixed and the matter tried. The benefits of a bind over ought to be explained to the defendant, as a guilty verdict will result in a criminal record and most probably an order that the defendant pays the prosecution's costs.

30.13 MENTALLY ILL OFFENDERS

The sentencing of mentally ill offenders is outside the scope of this text. In addition to the sentences already outlined, including a community order with a requirement of mental health treatment, there are other possibilities, including a hospital order under s. 37 Mental Health Act 1983. More information on the sentencing of mentally ill offenders can be found in *Blackstone's Criminal Practice*.

30.14 ANCILLARY ORDERS

30.14.1 PROSECUTION COSTS

It is common for courts to award some or all of the prosecution's costs in the event of a conviction. Priority is given to compensation orders and fines in the first instance.

The case of *R v Northallerton Magistrates' Court, ex p. Dove* [2000] 1 Cr App R (S) 136 provides the following guidance on awarding prosecution costs:

- The purpose of an award is to compensate the prosecution and not to punish the defendant.
- An award should not exceed the sum which the prosecutor has actually and reasonably incurred.
- Account must be taken of the offender's ability to pay, particularly having regard to any other financial penalties to be imposed, i.e. compensation/fine.

The amount sought by the prosecution depends on the nature of the offence and the degree of preparation that the prosecutor has had to undertake. The court may order all or part of the costs sought or make no order as to payment.

30.14.2 CONFISCATION AND FORFEITURE

We make brief mention of confiscation and forfeiture. The detail falls outside the scope of this text. The provisions are contained in the Proceeds of Crime Act 2002 and are notoriously complex. The Act gives the Crown Court powers to confiscate assets which are the result of the particular criminal conduct of which the defendant has been convicted. The most obvious example of this would be the proceeds of drug trafficking. However, the Act also permits a court to confiscate assets which it believes have been acquired as a result of general criminal conduct in circumstances where the offender is enjoying a 'criminal lifestyle'. There is a protracted procedure requiring the prosecution to provide a statement of information to which the defendant must respond. The provisions are not restricted to particular offences and can apply whenever a defendant is convicted before a Crown Court or if the defendant has been committed to the Crown Court for sentence. Although the court of its own motion can initiate the process, the application is likely to be made by the prosecution.

Section 143 PCC(S)A 2000 gives a court the power to order forfeiture of any property lawfully seized from the defendant (or which is in his possession or under his control at the time he was apprehended) which has been used for the purpose of committing or facilitating the commission of an offence or which was intended by him to be used for such purpose. In utilising this power, a court should have regard to the totality of sentence for the particular offence. Provision is included in s. 145 to allow the sale of property connected with an offence in order to pay compensation to the victim, but only where the offender's means are such that he would otherwise not be in a position to discharge the compensation figure.

30.14.3 ANTI-SOCIAL BEHAVIOUR ORDERS

ASBOs can be made on civil application or as an order ancillary to a criminal conviction, most usually at the invitation of the prosecutor. The power to impose an ASBO in criminal proceedings is contained in s. 1 Crime and Disorder Act 1998 and the Anti-Social Behaviour Act 2003. The behaviour complained of must be anti-social in that it causes alarm, harassment, or distress. The minimum duration of an ASBO is two years. There is no specified maximum.

A court should only make an order for as long as it considers necessary for the protection of the community from the named individual. The prohibitions expressed in the order must be specific in time and place and must be necessary to protect the public from further anti-social acts by the defendant in the locality. They must be reasonable and proportionate, clear, concise and enforceable. Guidance on the imposition of an ASBO in criminal proceedings was recently provided by the Court of Appeal in the case of *R v Parkin* [2004] Crim LR 490:

'In our judgment the following principles clearly emerge:

(1) The test for making an order is one of necessity to protect the public from further anti-social acts by the offender.

(2) The terms of the order must be precise and capable of being understood by the offender.

(3) The findings of fact giving rise to the making of the order must be recorded.

(4) The order must be explained to the offender.

(5) The exact terms of the order must be pronounced in open court and the written order must accurately reflect the order as pronounced. . . .

It will be readily observed from a consideration of the Home Office Guide to Anti-Social Behaviour Orders that the conduct primarily envisaged as triggering these orders was for a less grave offence than street robbery, namely graffiti, abusive and intimidating language, excessive noise, fowling the street with litter, drunken behaviour and drug dealing. Doubtless in drafting that report the Home Office had in mind that courts have considerable powers to restrain robbers. We do not go so far as to suggest that anti-social behaviour orders are necessarily inappropriate in cases with characteristics such as the present. But where custodial sentences in excess of a few months are passed, and offenders are liable to be released on licence, circumstances in which there is demonstrable necessity to make anti-social behaviour orders are likely to be limited.'

30.14.4 SEX OFFENDERS' REGISTER – NOTIFICATION REQUIREMENTS

Under the Sex Offenders Act 1997, the requirement to register is mandatory where an offender is convicted of a specified sexual offence. In accordance with the Sexual Offences Act 2003, the requirement to register has become a requirement to notify. The defendant must notify the police at a specified police station within three days of the notification order being made, or within three days of being released, if the defendant is sent to prison for the sex offence. The defendant must inform the police of his name, date of birth and home address and of any later change of address or absence from the country. The minimum period of notification is for five years (two years for a caution), increasing to ten years depending on the sentence imposed.

30.14.5 FOOTBALL BANNING ORDER

Football banning orders can be made as ancillary orders when a defendant is convicted of and sentenced for a relevant offence. The court may make such an order if it is satisfied that it will help to prevent violence or disorder at or in connection with any regulated football matches. If the defendant receives a custodial sentence for the substantive offence, the order can last for up to 10 years. Otherwise, the order will last for between three and five years. Football banning orders can also be applied for by the police on complaint.

30.14.6 RESTRAINING ORDER

Such an order is available where a defendant has been convicted of an offence under the Harassment Act 1997 either under s. 2 (harassment) or s. 4 (putting a person in fear of violence). The order will name the persons protected and clearly set out the behaviour that is prohibited. The order can be for a fixed period or until further order. Either the prosecution or the defendant can apply on a subsequent date to have the order varied or discharged.

30.14.7 DEPORTATION

We make brief mention of this. Section 3(6) Immigration Act 1971 permits a court to make a recommendation that an offender who is aged over 17 and who is not a British citizen and who has been convicted of an imprisonable offence be deported. The ultimate decision to deport must be taken by the Home Secretary. Where a court is proposing to make a recommendation, the defendant must be give at least seven days' written notice. A recommendation is more likely in relation to conviction for a serious crime.

KEY POINT SUMMARY

- Understand the range of sentencing options available to a court and the requisite criteria for each of them.

- Try to formulate a realistic sentencing objective for your client having regard to the offence your client has committed and the range of sentencing disposals available to the court.

- Try to think in terms of the worst case scenario for your client, and what you feel you can and would realistically like to achieve.

- If a custodial sentence is a distinct possibility, consider whether the custody threshold test is met: be prepared to cite supporting case law on this. Consider whether a community penalty would serve the interests of justice more effectively than a custodial sentence.

- Given that a financial penalty is common, be sure to have a statement of means from your client and be prepared to make appropriate representations based on your client's means.

- Anticipate an ancillary order such as prosecution costs.

- All of the above underscore the importance of researching the penalties for the offence you are considering and any specific sentencing guidelines.

SELF-TEST QUESTIONS

The following short scenarios are designed to test your knowledge and understanding of sentencing law. They concern aspects of sentencing law covered in this chapter and Chapters 28 and 29.

Consider the short scenarios below and try to answer the following questions:

1. What sentence do you feel the court is likely to pass, and why?

2. If you were the defence solicitor, what would you hope to persuade the court to do in terms of sentence?

Exercise 1

Celia appears in court represented by the duty solicitor. She pleads guilty to stealing a gold bracelet worth £150 from a counter display. Without trying to conceal anything she picked up the bracelet, tried it on her wrist and left the shop without paying, prompting the sales assistant to call shop security. She was stopped a few yards from the shop and admitted the theft. When interviewed by the police, she was co-operative but very tearful and frightened as to what her husband would say. She has no idea why she took the item. She had her credit cards on her at the time and could have paid.

Celia is married. She is 52. She has two grown-up children who live away from the family home. Her husband is a well-respected professional person. Celia has no employment. She has rheumatoid arthritis and has felt depressed of late. Celia is well thought of in her community and is an active member of a number of charitable concerns. Six months ago, Celia was conditionally discharged for 12 months for stealing items of underwear from a department store. She is in breach of this order by virtue of the current offence.

Exercise 2

Louise pleads guilty to theft. She worked as a trainee in a hairdresser's shop. She had access to the till and took small amounts (£150 in total) over a period of several weeks. The thefts caused a bad atmosphere as everyone in the salon was under suspicion. Louise says she took the money because an acquaintance was putting pressure on her to repay a debt. She says she fully intended to repay the money from her tips. Louise is 18, has no previous convictions and pleads guilty at the first opportunity. She is now unemployed and receiving income support and housing benefit. She lives in a bed-sit.

Exercise 3

Andrew was found cultivating five cannabis plants in his bedroom. He says he was growing them for personal use and for the use of his disabled partner who suffers from a chronic illness and finds the effects alleviate some of her discomfort. Andrew pleaded guilty at the first opportunity. He has several previous convictions for theft and possession of drugs. Andrew and his partner receive invalidity benefit of £130 per week.

Exercise 4

Darren is charged with assaulting a police constable in the execution of his duty. Darren and some of his friends had been celebrating their team's win. They had been drinking and were rowdy. They were stopped by police on the High Street who asked them to calm down. While most of the youths dispersed, Darren entered into an argument with one of the police officers. A scuffle ensued in which the police officer fell over. While the officer lay on the ground, he was kicked several times by Darren. The officer suffered bruising to his face and left arm. A pre-sentence report assesses Darren's risk of reoffending as being medium. It highlights Darren's alcohol consumption as being the motivation for the offence. Darren is deemed suitable for a community sentence including an unpaid work requirement.

Darren is 21 and has a previous conviction for possession of an offensive weapon. He completed a community order with a 60 hour unpaid work requirement for this last year. He pleads guilty to the assault on the officer and expresses his remorse. Darren is employed as a shop assistant and brings home £150 per week. He will lose his job if sent to prison. He lives with his mother and gives her £25 per week towards his keep. He owns a car and therefore has related car expenditure.

FIGURE 30.1 NON-CUSTODIAL SENTENCES

COMMUNITY SENTENCES UNDER THE CJA 2003

- Imposed where the court is satisfied the:

  - offence; or
  - combination of offences; or
  - associated offences

  is 'serious enough' to warrant it, s. 148(1) CJA 2003.

- S. 177 CJA 2003 creates a single community sentence which will impose one or more requirements on the offender, e.g.

  - unpaid work, s. 199 CJA 2003;
  - curfew requirement, s. 204 CJA 2003;
  - exclusion requirement, s. 205 CJA 2003;
  - residence requirement, s. 206 CJA 2003;
  - drug and/or alcohol rehabilitation requirement, ss. 209 & 221 CJA 2003.

- The requirement(s) imposed on the offender should be:

  - suitable for the offender; and
  - where the offender's liberty is restricted commensurate with the 'seriousness' of the offence, s. 148(3) CJA 2003.

- Sentencing discount for guilty plea will apply.

- Pre-sentence report will invariably be required.

FINES

- Court must consider offender's financial circumstances before imposing a fine, s. 162(1) CJA 2003.

- Fine must reflect the 'seriousness' of the offence, s. 164(2) CJA 2003.

- Sentencing discount will apply for a guilty plea.

- Fines are higher in the Crown Court.

OTHER TYPES OF SENTENCE

- conditional discharge;

- absolute discharge.

ANCILLARY ORDERS

- Compensation orders:

  - on conviction s. 130 PCC(S)A requires court to order compensation for any injury, loss, damage etc.;
  - court must give reason for not making compensation order;
  - magistrates can order compensation under to £5,000;
  - see Magistrates' Court Sentencing Guidelines for compensation for personal injury;
  - compensation in Crown Court is unlimited;
  - priority given to compensation orders over fines, prosecution costs etc.

FIGURE 30.1 (CONTINUED)

- Defendant pays prosecution costs:
  - purpose to compensate prosecution;
  - sum should not exceed costs reasonably incurred;
  - court must account for offender's ability to pay;
  - confiscation and forfeiture orders, see Proceeds of Crime Act 2002.
- ASBOs
- notification under sex offenders' register;
- football banning order;
- restraining order;
- deportation.

31 SENTENCING IN ROAD TRAFFIC CASES

31.1   INTRODUCTION

Road traffic cases occupy a considerable amount of time in magistrates' courts. Special sentencing considerations apply to such cases, which is why we have decided to devote a chapter solely to this aspect of sentencing. Driving offences range in seriousness, from documentary offences e.g. failing to display a road tax certificate, to causing death by dangerous driving.

There are aspects of road traffic sentencing that can be quite tricky. To be absolutely sure of the court's powers, you must research the sentencing options in relation to the offence your client is alleged to have committed. Once again, *Blackstone's Criminal Practice* and the Magistrates' Court Sentencing Guidelines provide an invaluable source of information in this regard. It is also important that you ascertain the details of your client's driving licence, as this may well affect the penalty the court can impose. For example, is your client the holder of a provisional driving licence or the holder of a full licence? Does your client have unexpired penalty points on his licence or a previous period of disqualification?

The importance of researching the penalties for the offence with which your client is charged cannot be overstated. Not all driving offences are endorseable with penalty points and a large number of driving offences, including careless driving, do not carry the possibility of a custodial sentence. Some offences (including careless driving) carry a variable number of penalty points. Conviction for certain offences requires the offender to undertake an extended driving test under s. 36(1) Road Traffic Act 1988 (RTA). An example of this disposal is the offence of dangerous driving, contrary to s. 2 Road Traffic Act 1988. In circumstances where obligatory endorsement of a driving licence is ordered, the court may disqualify the defendant until he has retaken and passed his driving test s. 36(4) RTA 1988. In addition to the imposition of penalty points and disqualification, a fine is likely to be imposed for the vast majority of less serious driving offences. You should consult the Magistrates' Court Sentencing Guidelines for an accurate indication of the likely penalty. If in doubt, consult the legal adviser to the court.

Fundamental to your understanding of road traffic law are the following terms:

- obligatory disqualification;
- discretionary disqualification; and
- obligatory endorsement.

31.2 OBLIGATORY DISQUALIFICATION

Some offences carry obligatory disqualification from driving. They include: driving with excess alcohol contrary to s. 5 RTA 1988; dangerous driving, contrary to s. 3 RTA 1988 and aggravated vehicle taking, contrary to s. 12A Theft Act 1968. Disqualification must be for a period of at least 12 months, unless special reasons apply (s. 34 RTA 1988). In some instances the period of disqualification will be longer. Where an offender commits an offence of drink driving within 10 years of having committed an excess alcohol offence, the minimum period of disqualification is three years. Where the defendant pleads guilty to an offence which carries obligatory disqualification, the court can impose an interim disqualification period pending the final resolution of sentence. The court has a discretion to disqualify until a test is passed where the offender has been convicted of an offence involving obligatory disqualification.

31.2.1 PROVISION FOR DRINK DRIVERS TO REDUCE THE PERIOD OF OBLIGATORY DISQUALIFICATION

Drink drivers who are disqualified for 12 months or more under the various driving offences involving excess alcohol or drugs are able to reduce their period of disqualification if they successfully complete a drink driver's rehabilitation course (s. 34A RTA 1988). The course is available in all areas. The defendant must pay for it privately. It has to be completed at least two months before the expiry of the period of disqualification. The reduced period of disqualification cannot be for less than three months and no more than a quarter of the entire period of disqualification.

31.3 PENALTY POINT ENDORSEMENT

A considerable number of offences oblige the court to endorse the driver's licence. These include: careless driving (s. 3 RTA 1988); failure to stop and report an accident (s. 170 RTA 1988) and having no insurance (s. 143 RTA 1988). In such circumstances the offender's driving licence must be endorsed with the appropriate number of penalty points unless, at the same time, the defendant is disqualified from driving either because the court has exercised its discretion to disqualify for the offence itself or because disqualification for the particular offence is mandatory.

31.3.1 PENALTY POINT ENDORSEMENT AND THE DISCRETION TO DISQUALIFY

Whenever a court endorses penalty points on a licence, it always has discretion to disqualify the offender from driving for the offence itself (s. 34(2) RTA 1988). Disqualification pending passing of a driving test may also be ordered where the safety of other road users is an issue (s. 34(4) RTA 1988). If a court chooses to disqualify in the exercise of its discretion for say, a particularly bad example of careless driving, no penalty points are actually imposed on the defendant's driving licence, although the particulars of the offence are endorsed. Where a court exercises its discretion to disqualify, the period of disqualification is entirely a matter for the court. Disqualification (whether obligatory or in the exercise of the court's discretion) for a period of 56 days or more, results in the defendant's licence being revoked and thereby wiping clear any existing penalty points.

31.3.2 NUMBER OF POINTS WHERE THE DEFENDANT HAS COMMITTED TWO OR MORE ENDORSEABLE OFFENCES

Where a defendant is convicted of two or more endorsable offences committed on the same occasion, the court will usually endorse the highest number of points, unless it thinks fit to order otherwise (s. 28 RTA 1988).

31.3.3 OFFENCES CARRYING A VARIABLE RANGE OF PENALTY POINTS

Where there is a variable range of penalty points, the actual points imposed should reflect the seriousness of the offence and the defendant's culpability. Careless driving carries a range of penalty points, from three to nine. Where the defendant is guilty of no more than a minor lapse in concentration, the endorsement of penalty points ought to be towards the lower end of the tariff. Conversely, a serious lapse in concentration or a prolonged course of bad driving will merit the imposition of penalty points towards the higher end of the tariff.

Sentencing for road traffic offences, in common with other general criminal offences, is based on seriousness. The Magistrates' Court Sentencing Guidelines usefully identify aggravating and mitigating features in relation to the most common road traffic offences. In relation to driving with excess alcohol, the guidelines provide an indication of the likely penalty and the likely period of disqualification based on the reading of the analysed specimen. This underscores the importance of researching any relevant sentencing guidelines before attempting to offer advice on likely sentence or indeed mitigating on behalf of a client.

31.3.4 SPECIAL PROVISIONS FOR 'NEWLY QUALIFIED' DRIVERS

Section 1 Road Traffic (New Drivers) Act 1995 introduced a probationary period of two years starting from the day on which a person became a qualified driver. If the newly qualified driver acquires six or more penalty points within the probationary period of two years, his licence will be revoked by the Secretary of State, requiring the driver to retake and pass an ordinary driving test before being eligible to apply for a full licence once more. The probationary period thereafter has no further application. Revocation of the driver's licence in these circumstances does not have the effect of wiping the licence clear, and the penalty points will remain on the licence for the statutory period of three years from the commission of the offence.

31.4 PROCEDURE ON SENTENCING IN CONNECTION WITH A ROAD TRAFFIC OFFENCE

In many instances of less serious driving offences, the defendant will take the opportunity of pleading guilty by post (see Chapter 18, paragraph 18.3). In some instances, the defendant may be subject to a fixed penalty at the road side (for qualifying offences see Sch. 3 to RTA 1988). In cases where the defendant denies the offence, he will be subject to a trial. A considerable number of the less serious road traffic offences are summary only. It is unlikely that a defendant will qualify for a representation order to cover the cost of legal representation at trial in such cases unless the sentencing consequences are serious.

Having been convicted of a road traffic offence, the defendant will be asked to produce his driving licence to the court. If his licence is unavailable, the court can request a print out from the Driver Vehicle Licensing Association (DVLA). Where the offender has a clean driving licence but is unable to produce it, a court can permit the defendant to swear to this fact on oath.

In any case where a magistrates' court is considering imposing a period of disqualification following conviction and the person to be disqualified is not present in court, the court must, by virtue of s. 11(4) MCA 1980, adjourn and notify the defendant that he is required to attend court as the court is considering a period of disqualification. If the defendant subsequently fails to attend, he can be disqualified in his absence, however the usual course of action will be to adjourn the proceedings and issue a warrant under s. 13 MCA 1980 to compel the defendant's attendance.

Where a court imposes penalty points or endorses a driving licence, the court will send the driving licence to the DVLA in Swansea.

31.5 DISQUALIFICATION UNDER THE TOTTING-UP PROCEDURE SYSTEM – S. 35 RTA 1988

A defendant will be liable to disqualification for at least six months if the penalty points to be taken into account for the current offence amount to 12 or more.

Where the defendant is convicted of an offence which carries obligatory endorsement, the penalty points to be taken into account are:

1. any points attributed to the offence in respect of which the defendant has just been convicted (except if disqualified for the offence itself under s. 34 RTA 1988); and

2. any points previously endorsed on his licence in respect of offences committed within the three years immediately preceding the commission of the present offence (if the defendant was disqualified in connection with an earlier offence, no penalty points would have been endorsed on his licence for that particular offence).

For the purposes of the totting-up procedure, it is the date of the commission of the offence which is the key date and not the date of conviction.

Where a person is disqualified from driving under the penalty points system, his driving licence is wiped clear of penalty points.

Disqualification under the totting-up provisions is mandatory unless there are mitigating circumstances, and must be for a minimum period of six months. The six month disqualification increases to 12 months if there has been a previous disqualification of 56 days or more within three years of the commission of the current offence. It increases to two years if there have been two or more disqualifications imposed within three years of the current offence. A court may order the offender to retake an extended driving test.

The minimum periods of disqualification under the totting-up provisions are subject to mitigating circumstances. If such circumstances are successfully argued, the court can reduce the minimum period of disqualification or not disqualify at all.

31.6 AVOIDING OBLIGATORY ENDORSEMENT OR OBLIGATORY DISQUALIFICATION – SPECIAL REASONS – SS. 34 AND 44 RTA 1988

To avoid obligatory endorsement or obligatory disqualification, a defendant must establish the defence of special reasons. What is a special reason? There is no statutory definition of special reasons. However, a substantial body of case law has built up over the years. We include here no more than a summary of the law. Further detail can be found in *Blackstone's Criminal Practice*. A special reason was defined in *Whittal v Kirby* [1947] KB 194 as:

> 'a mitigating or extenuating circumstance, which is connected with the commission of the offence but which is not personal to the offender and which does not constitute a defence to the charge.'

A finding of special reasons gives the court discretion as to whether to disqualify or endorse a driver's licence. In other words, a court can find that there are special reasons but can still choose not to exercise its discretion.

The onus of establishing special reasons rests on the defendant on the balance of probabilities. Invariably, the defendant will be expected to adduce evidence. An assertion of special reasons is likely to be scrutinised critically by the court.

The following have been held to amount to a special reason.

Emergency

Driving in an emergency may amount to a special reason if for example, the defendant had not intended to drive but, having consumed alcohol, was suddenly confronted with an emergency situation requiring him to drive. A court would enquire in such a case as to whether alternative transport might have been available. The test is whether the reasonable man would have regarded the situation as being one in which no other course of action was possible (*DPP v Whittle* [1996] RTR 154).

Laced drinks

Special reasons not to disqualify from driving can be found in a case where a defendant can establish that his drinks were laced, that he did not know or suspect that fact, and that if his drinks had not been laced, he would not have been above the legal limit (*DPP v O'Connor* [1992] RTR 66). Special reasons would not apply to someone who knew he was drinking alcohol but had been misled as to the nature and strength of the drink.

The shortness of the distance driven

An intention to drive only a short distance can be regarded as a special reason for not disqualifying. Guidance on this is provided in the Divisional Court's decision in *Chatters v Burke* [1986] RTR 396.

31.7 AVOIDING DISCRETIONARY DISQUALIFICATION

To avoid or reduce the period of discretionary disqualification the defendant can argue mitigating factors which are relevant to the offence and may be personal to the defendant, ie loss of employment and effect upon the defendant's faults.

31.8 AVOIDING DISQUALIFICATION UNDER THE TOTTING-UP PROCEDURE – S. 35 RTA 1988

To reduce or to avoid disqualification under the totting-up procedure, the defendant must argue mitigating circumstances which are relevant to the offence and may be personal to the defendant. Section 35(4) RTA 1988 specifically excludes the defendant from relying on:

- the fact the offence is trivial; or
- that loss of his licence would cause him hardship (unless the hardship is exceptional); or
- any mitigating circumstances which have been advanced and taken into account to avoid disqualification under the totting up procedure within the preceding three years.

31.8.1 THE DEFENCE OF EXCEPTIONAL HARDSHIP

In determining whether the defendant will suffer exceptional hardship in the event of his being disqualified under the totting-up procedure, regard will be had to all the circumstances. Hardship must be exceptional. The defendant has effectively got to prove that, if he loses his driving licence, he will suffer hardship of a very serious kind. The hardship can extend to those who are dependant on the defendant. Relevant factors will include: what type of job the defendant has; any other means of transport available to him (mere inconvenience is not enough); shift patterns; availability of public transport, etc.

It will invariably be necessary for the defendant to give evidence on oath to substantiate a defence of exceptional hardship and where appropriate, adduce evidence from an employer as regards the consequences of loss of licence.

31.9 FURTHER APPLICATION TO REDUCE PERIOD OF DISQUALIFICATION

Provision exists under s. 42 RTA 1988 for a person disqualified from driving to apply to the court to end the period of disqualification before its expiry date. The provisions apply to offenders subject to lengthy periods of disqualification. It is entirely a matter for the court's discretion. Under s. 42 the following factors are relevant: (a) the character of the person disqualified and his conduct subsequent to the order; (b) the nature of the offence; and (c) any other circumstances. A minimum period of disqualification must have expired before the offender is in a position to apply. In the case of an individual who was disqualified for less than four years, two years of disqualification must have expired.

31.10 ROAD SAFETY BILL

Looking Ahead

The Road Safety Bill is set to make a number of changes to the sentencing of road traffic related offences. It will also introduce new offences of causing death by careless driving and causing death by driving while being uninsured, unlicensed or disqualified. It will increase the penalties in relation to some offences and introduce variable penalty points for speeding offences. In certain circumstances, drivers will be able to reduce the number of penalty points on their licence by undertaking a driver improvement course. The legislation will require the worst drink-drivers to re-take their driving test and to undergo a medical assessment.

KEY POINT SUMMARY

- Ensure your client brings his driving licence to court.
- Ensure you have researched the penalties for the offence/s under consideration and any applicable sentencing guidelines.
- Ensure you have scrutinised your client's driving licence to see whether there are any past endorsements or disqualifications.
- Understand that special reasons apply only in relation to mandatory disqualification/endorsement and that special reasons are difficult to establish.
- Be prepared to make a submission and to adduce evidence in a case where your client may lose his licence under the totting-up procedure or in the exercise of the court's discretion to disqualify for the offence itself.

SELF-TEST QUESTIONS

Consider the following exercises designed to test your understanding of road traffic sentencing. Research the relevant sentencing guidelines and advise each client as to the likely outcome.

Exercise 1

Ian is summoned in connection with an offence of careless driving contrary to s. 3 RTA 1988. Ian was driving and approached a sharp bend in the road. His near-side wheel caught the kerb and the impact sent his car across the road onto the other carriageway. While spinning out of control, Ian's car clipped a cyclist riding on the other side of the carriageway, knocking him to the ground. The cyclist was not wearing a helmet. He sustained a fractured skull and died in hospital several days later. Ian pleads guilty at the first opportunity. He is deeply remorseful about the death of the cyclist and has had to take time off work and undergo counselling for depression. He has returned to his job where he receives a net salary of £2,500 a month. He is a married man with one dependant child. His wife does not work.

Exercise 2

Ruth is facing a charge of driving with excess alcohol, contrary to s. 5(1)(a) RTA 1988. She was observed by officers to be driving her car at 11pm in an erratic manner. She gave a positive specimen of breath at the roadside and was then arrested. She provided a further specimen which showed the level of alcohol in her breath as 111 mgs (against a legal limit of 35mgs), nearly four times over the legal limit.

Ruth pleads guilty. She admits to her solicitor that she has an alcohol dependency and that she is on anti-depressant medication. At present she is going through a traumatic divorce and feels that everything is spiralling out of control. Ruth is a nurse. She lives 25 miles from the hospital trust which employs her. She also works shifts. She is certain she will lose her job if she is disqualified from driving.

Exercise 3

Ben was involved in a minor road traffic accident which was attended by the police. It transpires that Ben was not insured to drive the particular vehicle he was driving. He is summonsed for driving without due care and attention (s. 3 RTA 1988) and for having no insurance (s. 143 RTA 1988). The lack of insurance was an oversight – he simply forgot to renew his policy. Ben had been pre-occupied because his wife had to go into hospital for an emergency operation leaving him with the care of their two school-age children. He expresses his regret and pleads guilty at the first opportunity. Ben has six points currently on his licence for speeding offences. Ben is a self-employed mechanic. He employs six others in his business. His business is 15 miles from his home. He works long hours. His work naturally involves him road testing vehicles. His wife cannot drive for the next six months due to her illness and the family is dependent upon Ben being able to drive. Ben draws £500 net per week from his business.

Exercise 4

Imran will plead guilty to an offence of driving without insurance (six to eight penalty points). He passed his test 18 months ago. His job requires him to drive and he does not wish to be without a driving licence. He earns £300 per week. The failure to have insurance was as a result of confusion as regards his mother's insurers. She had asked him to drive her car. He had checked her insurance cover with the insurance company and had been given the impression that his mother's policy extended to drivers under the age of 25. Imran is 23. When the insurance policy document was produced, the terms and conditions of the policy specifically excluded drivers under the age of 25.

Case study: *R v Roger Martin* (web-based only)

online
resource
centre

If you have accessed the *R v Roger Martin* case study from our Online Resource Centre, you will recall that Roger Martin has previously pleaded guilty to offences of common assault, careless driving and failing to stop. Research the relevant sentencing guidelines in relation to the road traffic offences with which Roger Martin is charged and consider what will be Roger's priority in terms of sentence.

You can access Roger Martin's plea in mitigation on our Online Resource Centre but we suggest that you do not do so at this stage until you have considered Chapter 32, which considers the role of the defence advocate in submitting a plea in mitigation.

Analysis of all the above can be found in Appendix 5.

FIGURE 31.1 SENTENCING IN ROAD TRAFFIC CASES

Offences reqiring obligatory disqualification

- Disqualification will be for a minimum period of 12 months.

- The driver's licence is revoked and wiped clear of penalty points where the period of disqualification is 56 days or more.

- The only way to avoid obligatory disqualification or to reduce the period of disqualification is to establish 'special reasons' for not disqualifying.

Offences for which there is discretionary disqualification

- Wherever penalty points have to be endorsed, a court has the discretion to order disqualification.

- Where the court disqualifies under its discretionary powers, the period of disqualification is a matter for the court.

- The driver's licence is revoked and wiped clear of penalty points where the period of disqualification in 56 days or more.

- The defendant can avoid discretionary disqualification by arguing mitigation relating to the offence and/or the defendant.

Offences requiring obligatory endorsement

- Specified offences require obligatory endorsement of a driver's licence.

- Where a range of penalty points can be imposed, the defendant's driving licence is endorsed; the number of penalty points the should reflect the 'seriousness' of the offence.

- The penalty points are aggregated with any other penalty points endorsed for offences committed within three years of the current offences.

- The only way to avoid obligatory endorsement is to establish 'special reasons'.

Disqualification under the 'totting-up' procedure – s. 35 Road Traffic Act 1988

- A defendant will be liable to disqualification for at least six months as a 'totter' if 12 or more penalty points have been endorsed on his licence for offences committed within the last three years;

- The court will take into account:

  - any points endorsed for the present offence; and

  - any points endorsed for offences committed within the last three years.

- Where a driver is disqualified as a totter for more than 56 days, his driving licence is wiped clean of points.

- Disqualification must be for a minimum of six months – longer in some cases.

- Defendant can avoid disqualification or seek to reduce the period of disqualification as a 'totter' by arguing mitigating factors including exceptional hardship.

32 SENTENCING IN PRACTICE

32.1   INTRODUCTION

The preceding chapters on sentencing have laid the foundations which enable us to consider the further aspects covered in this chapter. If you have not done so already, we invite you to work through Chapters 28–31 before proceeding.

In this chapter, we consider:

- the procedure on passing sentence;
- the importance of the plea in mitigation as a means of influencing the sentence that is passed by the court;
- how to construct a plea in mitigation.

32.2   THE PROCEDURE ON SENTENCING

The procedure is generally the same whether the offender is sentenced in the Crown Court or magistrates' court.

Sentencing occurs after a finding of guilt by the court or upon the offender pleading guilty to one or more offences. An adjournment may be necessary to obtain a pre-sentence report, or to await the conclusion of other outstanding criminal proceedings against the defendant where it would make good sense to sentence on the overall totality of the defendant's criminal behaviour.

32.2.1   PROCEDURE FOLLOWING A FINDING OF GUILT

Where a defendant has been found guilty by a verdict of the court, the court will be appraised of the circumstances of the offence and the involvement of the defendant. The defendant's solicitor will be invited to address the court by way of mitigation of sentence. If the defence solicitor, or the court of its own volition, feels further information about the defendant is required before sentence can be passed, the hearing will be adjourned and a standard delivery pre-sentence report (PSR) or a fast delivery sentence report will be ordered. In such a situation, the defence solicitor will reserve what he wishes to say by way of mitigation until the full sentencing hearing.

Where a court adjourns sentence for a PSR, it can remand the defendant in custody or on bail. Bail may be conditional or unconditional and can include a condition that the defendant cooperates with the probation service in the preparation of the report. A pre-sentence report should normally be available within three weeks where the defendant has been remanded in custody pending sentence, and within four weeks where the defendant is remanded on bail. For full consideration of the circumstances in which a PSR must be obtained see Chapter 28, paragraph 28.12.4.

32.2.2 PROCEDURE FOLLOWING A GUILTY PLEA

Before a guilty plea is entered, it is good practice to discuss the basis of your client's plea with the prosecution. As previously highlighted in Chapter 28, paragraph 28.14, a defendant's guilty plea does not necessarily imply acceptance of everything the prosecution states in outline of the circumstances relating to the offence. Where there is a significant dispute between the prosecution and the defence which would materially affect the sentence, a Newton hearing (*R v Newton* (1982) 77 Cr App R 13) may be required to determine the disputed fact. If a basis of plea can be agreed, this can be avoided.

Where a defendant pleads guilty, avoiding the need for a trial, the sentencing hearing will begin with the prosecution outlining the circumstances of the offence. This will be based on the evidence contained in witness statements and the defendant's interview. The prosecutor will refer the court to any victim impact statement that has been made in the case.

The prosecution will provide the court with a copy of the defendant's criminal record, drawing the attention of the court to any relevant convictions. If the current conviction places the defendant in breach of an existing order of the court, the prosecution ought to be in a position to provide details of the earlier offence. If the offence involves injury to an individual or damage to property, the prosecution should provide full details and hand in any documented applications for compensation. In the case of an injury, the prosecution may well refer the court to any sets of photographs taken of the injured party.

The prosecutor should present the facts fully and fairly. If there are any offences to be taken into consideration (see Chapter 28, paragraph 28.15) these will be referred to by the prosecution and an agreed schedule submitted to the court. Where it is confidently anticipated that a pre-sentence report will need to be ordered, the prosecution may present the court with an expedited version of the facts and allow the defence solicitor to make representations. Finally, the prosecution will ask for costs in a specified sum.

Having heard from the prosecution, it is the turn of the defence to submit a plea in mitigation. Once again, if the defence solicitor feels a PSR would be useful, he may immediately raise this point. If the court concurs, sentencing will be adjourned for the preparation of a report. Whether with a PSR or not, the principles of the plea in mitigation remain the same and are considered below.

Once the court has heard the outline of the facts from the prosecution and has listened to any representations by the defendant, the court is in a position to determine the appropriate sentence or penalty. In determining the appropriate sentence, the court will consider all the information before it and will apply any applicable sentencing guidelines in accordance with the principles outlined in Chapters 28–31 and apply any sentencing discount. It will then announce its decision in open court, explaining the sentence to the defendant and giving reasons for its decision.

32.3 **THE PLEA IN MITIGATION**

One of the most important functions a defence solicitor will be called upon to fulfill is to seek to mitigate sentence on his client's behalf. This is known as making a plea in mitigation. As previously explained, the sentence your client receives will largely be determined by the seriousness of the offence. However, in arriving at the most appropriate sentence for your client, the court will have regard to your client's personal circumstances and to any personal offender mitigation.

The plea in mitigation is important because it should assist the court to determine the seriousness of the offence and it should bring to the court's attention any relevant personal offender mitigation.

32.3.1 **COMPONENTS OF AN EFFECTIVE PLEA IN MITIGATION**

In order to deliver an effective plea in mitigation you need to combine a thorough knowledge of sentencing law and practice with good advocacy skills. There are, in our view, three fundamental requirements for a competent plea in mitigation.

Firstly, the defence solicitor must understand the theory of sentencing and the importance of researching any applicable sentencing guidelines (see Chapters 28–31).

Secondly, the defence solicitor must have in mind a realistic sentencing objective, having regard to the theory behind sentencing and having considered any applicable sentencing guidelines. Sentencing theory should be grasped during the vocational stage of training. Formulating a realistic sentencing objective is largely a question of common sense, although experience of sentencing in criminal courts will help to fashion it.

Thirdly, the defence solicitor needs good advocacy skills.

An effective plea in mitigation should be well thought through, carefully constructed and persuasively delivered. Preparation is the key.

32.3.2 **PREPARING A PLEA IN MITIGATION**

The starting point for any plea in mitigation is to ensure you are aware of the sentence a court can impose for the particular offence/s and whether there are any particular sentencing guidelines. This may require some legal research on your part.

You will be aware of the prosecution's version of the facts having considered the pre-trial disclosure of evidence (advance information) and having listened to the prosecutor's submission to the court outlining the circumstances of the offence. You will have taken your client's detailed instructions about the offence and will have considered and discussed with your client the content of any pre-sentence report that may have been ordered. You should therefore be in a position to assess the balance of aggravating and mitigating features in the offence and arrive at an assessment of the true seriousness of the offence.

Given that sentencing is based on the seriousness of the offence, you need to make an assessment of seriousness. You need to ask yourself 'What would I ideally like to achieve for my client?' Then put yourself in the position of the court and consider what sentencing objective the court is likely to follow. Will it want to punish your client/rehabilitate him/prevent the commission of further offences/protect the public/put your client on trust as to his future behaviour? By engaging in this exercise you will hopefully arrive at a realistic sentencing objective which gives you the basis upon which to build your plea in mitigation.

You might have concluded that a custodial sentence is a distinct possibility for your client. If it is, ask yourself whether the custody threshold test set out in Chapter 29 is met on the facts in this case. Consider *R v Howells* [1999] 1 WLR 307 and other cases that are relevant to the imposition of custodial sentence. Can you make use of them in your plea?

If your preparation leads you to the conclusion that the court might be amenable to imposing a community sentence, consider whether the requisite criteria for such sentence (as explained in Chapter 30), is met.

If a financial penalty or a compensation order is likely to be made, make sure you are in possession of an up-to-date statement of your client's financial means.

32.3.3 USING THE PRE-SENTENCE REPORT IN PREPARATION

In preparing your plea in mitigation you must of course discuss the content of any PSR or SSR with your client. There may be matters in the PSR with which your client disagrees or which are out of date. The probation officer who prepared the report is not usually available in court, but the defence can require the officer to attend if the defendant wishes to challenge what has been written. Advocates should be selective and refer the sentencing court to relevant portions of the pre-sentence report which assist the plea being put forward.

32.3.4 ADDUCING CHARACTER EVIDENCE OR OTHER EVIDENCE LIKELY TO BE OF ASSISTANCE IN YOUR PLEA IN MITIGATION

Will your client benefit from adducing testimonial evidence as to the sort of person he is? Your preparation should have alerted you to this possibility. If your client is a person of past good character and is charged with an offence likely to result in damage to his reputation, it is useful to be able to hand in a short written character reference to the court. If your client has a medical condition that is relevant to sentencing, consider obtaining a written note from your client's GP. Similarly, if your client has the offer of a job or a helpful letter from his employer, it is good mitigation to obtain written confirmation to this effect.

32.4 STRUCTURING A PLEA IN MITIGATION

There is no predetermined structure for a plea in mitigation. Every plea in mitigation must of course be tailored to the individual case. Having regard to all that has been said in this and the preceding chapters, we include a checklist of the possible factors an advocate might have regard to in constructing a plea in mitigation.

Introduction

If your client has pleaded guilty, you may wish to introduce yourself to the bench before beginning your plea in mitigation. You may also want to say a few words to introduce your client:

> 'Madam. . . my client is a young man. He is 24. He has a job and resides with his girlfriend . .'

Acknowledge the prosecution's presentation of the facts

Consider thanking the prosecution for its fair outline of the facts of the case, if this is appropriate:

> 'Madam, I am grateful to my friend for fairly outlining the facts in this case . . .'

If there are aspects of the prosecution's presentation with which you disagree, highlight them at this stage. The above sentence might continue:

> 'There is however one matter which I feel I ought to clarify/bring to your attention at the outset and before going any further . . .'

Using a pre-sentence report

If a pre-sentence report has been prepared, ascertain from the bench at an early stage in your plea whether they have had the opportunity to consider its content. If not, politely suggest that the bench may wish to do so before you continue with your plea. Think about court etiquette. Be polite:

'Madam, I wonder if you have had the opportunity to consider the pre-sentence report that has been prepared in connection with this matter? You have; I am grateful for that indication . . .'

Use the pre-sentence report selectively, if it is to your benefit:

'I wonder if I might direct Madam's attention to paragraph 12 of the pre-sentence report where Miss James speaks favorably of a community based disposal in this matter . . .'

Acknowledge your client's predicament

'Madam, let me say at the outset that my client is a deeply anxious individual . . . my client fully appreciates that he stands to be sentenced today for a serious offence/that he could be sent to prison for these offences today . . . he expresses his complete remorse for his wrongdoing . . . understands the need for punishment but also seeks the help of the court in dealing with his offending behaviour . . .'

Can you play down the seriousness of the offence?

Can you use the Magistrates' Court Sentencing Guidelines (or other applicable guidelines) to play down the seriousness of the offence? Consider the aggravating and mitigating factors. Are you absolutely clear as to the basis of your client's guilty plea if he is pleading guilty?

If your client has pleaded guilty to an offence of assault, relevant mitigating factors may include provocation, a minor injury, etc. If your client has been found guilty of a theft offence, relevant mitigating features would include the fact that it was committed spontaneously, the amount involved is small or that the theft or deception was not committed for personal gain. If the offence to be sentenced was burglary, relevant factors would include the fact that the property was empty or disused and that no damage was caused in the course of the burglary. Have the stolen items been recovered? Was the crime committed in a sophisticated way?

Be tactful when exploring the victim's role in the commission of the offence. You do not want to score an own goal. It is your client who stands to be punished for the offence, not the victim.

If custody is a distinct possibility

Consider the applicable criteria. Is the offence 'so serious' that only custody can be justified? Be prepared to make representations based on the aggravating and mitigating features. Once again, refer to sentencing guidelines and the case law considered in Chapter 29 and make the point that if a custodial sentence is to be imposed, its length should be commensurate with the seriousness of the offence (s. 153 CJA 2003). You might make reference to the current problems of prison overcrowding highlighted in *Kefford* [2002] 2 Cr App (S) R 106 and *Mills* [2002] 2 Cr App (s) R 229, with a view to trying to persuade the court to keep any custodial sentence to as short a length as possible.

As the new types of custodial sentence under the CJA 2003 become available, you might consider whether an intermittent custody term or a suspended sentence is more appropriate for your client.

Can you play down your client's role in the offence?

Was your client led into temptation? Perhaps your client was not the instigator or the 'ring leader'. Was your client provoked? Was your client intoxicated or under the influence of an unlawful substance? You have to be careful with regard to the aforementioned. Drink and drugs do not excuse an offender's behaviour, but they may go some way to explain why your client acted in the way he did.

Can you offer an explanation as to why your client has offended?

Do not seek to excuse the offence, but see if you can offer an explanation for your client's offending. Common factors include low self-esteem, mental health issues, complete lack of self-control, dire financial straits, homelessness and addictive behaviour such as alcoholism, drug abuse, gambling.

Are there any personal factors at work that might put the offending behaviour into context?

Is your client getting divorced? Maybe your client is in the grips of an acrimonious breakdown of a relationship? Perhaps your client is frustrated because he or she cannot gain access to their children resulting in a sense of frustration and anger. Is your client presently facing an uncertain future? Maybe he is ill, bereaved, redundant or about to be made redundant, being sued or going through some personal crisis. Consider whether any of the above can be substantiated by evidence, perhaps in the form of a short medical report or letter from an employer.

What is your client's attitude to the offence?

It is fair to say that some clients will give you more scope in this respect than others. Attitude may be reflected in a timely guilty plea and co-operation with the police. A guilty plea spares witnesses. You will want to remind the bench that it should give credit for a timely guilty plea.

Your client's attitude might be expressed in the pre-sentence report if one is ordered and you should highlight this and bring it to the attention of the court. How candid has your client been in engaging with the probation service?

Most advocates will express their client's regret and remorse and perhaps offer an apology. Of course, actions speak louder than words. If your client has sought to make reparation to his victim (by paying compensation or repairing any damage) or has personally expressed an apology this is very useful mitigation.

What effect will the conviction have on your client?

Will this conviction result in a damaged reputation? This will be of particular relevance in the case of a first-time offender, especially if convicted of an offence relating to dishonesty. A first-time conviction for a sexual offence will result in damage to your client's reputation.

What has been the effect of court proceedings on your client's family? Is the court sentencing a mother who has the sole care of her children? What effect have the proceedings had on your client? Has your client been put under stress by the court appearances? What were the circumstances of your client's arrest? Was it public? Did your client have to spend a night or two in a police cell? Is it an experience your client wishes to repeat? Does your client face the loss of his/ her job as a result of this conviction?

No previous convictions?

The fact that your client has no previous convictions is excellent mitigation. It means that this offence is completely out of character and is a one-off. The court may want to place your client on trust as to his future behaviour, depending on the seriousness of the offence.

What if your client has a criminal record?

Can you use your client's criminal record to your advantage? Perhaps the last conviction was some time ago? Consider whether your client has been subject to a community order and has found it to be beneficial. Has your client made brave attempts to rehabilitate himself in the meantime? Maybe steps have been taken to overcome drug addiction. Should your client be given the benefit of the doubt on this occasion? Can you detect a trend in the nature of the offences that have been committed that now needs to be addressed?

Do you have any character witnesses you might call to give evidence or to submit in written form to the court?

Your preparation for the plea in mitigation should have alerted you to this possibility. Ensure you have enough copies of any character references to distribute to the court.

What has your client done since to assist matters?

Has your client made good any damage or offered to pay voluntary sums of compensation? Has your client been able to obtain employment? Has your client begun to address the reason for his offending? If alcoholism or drug abuse is the problem, has your client sought help from professionals? If the offending behaviour is set against the backdrop of a marital or relationship breakdown, consider whether your client has come to terms with matters and is seeking help, perhaps from a solicitor or a counselling agency.

In short, is there evidence you can point to which suggests your client has some insight into his offending behaviour and wants to do something about it?

Finances

Given that the fine is a popular sentencing option in magistrates' courts (see Chapter 30), you must be in a position to provide the court with details of your client's finances, including weekly income and outgoings, savings and debts. A fine should always reflect an individual's ability to pay, and you may need to make representations on this basis. Imposing a fine could of course have a detrimental effect on your client's family. Where your client has an outstanding account with the court, you can expect the legal adviser to check whether your client's existing payments are up to date.

Miscellaneous considerations

Do not overlook the fact that if the current conviction puts your client in breach of an existing penalty, you will need to address this and the circumstances pertaining to that previous offence, as your client is likely to be re-sentenced or punished in some way for it. If your client has admitted an offence of absconding during the currency of the proceedings you will need to address the court on this as it constitutes a separate offence. Remember that if you are mitigating on a driving matter, different considerations might apply. You might need to argue special reasons or mitigating circumstances such as exceptional hardship (see Chapter 31).

Finally your conclusion . . .

What are you seeking to persuade the sentencing court to do? Are you looking for leniency, or a sentence to address your client's needs and the need to punish? Close your submission:

'Unless I can assist you further Madam . . . those are my submissions . . .'

The foregoing checklist assumes your client has pleaded guilty to the offence, obviating the need for a trial. If your client has been found guilty following a trial, whilst you can still address the court on the mitigating features of the offence, it is pointless to disagree with the verdict and to seek to minimise your client's role. By finding your client guilty, the court has already made up its mind about your client's involvement. You must, however, explain your client's personal circumstances so the court is appraised of the sort of individual it is sentencing.

32.5 ADVOCACY AND THE PLEA IN MITIGATION

Please refer to our comments in respect of advocacy skills in Chapter 4, paragraph 4.7. We highlight a handful of key features in relation to pleas in mitigation.

Use powerful words

Use words that are inclusive:

'Let us examine the circumstances surrounding the commission of this offence . . . you will see . . . you will no doubt appreciate the position my client found himself in . . .'

Use a structure

There is no pre-determined structure to a plea in mitigation. Consequently, you will need to devise a structure that gives coherence to your submission. Use the checklist at 32.4 above as your starting point. Consider ways in which you can link the various portions of your submissions:

'Madam, having looked at the circumstances of the offence, let us now turn to my client's personal situation . . .'

Remember, if you find yourself making a plea in mitigation before a district judge, you will need to be succinct. An experienced district judge may well indicate at the outset what sentence he or she is thinking of imposing on your client. Be prepared to hold your ground.

32.6 PROFESSIONAL CONDUCT

It would be unusual for you to be asked to confirm your client's list of previous convictions as part of the sentencing hearing. The Justices' Clerks' Society has advised its members that in relation to the citing of previous convictions, only one question should be put to the defence, namely: 'Have you seen this list?' What would you do if you were asked to confirm the accuracy of the list in circumstances where you know it contains errors or omissions that assist your client?

You are reminded of the importance of Rule 11.01 in that you must never knowingly deceive a court. Rule 11.10 provides:

'You might deceive or mislead a court by, for example:

(a) submitting inaccurate information or allowing another person to do so;

(b) indicating agreement with information that another person puts forward which you know is false . . . '.

Rule 10.12 provides that if you are acting for a defendant, you are not under any obligation to correct information given to the court by the prosecution or any other person which you know may lead the court to make an inaccurate assumption about the defendant or the case, provided you do not indicate agreement with that information.

The answer to the dilemma posed above depends for the most part on how the question regarding the accuracy of any list of previous convictions is phrased. In answering the question you must be careful not to violate client-confidentiality whilst at the same time being careful not to deceive the court. If the legal adviser follows the Justices' Clerks' Society advice, the dilemma should not arise.

SELF-TEST QUESTIONS

Case scenario: *R v William Hardy*

You will recall that William Hardy has pleaded guilty to the offence of unlawful sexual activity with a child. The magistrates decided to accept jurisdiction to sentence William Hardy summarily.

Your file to date (see Appendix 2) contains:

- William Hardy's proof of evidence;

- advance information;

- pre-sentence report;

- character references;

- an agreed basis of plea;

- your research of the relevant sentencing guidelines for an offence of this type (see analysis of self-test question in relation to Chapter 28.

In the light of all that we have considered in relation to sentencing, we invite you to draft a plea in mitigation on behalf of William Hardy.

You can see the full sentencing hearing in relation to *R v William Hardy* in the video section of our Online Resource Centre. In the video clips you will see the outline of the case presented by the solicitor for the CPS, followed by the plea in mitigation delivered by William Hardy's solicitor. A transcript (based for the most part on the plea) is included and analysis of the proceedings is provided on the

online resource centre

video. You will also see the magistrates pass sentence on William Hardy. We would ask you to note that this scenario was filmed before the Criminal Justice Act 2003 and the Sexual Offences Act 2003 came into force.

R v Roger Martin (web-based case study only)

Taking into consideration our study of sentencing theory and practice, it is your turn to draft a plea in mitigation on behalf of Roger Martin.

online resource centre

You are able to see the final determination of the *R v Roger Martin* case study by viewing his sentencing hearing in the video section of our Online Resource Centre. In the video clips you will see the outline of the case presented by the designated case worker for the CPS, followed by the plea in mitigation delivered by Roger Martin's solicitor. Analysis of the proceedings is provided in the video. You will see the sentence passed by the magistrates. The sentence concludes our consideration of this particular case study. We would ask you to note that this scenario was filmed before the Criminal Justice Act 2003 came into force. Were the same facts to be sentenced under the CJA 2003, Roger Martin would have been subject to a generic community order with specified requirements, which would include an element of supervision and unpaid work in the community.

FIGURE 32.1 SENTENCING PROCEDURE

Sentencing procedure where defendant found guilty

- Procedure generally same in Crown Court and magistrates' court.

- Court will be aware of facts of case and the defendant's role; defendant's criminal record is usually disclosed to the court.

- The case may be adjourned for pre-sentence report or specific sentence report.

- Defendant may be bailed or remanded in custody.

- Defence make a plea in mitigation.

- Defendant sentenced with court giving reasons.

Sentencing procedure where defendant pleaded guilty

- Procedure generally same in Crown Court and magistrates' court.

- Prosecution outline facts of the offence and the defendant's role.

- The case may be adjourned for pre-sentence report (PSR or specific sentence report (SSR)).

- Defendant's criminal record is usually disclosed to the court.

- Where dispute between prosecution and defence about facts of the offence, a Newton hearing (*R v Newton*) may be held.

- Defence make plea in mitigation.

33 APPEALS

33.1 INTRODUCTION

This chapter examines the practice and procedure involved in appealing against decisions of the magistrates' court or the Crown Court. In most cases, the defendant will appeal against the 'safety' of his conviction and/or the severity of the sentence. Some procedures for challenging the decision of the trial court, such as appeal by way of case stated or judicial review, are available to both the prosecution and the defence. There are also an increasing number of appeal procedures that are available only to the prosecution. The procedures explained in this chapter include:

- reopening a case, s. 142 Magistrates' Courts Act 1980;
- appeal from the magistrates' court to the Crown Court;
- appeal by way of case stated;
- judicial review;

- appeal to the Court of Appeal;
- Attorney-General's Reference;
- Criminal Cases Review Commission;
- appeals under the Criminal Justice Act 2003.

The rules of court relating to appeals are now contained in Parts 63–75 Crim PR.

33.2 REOPENNING A CASE – S.142 MAGISTRATES' COURTS ACT 1980

Following conviction by the magistrates, s. 142(2) MCA 1980 enables a defendant to ask the magistrates to set the conviction aside or to vary or rescind a sentence. The application may be made whether the defendant pleaded guilty or not guilty at the original trial and may be considered by the same bench who convicted the defendant or by a different bench.

In deciding whether to grant the application, the court will exercise its wide discretion under s. 142 MCA 1980 where it is 'in the interests of justice' to do so. Factors considered include the interests of the court and inconvenience to other parties of reopening the case.

There is no time-limit for making an application under s. 142 MCA 1980 but an unreasonable delay will be taken into account in determining the interests of justice test.

If the conviction is set aside, the case is reheard by a different bench of magistrates.

A common use of s. 142(2) MCA 1980 is to rectify an obvious mistake made during the defendant's trial. It is also used to reopen cases where a defendant has been convicted in his absence. When advising your client about potential avenues of appeal, you should consider whether an application under s. 142 MCA 1980 will provide a speedier remedy than an appeal to the Crown Court.

Section 142(1) allows a magistrates' court to vary or rescind its decision as to sentence if it is in the interest of justice to do so. This power is frequently used to reopen sentencing decisions (most notably the imposition of a fine) following a conviction in the defendant's absence.

Example

Kemal is charged with careless driving but unintentionally fails to attend for his trial at Stokeshire Magistrates' Court. He is convicted in his absence. He applies under s.142 MCA 1980 to have his conviction set aside. In deciding the interests of justice test, the bench will consider the inconvenience to the prosecution, the prosecution witnesses and to the court of the case being re-heard. These interests will be balanced against the defendant's general right to have the opportunity to defend himself.

If Kemal has strong mitigating reasons for failing to attend trial because, for example, he had to take his sick son to hospital, the bench will conclude that it is in the interest of justice to re-hear the case. If Kemal simply forget to attend court, it is likely that his application under s. 142 MCA 1980 will fail.

33.3 APPEAL TO THE CROWN COURT – S. 108 MAGISTRATES' COURTS ACT 1980 (PART 63 CRIM PR)

A defendant convicted before a magistrates' court may appeal against conviction and/or sentence to the Crown Court. Where the defendant pleaded guilty, he may only appeal against the sentence imposed. Appeal to the Crown Court is not available to the prosecution. The costs of the appeal will normally be met under a representation order if the defendant has been granted one (see Chapter 14 on funding). The defendant should ask the magistrates' court to extend its cover to include representation on appeal or make a fresh application before the Crown Court.

33.3.1 HOW TO APPEAL TO THE CROWN COURT

The notice of appeal must be given in writing within 21 days of the conviction and/or the sentence addressed to the chief executive to the justices of the magistrates' court that heard the case. There is discretion to extend this period.

The notice of appeal does not have to specify any detail other than by indicating whether the appeal is against conviction and/or sentence. It is usual to use a form of appeal which merely states that the 'defendant proposes to appeal on the ground that the magistrates erred in fact and in law in convicting him' or 'the defendant proposes to appeal against sentence on the ground that it was excessive in all the circumstances'.

There is no filter procedure and the court has no discretion to refuse to accept the appeal. Our case study *R v William Hardy* includes an appeal to the Crown Court against sentence.

Where the appellant received a custodial sentence in the magistrates' court, an application for bail until the hearing of the appeal may be made, although there is no prima facie right to bail. If the bail application is refused, a further application may be made to the Crown Court.

33.3.2 HEARING THE APPEAL

The appeal in the Crown Court takes the form of a complete rehearing of the case before a judge sitting with two lay magistrates. New evidence may be heard if it has become available since the original trial. The Crown Court can confirm, vary or reverse any part of the magistrates' original decision.

The defendant should be warned that if his appeal fails, the Crown Court can impose any sentence that was available to the magistrates. This may result in your client receiving a more severe penalty. An unsuccessful appeal can result in an order that the defendant pays some or all of the prosecution's costs.

33.4 APPEAL BY WAY OF CASE STATED – S. 111 MAGISTRATES' COURTS ACT 1980 (PART 64 CRIM PR)

Section 111 MCA 1980 provides:

'(1) Any person who was a party to any proceeding before a magistrates' court or is aggrieved by the conviction, order, determination or other proceeding of the court may question the proceeding on the ground that it is wrong in law or is in excess of jurisdiction by applying to the justices composing the court to state a case for the opinion of the High Court on the question of law or jurisdiction involved;

(2) An application under subsection (1) above shall be made within 21 days after the day on which the decision of the magistrates' court was given.'

Appeal by way of case stated to the Divisional Court may be made by any person who was party to the proceedings before the magistrates' court who seeks to challenge the conviction or any order or determination made by the court during the proceedings.

The grounds for making an appeal by way of case stated are that the magistrates' court was:

- wrong in law; or
- in excess of its jurisdiction.

The issues that are commonly raised in a case stated application includes whether:

- the justices had jurisdiction to try the case; or
- the justices were correct to find that there was a case to answer; or
- admissible evidence was excluded; or
- inadmissible evidence was admitted in evidence.

33.4.1 THE PROCEDURE FOR STATING A CASE

- Within 21 days of the acquittal or conviction or sentence, the aggrieved party must apply in writing (usually by letter), requiring the magistrates to state a case. The party should identify the question of law on which the Divisional Court's opinion is sought.

- A statement of case is prepared by the magistrates' adviser in consultation with the magistrates, which will:
  - outline the facts called into question;
  - state the facts as found by the magistrates;
  - state the magistrates' finding on the point of law being challenged, listing any authority cited, and
  - state the question for the Divisional Court to answer.

- Drafts of the case are then sent to the parties who may suggest amendments.

- The final form of the case stated is then sent to the appellant who must lodge it at the Crown Office of the Royal Courts of Justice in London. Notice and a copy of the case stated must be given to the respondent.

- The appeal is heard by the Divisional Court usually before three judges. Evidence is not called and the hearing takes the form of legal argument on the facts of the case as stated.

- The Divisional Court may reverse, amend or affirm the magistrates' decision or may remit the matter back to the magistrates with its opinion and a direction that the magistrates' court should, for example, convict the defendant or acquit him or the case should be tried again before a different bench.

- Costs may be awarded to either party out of central funds.

Magistrates may grant bail to a defendant who has received a custodial sentence pending the hearing of his appeal (s. 113 MCA 1980). If bail is refused, application can be made to a High Court judge in chambers.

33.4.2 IS FURTHER APPEAL POSSIBLE?

No – unless the matter can be appealed to the House of Lords on a point of law of public importance and either the Divisional Court or the House of Lords grant leave.

33.4.3 MAY THE SAME ISSUE BE APPEALED TO THE CROWN COURT AND BY WAY OF CASE STATED?

No – the right of appeal to the Crown Court is lost once an application is made to state the case. It is possible however to appeal by case of case stated to challenge the conviction but to appeal to the Crown Court against the sentence passed in the case. For this reason, the first avenue of appeal is usually the Crown Court (paragraph 33.3).

33.5 JUDICIAL REVIEW

Judicial review is available to a party in a criminal case where a magistrates' court as a 'public law' body has exercised its legal powers illegally or has failed to follow the correct procedure or has acted irrationally. Judicial review proceedings are governed by Part 54, Civil Procedure Rules. State funding for such an appeal would be way of the grant of a civil funding certificate.

Judicial review will be appropriate to challenge a decision where the magistrates' court acted in excess of its jurisdiction by failing to follow the statute which confers jurisdiction, or by acting in breach of the rules of natural justice, by, for example failing to allow an adjournment requested by a defendant on proper grounds or failing to give proper time to prepare a defence, see *R v Thames Magistrates' Court, ex p. Polemis* [1974] 1 WLR 1371, or where there are grounds for suspecting bias on the part of the legal adviser or one or more of the magistrates.

33.5.1 APPLYING FOR JUDICIAL REVIEW

Part 54 Civil Procedure Rules prescribes a two-stage procedure for applying for judicial review. The first stage is an application for leave to a High Court judge to obtain permission to proceed with judicial review. A notice of application on the appropriate claim form setting out the grounds for review must be filed by the defendant. The claim form must:

- identify the applicant; and
- the relief sought;
- the grounds on which the application is made; and
- an affidavit (i.e. a sworn statement) that verifies those grounds and adds further argument.

A single judge usually determines the application for leave without a hearing and in the absence of the other side (the respondent).

If leave is granted, the judicial review hearing will be before the Divisional Court which hears arguments from the applicant, the respondent and any other body affected by the magistrates' decision. In a criminal case this will usually be the CPS or the Home Office.

Bail pending the hearing of an application for judicial review may be granted by a judge in chambers.

At the end of the hearing, court makes its decision, and if the applicant's case is proven, will grant relief by making a mandatory order; and/or a prohibiting order or a quashing order.

33.6 APPEAL FROM THE CROWN COURT (PART 68 CRIM PR)

A person convicted of an offence on indictment may appeal to the Court of Appeal against his conviction and/or his sentence where he pleaded not guilty or against sentence only where he pleaded guilty (s. 1 Criminal Appeal Act 1968). The advice of counsel or a solicitor-advocate should always be sought before commencing an appeal against conviction and or sentence to the Court of Appeal.

33.6.1 OBTAINING LEAVE TO APPEAL

Leave to appeal against conviction and / or sentence to the Court of Appeal is always required. Leave may be given by the trial judge granting a certificate that the case is fit for appeal or the Court of Appeal can grant leave.

Where leave is required from the Court of Appeal, within 28 days of conviction or sentence, the appellant must serve on the Registrar of Criminal Appeals, a notice of application for leave to appeal, accompanied by draft grounds of appeal. The draft grounds will be settled by counsel.

33.6.2 FUNDING AN APPEAL TO THE COURT OF APPEAL

Where a defendant has been granted a representation order for trial on indictment, the order will cover both advice in connection with a possible appeal; drafting the grounds of appeal and seeking leave. Once leave to appeal has been granted, the representation order will need to be extended to cover representation at the appeal.

If the appeal is against conviction, a transcript should be provided, either of the judge's summing up or of some part of the evidence or where appropriate, the full transcript of the trial. The court's shorthand writer will then be asked by the registrar to transcribe the appropriate part of his notes. The papers are then put before a single judge.

This is a filtering stage at which a single judge considers whether leave ought to be given. If leave to appeal is given, public funding will be made available for the hearing itself.

If the single judge refuses leave to appeal, the appellant has 14 further days in which to serve notice upon the registrar that he wishes to renew the application before the full court. The papers are then put before the 'full' court, which considers the issue. If leave is refused, the application is lost and the appellant may be the subject of a loss of time order.

33.6.3 WHAT IS A DIRECTION FOR LOSS OF TIME?

Usually, any time spent in custody by an appellant between sentence being passed and his appeal being heard counts as part of any custodial sentence. A direction to the contrary called 'direction for loss of time' may be given by the court when refusing leave to appeal or dismissing an appeal purely on the grounds of law (s. 29 Criminal Appeal Act (CAA) 1968). This is a means of penalising an appellant for pursuing a frivolous appeal. In fact, directions for loss of time are very rarely made if counsel has advised on an appeal. A direction for loss of time would normally be made in respect of an appellant who, against counsel's advice, insists on proceeding with an appeal.

33.6.4 GRANTING BAIL ON APPEAL

The Court of Appeal has power to grant bail to an appellant pending the determination of his appeal. This may be exercised by the single judge when he considers the papers. Where the trial judge certifies that a case is fit for appeal, he may also grant bail pending determination of the appeal.

33.6.5 APPEALS AGAINST CONVICTION

The Court of Appeal may only allow an appeal against conviction if it thinks that the conviction is 'unsafe', s. 2(1)(a) CAA 1968 (as amended by Criminal Appeal Act 1995).

In deciding whether the conviction is 'unsafe', the Court of Appeal will listen to legal argument from each side and may, exceptionally, hear fresh evidence under s. 23 CAA 1968. The common practice is for an appellant to refer to specific legal or procedural errors that arose at trial, and then supplement these specific claims with the general ground that the conviction is unsafe.

The test to decide whether a conviction is 'unsafe' is subjective. Each member of the Court of Appeal must ask: 'Have I a reasonable doubt, or even a lurking doubt, that this conviction may be unsafe?' If the answer is affirmative, the appeal should be allowed (*Stafford v DPP* [1974] AC 878.). In *Pendleton* [2002] 1 WLR 72, the House of Lords held that the correct test in a case where the Court of Appeal receives fresh evidence on appeal under s. 23 CAA 1968, is whether the conviction was safe, not whether the defendant was guilty. In such cases the Court of Appeal must consider what effect the fresh evidence would have had on the minds of the jury had it been received at the original trial. If it might reasonably have affected the decision of the jury to convict, the conviction should be regarded as being unsafe.

There has been some concern that the amendment to the single ground of appeal by the CAA 1995, that the conviction is 'unsafe', has restricted the Court of Appeal's powers to quash a conviction. In *R v Chalkley; Jeffries* [1998] 2 Cr App R 79, the Court of Appeal confirmed that, following the amendment of s. 2(1) CAA 1968, the court had no power to allow an appeal if it did not consider the conviction to be unsafe but was in some other way dissatisfied with what had occurred at the trial, since the former tests of 'unsatisfactoriness' and 'material irregularity' were no longer available, except to determine the safety of a conviction.

In practice, however, the potentially restrictive interpretation of s. 2(1) CAA 1968 put forward in *Chalkley* has not been adopted, and in considering if a conviction is unsafe, the Court of Appeal is entitled to take into account whether:

- the conviction is unsatisfactory; or
- that the court made a wrong decision on a point of law; or
- there was a material regularity in the course of the trial.

As a consequence, grounds for appeal against conviction can include:

- wrongful admission or exclusion of evidence;
- failure to properly exercise judicial discretion;
- errors on the part of counsel;
- defect in the indictment;
- conduct of the trial judge;
- errors in the trial judge's summing-up;
- problems associated with jurors.

33.6.5 DISPOSALS AVAILABLE TO THE COURT OF APPEAL

In deciding whether the appellant's conviction was unsafe, the Court of Appeal court may:

- quash the conviction and, in effect, order an acquittal;
- quash the conviction and order a retrial; or
- find the appellant guilty of an alternative offence; or
- to allow part of the appeal; or
- dismiss the appeal.

33.7 APPEALS AND THE RIGHT TO A FAIR TRIAL – ARTICLE 6 ECHR 1950

In deciding whether the defendant enjoyed a fair trial under Article 6 ECHR, the European Court of Human Rights considers the whole trial process and not discrete elements such as whether the court should have exercised discretion to exclude a particular piece of prosecution evidence under s. 78 PACE 1984 on the ground of 'unfairness'.

This approach has led to uncertainty as to whether an 'unfair' trial under Article 6 would automatically lead to a conviction being overturned as 'unsafe.' This potential conflict was illustrated in *Condron v UK* (2001) 31 EHRR 1 where the ECtHR observed that there was a material difference between the review by the Court of Appeal on the grounds of the safety of a conviction and the review undertaken by the ECtHR on the basis that the applicant had not enjoyed a fair trial. According to the ECtHR the 'fair' trial test and the 'unsafe' conviction test were not the same.

The position is not completely clear. In *Togher* [2001] 3 All ER 463, Lord Woolf CJ suggested that if the accused had been denied a fair trial it was almost inevitable that the conviction would be regarded as 'unsafe' particularly in the light of the court's interpretive obligation under s. 3 Human Rights Act 1998. In *Davis, The Times*, 24 April, 2000, however, the Court of Appeal suggested that a finding by the ECtHR of a breach of Article 6 did not automatically lead to the quashing of a conviction. Although the Court of Appeal quashed the conviction in this case, it did so reluctantly. The authors of *Blackstone's Criminal Practice* cast doubt on the observations made by the Court of Appeal in this case. A safe conviction would, if it is submitted, necessarily imply a trial conducted in accordance with Article 6.

33.8 APPEAL AGAINST SENTENCE

An appeal against sentence follows the same procedure as an appeal against conviction except that an appeal against sentence only will not attract a loss of time direction. An appeal can be made on the basis that the sentence imposed was wrong in law, wrong in principle or was manifestly excessive. In considering an appeal against sentence, the Court of Appeal can:

- quash any sentence or order; or
- impose any sentence or order that could have been available to the Crown Court except the appellant should not be dealt with more severely than at the Crown Court.

33.9 APPEAL TO THE HOUSE OF LORDS (PART 74 CRIM PR)

Appeal from the Court of Appeal to the House of Lords may only be made where the Court of Appeal or the House of Lords certifies the case involves a point of law of general public importance.

33.10 ATTORNEY-GENERAL'S REFERENCES

Under s. 36 CJA 1988 (Part 74 Crim PR) the Attorney-General may, with leave of the Court of Appeal, refer to that court any sentence imposed by the Crown Court where he considers the sentence was unduly lenient. The Court of Appeal may then quash the original sentence and substitute such sentence (usually heavier) as it thinks appropriate for the case and which the court below had power to pass when dealing with the offender.

Under s. 36 Criminal Justice Act 1972 (Part 69 Crim PR) the Attorney-General has the power to refer a case to the Court of Appeal for its opinion on a point of law which arose in the case. The power relates to a case where the defendant was acquitted following trial on indictment. Whatever the outcome of the appeal, the defendant remains acquitted.

33.11 CRIMINAL CASES REVIEW COMMISSION

The Criminal Cases Review Commission, which was established by the Criminal Appeal Act 1995 is located in Birmingham and investigates and processes allegations of miscarriages of justice.

Under s. 9 Criminal Appeal Act 1995, the Commission may refer to the Court of Appeal:

- a conviction for an offence on indictment;
- a sentence imposed for an offence on indictment;
- a finding of not guilty by insanity.

Under s. 11 CAA 1995, the Commission may refer to the Crown Court a conviction and/or sentence imposed by the magistrates' court.

33.11.1 WHAT TEST MUST BE SATISFIED BEFORE THE COMMISSION CAN REFER A CASE?

The Commission may only refer a case to the Court of Appeal or to the Crown Court where, under s. 13 CAA 1995, the Commission considers that there is a real possibility that the verdict or sentence would not be upheld if the reference was made.

Section 15 CAA 1995 enables the Court of Appeal to direct the Commission to investigate a particular matter 'in such manner as the Commission thinks fit'. Sections 17–21 CAA 1995 provide the Commission with the power to obtain documents and direct officers to investigate and report on a relevant matter.

33.12 DOES THE PROSECUTION ENJOY A RIGHT TO APPEAL?

Until recently, the prosecution has enjoyed only limited rights to appeal. The prosecution had no right to appeal against acquittal of a defendant following a summary trial or trial on indictment. The only exception to this was the prosecutor's right to appeal a decision by magistrates by way of case stated in accordance with paragraph 33.4 above and by way of judicial review.

In relation to trials on indictment, the prosecution enjoys a right of interlocutory appeal against binding rulings made by a trial judge at a preparatory hearing in accordance with ss. 35 and 36 Criminal Procedure and Investigations Act 1996 (Part 65 Crim PR).

The 'right of the prosecution' to appeal against sentence is set out in paragraph 33.10 above. It requires a reference to be made by the Attorney-General.

The CJA 2003 has extended the prosecution's right of appeal in a number of important situations.

First, under s. 58 CJA 2003 the prosecution may appeal to the Court of Appeal against a terminating ruling made by the judge in relation to an issue at a trial on indictment and which cannot otherwise be the subject of an appeal to the Court of Appeal. The appeal can be against any judicial ruling made during the trial until the beginning of the summing-up to the jury. The procedure of appealing against a terminating ruling is described as a s. 58 application and includes where the prosecution appeals against:

- a successful submission of no case to answer by the defence; or
- a ruling on a PII application in favour of the defence; or
- a decision to stay the proceedings for an abuse of process; or
- a successful defence application to sever the counts on the indictment.

In making the application prosecution must agree that in the event of failing to obtain leave to appeal or if the appeal is abandoned, the defendant will be automatically acquitted.

Under the procedure, which is laid down in ss. 57–61 CJA 2003, the appeal can follow an expedited or non-expedited route. It is for the trial judge to decide which route is appropriate. In an expedited appeal, the trial may be adjourned to await the Court of Appeal's ruling. In a non-expedited appeal, the trial may be adjourned or the jury discharged.

Under s. 61 CJA 2003 the Court of Appeal may confirm or reverse or vary any ruling which the prosecution has appealed against. A ruling may only be reversed where the Court of Appeal is satisfied that –

- the ruling was wrong in law;
- the ruling involved an error in law or principle; or
- the ruling was not reasonable for the judge to make.

Where the Court reverses or varies the terminating ruling, it must order the resumption of the Crown Court trial or order a fresh trial or order the defendant's acquittal.

Second, the CJA 2003 has radically revised the traditional operation of *autrefois acquit*. Traditionally where a defendant has been found not guilty at trial and acquitted, the doctrine of *autrefois acquit* has prevented him from being retried for the same offence. Section 76 CJA 2003 allows the prosecutor to apply to the Court of Appeal for an order to quash the defendant's acquittal for a qualifying offence and to order a new trial. Generally a qualifying offence is any offence which carries a sentence of life imprisonment.

The Court of Appeal must order a retrial if there is new and compelling evidence in the case and it is in the interests of justice of the order to be made.

Looking Ahead

When in force, ss. 62 and 63 CJA 2003 give the prosecution the right of appeal on an evidential ruling made by the judge in relation to the admissibility of the prosecution evidence at trial. The appeal may be expedited or non-expedited and the Court of Appeal may confirm, reverse or vary the evidentiary ruling in question.

KEY POINT SUMMARY

- Ensure that you are know which avenue of appeal from the magistrates is appropriate to your client's case and be able to advise accordingly.

- Know the time limits and procedures for appealing.

- Be aware of the procedural steps in appealing from the Crown Court to the Court of Appeal.

- Understand what is meant by an 'unsafe' conviction under s. 2(1)(a) Criminal Appeal Act 1968.

SELF-TEST QUESTIONS

1. When might it be appropriate to apply for the case to be re-heard under s. 142 MCA 1980?

2. What is the potential danger to your client if appeals against sentence to the Crown Court?

3. Who may appeal by way of case stated?

4. Must leave be obtained to appeal from the Crown Court to the Court of Appeal?

5. On what ground may the Court of Appeal allow an appeal against conviction?

FIGURE 33.1 APPEALS

APPEALS FROM THE MAGISTRATES' COURT

- Rehearing the case, s. 142 MCA 1980
  - on the defendant's application, the magistrates' court may set the conviction/sentence aside;
  - the application will be granted where 'it is in the interests of justice';
  - any retrial will be reheard by a different bench of magistrates.

- Appeal to the Crown Court, s. 108 MCA 1980
  - against conviction/and or sentence;
  - within 21 days of conviction and / or sentence, defendant applies to magistrates' court which heard his case;
  - the appeal in the Crown Court takes the form of a rehearing;
  - the Crown Court can confirm, vary or reverse the magistrates' decision;
  - where the appeal fails, the Crown Court can impose any sentence which the magistrates might have imposed.

- Appeal by case stated, s. 111 MCA 1980
  - to the Divisional Court;
  - where the magistrates' court was wrong in law; or
  - acted in excess of jurisdiction;
  - application from any interested party within 21 days
  - appeal is heard by three judges in the Divisional Court;
  - the Divisional Court may reverse, amend or affirm the magistrates' court decision or may remit the case back to the magistrates.

- Judicial review, Part 54 CPR
  - application to the Divisional Court;
  - where a public law body acted in irrationally or illegally or did not follow the correct procedure;
  - where applicant proves the case, the court may make a mandatory order; or a prohibiting order; or a quashing order.

APPEAL FROM THE CROWN COURT

- Defendant may appeal to the Court of Appeal against conviction (where pleaded not guilty) and/or sentence;

- Leave must be obtained from the trial judge or the Court of Appeal;

- Appeal against conviction will be allowed where the conviction is 'unsafe', s. 2(1)(a) CAA 1968;

- Where conviction is 'unsafe', the court may:
  - quash the conviction and order an acquittal; or
  - quash the conviction and order a retrial;
  - find the appellant guilty on an alternative offence; or
  - allow part of the appeal; or
  - dismiss the appeal;

- In deciding an appeal against sentence, the Court of Appeal can:
  - quash any sentence or order; or
  - impose any sentence or order that was available to the Crown Court provided the appellant is not dealt with more severely than at his trial.

- Prosecution's right to appeal against:
  - rulings made by the trial judge at a preparatory hearing, ss. 35, 36 CPIA 1996;
  - appeal against a terminating ruling during a trial on indictment, ss. 57–61 CJA 2003;
  - application to the Court of Appeal for an order to quash the defendant's acquittal for a qualifying offence and to order a new trial, s. 76 CJA 2003.

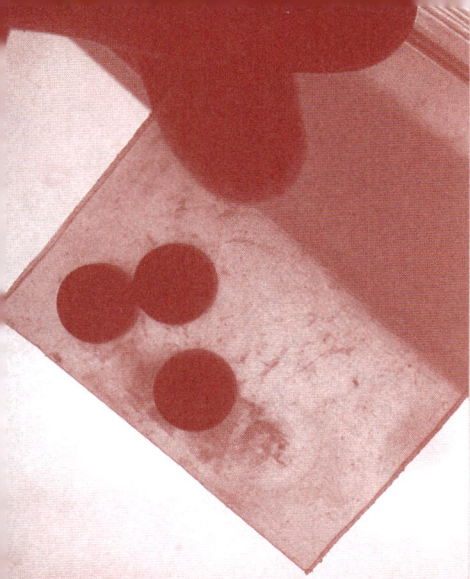

Part VI

YOUTH JUSTICE

Part VI comprises two chapters, which examine the special considerations that apply in relation to young offenders under the age of 18.

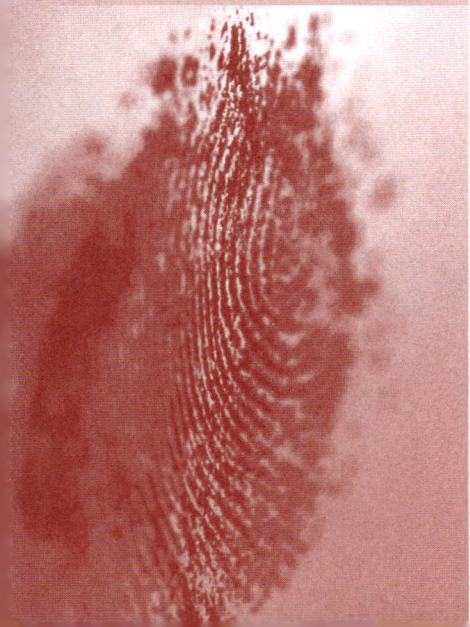

34 YOUTH JUSTICE

34.1   INTRODUCTION

The Audit Commission has estimated that approximately seven million crimes are committed each year by offenders under 18 years of age and that over £1 billon is spent annually dealing with offending by young people. Empirical research has also confirmed that approximately 17 per cent of all persons who are taken to the police station are aged under 18 years. Therefore juvenile offending has important political, economic and social implications as well as making important demands on the criminal justice system and those who work in it. The final two chapters of the *Criminal Litigation Handbook* have been written to acknowledge the growing importance of this increasingly specialist area of criminal practice.

While many of the practices and procedures of youth justice will be familiar to you and are based on the adult model, there are also important differences in recognition of the special position and vulnerabilities of young people in the criminal justice system. These special considerations are reflected, for example, in the relative informality of proceedings in the Youth Court and the requirement that all participants in the youth justice system are under a statutory duty to prevent offending by children and young people. Youth justice also has a number of specialist organisations that formulate policy and deal with young offenders and their families on a day-to-day basis. There is also a hierarchy of procedures and schemes which seek to divert juveniles from crime when they are in danger of offending for the first time through to pre-court orders and even after they have been charged and where there is suffi-cient evidence to prosecute. Therefore prevention from offending and the opportunities for the early rehabilitation of those who have offended are pervasive to the aims and procedures of youth justice, and, as a defence solicitor working in this area, you will need to have a good working knowledge of these issues.

We deal with youth justice in two chapters. Chapter 35, which follows, deals with the rules governing where the young person is to be tried and the disposals available to each court. This chapter deals with pre-trial issues and specifically covers the following areas:

* the terminology of youth justice;
* the youth justice organisations;
* the meaning of parental responsibility;
* the principal aims of the youth justice system;
* the early diversion procedures to prevent further offending;
* the juvenile at the police station;
* the alternatives to prosecution;
* the decision to charge.

34.2 THE TERMINOLOGY OF YOUTH JUSTICE

The terminology of youth justice uses a number of key words and phrases to categorise an offender who is not classed as an adult. It is important to be aware of the meaning of each term and to understand the context in which the term is used. A commonly used word is 'juvenile', which, while not defined in legislation, is generally applied to a person who is under 18 years of age. Section 29(1)(a) MCA 1980, for example, adopts this meaning. However, be aware that in relation to his detention at the police station and the powers of the custody officer under s. 37(15) PACE, an arrested juvenile is a person who is under 17 years of age or appears to be under 17 years of age.

You will also come across the word 'child'. Some legislation, for example s. 107 Children and Young Persons Act 1933, defines a child as a person under 14 years. However, in relation to a person in the care of the local authority, 'child' has an extended meaning to include a person aged under 18 years. The term 'young person' or 'young offender' or 'youth offender' is generally attributed to a person aged 14–17 years. This classification is relevant, for example, to sentencing powers where a distinction is drawn between the powers available over a child aged between 10 and 13 and a young person who is aged between 14 and 17.

In this chapter, as a matter of style, we adopt the generic terms of juvenile, youth, young person and young offender to mean a person under 18 years unless a different meaning is intended.

34.2.1 PERSISTENT YOUNG OFFENDER (PYO) AND PERSISTENT OFFENDER (PO)

Before leaving the terminology of youth justice, you should be aware that some of your clients will be formally classified as a persistent young offender (PYO). There is in fact no statutory definition of the term 'persistent young offender'. According to the Home Office (see *Tackling Delays in the Youth Justice System: A Consultation Paper*, October 1987), a PYO is:

* a young person aged between ten and 17 years;
* who has been sentenced by any criminal court in the UK on three or more separate occasions; and
* within three years of the last sentencing occasion is subsequently arrested or has an information laid against him for a further recordable offence.

While only approximately three per cent of youth offenders are classified as PYOs, they are responsible for committing a disproportionate amount of youth crime and special procedures aimed at their rehabilitation are in place. Where these initiatives are unsuccessful at changing the PYO's behaviour, Government targets require that the case be dealt with by the courts as expeditiously as possible and within 71 days from arrest to sentence.

A further classification relates to a persistent offender (PO). This classification is important when the Youth Court comes to sentence a young offender to a detention and training order (see Chapter 35). The term 'persistent offender' is not defined by statute. A PO may be a young person of previous good character or who may not have appeared in court before but is deemed a PO as he may have had numerous final warnings and/or reprimands, or may have committed a series of offences over a short period which are all charged on one occasion. It is up to the court to decide whether a young person is a PO. The classification may be relevant to the issue of deciding whether the young person should be tried summarily or on indictment, and where he is aged 14 years and over, the appropriate sentence that might be imposed.

34.3 THE YOUTH JUSTICE ORGANISATIONS

A number of specialist organisations operate in the youth justice system to develop and manage policies and resources or are involved in day-to-day contact with juveniles and their families. The Youth Justice Board for England and Wales (YJB) was created by the Crime and Disorder Act 1998 and exercises a supervisory function over the youth justice system by working to prevent juvenile offending, to address the reasons for their offending and to ensure that when a juvenile is committed to custody, the accommodation is safe and secure. In fulfilling this role the YJB:

- advises the Home Secretary on the operation and standards of the youth justice system;
- monitors the performance of the youth justice system;
- provides accommodation for young persons who are remanded into custody;
- identifies and promotes good practice in the youth justice service; and
- commissions research and publishes information on the youth justice system.

The YJB has an excellent website which can be accessed at: www.youth-justice_board.gov.uk.

The day-to-day administration of youth justice is undertaken by youth offending teams (YOTs), which are situated in every local authority in England and Wales. The multidisciplinary membership of each YOT is drawn from the police, probation service, social services and education, the health authority, housing and drug, alcohol and substance misuse agencies. The YOT identifies the needs of young offenders and manages specific programmes to prevent them offending or re-offending. The YOT also exercises the statutory responsibility of supervising young people in custody and on community orders.

It is important to establish a good working relationship with the member of the YOT who has been assigned to your client's case as often they are an invaluable source of information.

34.4 THE MAIN AIMS OF THE YOUTH JUSTICE SYSTEM

Section 37(1) Crime and Disorder Act 1998 states the principal aim of the youth justice system is to prevent offending by children and young people. In support of the principal aim, s. 37(2) CDA 1998 requires that:

> 'In addition to any other duty to which they are subject, it shall be the duty of all persons and bodies carrying out functions in relation to the youth justice system to have regard to that aim.'

As a defence lawyer, in common with the other participants in the youth justice system such as the police, the CPS, local authority and the courts, regard must be had to this overriding principle which runs alongside your professional conduct obligations as a solicitor.

A further duty is the 'welfare principle' imposed by s. 44(1) Children and Young Persons Act 1933 which requires:

> 'Every court in dealing with a child or young person who is brought before it, either as an offender or otherwise, shall have regard to the welfare of the child or young person and shall in a proper case take steps for removing from undesirable surroundings, and securing that proper provision is made for his education and training.'

When making submissions to the court about the appropriate action that should be taken against your client, you should always have the welfare principle in mind.

34.5 PARENTAL RESPONSIBILITY

To represent your juvenile client effectively, you must have an understanding of the concept of parental responsibility which was introduced by the Children Act 1989. Parental responsibility is defined by s. 3(1) of the 1989 Act as 'all the rights, duties, powers, responsibilities and authority which by law a parent of a child has in relation to the child and his property.' The concept relates to the person(s) who has (have) responsibility for looking after the young person on a daily basis and makes decisions about his life.

Married parents share parental responsibility for their child. If the parents are not married, parental responsibility is vested in the child's mother, although an unmarried father can acquire parental responsibility. Parental responsibility can be shared with or acquired by other legal bodies such as a local authority where, for example, the child is the subject of a care or supervision order.

You will need to work closely with the person(s) having parental responsibility over the juvenile and work together to ensure that the case has the best possible outcome for your client. The person having parental responsibility may also be involved in other aspects of the case, such as acting as the young person's appropriate adult at the police station or at the disposal of the case being made the subject of parenting order or a parental bind over, or paying the fine imposed on the young person.

34.6 PREVENTING JUVENILE OFFENDING

A key part of youth justice policies developed by the YJB are the early diversion procedures designed to deter a juvenile from getting into trouble in the first place or to seek the early rehabilitation of a juvenile who has already committed very low-level crimes or anti-social behaviour. Research commissioned by the YJB shows the peak age for juvenile offending is 14 years; so it is believed that if a juvenile can be diverted from offending before he reaches this age, the chances of him offending in the future will be much diminished. Therefore, a number of diversionary and intervention programmes have been developed to deter a young person from offending or re-offending. Some schemes are being piloted, while others are targeted at specific areas of social deprivation and high crime rates. A young person may be directed to participating in a scheme by the police or YOT member.

You should be aware of the schemes that are available in your local area to deal with the reasons for your client's offending and where appropriate suggest to the police or the CPS your client's willingness to attend such a scheme to divert him from being dealt with more formally.

The schemes include:

- youth inclusion programmes (YIPs);
- youth inclusion and support panels (YISPs);
- positive activities for young people (PAYP);
- positive futures (PF);
- safer school partnerships;
- mentoring;
- parenting skills.

34.7 PRE-COURT ORDERS

The next step in the hierarchy of responses to juvenile offending is provided by pre-court orders. When a juvenile first gets into trouble or engages in anti-social behaviour or is involved in very low-level crime, he may be dealt with outside the court system where an early diversion scheme (explained in section 34.6 above) is not available, or a scheme is not considered appropriate to the young person's needs. The police or local authority may use a range of pre-court orders to prevent the juvenile from offending and being dealt with more formally by the youth justice system. The following pre-court orders are available.

Acceptable behaviour contract
An acceptable behaviour contract is given to a juvenile when a local authority or YOT identifies a juvenile who is engaged in low-level anti-social behaviour. To address the reasons for the juvenile behaving in this way, the juvenile and his parent(s) or guardian(s) agree a contract to stop the patterns of behaviour that is causing the nuisance to the local community. If the terms of the contract are breached, the local authority may obtain an anti-social behaviour order against the juvenile.

Anti-social behaviour order (ASBO)
The infamous ASBO can be applied for by the police or a local authority in connection with any person aged ten years or over who is behaving in a way that causes distress or harassment to people who live in a particular locality. The ASBO prevents the young person from going to a particular place or from doing specified activities. A failure to comply with the terms of the ASBO can lead to prosecution.

34.8 POLICE DUTIES AND RESPONSIBILITIES AND JUVENILE SUSPECTS

A detailed explanation of the procedure in relation to detaining and questioning a person suspected of being involved in criminal behaviour is covered in Part II of this book. Below we highlight the special rules that apply to juveniles who have been arrested and detained at the police station.

34.8.1 DETERMINING THE YOUNG PERSON'S AGE

For the purposes of s. 37(15) PACE and Code C, a juvenile is any person who is aged under 17 years or who appears to be under 17 years of age. Code C para. 1.5 stipulates that anyone who appears to be under the age of 17 shall be treated as a juvenile in the absence of clear evidence to the contrary. Therefore, if a person who may be a juvenile refuses to give his age to the custody officer, or the officer believes the age the person has given is incorrect, the suspect must be treated as a juvenile. Remember that if the detained person is under ten years of age he has no criminal liability and therefore cannot be detained. In these circumstances, the custody officer will arrange for the child to be taken home, or if there is concern for the child's physical or moral welfare, the local authority social services department will be contacted.

While in police detention, a juvenile is classified as a 'vulnerable' suspect. Juveniles make up the largest number of suspects who fall into the category of a vulnerable suspect.

Where the person is identified as a juvenile aged ten years and over, he will be entitled to a range of special protections which are dealt with below.

34.8.2 THE CUSTODY OFFICER'S DUTIES

Code C requires the custody officer to identify the juvenile's needs and vulnerabilities (Code C 3.6–3.10). The custody officer must as soon as practicable identify the parent, guardian or local authority who has parental responsibility for the juvenile's welfare, and inform that person of the juvenile's arrest, the reasons for the arrest and the place where the juvenile is being held. As the person who is responsible for the juvenile's welfare will usually act as the appropriate adult, the person will be asked to attend the police station immediately.

34.8.3 THE APPROPRIATE ADULT

The role of the appropriate adult is to assist and advise the juvenile while he is in police detention. Code C, Note 1.7 requires that an appropriate adult for a juvenile should be:

- the juvenile's parent or guardian; or
- if the juvenile is in local authority care or in the care of a voluntary organisation, a person representing that organisation; or
- a social worker from a local authority social services department; or failing any of the above;
- a responsible adult aged 18 over who is not a police officer or employed by the police.

The suitability of a person to act as an appropriate adult is important because where the appropriate adult is considered incapable of effectively protecting the juvenile's interests or is incapable of assisting him, evidence obtained against the juvenile may be excluded at his trial. While it may appear that the juvenile's parent or carer will be the obvious choice, a parent may be incapable of acting through lack of experience or knowledge or through mental illness, or because the juvenile and parent are not on good terms. In these situations an alternative must be found. Depending on his age, the wishes of the juvenile as to who he wants to act as the appropriate adult should be taken into account. For example, in *R v Blake* [1989] 89 CR App R 179, the police ignored the juvenile's request that her social worker act as the appropriate adult, asking the girl's father to attend the police station directly against the girl's wishes. In *R v Morse* [1991] Crim LR 195, the juvenile's father had an IQ of below 70 and was incapable of appreciating the importance of his role. In both cases the confession made by the juvenile in the presence of the appropriate adult was excluded at their trials.

A solicitor should not act as an appropriate adult as it will lead to a conflict of interest between his role as a legal adviser and his role as an appropriate adult.

While the Codes of Practice provide only a general indication about the appropriate adult's role, some assistance is provided by the Home Office Guidance for Appropriate Adults, which states that the appropriate adult is required to:

- support, advise and assist the detained person, particularly while they are being questioned;
- observe whether the police are acting fairly and with respect for the rights of the detained person;
- advise the detained person to tell the truth if they believe that the juvenile is not telling the truth;
- assist with communication between the detained person and the police;
- ensure that the detained person understands their rights and that the adult has a role in protecting those rights.

It is also important to make a juvenile client aware that, unlike his legal adviser, the appropriate adult is not bound by any duty of confidentiality or professional privilege. The Law Society therefore strongly recommends that legal advisers at the police station should initially consult with their juvenile client in the absence of the appropriate adult to warn him about the dangers of disclosing information that would remain confidential between lawyer and client.

34.8.4 THE JUVENILE'S OTHER RIGHTS

In addition to his right to have an appropriate adult to support him, a juvenile is entitled to the full range of rights at the police station as other detainees. These include the right to inform someone of his arrest under s. 56 PACE and the right to legal advice under s. 58 PACE.

The juvenile has the same right to legal advice under s. 58 PACE as an adult. While the grounds for suspending the right to legal advice under s. 58(8) PACE apply to a juvenile in the same way as for an adult detainee, once the appropriate adult has been requested to attend the police station, it is very difficult for the police to justify that one or more of the reasons for delaying legal advice under s. 58(8) PACE applies. While the time limits for detention without charge are the same for both a juvenile and an adult, in view of the juvenile's vulnerabilities every effort should be made to keep detention to a minimum, especially in the case of a very young person. Generally a juvenile should not be held in a police cell unless there is no other way of guaranteeing his safety. In whatever place he is detained, the custody officer is required to monitor his detention more closely than in the case of an adult and to undertake regular risk assessments.

34.9 DEALING WITH A JUVENILE CLIENT

During your initial interview it is important that the young person gives you a full and coherent response to the allegations that have been made against him. You should advise him fully about the possible outcomes of the case, the consequences of him admitting his guilt and the possibility of him being given a reprimand or final warning. Young offenders (and often their parents or carers) are the most challenging clients that you will encounter; they will often have little respect for authority and are likely to test your patience. You need special skills to interview these clients and to get them to recognise that you are there to help and are not part of the law enforcement machinery.

Leanne Black, aged 14, is an infamous example of a young offender. In March 2006 Black, who is currently Britain's youngest drink-driver, attacked the CPS lawyer and threw a jug of water at the magistrates as she was sentenced to four months' custody for her second offence of drink driving. These dramatic events occurred shortly after her lawyer had submitted in mitigation that Leanne was a reformed character. The family's disruptive behaviour was not, however, limited to inside the courtroom. As she arrived at court Leanne hurled eggs at the media, and Nora Black, Leanne's mother flashed her bare bottom, inviting them to 'film this'.

Other infamous young offenders include twins Ben and Nathan Weeks, who became subject to ASBOs when they were just ten after the court heard they had made life hell for their neighbours in Norfolk by shouting, swearing and even shooting at residents' cars and windows with a ball-bearing gun.

34.10 DECIDING HOW THE CASE WILL PROCEED

Except in the most serious offences, the decision about how the case will proceed will not be taken immediately by the police or the CPS and a juvenile client will usually be bailed until the decision is made. The case file will often be referred to a youth offender specialist in the CPS to decide whether to prosecute or take alternative action.

In deciding how the case will proceed, the CPS lawyer will have in mind the 'welfare' principle under s. 44 CYPA 1933 and the statutory duty to prevent offending under s. 37 CDA 1998 explained at 34.4 above. The juvenile's right to a fair trial under Article 6 ECHR should also be taken into account. Further guidance is provided by paragraphs 8.8 to 8.9 in the Code for Crown Prosecutors for dealing with young offenders. Paragraph 8.8 of the Code requires the Crown Prosecutor to consider:

- the interests of the juvenile when deciding whether it is in the public interest to prosecute; and
- the juvenile's age should not preclude a prosecution where the seriousness of the present offence or the defendant's past behaviour justifies it.

Paragraph 8.9 states that generally a prosecution will only usually be appropriate where:

- the offence is so serious that a prosecution is justified; and/or
- the juvenile does not admit the offence; and/or
- the juvenile has failed to respond to a reprimand or final warning.

In addition to these specific considerations, both the evidential and public interest tests under the Code will need to be satisfied before the juvenile is charged or the prosecution continues.

34.10.1 ALTERNATIVES TO PROSECUTION

Where the sufficient evidence and public interest tests are satisfied under the Code para. 8.8 of the Code requires the Crown Prosecutor to consider the possibility of alternatives to prosecution. Your client may therefore be:

- given an informal warning; or
- given a reprimand; or
- given a final warning.

An informal warning will be given by a police officer usually in the presence of the person having parental responsibility and warning the juvenile about his future behaviour. An informal warning has the effect of discontinuing the proceedings.

An alternative to prosecution in more serious cases is provided by ss. 65 and 66 Crime and Disorder Act 1998 which provides a statutory system of reprimands and final warnings. The decision to deal with the young person by a reprimand or a final warning may be taken by a police officer without referring the case to the CPS (though consultation is highly likely) where the threshold test is met other than in an indictable offence. (See 13.5 for an explanation of the threshold test.)

Section 65(1)(2) CDA 1998 sets out the conditions for a reprimand or final caution to be administered:

- a police officer must have evidence that the young person has committed the offence;
- the police officer must consider that the evidence supports a realistic prospect of a conviction;
- the young person must admit to the police officer that he committed the offence;
- the young person must have no previous convictions; and
- the police officer must be satisfied that a prosecution is not in the public interest.

In addition to these factors which relate to the present offence, it will only be appropriate to reprimand a young person where he has not been previously warned or reprimanded, s. 65(2) CDA 1998. Section 65(5) CDA 1998 requires that a warning or reprimand should be given in the presence of an appropriate adult. It is also essential that to comply with the 'fair trial' provisions under Article 6 ECHR, the full and informed consent of the appropriate adult and the young person is required.

The main factor in deciding whether to charge, reprimand or warn the young person is the seriousness of the offence(s), including the nature of and circumstances in which the offence was committed. Reprimands and warnings do not count as convictions but can be cited in later criminal case in the same way as convictions. The warning or reprimand will be kept on record by the police until the young person reaches 18 years of age or for five years, whichever is the longer.

A reprimand is appropriate for a first-time offender; a final warning will be appropriate for second-time offenders and charging the young person will be appropriate for the most serious offences and persistent young offenders.

Detailed guidance on the Final Warning Scheme is available from the Home Office website. The web-links section of our Online Resource Centre will take you to it.

online
resource
centre

34.10.2 CHARGING THE YOUNG OFFENDER

Where the evidential and public interests under the Code for Crown Prosecutors are satisfied, the offence is sufficiently serious and the statutory duty under s. 37 CDA 1998 requires it, the young offender will be charged with the offence(s). The juvenile should be charged in the presence of the appropriate adult and his legal adviser. Having been charged, the custody officer must decide whether to release the young person on bail. As with an adult, the relevant criteria to be applied by the custody officer is set out under s. 38 PACE subject to an additional ground where it would not be in the young person's interests to be granted bail.

Where bail is refused, s. 38(6) PACE requires the custody officer to ensure that the young person is moved to local authority accommodation unless:

- it is impracticable to do so (in which case he must give reasons why this is so); or
- in the case of a child or young person aged between 12 and 17, no secure accommodation is available and it appears that local authority accommodation would not be adequate to protect the public from serious harm from that child or young person.

34.10.3 COMMENCING PROCEEDINGS AGAINST THE YOUNG PERSON

Commencing proceedings against the young person will follow the same procedure as for an adult. A summary offence will be commenced by laying an information and the issuing of a summons. In the case of either-way or indictable-only offence, the formal instigation of proceedings will begin by the police or CPS completing a charge sheet. The prosecuting authorities should also notify the juvenile's parent or guardian of the need for them to attend court. The court may impose a duty on the parent or guardian to attend court under s. 34A Children and Young Persons Act 1933.

34.11 FUNDING THE YOUNG PERSON'S RIGHT TO LEGAL REPRESENTATION

The cost of a young person's legal representation is based on the same eligibility criteria as for an adult, which were explained in detail in Chapter 14.

The cost of attending the young person at the police station will be met under the Police Station Advice and Assistance Scheme. The advice will be free of charge and there is no means test and there are no application forms. Post-charge you will apply for a representation order as soon as possible on Form A to cover the cost of any work not done in the police station and representing your client in court. As with an adult, a representation order will be granted where your client's case satisfies the interests of justice criteria under Sch. 3, Access to Justice Act 1999.

KEY POINT SUMMARY

- Always work in accordance with the statutory duties of the youth justice system under s. 37 CDA 1998 and the welfare principle under s. 44 CYPA 1933.

- Be aware of who has parental responsibility over your juvenile client.

- Be aware of the role of the YOT representative.

- Know the procedures the police have to follow under Code C when the juvenile is detained at the police station.

- Have a good working knowledge of the diversion procedures as alternatives to prosecution and be prepared to argue with the police and/or the CPS about their suitability for your juvenile client.

- Have good working knowledge of the approach taken by your local CPS office in applying the Code for Crown Prosecutors and other relevant matters when deciding whether to prosecute your juvenile client.

SELF-TEST QUESTIONS

1 Explain the role of the appropriate adult.

2. Is a youth offender entitled to publicly funded legal representation?

3. Explain the role of the Youth Offending Team.

4. Remi, aged 14, is a first-time offender charged with a minor offence of criminal damage contrary to s. 1 Criminal Damage Act 1971. Explain the factors the police and/or the CPS will take into account in dealing with Remi.

35.1   INTRODUCTION

Where formal criminal proceedings are instituted against the young person the general rule is that he will be tried and sentenced in the Youth Court. The Youth Court adopts more informal and less adversarial procedures to deal with the needs and vulnerabilities of young defendants. The procedures should also be compliant with the young person's right to a fair under Article 6 ECHR.

While juveniles/young defendants will usually be tried in the Youth Court, there are situations where the youth will be tried in the Crown Court or in the adult magistrates' court. The purpose of this chapter is to explain:

- the rules for deciding where a person under the age of 18 is to be tried;
- the rules for trying a young person in the Crown Court;
- the rules for trying a young person in the adult magistrates' court;
- the young defendant's right to court bail;
- the procedure in the Youth Court;
- the Youth Court's sentencing powers;
- the Crown Court's sentencing powers;
- the adult magistrates' court's sentencing powers.

35.2 THE YOUNG PERSON'S FIRST COURT APPEARANCE

In most cases the juvenile's first court appearance in connection with the offence will be in the Youth Court. If the case cannot be dealt with immediately, the court will either remand the young person in custody or release him on bail as explained in section 35.2.1 below.

If the young person pleads not guilty, the case is likely to be adjourned and a date set for trial in the Youth Court. If a guilty plea is entered, the court may proceed to sentence immediately (following an outline of the facts and any plea in mitigation), or it will adjourn sentence for the preparation of a pre-sentence report.

In most cases the young person will make his first appearance in the Youth Court, unless the case falls within one of the exceptions to this general rule. The exceptions are where the young person is:

- jointly charged with an adult, s. 46(1)(a) CYPA 1933; or
- charged with aiding and abetting an adult to commit an offence, s. 18(a) CYPA 1933, s. 46(1)(b) CYPA 1963; or
- charged with an offence which arises out of the same circumstances or are connected with the offence with which the adult is charged, s. 18(a) CYPA 1963.

In these cases the young person will make his first appearance in the adult magistrates' court.

35.2.1 COURT BAIL

As with adults, it is likely that the young person's entitlement to bail will be dealt with at his first court appearance. The law and procedure governing court bail under the Bail Act 1976 applies to a young person in the same way as to an adult defendant. (For a more detailed consideration of the law and procedure relating to bail, see Chapter 15.)

A young defendant therefore enjoys a presumption under s. 4 Bail Act 1976 of being granted bail. The presumption will be rebutted where the court finds that there are substantial grounds for believing that if granted bail, the youth:

- would fail to surrender to custody; or
- would commit further offences; or
- would interfere with witnesses or the course of justice; or
- has committed imprisonable offences while on bail; or
- as an additional ground, should be kept in custody for his own welfare.

In deciding whether to grant bail, the court will take into account the factors identified in para. 9 Sch. 1 Bail Act 1976 including the nature and seriousness of the offence, the young person's bail record and community ties, etc.

Where bail is refused, a defendant aged between 17 and 20 will be sent to a remand centre (known as a secure remand). A defendant under the age of 17 will be remanded into the care of the local authority subject to conditions of bail, including, in defined circumstances, electronic tagging. A young person aged 12 or over can be remanded into secure local authority accommodation, but only if the conditions laid down by s. 23(5) CYPA 1969 are met, including:

- where the young person is charged with a violent or sexual offence; or
- where the young person is charged with an offence punishable by 14 years or more imprisonment in the case of an adult and only remanding him into secure accommodation would protect the public from serious harm; or
- to prevent the commission by him of imprisonable offences.

When granted, bail may be unconditional or conditional. Conditions will be imposed where the court considers it necessary to ensure the young person attends court on the next occasion or prevents him from offending from while on bail or interfering with witnesses.

> **Looking Ahead**
>
> When in force, s. 14(2) CJA 2003 inserts para. 9AA into Sch. 1 Bail Act 1976, which applies only where the defendant is under 18 years. Bail may be refused where there are substantial grounds for believing he would commit an offence if he was granted bail, and the court will give particular weight to the fact that the present offence was committed while the young person was already on bail in connection with another offence. Similarly, when in force, s. 15(2) CJA 2003 inserts para. 9AB such that bail may be refused where there are substantial grounds for believing that if the young person was granted bail he would fail to surrender, and the court will give particular weight to the fact that the young person has without reasonable cause failed to surrender to custody when previously granted bail.

35.3 WHERE WILL THE YOUNG PERSON BE TRIED?

The general rule is that a young person will be tried in the Youth Court where:

- he is charged alone; or
- he is charged with another young person.

Most juveniles are therefore tried summarily in the Youth Court irrespective of the seriousness or the classification of the offence(s) with which they are charged. Section 24(1) MCA 1980 provides that this presumption applies even in the case of an indictable-only offence other than homicide.

Unlike an adult offender, the young person has no right elect trial. Therefore, if the magistrates are considering declining jurisdiction by sending the case to the Crown Court, the only course of action available to the juvenile's advocate is to make representations against having the case tried before a judge and jury. In contrast to the adult magistrates' court, the Youth Court has a maximum sentencing power of 24 months in custody.

As exceptions to the general rule, the young person may be tried in the Crown Court in the situations explained below.

35.3.1 TRIAL OF A YOUNG PERSON IN THE CROWN COURT

A defendant under the age of 18 will be tried in the Crown Court in the following circumstances:

- where he is charged with homicide or specified offences under s. 51A Firearms Act 1968, the Youth Court *must* send him for trial to the Crown Court, s. 24(1B) Magistrates' Courts Act

(MCA) 1980. The term 'homicide' is widely defined to include murder, manslaughter, attempted murder and attempted manslaughter.

- where the defendant is a 'dangerous' offender within ss. 226 and 228 Criminal Justice Act 2003, the Youth Court *must* send him for trial to the Crown Court, s. 51A CDA 1998;
- where the defendant is charged with a 'grave' crime and it is considered appropriate that the Crown Court should invoke its power under s. 91 PCC(S) A 2000 to pass a lengthy custodial sentence, he *may* be committed to the Crown Court for trial, s. 24(1) MCA 1980;
- where the young person is jointly charged with an adult and it is in the interests of justice to commit them both to the Crown Court for trial, s. 24(1)(b) MCA 1980.

The powers in relation to a 'dangerous' young offender, a young offender charged with a 'grave' crime and where a young offender is charged jointly with an adult, are considered below.

35.3.2 'GRAVE' CRIMES

Where the juvenile is charged with a 'grave' crime, he may be committed to the Crown Court for trial under s. 24(1) MCA 1980. It should be noted that s. 24 MCA is set to be subsumed under s. 51A(3)(b) CDA 1998 as a result of reforms under the Criminal Justice Act 2003.

A 'grave' crime is an offence which is punishable with at least 14 years' imprisonment in the case of an adult offender. Numerous offences carry a maximum custodial term in excess of 14 years, including the offences of rape, robbery and causing death by dangerous driving. Also included in the category of a 'grave' crime are certain offences under the Sexual Offences Act 2003 such as sexual assault under s. 3 of the 2003 Act.

The power to commit for trial under s. 24 MCA 1980 must be read in conjunction with s. 91(1) or (2) of the Powers of Criminal Courts (Sentencing) Act 2000, which allows the Crown Court to sentence a young person who has been convicted of a 'serious' offence. This section is required because of the Youth Court's limited sentencing powers. The maximum custodial term that can be passed by the Youth Court on a young offender is a 24-month detention and training order (DTO). Only the Crown Court is empowered to impose a longer custodial term on a young offender (s. 91 PCC (S) A 2000). The power of the Youth Court to impose a DTO is also restricted in the case of a young person under the age of 15 unless the young person is a persistent offender, s. 100 PCC (S) A 2000. There is no power to impose a DTO on an offender under the age of 12. Therefore, the power to commit under s. 24 MCA 1980 will only be exercised where there is a real prospect that the juvenile will receive a custodial sentence of two years or more. In addition, to overcome the presumption that a person under 18 years of age should be tried summarily, there has to be some unusual feature in the offence which justifies the Youth Court declining jurisdiction. These offences will usually be of a serious sexual or violent nature or the young person is assessed to present a serious threat to the public as a result of mental instability.

The basis upon which the Youth Court should make its decision about whether to decline jurisdiction to try the young person or to commit to the Crown Court for trial has been judicially considered in a number of cases. In *R (D) v Manchester City Youth Court* [2002] 1 Cr App R(S) 573, it was stated that the Youth Court should not decline jurisdiction unless the offence and the circumstances surrounding it and the offender are such as to make it more than a theoretical possibility that a sentence of detention for a long period may be passed.

An overriding consideration for the magistrates is that trial in the Crown Court for a defendant under the age of 18 is inherently less suitable than in the Youth Court. This is especially significant where the young person is under 15 years of age. This raises the question whether the young defendant's right to a fair trial under Article 6 ECHR can be secured at trial on indictment.

The most authoritative guidance on the issue of venue is provided by *R on application of H, O and A v Southampton Youth Court* [2005] 2 Cr App R (S) 30, in which Leveson J in the Divisional Court stated as follows:

'In an effort to assist hard-pressed magistrates to determine this issue and thereby prevent the constant diet of cases of this nature before the court and, at the same time, seeking to avoid the need to trawl through the ever-growing list of authorities which touch on this point, with the approval of the Vice President of the Court of Appeal Criminal Division, I will attempt to summarise the matter in a way that can properly be put before the Youth Court whenever the situation arises. The general policy of the legislature is that those who are under 18 years of age and in particular children of under 15 years of age should, wherever possible, be tried in the Youth Court. It is that court which is best designed to meet their specific needs. A trial in the Crown Court with the inevitably greater formality and greatly increased number of people involved (including a jury and the public) should be reserved for the most serious cases.

It is a further policy of the legislature that, generally speaking, first-time offenders aged 12 to 14 and all offenders under 12 should not be detained in custody and decisions as to jurisdiction should have regard to the fact that the exceptional power to detain for 'grave' offences should not be used to water down the general principle. Those under 15 will rarely attract a period of detention and, even more rarely, those who are under 12.

In each case the court should ask itself whether there is a real prospect, having regard to his or her age, that this defendant whose case they are considering might require a sentence of, or in excess of, two years or, alternatively, whether although the sentence might be less than two years, there is some unusual feature of the case which justifies declining jurisdiction, bearing in mind that the absence of a power to impose a detention and training order because the defendant is under 15 is not an unusual feature.'

In determining whether there is a real prospect of a custodial term in excess of 24 months, it will be necessary for the Youth Court to have regard to sentencing guidelines applicable in the Crown Court (see Chapter 28).

In the Southampton Youth Court case, the magistrates sitting in the Youth Court declined jurisdiction to try a 14-year-old youth who was charged with indecent assault. The youth was not a persistent offender and for this reason, and because he was under 15, he could not be sentenced to a DTO. The defendant applied to the Divisional Court by way of judicial review. The Divisional Court criticised the defence solicitor for not challenging the submissions made by the CPS and stressed the importance of ascertaining the seriousness of the offence and any relevant sentencing guidelines. The case was remitted to the Youth Court to continue to hear the matter.

Where jurisdiction to summarily try a young defendant is declined, the court may also commit him for trial for any other indictable offence with which he is charged which can properly be joined in the same indictment (s. 24(1A) MCA 1980).

While the procedure for deciding whether the magistrates should exercise their powers under s. 24(1)(a) MCA 1980 is not laid down, the general approach is that the CPS will invite the magistrates to consider the issue of venue at an early stage in the proceedings where the juvenile is charged with a 'grave' crime. The defence will also make representations, which in most cases will seek to persuade the magistrates to try the case summarily.

35.3.3 DANGEROUS OFFENDERS UNDER THE AGE OF 18 (SS. 226 AND 228 CRIMINAL JUSTICE ACT 2003)

Section 51A 3(d) CDA 1998 requires the Youth Court to send the juvenile for trial in the Crown Court where the pre-requisites of s 226 or 228 CJA 2003 are established, that is:

- the juvenile is charged with a specified offence as defined by s. 224 CJA 2003; and
- if convicted he would be classified as a dangerous offender within ss. 226 or 228 Criminal Justice Act 2003 in that;
- it appears to the Youth Court that if the juvenile were found guilty of the offence, there is a significant risk to the public of serious harm occasioned by the commission of further specified offences by him; and
- the juvenile satisfies the criteria for imposing a sentence of indeterminate detention for public protection under s. 226(3) CJA 2003 or an extended sentence under s. 228(2) CJA 2003.

A full list of the 153 specified offences is found in Sch. 15 CJA 2003, but includes 'violent' offences such as manslaughter, kidnapping, offences under ss. 18 and 20 OAPA 1861 and 'sexual' offences, including rape, under s. 1 Sexual Offences Act 2003.

35.3.4 **ASSESSMENT OF DANGEROUSNESS FOR THE PURPOSE OF DECLINING JURISDICTION**

The main issue as to the interpretation of the power to send to the Crown Court for trial under s. 51A(3)(d) CDA 1998 is in relation to the assessment of whether the young person falls within the definition of a 'dangerous' offender. In deciding this, the court is required to take into account all the information that is available about the nature and circumstances of the offence and any information about the offender. In many cases the court will not be in possession of sufficient details to make an informed decision at this early stage. A proper assessment of the dangerousness of the defendant is unlikely to be possible until a pre-sentence report has been prepared by the YOT which of course can only happen after a finding of guilt, (see 35.11.3 below).

Therefore, in considering whether to exercise its power under s. 51A(3)(d) CDA 1998 the court will be strongly influenced by judicial guidance in a number of cases, most recently in *R (on the application of H, O and A) v Southampton Youth Court* [2005] 2 Cr App R (S) 30 which is discussed above, that offenders under 18 years of age should be tried in the Youth Court, which is best designed to meet their specific needs. If, after summary conviction for a specified offence, the court forms the view that the 'dangerousness' criteria is satisfied, the Youth Court may commit the young person to the Crown Court for sentence under s. 3C Powers of Criminal Courts (Sentencing) Act 2000 as amended by the CJA 2003. (This provision is not fully in force at the time of going to press.)

A recent illustration of the operation of s. 51A(3)(d) CDA 1998 is provided by the *CPS v South East Surrey Youth Court and MG* [2005] EWHC 2929.

D was born on 16 September 1987. On 2 July 2005 D allegedly caused actual bodily harm to V by striking him in the face with a beer bottle, causing a wound which required five stitches. On 28 July 2005 D was interviewed by the police in connection with this incident. D stated that he had acted in self-defence. On the same day, 28 July, D was arrested in connection with an unrelated offence of robbery, which was said to have occurred on 25 July and charged with the offence on 29 July and remanded in custody by the Youth Court. It was alleged that D had used a knife during the robbery. On 3 August D was sent to the Crown Court for trial in connection with the robbery under s. 51A(3)(d) CDA 1998. On the same day he was charged with the earlier assault occasioning actual bodily harm. On 24 August the prosecution submitted that D should be sent to the Crown Court for trial in connection with the assault under s. 51A(3)(d) CDA 1998 on the basis that the offence was a specified violent offence under s. 224 CJA 2003 and there was a real possibility that the criteria for an extended sentence under s. 228 CJA 2003 would be met.

In rejecting the prosecution submission, the justices adopted the following approach which was tacitly approved by the Divisional Court. In deciding whether the offence should be tried summarily or on indictment, the court should first consider whether the offence comes within the meaning of a 'grave' crime (see 35.3.2 above). If the offence is a 'grave' crime, the court is required to consider whether the defendant is 'dangerous'. If he is 'dangerous', the court can send to the Crown Court for trial under s. 51A(3)(d) CDA 1998. If he is not 'dangerous' but is charged with a 'grave' crime, the court can consider committing him to the Crown Court for trial under s. 24 MCA 1980 (s. 51A(3)(b) CDA 1998) where the criteria outlined in the Southampton Youth Court case is satisfied. If the defendant is not charged with a 'grave' offence, the issue of 'dangerousness' should only be considered following the defendant's conviction at summary trial. It should always be borne in mind that wherever possible those under 18 should be tried in the Youth Court.

The decision in the South East Surrey Youth Court case is significant as it confirms that the courts are reluctant to send a 'dangerous offender' for trial at the Crown Court under s. 51A(3)(d) CDA 1998 without also invoking the 'grave' crime provision under s. 24(1) MCA

1980. In the vast majority of cases the dangerousness test will only be applied in conjunction with s. 24(1) MCA 1980 where the defendant is charged with a 'grave' crime and the conditions for committing him for trial under s. 24(1) MCA 1980 are satisfied.

Where either side seeks to challenge the decision of the Youth Court to either accept or decline jurisdiction to try a youth, it is necessary to seek judicial review of the decision in the Divisional Court.

35.3.5 COMMITTING THE YOUNG PERSON FOR TRIAL UNDER S. 24(1)(b) MCA 1980

Under s. 24(1)(b) MCA 1980, a defendant under the age of 18 may be committed to the Crown Court for trial where:

- he is jointly charged with an adult; and
- the adult is going to be tried in the Crown Court; and
- the court considers that it is necessary in the 'interests of justice' for the young person to be jointly tried with the adult in the Crown Court.

In applying the interests of justice test under s. 24(1)(b) MCA, the court considers a number of factors, including:

- the circumstances of the offence including the seriousness of the offence;
- the age and maturity of the accused;
- the representations made by the prosecution and the defence;
- the inconvenience and expense of witnesses having to give evidence twice.

The court must also take into account the guidelines laid down in Part IV, paras. 39.1–39.16 in the Practice Direction (Criminal: Consolidated) [2002] 3 All ER 904. In deciding the appropriate place of trial for the young defendant, the Practice Direction requires that the court must consider the following points:

- the trial process should not expose the young defendant to avoidable intimidation, humiliation or distress;
- all possible steps must be taken to assist the young defendant to understand and participate in the proceedings;
- regard should be had to the welfare of the young defendant as required by s. 44 Children and Young Persons Act 1933;
- if a young defendant is indicted jointly with an adult, the court should consider at the Plea and Case Management Hearing whether it is in the interests of justice for the young defendant to be tried jointly with the adult in the Crown Court.

The Practice Direction is a response to criticism from the European Court of Human Rights in *T and V v UK* [2000] 30 EHRR 121, which held that the boys accused of killing Jamie Bulger had not had a fair trial in the highly formal proceedings of Preston Crown Court. The trial, which lasted for three weeks in November 1993, was accompanied by widespread media frenzy and great public hostility.

In appealing to the European Court of Human Rights, T and V submitted that their trial in the Crown Court constituted inhuman and degrading treatment within the meaning of Article 3 ECHR and that they had been denied a fair trial under Article 6. While the Court of Human Rights rejected the submission that T and V's trial breached Article 3, it did accept that their right to a fair trial under Article 6 had been violated. The Court concluded that the formality and ritual of the Crown Court must have seemed incomprehensible to the young defendants making it impossible for them to effectively participate in the proceedings.

The power to commit under s. 24(1)(b) MCA 1980 will be made where the young person appears together with an adult in the magistrates' court or where the young person appears in the Youth Court and is jointly charged with an adult in connection with an indictable offence and the adult has already been sent for trial in the Crown Court. If the justices decide that it is not in the interests of justice to commit the young person to the Crown Court, the charge will be put to him. Where he pleads guilty, the magistrates will consider whether they have the power to sentence him from the limited range of sentencing disposals available to it. If none of them is appropriate, the defendant will be remitted to the Youth Court for sentencing. If the young person pleads not guilty, he may be tried in the adult magistrates' court, but the normal practice is to send the case to the Youth Court for trial.

It is now generally accepted that in recognition of the young person's right to a fair trial under Article 6 ECHR, only very rarely will it be in the interests of justice for the young person to be tried jointly with an adult and that the young person should not be exposed to the intimidating atmosphere in the Crown Court unless there are very strong and compelling reasons for overturning this presumption.

Looking Ahead

The Criminal Justice Act 2003 is set to make some important changes to the allocation of cases involving young persons. The detail is contained in the extremely complex Schedule 3 CJA 2003 which will see some significant changes to the conduct of mode of trial proceedings in relation to adults which are highlighted in Chapter 16. The changes are coupled with the abolition of committal proceedings for an adult charged with an either-way offence which is to be tried before the Crown Court. Schedule 3 will amend s. 24 MCA 1980 (introducing s. 24A–24D).

In future, defendants under the age of 18 will be subject to the same procedure at the mode of trial stage, including the plea before venue, as adult defendants in a case where there is a possibility of the juvenile being tried in the Crown Court, either because s. 91 PCC (S) A 2000 applies, or he is jointly charged with an adult whose case is to be tried before a Crown Court. If a guilty plea is indicated, the Youth Court will be able to commit for sentence where it is of the opinion that a lengthy custodial term under either s. 91 PCC (S) A 2000 or an extended sentence under the 'dangerousness' provisions should be passed (s. 3B and 3C PCC (S) A 2000). Where the juvenile defendant indicates a not guilty plea, the Youth Court will proceed to a mode of trial enquiry as outlined in 35.3.1–35.3.5 above. An amendment is made to s. 25 MCA 1980 to allow the prosecution to reopen a mode of trial decision before a summary trial commences.

Schedule 3 will further amend s. 51 Crime and Disorder Act 1998, which governs the sending of cases to the Crown Court. Cases involving young defendants will be sent for trial under the revised s. 51 CDA 1998, as opposed to s. 24 MCA 1980. The revised s. 51 CDA 1998 enables a young defendant's linked offences to be sent with him to the Crown Court (s. 51A(4) and (5)). A young defendant will also take with him to the Crown Court any adult who is jointly charged with him or who separately faces a related either-way or summary offence (s. 51A(6) and (7)).

35.4 SAFEGUARDING THE YOUNG PERSON'S RIGHT TO A FAIR TRIAL IN THE CROWN COURT

If the court decides that trial in the Crown Court is appropriate for the young defendant, the Practice Direction (Criminal: Consolidated) requires that:

- the young defendant should visit the courtroom out-of-court hours to familiarise himself with the layout;
- where practicable, the trial should be held in a courtroom where all the participants are on the same level;
- a young defendant should normally be permitted to sit with his family and to engage in informal communication with his legal representative;

- the court should explain the course of proceedings to the young defendant in terms he understands and remind his legal representatives of their continuing responsibility to explain each stage of the proceedings to him;

- the trial should be conducted to a timetable which takes account of the young defendant's inability to concentrate for long periods;

- robes and gowns should not be worn unless the young defendant requests or the court considers there are good reasons for wearing robes and gowns;

- the court should be prepared to restrict attendance at court to those who have a direct interest in the outcome of the proceedings and to restrict the reporting of the proceedings by the media. As a trainee solicitor, it is likely that your principal will obtain the court's permission for you to attend the trial.

Even with these requirements in mind, the procedure for trying a young person in the Crown Court is generally the same as for adult defendants. One important difference is the reporting restrictions that are imposed on the media. Section 39(1) Children and Young Persons Act 1933 permits the court to direct that no newspaper report shall reveal the name, address or school of the young defendant or publish a photograph. A further difference is that s. 34A(1) Children and Young Persons Act 1933 requires that where the young defendant is aged under 16 years, his parent or guardian must attend court. Where the young person is aged 16 or 17, his parent or guardian may attend court.

35.5 TRIAL OF A YOUNG PERSON IN THE ADULT MAGISTRATES' COURT

Where the young person is charged jointly with an adult in connection with a summary offence or either-way offence (where jurisdiction to try the offence summarily has been accepted), the case must be heard in the adult magistrates' court, s. 46(1)(a) Children and Young Persons Act 1933 and s. 29 MCA 1980. The case may be remitted to the Youth Court where:

- the adult pleads guilty; and

- the young person pleads not guilty; or

- where the adult is committed for trial or is discharged and the young person pleads not guilty.

In practice, if the adult pleads not guilty to a summary offence or he accepts summary trial in relation to an either-way offence, the young person will usually be tried jointly with the adult in the magistrates' court. If the adult pleads guilty, in view of the magistrates' restricted sentencing powers over young defendants, the case will generally be remitted to the Youth Court for trial. The relevant rules of court relating to the trial of young persons before an adult magistrates' court are contained in Part 38 Crim PR.

Consider the following examples of the factors to be taken into account in deciding the place of trial of a defendant under the age of 18.

Examples

Josh, aged 14, is charged with theft. As he is charged alone and is a juvenile, he will be tried in the Youth Court.

Josh, aged 14, is charged jointly with Sharon, who is 16, with theft. As both defendants are under 18, both will be tried in the Youth Court.

Josh, aged 14, is jointly charged with Graham, aged 33, with robbery. Assuming Josh appears at the same time as Graham, the magistrates' court will be required to send Graham to the Crown Court under s. 51 CDA 1998. Josh will also be sent for trial if the magistrates consider it is in the interests of justice that Josh be tried with Graham (regard being had to s. 24(1)(b) MCA 1980).

Josh, aged 14, is charged with rape. As rape is a 'grave' offence, the Youth Court is likely to decline jurisdiction to try the case in favour of the Crown Court's more extensive powers of sentence under s. 91 PCC(S)A 2000. Consideration will also be given to the 'dangerousness' provisions (s. 226 and 228 CJA 2003).

Josh, aged 14, is jointly charged with Graham, aged 33, with common assault. If both Josh and Graham plead not guilty, the trial will be held in the adult magistrates' court. If Graham pleads guilty but Josh pleads not guilty, Josh will be tried in the Youth Court.

35.6 PROCEEDINGS IN THE YOUTH COURT

Most young defendants will be tried in the Youth Court where proceedings are more informal than in the adult court. The informality extends to the layout of the court, which enables the young person to fully participate in the proceedings (unless the defendant is remanded in custody). The defendant sits in a chair facing the magistrates and not in the dock. The advocates and witnesses remain seated during the proceedings. The defendant will be addressed by his first name and the language used should be appropriate to his age and maturity. The words 'conviction' and 'sentence' will be avoided as the phrases 'case proven' or 'not proven' are preferred. Sentences are described as 'disposals' and before disposing of the case, the court is required to inform the young person and his parent or guardian of the way it proposes to deal with the case.

The following may be present in court:

- court officers, including members of the Youth Offending Team (YOT);
- the parties in the case including the young person, prosecutor and defence lawyers and witnesses;
- the defendant's parents or guardians;
- the victim, unless it is not in the interests of justice for him to attend (this would be a rare occurrence);
- news reporters – although reports of the proceedings are generally restricted so as not to reveal the young person's identity, address or school, etc.

Even allowing for the greater informality, where the defendant denies the offence, the trial in the Youth Court will follow the same procedure as in the adult court:

- the prosecutor makes an opening speech;
- the first prosecution witness is examined-in-chief;
- the witness is cross-examined by the defence.
- the prosecutor may re-examine his witness;

(Each prosecution witness gives evidence through this procedure)

- the prosecutor may also put before the court:
  – documentary evidence;
  – exhibits (known as real evidence); and
  – statements admissible under s. 9 Criminal Justice Act 1967, which permits the written statement of a witness who is not in court to be read to the bench;
- at the close of the prosecution case, the defence may make a submission of no case to answer where the prosecution has failed to prove an essential element of the offence or the prosecution evidence has been so discredited that the court could not find the case proven against the defendant;

- the first defence witness, usually the accused, is examined-in-chief;
- the witness is cross-examined by the prosecution;
- the defence advocate may re-examine his witness;

(Each defence witness gives evidence through this procedure)

- the defence advocate may also put before the court:
  - documentary evidence;
  - exhibits (known as real evidence); and
  - statements admissible under s. 9 Criminal Justice Act 1967, which permits the written statement of a witness who is not in court to be read to the bench;
- the defence makes a closing speech;
- the court decides whether the case is proven;
- if proven, the court will proceed to disposing of the case; or
- if the case is not proven the defendant is free to leave the court.

35.7 SENTENCING THE YOUNG OFFENDER IN THE YOUTH COURT

Where the case is proven against the young person, under Part 44 Crim PR he and/or his parent or guardian will be given the opportunity to make a statement, and the court is also obliged to consider any relevant information about the young person's general conduct, home environment and school record. If the information is not immediately available, the court must consider adjourning for enquiries. A report may be required from a probation officer, social worker or YOT member.

When the Youth Court is in possession of the necessary information, a range of disposals are available to it. Some disposals relate to the young offender only, while others can and sometimes will be imposed on his parent or guardian.

As with adults, the court is required to take a structured approach to sentencing and will refer to sentencing guidelines produced by the Sentencing Guidelines Council and the Court of Appeal's sentencing decisions. The provisions relating to the sentencing of young people are contained in the Powers of the Criminal Courts (Sentencing) Act 2000 and the Criminal Justice Act 2003.

35.7.1 DEFERMENT OF SENTENCE – S. 1 PCC(S) A 2000

The Youth Court can defer sentence for up to six months. It might choose to do so, for example:

- because of an imminent and significant change in lifestyle; or
- to allow the young person to save up to pay compensation to the victim.

The court must give reasons for the deferment and explain what is required of the young person during the deferred period. If another offence is committed during the deferred period, the offender may be sentenced for the new offence in addition to the previous offence.

35.7.2 DETENTION AND TRAINING ORDER – SS. 100–107 POWERS OF THE CRIMINAL COURTS (SENTENCING) ACT 2000

A DTO is the main custodial sentence for a young offender. The disposal will be available in the following circumstances:

- The offender is aged between 12 and 18 years; and has been convicted of an imprisonable offence which is so 'serious' that neither a fine alone nor a community sentence can be justified (s. 152 CJA 2003).

- Currently, a court may not pass a DTO in the case of an offender under the age of 12.
- A court may not pass a DTO in the case of an offender under the age of 15 unless the court is of the opinion that he is a persistent offender (PO).
- The length of the order must be for one of periods specified in the Act: four, six, eight, ten, 12, 18 or 24 months. (The term may not exceed the adult maximum term which a Crown Court could pass on an adult over 21, which in the case of a summary-only offence is six months – soon to be 51 weeks (unless the statute prescribes less));
- The young offender will be entitled to a sentencing discount where he pleads guilty and should be given credit for periods spent on remand (s. 144 CJA 2003/s. 101(8) PCC (S) A 2000);
- The young person will begin a period of supervision half-way through the sentence, which will cease when the full term expires, s. 103 PCC(S)A 2000.

> **Example**
>
> Josh, aged 14, is convicted of theft in the Youth Court. He has ten previous convictions. As the court is satisfied that the offence is so serious that only a custodial sentence is appropriate and that Josh is a PO, it imposes a four-month DTO on Josh. Under the terms of the DTO, Josh will spend two months in custody and two months in the community under supervision.

35.7.3 COMMUNITY ORDERS

Community orders in relation offenders aged 16–17 are currently in a state of transition. If the offender is under 18, a youth community order under the CJA 2003 will be passed. If the offender is 16 or 17, however, as an alternative to the youth community order under the CJA (and for the time being at least), the court may instead choose to impose an 'old style' community order under the PCC(S) A 2000.

'Old-style' community orders are covered at (a), (b), (c) and (d) below. The youth community order is considered at (e)–(i) below.

A community sentence may only be imposed against a young person where the offence is serious enough to warrant it (s. 148 CJA 2003). Youth community sentences will be supervised by members of the youth offending teams (YOTs). Breach proceedings in relation to community sentences are governed by Schedules 3 and 8 PCC(S) A 2000.

(a) Community punishment order – ss. 46–50 PCC(S) A 2000
  - The offender must be aged at least 16-years-old.
  - A CPO shall not be passed unless the offence is serious enough to merit it (s. 35(1) SA 2000).
  - The court should obtain and consider a pre-sentence report unless it is unnecessary (ss. 36(4) and (6) SA 2000).
  - The court must be satisfied that the offender is suitable to perform work under the order.
  - The hours of unpaid work should not be less than 40 and no more than 240 (s. 46(3) PCC (S) A 2000).
  - Before making the order the court should explain to the offender the effect of the order and the consequences of not complying with the requirements.

(b) Community rehabilitation order – ss. 41–45 PCC(S) A 2000
  - The offender must be at least 16-years-old;
  - A CRO shall not be passed unless offence is serious enough to merit it, s. 35(1) PCC (S) A 2000;

- Regard should be had to s. 41 SA 2000, in that the court must conclude such an order is desirable in the interests of securing the offender's rehabilitation and protecting the public from the commission by him of further offence.
- The court should obtain and consider a pre-sentence report unless it is unnecessary (ss. 36(4) and (6) SA 2000).
- Before making the order the court should explain to the offender the effect of the order and the consequences of not complying with the requirements;
- The order can last between six months and three years.

(c) Community punishment and rehabilitation order – s. 51 PCC(S) A 2000
- The offender must be at least 16-years-old.
- A CPRO shall not be passed unless the offence is serious enough to merit it, s. 35(1) S A 2000;
- The court should obtain and consider a pre-sentence report unless it is unnecessary (ss. 36(4) and (6) S A 2000).
- The rehabilitation element must be between 12 months and three years.
- The community punishment element must be between 40 and 100 hours.

(d) Drug testing and treatment order – s. 52 PCC(S) A 2000
- The offender must be at least 16 years.
- A DTTO shall not be passed unless offence is serious enough to merit it, s. 35(1) S A 2000.
- A pre-sentence report would be a pre-requisite.
- The DTTO must be between six months and three years.
- The court must be satisfied that the offender is dependant on drugs and may be susceptible to treatment.
- The offender will be subject to regular drug testing and will have regular review hearings before the court.
- The DTTO is a high-intensity community order.

Section 148 CJA 2003 permits a court to pass one or more youth community orders on offenders below the age of 18. The court must be satisfied that the order it is imposing is the most suitable for the offender any restriction on the offender's liberty is commensurate with the seriousness of the offence. A pre-sentence report will invariably be required to assess suitability. Youth community orders include:

(e) Action plan order – ss. 69–71 PCC(S) A 2000
- The order is supervised by the Youth Offending Team (YOT).
- It lasts three months and is tailored to the needs and specific risks of the individual offender. It can include reparation to the victim, education and training.
- The action plan order can include drug testing and treatment for offenders aged 14 and over in defined circumstances.

(f) Attendance centre order – ss. 60–62 PCC(S) A 2000
- The defendant must have been convicted of an imprisonable offence.
- The offender will be required to attend attendance centre for specified number of hours covering a specified time;
- Attendance is for not less than 12 hours unless young person is under 14 years and is up to maximum of 24 hours.

(g) Supervision order – s. 63 PCC(S) A 2000

- A Supervision order can last up to three years.

- A range of conditions can be attached to a supervision order when the sentence is used for more serious offences. These are called 'specified activities' and can last for up to 90 days.

- Specified activities can include drug treatment, curfew and residence requirements.

- As part of supervision, a court may require the offender to undergo an ISSP (intensive supervision and surveillance programme). ISSPs are reserved for the most prolific young offenders. It combines intense levels of community-based surveillance with a comprehensive and sustained focus on tackling the factors that contribute to the young person's offending behaviour.

- The order is supervised by the YOT.

(h) Curfew order – ss. 37– 40 PCC(S) A 2000

- This requires the convicted offender to remain at a specified place between specified times.

- The maximum period of the curfew between two and 12 hours on a specified day.

- The order is for maximum of three months if young offender is between ten and 15.

- It should seek to avoid conflict with educational establishments attended by the offender or his religious beliefs.

- It will include electronic tagging.

(i) Exclusion order – s. 40 A PCC(S) A 2000

The court can make an order prohibiting an offender from entering a specified place.

- The order can last for up to three months.

- It may specify different places.

- It should seek to avoid conflict with educational establishments attended by the offender or his religious beliefs.

- It will include electronic tagging.

35.7.4 REPARATION ORDER – SS. 73–75 PCC(S) A 2000

The court may impose a reparation order on the young offender as part of the sentence it passes. In deciding the issue, the court will obtain a report from the young person's YOT who will suggest a suitable form of reparation. Such an order is designed to get the offender to address the consequences of his offending behaviour. It cannot be imposed where a custodial sentence is passed or a supervision order, action plan order or referral order is made. Under a reparation order:

- the young person is required to give reparation to a specified person or to the community;

- the work to be carried out is under the supervision of a probation officer or social worker;

- no more than 24 hours work to be completed within three months of the order;

- the order is overseen by YOT;

- in a case where a reparation order can be made, the court must give reasons for refusing to make one.

35.7.5 REFERRAL ORDER – S. 16 PCC(S) A 2000

A referral order will be appropriate for a first-time offender who admits guilt and the offence is not suitable to be punished by a custodial sentence or absolute discharge. It will be appropriate to make a referral order in the following circumstances:

- The young person will have no previous convictions including a conditional discharge or a bind over.

- If the young person pleaded guilty, a referral order *is mandatory* as long as neither custody nor an absolute discharge are appropriate and the young person has never been convicted or bound over.

- If the young person pleaded guilty to one offence but is found guilty of another offence, a referral order is discretionary.

- The length of referral order to a Youth Offending Panel (YOP) will be between three and 12 months.

- The YOP is composed of members of the community and a member of YOT who meet with the young person and his parent/guardian and agree a 'contract' with the offender which seeks to address the reasons for his offending behaviour.

- The victim of the offence may attend the YOP.

- The conviction is spent once the 'contract' is completed.

35.7.6 FINE – PART VI PCC(S) A 2000

While imposing a fine on an offender is the most common sentence passed by the criminal courts (see 30.8), fining a young person is relatively rare, for obvious reasons. When the court considers a fine to be appropriate, the following considerations apply:

- The fine may be imposed as a disposal in its own right.

- The court must taken into account the financial circumstances of the offender and/or his parent/guardian.

- The parent/guardian must attend the court hearing if the court considers making them pay.

- Where the young offender is under 16, the parent/guardian will be ordered to pay, unless:

  – the parent/guardian cannot be found; or

  – it would be unreasonable to expect them to pay.

- The maximum fine that can be imposed where the young offender is aged between ten and 13 is £ 250.

- The maximum fine that can be imposed where the young offender is aged between 14 and 17 is £1,000.

35.7.7 CONDITIONAL DISCHARGE – S. 12 PCC(S) A 2000

A conditional discharge may be imposed on a young offender whatever the offence. In practice, they are reserved for the less serious offences. The offender must not commit any further offences during the operational period of the conditional discharge, which can be up to a maximum of three years. If the young offender re-offends during the conditional period, he may be punished for both the later offence and for the original offence. A conditional discharge may be imposed on a young offender in the following circumstances:

- where the case is proven against a the young offender;

- where the court considers that it is not expedient to punish;

- where the young offender has not received a final warning within the last two years.

35.7.8 ABSOLUTE DISCHARGE – S. 12 PCC(S) A 2000

As with a conditional discharge, an absolute discharge is appropriate in connection with very trivial offences where the court considers that punishment is not required. An absolute discharge may be imposed in the following circumstances:

- where the is case proven against the young offender; and

- where the court considers that no punishment is required; and
- where the court considers there is no risk of further offending by the young person.

35.7.9 ENDORSEMENT OR DISQUALIFICATION OF THE JUVENILE'S DRIVING LICENCE/RECORD

For further information on driving penalties, see Chapter 32. Even though a young offender may have no driving licence, his driving record can still be subject to endorsement and disqualification.

35.7.10 COMPENSATION ORDER – SS. 130–135 PCC(S) A 2000

A convicted young offender may be ordered to pay to compensation up to a maximum of £5,000 in either the Youth Court or the adult magistrates' court for any personal injury, loss or damage which resulted from his offence. The Magistrates' Court Sentencing Guidelines provide guidance as the appropriate level of compensation. An important consideration will be the offender's ability to pay.

35.7.11 PARENTING ORDERS (SS. 8–10 CRIME AND DISORDER ACT 1998)

As the name suggests, a parenting order is directed to improving the parenting skills of the young offender's parent or guardian. Where an offender under the age of 16 is convicted of an offence and the court considers that a parenting order would be desirable in the interests of preventing further offending by the young person, it *shall* make a parenting order. A parenting order requires the parent or guardian to attend parenting guidance sessions for up to 12 months. The sessions are supervised by a member of the youth offending team or a probation officer or a social worker.

35.7.12 PARENTAL BIND OVER (S. 150(1) PCC(S) A 2000)

The young offender's parent or guardian must be bound over to prevent the juvenile under the age of 16 from committing further offences wherever the court is satisfied that it would be in the interests of justice to do so. If a court chooses not to make an order, it must give reasons in open court. A bind over may not be given where a court passes a referral order.

35.8 ANTI-SOCIAL BEHAVIOUR ORDERS (ASBOs)

The Crime and Disorder Act 1998 introduced a wide range of measures which seek to divert young people away from offending by imposing sanctions on their anti-social behaviour. They include anti-social behaviour orders, child safety orders, local child curfew schemes and the powers of the police to deal with truancy from school. Breach of an ASBO is a criminal offence which caries imprisonment. It seeks to prevent a young person from going to a particular place or doing a particular thing. It can be imposed on application by the police or local authority and upon conviction where the court considers the offender has acted in a manner that caused or was likely to cause harassment, alarm or distress. A steady body of case law has started to emerge in relation to ASBOs (see *Blackstone's Criminal Practice*).

35.9 SENTENCING THE YOUNG OFFENDER IN THE ADULT MAGISTRATES' COURT

The adult magistrates' court has limited sentencing powers over a young offender. In the few situations where the young offender is sentenced in the adult magistrates' court, the following disposals are most commonly imposed:

- fine;
- referral order in certain circumstances;
- conditional/absolute discharge;
- disqualification from driving;
- endorsement of the young person's driving licence/record.

The young offender will usually be remitted to the Youth Court for sentence. Relevant rules of court relating to the sentencing of young person before an adult magistrates' court are contained in Part 44 Crim PR.

35.10 SENTENCING THE YOUNG OFFENDER IN THE CROWN COURT

While the Crown Court may pass any appropriate sentence on a young person, s. 8 Powers of Criminal Courts (Sentencing) Act 2000 requires that where the young person has been convicted on indictment, it shall remit the offender to the Youth Court for sentencing unless it is 'undesirable' to so. In applying the 'undesirable' test, the Crown Court judge may not remit to the Youth Court where doing so would cause:

- delay; or
- unnecessary expense; or
- unnecessary duplication of the proceedings.

As the judge will be familiar with the facts of the case, it is common for the young person to be sentenced in the Crown Court. The Crown Court has the full range of sentencing disposals available to it, with the obvious addition that it can impose an extended sentence in accordance with s. 91 PCC(S) A 2000 for a 'grave' crime where the defendant has been convicted on indictment and, when it is in force, upon committal for sentence under s. 3B PCC(S) A 2000. Where an extended custodial sentence is passed, the young offender will serve his time in a young offenders' institution or secure training centre.

Where the young person has been convicted of murder, s. 90 PCC(S) A 2000 prescribes the mandatory sentence of detention at Her Majesty's Pleasure. Guidance on setting the minimum term can be found in ss. 269–277 CJA 2003. The starting point for an offender under 18 is 12 years before taking into account any mitigating or aggravating factors.

35.11 SENTENCING A 'DANGEROUS' YOUNG OFFENDER

The Criminal Justice Act 2003 has introduced specific sentencing powers in the Crown Court to deal with a dangerous young offender convicted of a specified offence. These powers may be exercised following the young person's conviction in the Crown Court or where he has been remitted under s. 3C Powers of Criminal Courts (Sentencing) Act 2000 to the Crown Court for sentence following summary conviction in the Youth Court (not completely in force).

Schedule 15 CJA 2003 lists the 153 categories of violent or sexual offences which come within the definition of a specified offence. A specified offence is defined under s. 224 CJA 2003 as:

- a violent or sexual offence which carries a sentence of ten or more years imprisonment or detention in a young offender's institution or custody for life; or
- a violent or sexual offence which carries a sentence of between two years and ten years imprisonment.

A specified violent offence includes manslaughter, kidnapping, offences under ss. 18 and 20 OAPA 1861. A specified sexual offence includes rape under s. 1 Sexual Offences Act 2003. The sentencing powers available to the Crown Court depends on whether the young person has been convicted of a violent or sexual offence which carries a maximum of ten or more years imprisonment or a violent or sexual offence which carries a sentence of between two years and ten years imprisonment. If the offender falls within the first category *and* is assessed as being dangerous, he must be detained for life or detained for public protection. If the offender falls within the second category *and* is assessed as being dangerous, the court must pass an extended sentence of imprisonment.

35.11.1 DETENTION FOR LIFE OR DETENTION FOR PUBLIC PROTECTION

Under s. 226(1) CJA 2003, where a person under 18 has been convicted of a serious violent or sexual offence (carrying a maximum of ten or more years' imprisonment) and the court is of the opinion that there is a significant risk to members of the public of serious harm occasioned by the commission by him of further specified offences, the court *must* impose a life sentence if the offence he has been convicted of would be liable to a sentence of detention for life (s. 226(2) CJA 2003).

If the circumstances of the case do not justify a life sentence, the court must choose between a sentence of detention for public protection or an extended sentence. If the court considers that an extended sentence would not be adequate to protect the public, the court must pass an indeterminate sentence for public protection (s. 226(3)).

The factors the court considers in assessing the dangerousness test are considered below and in Chapter 29 (29.9.5).

35.11.2 IMPOSING AN EXTENDED SENTENCE

Under s. 228(1) CJA 2003, the court must pass an extended sentence on a person under 18 who has been convicted of a specified violent or sexual offence (carrying a sentence of between two years and ten years imprisonment) where the court considers:

- there is a significant risk to members of the public of serious harm occasioned by the commission of further specified offences; and
- where the specified offence is a serious offence, it is not one in which the court is required to impose a sentence of detention for life or to impose a sentence for public protection.

Where the conditions for imposing an extended sentence are met, the court will set the appropriate custodial term and a further extended period of supervision which the young offender is required to serve on licence. The extended period on licence should be for such period as the court considers necessary to protect the public from serious harm occasioned by the commission of further specified offences by the young offender. The custodial term must be at least 12 months but must not exceed the maximum term (which is 24 months). The extended period must not exceed five years in the case of a specified violent offence (s. 228(3) CJA 2003) or eight years in the case of a specified sexual offence (s. 228(4) CJA 2003).

35.11.3 ASSESSMENT OF 'DANGEROUSNESS'

In deciding whether to detain an offender under 18 for life or for public protection or to impose an extended sentence, the court must consider the seriousness of the offence and/or other offences associated with it (s. 229 CJA 2003) to determine whether the juvenile will constitute a danger to the public. The court will take careful note of the facts of the offence, the pre-sentence report and any other relevant report. In these kinds of cases a psychiatric report is commonly obtained.

Guidance on these complicated provisions has been given by the Court of Appeal in *R v Lang and Others* [2005] EWCA Crim 2864. The guidance is reproduced in Chapter 29 (29.9.5).Your attention is specifically drawn to paragraphs (vi) and (vii) in the judgment as they apply to offenders under the age of 18.

35.12 WHAT IF THE DEFENDANT REACHES THE AGE OF 18 DURING THE PROCEEDINGS?

Although the rules and the case law on this point are not absolutely clear, the position would appear to be as follows:

If the defendant is under the age of 18 at the time he enters his plea before the Youth Court he will be tried as a youth, notwithstanding the fact that he reaches 18 during the currency of the proceedings.

So far as sentencing is concerned, s. 29 Children and Young Persons Act 1963 would appear to allow the Youth Court to sentence a youth who has pleaded guilty or been found guilty while still aged 17, but who attains the age of 18 before being sentenced. In other words, it is the date of conviction which is the determining factor. The Youth Court has discretionary power under s. 9 PCC(S) A 2000 to remit a juvenile to sentence in the adult court where the defendant attained the age of 18 before conviction.

For further information on youth justice, consult the Youth Justice Board's website at http://www.youth-justice-board.gov.uk.

KEY POINT SUMMARY

- The rules governing which court a young person will be tried in are complex and have to be grasped.

- If possible a defendant under 18 should be tried in the Youth Court, which is specifically designed for the special needs of younger offenders.

- Understand the concept of a 'grave' crime and why this is important in relation to mode of trial considerations for a youth under the age of 18.

- Understand when the 'dangerousness' provisions under s. 224 CJA 2003 bite and why they are important in relation to mode of trial considerations for youths.

- Know the circumstances in which the Youth Court can impose a detention and training order (DTO).

- Know the range of community penalties available to the Youth Court.

- Be able to explain the differences in procedure between the adult court and the Youth Court.

SELF-TEST QUESTIONS

1. What is the general rule about where a young defendant should be tried?

2. What is the main custodial sentence for a convicted young offender and when can it be passed?

3. Tracey is 15. She has been charged with an offence of arson contrary to s. 1(1) and (3) Criminal Damage Act 1971. It is alleged that she and a group of other girls set fire to a mobile classroom in the grounds of a high school, resulting in £20,000 worth of damage. The fire began at around 10.30 at night. The classroom was unoccupied. Tracey has no criminal record but comes from

a family beset by social problems. She had recently been suspended from school. No one else has been charged in connection with the incident. Consider the following questions:

- In which court will Tracey appear?

- In which court is Tracey likely to be tried and dealt with?

- If Tracey is found guilty of the offence, what range of sentences are open to the sentencing court?

4. Barry, aged 15, is charged with causing death by dangerous driving. He denies the offence. He has several previous convictions, including convictions for robbery, violence and aggravated vehicle taking. What considerations will the Youth Court have regard to in deciding whether to accept jurisdiction to try Barry?

FIGURE 35.1 YOUTH PROCEEDINGS

WHERE WILL A YOUNG PERSON BE TRIED?

Youth Court (the vast majority of young defendants are tried before the Youth Court). This will be the case where:

- the youth is charged alone; or
- the youth is charged with another youth.

Crown Court – This will be the case where:

- a youth is charged with homicide, which includes both murder and manslaughter, s. 24(1) MCA 1980; or
- a youth is charged with a 'grave' offence, s. 24(1)(a) MCA 1980. ('Grave' offence includes an offence for which an adult could be punished with imprisonment for 14 years or more, or specific offences under the Sexual offences Act 2003 and the Firearms Act 1968); or
- the offence charged is a specified offence and the defendant would, it appears, if found guilty satisfy the test of dangerousness under ss. 226 or 228 CJA 2003; or
- a youth is jointly charged with an adult and the adult is to be tried on indictment and the court considers that 'it is in the interests of justice' for them to be tried together, s. 24(1)(b) MCA 1980.

Adult magistrates' court – This will be the case where the young person is charged jointly with an adult in connection with a summary offence **BUT**

- the summary case may be remitted to the Youth Court where:
  - the adult pleads guilty; and
  - the young person pleads not guilty; or
  - the adult is committed for trial or is discharged and the young person pleads not guilty.

  When charged with an either-way offence, the young person has no right of election.

Youth court proceedings are:

- more informal in terms of procedure and terminology;
- limited right of public access;
- subject to reporting restrictions; and
- tried before a specially trained 'mixed' bench.

Youth Court sentencing powers include:

- DTO for those over 15 (maximum 24 months);
- no DTO for under 12s and under 15s need to be a PO;
- community youth orders;
- reparation order;
- referral order;
- fine/compensation;
- conditional discharge;
- Parenting order.

APPENDIX 1

R v LENNY WHYTE

For reasons of space, we include only a selection of the documentation that forms the basis of the solicitor's file on this case study.

The complete documentation as listed overleaf can be accessed on our Online Resource Centre in the case studies section. The documents selected for inclusion in this appendix are shown in **bold type**.

R v LENNY WHYTE: INDEX TO DOCUMENTATION ON SOLICITOR'S FILE

DOCUMENT 1 Initial Statement of Lenny Whyte

DOCUMENT 2 File Note/Initial Attendance on Client

DOCUMENT 3 CDS 1

DOCUMENT 4 Application for Representation Order – Selected Portions

DOCUMENT 5 Letter to the CPS Requesting Advance Information

DOCUMENT 6 Letter Requesting Copy of Custody Record

DOCUMENT 7 Client Care Letter

DOCUMENT 8 CPS Letter Regarding Advance Information (specimen letter)

DOCUMENT 9 Lymeshire Police Custody Record – Selected Portions

DOCUMENT 10 Record of Intial Description

DOCUMENT 11 Antecedents of Lenny Whyte-Restricted Access to CPS only

DOCUMENT 12 List of Previous Convictions for Lenny Whyte

DOCUMENT 13 Record of Attendance at Second Appearance Hearing

DOCUMENT 14 Transcript of Bail Hearing – Submissions of Prosecution and Defence

DOCUMENT 15 Record of Decision to Withold Bail

DOCUMENT 16 Notice of Application Relating to Bail to be Made to the Crown Court

DOCUMENT 17 Record of Crown Court Bail Hearing

DOCUMENT 18 (A–P) Advance Information/Committal Bundle – Selected Portions Excluding Documents (I–N)

DOCUMENT 19 Additional Statement of Lenny Whyte – Comments on Advance Information

DOCUMENT 20 File Note – Consideration of Advance Information and Record of Attendance at Mode of Trial Enquiry

DOCUMENT 21 Note to Trainee Solicitor – Enquiry re: Possible Alibi

DOCUMENT 22 CPS Letter regarding Committal Proceedings (Specimen Letter)

DOCUMENT 23 Extracts from the Committal Bundle

DOCUMENT 24 File Note on Committal Preparation and Attendance

DOCUMENT 25 CDS 4-Application for Prior Authority to Incur Disbursement

DOCUMENT 26 Notice of Committal/Post Committal Case Management Form

DOCUMENT 27 Letter Requesting Expert Report for the Defence

DOCUMENT 28 Letter to Client

DOCUMENT 29 CPS Letter Regarding CPIA 1996 Disclosure (Specimen Letter)

DOCUMENT 30A Police Schedule of Non-Sensitive Unused Material

DOCUMENT 30B Police Schedule of Non-Sensitive Unused Material

DOCUMENT 30C Notice of Intention to Admit Evidence of Defendant's Bad Character under CJA 2003

DOCUMENT 31 Notice to Accused regarding CPIA 1996 Disclosure

DOCUMENT 32 Letter to CPS Dealing with CPIA 1996 Matters and Bad Character Notice under s. 101 Criminal Justice Act 2003

DOCUMENT 33 Notification of Witness Requirements

DOCUMENT 34A Defence Statement

TIMESCALE OF EVENTS – *R v LENNY WHYTE*

- 20 March – charged with an either-way offence.
- 20 March – initial appearance before magistrates' court (adjourned for advance information and remanded in custody).
- 27 March – second appearance before magistrates' court (further adjourned for advance information – remanded into custody).
- 4 April (bail appeal before Crown Court – conditional bail granted).
- 24 April – third appearance before magistrates' court. Not guilty plea entered followed by mode of trial enquiry. Summary jurisdiction declined. Case adjourned and a date set for committal hearing.
- 30 May – fourth appearance before magistrates' court at committal hearing. Case committed to the Crown Court and a date set for a Plea and Case Management Hearing (PCMH).
- 30 June – first appearance before Crown Court at the PCMH – date set for trial.
- 22 August – trial.

DOCUMENT 1   INITIAL STATEMENT OF LENNY WHYTE

Proof of Evidence

Lenny Whyte of Flat 4a, Lymewood Court, Parkdale, Lyme, will state:

1. I am 27 years old and of mixed race origin. My father is from the Caribbean and my mother (who is deceased) was white. My date of birth is the 26/7/- I have been charged in connection with a burglary at the home of an 84-year-old woman in Sunrise Road, Lyme which occurred on the 17th March at around midday. I will plead not guilty and am innocent of the charge. I was not represented at the police station prior to being charged and have been refused police bail. I am also charged with possession of a small quantity of cannabis. I intend to plead guilty to this.

2. I was arrested at home on the 19th March as I was leaving my flat. I could not believe it. The next thing I knew they were searching my flat. They seized some of my clothing and a pair of training shoes. I was taken to a police car and shoved in the back and taken to the police station.

3. I was taken to Lyme Street Police Station, and had to stay there overnight. I cannot remember if my rights were explained. The police told me I would be detained overnight because they wanted me to participate in an identification procedure and it would take time to organise. I have been in this situation before. I recall asking for an identification parade but was told I would have a video parade. I was photographed not long after arriving at the police station. I watched the officer put together a video parade but I did not have a clue what was going on. I understand that several witnesses have been shown the video and one of them has picked me out.

4. It was a difficult night in detention. I did not get much sleep and I was really worried about my dog Butch. I live on my own and there is no one to see to him. The police did try to ring my sister but she could not be reached. I was also craving a cigarette as I am a chain smoker. Additionally, I am a diagnosed manic depressive. I am prone to erratic behaviour and mood swings. Sometimes I get very depressed. My medication helps but it has side effects and I do not take it as regularly as I should. I cannot recall whether I was asked about this when I arrived at the police station as it is all a bit of a blur. I told the police the following morning that I needed my medication and that I felt unwell. When I told the officer that I needed my medication for depression, a police doctor was called. Somebody must have gone to my flat to get my pills. I was checked over by the police doctor who gave me my tablets. He said I was fit to be interviewed which I was happy about. I thought that once I was interviewed I would be able to get out and see to things.

5. I believe it was explained to me that I could see a solicitor if I wanted to. To be honest I did not think there was much point as the police were going to charge me whatever I said. When the police said they were going to interview me at last, I did not want to delay matters further by requesting a solicitor. I regret the decision now. I kept telling the officers that I needed a smoke. I was told that it was up to me. In the circumstances, I just told the police what they wanted to hear. I wish to retract my confession. It is untrue.

6. I understand that another man is alleged to have been involved in the burglary. His name is Lloyd Green. I know of Lloyd Green. He is a drug dealer and has supplied drugs to me in the past. He is no longer my supplier. Green has got rough with me in the past when I owed him money.

7. I have been trying to recollect my whereabouts on Tuesday the 17th between 11.30–12.30pm. I think I may have been in my bookmakers – Gladbrookes in the High Street – and there might be someone there who could verify the fact. I place a small bet most days at around lunch time and I am fairly certain that that was where I was.

8. I do know the area around Sunrise Road. It is quite close to where I live. I often walk my dog on fields near to the back of Sunrise Road. I know one or two of the residents in the street. Most residents are friendly, but one or two of them are a little suspicious of me. The rear gardens of the houses in Sunrise Road which back onto the fields are not fenced off so it is possible for a person to wonder onto the lawns at the back of the houses.

9. I do not understand how I have come to be identified as the man seen running away from the back of the burgled property. It was not me. I can only assume it must have been someone else who maybe looks similar in appearance to me. In actuality, I am 5' 10''. I am of slim build. I have medium length dreadlocked hair and a slight beard. The police mentioned something about the white training shoes being worn by the burglar. I do not own a pair of white trainers. The trainers recovered from my flat were left there by a friend. I have never worn them.

10. So far as my personal circumstances are concerned, I live on my own in a housing association flat. I have a girlfriend. Her name is Sonia. We have been seeing each other on and off for six months, although we have not been living together. Sonia is four months pregnant with my child. The pregnancy was not planned. Sonia already has a child of her own. She is hoping to move to better accommodation as her present flat only has one bedroom. I am anxious to see Sonia. I need to know if she and the baby are okay.

11. I do not work. I am in receipt of income support. With my criminal record and my medical condition, it is difficult for me to get work. Having said that, I have a job interview next week – something my probation officer has organised. It is with a floor laying company. The owner has taken on ex-offenders in the past and is prepared to give me an interview. This could offer me the first real prospect of a job leading to full-time employment.

12. I get on very well with my sister, Tessa. She is my half-sister. She is a single mother. I see my sister once or twice a week. She makes sure my flat is clean and that I have food in. My mother died when I was 14 and my father left us when I was three. I don't know where he lives. Tessa, who is six years my senior, looked after me when our mother died.

13. I have been smoking cannabis since the age of 15. I became addicted to hard drugs, including crack, in my early twenties. At this time I was mixing with a lot of low-life individuals and having to commit crimes in order to pay off debts and fund my drug habit. Prison was really hard. Drugs were available but I stayed off hard drugs. When I finished my prison sentence I got myself a girlfriend and some stability. However, it was at this time that I began suffering with mental problems which I assumed were due to my drug addiction. I wish to make it clear that I am no longer addicted to drugs and only smoke cannabis very occasionally when I am feeling really depressed and weird. I must get bail. I cannot face going back to prison. I had not smoked any cannabis in the 24 hours before my arrest.

14. My GP is Dr Shaw at the Havelock Medical Centre, Willow Lane, Lyme. I do see a consultant psychiatrist at the Royal Lyme Hospital but I cannot recall his name. I am happy for my medical notes to be released.

15. I am currently on probation for an offence of assault. As part of the probation order, I was ordered to undergo psychiatric treatment. It was as a consequence of this that doctors diagnosed my mental illness. I have a really supportive probation officer, Maxine, with whom I get on really well. She understands my problems and is the one who has secured me a job interview.

16. I do have previous convictions but I cannot recall them all. I have previous convictions for burglary, drug use and assault. My most recent offence of assault was committed 18 months ago. It was very much out of character for me. I am not a violent man. The assault stemmed from a breakdown of a relationship and was committed shortly before my illness was diagnosed and treatment for it began. Aggressive tendencies are not uncommon in sufferers of manic depression and this may have been a contributing factor in the commission of this offence.

17. I have convictions for possession of amphetamine and cocaine and convictions for theft. Most of the theft offences relate to shoplifting committed in order to obtain drugs. As far as I can remember the burglary offences were drug related. I have previous convictions for failing bail. I have no excuse. I simply did not turn up at court. I suspect I was so out of it while on drugs that I simply forgot. To the best of my recollection, I have always pleaded guilty.

Lenny Whyte
20th March

DOCUMENT 2   FILE NOTE/INITIAL ATTENDANCE ON CLIENT
DATE 20/3/-

Attending Lenny Whyte at Lyme Magistrates' Court in my capacity as Duty Solicitor. Lenny Whyte is charged with a domestic dwelling house burglary. In the course of the interview, Lenny was less than coherent and kept asking me for a cigarette. He looked rough, dishevelled and appeared incapable of concentrating during the interview. He was not represented at the police station. He appears in custody as bail is opposed. Lenny suffers from bipolar depression for which he receives medication. I took a detailed initial statement from him but before doing so I had a word with the CPS lawyer dealing with the case, who gave me what advance disclosure she has to date which included Lenny's previous convictions and several witness statements. The evidence linking Lenny seems to be based on admissions in interview and eye-witness evidence. A second person is suspected of being involved in the burglary but no charges have been brought against this individual. The CPS lawyer indicated bail would be opposed.

In the course of my interview with Lenny, I assisted him to complete an application for a representation order which was granted immediately by the legal adviser in Court 1. On speaking with the CPS they were not in possession of a full file. Attending before Lyme Magistrates where the CPS requested a one week adjournment period to review the file. The adjournment was granted. The CPS then opposed bail. An application for bail was made by me. Bail refused on the grounds of risk of absconding and commission of further offences. The case was adjourned for one week. Mr Whyte was remanded to HMP Shawbury. Date of next hearing is 27 March.

I spoke to Lenny afterwards – he was clearly agitated and somewhat bewildered. I explained he could apply for bail to the Crown Court but that I would be able to re-apply for bail before the magistrates in one week's time as he had one further opportunity to apply to the magistrates' court for bail. If bail was refused on that occasion we could apply to the Crown Court. He agreed to this course of action. I explained I would be writing to him while he was on remand and that he would be visited by me or a member of the firm in order to take his further instructions on the evidence. I also spoke to Lenny's sister who attended court and who is evidently concerned for her brother's welfare.

Time engaged:
Attending client 50 minutes (including completing an application for a representation order)
Advocacy 30 minutes

DOCUMENT 4   APPLICATION FOR REPRESENTATION ORDER

FORM A
APPLICATION FOR RIGHT TO REPRESENTATION IN CRIMINAL PROCEEDINGS

MAGISTRATES' COURT OR CROWN COURT

I apply for the right to representation:
For the purposes of proceedings before the:

> CROWN/MAGISTRATES'/YOUTH COURT*

> * DELETE AS APPROPRIATE

PERSONAL DETAILS

1.a. SURNAME

> WHYTE

1.b. FORENAME

> LENNY

1.c. USUAL ADDRESS

> 4a LYMEWOOD COURT, PARKDALE, LYME

1.d. PRESENT ADDRESS (IF DIFFERENT FROM ABOVE)

1.e. DATE OF BIRTH

> 27/6/- (AGED 27)

2. CASE DETAILS

2.a. WHAT CHARGES HAVE BEEN BROUGHT AGAINST YOU? Briefly describe what it is that you are accused of doing i.e. theft of a DVD player worth £150

> DOMESTIC DWELLING HOUSE BURGLARY 17/3/-
> POSSESSION OF CANNABIS

2.b. ARE THERE ANY CO-DEFENDANTS IN THIS MATTER? IF YES, NAME THEM. IF NO, THEN GO TO QUESTION 3.

2.c. GIVE REASON WHY YOU AND YOUR CO-DEFENDANTS CANNOT BE REPRESENTED BY THE SAME SOLICITORS.

3. COURT PROCEEDINGS

3.a. I AM DUE TO APPEAR BEFORE:

THE: LYME MAGISTRATES	MAGISTRATES'/YOUTH COURT*
DATE: 20TH MARCH	AT AM/PM

OR

3.b. I APPEARED BEFORE:

THE:	MAGISTRATES'/YOUTH COURT*
DATE:	AT AM/PM

AND (TICK WHATEVER APPLIES)

[ ] MY CASE HAS BEEN SENT TO THE CROWN COURT FOR TRIAL UNDER SECTION 51 OF THE CRIME AND DISORDER ACT

[ ] MY CASE HAS BEEN TRANSFERRED TO THE CROWN COURT FOR TRIAL

[ ] I WAS CONVICTED AND COMMITTED FOR SENTENCE TO THE CROWN COURT

[ ] I WAS CONVICTED AND/OR SENTENCED AND I WISH TO APPEAL AGAINST THE CONVICTION/SENTENCE*

4. OUTSTANDING MATTERS

If there are any other *outstanding* criminal charges or cases against you, give details including the court where you are due to appear:

5. REASONS FOR WANTING REPRESENTATION

To avoid the possibility of your application being delayed or publicly funded representation being refused because the court does not have enough information about the case, you must complete the rest of the form. When deciding whether to grant publicly funded representation, the court will need to know why it is in the interests of justice for you to be represented. If you need help in completing the form, you should speak to a solicitor.

	DETAILS	REASONS FOR GRANT OR REFUSAL (*FOR COURT USE ONLY*)
5a. IT IS LIKELY THAT I WILL LOSE MY LIBERTY *(You should consider seeing a solicitor before answering this question)*	I have been charged with an offence of domestic burglary. The aggravating factors are that the victim is an 84-year-old woman and I have previous convictions of a like nature. In the light of the Court of Appeal's decision in *R v McInerney* (2002), I am at risk of a lengthy custodial sentence if convicted.	
5b. I AM CURRENTLY SUBJECT TO A SENTENCE THAT IS SUSPENDED OR NON-CUSTODIAL THAT IF BREACHED MAY ALLOW THE COURT TO DEAL WITH ME FOR THE ORIGINAL OFFENCE. **PLEASE GIVE DETAILS.**	I am subject to a community order for an offence of common assault. It was imposed 18 months ago and has 6 months left to run.	
5c. IT IS LIKELY THAT I WILL LOSE MY LIVELIHOOD.	N/A	
5d. IT IS LIKELY THAT I WILL SUFFER SERIOUS DAMAGE TO MY REPUTATION.	N/A	
5e. A SUBSTANTIAL QUESTION OF LAW IS INVOLVED. *(You will need the help of a solicitor to answer this question)*	I intend to challenge the admissibility of incriminating admissions I made at the police station under ss. 76 and 78 PACE. I am a diagnosed bipolar-depressive. I was not represented by a solicitor or an appropriate adult and was unwell during interview. I will oppose any attempt to have my previous convictions admitted under s.101 Criminal Justice Act 2003.	

5f. I SHALL BE UNABLE TO UNDERSTAND THE COURT PROCEEDINGS OR STATE MY OWN CASE BECAUSE: i. MY UNDERSTANDING OF ENGLISH IS INADEQUATE. ii. SUFFER FROM A DISABILITY	I suffer from bipolar depression for which I receive medication. I am subject to mood swings and will be unable to follow the proceedings without the assistance of a solicitor.	
5g. WITNESSES HAVE TO BE TRACED AND/OR INTERVIEWED ON MY BEHALF **(State circumstances)**	I think I was in a betting shop at the time of the burglary and my solicitors will need to make contact with the betting establishment to see if anyone there can recall my presence.	
5h. THE CASE INVOLVES EXPERT CROSS EXAMINATION OF A PROSECUTION WITNESS **(Give brief details)**	I intend to plead not guilty. There are several elderly eyewitnesses who purport to have recognised me. They are mistaken and will need to be cross-examined. The case against me involves expert witness evidence involving shoeprint comparisons which I intend to challenge. The investigating officer and custody sergeant will need to be cross-examined.	
5i. IT IS IN SOMEONE ELSE'S INTERESTS THAT I AM REPRESENTED	The eyewitnesses are all elderly and will need to be cross-examined.	
5j. ANY OTHER REASONS: **(Give further particulars)**	The case is most likely to be heard at the Crown Court.	

6. LEGAL REPRESENTATION

6.a. If you do not give the name of a solicitor, the court will select a solicitor for you.

6.b. You must tell the solicitor that you have named him.

6.c. If you have been charged together with another person or persons, the court may assign a solicitor other than the solicitor of your choice.

THE SOLICITOR I WISH TO ACT FOR ME IS:

Miss R James

GIVE THE FIRM'S NAME AND ADDRESS (IF KNOWN):

Hannibal and Mountford Solicitors

DECLARATION TO BE COMPLETED ON BEHALF OF THE SOLICITOR NAMED ABOVE:

I certify that the named solicitor above has a crime franchise contract or a general criminal contract, or an individual case contract.

I understand that only firms with a general criminal contract or individual case contract may provide representation in the Magistrates' Court.

Signed: Hannibal and Mountford
Dated: 20th March

7. DECLARATION

IF YOU KNOWINGLY MAKE A STATEMENT, WHICH IS FALSE, OR KNOWINGLY WITHHOLD INFORMATION, YOU MAY BE PROSECUTED.

IF CONVICTED, YOU MAY BE SENT TO PRISON FOR UP TO THREE MONTHS OR BE FINED OR BOTH (SECTION 21 ACCESS TO JUSTICE ACT 1999).

I apply for representation for the charge(s) that are currently before the court.

I understand that should my case proceed to the Crown Court or any other higher court, the court may order that I pay for some or all of the costs of representation incurred in the proceedings by way of a Recovery of Defence Costs Order.

I understand that should my case proceed to the Crown Court or any other higher court, I will have to furnish details of my means to the Court and/or the Legal Services Commission.

Signed: L Whyte   Dated: 20th March

DOCUMENT 9   LYMESHIRE POLICE CUSTODY RECORD

Station: **Lyme Street**

Reasons for Arrest
Burglary of dwelling house

Comments made by person, if present when facts of arrest were explained. Y/N [N]. If Yes, comments on log.

Video Tape Ref. No. LT/369

DETAINED PERSON'S RIGHTS
An extract from a notice setting out my rights has been read to me and I have been given a copy. I have also been provided with a written notice setting out my entitlements while in custody.

Signature: **Lenny Whyte**
Date: 19/3/-   Time: 15.45

LEGAL ADVICE REQUESTED
DETAILS:
I want to speak to a solicitor as soon as practicable

Signature:
Time: Date:

LEGAL ADVICE DECLINED
I have been informed that I may speak to a solicitor IN PERSON OR ON THE TELEPHONE:

I do not want to speak to a solicitor at this time.
Signature: **Lenny Whyte**
Time: 19/3   Date: 15.45

Reasons given, for not wanting legal advice
None given

NOTIFICATION OF A NAMED PERSON
REQUESTED Y/N [Y]
Details of nominated person
Theresa Whyte (Sister)

APPROPRIATE ADULT Y/N [N]

INTERPRETER Y/N [N]
Notices served & grounds for detention explained in the presence of Appropriate Adult/Interpreter

Signature of A/Adult

Time: Date:

Surname: **WHYTE**

Previous Name:

Forenames: **LENNY**

Address: **4A
LYMEWOOD COURT
PARKDALE
LYME**

Telephone

Occupation: **NONE**
Age: **27**   Date of Birth: **27/6/-**

Place of Birth: **LONDON**

Height: **5** Feet: **11** Inches: Sex: **M**

Arrested by:
Name: DS S Farrington
ID. No: 4291
Station: Lyme Street
Place of Arrest: 4a Lymewood Court, Lyme

	Time	Date
Arrested at:	15.30	19/3/-
Arrived at Station	16.10	19/3/-

Officer In Case:
Id. No: 4291
Name: DS Farrington

Officer Opening Custody Record

Signature: Mike Williams

Id No: 4231
Name: Sgt M Williams

CHARGES(S)

Custody No. 2305/05

Surname **WHYTE**
Forename (s) **LENNY**
Address **4A Lymewood Court** 　　　**Parkdale** 　　　**Lyme**
Postcode

Station: Lyme

Sex M/F (M)

D.O.B 27/6/-

ID Code: 1

Language: None

You are charged with the offence(s) shown below. You do not have to say anything. But it may harm your defence if you do not mention now something which you later rely on in court. Anything you do say may be given in evidence.

Consec. No.	Charge(s)
1.	That on the 17th March having entered as a trespasser a building, being a dwelling known as 19 Sunrise Road, Lyme you stole £75 in money property belonging to Lillian Kennedy contrary to s. 9(1)(b) Theft Act 1968
2.	That on the 19th March you unlawfully had in your possession a controlled drug of Class C namely cannabis, contrary to section 5(2) Misuse of Drugs Act 1971

Time and Date of Charge: 20th March   12.45hrs
Reply (if any): "you are racist pigs you lot are."

Signed (person charged)	Signed (appropriate adult)			
Officer charging Surname Farrington	Rank DS	No.4291	Station: Lyme St
Officer in case Surname	Rank	No.	Station
Charge accepted Surname	Rank	No.	Station

Appearing at LYME REMAND COURT at LYME SQUARE, LYME on the 20/3/   at 1400 hours

LYMESHIRE POLICE
DETAINED PERSONS MEDICAL FORM

Custody Ref: 2305/05

Name: Lenny Whyte   DOB: 27/6/-   Time/Date: 20/3/-

Reason Doctor requested:
Detainee telling me he felt claustrophobic and needed to take medication for depression

VISUAL ASSESSMENT BY CUSTODY SERGEANT

Cut/Abrasion ~   Bruising o   Other Suspected Injury +

Front   Back

ADMINISTRATION AND MOVEMENT TIMES

	Time	Date
Doctor called	0700	20/3/-
Doctor replied		
Agreed Arrival Time		
Doctor Arrived	0745	20/3/-
Departure/Conclusion		
Ambulance Called		
Ambulance Arrived		
Detainee taken to Hospital		Time/Date

Police-Signs/symptoms & First Aid given:
Observed detainee seemed very fidgety

By whom:

DOCTORS OPINION OR TELEPHONE ADVICE (NON-CONFIDENTIAL)

Name of Doctor: Dr Ghulam

Time/Date of Examination: 20/3/- 0800 hrs

Opinion: Anxious but lucid in thought. Orientated in time and space. Takes regular medication for manic depression

Medical Advice: Medicate per prescription

Examination/Observation: Completed/Refused   Risk of Self Harm: High/Medium/Standard

Location of Examination: Medical room/Cell/Other   Station: Lyme Street

RECOMMENDATIONS

	Yes	No		Yes	No
Recommended appropriate adult:		*	Medical review Required		*
Fit to be detained:	*		Time/Date required:		
			Time/Date carried Out:		
Fit for interview:	*				
Fit for transfer					
Fit for charge:					

Doctors Signature:
Ghulam

LYMESHIRE POLICE

Station: **LYME STREET**	Detained Person Serial No: **2305/05**

Surname: **WHYTE**
Forenames: **LENNY**

Last Review of detention conducted at:

Date	Time	Details of Action/Occurrence	
19/3/-	1630	Phone call to DP's sister 821249 (no contact made no answering machine). DP informed.	MW
	1700	DP accepted hot drink.	MW
	1730	DP taken meal – refused.	MW
	1800	DP seen in cell – in order.	MW
	1815	DP consents to taking saliva swab-non-intimate	MW
	1816	'I consent to providing a sample of my saliva.' Lenny Whyte	
	1830	DP taken to Identification suite for photographing and parade compilation.	MW
	1930	DP returned to my custody – placed in Cell F4.	MW
	1935	DP given a cup of tea – asking for cigarette.	MW
	1955	DP uses toilet.	MW
	2015	In cell awake and pacing.	MW

LYMESHIRE POLICE

Station: **LYME STREET**	Detained Person Serial No: **2305/05**

Surname: **WHYTE**
Forenames: **LENNY**

Last Review of detention conducted at:

Date	Time	Details of Action/Occurrence	
19/3/-	2030	In cell awake – muttering to himself.	MW
	2100	Banging on cell – uses toilet.	MW
	2130	In cell-pacing – requests cigarette-refused.	MW
	2200	In cell – in order. Custody transferred to Sgt Tom Slater	MW
	2230	In cell – sitting on bed wringing hands.	TS
	2300	In cell – in order.	TS
	2330	In cell – pacing.	TS
	2345	Detention reviewed. DP informed. Given refreshment.	TS
	2359	DP – on bed awake.	TS
20/3/-	0015	DP in cell pacing. Requests cigarette.	TS
	0045	On bed – suspect rocking to and fro. Asked if okay to see if okay. Requested more blankets supplied. DP informed me he wanted to sleep.	TS

LYMESHIRE POLICE

Station: **LYME STREET**	Detained Person Serial No: **2305/05**

Surname: **WHYTE** Forenames: **LENNY**

Last Review of detention conducted at:

Date	Time	Details of Action/Occurrence	
20/3/-	0115	DP in cell – awake. In order.	TS
	0145	DP in cell – uses toilet.	TS
	0215	DP in cell – asleep.	TS
	0245	DP – awake lying on bed.	TS
	0315	DP seen pacing in cell.	TS
	0345	DP awake – humming to himself.	TS
	0415	DP lying on bed – in order.	TS
	0445	DP awake – sitting on bed.	TS
	0515	DP taken to toilet.	TS
	0545	DP in cell pacing.	TS

LYMESHIRE POLICE

Station: **LYME STREET**	Detained Person Serial No: **2305/05**

Surname: **WHYTE**
Forenames: **LENNY**

Last Review of detention conducted at:

<u>Date</u>	<u>Time</u>	<u>Details of Action/Occurrence</u>	
20/3/-	0603	DP complains of feeling unwell. Requests doctor.	TS
	0610	Transferred into custody of Sgt Brough.	DB
	0630	DP offered breakfast. Informed by DP that his regular medication for depression is at home. FME requested. Officer dispatched to DP's house to locate medication.	DB
	0645	DP uses toilet. Informed GP requested to attend.	DB
	0710	Review of detention. DP informed.	DB
	0740	DP taken to medical room for examination by Dr Ghulam	DB
	0800	Dr Ghulam completes report – medication administered to DP who is fit to be interviewed. DP taken back to cell F4.	DB
	0815	DP in cell. In order.	
	0900	DP offered refreshment. Requests cigarette.	DB
	0915	DP informed of intention to interview – asked if requires	

LYMESHIRE POLICE

Station: **LYME STREET**	Detained Person Serial No: **2305/05**

Surname: **WHYTE** Forenames: **LENNY**

Last Review of detention conducted at:

Date	Time	Details of Action/Occurrence	
20/3/-		solicitor – refused.	DB
	0930	DP in cell. In order.	DB
	1000	DP asking when interview will be.	DB
	1030	DP in cell – agitated-pacing.	DB
	1045	DP in cell – allowed to use toilet.	DB
	1100	DP in cell pacing.	DB
	1115	DP given to the custody of DS Farrington and taken to interview room 2.	DB
	1230	Returned to my custody.	DB
20/3/-	1245	DP charged and documented. Bail refused on grounds of risk of absconding and commission of further offences. DP's sister contacted and informed. DP allowed to speak with sister.	DB
	1300	Into custody of Premier for transport to Lyme MC.	DB

DOCUMENT 12   LIST OF PREVIOUS CONVICTIONS FOR LENNY WHYTE

Print of PNC Record-PNCID: 005/6593V

Print For: WHYTE, LENNY

Date of Birth: 27/6/-

Date	Court	Offence/s	Sentence
10 years previous	Lyme Youth Court	Burglary (domestic dwelling)	Supervision Order (12 months)
7 years previous	Lyme Magistrates	Theft	Conditional Discharge (12 months)
5 years previous (February)	Blurton Magistrates	Theft Possession of amphetamine Driving without insurance	Community Rehabilitation Order (15 months)/ Licence endorsed
5 years previous (December)	Lyme Magistrates	Burglary (non-dwelling) Possession of class B drug Resisting constable Failure to surrender Breach community order	Custody 5 months concurrent
4 years previous	Chorley Magistrates	Possession of class B drug Theft Obtaining property by deception	Community Rehabilitation Order (12 months)
3 years previous (August)	Lyme Crown Court	Burglary (domestic dwelling) Possession of class A drug Failure to surrender	Custody 12 months concurrent
2 years previous (April)	Blurton Magistrates	Theft Possession of class B drug	Custody 4 months concurrent + unexpired term 108 days
18 months previous	Lyme Magistrates	s. 4 Public Order Act 1986 Common Assault	Community Order (24 months)

DOCUMENT 13   RECORD OF ATTENDANCE AT SECOND APPEARANCE HEARING

File note – 7th March

Attending Lyme Magistrates' Court for Lenny's second appearance.

Prosecution not in a position to provide a full file so no progress made as to venue for trial.

I made a second full application for bail on Lenny's behalf. Bail was once more refused on the grounds of the risk of absconding and committing of further offences.

Spoke to Lenny after the hearing and we agreed I would appeal the refusal of bail to the Crown Court.

Time engaged:
Advocacy 30 minutes
Waiting 10 minutes
Attending client 30 minutes
Travel to and from court 15 minutes
Preparing Notice of Appeal 15 minutes

online resource centre

You can see Lenny's contested application for bail in the video section of our Online Resource Centre. A transcript, broadly based on the hearing, appears at Document 14. We would ask you to note that when filming the application for bail we had made the assumption that this was Lenny's second appearance before magistrates (having been remanded in custody for eight days following his initial appearance) and that the CPS had served advance information on the defence.

The documented version of this case study has the mode of trial enquiry coming later than Lenny's second appearance before magistrates which more accurately reflects the position in real life as it generally takes the prosecution longer than eight days to provide a full file!

DOCUMENT 17   RECORD OF CROWN COURT BAIL HEARING

File Note – 4th April

Attending Lyme Crown Court. Appearing before Mr Recorder Jay. Making a further application for bail on behalf of Lenny Whyte. Bail was opposed by the CPS. Lenny was granted conditional bail as follows:

1. He resides at 4A Lymewood Court.

2. He reports to Lyme Street Police Station Mon/Wed/Friday 2–3pm.

3. He does not attempt to contact in any way Lillian Kennedy, Shirley Lewis or Harold Finney.

4. He does not go in to Sunrise Road or on the fields at the back of Sunrise Road.

Telephoning Lenny's sister to relay the good news. Explained he would be released and that I would be writing to him to stress the importance of abiding by bail conditions. Reminded her that Lenny was due to appear before Lyme Magistrates' on the 24th April.

Time engaged:
Advocacy 30 minutes
Waiting 5 minutes
Travel to and from court 15 minutes.

NB: Solicitor would need to write to Lenny advising him of his change in bail status and the importance of abiding by the conditions of his bail.

DOCUMENT 18A   WITNESS STATEMENT: LILLIAN KENNEDY

WITNESS STATEMENT

(CJ Act 1967, s. 9; MC Act 1980, s. 5A(3)(a) and s. 5B; MC Rules 1981, r. 70)

Name	Lillian Kennedy
Address	Supplied
Age/Date of Birth	Over 18
Occupation	Retired

Who states:

This statement, consisting of one page signed by me, is true to the best of my knowledge and belief and I make it knowing that if it is tendered in evidence I shall be liable to prosecution if I have wilfully stated in it anything which I know to be false or do not believe to be true.

Dated: 18th March   Signed: L Kennedy

I live at number 19 Sunrise Road, Lyme. I am 85 years old. On Tuesday the 17th March, I went to fetch my pension from Lyme High Street. I drew £95.00. Once I had paid my weekly sums for gas and electricity I was left with around £75. I got home at around 11 am. As I was walking up the road, a man approached me and asked me if I wanted any help with my shopping. I told him, no thank you. I would describe him as being quite tall and thin. He had a gaunt face, was black and had long, black straggling hair and a small beard on his chin. I think he was wearing a short, dark coloured top and a pair of white sports shoes. I saw him walk off into the fields near the back of my house.

I know I had my purse with me when I went into my house, because a friend of mine called in for 10 minutes, shortly after I got back from the Post Office. She had her grandchild with her and I gave her a pound from my purse. A short time after this I was putting some rubbish out when I thought I heard the telephone ringing. When I came in, I realised it was my front door bell. I answered the door. There was a man standing there. I have never seen this man before. He was white but had a tanned complexion. He was dressed smartly, wearing a suit and tie. He was quite bald. He wasn't very tall. I recall he was wearing glasses. He told me his car had broken down and asked if he could use the telephone. I told him he could not as I didn't have a phone. Not long after this a friend of my neighbour came round. She told me she had seen a black man in my back garden and that my back door was open. I immediately checked my handbag and saw that my purse was missing. She telephoned the police. I realised that I had left the back door open when I came to answer the front door. It was silly of me. The only money I get is my pension. The incident has left me shaken and frightened.

Later in the afternoon of the 17th March, the police took me around the local area in one of their cars. They asked me if I could see the man who had knocked on my front door. I couldn't see the man who had called but I did see the man who had offered to help me with my shopping earlier that morning. The police car stopped outside the Co-op on the High Street. I had a good look at the man and I am sure it was him.

Signed: Lillian Kennedy

DOCUMENT 18B   WITNESS STATEMENT: SHIRLEY LEWIS

WITNESS STATEMENT

(CJ Act 1967, s. 9; MC Act 1980, s. 5A(3)(a) and s. 5B; MC Rules 1981, r. 70)

Name	Shirley Lewis
Address	Supplied
Age/Date of Birth	Over 18
Occupation	Retired Teacher

Who states:

This statement, consisting of one page signed by me, is true to the best of my knowledge and belief, and I make it knowing that if it is tendered in evidence I shall be liable to prosecution if I have wilfully stated in it anything which I know to be false or do not believe to be true.

Dated: 18th March   Signed: S Lewis

On Tuesday the 17th March, I was visiting my elderly aunt at 19 Sunrise Road, Lyme. She lives next door to Lillian Kennedy at number 17. At around midday on Tuesday 17th March, I went out the back of my aunt's property to bring some washing in that was pegged up on the washing line. The time was around midday.

I was facing Lillian's back garden. A low wall divides the gardens, it being largely open plan. I saw a man in her garden. I watched him for a good few seconds. In fact I nearly called out to him, to ask what he thought he was doing, but something stopped me. He didn't see me because I was behind a large sheet pegged on the line. I don't know where he came from but I watched him wander out of Lillian's garden and off down the back lane. At this point I noticed the back door to Mrs Kennedy's house was open.

I would describe the man as being of Afro-Caribbean origin. He was about 5ft 8/9 in tall. He was of slim build and was wearing a black hooded sweatshirt with the hood up, so I could not see his hair. The man I saw was wearing a pair of white training shoes. I went round to see Lillian almost straight away and she told me that her purse was missing. I am certain I would be able to recognise the man again. I had the distinct feeling I had seen the man before. In fact I have seen him walking his dog, a brown and white terrier, in the grassy area nearby, on more than one occasion.

Signed: Shirley Lewis

DOCUMENT 18C   WITNESS STATEMENT: HAROLD FINNEY

WITNESS STATEMENT

(CJ Act 1967, s. 9; MC Act 1980, s. 5A(3)(a) and s. 5B; MC Rules 1981, r. 70)

Name	Harold Finney
Address	Withheld
Age/Date of Birth	Over 18
Occupation	Retired Engineer

Who states:

This statement, consisting of one page signed by me, is true to the best of my knowledge, and belief and I make it knowing that if it is tendered in evidence I shall be liable to prosecution if I have wilfully stated in it anything which I know to be false or do not believe to be true.

Dated: 18th March   Signed: H Finney

I have lived in Sunrise Road for the past five years. I am a member of the local area neighbourhood watch scheme. On Tuesday the 17th March, at around 11.30am, I observed a black car drive into Sunrise Road, Lyme, and park. I could not see anyone in the car because the windows were dark. The car remained parked in the road for 15 minutes or so. I started to get suspicious and took a note of the registration number. It was DY 01 5JT. About five minutes after I first noticed the car I saw a man walking past my window. I watched him go over to the car and get in. The telephone rang at this point and I did not see the man again. I was on the telephone for some time. When I went to look out of my window at around midday, I saw the black car driving off.

I would describe the man I saw getting into the car as being black and in his twenties. He was tall and thin. He was black and had long, dark hair. He was wearing a short black top and a pair of white training shoes.

Signed: H Finney

DOCUMENT 18D   WITNESS STATEMENT SGT S FARRINGTON

WITNESS STATEMENT

(CJ Act 1967, s. 9; MC Act 1980, s. 5A(3)(a) and s. 5B; MC Rules 1981, r. 70)

Name	Steven Farrington
Address	Lyme Street Police Station
Age/Date of Birth	Over 18
Occupation	Detective Sergeant

Who states:

This statement, consisting of one page signed by me, is true to the best of my knowledge and belief, and I make it knowing that if it is tendered in evidence I shall be liable to prosecution if I have wilfully stated in it anything which I know to be false or do not believe to be true.

Dated: 20th March   Signed: S Farrington

On the 17th March I, in the company of Detective Constable Andrew Shaw, attended the home of Lillian Kennedy at 19 Sunrise Road, Lyme. Mrs Kennedy is an 85-year-old widow. From our enquiries it was ascertained that Mrs Kennedy's purse had been stolen, containing her pension money of £75.00 in cash.

As a result of our enquires, during the afternoon of March 17th, we took Lillian Kennedy on a tour of the locality in an unmarked police car, to see if she could possibly spot the person or persons suspected of carrying out the burglary. In the course of the tour of the local area, Mrs Kennedy drew our attention to a man of Afro-Carribean origin. The man was 5 ft 10 in and of slim build. He had shoulder-length, dreadlocked hair and a slight goatee beard. He was wearing a black hooded sweatshirt and black jogging bottoms. He was wearing a pair of brown training shoes. My colleague Detective Constable Shaw recognised the man as Lenny Whyte. Mrs Kennedy was quite adamant that Lenny Whyte was the man who had approached her in her street a short time before the burglary and who had offered to help her with her shopping before disappearing behind the back of Sunrise Road. Mrs Kennedy observed Lenny Whyte in good light for a minute or two before confirming his identification.

A decision was taken not to arrest Lenny Whyte at this time as further enquires were being pursued in connection with a possible accomplice.

At 09.30 hours on the 18th March, Lloyd Green was arrested in connection with the burglary. He was taken to Lyme Street Police Station where his detention was authorised. A video identification was convened but Mrs Kennedy failed to identify Lloyd Green. Mr Green was released on police bail at 15.30 hours on the 19th March.

At 15.15 hours on the 19th March, Lenny Whyte was approached by me and Detective Constable Shaw just outside his flat at 4a Lymewood Court. Mr Whyte was arrested and cautioned. A search of his flat was conducted pursuant to s. 32 PACE. In his presence, I seized a black hooded sweatshirt (Exhibit SF1) and a pair of size 9 white Nike training shoes were also seized (right shoe-exhibit number SF2 and left shoe exhibit number SF3). In the course of searching Lenny Whyte, a quantity of cannabis resin was found (exhibit SF4) in his trouser pocket.

Lenny Whyte became obstructive at which point he was handcuffed and placed in the back of a police car. He was then taken to Lyme Police Station where his detention was authorised in accordance with the Police and Criminal Act 1984. A sample of saliva was taken from Mr Whyte (Exhibit SF5).

Lenny Whyte was detained overnight. On the 20th March, Lenny Whyte was identified in the course of a video parade by a neighbour who lives near to the victim's burgled property, as the man she had seen in Lillian Kennedy's back garden at around midday on the 17th March.

Whyte was certified fit to be interviewed by a police doctor. Declining the services of the solicitor, Whyte was interviewed the following day. The interview lasted 46 minutes. One tape was used during the interview and a copy of the sealed tape is available (exhibit SF6).

In the course of the interview Whyte admitted he had entered Mrs Kennedy's house and stole £75. At the conclusion of the interview Leonard Whyte was charged with burglary and cautioned.

MrWhyte was denied police bail and was escorted to Lyme Magistrates' Court.

Signed: Sgt S Farrington 4291

RECORD OF INTERVIEW

Person interviewed: LENNY WHYTE

Place of interview: LYME STREET

Date of interview: 20/3/-

Time commenced: 1130 HRS

Time concluded: 1216 HRS

Duration of interview: 46 MINUTES

Interviewing officer(s): DS 4291 FARRINGTON/DC 2890 SARAH SHAW

Other persons present: NONE

Tape reference number: 21 /SF/59217/03/-

Exhibit Number: SF6

Policy Exhibit No:	
No of pages: (3, as reproduced)	
Signature of interviewing officer producing exhibit	
DS S Farrington	

Tape counter Times(s)	Person speaking	Text
0000		Normal introductions were made and the interviewee was reminded of his legal rights and cautioned.
		The officer said WHYTE was under arrest in relation to a burglary at 19 Sunrise Road in Lyme.
0148	Sgt Farr.	Before we begin, Lenny, I just want to check you feel well enough to be interviewed. Do you feel OK?
0159	R	Just tired, okay okay.
0210	Sgt Farr.	Are you happy to be interviewed without a solicitor?
0218	R	Yea.
0245	Sgt Farr.	I want to ask you about your whereabouts between 11 and 1pm on Tuesday the 17th March. Can you remember where you were and what you were doing?
0300	R	The usual routine. You know what I mean man?
	Sgt Farr.	What is your usual routine Lenny?
	R	(Suspect sits in silence)
0345	Sgt Farr.	I think lad, you'd better take the situation you're in a bit more seriously don't you?
0400	R	Yeah, yeah-you lot got it in for me.
0430	Sgt Farr.	You understand that you have been arrested in connection with a burglary at 19 Sunrise Road. The victim is an elderly woman and someone has stolen her pension.
0500	R	Yeah, yeah. (Suspect starts shaking his head.) Can I have a cigarette? I need a smoke. This needs sorting, right – got things that need sorting, right.
0525	Sgt Farr.	As soon as this interview is over and you start to answer my questions the sooner you can have a cigarette. Do you know the area around Sunrise Road?
0600	R	Yeah.
0624	Sgt Farr.	Did you go into Sunrise Road on the 17th March?
0635	R	No.

0702	Sgt Farr.	The old lady who was burgled has pointed you out as the man who approached her in Sunrise Road at around 11.30am and offered her help with her shopping. Was that you Lenny because she says it was?
0745	R	What day is it today?
0800	Sgt Farr.	It's Thursday – now just answer the question Lenny – the sooner we get your account the sooner this process will be over.
1100		Are we just going to sit here in silence Lenny?
1110		(Suspect stands up and starts pacing.) Sit down Lenny. The old lady describes the man who approached her in her street at around 11 or so as being a black youth, quite tall, with dreadlocks, wearing a short dark top and wearing white trainers. Would you accept that that description matches you?
1204	R	Don't know what you're getting at – don't know
1227	Sgt Farr.	The old lady was taken on a tour of the High Street to see if she could see the man who had approached her earlier that morning. She pointed you out to us. You were seen wearing a dark hooded top. I will ask you again were you in Sunrise Road at anytime on the morning of 17th March? (Suspect starts pacing.) Sit down Lenny and answer the question. (Reply inaudible.)
1312		We have another eyewitness, Lenny, who has identified you near the back door of the old lady's house at just after midday on the 17th March. She has given us a clear description of the person she saw. She states she saw a man of Afro-Caribbean origin in the old lady's garden near the open back door. She describes the man has having pointy features, wearing a black hooded top with the hood up. Her description matches your appearance. She has subsequently identified you at a video identification parade. I am going to ask you again, can you tell me where you were between 11 and 1pm on Tuesday the 17th March?
1506	R	(Suspect makes no reply. Refuses to look at me.)
1724	Sgt Farr.	Are these your trainers Lenny? (Suspect shown a pair of white Nike training shoes.) (Stop tapping the table Lenny.)
1806	R	Not mine, no way.
1815	Sgt Farr.	Well they were found in your flat, amongst your other footwear. You see, all the eyewitnesses describe seeing a man matching your appearance, wearing a pair of white trainers. They are all very clear about this, and it so happens that you have a pair of white trainers in your flat. Were you wearing these trainers on the morning of the 17th March?
1950	R	(Inaudible reply.)
2000	Sgt Farr.	You take a shoe size 9 don't you Lenny? These are a size 9. Are these your shoes?
2030	R	They ain't mine. Someone must have left them at my place.
2057	Sgt Farr.	Has anyone stayed at your flat recently?
2103	R	Come on, let's get this sorted. I've got big things to do.
2218	Sgt Farr.	When you were arrested you were found in possession of a quantity of cannabis. Are you using drugs at the moment Lenny?
2228	R	(No reply.) (Suspect rocking the table, asked to desist.)
2330	Sgt Farr.	Do you know a man by the name of Lloyd Green?
2400	R	I know who you are talking about right-he ain't no mate of mine.

2459	Sgt Farr.	Would it surprise you to learn that a car registered to him was seen in Sunrise Road at around 11.30am on Tuesday the 17th March?
2502	R	No reply
2613	Sgt Farr.	We have an eyewitness who describes a man just like you approaching Lloyd Green's car in Sunrise Road sometime before midday. I suggest that man was you. What do you have to say?
2640	R	Look – fuck you. I need a cigarette. I ain't into robbing no old woman right. I don't understand this. I don't understand all this.
2705	Sgt Farr.	Why did you need to speak with Lloyd Green, Lenny?
2804	R	(No reply.)
2905	Sgt Farr.	I will ask you again Lenny – was it you seen talking to Lloyd Green?
3000	R	(No reply.)
3104	Sgt Farr.	Is Lloyd Green putting pressure on you Lenny? Do you owe him money?
3219	R	(Suspect makes no reply.)
3315	Sgt Farr.	Look at me, Lenny. This is your chance to offer an explanation. Is there anything you wish to tell me?
3510	R	How much longer are you keeping me here? I've gotta go. I've got things to do – important things. You're fitting me up anyway like you always do.
3609	Sgt Farr.	I can't say how much longer you will be here Lenny. That's up to you.
3720	R	Don't know nothing right about Lloyd Green.
4010	Sgt Farr	Shall I tell you what I think? I think you owe Lloyd Green money. He wants it and wants it now. He tells you to get it or else. You don't have any so either you or he decides you should steal it. You know the area. You agree he will knock on the door of the old lady you saw earlier. When she is distracted, you will break in and see what you can get your hands on. Nice and easy. Is that how it happened?
4202	R	(No reply.)
4230	Sgt Farr.	Look Lenny – this is a serious matter. How do you explain the evidence against you? The eyewitness who has identified you, the white training shoes found in your flat which all the eyewitnesses makes reference to and the fact that you have admitted knowing Lloyd Green. Is it all coincidence Lenny?
44 06	R	Alright, I stole it from the old lady yea. I needed the money right. He wanted it. Now fucking charge me and let me get out of here.
4440	Sgt Farr.	Calm down Lenny and sit down. There is no need to get uptight. Who was your accomplice Lenny? Who distracted the lady at her front door?
4500	R	I am not saying anything more. Charge me if you are going to and let me out of here. I ain't saying nothing more.
4530	Sgt Farr.	Did someone put you under pressure to commit this burglary? Was it Lloyd Green? Is he your supplier?
4600	R	(No reply.)

Suspect continues to be uncooperative and verbally abusive. Interview terminated at 46 minutes.

DOCUMENT 18F FURTHER WITNESS STATEMENT OF SHIRLY LEWIS

WITNESS STATEMENT

(CJ Act 1967, s. 9; MC Act 1980, s. 5A(3)(a) and s. 5B; MC Rules 1981, r. 70)

Name	Shirley Lewis
Address	Supplied
Age/Date of Birth	Over 18
Occupation	Retired Teacher

Who states:

This statement (consisting of one page signed each by me) is true to the best of my knowledge and belief and I make it knowing that if it is tendered in evidence I shall be liable to prosecution if I have wilfully stated in it anything which I know to be false or do not believe to be true.

Dated: 20th March
Signature: S Lewis

I reside at the address shown overleaf.

I have been asked to view a video identification parade as a result of an incident that I witnessed on the 17th March, when at the home of my aunt at 19 Sunrise Road Lyme. The incident occurred at around midday on the 17th March.

On the 20th March, I was at the Identification Suite at Lyme Police Station when I was shown a Video Identification Parade.

- After viewing the Video Parade, I identified the person at position No 4 on the Video

I can confirm that before viewing the Video Parade I was supervised by WPC Khan who informed me that I was not allowed to discuss the incident with any other person, including any other witness, and that no such conversation took place. I have not seen any broadcast or published films or photographs, or any descriptions relating to the offence for which I am a witness.

Signature: S Lewis

DOCUMENT 18G   FURTHER WITNESS STATEMENT OF HAROLD FINNEY

WITNESS STATEMENT

(CJ Act 1967, s. 9; MC Act 1980, s. 5A(3)(a) and s. 5B; MC Rules 1981, r. 70)

Name	Harold Finney
Address	Withheld
Age/Date of Birth	Over 18
Occupation	Retired Engineer

Who states:

This statement, consisting of one page signed by me, is true to the best of my knowledge and belief, and I make it knowing that if it is tendered in evidence I shall be liable to prosecution if I have wilfully stated in it anything which I know to be false or do not believe to be true.

Dated: 20th March
Signature: H Finney

I reside at the address shown overleaf.

As a result of an incident that I witnessed on the 17th March when I saw a black man approach a car in Sunrise Road at around 11.50am. On the 20th March I was at the Identification Suite at Lyme Police Station when I was shown a Video Identification Parade.

- After viewing the Video Parade, I identified the person at position No 2 on the Video

I can confirm that before viewing the Video Parade I was supervised by WPC Khan who informed me that I was not allowed to discuss the incident with any other person, including any other witness, and that no such conversation took place. I have not seen any broadcast or published films or photographs, or any descriptions relating to the offence for which I am a witness.

Signature: H Finney

WITNESS STATEMENT

(CJ Act 1967, s. 9; MC Act 1980, s. 5A(3)(a) and s. 5B; MC Rules 1981, r. 70)

Name	Lillian Kennedy
Address	Supplied
Age/Date of Birth	Over 18
Occupation	Retired

Who states:

This statement, consisting of one page signed by me, is true to the best of my knowledge and belief, and I make it knowing that if it is tendered in evidence I shall be liable to prosecution if I have wilfully stated in it anything which I know to be false or do not believe to be true.

Dated: 20th March
Signature: L Kennedy

I reside at the address shown overleaf.

As a result of an incident that I witnessed on the 17th March when I was approached by a black man in the street where I live in Sunrise Road, I was at the Identification Suite at Lyme Police Station when I was shown a Video Identification Parade.

- After viewing the Video Parade, I identified the person at position No 2 on the Video
- I was unable to identify any person

I can confirm that before viewing the Video Parade I was supervised by WPC Khan who informed me that I was not allowed to discuss the incident with any other person, including any other witness, and that no such conversation took place. I have not seen any broadcast or published films or photographs, or any descriptions relating to the offence for which I am a witness.

Signature: L Kennedy

DOCUMENT 180   WITNESS STATEMENT OF SCIENTIFIC SUPPORT OFFICER

WITNESS STATEMENT

(CJ Act 1967, s. 9; MC Act 1980, s. 5A(3)(a) and s. 5B; MC Rules 1981, r. 70)

Statement of: Carol Jayne Lawton   Title

Age if under 18: Over 18   Occupation: Scenes of Crime Officer

This statement (consisting of 2 pages signed each by me) is true to the best of my knowledge and belief and I make it knowing that if it is tendered in evidence I shall be liable to prosecution if I have wilfully stated in it anything which I know to be false or do not believe to be true.

Dated: 20th March

Signature: Carol Lawton

I am a Scientific Support Officer employed by Lymeshire Police based at Lyme Street Police Station. At 14.30 hours on the 17th March, as a result of a message received, I attended 19 Sunrise Road, Lyme. The property is a house in a residential area and is occupied by an elderly female who lives alone. At the side of the house there is a concrete porch area which is covered from the elements by an enclosed carport. Access to the carport can be gained from the front of the property and from the rear. Access from the rear of the property involves waking through a garden which contains soil beds. The soil beds were wet from a heavy downpour of rain during the night and the preceding days. While I was in the garden area I noticed several footprints on soil beds. I conducted a visual examination of the concrete porch area leading up to the back door of the property and discovered several shoeprints bearing slight soil deposits.

While I was there I took certain photographs, some of which were duplicated, from which an album of prints has been produced marked CJL1, which I would describe as follows:

CJL1 (Shoe marks)   Album of Prints (Exhibit No)

Photo 1 View of the backdoor of the back door of 19 Sunrise Road, Lyme

Photo 2 View of the car port from the garden gate of 19 Sunrise Road, Lyme

Photo 3 View of concrete porch

Photo 4 View of shoe mark on concrete

Photo 5 View of shoe mark on concrete

Photo 6 View of shoe mark on concrete

Photo 7 View of shoe mark on concrete

Photo 8 View of CJL2 and CJL3 (Exhibit No   ) in place before being lifted.

All negatives are filed at the Chief Constables office bearing reference number LP-200510965-0971.

During the course of my examination, I retained the following items, and packaged and labelled them as follows:

CJL 2 Shoe mark 16 cm from backdoor of property electro statically lifted

CJL 3 Shoe mark 8 cm from backdoor of property electro statically lifted

The above items were retained in my possession until I retuned to the Scenes of Crime store. I placed items CJL 2 and CJL 3 into a laboratory sack and sealed it with a tag number B8760456. I placed the sack in the secure Scenes of Crime Store.

At 1700 hours on the 19th March, while on duty at Lyme Street police station, I attended the property store. There I took possession of the following items from reference number 256/789432:

SF2   Left white Nike training shoe (Exhibit No . . . .)

SF3   Right white Nike training shoe (Exhibit No . . . .)

I placed SF2 into a laboratory sack and sealed it with tag number B49304667. I placed the sack into the secure Scenes of Crime store. I placed SF3 into a laboratory sack and sealed it with tag number B49304668. I placed both sacks into the secure Scenes of Crime store.

At 1845 on the 19th March, I attended Lyme Street Custody Suite from where I collected the following item, labelled as:

SF5 (Exhibit no   ) DNA mouth swab (x2).

I placed this item into a transit sack which I then sealed with tag no B986740.

All the transit sacks collected in conjunction with this investigation were left in secure and appropriate storage within Lyme Street Scenes of Crime Department for collection and then onward delivery to the Forensic Science Laboratory.

Signature CJ Lawton SOCO 6512

DOCUMENT 18P   WITNESS STATEMENT OF FORENSIC SCIENTIST

Laboratory Reference: 500 679 4033
Order Reference: 400 593 1297
The Forensic Science Service

DS Steve Farrington
Lyme Street Policing Unit
Lymeshire Police

Client Reference: URN 05/2218

WITNESS STATEMENT

(CJ Act 1967, s. 9; MC Act 1980, s. 5A(3)(a) and s. 5B; MC Rules 1981, r. 70)

Statement of: Sarah Hardacker BSc (Hons)

Age of Witness: Over 18

Morley Laboratory, Forensic Science Service, Belfield House, Nile Street, Birmingham.

This statement (consisting of four pages signed each by me) is true to the best of my knowledge and belief, and I make it knowing that if it is tendered in evidence I shall be liable to prosecution if I have wilfully stated in it anything which I know to be false or do not believe to be true.

Date: 25th March   Signature: S Hardacker

DEFENDANT: LEONARD WHYTE

I hold the degree of Bachelor of Science with an Honours Degree in Applied Biochemistry and have worked as a Forensic Scientist since 1995. During this time I have dealt with many investigations involving footwear.

RECEIPT OF ITEMS

Records show that on the 20th March amongst other items, the 4 items described below relating to an investigation of a burglary at domestic premises in Lyme were received at the Morely laboratory of the Forensic Science Service from Lymeshire Police.

<u>From 19 Sunrise Road, Lyme</u>

CJL 2 Electrostatic shoeprint lift

CJL 3 Electrostatic shoeprint lift

<u>From Lenny Whyte</u>

FS 2   Left white training shoe

FS 3   Right white training shoe.

BACKGROUND INFORMATION

From the information provided by the Police, I understand the following:

On the 17th March a burglary occurred at 19 Sunrise Road, Lyme. Entry to the property was gained through an unlocked backdoor while the sole occupant of the property was distracted by a caller at the front door.

A subsequent Scene of Crime examination recovered footwear marks on a concrete surface near to the backdoor of the property. The shoeprints are believed to belong to the offender.

Lenny WHYTE was arrested on the 19 Sunrise Road and following a search of his home address 4A Lymewood Court, Lyme a pair of white size 9 white Nike trainers were recovered.

This is the information on which I have based my examination and have used in the interpretation of the findings.

PURPOSE OF EXAMINATION

To determine whether or not the recovered training shoes relating to Lenny WHYTE have made the footwear marks recovered from 19 Sunrise Road, Lyme.

LABORATORY EXAMINATION

With this aim in mind, the following items have been examined:-

Re: 4A Lymewood Court, Lyme (relating to Lenny WHYTE)

FS2 and FS3 – Pair of Nike white training shoes

Re: 19 Sunrise Road, Lyme

CJL 2 – Footwear lifts from concrete porch

CJL 3 – Footware lifts from concrete porch

These items have been examined with the help of scientific assistants, details of which are noted on the Forensic Examination Record, SH/FER/1 that accompanies this statement. Details of the examination are documented in the case notes which can be inspected at the laboratory under order number **400 593 1297**.

TECHNICAL ISSUES

When a person steps onto a surface, a mark may be left of the under-surface of their footwear. This footwear impression will persist for a long time if left undisturbed. It may be preserved, recovered and enhanced in order to facilitate a detailed comparison, at the Forensic Science Laboratory, between it and test impressions taken from the suspect's shoes. Details such as pattern, general size and degree of wear can be compared. Additionally, any marks in the scene impression that correspond to damage features on the under-sole of the shoe can provide conclusive evidence to connect that particular shoe to the scene. Any such footwear marks can be compared with any recovered items of footwear.

RESULTS OF EXAMINATION

Re: Lenny WHYTE

The training shoes (SF2 and SF3) are a pair of size 9 Nike with a sole pattern of zigzag fine bars and blocks. The soles of the training shoes are worn, with damage evident on both of the soles. The sole pattern of these boots is only one of a vast range of sole patterns available on sports/casual footwear and is one of the more frequently encountered patterns at the laboratory. On the right shoe there is a cut measuring 3 mm.

Re: CJL 2 and CJL 3

Items are two photographs of electro statically dust print lifted footwear marks. The clearest mark, depicted on photograph CJL2 corresponds in pattern, size/configuration and wear to the submitted right training shoe (SF3). In addition there are features in the mark that correspond to features of random damage on the sole of the same right shoe. There was one mark in the impression taken from the right shoe and while not clearly defined nonetheless corresponded to the feature of damage on the right training shoe.

There is a poor quality and poorly defined footwear mark depicted on the lift CJL 3 that corresponds in pattern and is appropriate in terms of size and configuration and wear to the submitted left training shoe SF2. However, given the quality of the mark and detail obtained from the footwear mark on the other lift (CJL2) this footwear mark has not been examined in any further detail.

INTERPRETATION

In my opinion, the degree of correspondence observed between the footwear mark on the concrete floor of the backdoor porch and the submitted right training shoe is of the utmost significance. Indeed, I consider the likelihood of the observed degree of correspondence occurring by sheer coincidence, if the training shoe did not make the respective mark on the concrete floor to be so remote as to be discounted on a practical basis. There was one mark in one of the impressions that corresponds to damage features on the under-sole of Mr Whyte's right training shoe. Damage features are acquired randomly on footwear and so I therefore consider this finding enhances the significance of the pattern match and in my opinion the overall degree of correspondence is much more likely if this shoe made the impression rather than some other footwear taken from the random population.

CONCLUSION

In my opinion, the results of this examination provide very strong evidence that the right training shoe relating to Lenny WHYTE has made a mark on the concrete floor close to the backdoor of 19 Sunrise Road, Lyme.

(Scale of Evidential Support: – no, limited, moderate, moderately strong, strong, very strong, extremely strong, conclusive.)

Signed: S Hardacker

DOCUMENT 19   ADDITIONAL STATEMENT OF LENNY WHYTE – COMMENTS ON ADVANCE INFORMATION

I have read the advance information provided by the prosecution and make the following observations.

Lillian Kennedy
I think I know this lady. I have seen her before when I have walked my dog Butch. If she says it was me who approached her on the day in question then she is mistaken. I do not recollect going into Sunrise Road on the 17th March.

Shirley Lewis
This witness is mistaken. There is no way she could have seen me at the back of the old lady's house. I was not there. She says the man she saw was wearing white training shoes. I do not wear white training shoes. She may have seen me in the area on one or two occasions. As I already said I walk my dog Butch (a terrier) in fields near to Sunrise Road. I am not the only black man who lives in the area. She is confusing me with some-one else.

Harold Finney
I did not see or approach any black car in Sunrise Road.

DS Steve Farrington
I dislike this police officer. On the way back from the interview room he said that I deserved everything the court would throw at me. Nobody explained to me why I could not have an identification parade. The police let me make a phone call to my sister, but she wasn't in when I rang. I was offered a solicitor but I honestly didn't think there was much point in one being there. The police were going to fit me up whatever. I was really desperate to get out of the police station. I seemed to have been there forever. I wanted a cigarette and I was worried about Butch my dog and about Sonia. I didn't feel very well during the interview and cannot honestly remember what I said. Looking back I should have had a solicitor present. All I wanted was for the interview to be over and done with, so that I could be charged and released on bail. The police got me to say what they wanted to hear. What I said to them in interview about my involvement is untrue. I wish to retract my statement.

I told the custody sergeant the following morning that I was on medication. He asked me why I hadn't mentioned it before. I cannot remember whether I was asked at the outset whether I was on medication. I just felt totally out of it. He called the police doctor who examined me. I believe an officer went back to my flat to collect my medication.

I was examined by a GP. He didn't seem much interested in me. He gave me my medication and told me I was fine.

I swear I have never worn the white trainers. They were given to me by a friend. I cannot remember who because I often have friends come to see me and sometimes they stay over. I have not worn the shoes.

Lloyd Green
I believe Lloyd Green has not said anything against me. I do know Lloyd Green. He is a drug dealer and loan shark. I have owed him money in the past. He can get a bit rough with you when you don't 'come up with the goods'. I cannot say whether Lloyd Green was involved in this burglary or not as I wasn't there.

Dated 24th April

DOCUMENT 20   FILE NOTE – CONSIDERATION OF ADVANCE INFORMATION AND RECORD OF ATTENDANCE AT MODE OF TRIAL ENQUIRY

10th April – Travelling to and from identification Suite. Viewing the DVD video identification compilation and the video film of the viewing process. The compilation seems fair. The witness Shirley Lewis appears confident in her identification of Lenny Whyte.

Travel 15 minutes
Attendance 30 minutes

11th April
Engaged considering the Advance Information.

Having considered the evidence, I am of the view that Lenny should indicate a not guilty plea at the plea before venue. It is unlikely (given the seriousness of the offence and the likely sentence in the event of conviction) that the magistrates would accept jurisdiction to try this matter. At the mode of trial enquiry the court must assume the prosecution's version of the facts is correct so there is no point in drawing the magistrates' attention to the weaknesses in the prosecution's case at this stage.

In the unlikely event of Lenny being presented with a choice, my considered opinion is that he would, in any event, be best advised to elect a Crown Court trial for the following reasons:

- He stands a better chance of being acquitted.

- There are areas of disputed evidence which are best dealt with in the absence of the jury.

- A qualified judge would be more confident about excluding evidence.
Against is:

- The risk of a higher sentence (although I suspect that magistrates would commit for sentence in any event).

- It will take longer to come to trial but Lenny does not seem unduly concerned by this.

- Defence statement is mandatory-but if the case is committed to the Crown Court we stand a better chance of flushing out further disclosure.

The advantages of the Crown Court outweigh those in favour of the magistrates' court in Lenny's case. In any event the exercise is likely to be academic since the magistrates will almost certainly decline jurisdiction and adjourn for committal proceedings.

Time engaged: 20 minutes

File note-24th April

Attending Lyme Magistrates' Court. Taking Lenny through the Advance Information and obtaining his comments thereon. I explained to Lenny that I had viewed the Video Identification Parade and considered that this had been fair.

I explained to Lenny and his sister that I did not feel that the magistrates would accept jurisdiction but that if they did he should elect trial by jury on the burglary charge in any event.

An indication of a guilty plea was entered in relation to the possession of cannabis charge and a not-guilty plea was entered in relation to the burglary matter. Mode of Trial Enquiry was held with the CPS inviting the magistrates to decline jurisdiction. No representations from us in relation to mode of trial. Jurisdiction declined-case adjourned to 30th May for preparation of committal papers.

The clerk to the justices did not feel that the cannabis charge should be committed to the Crown Court for sentence under s 4 PCC(S)A 2000 as there was an insufficient nexus. Consequently I briefly addressed the bench in terms of sentence and a 12 month conditional discharge was imposed.

Time engaged:
Advocacy 10 minutes
Waiting 10 minutes
Attending client 30 minutes
Travel to and from court 15 minutes.

You can see the plea before venue/mode of trial enquiry on the burglary charge in the Lenny Whyte video section of our Online Resource Centre. It precedes Lenny's contested application for bail. See note in connection with Document 13 for explanation of the chronological differences between the filmed portions of the Lenny Whyte case study and the documented version you are presently considering.

online resource centre

DOCUMENT 22 CPS LETTER REGARDING COMMITTAL PROCEEDINGS SEPCIMEN LETTER

CROWN PROSECUTION SERVICE
Queen's Chambers
Blackburn Street
Lyme
LY3 2BE

Date: 13/5/-

Ref: AH/IW
Your ref: RJ/SAW

Hannibal and Mountford Solicitors
20 High Street
Lyme Bank
Lyme
LY10 34 T

Dear Sirs,
R v Lenny Whyte
Lyme Magistrates' Court
Committal Hearing 30th May

I enclose by way of service, in accordance with section 5(b) Magistrates' Court Act 1980, committal papers for the above.

Committal papers have been prepared in accordance with the Practice Direction given by the Lord Chief Justice on the 3rd June 1986. I enclose one copy of the committal volumes for your client, together with a further copy for your own use.

If no depositions are taken, and there are no alterations to the Crown Court case papers now served, no further copies will be served on you. It will be for you to prepare any further papers for your counsel and your client. If there are any alterations, the Crown Prosecution Service will supply you with copies of depositions and an amended list of witnesses/ or exhibits. These arrangements will ensure that the judge and all parties at the trial will work form identically indexed volumes.

The written statements contained in the committal volumes will be tendered in evidence before the magistrates unless you object to any statement being tendered under section 5b Magistrates' Court Act 1980 and rule 70 Magistrates Courts Rules 1981. If you object to any statement being tendered in evidence, you should inform me as soon as possible.

Delay and expense may be caused if you fail to act promptly upon this letter in this regard. It is however, for the prosecution to decide what evidence to bring in support of the charge at committal stage.

Unless I hear to the contrary I will assume that the committal will be in accordance with the provisions of section 6(2) Magistrates' Court Act 1980.

Yours faithfully,

Andrew Hurst
Principal Crown Prosecutor

DOCUMENT 23   EXTRACTS FROM THE COMMITTAL BUNDLE

NOTE TO THE READER
We have included the front sheets of a typical committal bundle. In addition to the extracts we have included here, you would also receive typed versions of the prosecution's witness statements (comprising used material) as well as a full transcript of interview. Such documentation would be entirely comparable with the Advance Information. It would include any further statements that have not previously been disclosed as Advance Information which the CPS intends to rely on. We invite you to assume that typed versions of the Advance Information in this case study (Documents 18 A–P) have been served with the committal bundle.

The charge(s) set out on the Schedule(s) attached to the accompanying papers has/have been prepared in indictment form in consequence of the responsibility which the Crown Prosecution Service has in relation to the form and content of indictments.

This/these should be treated in exactly the same way as committal charges in traditional form unless 's. 40 CJA 1988' appears under a court number. In that case the charge is not a committal charge but indicates the intention that it should be included in an indictment under section 40 Criminal Justice Act 1988.

Schedules also serve as draft indictments following a committal but may be subject to amendments, or replaced by a new draft settled by Counsel, before being preferred for signature by the appropriate officer of the Crown Court. A copy of the indictment as signed will be supplied in the usual way.

<u>**DRAFT INDICTMENT / COMMITTAL CHARGES**</u>

INDICTMENT (No.   )

CROWN COURT AT LYME

THE QUEEN -V- LENNY WHYTE

LENNY WHYTE

Is charged as follows:

Count 1: <u>**STATEMENT OF OFFENCE**</u>

BURGLARY contrary to Section 9(1)(b) of the Theft Act 1968.

PARTICULARS OF OFFENCE

LENNY WHYTE that on the 17th March having entered as a trespasser a building, being a dwelling known as 19 Sunrise Walk, Lyme you stole £75 in money property belonging to Lillian Kennedy

Officer of the Court

REGINA

-V-

LENNY WHYTE

Statements

No.	Name of Witness	Date of Statement	Page No (s)
1.	L Kennedy	18/3/-	
2.	L Kennedy	20/3/-	
3.	S Lewis	18/3/-	
4.	S Lewis	20/3/-	
5.	H Finney	18/3/-	
6.	H Finney	20/3/-	
7.	S Farrington	20/3/-	
8.	A Khan	20/3/-	
9.	E Mason	20/3/-	
10.	C Sutton	20/3/-	
11.	J Bradbury	20/3/-	
12.	P Reynolds (x2)	19/3/-	
13.	C Lawton	20/3/-	
14.	S Hardacker	25/3/-	

REGINA

-V-

LENNY WHYTE

Exhibit List

No	Reference	Item
1.	SF2	Left size 9 Nike training shoe
2.	SF3	Right size 9 Nike training shoe
3.	SF6/a	Tape recorded interview/Whyte Tape Reference 21/SF/59217/03–*
4.	SF6/b	Transcript of interview/Whyte*
5.	CJL1	Album of photographs of shoeprints in situ
6.	CJL2	Shoe print lift
7.	CJL3	Shoe print lift
8.	SF5	Black hooded swearshirt
9.	PR1	DVD Compilation of Video Images Ref 05/01166/20A
10.	CS2	Video of Video Identification viewing process-film ref. no. 277/05

N.B. Exhibits marked * are served with the committal papers, other exhibits may be examined on suitable appointment.

REGINA

-V-

LENNY WHYTE

FORM 14A

<u>Notice to accused: right to object to written statement or deposition being read out at trial without further proof (CPIA Act 1996 Sch. 2, paragraphs (3)(c): MC Rules 1981, r. 8 (as amended by MC (Amendment) (No.1) Rules 1997).</u>

To: LENNY WHYTE of 4a, Lymewood Court, Parkdale, Lyme

If you are committed for trial, the Crown Court may try you in respect of the charge or charges on which you are committed or in respect of any other charge arising out of the same transaction or set of circumstances which may, with the leave of the Court, be put to you.

Written statements have been made by the witnesses named below and copies of their statements are enclosed. Each of the statements will be read out at trial without oral evidence being given by the witness who made the statement unless you want the witness to give oral evidence and to be cross-examined on such oral evidence. If you want any of these witnesses to give oral evidence, and to be cross-examined if necessary, you should inform the Crown Court and me within 14 days of being committed for trial. If you do not do so you will lose your right to prevent the statement being read out without oral evidence being given by the witness in question and you will only be able to require the attendance of the witness with the leave of the Court, but that will not prevent the prosecutor from exercising his discretion to call the witness to give oral evidence, and be cross-examined, at the trial if the prosecutor so wishes.

If you have a solicitor acting for you in your case, you should hand this notice and the statements to him/her at once so that he/she may be able to deal with them.

Address any reply to:

The Branch Crown Prosecutor
Crown Prosecution Service
Queen's Chambers
Blackburn Street
Lyme

DOCUMENT 24   FILE NOTE ON COMMITTAL PREPARATION AND ATTENDANCE

Case preparation – 25th May

Speaking with Lenny Whyte's consultant psychiatrist. He is happy to provide us with a psychiatric report. It will cost £750. Explained I would seek the prior authority of the LSC and would thereafter put our request in writing.

Considering the committal documentation in this matter and determining there is nothing to be gained from seeking a long style committal as the examining justices no longer have the power to exclude evidence at a committal hearing.

RJ
Time engaged 20 minutes

Attendance Note
30th May

Attending Lenny Whyte and his sister at Lyme Magistrates' Court. Explaining the nature of a committal hearing. Appearing before Lyme Magistrates. Lenny's case was committed via a short style committal. Conditional bail renewed and the PCMH fixed for the 15th June.

RJ
Attending client 15 minutes
Court hearing 5 minutes.

NOTE: Committal proceedings having concluded, solicitors for Lenny Whyte can submit a claim for costs under the standard fee arrangement on the CDS11 Form.

DOCUMENT 26   NOTICE OF COMMITTAL\POST COMMITTAL CASE MANAGEMENT FORM

<u>COMMITTAL IN ACCORDANCE WITH THE PROVISIONS OF SECTION 6(1) OF THE MAGISTRATES COURTS ACT 1980</u>

<u>LYME CROWN COURT</u>

Regina

-V-

<u>**LENNY WHYTE**</u>

DATE OF COMMITTAL	30th May
MAGISTRATES' COURT	Lyme Magistrates' Court
DATE OF PLEA AND CASE MANAGEMENT HEARING	30th June
FOR THE PROSECUTION	Crown Prosecution Service Lyme Branch
FOR THE DEFENCE	Hannibal Solicitors 20 High Street, Lyme Bank, Lyme Ref RJ
CHARGES	* See attached list
EXHIBITS	* See attached list
WITNESSES	* See attached list

DOCUMENT 27   LETTER REQUESTING EXPERT REPORT FOR THE DEFENCE

HANNIBAL AND MOUNTFORD SOLICITORS
20 High Street,
Lyme Bank, Lyme
LY10 34T

Telephone: 01576-455971
Fax: 01576-200345
Email: Hannibal@solicitors.co.uk

3rd June

Dear Dr Mayhew

Re: Lenny Whyte-Date of Birth 27/6/- aged 27

We write further to our telephone conversation on the 25th May. You will recall that we act on behalf of Lenny Whyte in connection with criminal proceedings. We understand that Mr Whyte is a patient of yours. Our client is pleading not guilty to an allegation of burglary and will stand trial before Lyme Crown Court on a date to be fixed.

In our telephone conversation you kindly indicated that you would be prepared to undertake a report for use in the case specifically addressing the reliability of incriminating comments made by our client while at the police station in the light of his medical condition. Your agreed fee for this report is £750. We would ask you note that Mr Whyte is legally aided and payment of your fees will therefore be requested by us from the Legal Services Commission which may take some time.

In this letter of instruction we enclose the following:

- Our client's form of authority to release information to us
- Our client's statement of events
- A copy of our client's custody record
- The tape recorded interview conducted in relation to our client
- A written transcript of the tape recorded interview
- A list of our client's previous convictions
- Extracts from Code C of the Codes of Practice

We intend to dispute the admissibility of Mr Whyte's confession at his trial on the legal grounds that it would be unfair to place reliance upon it and it is unreliable. You will most probably be aware that there are numerous safeguards in Code C of the Police and Criminal Evidence Act 1984 which are designed to safeguard against unreliable confessions by suspects in custody. We contend that these safeguards were not respected by the police in Mr Whyte's case.

Mr Whyte was not represented by a solicitor at the police station. He was detained overnight and was extremely anxious to escape the confines of legal custody. Crucially, for whatever reason, it was not appreciated from the outset that Mr Whyte suffers from bi-polar depression. In fact his condition did not come to light until some 15 hours after having been detained. Our client was examined by a police doctor who administered an appropriate dose of Mr Whyte's regular medication and pronounced him fit to be interview. Our client should of course have had an appropriate adult to look after his interests while in custody. This never occurred and is compounded further by the absence of a solicitor. We understand from Mr Whyte that he does not take his medication as regularly as he should and that upon his arrest he was found to be in possession of a small quantity of cannabis resin.

We would very much like to obtain a report from you that address the following matters:

1. The nature of Mr Whyte's condition
2. The nature of the medication Mr Whyte receives
3. The effect of the medication if taken regularly and any side-effects
4. The effect of the medication if it is not taken regularly
5. The effect of the medication if combined with drugs such as cannabis/alcohol
6. Our client's state of mind while in detention and why this most likely contributed to him making untrue incriminating admissions in order to relieve the pressure of the situation he found himself in.

Should you require any further information we should be pleased to assist.

We should be pleased to receive your report within four weeks. We may be forced to request you to give evidence on our client's behalf in due course and would therefore be grateful if you could give us an indication of any dates over the next six months when you would be unavailable to attend court. We need this information before the 15th June as the Crown Court judge will want to set a firm date on Mr Whyte's next appearance to address the question of the admissibility of his confession.

We thank you in anticipation of your assistance.

Yours sincerely
Rachel James
Rachel James
Hannibal and Mountford

Anthony Hannibal (BA Partner), Louise Mountford (LL.B Partner), Denis Davies
(LL.B Partner) Tim Howard (LL.B Associate Solicitor), David Temple (LL.B Associate Solicitor),
Rachel James (LL.B Associate Solicitor), Mike Tamworth (Fellow of the
Institute of Legal Executives), Lisa Hardy (Accredited Police Station Clerk),
Ali Khan (Accredited Police Station Clerk)
Regulated by the Law Society

**DOCUMENT 29   CPS LETTER REGARDING CPIA 1996
DISCLOSURE (SPECIMEN LETTER)**

CROWN PROSECUTION SERVICE
Queen's Chambers,
Blackburn Street,
Lyme
LY3 2BE

Date: 4/6/-
Ref: LR/JW

Hannibal and Mountford Solicitors
20 High Street,
Lyme Bank,
Lyme
LY10 34T

Dear Sirs,
Re: Lenny Whyte
Date of Next Hearing: PCMH 30th June

Disclosure of Prosecution Material under section 3, Criminal Procedure and
Investigations Act 1996 (CPIA).

Notice of intention to adduce evidence of your client's character under s 101 Criminal
Justice Act 2003

I am required by section 3 of the above Act, to disclose to you any prosecution material, which has not previously been disclosed, which might reasonably be considered capable of undermining the case for the prosecution or of assisting the case for the accused.

Attached to this letter is a copy of a schedule of non-sensitive material prepared by the police in compliance with their duty under part II CPIA and the provisions of the Code of Practice. The schedule has been prepared by the Police Disclosure Officer, who in this case is DS Hague.

Unless the word 'evidence' appears alongside any item, all the items listed on the schedule are not intended to be part of the prosecution case. You will receive a written notice should the position change.

Where indicated, copies of the items listed are attached. Material marked as available for inspection can be viewed by arrangement with myself.

This material is disclosed to you in accordance with the provisions of the CPIA, and you must not use or disclose it, or any information recorded in it, for any purpose other than in connection with these criminal proceedings. If you do so without the permission of the court, you may commit an offence.

If you supply a written defence statement to me and to the court within 14 days of the date of the receipt of this letter, material which has not been disclosed at this stage will be further reviewed in the light of that statement.

A defence statement is required by section 5 CPIA in Crown Court cases. In Magistrate's Court cases, section 6 CPIA makes a defence statement optional. Please bear in mind that we will rely upon the information you provide in the statement to identify any remaining material, which has not already been disclosed but which might reasonably assist in the defence case as you have described it. The statement will also be relied on by the court if you later make an application under section 8 CPIA.

If you do not make a defence statement where one is required, or provide one late, the court may permit comment and/or draw an adverse inference.

If you request access to any item which is marked for disclosure by inspection, it is essential that you preserve this schedule in its present form, as access will only be granted upon production of the schedule to the person supervising access.

I am also enclosing notice of my intention to adduce evidence of your client's bad character under s 101 Criminal Justice Act 2003.

If you have a query in connection with this letter, please contact myself.

Yours faithfully,

Lewis Rowe
Crown Prosecution Service

Form MG 6C

DOCUMENT 30A   POLICE SCHEDULE OF NON-SENSITIVE UNUSED MATERIAL

R v LENNY WHYTE   URN

Is there any material in this case which has not been examined by either the investigating or disclosure officer? Yes   No

The Disclosure Officer believes that the following material, which does not form part of the prosecution case, is NOT SENSITIVE.

Item No.	DESCRIPTION AND RELEVANCE (Give sufficient detail for CPS to decide if material should be disclosed or requires more detailed examination)	LOCATION	FOR CPS USE: * Enter: D = Disclose to defence I = Defence may inspect	
			*	COMMENT
1.	Tape recording of 999 call 17/3/– from witness S Lewis- description of suspect	Lyme Street Police Station control room		
2.	Incident (CAD) Log no. 3569/0/–(17/3/–details of witness S Lewis and description of suspects	Lyme Street Police Station control room		
3.	Pocket note-book entry–DC 2198 Shaw re details of crime report contains details of first description of suspects	With DC 2198 Shaw		
4.	Pocket note-book entry DS 4291 Farrington re: arrests and interview of GREEN and WHYTE	With DS 4201 Farrington		
5.	Pocket note-book details search of premises–DC 2198 Shaw, Flat 4a Lymewood Court, Parkdale, Lyme–home address of WHYTE	With DC 2198 Shaw		
6.	Custody record no. 2346/05/-GREEN	Lyme PS		
7.	Custody record no. 2305/05/-WHYTE	Lyme PS		Disclosed

Signature: David Hague DC 2486

Date:

Reviewing lawyer signature: L.Rowe

Print name: Lewis Rowe

Date:

Form MG 6C

DOCUMENT 30B POLICE SCHEDULE OF NON-SENSITIVE UNUSED MATERIAL

R v LENNY WHYTE   URN

Is there any material in this case which has not been examined by either the investigating or disclosure officer? Yes   No

The Disclosure Officer believes that the following material, which does not form part of the prosecution case, is NOT SENSITIVE.

Item No.	DESCRIPTION AND RELEVANCE (Give sufficient detail for CPS to decide if material should be disclosed or requires more detailed examination)	LOCATION	FOR CPS USE: * Enter: D = Disclose to defence I = Defence may inspect	
			*	COMMENT
8.	PNC printout of previous convictions of GREEN	On file		
9.	Submission forms to FSS dated	On file		
10.	Letter from FSS dated	On file		
11.	DNA swab sample taken from WHYTE	FSS Morley Street		
12.	Inspector C Sutton – contemporaneous hand written notes of Video Identification procedure (Form 116/2)	On file		

Signature: David Hague DC 2486

Date:

Name: David Hague DC 2486

Reviewing lawyer signature: L Rowe

Print name: Lewis Rowe

Date:

DOCUMENT 32   LETTER TO CPS DEALING WITH CPIA 1996 MATTERS AND BAD CHARACTER NOTICE UNDER S. 101 CRIMINAL JUSTICE ACT 2003

HANNIBAL AND MOUNTFORD SOLICITORS
20 High Street,
Lyme Bank, Lyme
LY10 34T
Telephone: 01576-455971
Fax: 01576-200345
Email: Hannibal@solicitors.co.uk

Crown Prosecution Service
Queen's Chambers
Blackburn Street
Lyme
LY3 2BE

Date: 13/6/-
Ref: LR/JW
Our ref: RJ/SW

Dear Sirs,
R v Lenny Whyte
Date of Next Hearing – Plea and Case Management Hearing – Lyme Crown Court 30th June

Please find attached notification of our requirements in respect of the evidence tendered at the committal hearing on the 30th May. We shortly intend to take counsel's opinion in this matter and if we are in a position to agree prosecution witness evidence we will notify you accordingly.

We further enclose our client's the defence statement under s. 5, Criminal Procedure and Investigations Act 1996.

We look forward to receiving further prosecution disclosure. In particular, we would like disclosure of Lloyd Green's interview.

We intend to dispute the admissibility of our client's interview with the police in connection with this matter. We hereby give you notice under s. 6D CPIA 1996 of the fact that we have instructed our client's consultant psychiatrist, Dr Oliver A Mayhew to provide us with an expert opinion as to our client's state of mind at the time of his interview. Consequently we will want to cross-examine the custody officers who were responsible for compiling the custody record in relation to our client. We will also want to cross-examine the police doctor who examined our client and Inspector Rushton who reviewed our client's detention. Please confirm that you will ensure the attendance of these witnesses. We will of course require our client's custody record and the transcript of interview to be admitted into evidence. For theses reasons we will require tape playing facilities in court. We anticipate that the point of law which arises in connection with the interview in this case will form the basis of a pre-trial hearing in connection with this matter as we do not consider either side will be in a position to resolve the matter at the PCMH.

We also enclose notice of our intention to oppose the admission of our client's past bad character at his forthcoming trial.

We look forward to hearing from you accordingly.

Yours faithfully
R James
Hannibal and Mountford

Anthony Hannibal (BA Partner), Louise Mountford (LL.B Partner), Denis Davies
(LL.B Partner) Tim Howard (LL.B Associate Solicitor), David Temple (LL.B Associate Solicitor),
Rachel James (LL.B Associate Solicitor), Mike Tamworth (Fellow of the
Institute of Legal Executives), Lisa Hardy (Accredited Police Station Clerk).
Ali Khan (Accredited Police Station Clerk)
Regulated by the Law Society

Note: A copy of this letter and its enclosures will also be sent to the Crown Court. We will also submit our completed Form B as judges in the Crown Court are required to consider making a Recovery of Defence Costs Orders (see Chapter 14) in the event of conviction. Such an order is unlikely in Lenny's case given that he is in receipt of welfare benefits.

DOCUMENT 34A   DEFENCE STATEMENT

Section 5, Criminal Procedure and Investigation Act 1996

REGINA v LENNY WHYTE

1. I, Lenny Whyte, deny that I was the person responsible for committing a burglary at 19 Sunrise Walk, Lyme between 11.45am–12.30pm on the 17th March this year.

2. I take issue with those prosecution statements which suggest that I was one of the two men involved in the burglary. I was not in the area at the relevant time. I take issue with Shirley Lewis's identification of me. She is mistaken.

3. I wish to retract what I said in interview on the 20th March regarding the circumstances of this offence. I intend to dispute the admissibility of my interview with the police. At the time of my interview I was and still am suffering from bipolar depression. I did not have the services of a solicitor or an appropriate adult. I will contend that my interview should be excluded under ss. 76(2)(b) and 78 PACE 1984.

4. I deny that the white training shoes recovered from my flat belong to me. I have never worn them.

Signed: Lenny Whyte   Date: 13th June

To: Crown Prosecution Service
     Lyme Crown Court

DOCUMENT 35   CPS SPECIMEN LETTER DEALING WITH FURTHER DISCLOSURE

CROWN PROSECUTION SERVICE
Queen's Chambers,
Blackburn Street,
Lyme
LY3 2BE

Date: 18/6/-

Our ref: LR/TY
Your ref: RJ/

Hannibal and Mountford Solicitors
20 High Street,
Lyme Bank,
Lyme
LY10 34T

Dear Sirs,

R v Lenny Whyte
Lyme Crown Court – Plea and Case Management Hearing: 30th June
Disclosure of Prosecution Material under section 3, Criminal Procedure and Investigations Act 1996.

I have considered your defence statement dated the 13th June provided under section 5, Criminal Procedure and Investigations Act 1996. Under section 7A, I am required to disclose to you any prosecution material, which has not previously been disclosed and which might reasonably be expected to assist your defence, as described in your statement.

A copy of a schedule of non-sensitive unusual material prepared by the police has already been sent to you. Having considered the schedule in the light of your defence statement, the items listed below are those which I consider might reasonably be expected to assist your client's defence. The numbers refer to the numbers on the schedule previously provided. Where indicated, copies of the items listed are attached. Material marked as available for inspection can be viewed by arrangement with myself.

Item	Description	Copy	Insp.
	Record of interview: Lloyd	Yes	N/A
	Letter S. Leighton FSS	Yes	N/A

This material is disclosed to you in accordance with the provisions of the CPIA, and you must not use or disclose it, or any information recorded in it for any purpose other than in connection with these criminal proceedings. If you do so without the permission of the court, you may commit an offence.

If you consider that there is other prosecution material, which might assist your defence and which has not already been disclosed, please let me know and I will reconsider my decision in the light of any further information that you provide. Alternatively, you may apply to court under section 8, Criminal Procedure and Investigations Act 1996. The court will assess your application in the light of your defence statement.

If you request access to any item which has been market for disclosure by inspection, it is essential that you preserve this letter in its present form, as access will only be granted upon production of this letter and the schedule previously provided to the person supervision access.

If you have any query in connection with this letter, please contact myself.

Yours faithfully,

Lewis Rowe
Crown Prosecution Service

DOCUMENT 36   FURTHER DISCLOSURE

RECORD OF INTERVIEW

Person interviewed: LLOYD GREEN

Place of interview: LYME STREET

Date of interview: 19/3/-

Time commenced: 1830 HRS

Time concluded: 1841 HRS

Duration of interview: 11 MINUTES

Interviewing officer(s): DS 4291 FARRINGTON/DC 2890 SARAH HILL

Other persons present: RICHARD BAKER (Baker + Co)

Tape reference number: 24 /SF/59218/04/-

Exhibit Number: SF

Police Exhibit No:
No of pages:
Signature of interviewing officer producing exhibit
DS S Farrington

Tape counter Times(s)	Person speaking	Text
0000		Normal introductions were made and the interviewee was reminded of his legal rights and cautioned.
0030	Farrington:	I am investigating a burglary at an old lady's bungalow, Lloyd. I would like to ask you some questions in connection with this.
0112	Baker:	Before you go any further Sergeant, my client wishes me to read out the following statement. Having read out my client's statement my client will not answer any further questions you may wish to put to him.
		'I categorically deny any involvement at a burglary at 19 Sunrise Road, Lyme, between midday and 12.30pm on the 17th March.
		I accept I was sitting in my car at this time in the street. My car is a black BMW, registration number DY01 SJT. I was having a spot of trouble with my car in that it kept cutting out on me. I pulled into the street to make a call on my mobile phone to my mechanic. While on the phone I recall I was approached by a black guy who asked me for a light I think. I do not know who this man was. I have not seen him before. I would describe him as being tall, black and clean shaven. I got out of my car once to check under the bonnet. I did not approach anyone in Sunrise Road. I did not knock on anyone's door seeking to make a phone call. I tried the ignition several times more and eventually managed to get the car started. I have since had the car checked out and have had the alternator replaced. I have a receipt for the work done. If you wish me to participate in any identification procedure I would providing it is fairly conducted.'
0700	Farrington:	It's a coincidence then Lloyd, is it? – Can you tell me whether you know a black man by the name of Lenny Whyte?
0745	Green:	I have said all I want to say. I refer you to my written statement.
0830	Farrington:	Why was you car parked in Sunrise Road? It's a street occupied by pensioners. What possible reason would you have for being there?

0905	Green:	I have said all I wanted to say in connection with this matter. I refer you to my written statement.
1000	Farrington:	You must have had a mobile telephone on you – why did you need to knock on the old lady's door?
1030	Green:	I make no comment.

Interview terminated.

DOCUMENT 37   FURTHER DISCLOSURE

Forensic Science Service
Crime Reporting Unit
Bellfield House
Nile Street
Birmingham

DS Steve Farrington
Lymeshire Police
Lyme Street Police Station
URN **05/221**
Lab Ref **500 679 4033/400 593 1297**

Date 28th March

Dear DS Farrington

Re: Burglary 19 Sunrise Road Lyme

Information

I understand that 19 Sunrise Road, Lyme was burgled at some time between 11.45 and 12.30 hours on the 17th March.

It is believed that the burglar may have been responsible for leaving footprints near to the back door of the burgled property. A pair of training shoes was recovered from 4a Lymewood Court, Lyme, the home address of LENNY WHYTE suspected of having left the shoeprints.

Items Received
The following are amongst items relating to this case submitted to the Morely laboratory of the Forensic Science Service on the

SF2 and SF3 (Ex nos.) – A pair of Nike white training shoes

SF5 (Ex no) – Reference mouth swabs from LENNY WHYTE

Purpose
My purpose was to determine if there is any scientific evidence to assist in addressing the issue of whether or not there is any cellular material from Lenny WHYTE to link him to the training shoes recovered from his property.

DNA swabs have been taken from the tongue and from the lace ends of the right and left training shoe (SF3 and SF2).

Results
An attempt to obtain a DNA profile from material swabbed from the tongue and lace ends (SF3) was unsuccessful. This is probably due to there being insufficient DNA present in the material tested.

In the absence of any DNA profiles, the findings do not assist in addressing whether or not the material from the tongue and lace swabs is from Lenny WHYTE.

Please do not hesitate to contact me should you require any further assistance.

Yours faithfully,

Dr Samantha Leighton
Forensic Scientist
Morely Laboratory

DOCUMENT 39 BRIEF TO COUNSEL TO ATTEND PCMH

<u>LYME CROWN COURT</u>   <u>LISTING NO.</u>

REGINA

-v-

LENNY WHYTE

- - - - - - - - - - - - - - - - -

BRIEF ON BEHALF OF THE DEFENDANT TO APPEAR AT THE PCMH – 30th JUNE AT 10am AND AT THE SUBSEQUENT TRIAL ON A DATE TO BE FIXED

- - - - - - - - - - - - - - - - -

Counsel receives herewith copies of the following:

1. Proof of evidence of Lenny Whyte dated 20th March
2. Draft Indictment
3. Committal bundle including:

    a) Statement of Lillian Kennedy (x2)
    b) Statement of Shirley Lewis (x2)
    c) Statement of Harold Finney (x2)
    d) Statement of DS Farrington
    e) Statement of WPC Anjuna Khan
    f) Statement of WPC Emma Mason
    g) Statement of Inspector Christopher Sutton
    i) Statement of WPC Josie Bradbury
    j) Statement of PC Peter Reynolds
    k) Statement of Carol Lawton SOCO
    l) Statement of Sarah Hardacker
    m) Transcript of interview: Lenny Whyte
    n) Previous convictions of Lenny Whyte
    o) Exhibit List

4. Statement of Lenny Whyte with comments on the prosecution evidence dated 24th April
5. Defence Psychiatric Report
6. Custody Record
7. Tapes of interview
8. Initial Prosecution Disclosure
9. Defence Statement
10. Notice of intention to adduce evidence of Lenny Whyte's previous convictions
11. Notice objecting to the admissibility of Mr Whyte's previous criminal convictions.
12. Further Prosecution Disclosure
     a) Record of interview with Lloyd Green
     b) Letter from Forensic Science Service
13. Copy letter to the CPS dated 13th June including witness requirements
14. Through Legal Aid Order
15. Plea and Case Management Form

Introduction

Counsel's instructing solicitors act on behalf of Lenny Whyte. As Counsel will see from the enclosed draft indictment, Mr Whyte is charged with burglary. It is alleged he broke into 19 Sunrise Road on the 17th March this year and stole £75. Mr Whyte intends to plead not guilty to the burglary allegation. Upon his arrest, Mr Whyte was found to be in possession of a small quantity of cannabis. He pleaded guilty to simple possession and was sentenced to a conditional discharge for 12 months by Lyme Magistrates on the 24th April.

Chronology

Mr Whyte was arrested on the 19th March. He appeared before Lyme Magistrates on the 20th March when bail was refused. He subsequently appeared again on the 27th March when bail was refused for a second time and jurisdiction to try the matter was refused. On the 4th April our client appeared before a Crown Court Judge in chambers at Lyme Crown Court and was granted bail subject to a number of conditions. Lyme

Magistrates' Court declined jurisdiction to try Lenny Whyte on the 24th April. Mr Whyte was committed to Lyme Crown Court via a short style committal on the 30th May.

The Plea and Case Management Hearing in this case has been listed for the 30th June. Counsel is instructed to attend. It is our intention to instruct counsel to represent Mr Whyte at trial and would ask you to take note of this fact when considering listing arrangements.

Prosecution Case and Evidential Matters

On the 17th March a burglary occurred at 19 Sunrise Road, Lyme (the home of 84 year old Lillian Kennedy) sometime between 11.45 hours and 12 midday. The prosecution contend that this was a distraction burglary. It is alleged that a man knocked on the door of 19 Sunrise Road on the pretence of having to use the telephone and while the occupier was distracted, the burglar gained entry to the property via an unlocked back door and proceeded to steal £75 from the victim's purse. The prosecution contend that the person entering the property was Mr Whyte. It is believed that the man responsible for distracting Mrs Kennedy at her front door is Lloyd Green. Although Green was arrested and interviewed he has not been charged with any offence arising out of this incident. In his interview with the police he denied any involvement in the burglary and did not implicate Lenny Whyte. Instructing solicitors do not act for Lloyd Green and did not represent him at the police station.

The principal evidence against Mr Whyte comprises eye-witness identification, confession evidence and forensic circumstantial evidence. We will deal with each in turn.

Counsel will see the statements of Lillian Kennedy contained in the committal bundle that she did not see the man who entered her property. She states however that she was stopped by a man in her street who offered to help her with her shopping. This was approximately 30–40 minutes before the burglary. On a subsequent tour of the local area the afternoon of the burglary she identified Lenny Whyte as being that person. The police did not immediately arrest Mr Whyte. At a subsequent VIPER identification procedure, however, Mrs Kennedy failed to identify Mr Whyte which rather casts her earlier street identification into doubt. Mrs Kennedy does however provide a description of the man who approached her which accords for the most part with the description of a man seen leaving the backdoor of the burgled property by another eye-witness. When Mrs Kennedy pointed Mr Whyte out to the police he was wearing the same attire save in one significant respect – he was not observed to be wearing white training shoes. In the circumstances it is difficult to see what Mrs Kennedy's evidence contributes to the prosecution's case. Counsel is asked to advise on this point and consider whether her evidence may be challenged on the basis of its relevance. Counsel will note that Mrs Kennedy spoke with the man who knocked on her front door. She was however unable to identify Lloyd Green at a VIPER identification procedure.

Of central importance to the prosecution's case is the evidence of Shirley Lewis. Counsel will see from her statement that she was in the back garden of a neighbouring property at midday when she saw a man behaving suspiciously near the back door of 17 Sunrise Road. She was hanging out some sheets on the washing line. She observed the man for a few seconds and was able to provide the police with a description of the man and his clothing. Her description accords with Mr Whyte's actual appearance. She observed the man was wearing white training shoes. At a subsequent VIPER identification procedure, Mrs Lewis identified Lenny Whyte as being that man. Her identification is based in part on recognition. She states she has seen Mr Whyte before in the area. Mr Whyte does not dispute this possibility as he lives near the victim and has, on occasion, walked his dog in fields near the burgled property. Mr Whyte is adamant, however, that this witness is mistaken and that it was not the man she saw.

A link in the chain of evidence is provided by the account of Harold Finney. Mr Finney lives in a property across the road from the burgled house. At 11.30am he observed a car drive along Sunrise Road and park. He was suspicious of the car and noted the registration number. The car is registered to Lloyd Green. Mr Finney states he observed a black man on foot approach the car. He describes a man who appearance is similar to that of Lenny Whyte. He also describes the clothing the individual was wearing which included a dark sweatshirt and white training shoes. At this point Mr Finney was diverted by a telephone call. He saws nothing more of any relevance. At a subsequent VIPER identification parade, he picked out someone other than Lenny Whyte. He never saw the driver of the car.

Counsel is asked to note that Mr Whyte was unrepresented at the police station. Consequently the identification procedure was conducted in the absence of legal advice. Having reviewed the DVD compilation and the video of the viewing process, instructing solicitors are satisfied that the procedure was conducted fairly in accordance with Code D. The DVD compilation is included should counsel wish to consider it.

Upon arrest and pursuant to a section 32 PACE 1984, a search of Mr Whyte's flat was carried out. The police recovered a dark hooded sweatshirt and a pair of white size 9 Nike trainers. Counsel will note that in the course of the investigation shoeprint evidence was gathered from just outside the backdoor of the burgled property. Subsequent forensic comparison of the shoeprint lifts and the soles of the shoes recovered from Mr Whyte's flat strongly suggest these training shoes were responsible for leaving the shoe prints. Mr Whyte cannot offer an explanation for this other than to state the shoes were left at his flat by a friend, whose name he cannot recall. In interview he stated he had not worn the shoes. Document 10 b disclosed by way of further disclosure is useful in this respect. Counsel is asked to see whether this statement can be agreed under s. 9 CJA 1976.

The prosecution will seek to rely on the account given by Mr Whyte in his interview with the police. It amounts to a confession. Counsel is referred to the transcript of interview in this regard. Mr Whyte wishes to retract his confession for reasons considered in detail below.

The prosecution have served notice of their intention to adduce evidence of Mr Whyte's previous criminal convictions.

Defence Case and Evidential Matters

Counsel will see Mr Whyte's comments on the prosecution evidence in document 4. Counsel will see that a defence statement has been filed in this case. Mr Whyte intends to plead not guilty. He wishes to strongly challenge the admissibility of his confession. He maintains that he is not the man responsible for the burglary. Despite our best efforts, Mr Whyte is unable to substantiate his precise whereabouts at the relevant time with an alibi.

Instructing solicitors feel there are strong grounds for seeking the exclusion of Mr Whyte's confession under ss 76(2)(b) and 78 PACE 1984. Counsel is referred at this juncture to Mr Whyte's statement and to the custody record. Mr Whyte was unrepresented at the police station, although on the face of it, it would appear that the police acted within the law of s. 58 PACE, albeit not the spirit. An attempt was made by the custody sergeant to contact Mr Whyte's sister once during our client's detention but no contact was in fact established. Counsel will note that Mr Whyte suffers from a diagnosed psychiatric condition for which he receives psychiatric care and medication. It is not altogether clear why this fact was not ascertained by the custody sergeant who should have undertaken a risk assessment having authorised the continued detention of our client. Our client is not always inclined to help himself and upon his arrest he was not found to be in possession of any medication. Our client states that he cannot recall being asked whether he suffered from a medical condition requiring medication. Our client states he was not suffering drug withdrawal symptoms at the time but is chronically addicted to nicotine. Counsel will see that he was detained overnight. The custody record suggests that Mr Whyte did not have much to eat and had little sleep.

It is evident from the custody record that some 14 or so hours after having first been detained, Mr Whyte mentioned the fact that he felt unwell and needed his usual medication. A police surgeon was called. Dr Ghulam examined our client and having administered his medication pronounced him fit to be interviewed. Crucially, Mr Whyte was not provided with an appropriate adult, contrary to Code C. As such he went into the interview completely unrepresented, craving a cigarette, desperate to relieve the pressure of the situation and suffering from a diagnosed psychiatric condition. In the circumstances, it is difficult to see how a court could regard Mr Whyte's confession as being admissible. Counsel is referred to the decision in *R v Aspinall* [1999] 2 Cr App R 115 as being a decision of the Court of Appeal which supports our contention that the confession is both unreliable and unfair to admit. The admission of a confession obtained in these circumstances would in our view represent a violation of Article 6.

Counsel will see that we have obtained a report from Mr Whyte consultant psychiatrist. The report is extremely helpful and we intend to place reliance upon it. The report has been disclosed to the CPS in accordance with the requirements of s. 30 CJA 1988. Dr Mayhew would be prepared to attend court to give evidence if necessary.

Clearly if the confession can be excluded in this case, a major component of the prosecution's case is lost and counsel may wish to consider whether a submission of no case to answer might be mounted in these circumstances

Instructing solicitors have notified the CPS of its intention to challenge the admissibility of the confession in this case. Unless the CPS decides to concede the point at the PCMH, we anticipate the issue will need to be listed for a judge's binding ruling on its admissibility. We would welcome Counsel's views on this point.

Instructing solicitors have served the appropriate notice on the prosecution objecting to the admissibility of Mr Whyte's criminal convictions. Counsel is asked to use her best endeavours to ensure that this very prejudicial evidence is excluded at the Plea and Case Management Hearing.

Counsel is requested to advise on all issues likely to arise at the PCMH and generally on the evidence and on preparation for trial. A PCMH form is enclosed for counsel's consideration. At present we have asked the CPS for all the witnesses it tendered at the committal hearing to attend. We suspect a number of witnesses can be agreed in this case and would ask counsel to specifically consider this point so that we may write to the CPS. Should Counsel require a conference we would ask her clerk to contact us.

Counsel is instructed to appear on behalf of the defendant at the PCMH on the 30th June at 2.30pm.

Rachel James, Hannibal and Mountford Solicitors
Date: 22nd June

DOCUMENT 41   FILE NOTE BASED ON PLEA AND CASE MANAGEMENT HEARING

30th June

Attending Crown Court for Plea and Case Management Hearing. Speaking with Ms Rhianna Stockley of counsel beforehand. There was considerable discussion between counsel on each side. Counsel for the CPS conceded breaches of Code C and indicated that the CPS would not be placing reliance upon Mr Whyte's confession which is extremely good news.

Argument was heard in relation to the admissibility of Lenny's previous convictions under s 101(1)(d) of the Criminal Justice Act 2003. The judge His Honour J Baker ruled in favour of admitting them. The case has been listed for trial on the 22nd August. Certificate for solicitor to attend was granted. Counsel and I explained the proceedings to Mr Whyte and his sister. Respective counsel agreed the following witness' evidence could be read at trial: WPC Khan/WPC Mason/Insp Sutton/Bradbury/PC Reynolds/WPC Lawton/Dr Hardacker/Dr Leighton.

Time engaged:

Travel 20 minutes
Waiting 60 minutes
Conference 40 minutes
Hearing 30 minutes

BW

DOCUMENT 47 FILE NOTE BASED ON TRIAL

22nd August

Attending Lyme Crown Court for Lenny Whyte's trial. Ms Stockley for Lenny Whyte and Parminder Singh for the prosecution. His Honour Thomas Shand presiding. Before the trial began, Ms Stockley asked the judge to reconsider the ruling by His Honour Judge Baker to allow evidence of the defendant's previous convictions to be admitted on the basis that their prejudicial effect would outweigh their probative value. It was agreed that the prosecution in its opening would not refer to the defendant's previous convictions but that the matter would be kept under review during the course of the trial.

The prosecution called Shirley Lewis who was extensively cross-examined with Mrs Lewis conceding that she could have been mistaken. CPS called Lillian Kennedy and Harold Finney. Before the investigating officer was called, Ms Stockley asked for confirmation that the officer would not be asked questions regarding the defendant's previous convictions as she was minded to make a submission of no case to answer. The judge ruled in her favour, without prejudice to any decision he might make as regards a submission being made. DS Farrington also gave evidence and was cross-examined. Prosecution read out a number of s. 9 statements which included the forensic evidence. Ms Stockley then made a submission of no case to answer. She explained that the most important eye witness linking Mr Whyte to the crime scene was Shirley Lewis and her evidence had been discredited. There was no concrete forensic evidence to link the defendant to the crime scene. The only remaining 'evidence' was the fact of his previous convictions and that it was clearly contrary to the defendant's right to a fair trial that a conviction could be based on this fact alone. The submission of no case to answer was upheld by the judge. The jury were directed to acquit on the burglary charge. Mr Whyte and his sister were immensely relieved and pleased.

Time engaged:
Travel 30 minutes
Waiting 40 minutes
Conference 30 minutes
Hearing 4 hours

BW

The case having now concluded, the defence solicitor can submit her final claim for costs from the Legal Services Commission via the Crown Court.

APPENDIX 2

R v WILLIAM HARDY

The complete documentation as listed overleaf can be accessed on our Online Resource Centre in the case studies section.

R v WILLIAM HARDY INDEX TO DOCUMENTATION ON SOLICITOR'S FILE

DOCUMENT 1 Initial Statement of William Hardy

DOCUMENT 2 File Note Based on Police Station Attendance

DOCUMENT 3 File Note Based on Initial Attendance in the Office

DOCUMENT 4 Form CDS 1

DOCUMENT 5 Letter to CPS Requesting Advance Information

DOCUMENT 6 Letter to Magistrates' Court

DOCUMENT 7 Representation Order Application

DOCUMENT 8 Client Care Letter

DOCUMENT 9 Specimen Letter from CPS Dealing with Advance Information

DOCUMENTS 10 A–E Advance Information

DOCUMENT 11 File Note of Interview Reviewing Advance Information with Client

DOCUMENT 12A File Note of Plea Before Venue (GUILTY PLEA ENTERED)

DOCUMENT 12B Agreed Written Basis of Plea

DOCUMENT 13 Pre-Sentence Report

DOCUMENT 14 Statement of Character Witness 1

DOCUMENT 15 Statement of Character Witness 2

DOCUMENT 16 Record of Attendance at Sentencing Hearing

DOCUMENT 17 Transcript of Plea in Mitigation based for the most part on the Filmed Video Version of the Sentencing Hearing on our Online Resource Centre

DOCUMENT 18 Letter to Client

DOCUMENT 19 Notice of Appeal Against Sentence

DOCUMENT 20 Brief to Counsel to Represent William Hardy at the Appeal Hearing before Lyme Magistrates' Court

DOCUMENT 21 Note of Crown Court Appeal Hearing

TIMESCALE OF EVENTS

- 7 December – charged with an either-way offence.
- 14 December – initial appearance before magistrates' court (adjourned for advance information).
- 14 January – second appearance before magistrates' court (plea before venue – guilty plea entered – adjourned for pre-sentence report).
- 18 February – third appearance before magistrates' court (sentenced).
- 13 March – appeal against sentence before Crown Court.

DOCUMENT 1   INITIAL STATEMENT OF WILLIAM HARDY

William Hardy, 10 Cambridge Place, Madeley, Lyme aged 24 (date of birth 14/2/-) will state:

1. I have been charged with an offence under s. 9(2) Sexual Offences Act 2003. I am alleged to have had sexual intercourse with a girl under the age of 16. I fully admit the offence. The girl in question is Rachel Coles. She is 15. Her date of birth is 3/6/-. Unfortunately, Rachel is three months pregnant. We have been having a consensual sexual relationship for the past six months. Rachel is a friend of my sister. The attraction was all one-sided to begin with and it was Rachel who took the initiative. Later the attraction became mutual. I would say that Rachel is emotionally mature for her age. Rachel and I were very much in love. However, our relationship is now at an end.

2. I am not clear yet what Rachel proposes to do about the pregnancy. I only found out she was pregnant about six weeks ago when Rachel's mother confronted me. I am prepared to stand by Rachel whatever her decision. Should she decide to have the baby, I am more than happy to shoulder my responsibilities, etc.

3. Until fairly recently, I was living at home with my mother and my younger brother and sister. For the past three years I have been studying BSc Sports Science with Biology at Manchester University commuting home most evenings. I am currently undertaking a Postgraduate Certificate in Higher Education at Manchester Metropolitan. I hope to qualify as a teacher. My A-level results were not too good, largely due to the tragic loss of my father in a car accident a few weeks before my A levels began. His death affected my family and me enormously. I worked for a couple of years and retook two of my A levels in order to get to University.

4. I will be totally honest about my relationship with Rachel. Rachel has been a friend of my sister for the past two years. Rachel had a problem with maths at school. It was agreed that I would provide her with some learning support. I had been helping my sister with her maths. The private tuition took place in the January of last year during my inter-semester break for a period of four weeks. I went to Rachel's house once a week and assisted her with her maths homework. Her mother paid me for the tuition. I formed the impression that Rachel was distressed about her parent's marital difficulties. Her father had left the matrimonial home a few weeks before. I offered her my perspective on the matter and we got into quite a lot of personal stuff. I gained the impression that Rachel was attracted to me. However, nothing inappropriate occurred. I then went back to University.

5. The next time we met up was in March at my brother's 18th Birthday party. Rachel attended it. She looked fantastic. She looked like a 17 or 18-year-old. She had makeup on and was wearing really sexy clothing. She was also drinking alcohol. I could tell she was interested in me. She kept throwing me looks. Basically she was flirting with me. I guess I was flattered. I had not long since finished with my girlfriend of the past two years and was feeling pretty sorry for myself. I was also a little drunk. We didn't really chat at the party but as she was leaving she squeezed past me and put something in my hand. When she had gone I looked at what it was. It was a mobile number written on a piece of paper with the words 'call me'. I called her the following day and asked her if she wanted to go out for a pizza. She didn't hesitate. We went out the following evening. We talked about this and that. On the way back we sat in my car and had a kiss and a cuddle. I told her to cool it as she wasn't old enough for any funny business. She just teased me and said she was. I told her I couldn't see her again and that I was going back to University. I did not see her again until the end of April. She did however send me a couple of text messages having obtained my number from my sister. The messages were innocuous enough stating how much she had enjoyed the meal out and that she hoped to see me again.

6. Towards the end of April, I returned home. On one evening my sister went out to a party. My mother asked me to collect her. I did so. She was with Rachel. She and my sister came back to the house. We called for some chips on the way home. We had coffee and then my sister asked if I would take Rachel home. I didn't feel there was anything else I could do. The atmosphere in the car was a little awkward. At one point (and as I was driving) Rachel started rubbing the inside of my thigh, moving up to my penis. I became aroused. By the time I had reached her house we had agreed that I would take her out the following night. I started to realise that I was really attracted to her. That is how our relationship began to develop. We dated a few times more and on the night before I was due to go back to University to sit my finals we made love in the back of my car. This would have been in early May. We had been kissing passionately. Rachel was insistent that I made love to her. She told me she had had sex before with someone older than her. I wore a condom. Rachel told me she intended to see her GP in order to go onto the pill and that I would not need to wear one again. Afterwards Rachel told me it had been her first time. I was surprised. I returned to University. I have to say that I was smitten with her. We were in constant touch by phone, text and email. When I returned home for the summer vacation we couldn't wait to see each other. No one else knew of our relationship. We decided it was best to keep it a secret.

7. Rachel told me that she was on the pill. Consequently I chose not to use any protection on the other occasions when we had sex. We had sex a few times over the summer in the back of my car. I accept it was rather sordid and I am ashamed but there was no where else we could go. On one occasion we had sex at her mother's house when her mother was out. Rachel explained my presence on the basis that I was providing her with extra maths tuition. I am deeply ashamed of this. During the last week of August my mother and sister went on holiday. My brother was away which meant we had the use of my house. I knew that each time we did it-it was wrong but she was very willing and we were in love with each other. Towards the end of the summer we were starting to plan a long-term future together. I was due to start my Postgraduate Certificate in Education (PGCE) at the end of September. I was going to look for a teaching post straight away and get a flat which would mean that Rachel could come and live with me when she was 16. We were full of optimism.

8. Unfortunately, Rachel's mother found out about our relationship. It was apparent that Sandra Coles was not happy about it. She was of the opinion that I was too old and was taking advantage of her daughter. She wrote me a letter, instructing me to stop seeing Rachel. Rachel tore the letter up but I could tell that she was greatly upset by her mother's interference. Rachel was absolutely adamant that she wanted to continue our relationship. In September I left home again to attend my Postgraduate Course. I came home on a couple of weekends. It was clear to me that things had changed. Rachel did not seem to be quite so keen on me. She wouldn't tell me what was wrong but she seemed jealous. I believe that my sister had told her I was seeing someone else at University. It wasn't true at the time but it is now.

9. I saw Rachel again in October. We had sex. This was the last occasion. It was consensual. After this I didn't hear from her for a good three weeks. The next thing I knew was that she was pregnant. I got a call from my mother. She had been confronted by Rachel's mother on the doorstep of our house. I was gutted and my mother was beside herself. Sandra Coles has forbidden her daughter to speak with me. It was she who involved the police and social services. I have been maligned as a child molester by Mrs Coles and have undergone a thorough investigation by the police and social services. I cannot imagine what state Rachel must be in. I have texted her since finding out about the pregnancy but she has not replied.

10. I realise that I have been an incredibly stupid fool. I don't know what possessed me. I am not attracted to younger girls. To look at Rachel you would think she was older than she was. I am ashamed of my conduct. I accept the relationship should never have occurred. I have caused my family a considerable amount of embarrassment. My mother and I have only recently been on speaking terms. She has had phone calls from the local press and anonymous phone calls branding me a paedophile. My sister Emma no longer associates with Rachel. Emma has found it very difficult at school. I sincerely wish I could turn back the clock. I am aware that I am at risk of a prison sentence and to say that I am scared of the prospect is an understatement. I have found the whole business of being arrested and interrogated deeply embarrassing. I accept I have done wrong.

11. My personal circumstances are as follows:

I completed my degree (a BSc in Sports Science and Biology) in July earlier this year. I gained an upper second from Manchester Metropolitan University. I am currently undertaking a PGCE at Manchester Metropolitan University with a view to qualifying as a teacher. I have had to undertake work experience in a school as part of this course, which I thoroughly enjoyed. I have the offer of a teaching job at a Sixth Form College in Telford, teaching Physical Education and Science. It is tenable from 1 August next year and will pay me £16,500 in my first year. I do not know how a conviction of this nature will affect the position.

12. I have no previous convictions.

13. I support myself on a student loan and have student debts totalling £15,000. However, my paternal grandmother died a couple of months ago. She left me a one third share in her house – my share will be worth approximately £16,000. The house is up for sale. I cannot say when I will receive my legacy.

   I work part time behind a bar and for this I earn approximately £100 per week.

   I have a student loan of £3,000 per year.

Out of this, I have weekly outgoings for:

Board and lodging £50
Car Loan £20
Petrol £30
Car Tax and Insurance £15

15. It is my intention to purchase a flat as soon as I am in a stable job. I have a new girlfriend. Her name is Amanda. She is 23 and is also training to become a teacher. She is aware of the current proceedings. We intend to live together when our course is concluded.

16. So far as my interests are concerned I enjoy contact sports such as football. I am a county hockey player. I have an FA recognised coaching qualification and have undertaken coaching with football academies during the summer holidays both in England and in France. Prior to attending University, I spent three months in Ghana as a volunteer with a charitable organisation coaching kids to play football. The kids were poor and underprivileged. I also took some English classes with the kids. I had a fantastic time and an amazing experience. It is something I would like to do again at some point in the future.

Dated: 11th December

DOCUMENT 2   FILE NOTE BASED ON POLICE STATION ATTENDANCE

Date: 7th DECEMBER

Attending William Hardy at Lyme Police Station. He has been arrested on suspicion of having had sexual intercourse with a child under the age of 16 (s. 9(2) Sexual Offences Act 2003). Speaking with DS Harper the investigating officer. She stated that a 15-year-old girl called Sandra Coles had made a statement in which she accused Mr Hardy of engaging in several acts of consensual sexual intercourse from the age of 14. Taking a detailed statement from Mr Hardy and forming the opinion that he was capable of answering questions. On the basis of what he disclosed I advised him that he would most probably have to plead guilty. He could not argue the statutory defence given his age and the fact that he knew the age of the girl concerned. I advised him that he was likely to be charged although I would see if a caution was an option.

Subsequently attending in interview with the police. Mr Hardy made a frank admission denying that any sexual contact or inappropriate behaviour had been engaged in during the private maths tuition he provided for the girl at the beginning of the year. Discussed with DC Harper the possibility of caution but to no avail. Subsequently attending Mr Hardy during the charging procedure. Agreed conditional bail – not to contact or approach Rachel Coles or her mother or go near their address. Informed Mr Hardy that he should make an appointment with Rachel James at the office in the very near future so that she could advise him.

Date of first appearance before Lyme Magistrates 14th January

Time engaged:
Attendance at police station 70 minutes.

AK

DOCUMENT 3   FILE NOTE BASED ON INITIAL ATTENDANCE IN THE OFFICE

File Note: 11th December

Attending William Hardy and his mother at the office. Taking a detailed statement from him (see Document 1). Assisting him to complete an application for a representation order and explaining the importance of obtaining Advance Information. I discussed the possible outcomes in terms of sentencing and explained the advantages of an early guilty plea coupled with remorse. I also explained there was a risk that the matter could be committed to the Crown Court for sentence. Date of first hearing is the 14th December. Once I am in possession of full Advance Information I explained we would be in a position to agree the basis of his plea.

Time engaged: 30 minutes
Preparation of attendance note 6 minutes

RJ

DOCUMENT 4-CDS 1

Client's Details Form   CDS1

Criminal Defence Service

Please complete in block capitals

Client's details

UFN: | 4 | 9 | 3 | 1 | 3 | 0 |╱| 5 | R | J |

Surname: HARDY

First name: WILLIAM

Date of birth: __14__ / __2__ /   National Insurance no: | Y | A | 2 | 4 | 8 | 5 | 3 | 7 |T|

Marital status: ☒ Single   ☐ Married   ☐ Cohabiting

☐ Separated   ☐ Divorced   ☐ Widowed

Current address: 10 Cambridge Place

Madeley

Town: Lyme

County: Lymeshire   Postcode: LY799 2RB

Data Protection Act - access to personal data

The personal data provided by you will be processed in accordance with the principles of the Data Protection Act 1998 and for the purposes of the Legal Services Commission's functions under the Access to Justice Act 1999. You have the right to make a formal request in writing for access to personal data held about you to inspect it and have it corrected if it is wrong. The Legal Services Commission may receive information about you from certain third parties, or give information to them; these third parties include some government departments. However, we will not disclose information about you unless the law permits us to.

Equal Opportunities Monitoring

a *Completion of this section is voluntary. This will be treated in the strictest confidence and will be used purely for statistical monitoring and research.*

Please tick the boxes which your client would describe themselves as being:

Ethnic Monitoring

White
☒ (a) British
☐ (b) Irish
☐ (c) White Other

Mixed
☐ (a) White and Black Caribbean
☐ (b) White and Black African
☐ (c) White and Asian
☐ (d) Mixed Other

Asian or Asian British
☐ (a) Indian
☐ (b) Pakistani
☐ (c) Bangladeshi
☐ (d) Asian Other

Black or Black British
☐ (a) Black Caribbean
☐ (b) Black African
☐ (c) Black Other

☐ **Chinese**

☐ **Other**

Disability Monitoring

The Disability Discrimination Act defines disability as: a physical or mental impairment with long term, substantial effects on a person's ability to perform day-to-day activities. Does your client consider himself or herself to have a disability?   ☐ Yes   ☐ No

---

CDS1   Page 1   Version 5 October 2003   (c) Criminal Defence Service

This page must be completed in full where freestanding Advice and Assistance is sought in any Class of Work (except Police Station Advice and Assistance/warrants/armed forces custody hearings/Duty Solicitor advice) or where Advocacy Assistance is sought in the Prison Law Class of Work only.

Capital details

Does your client or partner (if living with client as a couple) get Income Support, Income Based Job Seeker's Allowance or Guarantee State Pension Credit?

☐ Yes.   a *If you are applying for Advocacy Assistance, ignore the rest of this page*

a *If you are applying for Advice and Assistance, complete the rest of the page*

☐ No. Complete the rest of this page

How many dependants does your client have?
(partner, children or other relatives in the client's household) _____

Give the total savings and other capital which your client has *(and their partner, if relevant):*
(include equity in home above £100,000 after allowing for mortgage(s) up to the value of £100,000)

The client: £ _____

Partner (if living with the client as a couple): £ _____

Total: £ _____

Income details

Does your client or partner (if living with client as a couple) get Income Support, Income Based Job Seeker's Allowance, Guarantee State Pension Credit, Working Tax credit plus Child Tax credit* or Working Tax credit with disabilities element*

(*where gross income does not exceed £14, 213.)

☐ Yes. Ignore the rest of this section   ☐ No. Give the total weekly income of:

The client: £ _____

The client's partner (if living with the client as a couple): £ _____

Total: £ _____

Calculate the total allowable deductions:

Income tax: £ _____

National Insurance contributions: £ _____

Partner (if living with the client as a couple): £ _____

Attendance allowance, disability living allowance, constant attendance allowance and any payment made out of the Social Fund: £ _____

Dependent children and other dependants:

	Age	Number	
15 or under	_____		£ _____
16 or over	_____		£ _____

Less total deductions: £ _____

Total weekly disposable income: £ _____

Hannibal and Mountford Solicitors
20 High Street,
Lyme Bank, Lyme
LY10 34T

Telephone: 01576-455971
Fax: 01576-200345
Email: Hannibal@solicitors.co.uk

Crown Prosecution Service
Queen's Chambers
Blackburn Street
Lyme
LY3 2BE

Date: 11/12/-
Ref: RJ/SAW

Dear Sirs,

Re: Lyme Magistrates – 14th December
William Hardy – Sexual Activity with a Child

We are instructed on behalf of William Hardy who is due to make his first appearance before Lyme Magistrates' Court on the 14th December.

Please provide us with the following:

- Advance Information in accordance with Criminal Procedure Rules – Part 21.
- Details of our client's previous convictions.
- Details of any claim for compensation/restitution.
- A list of any offences to be taken into consideration
- A copy of our client's tape recorded interview

Yours faithfully,

R James
Hannibal and Mountford Solicitors

Anthony Hannibal (BA Partner), Louise Mountford (LL.B Partner), Denis Davies (LL.B Partner) Tim Howard
(LL.B Associate Solicitor), David Temple (LL.B Associate Solicitor), Rachel James (LL.B Associate Solicitor),
Mike Tamworth (Fellow of the Institute of Legal Executives), Lisa Hardy (Accredited Police Station Clerk),
Ali Khan (Accredited Police Station Clerk)
Regulated by the Law Society

Hannibal and Mountford Solicitors
20 High Street,
Lyme Bank, Lyme
LY10 34T

Telephone: 01576-455971
Fax: 01576-200345
Email: Hannibal@solicitors.co.uk

Date: 11/12/-

Ref: RJ/SAW

Clerk to the Justices
Lyme Magistrates Court
Lyme Square
Lyme

Dear Sirs,

Re: William Hardy – Date of First Hearing 14th December

We act on behalf of the above named client who is due to appear before Lyme Magistrates Court on the 14th December to answer charges of sexual activity with a child contrary to section 9(2) Sexual Offences Act 2003.

We enclose herewith an application for a Representation Order for your earliest attention.

Yours faithfully,

Rachel James
Hannibal and Mountford

DOCUMENT 7 REPRESENTATION ORDER APPLICATION

FORM A

APPLICATION FOR RIGHT TO REPRESENTATION IN CRIMINAL PROCEEDINGS

MAGISTRATES' COURT OR CROWN COURT

I apply for the right to representation:
For the purposes of proceedings before the:

CROWN/MAGISTRATES'/YOUTH COURT*

* HIGHLIGHT AS APPROPRIATE

PERSONAL DETAILS

1.a. SURNAME

HARDY

1.b. FORENAME

WILLIAM

1.c. USUAL ADDRESS

10 CAMBRIDGE PLACE, MADELEY, LYME

1.d. PRESENT ADDRESS (IF DIFFERENT FROM ABOVE)

1.e. DATE OF BIRTH

3/9/- Aged 24

2. CASE DETAILS

2.a. WHAT CHARGES HAVE BEEN BROUGHT AGAINST YOU? Briefly describe what it is that you are accused of doing e.g. theft of a DVD player worth £150

Sexual activity with a child (consensual sexual intercourse with a girl under the age of 16 but over the age of 13) contrary to s. 9(2) Sexual Offences Act 2003

2.b. ARE THERE ANY CO-DEFENDANTS IN THIS MATTER? IF YES, NAME THEM. IF NO, THEN GO TO QUESTION 3.

N/A

2.c. GIVE REASON WHY YOU AND YOUR CO-DEFENDANTS CANNOT BE REPRESENTED BY THE SAME SOLICITORS.

3. COURT PROCEEDINGS

3.a. I AM DUE TO APPEAR BEFORE:

THE: LYME MAGISTRATES	MAGISTRATES'/YOUTH COURT*
DATE: 4TH JANUARY	AT AM/PM

OR

3.b. I APPEARED BEFORE:

THE:	MAGISTRATES'/YOUTH COURT*
DATE:	AT AM/PM

AND (TICK WHATEVER APPLIES)

[] MY CASE HAS BEEN SENT TO THE CROWN COURT FOR TRIAL UNDER SECTION 51 OF THE CRIME AND DISORDER ACT

[] MY CASE HAS BEEN TRANSFERRED TO THE CROWN COURT FOR TRIAL

[] I WAS CONVICTED AND COMMITTED FOR SENTENCE TO THE CROWN COURT

[] I WAS CONVICTED AND/OR SENTENCED AND I WISH TO APPEAL AGAINST THE CONVICTION/SENTENCE*

4. OUTSTANDING MATTERS

If there are any other *outstanding* criminal charges or cases against you, give details including the court where you are due to appear:

5. REASONS FOR WANTING REPRESENTATION

To avoid the possibility of your application being delayed or publicly funded representation being refused because the court does not have enough information about the case, you must complete the rest of the form. When deciding whether to grant publicly funded representation the court will need to know why it is in the interests of justice for you to be represented. If you need help in completing the form you should speak to a solicitor.

	DETAILS	REASONS FOR GRANT OR REFUSAL (*FOR COURT USE ONLY*)
5a. IT IS LIKELY THAT I WILL LOSE MY LIBERTY *(You should consider seeing a solicitor before answering this question)*	I am charged with sexual activity with a girl under the age of 16. I am at real risk of a custodial sentence. The sentencing guidelines based on the old offence of unlawful sexual intercourse suggest a custodial sentence. Aggravating features include the fact that the girl is pregnant and it is alleged I was in a position of trust when I first met the girl.	
5b. I AM CURRENTLY SUBJECT TO A SENTENCE THAT IS SUSPENDED OR NON-CUSTODIAL THAT IF BREACHED MAY ALLOW THE COURT TO DEAL WITH ME FOR THE ORIGINAL OFFENCE. **PLEASE GIVE DETAILS.**		
5c. IT IS LIKELY THAT I WILL LOSE MY LIVLIHOOD.	I am training to become a teacher and have the offer of a job at a sixth form college. I stand to lose my job and future livelihood.	
5d. IT IS LIKELY THAT I WILL SUFFER SERIOUS DAMAGE TO MY REPUTATION.	I have no previous convictions. I am accused of an offence of a sexual nature. Conviction will seriously damage my reputation.	
5e. A SUBSTANTIAL QUESTION OF LAW IS INVOLVED. *(You will need the help of a solicitor to answer this question)*		

5f. I SHALL BE UNABLE TO UNDERSTAND THE COURT PROCEEDINGS OR STATE MY OWN CASE BECAUSE: **i. MY UNDERSTANDING OF ENGLISH IS INADEQUATE.** **ii. SUFFER FROM A DISABILITY**		
5g. WITNESSES HAVE TO BE TRACED AND/OR INTERVIEWED ON MY BEHALF (*State circumstances*)		
5h. THE CASE INVOLVES EXPERT CROSS EXAMINATION OF A PROSECUTION WITNESS (*Give brief details*)		
5i. IT IS IN SOMEONE ELSE'S INTERESTS THAT I AM REPRESENTED	As the offence involves a sexual intercourse with a child, it is clearly in the interest of the victim that I am represented.	
5j. ANY OTHER REASONS: (*Give further particulars*)		

6. LEGAL REPRESENTATION

6.a. If you do not give the name of a solicitor, the court will select a solicitor for you.

6.b. You must tell the solicitor that you have named him.

6.c. If you have been charged together with another person or persons, the court may assign a solicitor other than the solicitor of your choice.

THE SOLICITOR I WISH TO ACT FOR ME IS:

Miss R James

GIVE THE FIRM'S NAME AND ADDRESS (IF KNOWN):

Hannibal and Mountford Solicitors
20 High Street
Lyme Bank
Lyme

DECLARATION TO BE COMPLETED ON BEHALF OF THE SOLICITOR NAMED ABOVE:

I certify that the named solicitor above has a crime franchise contract or a general criminal contract, or an individual case contract.

I understand that only firms with a general criminal contract or individual case contract may provide representation in the Magistrates' Court.

Signed: R James

Dated: 11/12/-

7. DECLARATION

IF YOU KNOWINGLY MAKE A STATEMENT, WHICH IS FALSE, OR KNOWINGLY WITHHOLD INFORMATION, YOU MAY BE PROSECUTED.

IF CONVICTED, YOU MAY BE SENT TO PRISON FOR UP TO THREE MONTHS OR BE FINED OR BOTH (SECTION 21 ACCESS TO JUSTICE ACT 1999).

I apply for representation for the charge(s) that are currently before the court.

I understand that should my case proceed to the Crown Court or any other higher court, the court may order that I pay for some or all of the costs of representation incurred in the proceedings by way of a Recovery of Defence Costs Order.

I understand that should my case proceed to the Crown Court or any other higher court, I will have to furnish details of my means to the Court and/or the Legal Services Commission.

Signed: W Hardy   Dated: 11/12/-

FOR COURT USE ONLY

ANY ADDITIONAL FACTORS CONSIDERED WHEN DETERMINIGN THE APPLICATION, INCLUDING ANY INFORMATION GIVEN ORALLY.

DECISION ON THE INTEREST OF JUSTICE TEST

I HAVE CONSIDERED ALL AVAILABLE DETAILS OF ALL THE CHARGES AND IT IS/IS NOT IN THE INTERESTS OF JUSTICE THAT REPRESENTATION BE GRANTED FOR THE FOLLOWING REASONS:

The defendant is at real risk of a custodial sentence

The defendant will suffer serious damage to his reputation if convicted.

Signed: S Fisher   (Appropriate Officer)

Dated: 14th December

TO BE COMPLETED WHERE RIGHT TO REPRESENTATION EXTENDS TO THE CROWN COURT

STATEMENT OF MEANS FORM B GIVEN TO DEFENDANT ON: (DATE)

INDICATE TYPE OF CASE BELOW:

INDICTABLE ONLY   YES[ ] NO [ ]

SECTION 51 OFFENCE

EITHER-WAY OFFENCE AND ELECTED/NOT SUITABLE   YES [ ] NO [ ]
FOR SUMMARY TRIAL

FIRST DATE OF HEARING AT CROWN COURT:

FOR COURT USE ONLY

On reconsideration by a Legal Adviser/Magistrate/District Judge (Magistrates' Courts)/the Court, it has been determined that it is/is not on the interests of justice that the application be granted for the following reasons:

Signed:_____(Appropriate Officer)

Dated:

Hannibal and Mountford Solicitors
20 High Street,
Lyme Bank, Lyme
LY10 34T

Telephone: 01576–455971
Fax: 01576–200345
Email: Hannibal@solicitors.co.uk

Date: 11/12/-

Ref: RJ/SAW

Mr William Hardy
10 Cambridge Place
Madeley
Lyme

Dear Mr Hardy,

My name is Rachel James and I am an associate solicitor in the firm. As I explained in our initial meeting at the office, I will be responsible for and have the conduct of your case as it proceeds. Let me take this opportunity of thanking you for instructing us in this matter.

Nature of the case against you

As you are aware you have been charged with the offence of engaging in sexual activity with a child contrary to section 9 (1) Sexual Offences Act 2003. The girl in question is Rachel Coles. I understand she is 15 years. You were represented at Lyme Police Station by our Mr Ali Khan. Having discussed the matter with you, you made full and frank admissions in your interview with the police. As such you were charged with the offence outlined above and are due to make your initial appearance before Lyme Magistrates' Court on the 14th December. May I remind you that you were released from custody on police bail, subject to conditions not to contact Rachel Coles or her mother and not to approach their residence. It is important that you abide by these conditions. Should you fail to do so, you could find yourself being arrested and detained in custody.

Legal Aid

Your application for a Representation Order, which will enable you to be represented at court, has now been sent to the Lyme Magistrates' Court. I will inform you as soon as I know whether or not it has been granted.

If you are granted a Representation Order in your criminal proceedings you will not have to pay anything towards your legal costs providing your case remains in the magistrates court. If your case is committed to the Crown Court however, you could be asked to make a contribution towards your legal expenses in the event of your being convicted. If your case is committed to the Crown Court you will be required to complete a statement of your means on Form B. If this applies to your case, I will need you to complete Form B in good time. If you fail to provide this or any other financial information required by the Court you could face the risk of the Judge at the Crown Court ordering you to pay personally all or some of your legal costs under a recovery of defence costs order. If you are acquitted, you will not be required to pay anything.

If your representation order is withdrawn for any reason then your public funding ceases and you will be liable to pay your future legal costs in this case on a privately paying basis if you wish my firm to continue to represent you.

I would ask you to note that the Legal Services Commission will never pay the prosecution's cost (in the event of your conviction) even though you are a publicly funded party yourself. The level of costs ordered to be paid is normally assessed by the Court in a sum that is considered reasonable bearing in mind your means. This may not be the full amount of the prosecution's costs.

What will happen next?

Your case can be dealt with either in the Magistrates' Court or the Crown Court. We will advice you fully at the appropriate time as to which Court would be better for you if you are given the choice.

It is important that I obtain full copies of the prosecution's evidence against you. This is known as Advance Information. It will include a summary of your interview with the police and full particulars of Rachel Cole's evidence. Once I am in possession of this important information I will contact you with a view to taking your full instructions and determining your plea to the allegations made against you. Should the information I require from the prosecution not be received by me before your initial appearance before Lyme Magistrates on the 14th December, I will seek an adjournment of two to three weeks. Such a request is extremely common and in no way prejudices you.

If the case is adjourned for a committal for trial to the Crown Court it will normally be adjourned for between six and eight weeks. Once the case has been committed to the Crown Court you will be required to appear at a plea and case management hearing which could be another 4 weeks after committal. This is the hearing at which you would be expected to indicate your plea. If your case reaches the Crown Court, I will write to you again fully explaining the procedure.

If you plead guilty in the Magistrates' Court, the Magistrates' Court will have to decide whether it has sufficient powers to sentence you. If the Court does not feel that it has sufficient powers to sentence you, you will be committed for sentence in the Crown Court. It is likely that the National Probation Service would be required to prepare a pre-sentence report in any event to give the sentencing court much more information about you. I will advice you further as to sentence should the need arise.

Responsibility for the work

I will have the day to day responsibility for the conduct of your case together with overall supervision. Brian Lake, a trainee solicitor, will also be involved in helping me to prepare your case. He will work under my supervision. If I am unavailable for any reason, my secretary will either take a message or refer you to a colleague. If it becomes necessary for someone else to take over the conduct of your case you will be notified with an explanation of the reasons.

Should you wish to see someone else in the firm then we will with the best of endeavours try to accommodate your wishes. Persons dealing with matters within the firm are:

Anthony Hannibal (BA Partner)
Louise Mountford (LL.B Partner)
Denis Davies (LL.B Partner)
Tim Howard (LL.B Associate Solicitor)
David Temple (LL.B Associate Solicitor)
Rachel James (LL.B Associate Solicitor)

Complaints

The person with supervisory responsibility for your case is Mrs Louise Mountford. While we always endeavour to avoid problems, if there is any aspect of our service with which you are unhappy and which cannot be resolved between yourself and me, you should speak to Mrs Mountford.

Unless I contact you in the meantime, I will meet you at court on the 14th December at 9.30am.

If you have any queries at all about this letter please do not hesitate to contact me and I shall be happy to discuss it with you further.

Yours sincerely,

Rachel James

DOCUMENT 9   SPECIMEN LETTER FROM CPS DEALING WITH ADVANCE INFORMATION

CROWN PROSECUTION SERVICE
Queen's Chambers
Blackburn Street
Lyme
LY3 2BE

Date: 3/1/-

Ref: SS/IW

Hannibal and Mountford Solicitors
20 High Street
Lyme Bank
Lyme
LY10 34T

Dear Sirs,

Advance Disclosure Request
R v William Hardy
Date of hearing – 14th January

With reference to your letter dated the 11th December, requesting Advance Information in accordance with the Criminal Procedure Rules, Part 21, I enclose copies of the following documents:

(a) statements of witnesses

(b) copy of tape of interview

Tape-playing facilities are not available in court unless specifically required.

Yours faithfully,

Sonia Smith
Crown Prosecutor

DOCUMENT 10A STATEMENT OF RACHEL COLES

<u>WITNESS STATEMENT</u>

(CJ Act 1967, s. 9; MC Act 1980, s. 5A(3)(a) and s. 5B; MC Rules 1981, r. 70)

STOKESHIRE CONSTABULARY

This is a transcript of a video interview conducted at Lyme Police Station

Interview of:	**Rachel Coles**
Date of Birth:	**3/6/ (aged 15)**
Address:	**Supplied**
Interview at:	**Lyme Street Police Station**
Date:	**30/11/-**
Duration of Interview:	**60 minutes**
Interviewing Police Officer:	**D C Carol Harper 2365**
Other Persons Present:	**Rosie White, Social Worker**

Q. Rachel, I want to ask you some questions regarding your relationship with William Hardy. You understand that you don't have to answer any of my questions but that if you choose to do so it is very important that you speak the truth. We only want to find out the truth. It is not the case that you are in trouble – OK?

A. I understand.

Q. How old are you Rachel?

A. I am 15

Q. Which school do you attend?

A. Lyme Girls School.

Q. I understand that you are pregnant. Is that correct?

A. Yes (starts crying)

Q. Do you want to break?

A. No

Q. How many weeks pregnant are you?

A. 13 weeks

Q. Can you tell me who the father of your baby is Rachel?

A. It's William Hardy.

Q. You have been having a sexual relationship with William Hardy?

A. Yes I have.

Q. I am going to ask you some personal questions about your relationship with William Hardy – is that okay?

A. I suppose so.

Q. How do you know him?

A. My friend Emma – he is her brother

Q. So you have known William for some time?

A. Yes.

Q. Does William know how old you are?

A. Yes he does, although I lied to him about my age to begin with. I told him I was nearly 16.

Q: How did your relationship with William begin?

A. He gave me private maths lessons.

Q. I understand he is training to be a teacher?

A. Yes.

Q. Where did these lessons take place?
A. At my house.

Q. Did anything inappropriate occur?
A. What do you mean?

Q. Did you just focus on mathematics and nothing else?
A. Yes, but we talked a lot – he was a really good listener.

Q. What sort of things did you discuss?
A. Personal stuff.

Q. Personal stuff?
A. Yeah-he told me about his father and I told him about my parents that's all.

Q. When did these lessons take place?
A. In January this year.

Q. So you would be 14 at that time?
A. Yes.

Q. Did any sexual contact take place during these lessons?
A. This is embarrassing – we just kissed okay and hugged one another.

Q. Did you want him to hug you?
A. Look – I was upset over something, right – he just gave me a hug.

Q. Who initiated the kissing?
A. It was me. I just wanted to be close to him.

Q. Did he touch you anywhere else during these lessons?
A. I let him feel my breasts.

Q. Did sexual intercourse take place during any of your lessons?
A. No-nothing really happened okay. He said he couldn't get involved with me because I was too young and he had to go back to University.

Q. As far as you can recall when did you first have sexual intercourse with William?
A. Sometime at the end of April or start of May I think. I went out with him. We had a drink and on the way back home we made love in the back of his car.

Q. You said you had a drink? Was that an alcoholic drink?
A. Yes.

Q. Were you drunk?
A. I suppose I was a bit but not really drunk.

Q. Did William buy you the drink?
A. I asked for a drink with the meal and he paid, okay.

Q. Did you want to have sexual intercourse with William?
A. Yes.

Q. You said you felt a bit drunk-did you understand what you were consenting to Rachel?
A. Yes I did – I really wanted him to make love to me okay.

Q: What type of sex did you have?
A. What do you mean?

Q. Was it oral sex or vaginal sex?
A: Vaginal sex.

Q. Were any precautions taken?
A. William wore a condom. We agreed I would go on the pill.

Q. Did you suggest that you would go on the contraceptive pill, Rachel?
A. I think William mentioned it – he said he would prefer to do it without wearing a condom and I said I would see my doctor.

Q. How old were you when you first had sexual intercourse with William Hardy?
A. It was 14 – nearly 15.

Q. Was this the first time you ever had sex?
A. Yes.

Q. Did William know that you were a virgin, Rachel?
A. No – not before we did it – I told him afterwards.

Q. Did you have sexual intercourse on any further occasions?
A. Yes.

Q How many times did you have sex?
A. God I don't know, 10 or 12 times.

Q. Always with your consent?
A. Always.

Q. Were you under the influence of alcohol on any of these occasions?
A. I cannot remember – sometimes we would have a beer and stuff. Look, he really fancied me and I fancied him. We were in love, okay – it was that simple, okay. I cannot believe it's all got so messy.

Q. Did you subsequently go on the contraceptive pill, Rachel?
A. Yes, I did.

Q. When was this?
A. In April . . . I think.

Q. Have you had sex with anyone else?
A. No I haven't – I'm not some sort of slag.

Q. Did William wear a condom when you were having sex?
A. No – not when I went on the pill.

Q. You are certain William is the father of your baby?
A. I am certain – I didn't take the pill every day.

Q. Are you still seeing William?
A. No – he's got another girlfriend.

Q. Is there anything you wish to add or clarify?
A. No – except I am sorry he has got into so much trouble (starts crying).

Interview terminated.

DOCUMENT 10B STATEMENT OF SANDRA COLES

<u>WITNESS STATEMENT</u>

(CJ Act 1967, s. 9; MC Act 1980, s. 5A(3)(a) and s. 5B; MC Rules 1981, r. 70)

Statement of (name of witness) Sandra Coles

Age of witness (if over 18 enter 'over 18') Over 18

Occupation: Doctor's Receptionist

Address: Supplied

This statement (consisting of two pages, each signed by me) is true to the best of my knowledge and belief, and I make it knowing if it is tendered in evidence, I shall be liable to prosecution if I have wilfully stated in it anything which I know to be false or do not believe to be true.

Dated: 30/11/   Signed: S Coles

I am the mother of Rachel Coles who is 15 years old. My daughter's date of birth is the 3/6/- I am living apart from Rachel's father, my husband. I live with Rachel and her brother in the former matrimonial home. Rachel's father left home several months ago. It would be fair to say that Rachel has found his absence difficult to cope with.

My daughter is three months pregnant. The father of her baby is William Hardy. It is my understanding that he is 24 years of age. In January this year, I hired William Hardy to provide Rachel with some extra tuition in maths as she was struggling at school. On at least four occasions, he attended my home and was alone with Rachel in the study.

I first became aware that Rachel was having a relationship with William Hardy in August this year. I was appalled. I explained to Rachel at the time that I thought William was too old for her. I suggested to her that he would only be after one thing, namely sexual intercourse and that I was concerned that she was vulnerable. Notwithstanding my protestations, Rachel continued to see William Hardy behind my back. This led to further arguments between Rachel and me. I started to become more and more concerned for Rachel's well being by the end of August. She was regularly staying out until the early hours of the morning. On one or two occasions she came back in an intoxicated state. She told me she had been with her boyfriend at his own house and that they had had pizza and had shared a bottle of wine. She had been watching a video and had fallen asleep not realising the time. I was livid and wrote William Hardy a letter the next day making quite plain my objections to the relationship.

I was concerned the whole matter would affect Rachel's school-work. I tried to stop Rachel from having anything to do with William Hardy and directly appealed to him on several occasions, including writing the letter – it was all to no avail.

I noticed a change in Rachel's behaviour in October of this year. She became increasingly moody with me and tearful. I asked her if the relationship had ended and she told me quite firmly that it had not. One morning, two or three days later, I heard Rachel being sick in the toilet. I feared the worst and immediately challenged Rachel, asking her if she was pregnant. She told me she was and broke down in tears. I asked her if William Hardy was responsible. She refused to tell me at first but eventually admitted that it was William's child. I asked her if he had taken any precautions before having sex. I was told in fact that he had suggested Rachel go on the pill. Rachel told me she had consulted our family doctor and that respecting her confidence he had prescribed the pill without my knowledge and consent.

At this point I was absolutely devastated. I went over to William Hardy's home later that day and confronted his mother. I would have confronted him had he been there. I immediately involved the police, who in turn involved Social Services. As far as I am aware, Rachel is presently not seeing William Hardy. Rachel has undergone counselling and has yet to decide what to do about the pregnancy. She and I are both devastated by the pregnancy.

As far as I am aware, prior to Rachel's involvement with William Hardy she had had no previous boyfriend, and certainly no sexual contact.

Signed: S Coles

Taken by: Carol Harper DS 2365

DOCUMENT 10C   STATEMENT OF DR R FORREST

WITNESS STATEMENT

(CJ Act 1967, s. 9; MC Act 1980, s. 5A(3)(a) and s. 5B; MC Rules 1981, r. 70)

Statement of (name of witness) Dr. Richard Forrest.

Age of witness (if over 18-state over 18) Over18

Occupation: General Medical Practitioner

Address: Supplied

This statement (consisting of two pages signed by me) is true to the best of my knowledge and belief, and I make it knowing if it is tendered in evidence, I shall be liable to prosecution if I have wilfully stated in it anything which I know to be false or do not believe to be true.

Dated: 2/12/-   Signed: R Forrest

I am a General Practitioner.

Rachel Coles is my patient. I have treated Rachel since moving to the practice when Rachel was five.

This statement is made with the consent of both Rachel and her mother, Sandra Coles.

I had a consultation with Rachel according to my medical notes on the 18th June when she informed me that she wished to take the oral contraceptive pill for contraceptive purposes. I spoke at length with Rachel about the risks of sexual intercourse but she was firmly adamant that her sexual relationship was to continue and that she wished to be prescribed an oral contraceptive. Rachel asked me not to inform her mother. As she was 15 and appeared emotionally mature, I respected her confidence and prescribed her the oral contraceptive pill.

Rachel was prescribed a low risk contraceptive pill, Brevinor. Her blood pressure was taken before the prescription was given. She was informed that she should read carefully the explanatory leaflet and that her partner should take additional precautions to protect against sexually transmitted diseases etc.

On the 1st November last I had a further consultation with Rachel. She informed me that she thought she was pregnant. She had symptoms of morning sickness and tiredness. Furthermore she had missed two periods. It was agreed that she should undergo a pregnancy test. The test proved positive. A range of possibilities with regard to the pregnancy was discussed with Rachel.

I had a further consultation with Rachel three days later. She was extremely upset insisting that she did not wish to be pregnant. In consultation with Rachel's mother I referred Rachel to the Royal Lyme Hospital for the purposes of having her pregnancy terminated. The termination was confirmed to me by letter on the 13th December last. Rachel was also prescribed a pessary for the treatment of vaginal thrush. No further medical problems were encountered and Rachel left hospital the day after the termination.

Signed: R Forrest MD

Taken by: DC S Brown 3954

DOCUMENT 10D   STATEMENT OF DC C HARPER

WITNESS STATEMENT

(CJ Act 1967, s. 9; MC Act 1980, s. 5A(3)(a) and s. 5B; MC Rules 1981, r. 70)

Statement of (name of witness) DC Carol Harper 2365

Age of witness (if over 18 enter 'over 18') Over 18.

Occupation: Detective Constable 2365

Address Lyme Street Police Station

This statement (consisting of one page signed by me) is true to the best of my knowledge and belief, and I make it knowing if it is tendered in evidence, I shall be liable to prosecution if I have wilfully stated in it anything which I know to be false or do not believe to be true.

Dated: 8/12/   Signed: C Harper

I am a Detective Constable in the Stokeshire Constabulary stationed at Lyme Police Station.

Acting upon information received and in the presence of DC Simon Brown I went on Friday, 4th December to William Hardy at his address of 10 Cambridge Place, Madeley, Lyme. On answering the door, William Hardy confirmed his identity to me. I informed Mr Hardy that I wished to ask him some questions regarding his relationship with a Miss Rachel Coles. He replied 'I've been expecting you'. I cautioned Mr Hardy and asked if he had a relationship with Rachel Coles. He confirmed that he had. I asked him if he would be prepared to answer some questions at Lyme Street Police Station the following Monday. He agreed. At 1000 hours on Monday 7th December, William Hardy presented himself at Lyme Street Police Station. He was arrested on suspicion of having engaged in sexual activity with a child, namely a girl under the age of 16. He was subsequently interviewed on tape by me in the presence of his legal adviser. Two tapes were used and a sealed master tape is available as exhibit 'CH1'.

At the conclusion of the interview William Hardy was charged with an offence contrary to s. 9(2) Sexual offences Act 2003. He was cautioned and released on conditional bail pending his initial appearance before Lyme Magistrates.

Signed: Carol Harper DC 2365

DOCUMENT 10E   RECORD OF INTERVIEW

Person interviewed: WILLIAM HARDY

Place of interview: LYME STREET

Date of interview: 7/12/-

Time commenced: 1030 HRS

Time concluded: 1100 HRS

Duration of interview: 30 MINUTES

Interviewing officer(s): DC CAROL HARPER 2365
                        DC SIMON BROWN 3954

Other persons present: ANJUNA KAHN-POLICE STATION ADVISER

Tape reference number: 21 /CH/45937/05/-

Exhibit Number: CH1

Policy Exhibit No:	
No of pages:	
Signature of interviewing officer producing exhibit	
DC C Harper	

Tape counter Times(s)	Person speaking	Text

Introduction and caution given. Reminded of the reason for his arrest

Tape counter Times(s)	Person speaking	Text
0035	Harper	William, I want to ask you some questions regarding your relationship with Rachel Coles. Do you accept you have been having a sexual relationship with Rachel Coles?
0040	R	Yes, I do
0100	Harper	Can you confirm your age?
0114	R	I am 24.
0125	Harper	Do you know how old Rachel Coles is?
0130	R	Yes – she is 15.
0140	Harper	Rachel alleges you and she have been having a sexual relationship. Is that correct?
0160	R	What you mean is that her mother is making the allegation, and yes I accept that I have been having a sexual relationship with Rachel.
0200	Harper	Have you known Rachel for some time?
0230	R	I have known her for a while – she is a friend of my sister.
0240	Harper	And your sister is how old?
0250	R	She is the same age as Rachel – she is 15.
0300	Harper	You know it is a criminal offence to have sexual intercourse with a girl under the age of 16?
0330	R	Yes I do, and I sincerely regret it.
0340	Harper	When did you start to get interested in Rachel?
0400	R	God, I don't know – sometime in March this year.
0422	Harper	I understand that you are training to become a teacher and that in January this year you provided Rachel with extra maths tuition at her home?
0450	R	Yes.
0500	Harper	Did any sexual contact take place during these lessons?
0528	R	Absolutely not.
0540	Harper	So you deny fondling Rachel's breasts and kissing her during these lessons.
0600	R	Absolutely – has she said that? She knows that is not true.
0640	Harper	Rachel has stated that you and she talked about personal matters during these lessons. Is that correct?

0713	R	Look – I don't know where you are going with this. Nothing inappropriate occurred while I was engaged in providing Rachel with maths tuition. I knew she fancied me – it was obvious but I did not take advantage. There was one occasion when she got upset talking about her dad. I told her that my dad had been killed in a car accident and how tough it had been. She became upset and I just gave her a reassuring hug and that was it. If she took it to mean something else, it wasn't.
0830	Harper	When do you say sexual contact first took place?
0850	R	It was in April, I think, I cannot be too sure of the dates.
0930	Harper	Did you initiate this sexual contact?
1003	R	It was a mutual thing. We had fallen in love.
1020	Harper	Do you accept that sexual intercourse occurred sometime toward the end of April in your car?
1035	R	Yes.
1100	Harper	And that when you had sex with her you knew she was only 14?
1115	R	She was 14 but I have to say she is an emotionally mature young woman – she knew exactly what she wanted and what to do. It was Rachel who initiated sex. She behaved more like a 21-year-old. When I first met her she told me she was nearly 16. Did she tell you that?
1200	Harper	Did you ply her with alcoholic drink before having sex with her?
1210	R	No. I resent the tone of your questions – you are making me out as some sort of sexual predator who has got a thing for young girls, and I'm not. I accept it was totally wrong and should never have happened but we were in love. I did not ply her with drink. I brought her a beer to go with her pizza. It is what she asked me for. When I saw her at my brother's birthday party earlier in the year she was pretty drunk. I do not think she is a stranger to the odd alcoholic drink. No, I did not ply her with drink with a view to getting her into bed, if that it was you are intimating.
1340	Harper	Did you know she was a virgin before having sex?
1405	R	She told me she had had a previous sexual experience with someone older than her so no, I didn't think she was a virgin.
1430	Harper	But you realised afterwards that she had lied to you but that didn't stop you having sex with her again did it?
1500	R	No reply.
1546	Harper	Was it your suggestion that Rachel should see her GP and go on to the contraceptive pill?
1600	R	No it wasn't – she said she would see her GP, it was her idea.
1635	Harper	Nevertheless you had unprotected sexual intercourse with Rachel on further occasions?
1718	R	Yes.
1800	Harper	Rachel states that sexual intercourse took place between 10 or 12 times between April and October. Is this correct?
1900	R	You must be kidding – I wasn't at home all that often. I would say it was five or six times at the most.
2000	Harper	Are you aware that Rachel is three months pregnant?
2100	R	Yes I am.
2140	Harper	Are you the father of her baby?
2200	R	I understand that I am.
2245	Harper	Given that you intend to qualify as a teacher do you accept that your conduct was entirely inappropriate and morally reprehensible?

2300	R	Look, I am not taking a lecture from you. I accept that I have been a complete and utter fool – what can I say?– it should not have happened but it did. I really liked her, fancied her, and no way was she shy or anything – she pursued me and everything we did together was consensual. I regret getting involved with Rachel but it was difficult to resist her charms and that is something I am going to be paying for, for some time. I do not wish to add anything further.

Interview terminated 30 minutes.

DOCUMENT 11   FILE NOTE OF INTERVIEW REVIEWING ADVANCE INFORMATION WITH CLIENT

File note: 5/1/

Attending Mr Hardy at the office. Taking him through the Advance Information. Accepting the substance of what is said in the statements. However, William vehemently denies that he reciprocated any sexual advances made by Rachel during the private maths tuition sessions. William is adamant that sexual intercourse occurred on no more than 5 or 6 occasions. He has learnt that Rachel has had an abortion.

William continues to undertake his teacher training course. He has checked with the Department of Education and will definitely be unable to teach children below the age of 16 in the event of conviction. He is resigned to the fact that a number of career avenues will be closed for him.

I explained that the next stage of the case would be the plea before venue/mode of trial. Based on the evidence William will plead guilty. However this is on the basis that he was not in a position of trust when the sexual relationship began and that intercourse took place on a small number of occasions and was consensual at all times. I explained that if this was not acceptable to the CPS, a 'Newton Hearing' might be required. I further explained to William that the magistrates could send him to the Crown Court for sentence and that they would almost certainly order a pre-sentence report, necessitating a three to four week adjournment. William sought specific advice on sentencing. Based on my research and my experience I told him that he was at a serious risk of imprisonment although I would do my best to mitigate the risk. I asked him to give me with the names of persons who might be prepared to provide him with a character reference.

William tells me he has had a consultation with his GP who has diagnosed him as having depression. I obtained William's written consent to write to his GP to obtain confirmation.

I explained that I would write to the CPS indicating the basis of his guilty plea to see if agreement could be reached. Date of next hearing is 14th January.

Time engaged: 40 minutes

DOCUMENT 12A FILE NOTE OF PLEA BEFORE VENUE (GUILTY PLEA ENTERED)

File note: 14th January

Attending Lyme Magistrates' Court.

Speaking with Clara Bailey CPS lawyer. Explaining the basis on which William Hardy was prepared to plead guilty. After due consideration, Ms Bailey indicated that she was prepared to accept Mr Hardy's plea on the basis that no sexual behaviour occurred during the time at which Mr Hardy was providing Rachel Coles with private maths tuition. An agreed basis of plea was subsequently drafted at court (copy attached on file).

William Hardy duly entered a guilty plea. CPS outlined the facts. Submission made to request the magistrates to accept jurisdiction to sentence. This was agreed and an all options pre-sentence report was ordered with the case being adjourned for four weeks. Mr Hardy was placed on conditional bail not to approach Rachel Coles or her mother or to contact them in any way and not to approach their home.

Spoke to Mr Hardy after the hearing. He handed me the name and address of a possible character witness. Explained the importance of him abiding by the condition of his bail and being completely open with the probation service in the preparation of the report, the contents of which I will discuss with him in due course.

Date of next hearing: 18th February

Time engaged:
Preparation 10 minutes
Attendance with client 10 minutes
Court hearing 10 minutes
Waiting 30 minutes
Travelling 20 minutes

Note – You can view the plea before venue hearing in relation to William Hardy in the video clip section of our Online Resource Centre. When viewing this scenario, please bear in mind that when filming took place the provisions of the Sexual Offences Act 2003 were not in force and William Hardy was charged with the old offence of unlawful sexual intercourse with a girl under the age of 16 contrary to s. 6 Sexual Offences Act 1956.

**online
resource
centre**

LYME MAGISTRATES' COURT CHARGES CONTRARY TO S. 9(2)
SEXUAL OFFENCES ACT 2003

I, William Hardy, intend to plead guilty to the charge of having engaged in unlawful sexual activity with Rachel Coles. The basis of my guilty plea is agreed with the Crown Prosecution Service. In pleading guilty, I accept that I had full, penetrative sexual intercourse with Rachel Coles on five or six occasions and that I knew her to be 15 years old. Ms Coles's consent was freely given on each and every occasion when sexual intercourse occurred and was in the context of a loving relationship. At no time did I abuse my position of trust on the small number of occasions when I was paid to provide Ms Coles with extra maths tuition. Such tuition took place many weeks before our sexual interest in each other began.

Signed: William Hardy

Signed: Clara Bailey
For and on behalf of the Crown Prosecution Service

Dated: 14th January

DOCUMENT 13   PRE-SENTENCE REPORT

SPECIMEN PRE-SENTENCE REPORT
This is a Pre-Sentence report as defined in
Section 158 of the Criminal Justice Act
and has been prepared in accordance
with the requirements of the National
Standard for Pre-Sentence Reports

National Probation Service
for England and Wales

THIS REPORT IS A CONFIDENTIAL DOCUMENT

OFFENDER'S DETAILS

Name	William Hardy
Date of Birth	14/2/– (aged 24)
Address	10 Cambridge Place
	Madeley
	Lyme
Post Code	

COURT DETAILS

Sentencing Court	Lyme Magistrates
Date of hearing	18/2/-
Local Justice Area	Lymeshire
Date report requested	14/1-

OFFENCE DETAILS

Offence(s) (dealt with in this PSR):	Date of offence
Unlawful sexual activity with a child (15-year-old)	May–October

PSR WRITER'S DETAILS

Name	Tom Finn
Official Title	Probation Officer
Office Location	Festival Lane, Lyme

Date report completed and signed:	10th February

1. SOURCES OF INFORMATION

This report is underpinned and informed by an Offender Assessment System (OASys) in the identification of the risk of reconviction and the risk of harm presented by this defendant.

In the preparation of this report I have undertaken one interview with Mr Hardy. I have also read the Advance Information provided by the Crown Prosecution Service. I have also discussed Mr Hardy with the group leader for the Sex Offender Treatment Programme.

2. OFFENCE ANALYSIS

Mr Hardy does not refute the Prosecution's version of events for the most part. The complainant was a friend of Mr Hardy's sister. Mr Hardy accepts that he was in a position of trust vis a vis the complainant, having regard to his age and more importantly to the fact that he provided extra maths tuition to the complainant last January. These lessons were paid for by the complainant's mother and took place over a period of four weeks at her home. Mr Hardy denies that any sexual contact took place during these lessons. The complainant maintains that it did, although it did not amount to sexual intercourse. Mr Hardy admits to being aware of the complainant's interest in him during these lessons and admits a number of conversations of an intimate nature took place. It seems apparent that the prelude to subsequent intercourse occurred during these lessons.

Mr Hardy maintains that he thought the complainant was a year older than she said she was. He also states that she seduced him from the outset and was clearly intent on pursuing him. He accepts that this does not excuse his behaviour and that for someone who nurtures the ambition of becoming a teacher, his conduct was grossly inappropriate. Mr Hardy maintains that sexual intercourse took place on a handful of occasions only.

In the course of our interview, Mr Hardy found it difficult to explain why he became involved. He maintains he is not attracted to young girls and that his previous relationships have all been with females of the same age as himself. He admits to being flattered by the complainant's determined attention and believes that to begin with he simply gave in to his sexual urges. Having crossed the rubicon, Mr Hardy states he came to care for the complainant and found himself falling in love with her. At the height of their relationship, he maintains he genuinely saw some future in it.

The relationship was brought to an end when the complainant's mother discovered that the her daughter was two months pregnant. The pregnancy has since been terminated. Mr Hardy expressed his deep remorse for the outcome of events in our interview and his concern for the future wellbeing of the complainant. He fully understands the risks associated with underage sex. He is extremely embarrassed by his conduct. He maintains he has been very naive and that his conduct will not be repeated.

3. OFFENDER ASSESSMENT

This OASys summarises the relevant factors which have been identified as contributing to the defendant's risk of reconviction. The indicators which reach or exceed the mid-way point on the chart are those which need to be addressed in order to reduce the likelihood of further offences being committed.

Factors Contributing to Offending

Below 50%=Below threshold of concern. 50% and above = Above threshold of concern

	0%	50%	100%

Offending information	———
Accommodation	———
Education, training, employment	———
Financial management	———
Relationships	—————————
Lifestyle and associates	———————
Drug misuse	—————
Alcohol misuse	—————
Emotional wellbeing	———————————
Thinking and behaviour	———————————
Attitudes	—————————

Mr Hardy is a young man aged 24. He is local to the area. He lives, for the most part, with his mother in a privately owned detached house. Mr Hardy has a younger brother who is 18 and a sister, Emma, aged 14, who had been a friend of the victim in this matter. Mr Hardy's father died tragically in a car accident when he was 19. Mr Hardy explained that this had a profound effect on him and his family. He describes his world as having been turned upside down. He was due to attend University but deferred his place in order to be with his mother and siblings.

Prior to this tragedy Mr Hardy describes a normal upbringing in a loving, if not strict environment. His mother is a committed Christian and Mr Hardy was a regular church attendee until the age of 15. He completed his secondary education with nine GCSEs and went on to complete three A Levels. His grades were disappointing, prompting Mr Hardy to attend night school in order to better his grades. Mr Hardy states he found his father's death motivated him to take control of his life and to try and enjoy it to the full. He has a wide circle of friends. He attended the Manchester Metropolitan University when he was 21 and gained an upper second class honours degree in Sports Science. He is currently enrolled on a Postgraduate Certificate in Education, which he intends to complete. His ultimate ambition is to teach, preferably at sixth form level. This conviction, however, puts a teaching career in jeopardy.

Mr Hardy is a man of past good character. He currently receives a student loan worth about £3,000. He works part time in a bar earning approximately £100 per week. From this he has to pay tuition fees, board and lodging, a car loan and car related expenses. He is a beneficiary under his late paternal grandmother's will. Her property is on the market for £120,000. Mr Hardy expects to receive a third share along with his siblings.

Mr Hardy is currently in a new relationship with a fellow student. She is 23. He hopes that they will be able to set up home together at some stage. She is aware of the court proceedings.

4. ASSESSMENT OF THE RISK OF HARM TO THE PUBLIC AND THE LIKELIHOOD OF RE-OFFENDING

Likelihood of reconviction:	Low	Low–Medium	Medium	Medium–High	High
Likelihood of re-offending	Low	Low–Medium	Medium	Medium–High	High

Mr Hardy presents a low risk of reconviction for an offence of a sexual nature, or indeed any other type of offence. He has shown some understanding of the motivation behind his offending and the risks that such conduct can cause. Despite suffering a recent bout of depression, Mr Hardy does not pose a risk of self-harm.

5. CONCLUSION

The nature of this offence is concerning. The complainant was in a relationship of quasi-trust with Mr Hardy. She was only 14 and has undergone the trauma of an abortion as a result of the sexual activity she engaged in with Mr Hardy. Although sexual intercourse took place in the context of a loving and consensual relationship, it was still a corrupting experience for her. Mr Hardy is very concerned about the prospect of a custodial sentence. It is difficult to see what would be achieved by the imposition of a custodial sentence. The potential loss of Mr Hardy's future career might be considered punishment enough. Mr Hardy would be suitable for a Community Order with requirements. Mr Hardy is capable of undertaking unpaid work in the community. In particular the Court may wish to consider the merits of a supervision requirement combined with a Sex Offender Treatment Programme requirement.

Proposal: Community Order with a supervision requirement to last two years. Under section 42 Schedule 2, paragraph 2 of the Powers of Criminal Courts (Sentencing) Act 2000, you are required to participate in individual and group programmes as and when you are directed by your supervising officer to do so. Attendance at these programmes shall be for not more than 60 days in the aggregate.

Signed: Tom Finn

Date: 10/2/-

DOCUMENT 14   STATEMENT OF CHARACTER WITNESS 1

STATEMENT OF EVELYN HARDY

I have been asked by my son's solicitor to put down my thoughts on paper. I am absolutely devastated by William's involvement with Rachel Coles. I am surprised by his conduct. William has been brought up to know better. We come from a close knit family. I am a regular worshipper at Church. William's father died tragically in a car accident five years ago. His death had a profound effect on us all. William has a younger brother Stephen aged 18 and his sister Emma, who is 14.

I was unaware that William had been seeing Rachel Coles. Had I been aware of the relationship I would have done my best to put a stop to it. The relationship was evidently conducted in secret. Rachel is a friend of my daughter, and not even she knew.

The past eight weeks or so have been an absolute nightmare. William's actions have caused us a great deal of distress. We stand by him, however. He has our love and support. Naturally, as a Christian I am disappointed by Rachel's decision to terminate the pregnancy. I understand her reasons for doing so. I have no doubt that William would have accepted the responsibilities of fatherhood. I do not understand what possessed William to become involved with Rachel. Evidently they were in love and saw some future in the relationship. Rachel must accept some share of the blame for what has occurred.

William has always been a dutiful son. I am very proud of his achievements. He has been involved with charitable work since he was 18. Two years ago he spent six months in Ghana coaching and working with underprivileged children. That is what is so frustrating, as William has such a good rapport with children. He has studied hard and that is why I find it so hard to accept that he could be throwing it all away. I have been concerned by his state of mind in recent weeks. He seems very depressed. He is normally such a positive person with an abundance of energy. The entire episode has been a sobering experience for William.

Signed: Evelyn Hardy

31/1/-

DOCUMENT 15   STATEMENT OF CHARACTER WITNESS 2

The Bothy
Wengard Lane
Southfields
Lyme

28/1/-

Dear Sirs,

Re: William Hardy

I have been asked to provide a reference on behalf of William Hardy.

I was a good friend of Charles Hardy, William's father. Charles tragically died in a car accident five years ago. I have remained a friend of the family ever since.

I have known William since he was five years old. I have always found William to be a sensitive, sensible and honourable young man. There is no doubt that the death of his father affected him greatly. In the months following his father's death, William assumed the responsibilities as head of the family until his mother felt she could cope. He has remained a very attentive and dutiful son and a tremendous brother to Stephen and Emma.

I have never known William to be in trouble of any kind. He never went through a rebellious stage. He has worked hard at school and for his degree. He has also undertaken a lot of charitable work for one so young.

I am aware of the court proceedings against William. He has been extremely naive and I am surprised by his lack of judgment in the matter. I have discussed the matter with him. He is most contrite and extremely worried about the outcome of the proceedings. I cannot speculate as to what William's motives were for getting involved with a girl so young. I sincerely believe that he has learned from this experience and will be all the wiser for it.

Yours sincerely

Major Tim Henderson

DOCUMENT 16   RECORD OF ATTENDANCE AT SENTENCING HEARING

18th February

Attending Lyme Magistrates' Court for sentencing hearing.

I took Mr Hardy through the pre-sentence report, the content of which he was prepared to accept.

Outline of the facts was presented by the CPS. Making a lengthy plea in mitigation and guiding the bench through the pre-sentence report. William was given a four-month term of imprisonment. The Chair of the Magistrates explained that the right message had to be sent out to the public and that an offence of this nature was so serious that only custody was justified. Credit had been give for Mr Hardy's timely guilty plea. Mr Hardy was placed on the Sex Offender's notification register for five years.

Speaking to Mr Hardy and his mother after the hearing. Mrs Hardy was in tears and William looked bewildered. I discussed the possibility of an appeal against sentence to the Crown Court. I explained that I thought he was in with a chance and that I would consider drafting a notice of appeal and a possible bail application when I returned to the office.

Mr Hardy will be transferred to HMP at Shawbury.

Time engaged:
Travel 20 minutes
Waiting 30 minutes
Preparation 30 minutes
Attending client 20 minutes
Advocacy 35 minutes

online resource centre

The actual sentencing hearing in relation to this case can be viewed in the video section of our Online Resource Centre. Document 17 contains a transcript of the prosecutor's outline of the facts and the plea in mitigation submitted by Mr Hardy's solicitor. *

The magistrates' court work can now be billed on the lower standard fee category and would be put on the CDS6 which is the monthly return.

* We ask you to note that when filming took place, the new sentencing provisions under the Criminal Justice Act 2003 were not in force. Whilst we have been able to amend the documentation in the case study to reflect the changes, we were unable to undertake re-filming. On the video you will therefore see Mr Hardy sentenced under the old law.

DOCUMENT 17   TRANSCRIPT OF PLEA IN MITIGATION BASED FOR THE MOST PART ON THE FILMED VIDEO VERSION OF THE SENTENCING HEARING ON OUR ONLINE RESOURCE CENTRE

R v WILLIAM HARDY

Prosecution outline of the facts

Your worships – the defendant Mr. Hardy is a 24-year-old postgraduate student and at the time of the offence was training to become a teacher. In January of last year he was invited by the victim's mother to provide the victim with some extra tuition in maths and he was paid for this. No sexual intercourse took place at this time. It appears that the defendant first engaged in the act of sexual intercourse with the young lady in April or May of last year. At that time the defendant believed her to be 15 and on the first occasion when sexual intercourse took place she was in fact on 14. It soon became apparent that the young lady had not had prior sexual experience. The defendant insisted the victim subsequently went on the contraceptive pill however sexual intercourse of an unprotected nature took place on further occasions. The relationship continued until October of last year despite much opposition from the young lady's mother. Shortly after the relationship ended the young lady realised that she was 12 weeks pregnant. Since that time she has undergone a termination of that pregnancy. As I am sure you can imagine your worships, the past few weeks have been especially difficult for the young lady and her family.

When the defendant was interviewed he admitted that sexual intercourse had taken place approximately six times over an eight or nine month period. There was an allegation made by the victim that the defendant had intercourse on an occasion when she was intoxicated with alcohol bought for her by the defendant. This was denied by the defendant in an interview. It should be made clear that the young lady is adamant that all sexual acts that took place between her and the defendant took place with her express consent and encouragement for the most part. In interview the defendant stated that as far as he was aware the young lady had wanted to be involved in intercourse each time it took place and they had enjoyed both a happy and fulfilling experience. In fact, at the time of the relationship the defendant hoped that the relationship would continue and that the couple would be able to live together legally when the young lady was 16. Your worships, when the defendant was interviewed he was not exactly contrite during the interview. However, he did express some concern of the young lady's welfare. Mr Hardy is a man of past good character.

Madam, those are the facts. There is no formal claim for compensation although it is something that you may wish to consider in the exercise of your discretion today. Prosecution costs are applied for in the sum of £135.

Defence plea in mitigation

Ma'am, I wonder whether at this stage you have had an opportunity to read the pre-sentence report (yes, we have). I am grateful for that indication. Ma'am, as you have heard, Mr. Hardy is a young man of 24 years of age. He is deeply remorseful and he clearly regrets this offence. I would ask you to give Mr Hardy full credit for his early guilty plea and that credit would also include his co-operation with the police investigation.

Mr Hardy certainly accepts that there was a sexual relationship between him and Miss Coles which initially started at the end of April of last year. The first contact Mr Hardy had with Miss Coles was through his sister who is of a similar age. Mr Hardy had come to know Miss Coles through his sister and it was through the family that they had arranged for Mr Hardy to provide some private tuition for some maths lessons. Mr Hardy is adamant that no inappropriate behaviour took place during those tuition lessons and it is accepted by the prosecution that that is the case. Strictly speaking, Mr Hardy was not in a position of trust at the time of sexual intercourse later when that did take place.

Ma'am, a rapport began to develop between Mr Hardy and Miss Coles, and that was all at that stage. Mr Hardy then returned to university to review his studies in the final year of his degree. It was later in March that the relationship resumed. Mr Hardy returned home to an eighteenth birthday party of his brother and he then came across Miss Coles in a social scene. Ma'am, Mr Hardy accepts that on this occasion Miss Coles was intoxicated with alcohol and that she was very flirtatious on that evening and essentially that is how the relationship started.

Ma'am, at the point of sexual intercourse Mr Hardy actually believed that Miss Coles was a year older. He believed that she was 15 years of age at that point. Ma'am, by the time that Mr Hardy and Miss Coles had embarked on a sexual relationship they were essentially a young couple in love. The relationship was a consensual and loving one, and you have heard from the prosecution that indeed Miss Coles accepts that it was a consensual relationship. The relationship continued on an ad hoc basis because Mr Hardy was continuing his studies at University. The couple became more involved when he returned during the summer. Mr Hardy is adamant that sex only took place on approximately five or six occasions and the prosecution have accepted that that is the case.

Mr Hardy is certainly very regretful about the pregnancy. Mr Hardy did not take precautions during sexual intercourse because the injured party herself had insisted that she was taking the contraceptive pill. Mr Hardy would have wished to have remained by her side and helped her through these problems, particularly because she has had a termination, but clearly you will be aware of the bail conditions that were imposed by the Court initially and Mr Hardy has been unable to have any communication with her whatsoever but certainly would have stood by her.

Ma'am, Mr Hardy does not wish to seek to minimise the seriousness of this offence. He realises that it is a highly serious offence and once for which he is at risk of a custodial sentence. But I would ask you this question 'is his offence so serious that only custody is the option available to him today?' Is custody justified in these circumstances? I would suggest to you that Mr Hardy was not in a position of trust at the time that sexual intercourse took place and he is not a sexual predator. Indeed, he has had previous relationships with girlfriends who have only been a similar age to himself, and currently has a relationship with his girlfriend who stands by him.

Ma'am, you will have read the pre-sentence report and you will have seen from paragraph 9 of that report that Mr Hardy presents a low risk of reconviction for offences of a sexual nature, or indeed any other type of offence. He has shown some understanding of the motivation behind his offending and the risk that such conduct can cause. Ma'am, the probation service has clearly indicated a proposal of a community penalty with a number of specified requirements for which Mr Hardy would be eligible.

Ma'am, there has been particular stress upon the family during these proceedings. Certainly Mr Hardy's mother has found it particularly difficult because her son has been branded a paedophile. Also Mr Hardy's sister has found it considerably difficult, still being at school with the injured party herself and the problems that have resulted from these proceedings. Mr Hardy is deeply regretful that his actions have caused some much upset.

Ma'am, Mr Hardy has now completed his degree and has to his credit attained an upper second class degree in sports science and biology. He is currently taking a PGCE in teaching. Ma'am, you will understand the difficulties with Mr Hardy will face in becoming a teacher with a conviction of this nature. Indeed, a lot of the avenues that would have been open to him will certainly now be closed. At present Mr Hardy has actually been offered a job at sixth form college teaching physical education and science. It is assumed that that particular position will no longer be available once Mr Hardy is convicted of this offence and has received a sentence. That sentence will include a requirement to register, of course, on the Sex Offender's Register. It is a tentative hope that Mr Hardy could gain employment in the teaching field in the sixth form area but certainly he will not be in a position to teach children under the age of 16 years. Mr Hardy did have a great career ahead of him. Clearly he hopes to become a teacher. He has a great rapport with children as I will indicate to you in a moment through his voluntary work. Through this very, very foolish relationship that he embarked on, his chosen career will most probably now be at an end.

You may consider in the circumstances Ma'am, that the fact that his career may well be at an end is sufficient punishment.

Ma'am, you will also have read from the report about Mr Hardy's involvement in voluntary work and football. Prior to university, he spent three months in Ghana at a charitable organisation teaching football to the poor and underprivileged and clearly this is a great credit to him and the community.

Ma'am, at present Mr Hardy is undertaking bar work. He earns £100 per week he has a student loan of £3,000 per annum and he would roughly take home from that about £57 per week. His outgoings are roughly £95 per week.

Ma'am, I do have two references to hand into the court. These are from his mother who has provided a detailed reference and also a family friend Major Tim Henderson.

Ma'am, in the circumstances you are aware that this matter may result in a custodial sentence being justified but I would seek to persuade you to impose a community penalty today. As you have seen from the pre-sentence report, Mr Hardy is eligible for community penalties. A community order would give Mr Hardy the opportunity to reflect on his actions and he would be in a position to become fully involved with the probation service and in particular with the sex offender treatment programme. Ma'am, I would urge you in those circumstances to impose a community penalty. Ma'am, it is difficult to see what a custodial sentence would achieve in these circumstances.

Ma'am, those are my representations at this stage, unless you have any specific questions for me.

DOCUMENT 18   LETTER TO CLIENT

Hannibal and Mountford Solicitors
20 High Street,
Lyme Bank, Lyme
LY10 34T

Telephone: 01576-455971
Fax: 01576-200345
Email: Hannibal@solicitors.co.uk

Date: 25/2/-

Ref: RJ/SAW

Mr William Hardy
HMP Shawbury
Lymeshire

Dear Mr Hardy,

Re: Appeal against sentence

I am pleased to be able to tell you that your appeal against sentence has been listed for hearing on the 13th March at 2.30pm. This is the earliest date Lyme Crown Court could accommodate. I have briefed a barrister to represent you before the Crown Court.

The prison authorities will make the necessary arrangements to transport you to the Crown Court. A member of staff from the firm will meet you there on the 13th March.

Do not hesitate to contact me if you need any help or advice in the meantime.

Yours sincerely,

Rachel James
Rachel James
Hannibal and Mountford

Anthony Hannibal (BA Partner), Louise Mountford (LL.B Partner), Denis Davies (LL.B Partner)
Tim Howard (LL.B Associate Solicitor), David Temple (LL.B Associate Solicitor), Rachel James
(LL.B Associate Solicitor), Mike Tamworth (Fellow of the Institute of Legal Executives),
Brian Lake (LL.B Trainee Solicitor), Lisa Hardy (Accredited Police Station Clerk),
Ali Khan (Accredited Police Station Clerk)
Regulated by the Law Society

DOCUMENT 19   NOTICE OF APPEAL AGAINST SENTENCE

MAGISTRATES' COURTS PROCEDURE

Notice of Appeal to Crown Court against conviction, order or sentence (Magistrates' Courts Act 1980, s. 108: Crown Court Rules 1982, r. 7).

To: Clerk to the Justices for Lyme Magistrates' Court sitting at Lyme AND to the Crown Prosecution Service.

On the 14th January, William Hardy was convicted by the above magistrates' court as follows: for an offence contrary to s. 9(2) Sexual Offences Act 2003 for which William Hardy pleaded guilty and for which the court on the 8th February sentenced William Hardy to four months imprisonment.

I give notice that I intend to appeal to the Crown Court at Lyme against sentence.

The general grounds for appeal are: the imposition of a custodial sentence for this offence was wrong in principal in the light of strong personal mitigating factors.

Dated: 22nd February   Signed: W Hardy

DOCUMENT 20 BRIEF TO COUNSEL TO REPRESENT WILLIAM HARDY AT THE APPEAL HEARING, BEFORE LYME MAGISTRATES' COURT

IN THE LYME CROWN COURT

R

v

William Hardy

BRIEF TO COUNSEL TO APPEAL AGAINST SENTENCE

Counsel receives herewith the following:

1. Statement of William Hardy

2. Prosecution witness statements comprising:-
   a) Rachel Coles (victim)
   b) Sandra Coles (victim's mother)
   c) DC Carol Harper
   d) Dr R Forrest

3. Transcript of tape recorded interview

4. Pre-sentence report

5. Character witness statement-Evelyn Hardy

6. Character witness statement-Major Henderson

7. Copy of attendance note

8. Notice of Application to Appeal

9. Copy Representation Order

1. Counsel's instructing solicitors act on behalf of William Hardy. Mr Hardy is 24. He pleaded guilty before Lyme Magistrates to an offence of sexual intercourse with a child under the age of 16, contrary to s. 9 Sexual Offences Act 2003 on the 14th January. Jurisdiction to sentence Mr Hardy was retained by Lyme Magistrates and on the 18th February. Mr Hardy was sentenced to a period of four months imprisonment and placed on the Sex Offender's Register for a period of five years. He wishes to appeal against his sentence.

2. Counsel is referred to Document 1 which contains Mr Hardy's proof of evidence. The prosecution's case is contained in Documents 2(a–d). Counsel will note that Mr Hardy has never denied having a sexual relationship with Ms Coles and that all incidents of sexual intercourse took place within the context of a loving, consensual relationship. Ms Coles and Mr Hardy came to know each other through Mr Hardy's younger sister. In January last year, Mr Hardy provided Ms Coles with some extra maths tuition. There was no ulterior motive. Ms Coles was struggling with maths. Mr Hardy had been able to provide assistance to his sister. At the invitation of Ms Coles's mother, Mr Hardy agreed to provide extra tuition at the home of Ms Coles. It was an agreed basis of plea that Mr Hardy had not engaged in any inappropriate sexual behaviour during these lessons. It is accepted however that Ms Coles became attracted to Mr Hardy at this time.

3. A sexual relationship did not begin until April/May of that year. It seems clear from Ms Coles's interview that it was she who took up the initiative. Sexual intercourse took place on a handful of occasions during the summer. Mr Hardy states that he had fallen in love with Ms Coles and that they were planning a future together when she came of age. Mr Hardy accepts that he was completely wrong and very naïve.

4. The relationship broke down in October of last year when Ms Coles's mother discovered the relationship and Ms Coles fell pregnant.

5. Counsel will see from Document 4 that a helpful pre-sentence report was prepared on Mr Hardy's behalf. In addition, the court was referred to two written character reference – Documents 5 and 6. In spite of instructing solicitor's best efforts, Mr Hardy was sentenced to four months in custody. Credit was given for his timely guilty plea. Since sentence, Mr Hardy has been inside HMP Shawbury and is by all accounts finding it very difficult.

6. Instructing solicitors take the view that the imposition of a custodial sentence upon Mr Hardy was exceptionally hard. In the absence of a Newton hearing, the court is presumed to have accepted that Mr Hardy was not in a strict position of trust vis a vis the victim when he engaged in sexual intercourse with her.

7. In passing sentence the magistrates took the view that the offence was so serious that only custody could be justified and that the right message had to be sent out to the public. The predecessor of s. 9(2) Sexual Offences Act 2003 is of course s. 6 Sexual Offences Act 1956 – engaging in unlawful sexual intercourse with a girl under the age of 16. There are no specific Magistrates' Court Sentencing Guidelines on this offence although reference might be made to the National Mode of trial Guidelines 1995 and the offence of indecent assault. Counsel is referred however to the Court of Appeal's decision in *R v Taylor* [1977] 1 WLR 612 where Lawton LJ talked of virtuous friendships ending in unlawful sexual intercourse as not meriting a sentence of a punitive nature. Lawton LJ went on to say however that a man in a supervisory capacity who abuses his position of trust for his own sexual gratification should get a sentence somewhere near the maximum (two years under the 1956 Act). In between there come many degrees of guilt. Instructing solicitors are unaware of any new sentencing guidelines that have been issued in connection with the Sexual Offences Act 2003, although the matter is subject to a consultation exercise being undertaken by the Sentencing Advisory Panel.

8. Instructing solicitors would concede that Ms Coles was a vulnerable individual. However, to a certain extent so too was Mr Hardy. Counsel will see from his statement and from the pre-sentence report and character witness statements that the death of Mr Hardy's father affected him enormously. The age disparity between Mr Hardy and Ms Coles was not huge. Mr Hardy was not in a position of trust when their relationship began to develop. It is accepted that Ms Coles was a virgin but she had led Mr Hardy to believe she had had a prior sexual experience. It is accepted that sexual intercourse occurred more than once.

9. In terms of mitigation, Mr Hardy has no previous convictions and pleaded guilty at the earliest opportunity. He has showed his complete remorse and very deeply regrets the fact that Ms Coles became pregnant and subsequently underwent an abortion. Mr Hardy is not a sexual predator. This was a one-off offence in which the victim was a willing participant. Mr Hardy is assessed as presenting a low risk of re-offending. He has learned a very hard lesson. The conviction has cost Mr Hardy his career. He was well on his way to qualifying as a teacher. His reputation is in ruins and the impact on his family cannot be understated.

10. Instructing solicitors would probably concede that on the face of it the offence was so serious as to justify a custodial sentence. However, the court seems to have ignored the strong mitigating factors raised by instructing solicitors and referred to in the pre-sentence report. Instructing solicitors believe a community disposition coupled with the payment of compensation to Ms Coles to be the most sensible outcome and one that meets the requirements of justice.

11. Counsel is asked to represent Mr Hardy before Lyme Crown Court on his appeal against sentence on the 13th March.

Rachel James
Hannibal and Mountford Solicitors
28th February

DOCUMENT 21   NOTE OF CROWN COURT APPEAL HEARING

13th March

Attending Lyme Crown Court. Mr Hardy was represented by Ben Knight of counsel. The sentencing hearing was heard before Mr Recorder Dawson and two lay magistrates. The court determined that a custodial sentence was right in principal for this particular offence but that the term should be suspended for 12 months.

Time engaged:
In conference 30 minutes
Hearing 30 minutes
Travel 20 minutes
Waiting 20 minutes

The proceedings having finally concluded, a claim for costs can now be submitted to the Crown Court on a Standard Fee Form.

APPENDIX 3

EXTRACTS FROM MODE OF TRIAL GUIDELINES 2004

The purpose of these guidelines is to help magistrates decide whether or not to commit defendants charged with 'either way' offences for trial in the Crown Court. Their object is to provide guidance not direction. They are not intended to impinge on a magistrate's duty to consider each case individually and on its own particular facts. These guidelines apply to all defendants aged 18 and above.

GENERAL MODE OF TRIAL CONSIDERATIONS

Section 19 of the Magistrates' Courts Act 1980 requires magistrates to have regard to the following matters in deciding whether an offence is more suitable for summary trial or trial on indictment:

(a) the nature of the case;

(b) whether the circumstances make the offence one of a serious character;

(c) whether the punishment which a magistrates' court would have power to inflict for it would be adequate;

(d) any other circumstances which appear to the court to make it more suitable for the offence to be tried in one way rather than the other;

(e) any representations made by the prosecution or the defence.

Certain general observations can be made:

(a) The court should never make its decision on the grounds of convenience or expedition.

(b) The court should assume for the purpose of deciding mode of trial that the prosecution version of the facts is correct.

(c) The fact that the offences are alleged to be specimens is a relevant consideration (although, it has to be borne in mind that difficulties can arise in sentencing in relation to specimen counts see *R v Clark* [1996] 2 Cr App R (S) 351 and *R v Canavan and others* [1998] 1 Cr App R (S) 243); the fact that the defendant will be asking for other offences to be taken into consideration, if convicted, is not.

(d) Where cases involve complex questions of fact or difficult questions of law, including difficult issues of disclosure of sensitive material, the court should consider committal for trial.

(e) Where two or more defendants are jointly charged with an offence each has an individual right to elect his mode of trial.

(f) In general, except where otherwise stated, either way offences should be tried summarily unless the court considers that the particular case has one or more of the features set out in paragraphs 51.4 to 51.18 (see below) and that its sentencing powers are insufficient.

(g) The court should also consider its power to commit an offender for sentence under sections 3 and 4 of the Powers of Criminal Courts (Sentencing) Act 2000, if information emerges during the course of the hearing which leads it to conclude that the offence is so serious, or the offender such a risk to the public, that its powers to sentence him are inadequate. This means that committal for sentence is no longer determined by reference to the character and antecedents of the offender.

FEATURES RELEVANT TO INDIVIDUAL OFFENCES

Where reference is made in these guidelines to property or damage of 'high value' it means a figure equal to at least twice the amount of the limit (currently £5,000) imposed by statute on a magistrates' court when making a compensation order.

BURGLARY: DWELLING-HOUSE

Cases should be tried summarily unless the court considers that one or more of the following features is present in the case and that its sentencing powers are insufficient. Magistrates should take account of their powers under sections 3 and 4 of the Powers of Criminal Courts (Sentencing) Act 2000 to commit for sentence.

(a) Entry in the daytime when the occupier (or another) is present.

(b) Entry at night of a house which is normally occupied, whether or not the occupier (or another) is present.

(c) The offence is alleged to be one of a series of similar offences.

(d) When soiling, ransacking, damage or vandalism occurs.

(e) The offence has professional hallmarks.

(f) The unrecovered property is of high value.

(g) The offence is racially motivated.

NOTE: Attention is drawn to paragraph 28(c) of Schedule 1 to the Magistrates' Courts Act 1980 by which offences of burglary in a dwelling cannot be tried summarily if any person in the dwelling was subjected to violence or the threat of violence.

BURGLARY: NON-DWELLING

Cases should be tried summarily unless the court considers that one or more of the following features is present in the case and that its sentencing powers are insufficient. Magistrates should take account of their powers under sections 3 and 4 of the Powers of Criminal Courts (Sentencing) Act 2000 to commit for sentence.

(a) Entry of a pharmacy or doctor's surgery.

(b) Fear is caused or violence is done to anyone lawfully on the premises (e.g. night-watchman, security guard).

(c) The offence has professional hallmarks.

(d) Vandalism on a substantial scale.

(e) The unrecovered property is of high value.

(f) The offence is racially motivated.

THEFT AND FRAUD

Cases should be tried summarily unless the court considers that one or more of the following features is present in the case and that its sentencing powers are insufficient. Magistrates should take account of their powers under sections 3 and 4 of the Powers of Criminal Courts (Sentencing) Act 2000 to commit for sentence.

(a) Breach of trust by a person in a position of substantial authority, or in whom a high degree of trust is placed.

(b) Theft or fraud which has been committed or disguised in a sophisticated manner.

(c) Theft or fraud committed by an organised gang.

(d) The victim is particularly vulnerable to theft or fraud, e.g. the elderly or inform.

(e) The unrecovered property is of high value.

HANDLING

Cases should be tried summarily unless the court considers that one or more of the following features is present in the case and that its sentencing powers are insufficient. Magistrates should take account of their powers under sections 3 and 4 of the Powers of Criminal Courts (Sentencing) Act 2000 to commit for sentence.

(a) Dishonest handling of stolen property by a receiver who has commissioned the theft.

(b) The offence has professional hallmarks.

(c) The property is of high value.

SOCIAL SECURITY FRAUDS

Cases should be tried summarily unless the court considers that one or more of the following features is present in the case and that its sentencing powers are insufficient. Magistrates should take account of their powers under sections 3 and 4 of the Powers of Criminal Courts (Sentencing) Act 2000 to commit for sentence.

(a) Organised fraud on a large scale.

(b) The frauds are substantial and carried out over a long period of time.

VIOLENCE (SECTIONS 20 AND 47 OF THE OFFENCES AGAINST THE PERSON ACT 1861)

Cases should be tried summarily unless the court considers that one or more of the following features is present in the case and that its sentencing powers are insufficient. Magistrates should take account of their powers under sections 3 and 4 of the Powers of Criminal Courts (Sentencing) Act 2000 to commit for sentence.

(a) The use of a weapon of a kind likely to cause serious injury.

(b) A weapon is used and serious injury is caused.

(c) More than minor injury is caused by kicking or head-butting.

(d) Serious violence is caused to those whose work has to be done in contact with the public or are likely to face violence in the course of their work.

(e) Violence to vulnerable people, e.g. the elderly and infirm.

(f) The offence has clear racial motivation.

NOTE: The same considerations apply to cases of domestic violence.

PUBLIC ORDER ACT OFFENCES

Cases should be tried summarily unless the court considers that one or more of the following features is present in the case and that its sentencing powers are insufficient. Magistrates should take account of their powers under sections 3 and 4 of the Powers of Criminal Courts (Sentencing) Act 2000 to commit for sentence.

(a) Cases of violent disorder should generally be committed for trial.

(b) Affray.

(c) Organised violence or use of weapons.

(d) Significant injury or substantial damage.

(e) The offence has clear racial motivation.

(f) An attack on police officers, ambulance staff, fire-fighters and the like.

VIOLENCE TO AND NEGLECT OF CHILDREN

Cases should be tried summarily unless the court considers that one or more of the following features is present in the case and that its sentencing powers are insufficient. Magistrates should take account of their powers under sections 3 and 4 of the Powers of Criminal Courts (Sentencing) Act 2000 to commit for sentence.

(a) Substantial injury.

(b) Repeated violence or serious neglect, even if the physical harm is slight.

(c) Sadistic violence, e.g. deliberate burning or scalding.

INDECENT ASSAULT

Cases should be tried summarily unless the court considers that one or more of the following features is present in the case and that its sentencing powers are insufficient. Magistrates should take account of their powers under sections 3 and 4 of the Powers of Criminal Courts (Sentencing) Act 2000 to commit for sentence.

(a) Substantial disparity in age between victim and defendant, and a more serious assault.

(b) Violence or threats of violence.

(c) Relationship of trust or responsibility between defendant and victim.

(d) Several more serious similar offences.

(e) The victim is particularly vulnerable.

(f) Serious nature of the assault.

UNLAWFUL SEXUAL INTERCOURSE

Cases should be tried summarily unless the court considers that one or more of the following features is present in the case and that its sentencing powers are insufficient. Magistrates should take account of their powers under sections 3 and 4 of the Powers of Criminal Courts (Sentencing) Act 2000 to commit for sentence.

(a) Wide disparity of age.

(b) Breach of position of trust.

(c) The victim is particularly vulnerable.

DRUGS

Class A:

(a) Supply; possession with intent to supply: these cases should be committed for trial.

(b) Possession: should be committed for trial unless the amount is consistent only with personal use.

Class B:

(a) Supply; possession with intent to supply: should be committed for trial unless there is only small scale supply for no payment.

(b) Possession: should be committed for trial when the quantity is substantial and not consistent only with personal use.

DANGEROUS DRIVING AND AGGRAVATED VEHICLE TAKING

Cases should be tried summarily unless the court considers that one or more of the following features is present in the case and that its sentencing powers are insufficient. Magistrates should take account of their powers under sections 3 and 4 of the Powers of Criminal Courts (Sentencing) Act 2000 to commit for sentence.

(a) Alcohol or drugs contributing to the dangerous driving.

(b) Grossly excessive speed.

(c) Racing.

(d) Prolonged course of dangerous driving.

(e) Other related offences.

(f) Significant injury or damage sustained.

CRIMINAL DAMAGE

Cases should be tried summarily unless the court considers that one or more of the following features is present in the case and that its sentencing powers are insufficient. Magistrates should take account of their powers under sections 3 and 4 of the Powers of Criminal Courts (Sentencing) Act 2000 to commit for sentence.

(a) Deliberate fire-raising.

(b) Committed by a group.

(c) Damage of a high value.

(d) The offence has clear racial motivation.

APPENDIX 4

MAGISTRATES' COURT SENTENCING GUIDELINES*

* Reproduced with the very kind permission of the Magistrates' Association. A complete copy of the guidelines may be accessed via password on our Online Resource Centre.

<table>
<tr><td>

Assault –
actual bodily harm

</td><td>

Offences Against the Person Act 1861 s.47
Triable either way – see Mode of Trial Guidelines
Penalty: Level 5 and/or 6 months

</td></tr>
</table>

CONSIDER THE SERIOUSNESS OF THE OFFENCE
(INCLUDING THE IMPACT ON THE VICTIM)

IS DISCHARGE OR FINE APPROPRIATE?

IS IT SERIOUS ENOUGH FOR A COMMUNITY PENALTY?

GUIDELINE: → *IS IT SO SERIOUS THAT ONLY CUSTODY IS APPROPRIATE?*

ARE YOUR SENTENCING POWERS SUFFICIENT?

THIS IS A GUIDELINE FOR A FIRST-TIME OFFENDER PLEADING NOT GUILTY

⊕ CONSIDER AGGRAVATING AND MITIGATING FACTORS ⊖
AND THE WEIGHT TO ATTACH TO EACH

for example	for example
Abuse of trust (domestic setting) Deliberate kicking or biting Extensive injuries (may be psychological) Headbutting Group action Offender in position of authority On hospital/medical or school premises Premeditated Victim particularly vulnerable Victim serving the public Weapon *This list is not exhaustive*	Minor injury Provocation Single blow *This list is not exhaustive*

If offender is on bail, this offence is more serious
If offender has previous convictions, their relevance and any failure to respond to previous sentences should be considered – they may increase the seriousness. The court should make it clear, when passing sentence, that this was the approach adopted.

TAKE A PRELIMINARY VIEW OF SERIOUSNESS,
THEN CONSIDER OFFENDER MITIGATION

for example
Age, health (physical or mental)
Co-operation with police
Evidence of genuine remorse
Voluntary compensation

CONSIDER YOUR SENTENCE

Compare it with the suggested guideline level of sentence and reconsider your reasons carefully if you have chosen a sentence at a different level. Consider a reduction for a timely guilty plea.

DECIDE YOUR SENTENCE
NB. COMPENSATION – Give reasons if not awarding compensation

Burglary (dwelling)	Theft Act 1968 s.9 Triable either way – see Mode of Trial Guidelines Penalty: Level 5 and/or 6 months

CONSIDER THE SERIOUSNESS OF THE OFFENCE
(INCLUDING THE IMPACT ON THE VICTIM)

IS DISCHARGE OR FINE APPROPRIATE?

IS IT SERIOUS ENOUGH FOR A COMMUNITY PENALTY?

IS IT SO SERIOUS THAT ONLY CUSTODY IS APPROPRIATE?

GUIDELINE: →   **ARE YOUR SENTENCING POWERS SUFFICIENT?**

THIS IS A GUIDELINE FOR A FIRST-TIME OFFENDER PLEADING NOT GUILTY

⊕ CONSIDER AGGRAVATING AND MITIGATING FACTORS AND THE WEIGHT TO ATTACH TO EACH ⊖

for example	for example
Force used or threatened Group enterprise High value (in economic or sentimental terms) property stolen More than minor trauma caused Professional planning/organisation/ execution Significant damage or vandalism Victim injured Victim present at the time Vulnerable victim *IF ANY of the above factors are present you should commit for sentence.*	First offence of its type AND low value property stolen AND no significant damage or disturbance AND no injury or violence Minor part played Theft from attached garage Vacant property *ONLY if one or more of the above factors are present AND none of the aggravating factors listed are present should you consider NOT committing for sentence.*

If racially or religiously aggravated, or offender is on bail, this offence is more serious
If offender has previous convictions, their relevance and any failure to respond to previous sentences should be considered – they may increase the seriousness. The court should make it clear, when passing sentence, that this was the approach adopted.

TAKE A PRELIMINARY VIEW OF SERIOUSNESS, THEN CONSIDER WHETHER THE CASE SHOULD BE COMMITTED FOR SENTENCE, THEN CONSIDER OFFENDER MITIGATION

for example
    Age, health (physical or mental)
    Co-operation with police
    Evidence of genuine remorse
    Voluntary compensation

CONSIDER COMMITTAL OR YOUR SENTENCE

Compare it with the suggested guideline level of sentence and reconsider your reasons carefully if you have chosen a sentence at a different level. Consider a reduction for a timely guilty plea.

DECIDE YOUR SENTENCE
NB. COMPENSATION – Give reasons if not awarding compensation

Common assault	Criminal Justice Act 1988 s.39 Triable only summarily Penalty: Level 5 and/or 6 months

CONSIDER THE SERIOUSNESS OF THE OFFENCE
(INCLUDING THE IMPACT ON THE VICTIM)

IS DISCHARGE OR FINE APPROPRIATE?

GUIDELINE: → *IS IT SERIOUS ENOUGH FOR A COMMUNITY PENALTY?*

IS IT SO SERIOUS THAT ONLY CUSTODY IS APPROPRIATE?

THIS IS A GUIDELINE FOR A FIRST-TIME OFFENDER PLEADING NOT GUILTY

➕ CONSIDER AGGRAVATING AND MITIGATING FACTORS AND THE WEIGHT TO ATTACH TO EACH ➖

for example	for example
Abuse of trust (domestic setting) Group action Injury Offender in position of authority On hospital/medical or school premises Premeditated Spitting Victim particularly vulnerable Victim serving the public Weapon *This list is not exhaustive*	Impulsive Minor injury Provocation Single blow *This list is not exhaustive*

If offender is on bail, this offence is more serious
If offender has previous convictions, their relevance and any failure to respond to previous sentences should be considered – they may increase the seriousness. The court should make it clear, when passing sentence, that this was the approach adopted.

TAKE A PRELIMINARY VIEW OF SERIOUSNESS, THEN CONSIDER OFFENDER MITIGATION

for example
Age, health (physical or mental)
Co-operation with police
Evidence of genuine remorse
Voluntary compensation

CONSIDER YOUR SENTENCE

Compare it with the suggested guideline level of sentence and reconsider your reasons carefully if you have chosen a sentence at a different level. Consider a reduction for a timely guilty plea.

DECIDE YOUR SENTENCE
NB. COMPENSATION – Give reasons if not awarding compensation

Sexual Offences Act 1956 ss.14&15
Triable either way – see Mode of Trial Guidelines
Penalty: Level 5 and/or 6 months
Entry in Sex Offender's Register (consult legal adviser)

Indecent assault

CONSIDER THE SERIOUSNESS OF THE OFFENCE
(INCLUDING THE IMPACT ON THE VICTIM)

IS DISCHARGE OR FINE APPROPRIATE?

IS IT SERIOUS ENOUGH FOR A COMMUNITY PENALTY?

GUIDELINE: → IS IT SO SERIOUS THAT ONLY CUSTODY IS APPROPRIATE?

ARE YOUR SENTENCING POWERS SUFFICIENT?

THIS IS A GUIDELINE FOR A FIRST-TIME OFFENDER PLEADING NOT GUILTY

➕ CONSIDER AGGRAVATING AND MITIGATING FACTORS AND THE WEIGHT TO ATTACH TO EACH ➖

for example	for example
Age differential	Slight contact
Breach of trust	*This list is not exhaustive*
Injury (may be psychological)	
Prolonged assault	
Very young victim	
Victim deliberately targeted	
Victim serving the public	
Vulnerable victim	
This list is not exhaustive	

If racially or religiously aggravated, or offender is on bail, this offence is more serious
If offender has previous convictions, their relevance and any failure to respond to previous sentences should be considered – they may increase the seriousness. The court should make it clear, when passing sentence, that this was the approach adopted.

TAKE A PRELIMINARY VIEW OF SERIOUSNESS, THEN CONSIDER OFFENDER MITIGATION

for example
 Age, health (physical or mental)
 Co-operation with police
 Evidence of genuine remorse
 Voluntary compensation

CONSIDER YOUR SENTENCE

*Compare it with the suggested guideline level of sentence and reconsider
your reasons carefully if you have chosen a sentence at a different level.
Consider a reduction for a timely guilty plea.
Entry in Sex Offender's Register (consult legal adviser).*

DECIDE YOUR SENTENCE
NB. COMPENSATION – Give reasons if not awarding compensation

Theft	Theft Act 1968 s.1 Triable either way – see Mode of Trial Guidelines Penalty: Level 5 and/or 6 months May disqualify where committed with reference to the theft or taking of a vehicle

CONSIDER THE SERIOUSNESS OF THE OFFENCE
(INCLUDING THE IMPACT ON THE VICTIM)

IS DISCHARGE OR FINE APPROPRIATE?

GUIDELINE: → *IS IT SERIOUS ENOUGH FOR A COMMUNITY PENALTY?*

IS IT SO SERIOUS THAT ONLY CUSTODY IS APPROPRIATE?

ARE YOUR SENTENCING POWERS SUFFICIENT?

THIS IS A GUIDELINE FOR A FIRST-TIME OFFENDER PLEADING NOT GUILTY

⊕ CONSIDER AGGRAVATING AND MITIGATING FACTORS AND THE WEIGHT TO ATTACH TO EACH ⊖

for example
- High value
- Planned
- Sophisticated
- Adult involving children
- Organised team
- Related damage
- Vulnerable victim
- *This list is not exhaustive*

for example
- Impulsive action
- Low value
- *This list is not exhaustive*

If racially or religiously aggravated, or offender is on bail, this offence is more serious
If offender has previous convictions, their relevance and any failure to respond to previous sentences should be considered – they may increase the seriousness. The court should make it clear, when passing sentence, that this was the approach adopted.

TAKE A PRELIMINARY VIEW OF SERIOUSNESS, THEN CONSIDER OFFENDER MITIGATION

for example
- Age, health (physical or mental)
- Co-operation with police
- Evidence of genuine remorse
- Voluntary compensation

CONSIDER YOUR SENTENCE

Compare it with the suggested guideline level of sentence and reconsider your reasons carefully if you have chosen a sentence at a different level. Consider a reduction for a timely guilty plea.

DECIDE YOUR SENTENCE
NB. COMPENSATION – Give reasons if not awarding compensation

| Theft Act 1968 s.1
Triable either way – see Mode of Trial Guidelines
Penalty: Level 5 and/or 6 months | **Theft in breach of trust** |

CONSIDER THE SERIOUSNESS OF THE OFFENCE
(INCLUDING THE IMPACT ON THE VICTIM)

IS DISCHARGE OR FINE APPROPRIATE?

IS IT SERIOUS ENOUGH FOR A COMMUNITY PENALTY?

GUIDELINE: → IS IT SO SERIOUS THAT ONLY CUSTODY IS APPROPRIATE?

ARE YOUR SENTENCING POWERS SUFFICIENT?

THIS IS A GUIDELINE FOR A FIRST-TIME OFFENDER PLEADING NOT GUILTY

⊕ CONSIDER AGGRAVATING AND MITIGATING FACTORS AND THE WEIGHT TO ATTACH TO EACH ⊖

for example	for example
Casting suspicion on others Committed over a period High value Organised team Planned Senior employee Sophisticated Vulnerable victim *This list is not exhaustive*	Impulsive action Low value Previous inconsistent attitude by employer Single item Unsupported junior *This list is not exhaustive*

If racially or religiously aggravated, or offender is on bail, this offence is more serious
If offender has previous convictions, their relevance and any failure to respond to previous sentences should be considered – they may increase the seriousness. The court should make it clear, when passing sentence, that this was the approach adopted.

TAKE A PRELIMINARY VIEW OF SERIOUSNESS, THEN CONSIDER OFFENDER MITIGATION

for example
Age, health (physical or mental)
Co-operation with police
Evidence of genuine remorse
Voluntary compensation

CONSIDER YOUR SENTENCE

Compare it with the suggested guideline level of sentence and reconsider your reasons carefully if you have chosen a sentence at a different level. Consider a reduction for a timely guilty plea.

DECIDE YOUR SENTENCE
NB. COMPENSATION – Give reasons if not awarding compensation

| Road Traffic Act 1988 s.3
Triable only summarily
Penalty: Level 4
Must endorse (3-9 points OR may disqualify) | **Careless driving** |

CONSIDER THE SERIOUSNESS OF THE OFFENCE

GUIDELINE: →
IS DISCHARGE OR FINE APPROPRIATE?
IS IT SERIOUS ENOUGH FOR A COMMUNITY PENALTY?

(COMMUNITY REHABILITATION AND CURFEW ORDERS ARE THE ONLY
AVAILABLE COMMUNITY PENALTIES FOR THIS OFFENCE)

THIS IS A GUIDELINE FOR A FIRST-TIME OFFENDER PLEADING NOT GUILTY

GUIDELINE FINE – STARTING POINT B

✚ CONSIDER AGGRAVATING AND MITIGATING FACTORS AND THE WEIGHT TO ATTACH TO EACH ➖

for example	for example
Excessive speed	Minor risk
High degree of carelessness	Momentary lapse
Serious risk	Negligible/parking damage
Using a hand-held mobile telephone	Sudden change in weather conditions
This list is not exhaustive	*This list is not exhaustive*

Death, serious injury or damage is capable of being aggravation

If offender is on bail, this offence is more serious
If offender has previous convictions, their relevance and any failure to respond to previous sentences should be considered – they may increase the seriousness. The court should make it clear, when passing sentence, that this was the approach adopted.

TAKE A PRELIMINARY VIEW OF SERIOUSNESS, THEN CONSIDER OFFENDER MITIGATION

for example
Co-operation with police
Evidence of genuine remorse
Voluntary compensation

CONSIDER YOUR SENTENCE

Endorse (3-9 points OR period of disqualification)
Consider other measures (including disqualification until test passed if appropriate –
for example, age, infirmity or medical condition)
Compare it with the suggested guideline level of sentence and reconsider
your reasons carefully if you have chosen a sentence at a different level.
Consider a reduction for a timely guilty plea.

DECIDE YOUR SENTENCE

Road Traffic Act 1988 s.170(4) Triable only summarily Penalty: Level 5 and/or 6 months Must endorse: (5-10 points OR disqualify)	**Failing to stop** **Failing to report**

CONSIDER THE SERIOUSNESS OF THE OFFENCE

GUIDELINE: →   *IS DISCHARGE OR FINE APPROPRIATE?*
IS IT SERIOUS ENOUGH FOR A COMMUNITY PENALTY?
IS IT SO SERIOUS THAT ONLY CUSTODY IS APPROPRIATE?

THIS IS A GUIDELINE FOR A FIRST-TIME OFFENDER PLEADING NOT GUILTY

GUIDELINE FINE – STARTING POINT C

⊕   CONSIDER AGGRAVATING AND MITIGATING FACTORS AND THE WEIGHT TO ATTACH TO EACH   ⊖

for example Evidence of drinking or drugs Serious injury Serious damage *This list is not exhaustive*	for example Believed identity to be known Failed to stop but reported Genuine fear of retaliation Negligible damage No one at scene but failed to report Stayed at scene but failed to give/left before giving full particulars *This list is not exhaustive*

If offender is on bail, this offence is more serious
If offender has previous convictions, their relevance and any failure to respond to previous sentences should be considered – they may increase the seriousness. The court should make it clear, when passing sentence, that this was the approach adopted.

TAKE A PRELIMINARY VIEW OF SERIOUSNESS, THEN CONSIDER OFFENDER MITIGATION

for example
Co-operation with police
Evidence of genuine remorse
Voluntary compensation

CONSIDER YOUR SENTENCE

Endorse (5-10 points OR period of disqualification)
Compare it with the suggested guideline level of sentence and reconsider your reasons carefully if you have chosen a sentence at a different level.
Consider a reduction for a timely guilty plea.

DECIDE YOUR SENTENCE

APPENDIX 5

ANSWERS TO SELF-TEST QUESTIONS

CHAPTER 2

1. (i) Where the value of damage in a criminal damage case is less than £5,000, the case will be tried summarily. (ii) Where the value of damage in a criminal damage case is more £5,000, the case is triable either way. (iii) Possession of a controlled drug is an either-way offence. (iv) Careless driving is a summary offence. (v) Murder is an indictable only offence.

CHAPTER 3

1. The Crown Prosecutor decides whether there is sufficient evidence to charge or in some offences, the custody officer.

2. Yes – the prosecution has extensive obligations to provide pre-trial disclosure of its evidence in all cases, including summary matters. The Attorney-General's Guidelines on Disclosure provide that the prosecution should disclose the evidence it intends to rely on at a summary trial.

3. A mode of trial hearing will be held in an either-way offence where the defendant indicates at the plea before venue that he intends to plead not guilty.

4. The defendant's first appearance in an indictable-only offence will be before the magistrates.

5. The Crown Court generally hears the defendant's appeal against conviction.

CHAPTER 4

1. Section 3 of the Human Rights Act 1988 places an obligation on the criminal courts to interpret all legislation 'as far as possible' to comply with ECHR law. In determining Convention rights the courts must apply ECHR law determined by the decisions of the European Court of Human Rights. The HRA 1998 does not give the courts the power to strike down legislation which is contrary to the ECHR. So, where it is not possible to give effect to the ECHR law in a case, s. 4 HRA 1998 requires the superior courts such as the Court of Appeal and the House of Lords to make a declaration of incompatibility. The declaration gives Parliament the opportunity to amend the domestic provision which conflicts with Convention law. It is a matter for Parliament to decide whether or not to amend the offencing legislation.

A defence solicitor might rely on Convention rights (most obviously Article 6) in support of a legal submission to have prosecution evidence excluded in a case. It could also be relied on to challenge an aspect of procedure; to stay proceedings for an abuse of process and on appeal against conviction. Under its interpretive obligation in s. 3 HRA 1998, the court must take into account the ECHR when making its decision.

Additional protection is provided to the defendant by s. 6 HRA 1998, which places a duty on a public authority such as the police, the Crown Prosecution Service and the courts to discharge its legal duties in compliance with the ECHR.

2. The consequences of failing to abide by the rules of professional conduct include an appearance before the Law Society's disciplinary panel for breach of the code. The Law Society's powers of punishment range from giving a reprimand, to striking a solicitor off the role. In relation to non-qualified staff, it can make a direction that no firm employ that person. Your actions may cause your firm to have a complaint made against it to the Office for the Supervision of Solicitors (OSS). You may also be censured in court by the judge/bench and by your peers. You must always be on your guard!

CHAPTER 5

CASE STUDY *R v LENNY WHYTE*

The prosecution will contend that Lenny is the man responsible for unlawfully entering the home of Lillian Kennedy and stealing money from her. The prosecution will allege that Lenny was assisted in the burglary by another individual – most probably Lloyd Green. The police have not charged this second individual. The prosecution will contend that this person deliberately distracted Lillian Kennedy at her front door to enable the burglar to obtain access to her property in order to steal. We must speculate on the motives for the burglary. It may well be the prosecution's theory that Lloyd Green was most probably putting Lenny Whyte under pressure to pay off a debt owed to him. The person who entered Lillian Kennedy's property via an unlocked backdoor is said to be Lenny Whyte. What evidence links Lenny to the crime?

Witness – Lillian Kennedy. She states she saw Lenny in the vicinity of her home an hour or so before the burglary and that he offered to assist her with her shopping. She describes the man as wearing white training shoes. She identifies Lenny to the police when she is taken by them on a tour of the immediate vicinity. She is subsequently unable to identify Lenny at a video identification parade and she is unable to identify Lloyd Green.

Witness – Shirley Lewis. She was in the garden next to the burgled property and gives a description of the man which corresponds with Lenny's actual appearance and mentions the white training shoes. She subsequently identifies Lenny as being that man at a video parade.

Witness – Harold Finney. This witness provides the police with a registration number of a car parked in Sunrise Walk which leads to Lloyd Green being arrested. He describes a man similar to Lenny approaching the car. This witness is unable to identify Lenny at the subsequent video identification parade.

Lenny's incriminating admissions made during the police interview satisfy the definition of a confession.

Real evidence of the white training shoes found in Lenny's flat.

Forensic opinion evidence that shoeprints located and lifted at the rear of the burgled property can be said to match the soles of the training shoes found in Lenny's flat.

Lenny has several previous convictions and a drug habit which places him in a category of persons more likely to have committed this crime. The prosecution will want to adduce evidence of Lenny's past bad character, specifically in relation to his past offences of theft and burglary. Can the defence prevent this?

Lenny will plead not guilty. His defence is that it was not him. If it was not him, it must be someone else. The defence theory in this case means the following evidence will have to be challenged:

- eye-witness identification;
- Lenny's confession;
- forensic evidence.

If Lenny is able to advance an alibi, this will strengthen the challenge to the prosecution's case if the alibi evidence is accepted. The second person alleged to have been involved has not been charged and at this stage, Lenny is not implicated by the involvement of any co-accused which might require a corroboration warning to be given.

Having regard to this introductory chapter on criminal evidence and having identified the areas of criminal evidence involved in this scenario, consider how you might challenge the eye-witness identification in this case. There may be a possible application of s. 78 PACE in this regard, given Lenny was unrepresented at the police station. You will certainly be talking about the Turnbull Guidelines, as this is a case of mistaken identity and there are several weaknesses in the eye-witness identification. You will have concerns about the manner in which Lenny's confession was obtained and so you will want to make an application to have the confession excluded under ss. 76 and 78 PACE. Might a report from Lenny's psychiatrist assist in this respect?

The opinion evidence of the forensic scientist will be admissible as expert opinion evidence. You will want to undermine the weight to be attached to the opinion, given the popularity of Nike training shoes. Lenny states he has never worn the shoes. You will no doubt wish to oppose the admission in evidence of Lenny's past bad character.

You are on your way to securing an acquittal in this case. You have identified the main points of contention. When you have worked through the later chapters on criminal evidence you will be able to fully discuss and apply the principles of evidence law that arise in this case.

CHAPTER 6

1. Judicial guidance on the reasonable suspicion or belief test is provided by *O'Hara v Chief Constable, RUC* [1997] AC 286. Further, important guidance is located in (Code A 2.2–2.11).

2. On arrest, the suspect will be cautioned in the following way: 'You do not have to say anything. But it may harm your defence if you do not mention, when questioned, something which you later rely on in court. Anything you do say may be given in evidence', Code C para. 10.

3. The powers to search a person after arrest are contained in s. 32 PACE. The power to search the premises in which a person was at the time of his arrest or immediately before his arrest is also contained in s. 32 PACE. The power to search premises occupied or controlled by a suspect after arrest are contained in s. 18 PACE.

4. The police will apply to a justice of the peace to search premises under s. 8 PACE where it is not possible to contact the person who could allow the police to enter premises to search for evidence in connection with an indictable offence.

5. On the facts, the police could stop and search Trevor under s. 1 PACE 1984, provided the officer has reasonable grounds for suspecting Trevor may have on his person a prohibited article. Given the intelligence provided by CCTV operators, reasonable suspicion could easily be established in this case. Based on the information provided and Trevor's reaction when approached, the police would have reasonable grounds for suspecting Trevor to have been involved in an offence and that it is necessary to arrest him (s. 24 PACE). Having arrested him and cautioned him, the police officer would be entitled to search Trevor under s. 32 PACE if he had reasonable grounds for believing Trevor may have evidence on him relating to an offence. The officer may choose to take Trevor into custody or possibly release him on 'street bail'.

6. Suggested solution can be found in the answers to the self-test questions supporting Chapter 9.

CHAPTER 8

SCENARIO 1

If the jury concludes it was reasonable for Karl to have mentioned he acted in self-defence while being questioned at the police station, he is at risk of an adverse inference being drawn under s. 34 CJPOA 1994 against him at his trial.

SCENARIO 2

Although Stan has put forward facts in support of a possible defence at trial, he failed to mention the possibility that he acted in self-defence. This is a fact he now relies on at court in his defence. If the jury finds he could reasonably have been expected to mention this fact, this could weaken his defence of self-defence (s. 34 CJPOA).

SCENARIO 3

Jason is at risk of a double adverse inference. Providing the circumstances set out in s. 36 CJPOA are met, he risks an adverse inference in that he has failed to give an explanation for scratch marks visible on his face. The marks are on his person. The arresting constable or other investigating officer must reasonably have believed the presence of the marks might have been attributable to Jason's participation in a crime. The officer must have made Jason aware of his belief before requesting Jason to give an account, explaining in ordinary language the risk he faces from his failure to do so. In addition, Jason risks an adverse inference under s. 34.

SCENARIO 4

In this instance Rio too is at risk of an adverse inference under s. 36 CJPOA. Subsection 36(3) makes it clear that the section applies to the condition of clothing as it does to footwear.

SCENARIO 5

Providing the conditions set out in s. 37 CJPOA 1994 are met, Jane risks an adverse inference being drawn against her, in that she has failed to give an explanation for her presence near the scene of a crime. The arresting constable or other investigating officer must reasonably have believed Jane's presence might have been attributable to her participation in a crime. The officer must have made Jane aware of his belief before requesting her to give an account, explaining in ordinary language the risk she faces from her failure to do so. Under s. 37 CJPOA a 'place' is widely defined and includes buildings, vehicles and vessels. By refusing to give evidence at her trial, Jane risks an adverse inference being drawn against her under s. 35 Criminal Justice and Public Order Act 1994 (see Chapter 26) as well.

SCENARIO 6

The fact that Carley remained silent on the advice of her solicitor does not immunise her against the jury drawing an adverse inference. In order to persuade the jury not to draw an adverse inference, Carley is best advised to waive legal professional privilege and explain her reasons for not putting her defence at the police station. This could be done in a number of different ways:

- Carley's solicitor could have explained his reasons on the tape recorded interview;
- Carley may give evidence of the reasons herself;
- There may be evidence from the solicitor (either in person or in agreed written hearsay form).

The reasonableness or otherwise of Carley's decision to remain silent will be a matter for the jury. If this were a Crown Court trial, the judge would be required to carefully direct the jury on s. 34 CJPOA, in accordance with the requirements in *R v Argent* and the Judicial Studies Board specimen direction.

CHAPTER 9

SCENARIO 1

This scenario raises the matter of unlawfully obtained evidence. The illegality relates to the manner in which Ranjit was stopped and searched under s. 1 PACE 1984 (see Chapter 6). The search could well be illegal for a number of reasons:

- Was the decision to stop and search Ranjit based on reasonable suspicion as required by Code A (paras. 2.2–2.11)? This seems doubtful.
- Did the officers provide Ranjit with the required information before commencing the search as required by Code A para. 3.8?
- Was the manner in which the search was conducted (removal of outer clothing, socks and shoes in public) lawful, having regard to Code A para. 3.5?

As a result of the actions of the police, a quantity of cocaine is found. If the search was unlawful, can the evidence obtained as a consequence be excluded under s. 78 PACE? Certainly the defence advocate should consider such an application. Given the restrictive interpretation of s. 78, however, it is highly questionable whether the evidence would be excluded since it is relevant and reliable.

Ranjit may have a defence to the allegation that he assaulted a police officer in the execution of his duty if it can be established that the officer was not in fact acting in the execution of his duty at the time he initially approached Ranjit and grabbed him by the shoulder. Additionally, Ranjit may state that he acted in self-defence.

SCENARIO 2

This scenario raises the spectre of entrapment by the prosecuting authorities. Entrapment does not provide a defence in substantive law, but Stan might argue the evidence should be excluded under the abuse of process doctrine as defined by the House of Lords in *R v Loosley* [2001] 1 WLR 2060. The application of the various factors identified in the various judgments would need to be applied to the specific factors in this case for a decision to be reached. Relevant factors would include Stan's lack of a criminal record and the fact that he was not immediately in possession of drugs when initially approached by the officers. The suggestion that the officers caused Stan to commit the offence is, on the face of things, made out. If it did, this would constitute state created crime and would be an abuse of process.

CHAPTER 10

EXERCISE 1: ANSWERS TO THE QUESTIONS TESTING YOUR KNOWLEDGE OF CODE C SAFEGUARDS

Question 1

In accordance with Code C 10.1 a caution must be given to any suspect who the police wish to question in circumstances where there are grounds to suspect that person of involvement in an offence and whose silence or answers to any questions may be given in evidence against him. An individual must also be cautioned on arrest and on being charged (C 10.5) or informed that they might be prosecuted. A caution must also be given at the commencement of each interview (Code C 10.1) and where there is a break in an interview the suspect should be reminded that they are under caution (C 10.8). It is the duty of the interviewing officer to ensure that the suspect understands the caution (Code C 10D). Where access to a solicitor has been delayed in accordance with s. 58(8) PACE/ Code C 6.6, s. 58 Youth Justice and Criminal Evidence Act 1999 prohibits a court from drawing an adverse inference from silence. In these circumstances the police are obliged to caution the suspect in the following terms: 'You do not have to say anything, but anything you do say may be given in evidence against you'.

The caution reminds the suspect that he has the right not to incriminate himself. Incriminating admissions obtained in circumstances where a caution has not been properly administered are vulnerable to challenge under s. 76(2)(b) and s. 78 PACE. In *R v Armas-Rodriguez* [2005] EWCA Crim 1981, while acknowledging that a failure to caution a suspect at the commencement of an interview constituted a 'significant and substantial' breach of Code C, on the facts in this particular case, it had not been unfair (in accordance with s. 78 PACE 1984) to admit the interview. In particular, the Court of Appeal observed that the police had cautioned D on arrest; there had been no bad faith on the part of the interviewing officer, the defendant had been represented by a solicitor throughout; the interview had been tape recorded and the questions put fairly. Furthermore, the defendant had been interviewed a second time under caution and had given a substantially similar account.

Question 2

Upon arrival at the police station and in accordance with Code C 3.1, the custody officer should explain to the suspect that he has the following rights which may be exercised at any stage:

(i) the right to have someone informed of his arrest;

(ii) the right to consult in private with a solicitor, such advice being free (save in isolated categories) and independent;

(iii) the right to consult the Codes of Practice.

Furthermore, under Code C 3.5, the custody officer is required to ask the suspect on his arrival at the police station whether s/he:

- wants legal advice;
- wants to inform someone of his arrest;
- might be in need of medical treatment;
- requires the presence of an appropriate adult; or
- requires an interpreter.

Question 3

A number of individuals might be considered vulnerable. Under Code C 3.6–3.10 the custody officer must undertake a risk assessment of all detainees. Detainees who would clearly require assistance include those with learning difficulties or communication difficulties, those requiring an interpreter, those on medication, juveniles; the mentally disordered or mentally vulnerable. In some instances the detainee will require the services of an appropriate adult (C 3.15).

Questions 4 and 5

Some very important safeguards are contained in paragraph 6 of Code C. C 6.4 stipulates that no police officer should, at any time, do or say anything with the intention of dissuading a detainee from obtaining legal advice. If the detainee refuses legal advice Code C 6.5 requires the custody officer to explain that he may seek advice over the telephone and if the detainee continues to decline the services of a lawyer, the custody sergeant should ask the detainee why and record the reasons. The effect of these paragraphs is to encourage the police to be proactive in securing suspects access to legal advice.

Access to legal advice may be delayed but only in the circumstances set out in Code C 6.6. If C 6.6 does not apply a detainee wanting legal advice may not be interviewed or continue to be interviewed until they have received legal advice.

The decision to delay access to a solicitor is a serious matter and will require justification by the police. A confession obtained in violation of s. 58 PACE is particularly vulnerable to challenge under both s. 76 and/or s. 78 PACE.

A suspect should be reminded at the start or re-commencement of any interview that the suspect is entitled to free legal advice and that the interview can be delayed for that purpose.

Question 6

Custody time limits are set out in s. 42 PACE as amended by s. 7 CJA 2003. The maximum period of detention for any individual arrested but not charged in connection with an indictable offence is 36 hours. This period can be extended up to 96 hours on the authority of a magistrates' court for an indictable offence. The detention of any individual must be justified at all times under s. 37(2) PACE. The custody officer must be satisfied that detention is necessary to secure or preserve evidence relating to an offence for which the person is under arrest or to obtain such evidence by questioning. If the detention grounds are not made out, the detainee must be released immediately either with or without bail (s. 34 PACE). Where there is sufficient evidence to charge an individual, s. 37(1) PACE provides the individual must be charged and either released on bail or remanded into police cells pending an appearance before magistrates within 24 hours. Detention is subject to regular reviews, initially at six hours and thereafter at nine-hourly intervals (s. 40 PACE).

Question 7

The basic human rights to which a suspect is entitled are set out in Code C paras. 8 and 9. They include the right to an adequately heated, cleaned and ventilated cell. Access to toilet facilities must be provided. If a detainee's clothing needs to be removed, he should be supplied with adequate replacement clothing. The detainee should be provided with two light meals and one main meal in any 24-hour period. Drinks should be provided at meal times and upon reasonable request. The above safeguards underline the importance of the custody record in evidential terms. It should be a complete record of the detainee's time in detention and it should record any complaints made by the detainee (C 9.2).

In accordance with Code C 12.2, in any period of 24 hours, a suspect is entitled to a continuous period of eight hours' rest, normally at night, and under C 12.8, a suspect is entitled to breaks from interviewing at recognised meal times. Interviews should break for refreshments at two-hour intervals.

Question 8

An interview, according to Code C para. 11.1A, is the questioning of a person regarding their involvement or suspected involvement in a criminal offence which, under Code C para. 10, must be carried out under caution. Such an interview must be carried out at a police station unless the very strict conditions in Code C 11.1 are made out.

Question 9

Paragraph 9.5 of Code C is important. If a detainee appears to be suffering from physical illness, or is injured, or appears to be suffering from a mental disorder, or appears to need clinical attention, the custody officer must make sure the detainee receives appropriate attention as soon as reasonably practicable. Paragraph 9.13 provides that where a health care professional is called to examine or treat the offender, the custody officer shall ask for their opinion about any risks or problems the police need to take into account when making decisions about the detainee about when to carry out an interview and the need for specific safeguards. Note 9C offers the following guidance:

'A detainee who appears drunk or behaves abnormally may be suffering from illness, the effect of drugs or may have sustained injury, particularly a head injury which is not apparent. A detainee needing or dependent on certain drugs, including alcohol, may experience harmful effects within a short time of being deprived of their supply. In these circumstances, when there is any doubt, police should always act urgently to call an appropriate health care professional.'

Code C 12.3 is all important. Before any detainee is interviewed the custody officer shall assess whether the detainee is fit to be interviewed. In appropriate cases, the custody officer will take this decision in conjunction with a health care professional.

An omission on the part of the police to spot and deal with a particular vulnerability renders any resulting confession vulnerable to challenge under ss. 76 and 78 PACE.

Question 10

Code C para. 11.5 provides an important safeguard in relation to confession evidence by prohibiting officers from offering inducements to the suspect. It provides that no officer interviewer shall indicate, except to answer a direct question, what action the police may take if the suspect adopts a particular course of action. If the suspect asks a direct question, the interviewer may inform the suspect of what action the police propose to take, provided the action is itself proper and warranted.

The safeguards associated with the conduct of interviews of mentally vulnerable individuals are covered by Code C 11.5. Note 11 C is worth considering:

'Although juveniles or people who are mentally vulnerable are often capable of providing reliable evidence, they may, without knowing or wishing to do so, be particularly prone in certain circumstances to provide information that may be unreliable, misleading or self-incriminating. Special care should always be taken when questioning such a person, and the appropriate adult should be involved if there is any doubt about a person's age, mental state or capacity. Because of the risk of unreliable evidence it is important to obtain corroboration of any facts admitted wherever possible.'

Aside from the numerous safeguards already identified, juveniles and the mentally ill and mentally vulnerable are entitled to have an appropriate adult present during an interview (Code C 11.5).

EXERCISE 2: ANALYSIS OF LENNY WHYTE'S CONFESSION

The admissibility of Lenny's confession should be challenged under s. 76(2)(b) PACE (unreliability) and s. 78 PACE (unfairness).

The admissibility of Lenny's confession would be determined at a pre-trial hearing. A *voir dire* would need to be conducted, at which the judge would hear evidence as to how Lenny's confession was obtained. The prosecution would have the burden of proof under s. 76(2)(b). The prosecution would need to call the custody officers who supervised Lenny's detention, as well as the interviewing officers. In this instance, the prosecution would also need to call Dr Ghulam, who examined Lenny while he was in detention. The custody record would be an important piece of evidence at this hearing.

Given Lenny's recent psychiatric history, the defence might explore the possibility of obtaining a psychiatric report to shed light on Lenny's state of mind during his detention and in interview.

The burden of proof under s. 76(2)(b) rests on the prosecution. The prosecution would point to the fact that Lenny was offered a solicitor but declined. Furthermore, attempts were made to contact Lenny's sister. Lenny was fed and refreshed. He was given rest and his detention was properly reviewed. When the officer in charge was made aware of Lenny's mental state, he was allowed to see a doctor, who subsequently administered Lenny's medication and pronounced him fit to be interviewed. On the face of it, the prosecution would have to concede there had been a breach of the requirement to ensure access to an appropriate adult, under Code C paragraph 3.15, having been made aware of Lenny's mental condition. However, they can still contend that the breach did not result in an unreliable confession, nor is it one that would be unfair to admit. It is not Lenny's first experience of custody and he may be taken to know the procedures.

The defence would make much of the fact that Lenny was unrepresented at the police station and did not have the services of an appropriate adult. On oath, you would need to ask the custody officer who opened the custody record if he undertook a risk assessment of Lenny Whyte in accordance with the requirement under Code C paras 3.6–3.10 and if he did, why Lenny's vulnerability was not spotted immediately. It may be that Lenny lied to the officer and simply did not make the officer aware of his particular needs. When searched, Lenny was not found to be in possession of his medication.

The defence would want to explore whether the police fully complied with s. 58 PACE. Code C, para. 6.5 requires the police to be proactive in ensuring access to a solicitor. The absence of a solicitor is made worse by the fact that Lenny was not provided with the services of an appropriate adult. Having made the police aware of his mental condition, and having been examined by a police doctor, it must be put to the custody officer that there was a blatant breach of Code C 3.15. A suitable appropriate adult in this case would have been Lenny's sister. The police only tried her number once while Lenny was in custody. Furthermore, the defence would be able to point to a breach of Code C 11.15 which stipulates that a vulnerable suspect should not be interviewed in the absence of an appropriate adult for the reasons highlighted in Note 11 C.

The defence would need to explore Lenny's behaviour while in custody. Did no one pick up on the fact that Lenny did not sleep and had very little to eat? Such behaviour is indicative of someone with depression. In addition, it should be put to the officers that Lenny made it clear he wanted a cigarette and that it was suggested to him that if he cooperated, his release from custody would have been speeded up. Reliance might be placed by the defence on the case of *R v Aspinall* [1999] Crim LR 741. The facts are not dissimilar.

The defence can easily establish a link in terms of cause and effect. Had a solicitor been present, the outcome for Lenny would have been different. Given Lenny's metal state and the fact that he was desirous of escaping the confines of his custody, coupled with the very serious omission to ensure access to an appropriate adult, further compounded by the lack of legal advice, Lenny's confession is both unreliable and unfair to admit. If the confession were to be excluded, a principal component of the prosecution's case would be lost.

You can chart the progress of Lenny's case through our case study, the complete version of which can be accessed from our Online Resource Centre.

CHAPTER 11

OBSERVATIONS ON THE IDENTIFICATION ISSUES RAISED BY *R v LENNY WHYTE*

There are three eyewitnesses in Lenny's case. We will deal with each of them in turn.

Lillian Kennedy

It is important to realise that Mrs Kennedy cannot assist the prosecution in providing any evidence as to the identity of the man who entered her property by the unlocked back door. She is able to provide a description of the burglar's accomplice, but she is not able to identify him. She does identify Lenny in a street identification. This would appear to be in compliance of Code D 3.2 as the police would not have had a known suspect in mind at this point in time. Mrs Kennedy's evidence will be that a man (whom she states was Lenny Whyte) approached her some 30 to 60 minutes before the burglary and offered her assistance with her shopping bags. This evidence (assuming she correctly identifies Lenny as being that man) does no more than place Lenny in the vicinity, though crucially not at the relevant time. Her evidence is of marginal relevance. She is able to describe what the man who offered her help was wearing, and makes specific reference to the white trainers. When she points Lenny out to the police, he is not, however, wearing white training shoes. A pair of white training shoes were subsequently recovered from Lenny's flat.

Having a known suspect in mind, the police acted correctly in arresting Lenny Whyte and arranging an identification procedure. It would have been wholly wrong for the police to have shown Mrs Lewis photographs of convicted offenders (including Lenny), having a known suspect in mind.

The evidence of Shirley Lewis is important. She purports to be able to identify Lenny Whyte as being the man she saw in Mrs Kennedy's back-garden at the relevant time. She provides the police with a description of which a written record is kept in accordance with Code D 3.1. She specifically mentions the white training shoes worn by the man she observed in the garden. She subsequently attends a video identification procedure which the police state was conducted in accordance with Code D Annex A. In the course of the video identification procedure, Mrs Lewis picks out Lenny Whyte. He is number 7 in the video line-up. Look through the video identification parade record (and remember you would be entitled to a copy of the video images). Look at the words used by Mrs Lewis when she selects Lenny's image: 'I think it is number 7. I can't be one hundred percent sure – yes 7 – I recognise him now. I have seen him before.'

Was the video parade compiled in accordance with Code D Annex A? Can you point to specific breaches of Code D which could form the basis of a challenge under s. 78 PACE to the admissibility of Mrs Lewis's identification evidence? Lenny states he did not understand what was happening as regards the video parade, and that no one explained to him why he could not have an identification parade. The most disturbing aspect of Lenny's detention is that he did not have access to legal advice. He does not appear to have been present when the video parade was compiled and, as such, it will be extremely important for you to review the parade's composition in an attempt to assess its fairness.

The final eyewitness is Harold Finney. Again, he is able to provide a description of the man he observed close to the time of the burglary walking past his window and going over to a black car in the street (which the prosecution contend belongs to Lloyd Green, the suspected accomplice). Mr Finney's description is consistent with Lenny's appearance. He also mentions that the man was wearing distinctive white training shoes. Mr Finney also attends the video identification parade. Significantly, he is unable to identify Lenny.

The other evidence linking Lenny to the crime is of course his interview with the police which is considered in the context of Chapter 10 self-test questions and the circumstantial evidence relating to the footwear found in his flat. This constitutes expert opinion evidence, which is considered in Chapter 24.

CHAPTER 13

1. It is likely that, on the facts, the evidential test is satisfied assuming the prosecution is satisfied that each witness is capable of giving reliable, independent evidence. A common defence submission in a historic sexual abuse case such as this is to challenge the reliability of the witness's recollection of the incidents giving rise to the charges. The prosecution case may also be challenged by the possibility of collusion between the prosecution witnesses. If these potential difficulties are overcome, in view the seriousness of the charges it appears to be in the public interest for Gerald to be charged and prosecuted even after taking into account Gerald's age.

2. In Debbie's case, the evidential test appears to be satisfied as the store detective will testify at trial and there is a security video tape of the alleged offence. Debbie's solicitor may however submit that given her domestic circumstances, it is not in the public interest for the prosecution to continue. You might also argue that this case is suitable for a conditional caution. If Debbie is prosecuted and she pleads guilty or is found guilty, her difficult domestic circumstances provide persuasive material to be used in your plea in mitigation before sentencing if she pleads guilty or is found guilty.

3. While it is probably in the public interest for Jim's case to continue, as disputes between neighbours should not be settled by violence, the evidential test appears not to be satisfied as the only witnesses are Sally's husband and her sons aged 19 and 21. When making representations to the CPS, Jim's solicitors would submit Jim should not be charged, because of the lack of independent, credible witnesses.

4. It is clearly in the public interest for Kyle to be charged and prosecuted. Did you identify the aggravating factors? The evidential test would have to be reviewed carefully to ensure that sufficient independent, reliable evidence was available to provide a realistic prospect of a conviction.

5. This is clearly a case of domestic violence as it comes within the term used to describe a range of behaviour often used by one person to control and dominate another, with whom they have or have had a close or family relationship. The offence includes physical, sexual, psychological and emotional violence on Patrick, by Frank, his father. Even though Patrick does not want any further action to be taken against Frank, there might be a danger that if a prosecution is not undertaken, Frank may commit further serious offences against Patrick. It is likely that both the public interest and the evidential tests are satisfied, unless Frank's solicitor can persuade the CPS that the matter might be constructively settled by reference to a third party mediation agency.

CHAPTER 15

ANALYSIS OF EXERCISES 1 AND 2

You were asked to consider two examples which will require a decision of magistrates as to whether or not bail should be granted. In each case you were asked to consider the facts from the point of view of the prosecuting solicitor and the defence solicitor. Below is a summary of the arguments likely to be advanced. The prosecution will begin each submission with an explanation of how each defendant came to be charged with the offence for which he appears and an outline of the evidence linking him to that charge. Note the inter-play between the grounds for objecting to bail and the factors relied on to substantiate those grounds.

Prosecution submissions in relation to Karl Green – Exercise 1

In relation to Exercise 1, the prosecution is likely to oppose bail on the grounds that Green will abscond, commit further offences and interfere with witnesses.

The prosecution will point to the evidence and to the fact that this is a very serious offence that could still result in a murder charge and that the defendant is subject to a suspended prison sentence. What is more, the defendant is already on bail for an earlier serious offence of violence. The risk of conviction is high, so too is a lengthy custodial sentence. The prosecutor will highlight a fairly recent conviction for failing to surrender and Green's poor community ties. Taken together, these all point to a substantial risk that this defendant will abscond if released on bail.

The prosecution will further suggest that Green is likely to commit further offences if released on bail. The prosecution can argue there is no right to bail in this case (see 15.5.1). The CPS will invite the court to consider his lengthy criminal record for violence. The defendant lives on the same estate as the injured party and his family. Such a serious assault is likely to engender feelings of hostility on the estate and the risk of Green being drawn into further confrontations cannot be ignored. Special weight will be attributed to the fact that Green is already on conditional bail for an earlier, unrelated serious allegation of assault and has already answered an allegation that he breached one of his bail conditions. In short, Green is not a man to be trusted.

Finally the prosecution is likely to argue that the defendant will interfere with prosecution witnesses. The defendant has a lengthy record consisting of violent assaults and is evidently easily provoked. One of the witnesses is a friend of the injured party who lives in close proximity to the defendant.

Defence submissions in relation to Karl Green – Exercise 1

The defence solicitor would be faced with an uphill task in this case. One thing the solicitor should have done is to contact Green's sister, who lives some ten miles outside the area for confirmation of an offer of alternative accommodation. We will assume such an offer has been made.

The defence solicitor would remind the magistrates of the fact that they have heard only one side of the case. Green's intention is to plead not guilty, maintaining he acted in self-defence. It is a defence he put forward at the police station and he has a witness to substantiate his version of events.

Taking each of the prosecution's objections in sequence and dealing with the risk of absconding, the defence solicitor would point out that Green has had ample opportunity to run and hide between the occurrence of the incident and his subsequent arrest. He has strong community ties, having been born in the area. He has a son he sees regularly and a job which will be lost if he is remanded into custody. He has only one previous conviction for failing to surrender. The defence solicitor should explain the circumstances surrounding this and stress the fact of Green having voluntarily surrendered at the time and in turn receiving a fine.

So far as the danger that he might commit further offences is concerned, again he denies intentionally assaulting the injured party and has not of course been convicted of any offence arising out of the incident at the pub. He cannot deny the fact that he is on conditional bail for a further assault. All the defence solicitor can say about that, is that he accepts some level of criminal responsibility and awaits his deserved punishment. The offence was unforgivable but was committed while Green was very drunk. The defence solicitor will have to try to put a positive spin on Green's criminal past, highlighting what, if anything, has changed since they were committed. Unfortunately some of his previous convictions are fairly recent. The defence solicitor should deal with the earlier breach of bail conditions, stressing the mitigating factors that were obviously accepted by the court. It is not evident that Green is in the habit of committing offences while on bail.

So far as interfering with witnesses is concerned, the defence solicitor will put forward an adamant denial that this would happen, as Green would not wish to make matters worse for himself.

The best that Green could possibly hope for in this case is the grant of bail subject to stringent conditions. The defence solicitor might suggest a condition of residence at the sister's address. This would deal in part with the risk of failing to surrender and the risk of the commission of further offences due to possible confrontations. It would also help to deal with the risk of interference with witnesses. No doubt, Green would be prepared to agree with any condition that kept him out of prison including a condition of reporting to his local police station, a condition of no contact with prosecution witnesses and a curfew. In the cirumstances, however, bail is likely to be refuced.

Exercise 2 – Prosecution submissions in relation to Daniel Phillips

In relation to Exercise 2 the prosecution is likely to argue that Daniel may abscond, commit further offences and interfere with the injured party. The allegation against Daniel is extremely serious and he is currently subject to a suspended sentence of imprisonment. The CPS will point to the circumstantial evidence against Daniel Phillips linking him to the crime scene and his no comment interview at the police station. It took three days in which to locate Mr Phillips, as he was not residing at his mother's address. The risk of conviction is high, as is the prospect of a prison sentence.

So far as the commission of further offences and interference with prosecution witnesses is concerned, the prosecution will make plain the injured party's feelings in this case. The defendant's behaviour would suggest he is an obsessive individual with little respect for authority. He is charged with resisting arrest on this occasion and has previously breached a court order. He is subject to a restraining order preventing him from harassing Ms Hughes. He clearly cannot leave her alone. With the restraining order in force there would seem to be little point in imposing a condition that he does not contact Ms Hughes. The risk that he may seek to harm Ms Hughes or interfere with her is extremely high.

Defence submissions in relation to Daniel Phillips

On a practical point, if the defence solicitor can persuade Daniel's new girlfriend and her mother to attend court, so much the better.

The defence solicitor should remind the magistrates of the presumption in favour of bail. The defence advocate should challenge the nature of the prosecution's case against Daniel. He will no doubt point out that there is no forensic evidence to connect him to the crime scene and that he was advised not to answer questions at the police station on legal advice. The only evidence against him is the tenuous nature of a voice identification by a witness who is not certain. He is likely to stress that the earlier access visit went off without any difficulties and that he would have no reason to want to burn down Ms Hughes's house. What is more, he has an alibi (his girlfriend and her mother) who will say he could not possibly have been setting fire to his former girlfriend's home. Consequently, he will not abscond because he has little fear of being convicted. He is able to offer a fixed address and has a job, which will be lost if he is remanded into custody. He will not abscond because his son is important to him. Furthermore, his new girlfriend is pregnant with his child and needs his support.

So far as the risk of him committing further offences is concerned, the defence solicitor will say that these are a thing of the past. He is abiding by the terms of his restraining order, which remains in force. He is benefiting from the input of the probation service and is addressing the reasons for his past offending.

The defence solicitor is likely to offer bail conditions to include residing at his current address, reporting to his local police station and a condition that he does not contact Ms Hughes or her friend.

Decision of the court in each case

In relation to Karl Green, the magistrates remand him into custody and send the case forthwith to the Crown Court. Their reasons for doing so are the substantial risk that the defendant will abscond having regard to the very serious nature of the allegation and the risk of him committing further offences, in the light of his criminal record and the fact that he is already on bail for a similar serious allegation of assault. They are not convinced that the imposition of conditions would alleviate their concerns. Karl Green may consider making an application for bail to a Crown Court judge in chambers.

In relation to Daniel Phillips, after some deliberation the magistrates decide to grant him bail conditional on him residing at the address of his girlfriend's mother, reporting to his local police station three times a week and a further condition that he should keep away from and not try to contact Rachel Hughes or her friend. In their view, the imposition of conditions would alleviate the risk of Mr Phillips committing further offences and interfering with prosecution witnesses.

CHAPTER 16

EXERCISE 1

Gordon Davey should be advised to elect trial by jury in any event. He stands a greater chance of being acquitted of this offence before a jury of his peers. However, Gordon Davey may feel he would rather the matter be tried summarily as his ordeal will be over more quickly and with less publicity.

There are no current National Mode of Trial Guidelines specifically on the offence with which Gordon is charged. However its predecessor is the offence of indecent assault and there are Mode of Trial Guidelines on this.

It is likely that the CPS will represent that this case is suitable for summary trial. Although there are the presence of some aggravating features identified in the National Mode of Trial Guidelines – see Appendix 3 (the age disparity between the perpetrator and his victim and the defendant's position of trust as the uncle of the girl) this would appear to be a one-off offence where the nature of the indecent assault is relatively minor and no injury has been caused. In these circumstances a maximum sentence of six months' imprisonment is likely to be sufficient.

If Gordon wishes to consent to summary trial, it would be unnecessary for you to make any representations save to agree with the CPS that in your view, the matter is suitable for summary disposal. Only if the CPS were to invite the Bench to decline jurisdiction, with Gordon wishing to have the matter tried summarily, would it be necessary for you to make representations as to why the case can be dealt with summarily. This would require you to play down any aggravating features of this indecent assault.

It is likely that the magistrates will accept jurisdiction on the basis that there are few aggravating factors and their power to impose a current maximum custodial sentence of 6 months on a finding of guilt is likely to be adequate.

The magistrates' decision

If the magistrates decide that the offence is suitable for summary trial, the clerk will tell Gordon of the court's view and inform him that if he consents, he can be tried summarily but, if he chooses, he may elect to trial by jury instead.

Gordon must also be told that if he is tried by the magistrates and found guilty, information about his character and antecedents will be obtained, and that if, because of these, the magistrates consider their powers of punishment are inadequate, he may be committed to the Crown Court for sentence. This procedure is mandatory and failure to follow it amounts to procedural *ultra vires*. Any conviction obtained in breach of the legal adviser giving this warning is liable to be quashed when challenged in judicial review proceedings.

The legal adviser will then put Gordon to his election by asking him whether he wishes to be tried by the magistrates or before a jury. Only if Gordon consents to trial in the magistrates' court may the magistrates proceed to summary trial. If Gordon does not give his consent, MCA 1980, s. 20 requires the case to be tried in the Crown Court.

EXERCISE 2

All the offences are triable either way. The magistrates' maximum powers of sentence on conviction for two or more either-way offences would currently be 12 months. It is most likely that the CPS will invite the magistrates to decline jurisdiction on the basis that their powers of sentence will be insufficient and that there are likely to be factual complexities in this case. Given Simon's denial and his complete lack of any previous convictions, he would be best advised to elect trial by jury in the Crown Court in any event.

As this is theft in breach of trust committed over a period of months, totalling a not insubstantial amount of money, the magistrates are likely to decline jurisdiction, in which case Simon will have no choice and the matter will be adjourned and a date set for his committal to the Crown Court.

EXERCISE 3

Wayne Mason is charged with an either-way offence and two summary-only offences which will mean that, in the event of conviction, magistrates could impose a maximum sentence of six months only. The CPS might take the view that the magistrates' powers of sentence in this instance are likely to be sufficient, notwithstanding the presence of aggravating features in the dangerous driving offence. However, this is a borderline case and the CPS could invite the court to decline jurisdiction on the basis of those aggravating features.

At present Wayne Mason intends to plead not guilty. He is faced with a tricky choice if the magistrates accept jurisdiction. His chances of acquittal are higher in the Crown Court than in the magistrates; however, the

Crown Court is likely to impose a harsher sentence in the event of conviction. If he wishes to be tried summarily in the face of contrary views from the CPS, his solicitor will have to make representations as to why the either-way offence of dangerous driving can be dealt with summarily. In this regard, the solicitor would need to play down the aggravating features in order to persuade the Bench that their sentencing power of six months for all offences would be sufficient. If Wayne is intent on trial in the Crown Court in any event, defence representations are unnecessary in this instance.

Were Wayne to indicate a guilty plea he would be tried summarily with the possible risk of a committal to the Crown Court for sentence (s. 3 PCC(S)A 2000.) However, with the availability of a six-month maximum sentence and a one-third discount for a timely guilty plea, the magistrates would arguably have sufficient powers to sentence.

In the event of Wayne maintaining his not guilty plea, the decision would be that of the magistrates. Applying the National Mode of Trial Guidelines, the presumption would be in favour of summary disposal. However there are some aggravating factors in relation to the either-way matter, including grossly excessive speed and the presence of alcohol. It would be a debateable decision in this case.

When the increased powers of sentence available to magistrates contained in the CJA 2003 are implemented there would be no question that their powers of sentence would be sufficient. If the dangerous driving allegation was committed to the Crown Court, the TWOC offence could be included for trial on the indictment in accordance with s. 40 Criminal Justice Act 1988 (CJA) and the driving with no insurance could be sent for plea under s. 41 CJA 1988 – see paragraph 16.19.

CHAPTER 17

To ascertain the disclosure requirements, firstly determine the classification of the offence Barry is charged with. Rape is an indictable-only offence.

Advance information is likely to be forthcoming in the early stages of this case. Following Barry's initial appearance before magistrates his case will be sent forthwith to the Crown Court. Within 70 days of the case being sent you are entitled to disclosure of the prosecution's case (used material). This is likely to comprise the witness statements of Tina, Kelly, Leroy, relevant staff at the care-home to whom she made the complaint, the medical and forensic evidence, the statement of the investigating officers, the record of interview with Barry and any items of real evidence.

Let us say that the medical/forensic evidence reveals traces of seminal fluid inside Tina and on her clothing. DNA extracted from the seminal fluid matches the known sample of DNA taken from Barry. The medical evidence also shows Tina to be eight weeks pregnant at the time when the alleged incident occurred.

On taking Barry's further instructions in the light of this evidence, Barry now admits to having had sexual intercourse with Tina, but only with her consent and in return for payment in the public toilets. After having sex, Barry states Tina rejoined her friend, Kelly. Barry denies pestering Tina for sex. His reason for lying to you in the first place is that he is embarrassed to admit to having had under-age sex with the girl. He did not think she would make a complaint.

Having served you with the 'case sent bundle', the CPS provide you with a schedule of 'unused' material as defined under s. 3 CPIA 1996. At this stage the prosecution discloses to you that Kelly, Tina's friend, has a previous conviction for theft and that Leroy has previous convictions for public order offences and theft. Such information satisfies the test of evidence that might reasonably be considered capable of undermining the case for the prosecution.

The pre-trial disclosure of the evidence in this case has helped to narrow the facts in issue in that the act of sexual intercourse is admitted but what is in dispute is whether Tina consented.

As this matter is indictable only, Barry will need to file a defence statement (s. 5 CPIA 1996). You will need to draft this carefully. Clearly he will indicate his intention to plead not guilty to rape on the basis that Tina consented to sexual intercourse and that sexual intercourse was offered to him by Tina in return for payment on one occasion only. He will deny any suggestion that he has been pestering Tina for sex. Will you go so far as to suggest Tina is falsely accusing Barry of rape and that you have reason to believe she has made a proven false allegation against another male in the past? If you want to obtain further disclosure on this, you will need to articulate it.

Service of the defence statement will cause the prosecution to look again at disclosure to see if there is anything that might reasonably assist Barry's defence as articulated in his statement (s. 7A CPIA 1996).

Barry defence statement clearly raises issues to do with Tina's credibility. As a child in the care of the local authority there will be a social service file on her which should contain an account of the alleged incident involving the male care-worker together with an assessment of Tina's personality. This is information which lies in the hands of a third party that you would presumably like to have access to? It may in fact be in the hands of the prosecution if the prosecution has sought access to it.

The prosecution and social services are likely to oppose disclosure on the ground of public interest immunity. The information is sensitive. It concerns a child and there are clearly issues of confidentiality. If the material is in the hands of the prosecution, it will need to apply to the court to sanction the withholding of such material. Notice of the application should be given to the defence to enable you to make representations. Representations may also be made by social services. Disclosure will be ordered if the judge concludes the information contained within the file would help to avoid a miscarriage of justice. If the material is in the hands of social service with disclosure being resisted, the defence will need to apply for a witness summons against social services. The same issues as regard public interest immunity will apply *R v Brushett* [2001] Crim LR 471.

CHAPTER 18

1. Two or more informations may be tried together in circumstances where the court considers it is in the interest of justice. Guidance on the application of the interest of justice in this context is provided by the decision of the House of Lords in *Chief Constable of Norfolk v Clayton* [1983] 2 AC 473.

2. The defence advocate will be aware of the prosecution's case because he will have sought disclosure of used material under Part 21 Crim PR. Where a defendant pleads not guilty to a case that is to be tried summarily, the CPIA 1996 requires the CPS to make disclosure of unused material (s. 3 CPIA 1996) that would reasonably be considered capable of undermining the case for the prosecution or assisting the case of the accused. The defendant has the option of submitting a defence statement in a summary case (s. 6 CPIA). Any further disclosure which might assist the defence articulated will only be forthcoming if a defence statement has been served (s. 7A CPIA).

3. The attendance of a witness can be secured by the issue of a witness summons under the procedure set out in s. 97 MCA 1980 and Part 28, Crim PR.

4. The role and responsibilities of the legal adviser or justices' clerk are briefly outlined in Chapter 2, paragraph 2.6.3. The role of the legal adviser is to advise the magistrates on law, practice and procedure. The legal adviser plays no part in decisions on fact. The legal adviser will effectively run the court, keeping a written record of the proceedings and offering assistance to unrepresented defendants.

5. A submission of no case to answer is usually made at the close of the prosecution's case in circumstances where the defence contends there is no evidence to prove an essential element of the charge against the defendant or the evidence adduced by the prosecution has been so discredited as a result of cross-examination or is so manifestly unreliable that no reasonable tribunal could safely convict upon it.

CHAPTER 19

1. All defendants appear initially before a magistrates' court. In a case where the defendant is alleged to have committed an indictable-only offence, the magistrates will send the case forthwith to the Crown Court. Matters relating to representation orders and the defendant's bail status in the meantime will be determined at the initial appearance before magistrates.

2. The prosecution must make disclosure of all used material in its case sent bundle or committal bundle. Thereafter it comes under obligations to make available unused material in accordance with the requirements of the Criminal Procedure and Investigation Act 1996. The requirement to file a defence statement is compulsory in cases to be tried on indictment (s. 5 CPIA 1996).

3. Where the defence concludes that the prosecution's pre-trial disclosure does not disclose a case to answer, written or oral application can be made under Sch. 3 CDA 1998 (see Part 13 Crim PR). Oral evidence may be given at this hearing only with leave of the judge.

4. The primary purpose of the PCMH is to allow the Crown Court to engage in effective trial management of the case. The hearing will identify the issues that are in dispute. A defendant will be required to enter a plea. In the event of the plea being not guilty, the judge ought to be in a position to set a firm trial date and to make binding rulings on any points of law that are in dispute.

5. Preparatory hearings are reserved for long and complex cases to be tried in the Crown Court.

CHAPTER 20

1. The bill of indictment is the document that contains the charges against the defendant on which he is arraigned at the commencement of a trial on indictment.

2. More than one offence may be charged in the same indictment where the offences are either founded on the same facts; or form or are part of a series of offences of the same or similar nature, r. 9, Indictment Rules 1971. *In Ludlow v MPC* (1970) 54 Cr App R 233, the House of Lords held that for offences to be similar there must be some nexus between them both in terms of law and fact.

3. For a submission of no case to answer to succeed before a Crown Court judge, the defence advocate must satisfy the test laid down in *R v Galbraith* [1981] 2 All ER 1060 (see paragraph 20.10).

4. There is a strict separation of function between judge and jury in the Crown Court. The jury determines all issues of fact, while the judge determines all issues of law. Whenever a point of law arises it must be aired in the absence of the jury. This protects the jury from hearing what might be prejudicial information regarding the defendant. Generally speaking, most issues of law, particularly disputed evidence, are resolved before trial at a pre-trial hearing. Sometimes, a *voir dire* (or trial within a trial) is required to determine admissibility of evidence.

5. The trial judge oversees the trial process. It is the duty of the trial judge to ensure the defendant enjoys a fair trial. At the conclusion of the trial the trial judge sums up the case for the jury. The summing-up is important because it represents the last words said in the trial. The judge will remind the jury of the evidence they have heard and crucially, he will direct them on the law. Any errors or omissions during the summing-up may provide a convicted defendant with grounds for appeal.

6. An attendance certificate is granted by a judge in the Crown Court and ensures payment by the LSC for the services of a solicitor or other legal representative at the Crown Court attending counsel.

CHAPTER 21

QUESTION 1

The general rule in a criminal case is that the prosecution bears the burden of proving a defendant's guilt beyond reasonable doubt. It is known as the legal burden of proof and it requires the prosecution to prove the essential elements of the offence charged. The principle is enshrined in *Woolmington v DPP* [1935] AC 463 and is consistent with the presumption of innocence safeguarded by Article 6(2) ECHR.

QUESTION 2

Reverse onus clauses refer to those instances in which a legal burden of proof is cast on a defendant to effectively prove his innocence. A statutory section may impose a legal burden of proof on a defendant expressly or by implication. A number of different statutes impose a legal burden of proof on a defendant. For this reason, it is always important to research the elements of the offence with which your client is suspected of or with which he is charged.

QUESTION 3

The current guidelines are contained in the Court of Appeal's judgment in *Attorney-General's Reference (No. 1 of 2004)* [2004] 1 WLR 2111. Relevant factors include:

- the definition of the offence and the elements the prosecution must prove;
- the ease with which a defendant can establish a particular defence;
- whether the offence is of a regulatory nature;
- the severity of the penalty that conviction carries;
- whether the imposition of a legal burden of proof is proportionate to the aim of the legislation and if it is not, whether it can be read down to impose an evidential burden of proof only.

QUESTION 4A

We have deliberately chosen to include a rape offence as the law in relation to rape has been redefined by the Sexual Offences Act 2003. To answer this question it is necessary to research the new offence of rape as defined by s. 1 SOA 2003. The relevant sections are reproduced below.

'**(1)** A person (A) commits an offence if—

   (a) he intentionally penetrates the vagina, anus or mouth of another person (B) with his penis,

   (b) B does not consent to the penetration, and

   (c) A does not reasonably believe that B consents.

(2) Whether a belief is reasonable is to be determined having regard to all the circumstances, including any steps A has taken to ascertain whether B consents.

(3) Sections 75 and 76 apply to an offence under this section.'

'75. **Evidential presumptions about consent**

(1) If in proceedings for an offence to which this section applies it is proved—

   (a) that the defendant did the relevant act,

   (b) that any of the circumstances specified in subsection (2) existed, and

   (c) that the defendant knew that those circumstances existed, the complainant is to be taken not to have consented to the relevant act unless sufficient evidence is adduced to raise an issue as to whether she consented, and the defendant is to be taken not to have reasonably believed that the complainant consented unless sufficient evidence is adduced to raise an issue as to whether she reasonably believed it

(2) The circumstances are that—

   (a) any person was, at the time of the relevant act or immediately before it began, using violence against the complainant or causing the complainant to fear that immediate violence would be used against him;

   (b) any person was, at the time of the relevant act or immediately before it began, causing the complainant to fear that violence was being used, or that immediate violence would be used, against another person;

   (c) the complainant was, and the defendant was not, unlawfully detained at the time of the relevant act;

   (d) the complainant was asleep or otherwise unconscious at the time of the relevant act;

   (e) because of the complainant's physical disability, the complainant would not have been able at the time of the relevant act to communicate to the defendant whether the complainant consented

   (f) any person had administered to or caused to be taken by the complainant, without the complainant's consent, a substance which, having regard to when it was administered or taken, was capable of causing or enabling the complainant to be stupefied or overpowered at the time of the relevant act.

(3) In subsection (2)(a) and (b), the reference to the time immediately before the relevant act began is, in the case of an act which is one of a continuous series of sexual activities, a reference to the time immediately before the first sexual activity began.'

In this case the prosecution has the legal burden of proving (beyond reasonable doubt that) intentional penile penetration of the women by the defendants without the women's consent. These are the *actus reus* and *mens rea* elements of the offence.

Robert and Pete do not deny the *actus reus*. They may make a formal admission under s. 10, CJA 1967 to this effect. They contend however that their victims consented. The defendants will need to show that they believed the women were consenting and that they had reasonable grounds for believing. Section 1(3) provides that whether a belief is reasonable is to be determined having regard to all the circumstances, including any steps the defendant has taken to ascertain whether his victim consented. The overall legal burden of proof rests on the prosecution. However, in this case it is assisted by the evidential presumption in s. 75.

The evidential presumption in s. 75(2)(f) will apply in this instance as the women are claiming that a substance was administered to them which impaired their ability to consent to sexual intercourse. The effect of s. 75 is that the complainant is taken not to have consented and the defendant is to be taken not to have reasonably believed that the complainant consented. An evidential burden is placed on the defendant to adduce sufficient evidence to raise an issue as to whether the defendant reasonably believed in consent. In order for the presumption not to apply, the defendant will need to satisfy the judge from the evidence that there is a real issue about consent that is worth putting to the jury. In practice the evidence produced may be from evidence that the defendant himself gives in the witness box, or from evidence given on his behalf by a defence witness, or resulting from evidence given by the complainant during cross-examination. If the judge is satisfied that there is sufficient evidence to justify putting the issue of consent to the jury, he will so direct.

Given s. 75 imposes an evidential burden only on the defendant, it is arguably compatible with Article 6(2) ECHR.

QUESTION 4B

The relevant section is s. 139(1) Criminal Justice Act 1988. Under this section, it is an offence for a person to have with him in a public place an offensive weapon as defined by the Act. Sections 139(4) and (5) provide it is a defence for the defendant to prove that he had good reason or lawful authority for having the article with him in a public place. The relevant case law on what constitutes a good reason or lawful excuse may of course be researched. As drafted, s. 139(4) imposes an express legal burden of proof on the defendant. If Lee is to secure an acquittal in this case, he must adduce evidence which is sufficient on the balance of probabilities to prove he had a good reason for being in possession of the article in question. If he fails to do so and the prosecution prove possession of the relevant article, Lee will be convicted.

Given the section imposes a legal burden of proof on Lee, is it compatible with Article 6(2) ECHR? In fact, this statutory section has been considered by the Divisional Court which held the section was a proportionate response to the social problem of people carrying knives in public about which there was a public need a to take action (*R v Matthews* [2004] QB 690 and *L v DPP* [2002] 1 Cr App R 32).

CHAPTER 22

David is charged with indecent assault on his step-daughter, Florence aged 14. Florence has learning difficulties. David is pleading not guilty. The prosecution have witness statements from Susie, David's wife and their son Aaron aged seven.

(a) Susie is a competent witness for the prosecution and in view of the offence with which David is charged is also compellable – see s. 80(3) PACE.

(b) Florence will be presumed competent to give sworn evidence under s. 55(3) YJCEA as she is aged 14.

(c) We are told that Florence has learning difficulties. If there is reason to doubt her competency to give evidence, the test that needs to be satisfied is laid down in s. 53(3). The court will need to ascertain whether Florence can understand questions put to her and give answers that can be understood. In

determining these questions, the court must treat Florence as having the benefit of a special measures direction under s. 19. As Florence is over 14 she will give sworn evidence. If it transpires however that she is competent in accordance with s. 53(3) but is unable to satisfy the test for sworn evidence (she does not have sufficient appreciation of the solemnity of the occasion and the added responsibility to tell the truth – s. 55(2)) she will be permitted to give unsworn evidence under s. 56 YJCEA.

(d) As Aaron is under 14, s. 53 YJCEA presumes that he is competent to give unsworn evidence under s. 56 YJCEA.

(e) Both witnesses will be eligible to give evidence under a special measures direction under s. 16 YJCEA. Aaron is a witness under 17, as is Florence. In addition, Florence suffers from a mental disorder with the result that her evidence is likely to be diminished as a consequence. Where the court considers that a special measures direction is likely to improve the quality of the evidence given by the witness, the court must make the appropriate order (s. 19(2)). Additionally, both fall within the definition of a child witness requiring special protection within the meaning of s. 21. This provision makes video-recorded examination-in-chief and further examination via live link a requirement of the special measures direction.

(f) Even though David may come be classified as an intimidated witness as he is the defendant, he cannot give evidence under a special measures direction in accordance with the decision in *R. (On the application of S) v Waltham Forest Youth Court and (1) Crown Prosecution Service and (2) Secretary of State for the Home Department* [2004] 2 Cr App R 21.

CASE STUDY *R v LENNY WHYTE*

The only witness, who on the face of it, might be considered eligible for a special measures direction is Lillian Kennedy, the 84-year-old victim of the burglary offence. She might come within the definition of an intimated witness if the court considers that the quality of her evidence is likely to be diminished by reason of fear or distress in connection with testifying in the proceedings. Regard will be had to Mrs Kennedy's age in determining this. If the court considers a special measures direction is likely to improve the quality of the evidence given by the witness, the court must make the appropriate order (s. 19(2)).

CHAPTER 23

1. Generally no – leading questions are not permitted in examination-in-chief except by agreement and most often in relation to introductory matters at the beginning of a witness's evidence.

2. Under s. 139 Criminal Justice Act 2003, a witness is entitled to refresh his memory from a document while testifying provided the document was made or verified by the witness on an earlier occasion and the witness states in his oral evidence that the document records his recollection of the matter at the earlier time; and his recollection of the matters about which he is testifying is likely to have been significantly better at that time than it is at the time of his oral evidence.

3. A hostile witness is a witness who shows no desire to tell the truth at the behest of the party calling him.

4. Cross-examination has a number of purposes including obtaining factual evidence from the witness that supports the case of the cross-examiner. It also enables the advocate to test the truthfulness of the evidence the witness has given in examination-in-chief or to cast doubt on the witness's evidence; and to undermine the witness's credibility.

5. A collateral issue (such as an issue relating to a witness's credibility) runs alongside the main issues in the case.

6. An allegation of recent fabrication on the part of a witness can be rebutted during re-examination by adducing evidence of a previous consistent statement made by the witness.

7(a). Unless the prosecution agree to the defence adducing evidence of Ben and Chris's previous convictions, leave of the court under s. 100 CJA 2003 will need to be sought. Arguably, the evidence does have substantial probative value in relation to a matter of substantial importance having regard to Kyle's defence.

7(b). Yes. The main protagonists contradict each other. Their respective veracity is therefore a matter of substantial importance. A conviction for perjury arguably shows a propensity to lie on oath. Account would have to be taken perhaps for the reasons why the offence was committed. Nevertheless, it substantial high probative value.

CHAPTER 24

SCENARIO

Stefan was represented at the police station. However, there does not seem to be any dispute arising out of the composition of the video parade. The only concern is that the victim was shown photographs prior to the video identification procedure. If (as it seems) Stefan was a known suspect, Code D 3.3 prohibits a witness from being shown photographs where the suspect is known and available. The police may suggest that they were concerned about the victim's condition and the delay in securing a positive identification; however, this would appear to be a *prima facie* breach of Code D. The defence advocate will want to make a submission under s. 78 PACE, that the victim's evidence of identification be excluded (see Chapter 11).

The CCTV footage constitutes real evidence from which the jury is able to draw its own conclusion. Is this a situation in which the jury would benefit from having expert evidence? It depends on the quality of the CCTV stills. If the footage is blurred, expert evidence may be admitted to assist the jury. Would Sergeant Taylor be deemed competent? This would be a matter for the judge. It will depend on the sergeant's experience (see *R v Clare and Peach* [1995] 2 Cr App R 333). It will be a matter for the jury as to how much weight it choose to attribute to the sergeant's opinion evidence.

Assuming the trial judge refuses to exclude the evidence and the matter is left to the jury, a full Turnbull warning will need to be given. This is a case in which Stefan disputes the identification of him. He relies on alibi to suggest he was somewhere other than at the scene of the crime at the relevant time. If the judge concludes the evidence of identification is weak but is supported or indeed, if the evidence is good, he can safely leave it to the jury directing them in accordance with the Turnbull guidelines. Evidence that supports the correctness of the victim's identification in this case, could come from the evidence of Andrew, the co-accused and from the refusal by Stefan to answer questions at the police station (s. 34 CJPOA 1994 – see Chapter 8). A specific weakness with regard to the evidence in this case would include the fact that it had been obtained in breach of Code D. The judge would need to explain why this is an important factor for the jury to have regard too (see *R v Forbes* [2001] 1 AC 473 – Chapter 11).

Is this a case which calls for a corroboration warning? Did you consider that Andrew's evidence might be regarded as tainted? Andrew is an accomplice. He is jointly charged with the offence but has chosen to plead guilty to a less serious offence and has given evidence for the prosecution, directly implicating Stefan in the more serious offence. Stefan suggests Andrew is lying and that in addition, because of his sister's involvement with an officer in the case, he is motivated to give false evidence against Stefan. The defence advocate will no doubt suggest to the judge that there is an evidential basis in this case, in accordance with the principles in *R v Makanjuola* [1995] 3 All ER 730 for a corroboration warning to be given. It is a matter for the trial judge as to whether he gives such a warning and what form that warning will take.

R v LENNY WHYTE

This is a case par excellence where a Turnbull warning would be appropriate if the matter were to be left to the jury. You will recall that we have previously considered the evidence of identification in this case (see Chapter 11).

As Lenny disputes the eye-witness identification of him, the trial judge would be required to direct the jury in accordance with *R v Turnbull* [1977] QB 224.

Expert evidence features in this case. Consider the statement of Sarah Hardacker (disclosed in the committal bundle) and the statement of Dr Samantha Leighton (disclosed as part of unused material under the CPIA 1996). Both of these witnesses are experts in their particular field. Ms Hardacker's s. 9 CJA 1967 statement lists her qualifications and experience. The primary facts from which Ms Hardacker provides her opinion (the lifted set of prints) are proved by the evidence of Carol Jane Lawton, a scene of crime officer. Ms Hardacker's evidence is required in this case as the process of comparing the print with the shoes found in Lenny Whyte's property is a matter falling outside the competency of the court. Ms Hardacker's conclusion that the shoes are responsible for leaving the prints outside the burgled property is strongly expressed. However, the evidence of Dr Leighton must be bourne in mind. Lenny Whyte states he has never worn the shoes found at his flat. Dr Leighton, an expert in DNA evidence was unable to find any of Lenny's DNA in the shoe.

CHAPTER 25

For the prosecution to rely simply on Duane's written statement creates a problem of hearsay. Hearsay evidence is generally inadmissible unless it can be brought within a common law or statutory exception.

The relevant statutory provision would be s. 117(4) CJA 2003 as this is a statement prepared in contemplation of criminal proceedings. The reason for the witness's unavailability would be due to the witness's fear. Duane is clearly an identifiable witness and we will assume he had the requisite capability at the time he made the statement. As the prosecution would be relying on fear as the condition for admitting Duane's written statement, fear needs to be proved and leave to admit the statement would be required. Under s. 116(4) CJA 2003, leave will only be granted if the court considers that it would be in the interests of justice to admit the statement having regard to:

(a) the statement's contents;

(b) to any risk that its admission or exclusion will result in unfairness to any party (with particular reference to how difficult it will be to challenge the statement if the relevant person does not give evidence);

(c) in appropriate cases to the fact that a special measures direction could be made in relation to the relevant person;

(d) any other relevant circumstance.

If leave is granted, Duane's written statement will be admissible under s. 117(4). We are told that Duane is an important witness in this case. Would the admission of his evidence prejudice a fair trial? Regard would be had to the safeguards applicable. The defendants can of course give evidence themselves or call evidence of alibi. Wayne's credibility can still be attacked if there is evidence available to undermine his credibility. The judge retains discretion under s. 78 PACE 1984 to exclude the evidence if he concludes its admission would prejudice a fair trial and in directing the jury, the judge will stress the limitations of evidence that has not been subject to cross-examination. The prosecution would need to establish and the court would need to be satisfied that every effort has been made to persuade Duane to give evidence with the benefit of special measures. On the assumption that Duane's evidence is not the only evidence in the case against the defendants, his evidence is likely to be admitted as hearsay.

CHAPTER 26

1. The prosecution will seek to adduce Ben's criminal record under s. 101(1)(d) CJA 2003. They will argue that the Ben's previous caution and conviction for possession of Ecstasy makes his suggestion that he was unaware that the car contained drugs less plausible. Ben's knowledge is an important matter in issue between the prosecution and defence. They might also argue that his conviction for handling stolen goods is indicative of a propensity to be untruthful.

The defence should oppose the admission of such evidence under s. 101(3). *Hanson* should be applied. Does the history of convictions establish a propensity to deal in drugs? He has a caution and one conviction for possession of drugs only. It would be necessary to examine the circumstances of the previous offences. If the quantities were small and of a recreational nature for personal use only, the defence might argue that they have little or no relevance to an allegation of conspiracy to import a large quantity of a Class A drugs and that their admission would have an adverse effect on the fairness of the proceedings. The caution and conviction date back some five and three years respectively. In the light of the statements made in *Hanson*, the defence would contend that a single previous conviction for handling stolen goods does not indicate a propensity to be untruthful. It would be important to find out whether Ben pleaded guilty or was found guilty of the handling charge. A further relevant consideration would be the strength of the prosecution's case and the fact that he was acquitted of the offence of possession with intent to supply.

2(a). The prosecution could argue that Brian's previous conviction for unlawful sexual intercourse is an offence in the same category (see Secretary of State's Order in relation to child sex offences) and that it shows a predisposition on Brian's part towards a sexual interest in young girls giving him a motive for the commission of this offence. The conviction is relatively recent.

Would the defence advocate apply to have the earlier conviction deemed inadmissible? The defence advocate ought to. In what sense does Brian's earlier conviction show a predisposition on his part towards rape? Rape implies the use of force. It is not suggested that Brian is predisposed towards the use of violence. It is not suggested that he used violence in relation to his earlier offence. Having been charged and convicted of unlawful sexual intercourse, the sexual acts would have taken place with his victim's consent. Arguably the conditions of s. 101(1)(d) are not met, and even if they are, the defence would strongly argue that the probative value of such a previous conviction in this context would be outweighed by its prejudicial effect, (s. 101(3)). It would be pertinent to ask how old Brian was when he committed the offence of unlawful sexual intercourse. If he was a young man, the point made by the prosecution that it shows he has a sexual interest in young girls is not entirely accurate.

The criteria for admission under s. 101(1)(d) is whether the evidence is relevant to an important matter in issue. The matter in issue is whether Brian's victim consented. The question the advocate should require the court to ask itself is: Does the earlier previous conviction make it more likely that Brian is guilty of the current charge? The answer the defence advocate will be seeking in this instance is – no.

2(b). The prosecution would strongly argue that it should be. It is an offence of the same description and it arguably shows a predisposition on Brian's part to the use of sexual violence against females. It is relevant to a crucial fact in issue, namely whether the victim did consent. Equally, the prosecution could argue that Brian's previous conviction shows a propensity to be untruthful as his defence was disbelieved on an earlier occasion.

In this instance, the defence would have to stress the prejudicial effect such knowledge would have on the jury. The circumstances of each rape would need to be very carefully examined and an important consideration would be the strength of the prosecution's case without the evidence of bad character (applying *Hanson)*.

3. An accused person cannot be forced to give evidence in support of his defence. If he chooses not to give evidence without good cause, an adverse inference can be drawn against him under s. 35 CJPOA. Given the nature of Tina's defence, there is an argument for suggesting that Barry needs to give evidence in order to advance his account. Barry stands to have his previous convictions exposed under s. 101(e) as defined by s. 104 CJA 2003, irrespective of whether he choose to give evidence or not. Tina's advocate would argue that Barry's previous convictions have substantial probative value in relation to an important matter in issue, namely who inflicted the injury to the child and who is more likely to be telling the truth. Given the inevitable prejudice to Barry, the trial judge would have to be satisfied that his previous convictions do have substantial probative value in the context of the case. It would be entirely up to the jury what inference they choose to draw from the knowledge of Barry's previous convictions if they are admitted.

4. Danielle is entitled to a good character direction in accordance with the decision in *R v Vye*. It is relevant to the likelihood of her having committed the offence and, if she gives evidence on oath, it is also relevant to her credibility as a witness. The evidential effect of good character would have to be made clear to the jury in the judge's direction.

R v LENNY WHYTE

You will recall that Lenny Whyte faces an allegation of burglary, which he denies. His defence is mistaken identity. Lenny has several previous convictions for burglary and theft related offences. Under s. 101(1)(d) CJA 2003 the prosecution could argue that Lenny's previous convictions show a propensity on his part to commit offences of a dishonest nature and a propensity to be untruthful. They place Lenny in a class of people more likely to have been in Mrs Kennedy's back garden at the relevant time than the average member of the public. Lenny's propensity gives context to his defence.

The defence would need to argue that propensity evidence is simply not relevant to the facts in issue in this case, namely whether the evidence of identification is correct. Even if they assume some relevance, their admission would have an adverse effect on the fairness of the proceedings (s. 101(3)) that they should be excluded. The defence will want to place reliance on *Hanson*. The defence will need to examine the circumstances of Lenny's earlier offences and whether he pleaded guilty or was found guilty having given evidence at trial. A relevant consideration would be the strength of the prosecution's case. *Hanson* stipulates that bad character evidence should not be admitted to bolster a weak prosecution case. The question of admissibility would be determined at the pre-trial hearing. Lenny's case illustrates the potential danger of the new law. If Lenny's previous convictions are admitted, his chances of being convicted are greatly increased.

CHAPTER 27

1. No – only those communications between a solicitor and client that involve the giving or obtaining of legal advice.

2. The test requires the dominant purpose of the communication to be in connection with pending or actual litigation.

3. Legal privilege vests in the client.

4. The privilege against self-incrimination allows a witness to refuse to answer a question, which in the opinion of the judge, would expose the witness to the possibility of any criminal charge under United Kingdom law. It also extends to a defendant who has been compelled to answer questions as part of an extra judicial- investigation where, at a subsequent criminal prosecution, the prosecution seeks to use the answers given in evidence against the defendant.

CHAPTER 28

The starting point in terms of sentence upon conviction for s. 47 OAPA 1861 assault, according to the Magistrates' Court Sentencing Guidelines, is a custodial sentence. Applying the principles in the Criminal Justice Act 2003 under s. 143(1), Scott should be sentenced on his culpability in committing the offence and the harm he has caused. His actions would appear to be intentional and injury has resulted as a consequence of his actions. Statutory aggravating factors in Scott's case include:

- s. 143(2) CJA 2003 – he has previous offences of a like nature;
- s. 143(3) – he committed this offence while on bail;
- s. 145 – the offence would appear to be racially motivated.

Having regard to the Magistrates' Court Sentencing Guidelines, the relevant aggravating factors specific to this offence are the fact that the disturbance involved a group and that the victim was kicked. This is a case where the magistrates might consider their power to impose a maximum sentence of six months to be insufficient. They could consider committing Scott to the Crown Court for sentence. It is likely that an 'all options' pre-sentence report would be requested. Regard would be had to any personal offender mitigation Scott might put forward. He would not be entitled to a sentencing discount because he did not plead guilty.

ANALYSIS OF CASE STUDIES

R v William Hardy

Section 9(2) Sexual Offences Act 2003 is a new offence. There are no current sentencing guidelines on this offence. The maximum sentence a magistrates' court could impose is six months (this will increase when s. 154 CJA 2003 comes into force). In the Crown Court however, the maximum penalty is 14 years. Under the previous law (s. 6 Sexual Offences (Amendment) Act 1956 – unlawful sexual intercourse with a girl under the age of 16) William would have faced a maximum custodial sentence of six months in the magistrates' court and a maximum sentence of two years in the Crown Court.

Did you spot the fact that William Hardy will also be subject to notification requirements under the SOA 2003 (previously the Sex Offenders' Register) for a statutory period, the duration of which depends on the sentence that he receives? Credit must of course be given for his timely guilty plea (s. 144 (CJA 2003).

There are in fact no sentencing guidelines on this specific offence in the Magistrates' Court Sentencing Guidelines. Sentencing guidelines were issued under s. 6 SOA 1956 and can be found in pre-2005 editions of *Blackstone's Criminal Practice*. An important case in this regard is the Court of Appeal's decision in *R v Taylor* [1977] 1 WLR 612. It provides:

> '. . . when there is a virtuous friendship which ends in unlawful sexual intercourse, it is inappropriate to pass sentences of a punitive nature. What is required is a warning to the youth to mend his ways. At the other end [of the spectrum], a man in a supervisory capacity who abuses his position of trust for his sexual gratification, ought to get a sentence somewhere near the maximum allowed by law, which is two years' imprisonment. In between there come many degrees of guilt.'

The closest we have in terms of guidance for offences of this type under the SOA 2003, is draft guidelines that have been produced by the Sentencing Advisory Panel: http://www.sentencing-guidelines. gov.uk/docs/consult_sexual_offences.pdf. In relation to the assessment of seriousness of consensual sexual offences against children, the Panel makes the following observations:

> 'The nature of the sexual activity will be the main factor in assessing the seriousness of an offence . . . other factors will include the age and degree of vulnerability of the victim. As a general indicator, the younger the child the more vulnerable he or she is likely to be. The age gap between the child and the offender is also relevant as is any breach of trust arising from a family relationship between the child and the offender or from the offender's professional or other responsibility for the child's welfare.'

Offences of this nature are clearly serious – more so now that the tariff has increased to a potential maximum of 14 years' imprisonment on indictment. The aggravating feature in this case is the suggestion that the prelude to sexual activity between William Hardy and his victim began when he was providing private tuition to the girl. Arguably he was in a position of trust as regards his victim. This is however denied by William Hardy. A Newton hearing could potentially be triggered, unless the CPS are prepared to accept the basis of William Hardy's plea that while sexual intercourse did occur on occasions, it was not while he was in a position of trust. In terms of mitigating features, the age disparity between the two is not that great and their sexual relationship would appear to be within the context of a loving and consensual relationship and had been initiated by the victim.

This is a finely balanced case in terms of possible committal to the Crown Court for sentence. Much will depend on the agreed basis of plea, the defence advocate's submission and the magistrates' personal point of view.

If you look at the video clips of this scenario, you will see William Hardy's appearance before magistrates at the plea before venue hearing. At his hearing, William pleads guilty. There is a brief outline of the facts presented by the prosecutor, followed by a brief submission by the defence advocate, asking the court to consider adjourning the matter for a pre-sentence report. You will see that after some discussion, the magistrates indicate that they are prepared to accept jurisdiction but order a pre-sentence report, keeping all their sentencing options open.

We ask you to complete your reading of the chapters on sentencing before viewing the final sentencing hearing in relation to William Hardy.

R v Roger Martin

Aside from the road traffic offences committed by Mr Martin, he faces the potential of six months in custody for the offence of common assault. As he intends to plead guilty, he will of course receive a discount. If one looks at the offence of common assault in the Magistrates' Court Sentencing Guidelines, the guideline sentence for a first time offender is a community penalty. Aggravating factors would include the injury caused to the victim. It should also be borne in mind that this assault was committed in the context of road rage. A little research on this point will reveal that such matters are taken very seriously by the courts. Consider paragraph B 2.3 in *Blackstone's Criminal Practice*:

> 'In *Fenton* (1994) 15 Cr App R (S) 682 the offender pleaded guilty to common assault (charges of assault occasioning actual bodily harm and dangerous driving were not proceeded with). In the course of an altercation between motorists, the offender pushed the victim in the chest. The Court of Appeal said that almost all cases of violence between motorists would be so serious that only custody could be justified. The appropriate sentence was seven days' imprisonment. See also *Ross* (1994) 15 Cr App R (S) 384.

The above underlines the importance of researching any available sentencing guidelines. In terms of mitigating factors, the fact that Roger Martin's actions were impulsive, that he was provoked and that it was a single blow would be relevant. Given the distinct possibility of a custodial sentence, a pre-sentence report should be ordered.

We will assume that having entered a guilty plea, the magistrates adjourn sentence and order a pre-sentence report, keeping all of their sentencing options open. We ask you to complete the chapters on sentencing before viewing the final sentencing hearing in relation to Roger Martin.

R v Lenny Whyte

Had Lenny been convicted, the maximum penalty he would face is seven years' imprisonment. This is a case where a pre-sentence report should be ordered to explore relevant personal offender mitigation and to consider what might be regarded as the most appropriate sentence for Lenny given his personal circumstances.

The relevant sentencing guidelines for this offence are found in the Court of Appeal's decision in *R v McInerney and Keating* [2003] 1 Cr App R 36. This is a leading case offering guidance on sentencing in burglary cases and urges courts to consider non custodial sentencing options for less serious burglaries. This particular offence of burglary is arguably one in which there are medium level aggravating features, as set out in the judgment. They include:

- a vulnerable victim;
- the fact that the victim was at home;
- the fact that the burglars worked as a group.

Additionally Lenny has a relatively recent previous conviction for burglary and numerous previous convictions for theft. As Lenny pleaded not guilty, he would not be entitled to a reduction in sentence.

CHAPTER 29

1. A custodial sentence is a sentence of last resort and is reserved for the most serious offences. The custody threshold test must be met before a custodial sentence can be imposed. The test under s. 152 CJA 2003 is whether the offence is so serious that neither a fine alone, nor a community sentence can be justified. A court can also impose a custodial term on an offender who refuses to comply with a requirement imposed as part of a community sentence or who fails to comply with a pre-sentence drug-test under s. 161(2) of the 2003 CJA. For the majority of offences that are sentenced in magistrates' courts, the key to determining the seriousness of the offence is the balance of aggravating and mitigating factors in the offence, informed by sentencing guidelines, such as those contained in the Magistrates' Court Sentencing Guidelines 2004. Likewise in the Crown Court, regard should be had to sentencing guidelines which provide guidance to the court on the appropriateness of custodial sentences (see Chapter 28).

2. The easy answer to the question is the seriousness of the offence to be sentenced. Section 153(2) CJA 2003 provides that the custodial term should be the shortest term commensurate with the seriousness of the offence. The picture is complicated however by a number of factors discussed in Chapter 29, including:

- credit for guilty plea;
- restrictions on magistrates' court's sentencing powers;
- early release schemes;
- the decision to impose consecutive or concurrent terms in a case where the defendant stands to be sentenced for two or more offences, or is currently subject to a suspended sentence;
- some statutes require the imposition of mandatory terms of imprisonment;

- special provision is made under the CJA 2003 for those who are deemed 'dangerous' offenders and those who qualify for extended sentences because of the nature of the crimes they have committed.

3. Under the CJA 2003, a court can choose to impose an immediate custodial term, a suspended term of imprisonment or an intermittent custodial term.

CHAPTER 30

EXERCISE 1

Start by looking at the Magistrates' Court Sentencing Guidelines for theft. The suggested guideline is a community penalty. Assess the seriousness of this particular theft and Celia's culpability. The mitigating features would be that it was impulsive and unsophisticated. The offence is aggravated by the fact that Celia is subject to a conditional discharge for an identical offence imposed only six months ago. It would be unrealistic to expect a fine or a conditional discharge on this occasion. Celia also stands to be sentenced for the original theft for which she was given a conditional discharge.

Celia will most probably be subject to a community order with a supervision requirement for both offences which may well benefit her. A pre-sentence report or a specific sentence report may be ordered in this case. She will be ordered to pay some or all of the prosecution's costs. On the assumption that the bracelet was returned to the shop, there will be no compensation to pay. In arriving at the eventual sentence, the court should give her credit for her guilty plea.

EXERCISE 2

Louise is also charged with theft, but there is a crucial difference between her offence and that of Celia. Louise's theft involves a breach of trust. She has stolen from her employer. The suggested guideline for theft in breach of trust is custody. Try to assess the relative seriousness of the theft and Louise's culpability.

The aggravating features include the fact that suspicion would have been cast on the other employees and that the offence was committed over a period of time. On the mitigating side of things the amount involved is small. Applying the test in *R v Howells* [1999] 1 WLR 307, the theft would not appear to be so serious that only custody can be justified. Realistically, you should be urging the court to impose a non-custodial alternative. Even though this is Louise's first offence, it would be unrealistic to expect a fine or conditional discharge, as this is two steps down from the guideline sentence.

This is a case where a pre-sentence report should be ordered. Louise has plenty of personal offender mitigation and could well be looking at a community order in the middle seriousness category combining a supervision requirement with an unpaid work requirement. She can expect to be ordered to pay £150 in compensation and some or all of the prosecution's costs. Given her limited means, priority would be given to the compensation. In arriving at the eventual sentence, the court should give a discount for her guilty plea perhaps reflected in the number of hours imposed as part of the requirement/s under the community order.

EXERCISE 3

The guideline sentence for possession of a Class C drug is a conditional discharge or fine. On the mitigating side, five plants are not a commercial industry. There is personal offender mitigation. Although Andrew has previous convictions, there would seem little point in doing anything save to fine him or to give him a conditional discharge on this occasion. He will probably be ordered to pay some or all of the prosecution's costs and an order will be made for the destruction of the plants. Credit should be given for Andrew's guilty plea, perhaps reflected in the level of fine or the duration of a conditional discharge.

EXERCISE 4

The sentencing guidelines for assaulting a police constable indicate the starting point is a custodial sentence. Assess the seriousness of this particular assault, including Darren's culpability and the harm his actions caused. This was an intentional assault. The assault resulted in injuries being sustained and it would appear that it was deliberate, sustained and involved kicking the officer while he was on the ground. Darren has a previous conviction for possession of an offensive weapon. This is not a case where the court would have the power to commit Darren to sentence in the Crown Court under s. 3 PCC(S)A 2000. Do you know why? The answer is because it is a summary only offence.

A realistic sentencing objective in this case would be to avoid a custodial sentence and secure a community order. This will not be easy. There is evidence of regret and it would appear that the incident was fuelled by excessive alcohol consumption. You should certainly refer to *R v Howells* [1999] 1 WLR 307 and the question of whether a prison sentence would serve any useful purpose in this case. A custodial sentence would probably result in Darren losing his job and being unable to pay compensation. Darren should be given credit for his early guilty plea. Darren could well be given a custodial sentence in the region of three months. This was a nasty assault on a serving police officer trying to fulfil his public duty. The court will feel the need to punish Darren and send out the right message. If the bench was feeling lenient, Darren might be made the subject of a community order with a lengthy unpaid work requirement and/or curfew requirement and/or a prohibited activity order. If this were imposed, he would be in a position to pay compensation to the police constable as well as prosecution costs.

CHAPTER 31

EXERCISE 1

Research the offence of careless driving in the Magistrates' Court Sentencing Guidelines or in *Blackstone's Criminal Practice*. Conviction requires the court to endorse Ian's licence with 3–9 penalty points. He will almost certainly be fined for the offence and the suggested starting level for any fine is Level B. Ian should be sentenced according to the seriousness of the offence and his level of culpability. This was not an example of blatant bad driving. The only aggravating factor is the tragic death that has resulted from what might be described as a minor lapse in concentration. Ian may be disqualified for the offence, as the discretion to disqualify exists whenever a court is required to endorse a driver's licence. If disqualification is ordered, no penalty points will in fact be placed on Ian's driving licence, but details of the endorsement will be included. If a Level B fine is imposed, Ian is looking at a fine in the region of £650. This will be reduced to take account of his timely guilty plea. If the court decided to exercise its discretion to disqualify from driving for the offence, there would be an argument, based on the lack of aggravating factors, that it should be kept to a minimum, perhaps three months.

EXERCISE 2

Did you research the offence of driving with excess alcohol? The bad news for Ruth is that disqualification from driving is mandatory for this offence. The Magistrates' Court Sentencing Guidelines suggest that for a reading of 111 mgs in breath, the period of disqualification should be in the region of 28 months and a community penalty should be considered. Ruth will be entitled to a one-quarter reduction in the period of disqualification if she successfully completes the drink driver's rehabilitation course. She has no grounds to argue special reasons for not disqualifying her. The court might consider fining her, but the guidelines suggest a community penalty. Given Ruth's admitted problems, a community order with a supervision requirement would appear to be the most constructive sentence. In determining the period, the court should have regard to Ruth's timely guilty plea.

EXERCISE 3

Ben has pleaded guilty to two endorseable offences. Careless driving carries an endorsement of 3–9 penalty points and driving with no insurance carries an endorsement of 6–8 penalty points. Ben will receive only one endorsement based on the offence attracting the highest number of points (s. 28 RTA 1988). If the magistrates decide to impose five penalty points for the offence of careless driving but seven penalty points for having no insurance, Ben's licence will be endorsed with seven penalty points in total. He can expect to be fined for each of the offences. The starting point for the fine is Level B. Account will be taken of Ben's means and a reduction should be made for his guilty plea. If a Level B fine is imposed, Ben will be looking at a figure of £500 for each offence, perhaps reduced to £400 for his timely guilty plea. If the court decides to apply a Level A fine, he will be looking at a financial penalty in the region of £250. Ben will be disqualified from driving because he already has six current penalty points on his licence. If six or more penalty points are imposed, he will have 12 or more points on his licence. To avoid disqualification under the totting-up procedure, he must establish that the loss of his licence would cause exceptional hardship (s. 35(4) RTA 1988). He would point out that his business is dependant upon his being able to drive and that any other form of transportation would be completely impractical.

EXERCISE 4

Imran is in a very unfortunate situation. As he is a 'newly qualified' driver within the definition of s. 1 Road Traffic (New Drivers) Act 1995, his licence will be revoked and he will have to pass his driving test all over again because of the imposition of at least six penalty points. This may take many weeks. The most pragmatic solution for Imran would be to argue for a very short period of discretionary disqualification under s. 34 RTA 1988, as this will mean no penalty points are in fact endorsed. He can expect to be fined and to have to pay prosecution costs. However, the fine should reflect the seriousness of the offence and there would appear to be plenty that the defence solicitor can say in mitigation of the offence itself.

CASE STUDY *R v ROGER MARTIN* (WEB-BASED ONLY)

In addition to the offence of common assault, Roger Martin has also pleaded guilty to careless driving (s. 3 Road Traffic Act 1988) and failing to stop and report (s. 170(4) RTA 1988.) His priority will be to keep his driving licence as his livelihood depends upon it.

Careless driving is punishable with penalty points ranging from 3–9. The guideline sentence, according to the Magistrates' Association Sentencing Guidelines, is a fine (Level B) or discharge. Careless driving is most commonly sentenced by way of a fine. The magistrates could choose to exercise their discretion to disqualify Roger for the offence itself (s. 34(2) RTA 1988). In this case however, the court is more likely to endorse his driving licence. The offence of careless driving in this case was prolonged and injury, albeit slight, resulted. The offence was committed in the context of what is commonly referred to as being 'road rage'. If the magistrates endorse Roger's driving licence, they are likely to be looking at the higher end of the tariff (eight or even nine penalty points) to reflect the seriousness of Roger's behaviour. Furthermore, Roger can expect a high fine for the same reason. Credit will be given for his timely guilty plea. However, the credit is applied to the size of the fine and has no application to the endorsement of penalty points.

The offence of failing to stop and report carries endorsement of 5–10 penalty points and the theoretical risk of a custodial sentence. The guideline sentence is in fact a fine or discharge. As these offences were committed on the same occasion, Roger's driving licence will be endorsed with the highest number of points (s. 28 RTA 1988). He can expect to be fined for this offence. Prosecution costs will also be ordered.

Roger already has six penalty points currently on his licence. If he receives (as is likely) six or more penalty points for the offences he has been convicted of today, he will be disqualified under the totting-up procedure (s. 35 RTA 1988), unless he is able to argue that the loss of his driving licence in these circumstances would cause him exceptional hardship. Having regard to his personal circumstances, you will see that Roger is heavily dependant

on his driving licence. He is a salesman by occupation. He has extensive financial outgoings, including child maintenance. He has a strictly-defined court contact order with his children which will be lost if he is unable to collect them on time. Furthermore, his youngest son is disabled and relies on his father being able to drive. Roger's former wife is unable to assist as she does not drive. It may not be reasonably practicable for Roger to use public transport. Roger can expect to give evidence on oath to substantiate his defence of exceptional hardship.

CHAPTER 33

1. A common use of s. 142 MCA 1980 is to rectify an obvious mistake during the defendant's trial and in cases where the defendant was convicted and sentenced in his absence.

2. The Crown Court may impose any sentence which the magistrates could have imposed. This might mean your client could receive a harsher sentence.

3. Any party to the proceedings may appeal by case stated.

4. Yes – leave must be obtained from either the trial judge or from the Court of Appeal.

5. An appeal against conviction will only be allowed where the conviction is 'unsafe' under s. 2(1)(a) Criminal Appeal Act 1968.

CHAPTER 34

1. The appropriate adult's role is to support, advise and assist the juvenile and to ensure that the police are acting fairly with respect to the detainee's rights.

2. Yes – subject to the same conditions as an adult offender.

3. YOTs undertake the day-to-day administration of youth justice. A YOT is situated in every local authority in England and Wales. The multidisciplinary membership of each YOT is drawn from the police, Probation Service, social services and education, the health authority, housing and drug, alcohol and substance misuse agencies. The YOT identifies the needs of young offenders and manages specific programmes to prevent them offending or re-offending. The YOT also exercises the statutory responsibility of supervising young people in custody and on community orders.

4. If it is decided not to prosecute Remi and evidential and public interest tests are satisfied under the Code for Crown Prosecutors, para. 8.8 of the Code requires the Crown Prosecutor to consider the possibility of alternatives to prosecution. Remi may therefore be given an informal warning or a reprimand. An informal warning will be given by a police officer usually in the presence of the person having parental responsibility and will warn Remi about his future behaviour. An informal warning has the effect of the proceedings being discontinued. An alternative approach would be to reprimand Remi where the officer has evidence that Remi committed the offence and evidence in the case discloses a realistic prospect of a conviction. Remi must admit to the police officer that he committed the offence and the officer is satisfied that a

online resource centre

prosecution is not in the public interest. A reprimand (and not a final warning) will be appropriate as Remi has not been previously warned or reprimanded, s. 65(2) CDA 1998.

CHAPTER 35

1. The young person should generally be tried in the Youth Court, but there exceptions to this, depending on whether the young person is facing a charge of homicide or a 'grave' crime, or is jointly charged with an adult facing an offence which is to be tried on indictment or may come within the 'dangerousness' provisions (see diagram at the end of Chapter 35).

2. The main custodial sentence for a young offender is a detention and training order. The maximum term is 24 months. It cannot be imposed on an offender under the age of 12. In relation to an offender under the age of 15, they have to be a persistent offender (see definition in Chapter 34). The custody threshold test must be met.

3. Tracey is 15 and will therefore appear before the Youth Court. She faces an offence that is triable either way. Tracey will have no right of election. The Youth Court will consider whether this case should be sent to the Crown Court under s. 24(1)(a) MCA 1980 as a 'grave' crime, having regard to the seriousness of the offence and its maximum power of punishment, which is a two year DTO. The justices' legal adviser will need to give advice on sentencing guidelines for this type of offence. Tracey is not charged with an aggravated offence of arson with intent to endanger life. However, the offence is serious and merits a custodial sentence on the face of it. The Youth Courts' maximum sentencing power in this case ought to be sufficient. If Tracey pleads guilty and expresses her remorse (and depending on the content of the pre-sentence report), it is possible that she may receive a community sentence. She is not old enough to be placed on a community rehabilitation order or community punishment order. The court might consider an action plan order with an element of reparation or perhaps a supervision order to address her needs. The offence is too serious to warrant a referral order. The Youth Court must bind over Tracey's parents or guardian unless it is not in the interest of justice to do so. It is unlikely that the court will consider a fine or an award of compensation given the social problems Tracey and her family face.

If the court considers the offence is so serious that a community sentence cannot be passed, Tracey will be sentenced to a DTO. The minimum order is four months. She will serve half her sentence in custody and the remaining half under supervision in the community.

4. Barry faces a charge which carries a maximum custodial sentence of 14 years in the case of an adult. It therefore falls within the definition of a 'grave' crime. It is also a 'specified' offence for the purposes of the 'dangerousness' provisions. It is likely that the Youth Court will decline jurisdiction in this case. The Youth Court would need to consider whether Barry would qualify as a dangerous offender, applying the complex provisions under ss. 226 and 228 of the Criminal Justice Act 2003. If they conclude that he is not 'dangerous' within the application of the provisions, they will go on to consider whether this is a 'grave' crime likely to result in a lengthy custodial term under s. 91 PCC(S) A 2000. The sentencing guidelines for causing death by dangerous driving suggest a lengthy custodial. On this basis and applying the Southampton Youth Justices' decision, the Youth Court could easily conclude that there is a more than theoretical risk of Barry receiving a custodial term in excess of 24 months.

INDEX